PERPETUAL EXPERIENCE™

Carl Lyon unravels the mysteries
of customer experience

perpetualexperience.com

PERPETUAL EXPERIENCE™

Copyright © 2016 Carl Lyon

perpetualexperience.com

ISBN 978-1-5262-0447-9

First published in Great Britain in 2016 by Carl Lyon.

All rights reserved.

Printed by The Lavenham Press, Suffolk, United Kingdom
Artwork by Steve Abbey, Woodley, United Kingdom

About the Author

Carl Lyon is a thought leader in customer experience. Having started his career as a sales engineer, he soon realised that he was just as passionate about the part people play in successful businesses as he was about engineering excellence.

His ability to engage with people and enthuse them about technical concepts led him to become involved in the Channel Tunnel project, when his employer sent him to explain a product to a company involved in the construction. After a successful sales pitch, the complexity of aligning both companies in support of the resulting business case kick started a fascination with how knowledge is shared and decisions are made in large organisations.

This fascination led him to become involved with the emerging field of customer experience, and a determination to help businesses find new and better ways of engaging with customers. In 2005, Carl launched the Quality of Experience Company (The QoE), a debating group for senior and middle managers to help them make sense of the transition from customer service to customer experience. The success of The QoE has given Carl a privileged insight into the inner workings of many large and complex organisations, and The QoE continues to yield cutting-edge insights about the increasingly experience-driven economy.

The outputs from The QoE sessions have helped many businesses develop effective responses to the evolving business landscape, particularly in the face of digital disruption. The knowledge that has been acquired through The QoE has also been instrumental in developing the concept of perpetual experience.

Acknowledgements

Any book is the product of a vast number of conversations, discussions, insights and contributions, and this book is no different. Many people have helped me shape the ideas and thoughts that have led me to develop the concept of perpetual experience and I am hugely grateful to all for their generosity, frankness, and interest in the topic.

In particular, there have been many people without whose input this book would not have been possible. Stewart Bromley, currently COO at Atom Bank, is a long-time associate and his knowledge and experience have been instrumental in helping me understand the logical progression of customer experience, through people experience and on into perpetual experience. And in addition to all those who are quoted in the book, I would also like to thank Bob Dunn, BskyB, Steve Dyer, Jaguar Land Rover, Nikolina Glamoclija, Vodafone, James Kaye, Home Group, Nigel Keys, HSBC, Steve Lawrence, Airbus Defence and Space, Andrew Lofts, Ricoh, Maria McCann, Jo Ho Ventures, Jo Moran, Marks and Spencer, Denisa Spinkova, Carlson Rezidor and Ed Thompson, Gartner, for sharing their experiences.

And of course, no author completes a project of this nature without the support of a close team of people. My thanks go to Chris and Christine Clarke without whose practical support the book would still be on the to do list. Deb Bradley for the design and production and, most importantly, her patience and guidance through some difficult times. Tony Reeves who has helped me translate my thoughts into this book through his unnerving ability to ask the right questions and make sense of my answers. And finally, to the rest of The QoE team for their continuing support and dedication.

You could say that I am, and shall be, perpetually grateful.

Contents

$$(CX + PX)^i = X^\infty$$

Customer experience plus people experience to the power of information = perpetual experience

Customer Experience (CX)

When a product or service is purchased and used by a customer, each individual outcome, good or bad, is expressed as an experience. Customer experience can therefore be viewed as a real-world, real-time assessment of a product or service that develops into an individual's perception of the company or brand.

People Experience (PX)

When a person is employed to work for a company, each individual task they undertake has an outcome, good or bad, and is expressed as an experience. People experience can therefore be viewed as a real-world, real-time assessment of the task or tasks an employee is asked to complete. Individually this drives behaviours, collectively these behaviours become a culture.

Information (i)

Customer and people experience generate contextual information that, when shared, stimulates knowledge and understanding that drives more informed decisions and actions. Shared information both empowers individuals and constitutes an invaluable resource for any business.

X^∞

Infinite experiences are produced by the continuously evolving needs of people, society and technology. To sustain its position, a business must therefore find a method of providing perpetually evolving experiences.

Perpetual Experience™

Perpetual experience is a business methodology that harnesses the complexity of the modern business environment, enabling organisations to deliver authentic, personalised, cutting-edge customer experiences.

By allowing themselves to be perpetually shaped by people and customers, businesses become more responsive, more innovative, more authentic, and more efficient through the liberation of experience and knowledge.

An everlasting emotional experience fuelled by the ongoing, increasingly personalised interactions with the company makes perpetual experience as relevant to early adopters as it is to seasoned practitioners.

Foreword

Our life is a concatenation of our experiences. Some good, some bad. Some memorable for all the right reasons, and some for the wrong. Some that we thought were great ten years ago, may only be perceived as mediocre today. Our individual expectations continue to evolve incrementally but, for new generations, the basis for great experience can be vastly different from previous generations. Revolutionary.

And so it is for business. Customer experience is as old as trade itself. Albeit it is only since the 1980s that businesses have explored it as a discipline. Many today state that they are customer centric or focused on customer experience. In reality many struggle to design or deliver an experience that differentiates and therefore fail to capitalise on the sustainable value that great experience creates.

If you run a business that cares about experience, whether that of its customers or employees, you will find the insight in this book useful. Carl challenges your thinking, captured in easy to follow concepts and defines a new approach to experience mastery. The current pace of change necessitates a new way of thinking and this book pulls together a number of strands into one comprehensive idea, Perpetual Experience™. You can digest the content in a few hours, and enjoy delivering a revolution in experience for years to come.

Stewart Bromley
Chief Operating Officer
Atom Bank

Preface

I've written this book to stimulate new ideas on the evolution of customer experience. It is presented as a conversation.

Customer experience, as we see it today, is predominantly the responsibility of senior managers and leaders in large organisations. However, as our conversation unfolds, I hope you will also see that the ideas in this book provide a way of stimulating conversation with a much wider business audience.

Origins of the book

You might be wondering how the concept of perpetual experience has been conceived and developed. The theories and practices that inform perpetual experience are the product of the challenges and developments that you and I have faced in our work and personal lives. The concept has also been refined by the views of countless others who have willingly shared their experiences, debated theories and explored a range of situations, and I am extremely grateful for their input.

The opportunity to develop perpetual experience has come about through the privileged access to individuals, companies and ideas that I have enjoyed through facilitating the Quality of Experience (The QoE) group. Since its formation in 2005, this community of professionals has learnt, re-learnt, practiced and re-practiced customer experience in all its various forms, from the very good to the very bad. Of course, over this time I've developed my own ideas and philosophy about customer experience, and the time has now come to put those ideas and philosophy into book form.

This doesn't mean the learning and development stops here. But I believe we are at a pivotal point where both the understanding and tools exist that can have a real impact on moving companies to a more proactive, inclusive and profitable future. Yes, experience, customers, people and profit are all in the same conversation. If the last ten years have shown us anything, it is that this combination has to work if we are to develop successful businesses to keep pace with our rapidly changing world.

This book tackles some of the key mysteries of customer experience in its wider context. I'll also be introducing common themes from The QoE group and the wider business community that have contributed so generously. These themes include building influence, delivering real-time benefits, engaging with technology, responding to disruption and preparing for the future.

Chapter one, the introduction to this book, is effectively a 'book within a book'. Within ten minutes of reading and thinking, you'll know where I stand on key issues regarding the development and evolution of customer experience. The four chapters in Part 1 identify and discuss the main challenges that I believe are the cause of much of the disruption currently affecting businesses in many sectors. Part 2 of the book then goes on to explain how perpetual experience can help businesses develop effective responses to - and capitalise on - technical and behavioural evolutions.

Chapter two, three, four and five examine the main trends that have affected experiences and will (in my view) continue to affect businesses over the next decade. Chapter two explores the significant impact of disruptive innovation and its effect on people, and how the combination of searchable knowledge and connectivity are changing people's behaviours and how they make decisions. Chapter three considers how new and emerging technologies are shaping the digital landscape and highlights the opportunities that this provides for both businesses and customers.

We then move to an investigation in chapter four into how digital has unleashed the power of 'many voices', and how this diversity of opinion can help us better understand needs and experiences. This chapter also builds a case for why a more inclusive approach to people and customers is required in order to inform effective decision-making. Chapter five digs deeper into the challenges of the connected society, how it is bringing a greater focus on individual needs rather than simply 'customer' needs, and the implications for people's expectations of businesses.

We then move into Part 2 of the book and an exploration of how perpetual experience can provide an effective response to the challenges identified in Part 1. Chapter six explains how customer experience develops into people experience, and then evolves into perpetual experience. This chapter also explains how perpetual experience can provide the information and knowledge needed to drive effective self and assisted service, a challenge with which many companies continue to grapple.

In chapter seven I move to the proposal that we should be placing a greater focus on people, rather than simply customers, employees or partners. If a business has the ambition to 'put the customer first' then it should also strive to 'put the employee first'. Of course, both can't be first, so this means that we should be seeking to influence behaviours through experiences for both employees and customers. Chapter seven also introduces the 'people experience journey', a key aspect of perpetual experience that enables companies to identify and address the weak links in products and service that lead to poor experiences.

Chapter eight examines the benefits of leading by influencing rather than by authority, but also why effective influence is difficult to achieve. I argue that exerting a continuous influence is a more effective way to manage businesses, teams and projects, as it encourages people to be more proactive in responding to the unforeseen yet inevitable challenges that will emerge from an environment that is perpetually changing.

This chapter also notes the dangers of only using a single measure to evaluate customer satisfaction, and how using a blend of measures is a better way to influence the desired behaviours of the people in the business.

However, effective influence is only achievable if the influencer is perceived as authentic. Chapter nine therefore explains why authenticity is the holy grail for businesses and how perpetual experience can provide the information to drive more authentic interactions. I explore how experiences, more than values, morality, ethics and culture, shape the behaviour of people and companies. I discuss how experiences influence decisions, and how bringing people together in an authentic environment can produce more customer-focused decision making.

The final chapter focuses on the practicalities of perpetual experience and how it is implemented. In chapter ten, I describe each element of perpetual experience - perpetual thinking groups, people experience journeys, incubation hubs, and experience engines - and how these elements come together to produce an exponential leap in effectiveness.

One final thing - at the end of each chapter you will find a summary of the key points and a place for you to jot down how the issues we have been discussing play out in your business context. As we work through the book you may wish to re-visit your notes as patterns and themes start to emerge.

I hope you enjoy reading this book as much as I have enjoyed writing it. I am confident that it will lead you to new insights that will benefit both you and your organisation, and enable you to establish perpetual experience as a way to achieve personal and collective success.

1 | INTRODUCTION

CHAPTER 1

Introduction

Mystery: $(CX + PX)^i = X^\infty$

Let's start our conversation with a common explanation of customer experience: putting the customer first.

Are we really saying all companies have to do is put the customer first? Can companies hand over that much control - and would customers actually benefit if they did?

A famous line is 'Henry Ford's customers wanted faster horses'. Did customers want a smartphone before they understood what it could do for them? Even 5-star hotels have to say "sorry, we can't" at some point, and their employees certainly have a right to say no when a customer request is beyond reasonable. The same can be said for the people involved - can the customer always be in control when it is the employees who need to carry out the tasks required for the business to function?

The understanding of customer experience as 'putting the customer first' has, in my view, many flaws that cause confusion, dissatisfaction and distrust - particularly if the message becomes part of the brand promise. Escalate this through the many transactions of the customer and it isn't long before customers and employees have little trust in the company. Take this further into the functional and interpersonal relationships within organisations, and then on into partner relationships, and the perpetuation of confusion and distrust becomes a powerful force.

There is no doubt that the ambition to put the customer first was to readdress the balance of power between organisation and customer and, in many cases, it has been a positive and effective message. But it could also be argued that this ambition has limited the potential of customer experience over the last decade. People increasingly assert their individuality through greater access to information, knowledge and opinion. Customers and employees are people first, and all expect to be treated with honesty and respect.

Access to knowledge, information and opinion is becoming easier all the time, further highlighting the need for transparency and authenticity. Our conversation will unpack both these terms and the opportunities they present for companies. It would seem that putting the customer first needs to evolve if companies are to prosper now and survive in the future.

But what is perpetual experience? And why do I believe that it can help customer experience evolve? To answer these questions, we must begin by tracing the evolution of customer experience, through people experience, and into perpetual experience.

Customer experience (CX)

When a product or service is purchased and used by a customer, each individual outcome, good or bad, is expressed as an experience. Customer experience can therefore be viewed as a real-world, real-time assessment of a product or service that develops into an individual's perception of the company or brand.

In principle, and at its broadest, customer experience is the evaluation of all the factors that affect a customer's feelings, emotions, opinions, decisions, behaviours or actions. From sales pitches to advertising, from public relations to social media, from product design to customer service, from strategy to accounts - all of these (and others) result in contact with customers and all generate individual experiences.

So, customer experience is a very broad topic that companies tend to exploit in discrete areas such as customer interface functions, call centres, service departments, complaints, or as part of a marketing strategy. Interestingly, the attitude of small businesses is the complete opposite, where good experiences are seen as a way to engage, sell to and retain customers. But whatever the company size or its practical definition of customer experience, one thing is definite - its impact on an organisation is immense. In a business, it directly affects sales and future sales, as well as net profits and net worth. And in a public organisation subject to regulation and pressure from external stakeholders, it directly affects the levels of satisfaction that service users receive.

Customer experience also attempts to expand an organisation into the world of emotional engagement, which goes beyond the simple interaction between company and customer. This brings in the effects of loyalty and advocacy: customer experience is the emotion that remains with the customer through the periods during which they are not in contact with the organisation. It can be said that this is both a strength and a weakness, as it has led companies away from the realities of what actually happens.

People experience (PX)

When a person is employed to work for a company, each individual task they undertake has an outcome, good or bad, and is expressed as an experience. People experience can therefore be viewed as a real-world, real-time assessment of the task or tasks an employee is asked to complete. Individually this drives behaviours, collectively these behaviours become a culture.

The early thoughts on people experience were based around the idea of 'happy employees, happy customers' and this is a good way of looking at it. The mood of employees interacting with customers affects the experience that customers receive, and acknowledging this has contributed significantly to the evolution of customer experience.

Some companies have taken this idea further by acknowledging that good employee experience will also increase creativity and ownership of problems. This has helped move customer experience into a more insightful and proactive, rather than purely reactive, role. A few companies have taken people experience much, much deeper into the organisation to enable their employees to use more emotional and intuitive thinking when dealing with customer issues. Very few have truly taken it into the ethos of the company and given it a substantial role in shaping the organisation. One of the reasons for this is the failure to recognise the difference in expectations in people who pay for products and services and people paid to carry out a task. For the foreseeable future these expectations will be considerably different, but what we often witness today is an unsustainable gap between the quality of experience delivered to customers and employees - especially as they may often be the same people. For example, you may own a car but also work for the car's manufacturer, or own a mobile phone and work for the network provider.

At its best, people experience is the first shift towards companies becoming proactive rather than reactive, and acknowledging that a balance of logic and emotional intelligence is a better guide to predicting needs. These companies are also in a better position to tackle the challenges of disruption as they are by nature more creative, and so better able to innovate new products and services.

What is perpetual experience?

Perpetual experience is a business methodology that harnesses the complexity of the modern business environment, enabling organisations to deliver authentic, personalised, cutting-edge experiences. By allowing themselves to be perpetually shaped by people and customers, businesses become more responsive, more innovative, more authentic, and more efficient through the liberation of experience and knowledge. Implementing perpetual experience enables businesses to benefit from disruption by learning and adapting more effectively to the rapidly changing ecosystem that is today's hyper connected global economy.

$$(CX + PX)^i = X^\infty$$

Customer experience plus people experience to the power of information = perpetual experience

The above equation forms the basis of the theory of perpetual experience. We take customer experience and include the dynamics of people experience. We then add the power of information, technology and searchable knowledge, and the outcome is an experience. However, the changes in customers' needs and expectations are infinite. Therefore, to sustain a quality experience a company's response must be perpetually evolving.

How do we get there?

In my view, it is becoming clear that customer experience is even more about people than it has been in the past. Sometimes we forget that employees are customers and customers are employees. At critical times, each party often has little understanding of the difficulties the other is facing. The default position can be to blame culture or values, when more often than not this isn't the case. This isn't intended as a criticism, but rather as an acknowledgement of circumstances and human behaviour.

Perpetual experience is something that helps the evolution of customer experience, not replaces it. What it may replace is customer experience management (CEM). My view is similar to that of putting the customer first, as CEM is often an over-statement. We cannot 'manage' someone's experience, we can at best influence it. Having said that, a lot of great work is done under the banner of CEM. Whether perpetual experience will replace CEM is for you to decide as it will largely depend on your own thoughts and professional environment.

So, the first task is to build up an in-depth understanding of customer needs to clearly establish the purpose of a product or service. The next is to contextualise how it is used and to develop the product or service accordingly. The final task is to personalise the product or service for the individual user. The company can then be confident of the customer experience and the actions that the experience drives. Whilst this may sound like a tall order we now know it is achievable, and anything else will inevitably lead to dissatisfaction and an inflated cost-to-serve model. Companies should - and could - have a clear view on all these issues before they decide to invest, but too often customer experiences are only seen as an outcome.

As I get deeper into the theories and practice of perpetual experience, you may find yourself questioning whether it is about the customer. Let me reassure you that it is, just as it is also about the reputation of the business, its sales, profit margins and balance sheet. It is often noted that customer-focused companies out-perform stock market indices quite substantially. Of course, it's not just customer experience that drives this performance, these companies are strong and efficient businesses on many levels. However, the customer focus and the company's performance are inseparable. Unfortunately, I've witnessed too many businesses concentrating on looking fit rather than on being fit for purpose.

The approach I take in this book is perhaps more pragmatic than many on the subject - I argue that we need to balance the needs of the business with those of the customer. We also need to acknowledge that customer relationships can be very different in the business to business (B2B) environment than in the business to consumer (B2C) environment.

Combinations of B2B and B2C markets that cover the whole delivery cycle emphasise the need for a practical approach to aligning efforts. Even within discrete markets, the experience can vary enormously due to differing technologies, culture and price orientation. Perhaps one of the most important things I've learnt, particularly in larger companies, is that for customer experience initiatives to be effective they have to be highly adaptable. If companies are to be sustainable, customer experience has to move from a reactive recovery position to a proactive, benefits-led approach, similar to that of smaller competitors and disruptors entering the marketplace. To achieve this, I believe customer experience needs to come to terms with the reality of why it is so difficult to deliver effectively, particularly for large organisations. If we think of customer experience as an outcome, it is a reflection of the company and its performance in satisfying all the relevant needs of its customers.

Why now?

An inspiration for my ambition to develop perpetual experience was the notion that the digital revolution, combined with the corresponding changes in how people go about managing their daily lives, could be used to improve businesses. One of the many conversations I had on this theme was a discussion with a senior manager in the insurance industry regarding a social media rant that escalated into a global industry debate. As we talked through the comments, it became apparent to both of us that the knowledge that had been shared meant that people working in the industry made up a large proportion of those involved in the debate. It made us question the basic premise that social media debates were purely representative of the customer voice.

I am convinced that the expertise that allows us to understand and change customer behaviours can also assist with improving our companies. Rather than changing the focus of customer experience, it seems clear that the way forward is to include employees and partners in discussions about experiences. Doing so will reveal, not only the root cause of poor experience, but also the creative solutions to fix the issues. This increased scope will drive efficiency and agility as businesses develop a clearer understanding of all the factors affecting the delivery of experiences.

Although I will be taking you through the thinking that led to perpetual experience, I would like to bring forward a few key points now.

The conversation will then move on to the advantages perpetual experience can bring to companies, wherever they are in their development of customer experience. The visuals I use throughout the book are intended to highlight how key aspects of customer experience change as it evolves. Each visual contains the same basic components - the central business function, products and services, customer service and customers. In reality there are of course many interlocking components, but it isn't uncommon to see companies described in this way on meeting room flipcharts, so I show them there here as an aid to our conversation. The two we are using at this stage represent customer service before the introduction of customer experience, and then perpetual experience in practice.

Figure 1 below depicts customer service as it has historically been deployed, with customers outside an impervious business boundary. Under such a model, customers' needs, views and opinions rarely affect decision makers deep within the company.

Figure 1: The service buffer

The main point of customer contact was with customer facing departments, often described as customer services or the customer interface. With a focus on resolving customer problems and handling complaints, it was frequently referred to as the service buffer and related to the cost of service. Over the years there have been three more main evolutions, and these are explained later on in chapter six.

You can't afford to wait

Today, even some of the best exponents of customer experience face challenges in adapting to fast changing multi-channel or omni-channel expectations. This is understandable as it is harder to reduce or re-direct an award-winning service centre than one that is failing and costly. However, it is good news for the many companies that are behind the curve as they have the opportunity to make quick advances without incurring as much cost along the way. The difficulty is identifying how and where to deploy efforts and resources, and to stop reinventing the wheel as customers' needs and expectations evolve. This is something we are now able to do.

What does perpetual experience look like?

I would like to give you a preview of how companies can evolve as perpetual experience is introduced. I'm not proposing that this can be achieved overnight - such rapid transformation is usually only accomplished by small start-ups and occasionally a substantial market disruptor. Atom bank, the fully digital, app-driven bank, is a good example of this, and I am proud that The QoE has been involved in assisting with their approach to customer experience. Even in these cases of successful disruptors, I have come to the conclusion that it is just as, if not more, difficult for them to scale up as it is for larger companies to mimic and then adopt the key elements of their success. But what am I proposing is a methodology that can accelerate the transformation that is required to cope with the increasing disruption.

The visual below shows perpetual experience in action. In the visual, the whole company has been reoriented and focused on experience. In such a model, there are no impervious boundaries - you will see people in sharing groups that are drawn from the business, its partners, customer services, customers and the wider society. Their contributions are driven by a range of motivations, extending from self-interest to a desire to help others with whom they now feel connected.

Large organisations need structure and certainly don't need the cost of re-designing. Perpetual experience avoids the need for restructuring by connecting people in innovative ways to empower the existing structure. Customer services still addresses customer problems but now feeds contextual solutions into self-serve and assisted channels enhanced by artificial intelligence (AI). It also acts as a diplomatic channel, sucking direct customer insight, as well as co-created solutions, into decision making functions. But customer services doesn't do this in isolation - it participates in cross company, partner, customer and wider experience communities. How these communities differ, we will discuss later. Customer experience now becomes perpetual experience, a value centre, rather than a cost to serve overhead.

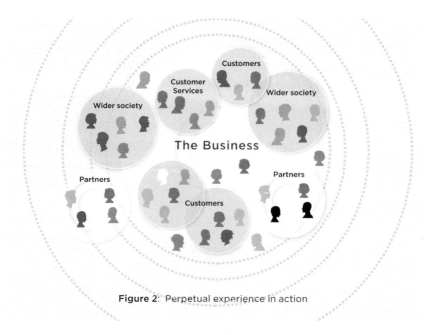

Figure 2: Perpetual experience in action

When looking at the day to day challenges facing large companies, it occurred to me that these communities have always existed. The connected society has only increased their scope and power and led us to a better understanding of how they work. My company, The QoE, has been doing this for many years, and we are now in a position where we know how to create and sustain both online and offline groups and communities. These can reduce and even eradicate the complications brought about by scale, and the silos and isolation that often result.

Why the change of focus?

Why are businesses changing their focus from customer experience to perpetual experience? They're realising that they need to be faster, more efficient, more innovative, and more agile - all while retaining the commitment of their customers, employees and stakeholders. They have the opportunity to take advantage of technological innovations and the subsequent changes in attitudes to sharing and co-creation. The challenge many businesses now need to overcome is how to release these attitudes and behaviours in their own people. If they are able to do this, they have a great opportunity, not only to improve the performance of their existing products, services and operations, but also to access the full potential of technologies, such as self and assisted service, that can deliver real-time benefits. Perpetual experience can be the stimulus that people and companies need.

Customer experience remains a business enigma that few have mastered and many are struggling to tame. Perpetual experience is a significant step forward and worthy of consideration for all directors and managers, and people like you, as we move into the future.

YOUR REFLECTIONS

What does CX mean to you?

What does your company want from CX?

What or who could help deliver CX?

Part 1

THE EVOLVING ENVIRONMENT

2

DISRUPTIVE INNOVATION

CHAPTER 2

Disruptive innovation

Mystery: Why do we value innovation but not disruption?

This and the next three chapters are focused on the major trends that are creating and shaping the environment, and the wider implications for experience. In this chapter, I look at disruptive innovation over the last decade and how it has driven substantial change.

The pace of change

As we know, the rate of technical innovation is classically referred to as Moore's Law. It was first stated by Gordon Moore, the co-founder of Intel and Fairchild Semiconductors, in 1965. It predicts that the number of transistors in computer chips doubles approximately every one to two years. This prediction has held for over 50 years. In 2015, Brian Krzanich, CEO of Intel, reported that the rate was slowing to two and half years, and over the next decade it is predicted to slow further, unless there is a radical change in chip technology. Even if the rate slowed to a doubling in every three years, it is still a very rapid rate of innovation.

Chips are now smaller, more powerful, and more energy efficient than ever before. But even as we begin to contemplate whether Moore's Law will continue to stand, we already know that developments such as quantum computing have the potential to increase processing power to unimaginably new heights. What we are interested in for the purposes of our conversation, however, is how these changes will affect our society and individual behaviours in ways that we are only beginning to understand and appreciate.

The technology is of course only one element of disruptive innovation. From a business perspective, innovation is often driven by new business start-ups that are able to combine their more intimate knowledge of customers with new technologies, and are less restricted by legacy systems, technologies, and indeed, thinking. This digital technology, combined with the power of social media, 'disrupts' established markets by offering better products or services that have greater functionality and more options for customisation. This fact alone means that many of the established market leaders are under threat, and in some cases already on a road to failure.

Uniquely perhaps, innovation is now being driven by customers and the wider society, rather than businesses. This shift in power has occurred partly due to the low cost of accessing both digital technologies and the marketplace, but also through the ability of individuals and groups to see and seize new opportunities in their world. For example, a group of students realised that an app to spread a restaurant bill across many credit cards would be very popular so they went ahead and built it. We can say with some degree of confidence that such innovative thinking will lead to the development of new products and services at an unprecedented rate. The pace of change is being further exacerbated by the ability of small companies to crowd fund their endeavours.

I also believe that large companies are able to innovate just as effectively and quickly as their smaller counterparts. It is only a matter of releasing the untapped creativity contained within their diverse and knowledgeable workforce.

Disruptive innovation

The term 'disruptive innovation' was first coined by Clayton M. Christensen in 1995. He found that disruptive innovations tended to be produced by outsiders using novel combinations of cheaper components for products and/or clever ideas for services. Christensen noted that established market leaders were rarely disruptors because any innovation would not be profitable at first, and to pursue a disruption would take resources away from innovations that were required to compete with current competitors. The back door was left open for the new start-ups.

The list of disruptive innovations is now endless. Self-service has become a reality for a wide variety of scenarios. The way we shop, buy holidays, and order many complex products and services has changed considerably in a relatively short space of time. One of the most prominent and disruptive innovations has been the ability for people to download music and film. This development may well be cheaper and more convenient for the customer, but it has decimated the value for artists, distributors and manufacturers in respect of CD and DVD sales. Interestingly, the physical experience of live performance is making a comeback, as is its economic viability. A great many industries, whether consumer, professional services or industrial, have now been disrupted by innovations that have permanently changed their market sector.

However, it is important to note that disruptive innovations are not individual, self-contained events. They are like pebbles dropping in water, each one creating more disruptive innovations that spread out in ripples. Each innovation creates another innovation and then another, and their spread is relatively rapid. Within just a few years, whole industries have been disrupted. We can look back from the point we have reached and say with some confidence that we have experienced, and still are experiencing, a revolution.

I want to spend a little time on one type of disruptive innovation that has changed customer experience almost beyond recognition over the last decade, and promises even more disruption in the next. Online communities have empowered individuals and groups, not only by virtue of scale but also through connected debate and consensus building. Their influence is growing and evolving at a phenomenal pace. It is only necessary to look at how news is gathered and reported to see how journalism has been fundamentally disrupted as everyone has now become a potential source of information, often with video footage.

This new world of knowledge and opinion has had a huge impact on our lives. The ability to use emails, download apps, access social networks, utilise GPS and maps, access digital entertainment, take, send and receive photographs, search for information and use e-commerce to make purchases - all from a single device - has put the world in our hands. Thanks to technology, information now effortlessly crosses social and professional boundaries.

The same can be said for the way in which information can now cross functional boundaries within organisations. I recently worked with a large multinational that, for the first time, has the ability to integrate its physical stores with the rest of the business. The stores are now digitally enabled and so connected to the systems and processes of the company, providing real-time data back into the organisation. The disruption this has caused has positive and negative repercussions for the management of the stores as their performance is now exposed in real-time. While this allows for more realistic and timely interventions by the group function, it also generates a more objectives-driven management style. Whether this is good or bad depends on your point of view.

Searchable knowledge

Specifically, I want to look at how the how the availability of knowledge - and how we access it - has changed. It is this transformation that I am suggesting is now at the heart of the challenges and the solutions that lie ahead. By the mid '90s, desktops and laptops at work were linked with home computers. The concept changed from 'corporate computing' to 'distributed computing'. By the new millennium, and for the very first time, technology was empowering individuals by allowing knowledge to be distributed, and more importantly, making it easily searchable.

Searchable knowledge has not only allowed people to increase the knowledge on a subject they already understand, or have an affinity with, it allows people to access knowledge on almost any subject. As they explore an issue and encounter something new, people can instantly search on that new subject. The effects then become exponential. It can be argued that this is not always a good thing as people confuse a little knowledge with expertise. It does, however, provide huge opportunities for companies that are able to make their expertise discoverable through searching.

As far back as 2005 when I was working at Lloyds they recognised the benefits of agents searching for knowledge, rather than retaining knowledge, as it would allow the circulation of new information to be real-time and advice up to date. At the time the technology wasn't sufficiently developed or scalable to achieve this. But it is of course today.

Lewis Ryden
Partner
Sybaris Chauffeurs

Lewis Ryden was Head of Call Management, Lloyds Banking Group from 2006 to 2008

Knowledge in the hands and minds of individuals leads to freedom to choose, freedom to learn, freedom to innovate and an increase in spontaneity, independence and self-reliance. At some point during this innovation, and it's difficult to identify exactly when, a shift of power occurred. Individuals became the source of information and knowledge as well as the recipients. The ability to retain power by controlling knowledge slipped quietly out of the back door of the business.

Along with freedom and self-empowerment, we started to see real evidence of the effects of reducing effort. However, this hasn't given us more free time as we may have expected and desired. In fact, the opposite has happened - available head space has become a scarcity as our attention is increasingly split between multiple information sources and distractions. The concept of head space came into the language of the business world relatively recently, but in effect reflects the challenges in the wider society. In essence, while connectivity gave us access to more information to tackle different situations, it simultaneously reduced the amount of effort we are prepared to spend in locating and verifying information.

Figure 3: Headspace doesn't change

And far from making our lives less busy, it can be said that technology, knowledge and information have extended the working day. Train journeys to and from home have been revolutionised by smart devices and many people now dedicate such time to reading emails and doing other work-related tasks. The subsequent increase in stress is something that companies are now taking very seriously and with good reason. We now hear the term 'flight mode' time, as we crave disconnection.

Inherent in these changes is a sense of confusion. It's early days - we see good and we see bad, we see things clearly one day and then it's opaque the next. This is the nature of change, heightened by the connectedness and information overload of the digital revolution.

An increasing percentage of our society has been disrupted by these innovations. We are now able to cross-reference information to verify who and what we trust, even though the ability to reinforce our original conclusion is not always a good thing. We get round this problem by seeking the opinion of 'people like us', people we in some way connect with on a personal level, even though we may not have met them in person. But the connection feels personal. It seems to have its basis in authenticity, to be derived from a shared passion or circumstance.

What fascinates me is that we are only in the very early stages of a shift from an industrial to a networked mind set. We are only just beginning to grasp the disruptive power of hyper connectivity for both large organisations and the wider society, and this disruption will only increase as technology becomes more deeply integrated into our everyday lives. Our reality is increasingly networked, and 'search' and 'share' are the two pillars upon which this reality is constructed.

This presents immense implications for what we expect from organisations, both as customers and employees. We are experiencing the merging of the digital and the physical before our very eyes, and with it the digital transformation of society. The networked era will disrupt almost every aspect of our lives as our understanding of the concept of organisation evolves in response to a hyper connected reality.

Tony Reeves[1]
UCA

---

[1] 'Work with me: the experience of Computer-Supported Cooperative Working in large organisations and implications for leadership.' 2016. The University of Lancaster.

Sometimes this can be random, but often is very effective, especially when we start to include the context provided by images or video.

Recently I searched YouTube to see if I could change a central heating pump. Seeing a man of my stature with a boiler identical to mine in a similarly small cupboard gave me the answer - call a plumber! Watching someone gave me the contextual knowledge I needed - reading a manual could not have fulfilled all the different criteria of that situation. When I faced another plumbing problem, I naturally went back to the videos to see if I could find any more advice. The man in the video has now made me part of his community, and when I have a need I will go back again. This kind of scenario will be played out many thousands, indeed millions of times a day in a whole range of social, and increasingly business related issues as people experience a need and then search for information and knowledge.

The power of search is now driving some of the world's most successful companies and threatening the very existence of others. It's no longer something we can ignore, in fact it's something I'll be proposing we can harness and use to our advantage.

The smart device

The smart device has revolutionised how people engage with the world and has taken search to a whole new level. We can now search wherever we are in real-time and be presented with information that reflects our location. Even more significantly, as I experience something I can share it instantly. For example, a lady uses a fashion app, checks for fitting using a 3D app, compares the price online with another app, checks the store location using a geolocation app so she can go and view the physical item, or just clicks to buy instantly if she trusts the fashion brand. All within minutes. Buy before lunchtime and her new dress could be delivered to her work location before 5 o'clock - in time for her night out. This highlights the need for companies to respond to the real-world, real-time experiences of customers.

Apps have fundamentally changed people's expectations of technology - we just expect an app to work very simply and intuitively. Apps have also introduced a plethora of new products and services that have the potential to disrupt whole industries, Hailo and Uber being just two examples. We see the effects of reduced effort and increased spontaneity in 1-click e-commerce. From a business perspective, apps have multiplied the points of contact, and changed both the point of purchase and the point of information. Billing is a good example. Smartphones have also opened the door to services driven by algorithms and artificial intelligence (AI) in everything from retail to banking.

For the smart device to have grown so quickly, it must be satisfying the needs of its users. Another good example is the mobile Facebook app that has made over a billion people more connected. Whether this connection is genuine or artificial is of course open to debate, but the truth is that the app is being used so it must satisfy a need. Who are we to judge the authenticity of that need?

We now see the phenomena of searchable knowledge and apps moving into the business environment, and although the dynamics are slightly different, the basic principles are still the same. A law practice in America recently discovered that LinkedIn had a more accurate employee directory than its own internal resource. Another insurance company, to its embarrassment, discovered that a similar online resource was the only way for it to establish how many people it actually employed globally.

There is another important aspect to the smart device that goes beyond just the ability to search, and that is the ability to share an opinion with a personal or professional network. For example, the lady buying her dress in the earlier example will 'like' the service she received from the fashion app and probably post a picture of the evening with her opinion of both the dress and the evening itself. Trusted social media sites, and in particular Facebook, have tremendous power and are as critical to the development of customer experience as the behaviour trends they set, more than anything else we have discussed. Similarly, the sharing of opinion is now a central feature of almost every online platform, whether used for social or business interactions. The opinion may be less personal but equally, if not more, powerful.

What does this mean for business?

It is clear that technology is already disrupting businesses from the inside out. For many employees the lure of intuitive technology, limitless information, finding quick opinions and guidance, is too much to resist. Of course we can, and should, defend data protection rights. But it appears that people are searching for an understanding of how things work in context, rather than simply searching for pure data or information.

Clearly businesses need to take notice and respond to these technical, social and behavioural innovations. In theory the smart device can, and may well, transform every market and industry - and in more ways than just at the point of access. There is no doubt that any disruption gives companies the opportunity to differentiate their products and service to either expand market share or increase margins, and ideally both. The question is how does the disruption itself help businesses achieve this? And what can they learn, and how?

In my view the disruption we have been discussing offers plenty of advantages, especially for people focused companies. Never before has so much information and opinion been so readily available to help companies identify customer needs, wants and desires. The same can be said for creativity, collaboration and innovation, where the combination of connectivity, reduced effort and rapid rewards has seen an explosion in enthusiasm to participate. Our conversation will now turn to the digital landscape, and we will explore in more detail how perpetual experience enables companies to both learn from and participate in positive disruption.

DISRUPTIVE INNOVATION

Key points

- Technology and connectivity have made disruption, and so the need for innovation, inevitable

- Searchable knowledge has empowered people and fundamentally changed how they behave and make decisions

- Information overload has reduced the effort people are prepared to invest when dealing with companies that don't provide intuitive access to the knowledge they require

- Harnessing disruption is the key to better experiences

In summary, perpetual experience will

- Act as an early warning system, enabling businesses to monitor the horizon

- Enable leaders to cut through the noise and find what people (customers and employees) actually need and want, then build effective strategies to deliver this

- Provide organisations with real-time information and the understanding that influences decision-making

- Move businesses into a position where they are driving, rather than responding to, innovation

YOUR REFLECTIONS

Who or what technology is disrupting your market, your business, your life?

For those of you who prefer to start with a clean sheet . . .

. . . to Mind Map

3 | THE DIGITAL LANDSCAPE

CHAPTER 3

The digital landscape

Mystery: If customers and companies want self and assisted service, why do people still pick up the phone?

This book and perpetual experience is fundamentally about people, and there is no denying that the digital landscape is changing people - even mimicking them. But before we explore how digital technologies are impacting people and businesses, let us begin by examining the digital landscape and how it may develop.

The unfolding landscape

Ever heard of a Technology Futurologist? Well, they do exist! I met Bruce Everest, Futurologist at Avaya and then later at Vodafone. He quickly illustrated how you can stimulate great ideas by articulating what will soon be possible, bringing to life the phrase 'you have to be able to see it before you can build it'. This visualisation or imagination is a key element of the digital transformation that we're currently living through, and this transformation is proving to be a challenge for many large organisations. Think tanks, management consultancies and technology companies have been mapping out likely developments, some of which are occurring now while others are still in the embryonic stage.

New tools

When deciding which new tools to adopt, the traditional view is that businesses need to determine those that will have the most impact on their business. But perhaps this view also needs to accommodate the impact that these tools will have on people. Business is about people, and customers are people, so shouldn't people be the primary focus, not the business? Following this logic, companies should be looking at what the technology will enable people to do differently, more accurately, faster or with less effort.

Let's consider a utility company's billing system from this perspective. Its primary role is to deliver an accurate and understandable bill to customers so they pay without the need to query the amount. The system also needs to reassure people working in the business that the bills are accurate. Lastly, the system needs to provide accurate and relevant information to answer any queries from customers or the business. The most important outcome is the provision of good experiences that generate trust in the system. As this utility billing example shows, although the people involved fall in two categories - customers and employees - their basic needs are the same. What can the technology do for me? Does it work? Can I use it easily? How much effort will it take? What is the experience like? And will it adapt in response to an evolving environment?

When considering the employee, the instinctive answer to the question 'what can the technology do' is often perceived as 'replace the person'. A significant factor contributing to this mind set is the use of short-term and over-simplified business cases that default to reducing headcount as the predominant financial outcome. Customer experience of course makes the case on behalf of the customer, but this is only part of the equation - it could be argued that employee experience has a more significant financial impact.

The direction therefore seems to be clear: the overall consideration should be what can the technology do for the people involved. The resulting quality of the experiences will determine the factual return on investment.

As employees and customers readily adopt the technology, the company reputation is enhanced, and loyalty and advocacy are a natural outcome.

I appreciate this may quite a different perspective from the normal approach, and this thinking will be developed as our conversation unfolds. At this stage I would like to consider a few of the technologies that are most likely to impact experience over the coming decade: artificial intelligence (AI), the internet of things (IoT) and virtual reality (VR). Each will have its own development path but they are likely to converge in the near future and potentially change the experience landscape considerably.

Artificial intelligence

AI is not new, and is already used in many products and services, such as Apple's Siri voice recognition or Google's increasingly reliable search results. IBM's Watson 'big blue' computer regularly beats the best human brains on complex strategy and games like Chess and Go, and Google has made a large investment to move AI forward with its DeepMind project.

AI often takes the form of specialist algorithms that are applied to masses of structured and unstructured data - or 'big' data. These algorithms are used for a multitude of commercial purposes, such as driverless cars and fraud detection in bank and stock trading. AI no longer just mimics humans, it does some things humans can't do, and AI-driven bots are designed to augment human behaviours. So AI is now in a position to influence new market opportunities and address some of the practical problems that the world faces. In essence it is producing completely new experiences.

Gartner, the technology research company, has calculated that the world's information will grow by 800% over the next five years. However, 80% of this information is in unstructured form - emails, text, images, voice, sounds and so on - all of which can be mined, sorted and analysed by AI. As Mr Kelly at Gartner says, "this data represents the most abundant, valuable and complex data in the world. And until now, we have not had the means to mine it."

One of the things we will be looking at in chapter ten is how the incubation hubs of perpetual experience can generate this valuable data, and how perpetual thinking can help us understand it.

Figure 4: Potential applications of artificial intelligence

The potential uses for AI are vast, as we can see from Figure 4 above. AI is likely to have a substantial impact in areas ranging from medicine to energy exploration, consumer behaviours to finance, military to social care. All technology revolutions are propelled not simply by discovery, but also by the needs of business and society. Millions of bright minds are, and will be, focused on using AI as it develops further. This phenomenon will not stop, nor should it. Yes, there are fears, concerns and perils with AI, but the benefits are huge. McKinsey has calculated the economic impact could be as much as $6.7 trillion by 2025. However, for most businesses the reality is that while they will gradually move in this direction they are currently falling short of reaping the full benefits that AI can yield.

How is AI impacting experiences?

From the customer perspective, one of the most compelling and widely used AI-enhanced virtual personal assistants (VPAs) is Apple's Siri. Android and other devices have similar applications and, as we know, these VPAs can send messages, schedule meetings, make phone calls, and track package deliveries for us. Others can file documents, answer queries, warn of bad traffic, plan holidays, find and book restaurants.

AI is something that will catch up with us all and become a standard business asset required, just to be able to operate alongside the competition. Big Data has been around for decades, but that is largely focused on ensuring data can be quickly consolidated in a central store. How to use that data effectively to produce automatic, insightful and intellectually correct assessments is where companies continue to struggle: the end result is not always tangible, the incoming data is not always dependable - especially in long standing firms with ageing systems.

On the one hand companies need to spend money on grabbing and cleansing data first but, on the other, senior leaders are still reluctant to spend money without clear financial return. Although the tide is turning on both counts.

In my area I now see innovation through data analytics being given a longer leash to roam, and the pressure to even produce accurate 'static' data on customer dashboards and reports is driving a data quality attitude behind the scenes.

Woe betide if a company changes their business approach on the back of inaccurate data.

Warwick Bailey
VP Head of Global Product Development
Carlson Wagonlit Travel

These VPAs have had mixed responses from consumers and businesses and limited impact, so it's worth taking a moment to think about why this is. One of the main causes has to be the lack of a real need. For example, an app that can give you an accurate reading of how many passengers are in the plane above you would be not be satisfying a need. But an app that tells you how many people are in each carriage of the approaching train when you are standing on the station platform is fulfilling a very real and personal need.

VPAs now have AI-driven speech interpretation and recognition interfaces, making it possible to control anything from search requests to controlling household appliances, using just our voice. With advances in AI, these VPAs will be capable of answering relatively complex questions almost instantly, as they are better able to understand what the user really wants based on their history of needs and preferences.

Google claims that only 8% of voice queries don't work, and within a relatively short time the error rate will be 1% at most - much better than the human error rate on the same query. In fact, Gartner now predicts that these smart machines will be 'the most disruptive in the history of IT'. This will drive substantial changes in how businesses approach satisfying queries from customers. Why not also queries from employees and partner communities?

Moving into a world where machines can out-perform people raises some interesting questions, not least what is the role of people in this technology-enabled future? Perhaps the blending of intelligent machines with human physical and mental dexterity is the way forward - as seen in industries such as car manufacturing. Where one ends and the other takes over is down to a combination of technical capability, cost and social acceptance. The social acceptance issue is an interesting one and currently being played out with driverless cars, a phenomenon to which people were initially resistant, but which seems set to revolutionise the motor industry as people gradually accept handing control of their vehicles over to AI.

If an AI-enabled call centre could handle customers' queries with 100% accuracy then it would out-perform the traditional call centre.

Or would it? Where would the knowledge and understanding of the interplay between the customer, product and service come from? Basic AI is now in place in many call centres, but the challenge is to interpret complicated or unique customer queries accurately. Predictions of the call centre vanishing are, at the very least, premature, and my view is that they are fundamentally wrong. But self and assisted service has many guises. From full VPAs, such as Apple's Siri, to voice chat, to Frequently Asked Questions (FAQs), and a multitude of others in between. For many companies and customers, self-service has huge potential for increased accuracy, reduced effort and cost. Too often companies view the objective as cost for the company and effort for the customers. In reality, accuracy - or, more importantly, effective query resolution - decreases cost and effort for everyone.

But what about the emotional content? This depends on the need - if a customer needs a resolution he or she will opt for self or assisted service. On the other hand, if they need to express disappointment, anger or frustration, then they are likely to choose a voice option.

VPAs can be considered the ultimate ambition for self-service, but there will always be - and always should be - a place for human interaction. Yes, we can use automation, and we should because both customers and businesses want the cost reduction and ease of self and assisted service. I have done a great deal of work on self and assisted service over the last few years and it is becoming clear that the reasons for poor adoption are the associated attitudes and behaviours of the people involved. This has very little to do with the individuals or group not wanting it to happen, but behaviour patterns perpetuate the dependence on voice channel. There is also an inability to extrapolate knowledge from the customer and service interactions. Valuable ideas and work-arounds for resolving persistent customer queries often remain within teams, but if these could be harnessed and shared effectively they could be used to drive a truly exceptional self and assisted service experience.

We have seen predictions of technology-led business revolutions for many years. Some become reality, others hit unexpected challenges, and some of the biggest challenges are often people (customer or employee) related. Understanding how these technological developments affect us as human beings, especially in areas such as decision-making, is vital to both the health and potential survival of large organisations. Once again I'm talking about people, not just customers. The field of psychology is making substantial breakthroughs in decision-making and it is something I see as crucial in today's business world. Decision-making at all levels is being affected by effort, knowledge and the effects of being isolated from the audience. Cultural trends and behaviours are in many cases pre-determining outcomes in ways we are only just beginning to understand. This is an area I will return to in chapter eight as, in many cases, the fallibility of discrete decisions is being amplified by automation.

As I mentioned earlier, Big Data drives AI. More specifically, rapidly scaled 'data crunching' or analytics drives AI. What we are seeing now is "just the tip of the iceberg" says, Josh Sutton, Global Head of AI Practice at Publicis. He goes on to say "I think about AI in terms of three categories: first, Big Data tools, second, machine-learning and third, causal AI, otherwise known as common-sense AI - platforms that can determine why things are happening." We are seeing ever-expanding data sets, and it is now crucial to think critically about how we collect and leverage data - especially unstructured data - to move into a more proactive position and make more informed decisions. We will witness the ability to use voice-activated machine learning to understand what is happening, and then use common sense to understand why things are happening. In the very near future, customer experience will not only be mobile, it will also be AI, voice and video enabled.

In my opinion, this technological revolution also presents another serious challenge for large organisations. In many cases, the disparity between the digital tools we use at home and those we use in the workplace is exacerbating disruption. Our personal technologies often require less effort to use than those in the office. Is this gap sustainable? And what does this mean for businesses?

The internet of things

I'm travelling to Los Angeles tomorrow and have a simple question: "what is the smog level likely to be?" Until recently, the answer was not easy to find. Now, however, the information is available and immediately accessible because there are smog sensors across the city that are connected to the internet. This is the internet of things (IoT), a network of interconnected, web-enabled devices and sensors embedded in cars, oil pipes, meters, buildings and infrastructure.

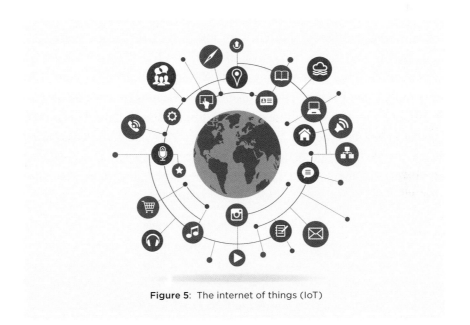

Figure 5: The internet of things (IoT)

Thanks to the IoT, I can turn on my heating at home remotely so that it reaches a comfortable temperature by the time I get back. But the IoT is much bigger than these simple tasks, and it holds huge promises, both for people and businesses. Gartner, the research company, says that by 2020 the IoT will comprise 26 billion devices, up from 900 million in 2009. When compared to the approximately 7.3 billion computers, smartphones and tablets that will be in existence by 2020, the growth of the IoT is mind-boggling. Peter Middleton at Gartner says that, "connectivity will become a standard feature . . . opening up the possibility of interconnecting just about everything, from the very simple to the very complex, to offer remote control, monitoring and sensing." In fact, Gartner believes that about 43% of large businesses have, by 2016, implemented the IoT in some way. It's here and is growing rapidly. The market is estimated at $300 billion.

I come back to the question of whether the IoT will be deployed to address real needs, both in business and from a customer perspective. As its implementation becomes easier, the battleground for business will be in identifying the most important - in other words the most satisfying - needs that have a real-world economic benefit. Tom Rebbeck, a digital economist at Analysys Mason says, "M2M* implies a closed system. The IoT is more about the sharing and opening up of data". He cites the 'smart city' as an example of the future where all the interconnected devices come together or can be accessed, and notes the growing interest in consumers connecting their mobile devices to the IoT. It is perhaps the exponential growth of new connections and associated products and services where the economic opportunities of the IoT will be realised.

The idea of smart cities, where all community services such as transport, schools and hospitals are connected, is both appealing to some and an abomination to others. The key elements contributing to their success or failure will be how they are accepted by society. This relates back to our previous conversation on identifying and satisfying actual needs - there will be a huge temptation for the technology to do clever things for the sake of doing clever things.

Virtual reality

Virtual reality (VR) is another area of technology that has made great promises but as yet has delivered very little. It's been around for a while, mainly in gaming, but its applications for business use are now developing quickly, and analysts are tipping 2016 to be the year of VR. The current

---

* machine to machine

drivers are the visual industries and big movies like Star Wars: The Force Awakens with their VR trailers. The digital media and broadcasting company Sky has been investing in a company called Jaunt to prepare for a world where news broadcasting is virtual. The important point here is that companies are beginning to use VR as a differentiator in their marketplace, and this trend will no doubt increase over the coming years.

Investment in VR is also reaching fever pitch, with potential applications emerging in space stations, nuclear power, medicine, education, military, aerospace. We're also not far away from being able to immerse ourselves in the real-time VR of shopping centres or taking the 90 day Cunard world cruise in our own home, and so on. The list is endless, limited only by the developing technologies and one's own imagination. However, once again we need to consider needs and the reality of when and where VR will actually deliver a good experience. To be satisfying, a cruise in your living room would really need sea air and movement! Developing the applications that people will be prepared to pay for beyond the novelty effect is where the smart money should be invested, and as choice increases, identifying real needs will become a key challenge.

Digital is changing people

We've now covered several predictions regarding the future of technology and their potential economic performance, and it is inevitable that they can't all be correct. A key benefit of perpetual experience is in helping businesses identify the real needs, as well as predict future needs, so they can respond effectively by designing appropriate experiences. It is also no longer realistic to think about technology, people, and society independently from each other, so we now need to examine the relationship between them.

The book 'Reinventing Organisations'[2] by Frederic Laloux traces the evolution of human consciousness and the parallel changes to organisational design. Through his research, Laloux observes that every time humanity moves to a higher level of consciousness there is a corresponding breakthrough in the ability to collaborate and organise.

Even more importantly, these breakthroughs have either been caused by, or accompanied by, a corresponding evolution in technology and working practices. There is no doubt in my mind that we are going through one such breakthrough as the levels of collaboration, creativity, empowerment and technological progress have never been so high.

Evolutionary breakthroughs in human collaboration

Organisation	Description	Key Breakthroughs	Current Examples
Wolf Pack (Red)	Constant exercise of power by chief to keep foot troops in line. Fear is the glue of the organisation. Highly reactive, short-term focus. Thrives in chaotic environments.	Division of labour Command authority	Mafia Street gangs Tribal militias
Army (Amber)	Highly formal roles within a hierarchical pyramid. Top-down command and control (what and how). Stability valued above all through rigorous processes. Future is repetition of the past.	Formal roles (stable and scalable hierarchies) Processes (long-term perspectives)	Catholic Church Military Most government organisations Public school systems
Machine (Orange)	Goal is to beat competition, achieve profit and growth. Innovation is the key to staying ahead. Management by objectives (command and control on what; freedom on the how)	Innovation Accountability Meritocracy	Multinational companies Charter schools
Family (Green)	Within the classic pyramid structure, focus on culture and empowerment to achieve extraordinary employee motivation.	Empowerment Egalitarian management Stakeholder model	Culture driven organisations (Ben & Jerry's, Southwest Airlines, ...)
Teal organisations*	?	?	?

*The central principle of Teal organisations is that they function as complex adaptive systems. They are adaptive in that the individual and collective behaviours mutate and self-organise corresponding to the change-initiating micro-event or collection of events

Figure 6: Evolutionary breakthroughs in human collaboration (adapted from Frederic Laloux, *Reinventing Organisations*.)

[2] Frederic Laloux: Reinventing organizations, a guide to creating organizations. Inspired by the next stage of human consciousness. 2014.

Laloux tracks human organisation from the earliest stages of humanity where people lived in small groups, through to larger tribes, and on into societies. Each shift brings new advances, such as the development of farming and the associated food security that this brings, followed by the evolution of complex mechanisms of law and accountability. As society becomes more complex, there are new issues to be addressed such as social inequality and materialism that drives a loss of community. But conversely, these evolutions raise our personal sensitivity and we become more conscious of others' feelings about us.

The last stage he describes is 'Evolutionary-Teal', and it is certainly the most important for the context we are discussing. One of the key developments in human consciousness at this stage is the ability for individuals to accept and validate multiple world views, rather than believing the current view to be the correct view. This is largely driven by an improved ability to separate ourselves from our ego, an ability that enables us to assess ourselves from a distance. According to Laloux, the impact of this on businesses is that, rather than individuals having to put on a professional 'mask' at work, organisations need to encourage people to bring their whole selves to work. People interacting in these organisations are likely to have, and desire, a more authentic experience as they are able to truly be themselves while at work. The benefit of such an approach to businesses are that it unleashes employees' creativity and innovation as they feel less restricted, and so are more likely to use the initiative that they would use in their personal lives.

One of the biggest challenges this presents is the reduced perception of control, leading to a corresponding increase in the need for trust. Arguably the most effective response to this challenge is the development of authentic working environments, and authenticity is a topic that we will explore in detail in chapter nine.

Joining the dots

AI, the IoT and VR are happening now and all three developments offer valuable benefits and opportunities. Not only are these technologies exciting in their own right but, when combined with other developments such as cloud computing, 'Big Data', 'smart cities', holography and robotics, the potential for generating new experiences is immense. But the important questions to consider when evaluating these new developments are - do the technologies satisfy a clear need? And is the real-world experience going to be good enough to change people's behaviour?

It can be hard to fully grasp this evolving landscape. It will be radical and hopefully useful and, while it will undoubtedly present new problems and challenges, these will be addressed by people, businesses and society. Hopefully you are now beginning to see that this book is about how people, companies and society participate, adapt to and profit from this new landscape.

One thing we can be sure of is that drawing meaningful insights from the combination of structured and unstructured data will be at the heart of what is to come. We're likely to acquire much more knowledge from our customers, but perhaps we need to extend our analysis to a wider audience in order to identify future needs. Certainly it seems that we can make much more use of the data that machines can obtain from human interaction, and this raises the issue of how we collect unstructured data from across our partners and internal functions, as well as what type of data we can share and why.

There are some elegant paradoxes ahead. Companies will have an increased number of touchpoints with customers, but be challenged to deliver consistent information and opinions. Customers will live in a perpetual environment that never stands still as they are surrounded by continuous change. And yet, at the same time they will be powerfully static as they increasingly use technologies such as voice-control to create new and powerful experiences from their lounge and share thoughts and opinions at the touch of a button. As the gap between personal and work technology narrows, organisations will have little choice but to empower and trust their workforce, and individual employees will need to be more responsible for the opinions they share.

For customers, disruptive innovation will lead to a world of perpetual experience. The question is, which companies will be joining them in this new environment? While the extent of disruption will vary from industry to industry, there is a fundamental truth in the saying that experience knows no boundaries. It is unlikely that this new world of perpetual experience can be leveraged by businesses whose mind set is even just a few years behind the curve.

THE DIGITAL LANDSCAPE

Key points

- Experience provides the context that data alone cannot provide

- Customers and employees want technology to provide increasingly effortless experience

- Enabling employees with intuitive and sharing technologies has the potential to generate new knowledge

- The customer interface/service buffer contains valuable knowledge that can be used to drive innovation and better self and assisted service

- Connectivity is changing how people think and behave

In summary, perpetual experience will

- Identify the advantages of digital for specific business and customer needs

- Make effective self and assisted service an achievable and sustainable reality

- Move a business into a mind set where it can disrupt its own thinking

- Enable organisations to move away from 'what has always been done' and towards 'what can be done'

- Provide companies with a mechanism to share knowledge more fluidly and effectively in order to deliver one version of the truth to the customer

YOUR REFLECTIONS

What would you pick from the digital revolution to help you improve CX?

How would you implement it?

For those of you who prefer to start with a clean sheet . . .

. . . to Mind Map

4 | MANY VOICES

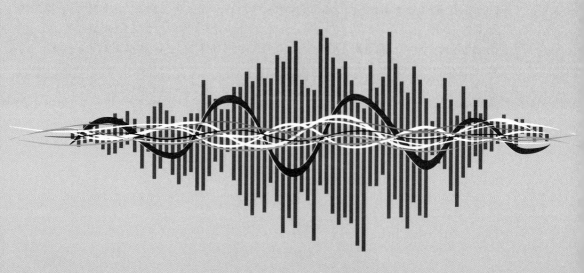

CHAPTER 4

Many voices

Mystery: *Why do so many voices say so little?*

Building a voice

The many voices of social media represent all the good and bad of humanity. In the early days, commentators and companies would be drawn to the extreme voices, or the voices of people with existing influence or perceived authority. What is now being recognised is that it is the middle ground that contains the vast majority of voices and opinions, and in this middle ground lies the greatest potential for creativity and innovation.

A great example of a person coming out of this middle ground to build a significant voice is the vlogger Zoella. Let me provide you with some context to this social media phenomenon. If you haven't heard of Zoella - real name Zoe Sugg - she is a young lady of 25 and a fashion and beauty icon to her followers. In 2009, at the age of 19, she posted her first video on YouTube. In January 2016, she had 10 million followers and her videos had more than 665 million views, putting her in the top 50 of YouTube's contributors.

How has she achieved this? Zoella's platform of choice has been the video sharing platform Youtube, which is available in over 76 languages in more than 87 countries. According to web analytics company Alexa, as of June 2015 YouTube was the third most visited website in the world and the top video website globally with 15 billion visitors per month. It's worth reiterating that YouTube is almost exclusively video only content. Video provides context and brings another dimension to 'people like me' that we will discuss later. Instead of her voice being just the written word, Zoella's voice is more powerful because people can see and hear what Zoella stands for. She appeals to the generation that now lives in a multi-screen world - a generation that will frequently be sitting in front of the television while playing a game or connecting with friends on their smart devices.

This is the background to Zoella. In addition to building a large following of mainly young women, she has also built a very sound social reputation. In 2003, The Telegraph considered her to be "one of Britain's most influential Tweeters" with over 4 million Twitter followers and over 7 million Instagram followers. A year later, she was named as the first 'digital ambassador' for Mind, the mental health charity, and in 2014 she published her first book with Penguin Books. It achieved the highest first week sales for a debut author and became the fastest selling book of the year. Why? That's what happens if you have a combined total of over 20 million followers across multiple social media platforms. No doubt you will know of Zoellas in your own areas of interest and their associated communities.

What does this mean for businesses?

Why am I telling you this? Well, Zoella is an example of how a voice builds in a truly 'social' community. Her voice has grown because it resonates with an increasing number of individuals. But more importantly, if we study what she is saying and what she represents, her popularity clearly identifies a need within her followers.

What do I mean by 'identifies a need'? Of course, Zoella has personality and likeability, and people perceive her to be 'one of us'. But what made people follow her is that they had a need that was being satisfied by her advice. A business in this market has undoubtedly looked at the advice she is offering and either associated themselves with it, or tried to replicate it. If they could, they would probably sell it, or at least try and derive a revenue stream from it.

There are three dimensions to Zoella's success: the individual voice, the followers and the content. Businesses can learn from all three. Her voice provides power through influence, which we will look at more closely in chapter eight. Her followers are a quantitative measure of the need that her content is addressing. The content itself is real-world, real-time knowledge, and the companies in the market do not currently have the contextual knowledge that she possesses, or she would not exist. This phenomenon is replicated in many industries. For example, there will be pockets of users that have a particular set of circumstances that generate a specific need. From a company perspective, this can be almost impossible to identify, but if the company could track the amount of people following a particular voice, this would clearly point to the source of the need.

This leads us to a point where we are not only able to better identify real-world needs, but also understand how to resolve them. Such a position can yield a goldmine of information that could be used in self and assisted service channels, but more often than not this information is lost.

The same dynamic of voice, followers and content can be used to identify the source of poor experiences within a company. To allow this to happen, companies need to accept that a voice will gain momentum around an important need. But, there is one very important difference in the Zoella effect when compared with 'traditional' business: Zoella is a real person with hopes and fears. She is transparent and talks of her depression just as openly as she talks about great days out with her boyfriend. Without doubt, her followers know that she is 'one of us and we trust her'. This authenticity is something that can be of great value to a business - authenticity builds followers and so influences power.

To help businesses, the lessons from Zoella's story need to be taken into the context of a company. In the past, companies would listen to the voice of the regulator, the industry, employees, society, or customer pressure groups. But many of these voices are now being drowned out by the new and powerful voices of the connected world. These are not voices of facts and figures, they are voices of diverse opinions, shared beliefs, real honesty, real trust, real authenticity, real passions and real dreams. Of course, the many voices emanating from social media can be irreverent and provocative, just as much as they can be challenging and creative. But these two perspectives are clearly linked: if we have heard anything from companies over the last twelve months, it has been how do we instil creativity and innovation. Including many and varied voices in order to identify needs and develop new experiences is undoubtedly part of the answer.

It is worth reiterating that it is the 'dynamics' of social communities that are important to businesses. The scale or the platform are not the issue. What is important is how people can identify and create the content that will satisfy needs. In the real world, the needs of the individual will always evolve, and communities will always develop around these needs. In essence, this generates a state of perpetual thinking.

The benefits of perpetual thinking

Psychology and marketing literature are awash with various models that can be used to understand the processes people go through to reach individual outcomes from collective knowledge sharing. For the purposes of this book, I'm going to introduce my thoughts on how this happens.

Perhaps I ought to explain myself a little more. The dynamics we're about to discuss exist in the smallest group, and are magnified as the group grows into what we would commonly describe as a community. These dynamics apply equally to online and offline groups and communities. To avoid confusion, I'll use 'group' for anything up to twenty-five people meeting face to face, and 'community' when talking about a potentially infinite number of people brought together in the connected world.

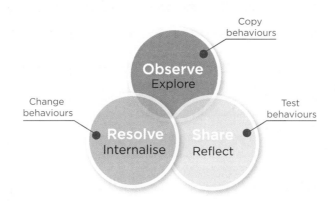

Figure 7: Changing behaviour through deliberately constructed debate

This model (illustrated above) is my representation of how people engaged in deliberate debate internalise new knowledge and choose to modify their behaviour. It has been developed through my observations of The QoE Group and individual participants' observations of under-performing meetings in their own business environment. Let's take a moment to consider external communities from a buying and feedback perspective. From the buyer's point of view, the online community that surrounds a product or service has everything the buyer needs. He or she can explore their options, observe others' reactions, and share their own thoughts. Others will comment, either endorsing or challenging the buyer's opinion, which enables the buyer to reach a decision, internalise it, take action and buy. When the buyer receives the product or service he or she can choose to re-engage with the community to complain, praise or resolve an issue. Whatever they do influences others in the community, and the community is a mechanism to observe, share and resolve. The next person will have a different view on the product or service: the process is therefore perpetual.

In a real-world situation, it's important to recognise that people move around this model in iterative circles. They may observe a possible solution, explore it, but on reflection find that it doesn't resolve their issue. Unsuccessful solutions are just as likely to be shared and are often just as valuable as successful ones, adding more to the process. For example, people may identify a need but this need may change or develop as they continue to search and evaluate their progress.

If we move this model inside a business, we simply replace the buyer with an employee. The product is replaced by an issue or task that needs to be resolved. The community is made up of people across the business, partners, and customers, and the same dynamics of observe, share, resolve apply. Most importantly, the individuals 'buy' into the resolution. When the resolution is implemented they can choose to return to the group to share their opinion and possibly improve on the proposition. The process is perpetual.

During this exercise, we have established a working model for innovation and ownership, two of the most sought after ambitions for businesses. But the very fact that many companies find this difficult is a clear indication of how out of touch they are with what is happening in the real world.

Tim Kitchener's and KCOM's example seen opposite shows that without a genuine need, participants will soon fade away through disinterest. Although a short-term community was established, it did not initially lead to perpetual thinking. But once a clear need was established, the opportunity for perpetual thinking presented itself.

This example also brings us to a point where we are discussing internal groups that have the same dynamics as social communities, rather than communities as they are perceived in the world outside the business.

In 2008 Yammer was a stealth deployment by KCOM's IT department as a 'cool tool'. For several years it lay dormant. Only 27 people signed up, with zero activity. I suspect those that did sign up did so because of 'shiny new toy syndrome'. The problem was, once people signed up to 'it', they expected 'it' to do something. They prodded it but it didn't move, so they got bored and left it alone.

It needed a reason for being.

In 2012 that reason arose. Improved collaboration technology led to KCOM closing some of its smaller offices and embracing home working. With hundreds of home workers and the rest of KCOM's 2,000 people spread across eight locations, sharing knowledge and generating new ideas through face to face interaction was simply not possible. It took just one person to collaborate with another using Yammer for the benefits to become apparent. Then, like the guy on the hill at the Sasquatch music festival in 2009 (YouTube it), one became two, two became three, three became half a dozen, and finally a hill full of people. In one month alone, 539 users registered.

But until 2015, KCOM's Yammer users remained concentrated among distributed communities, those that had previously worked in the same location. Most employees at KCOM's largest offices who still had daily face to face contact with colleagues, were invisible on Yammer and oblivious to its existence. What transformed the platform into a business-wide collaboration tool was KCOM's integration of it within the home page of its intranet and its decision to make information about a topic of wide interest - an impending re-brand - available only on Yammer. The result was a platform that hundreds more employees joined and are now still using, setting up their own groups of interest, sharing information and asking questions - simply because it's both more usable and more useful to them.

Kay Stevenson	Tim Kitchener
Head of Communications	Director
KCOM	Purple Panda

Tim was Customer Experience Manager at KCOM from January 2011 until December 2014

The difference is only one of scale: an internal group requires fewer participants to generate the same quality of outcome.

The power of many voices

Having explored the ways in which the power of many voices can provide a valuable source of new ideas, let me summarise the key advantages that this rich source of data presents for businesses.

Influence

We understand the power of influence, but in the digital world it seems that it is easier to quantify, using measurements such as numbers of followers, or numbers of likes. However, digital also makes it possible for this influence to extend beyond traditional boundaries. The implication for cross-functional, departmental or company boundaries is clear to see, as is the challenge to leadership, where we can now see that influence is different from designated authority. We can also see how influence builds around expertise and knowledge and then fades when the conversation moves to a different topic. Influence can therefore be understood as emergent rather than static.

Content

Companies are not short of issues that need to be addressed on behalf of the customer or the running of the company. What is difficult is getting to the issues that are sometimes hidden from them, and then to quantify which are the most important. The dynamics involved in building influence are a good indicator as to what these issues are, and the priority in which they need to be addressed. If you have many voices engaged in a free and open discussion, the real-world needs and experiences will emerge as the conversation unfolds. These real-world issues and resolutions have been validated by many voices, and they constitute the content that can elevate self and assisted service to new levels.

Innovation

Innovation and creativity are inevitable when there are many voices, and resolving issues is a natural consequence if you have the right mix of participants. This brings us to the importance of getting the right mix of people into our internal groups. The search for participants needs to cross the inevitable silos and company boundaries, and importantly, the participants need to have a genuine need to participate.

Perpetual thinking

When many voices are focused on real-world issues, they generate a different mind set. If someone is bringing in customer insight, or Big Data, or customer satisfaction scores, or any tangible proposition, exposing this data to many voices helps to separate the real-world issues from the noise. There is inevitably a mix of logical and emotionally intelligent analysis that goes a long way to delivering more rounded, and perhaps more people-oriented, decision-making. Inviting comment and debate on real-world issues generates an endless, perpetual creativity. This creativity extends into decisions involving Big Data and a plethora of other inputs.

We can now see that the power of many voices has many dimensions to it. Increased influence, the ability to identify and quantify real-world needs, and the potential to arrive at innovative solutions. Perhaps the biggest mystery is why this doesn't happen consistently within companies, a question that will be explored further in chapters seven and eight on influence and authenticity.

MANY VOICES

Key points

- Digital has unleashed the power of individuals and collaborative thinking

- The connected society is putting more power into the hands of individuals

- People are more likely to trust the opinions of their communities than they are the knowledge provided by the organisation

- The dynamics of 'observe, share, resolve' are increasingly shaping the behaviour of both customers and employees

In summary, perpetual experience will

- Harness the power of many voices to drive effective and collaborative innovation

- Contextualise the output from sources such as voice of the customer and AI through collaborative observation and resolution-building

- Prioritise and ratify information through the many voices of the real world

- Extrapolate contextual information and understanding to improve self and assisted service

- Make it possible for businesses to access previously untapped reserves of creativity in the workforce, and use these to drive innovation

YOUR REFLECTIONS

Who has the loudest voice in your market? Customers or the business environment?
Who has the information or knowledge you would most like to hear?

For those of you who prefer to start with a clean sheet . . .

. . . to Mind Map

5

I'M AN INDIVIDUAL

CHAPTER 5

I'm an individual

Mystery: *If companies fully appreciate that people are individuals, why do people rarely feel treated as such by companies?*

So far in the book I've looked at three major trends: technology, innovation and its effect on people. This chapter focuses on a fourth trend that promises to be the most important - the inevitable move towards individuality and personalisation.

It may be an inconvenient truth, but customers are real people. You might have experienced, as I have, the word 'customer' being treated as if describing an abstract concept. What do I mean by this? At its worst, the term 'customer' doesn't even reflect an individual or group of customers - it becomes something similar to a component of a machine, like a nut or a bolt, something logical and predictable, when of course it is anything but. At its best, 'customers' is a phrase that is intimately entwined with the needs and emotions of people.

The difference between the abstract 'customer' and customers often typifies the battle between parts of the business that consider themselves to be purely logical, and others where they are - you could argue - overly emotional. This friction between a healthy mix of logic, emotion or tangibles and intangibles, is in many cases the fault line between the two. The truth is that companies need a healthy mix of logic, emotion and intelligence in order to respond to situations effectively.

Once again, the digital revolution is coming to our rescue. Everything we have explored so far indicates that the connected world has empowered the individual. We no longer have customers, we have individuals. Think about it. All the digital trends are pointing to this as technology and searchable knowledge puts perceived power in the hands of the individual.

The trend towards 'individuals' not 'customers' rides on the back of the others and promises a wholly new way of going about business. I think it will be the most powerful disruptive trend we will experience.

The effects of personalisation and customisation

In its Predictions 2015 report, the independent technology and market research company, Forrester, highlighted that companies could historically differentiate themselves by factors such as price, product or supply chain. But now everyone has reached the same point. Today, the battleground is experience.

Not only is experience a feel-good factor for customers and a competitive edge for companies, it also leads to increased profitability and consistency of earnings. Experience and other anecdotal evidence is pointing to the fact that companies on the Dow Jones Index with the highest customer experience reputation are out-performing the index.

Gartner, the digital consultancy group, found in a recent survey that, unprompted, Amazon and Apple were top for customer experience in 30 countries. Amazon for its breadth and depth of the marketplace, its ease of use and payment and its search facility, and Apple for its brand image, products and innovation. In a way, I think this undersells their achievements. Both have reached a level of personalisation, both are subtly different and powerful.

Let's analyse the Amazon model for a moment. They offer a vast product range that seems to provide something for every need and budget, an intuitively searchable inventory and phenomenal delivery service. Up to this point it's an online shop on steroids and the customer can make his or her personal choice. The next level of innovation comes when they offer suggestions based on customers' searches, views and purchases. The customer is, in effect, personalising the inventory. They can take their time to reflect on their options and seek the opinions of others, and are even offered comparable alternatives. What strikes me, is that Amazon have built in all the attributes of a community without bringing people together - an impressive achievement.

Now let's consider Apple, who I believe have taken customisation to a whole new level and given us an approach that will transform more than just customer experience. Their designs are appealing, the branding is strong and the quality is good. But where they excel, and in my opinion are currently leading the market, is in the intuitiveness of their products and services and the ability to personalise. While others are now beginning to close the gap in both these areas, Apple has arguably set the standards.

Usability is a whole subject in its own right and not one that I intend, or am indeed qualified, to explore in sufficient depth. I do however appreciate its effects. Improved usability has led to a reduction in effort and associated stress, and has turned complicated tasks into pleasurable chores, even into games. Again, for me, Apple's introduction of apps to the world is a truly disruptive innovation. They turned what used to be a device for contacting people into an indispensable life-changing tool and, not only that, they have allowed me to personalise it to accommodate my own personal and professional circumstances. The smartphone is part of my life, and not just my work or home life, my whole life. But I am still an individual.

Of course, Apple and Amazon are amongst the beacons of the digital age that are offering multiple products to multiple customers. Can all companies take their offering to the same level? No, and they shouldn't try to, but there are valuable lessons to be learned. Offering choice facilitates personalisation, and when linked to intuitiveness the experiences become self-fulfilling - a state of perpetually good experiences.

Personalisation in the B2B environment

Let's flip to the B2B market. The same dynamics exist, but now different people are involved - the end users of the product or service, the project managers responsible for deployment, strategists, purchasing and quality control. And finally the decision-makers or customers that represent the needs of the end users.

In the B2B environment individuality and personalisation now assume a different look. In a B2B scenario a company will have many layers of people involved in finding, selecting and purchasing products and services. Companies wishing to sell to them build their own layered response. Let me explain what I mean by this, using a personal example. If you've read the notes on the author section of this book, you will already be familiar with my experience of the construction of the Channel Tunnel. Of course my role wasn't a significant factor, but re-telling and discussing the story retrospectively has helped shape my thoughts and conclusions. Observe, share, resolve in action I guess.

In my days as a sales engineer I was sent to the Channel Tunnel construction site to assist with discussions on a particular product. The meeting took months of patient work with the reciprocal customer/buyer layers to arrange. I arrived and found myself in an engineer's playground - massive machines, colossal construction and a huge hole in the ground that was getting bigger by the second. Other site engineers could sense my enthusiasm and soon I was invited into the tunnel where I was taken right down to the cutting machine itself. This is not what the other layers expected, and there was potential for them to be rather unhappy with this arrangement. But the site engineer had an ongoing problem, I had a head full of potential solutions. Moreover, the problems were real-world, real-time. The problem with the cutting tool was literally lying my feet, I had the solution in my bag.

What followed was three hours of fun for everyone, a business case was jointly written and approved, project managers given the go-ahead, the purchase department found the relevant specifications and business heads agreed terms over lunch.

The system worked brilliantly, and everyone in the layers played their part. Eventually the problem and the solution met in a personally collaborative environment. But - and you may already have guessed - the knowledge and information sharing up to the key interaction was appalling and very costly. As myself and others in my position progressed through the business, it was something we tried hard but ultimately failed to address as this was before even the earliest acknowledgement of customer experience.

Generally speaking, a layered response can be very effective. So, successful large B2B organisations do as much personalisation as consumer companies, but the personalisation takes a very different form.

From reactive to proactive

For another view on personalisation, let's return to a consumer model. KLM, acclaimed as a leader in customer experience, have built a reputation on small but very meaningful activities. A spoof story reached the press that they had a Beagle sniffer dog, Sherlock, who accompanied cabin crew when they were tidying aircraft after passengers had disembarked. The story described how Sherlock sniffed any items left on board - your scarf, your coat, or even your daughter's teddy bear - and once he was attached to his harness, he followed the scent through immigration to locate the passenger and return the item. It was, however, just a publicity stunt, which makes it easier for me to use the story as a strawman to help me construct several key points.

In the story, KLM are saying that you, the customer, are very important to us and we will take the initiative to do the little things that matter. As we know, customer experience is awash with such stories, and they're good examples of a personal response to a personal need. My intention isn't to criticise this approach but to highlight its reactive nature.

You can easily imagine how the KLM scenario would play out many times in the child's and parents' lives. We don't even think about the emotional value of this story, it's intuitive. On the face of it, it's a great story for KLM. But, as we said earlier, only from an emotional perspective. Let's explore this further. In reality a group of people would have had to come together at some point, brainstormed ideas, come up with Sherlock and put the idea into action. And it wouldn't have simply been an off-the-cuff action plan. The idea would have had to be signed off, a budget agreed, airport security regulations met, Sherlock found and trained, cabin staff trained, pilot schemes organised, and so on. So from KLM's perspective it would have been perceived as a big commitment to do the right thing. In fact, in the hearts and minds of everyone in KLM it would have represented their passion for great customer experience.

But my question is, why did the thinking stop at Sherlock? Why was the thinking only emotional? What happened to the logical argument? The commitment to a very expensive service recovery process was unlikely to achieve a good return on investment. The next stage would be for the group discussing the problem to find ways to prevent the teddy leaving the plane without its owner. Let's say we could introduce a simple and amusing sticker for child and teddy that beeps if one leaves without the other. Even better the child's sticker vibrates at more than a metre's separation. The teddy will never be lost. The sticker costs very little so everyone gains. The only problem is that KLM wouldn't have achieved the highly emotional recovery that made such a good story, one that would also have cost a considerable amount of money.

The dilemma is, which is more authentic? The recovery or the prevention? The expenditure on enhanced reputation or the reduction of cost for the same practical outcome? Who decides? How do companies hope to reach a balance between cost and quality of experience? It's this that concerns me. Are we looking for gestures or for consistency? Now that companies are open to increasing scrutiny afforded by the connected society, it would seem that consistency is becoming more important. For example, imagine the headline or Twitter rant: "they can find a child's teddy but ignored my new laptop as it didn't smell like me". How would this be perceived?

Companies who excel have a way of finding and delivering a consistent level of experience across different products and services and a multitude of customer interactions. As a result, they are both intrinsically authentic and perceived as authentic by their customers and the wider society. They seem to operate using a form of collective consciousness, and I believe this must originate from more than just the frontline employees.

The above scenario highlights the importance of authenticity in the debate between the emotional and logical approach to customer issues. Authenticity is a key aspect of perpetual experience, and we will explore it in depth in chapter nine.

Why be proactive?

From an economic perspective, being reactive is correctly associated with service recovery costs, with loyalty and advocacy as rewards. Being proactive, on the other hand, is more commonly associated with sales and consistent service delivery. The majority of companies currently need to deploy both strategies but would like to move towards the proactive because of the associated economic advantages. The example from Derek Allison overleaf articulates this well, drawing on his experience at Sony.

This is where perpetual experience can help by enabling companies to balance being reactive with proactive, and logic with emotion. As we have discussed in earlier chapters, one of the key elements in this balancing act is the inclusion of a range of individual opinions and voices in order to develop a consistent long-term proactive approach. The underlying theme is the need to influence the behaviours of individuals, even if this is for collective gain. What people say they will do and what they actually do can be very different and, even in this world of community and opinion, what really counts is actions.

At Sony Europe we worked with our Sony Centres to enable them to go beyond the traditional reactive minimal service levels. Opening up a customer centric approach soon started to challenge some of the preconceptions of what could be achieved. As goodwill became valued, we introduced a new proposition where carrying out Sony repairs on the spot became the norm. And the inevitable happened, grateful customers responded by purchasing other instore products.

In one example a customer brought a Dell computer into one of the stores. The member of staff advised that the service was for Sony laptops but helped the customer and resolved their problem free of charge there and then. The customer was so happy with the service that the following week they returned to the store to buy a Sony Vaio laptop computer.

The key factor was the natural willingness of the staff to help. It was authentic with no overtones of a purchase in return.

Derek Allison
Head of Customer Excellence
L-3 Communications

Derek Allison was Head of Customer Centricity at Sony Europe Ltd
from September 2009 to June 2014

With perpetual experience, what we now have is an ability to better understand the gap between what people say they will do and what they actually do. For example, a customer can leave a call to a company saying, 'I'm happy with this resolution', but we now have access to data that can either confirm or contest this. The implications are that either the customer gave up on a resolution, or another issue arose. Once again the data is available to identify the reason for their next interaction.

This takes us to a point where we can appreciate the power of many voices in designing and delivering experiences. These individual voices influence behaviours to provide, not only a competitive edge for products and services but also significant image and reputational gains. Something that is becoming increasingly important for both the consumer market and for regulated industries. In the latter, consumers are often replaced by interactions between large organisations and the general public, who may not have requested or see any value in the contact. National Grid is a great example of this, as Richard Court explains overleaf.

This leads us to the inevitable conclusion that whatever the business model and the people interactions are, we are still more able to influence decisions and behaviours by treating people as individuals. In doing so, the motivations become more personal and effective in driving lasting behaviour change.

We can only get to perpetual experience if we treat people as individuals.

Galvanising the organisation around delivering positive experiences to our customers and our employees has become increasingly vital to National Grid's success. This can be challenging in a regulated environment where your customers cannot choose you, you cannot choose them and some of your services (such as replacing gas mains) are, by their nature, disruptive.

The need to ensure alignment on the desired experience, as well as making sure we create the right environment for our people and partners to deliver, is key. This involves confirming that we are measuring the right things and getting to the root cause of what drives a good experience, rather than leaping to a quick fix.

We have seen the power of making customer service more personal by asking questions such as, "how would it feel to you?" and "what is stopping me from providing the experience I would like to deliver?".

We also involved our teams and partners in changing our connections process to move from an experience where the customer had 22 touchpoints and complicated information, to just 6 and a single point of contact.

This has defined a much better process where we can monitor key health metrics. But ultimately success still relies on the people delivering within the new process.

Richard Court
Head of UK RIIO Delivery
National Grid

I'M AN INDIVIDUAL

Key points

- We are moving from 'customers' and 'employees' to 'individuals'

- The connected society has increased both the influence and the importance of the individual, and the individual now has more power to challenge authority

- People expect increasingly personalised and emotional interactions with a company

- The engagement model has changed: people are now used to 'opting-in' to a group, service, or organisation, and this dynamic becomes more pronounced within companies

- For businesses, engaging with people as individuals is easy to say but hard to do

In summary, perpetual experience will

- Help an organisation develop the knowledge to speak with one voice

- Enable a business to genuinely engage with people as individuals by recognising their needs and valuing their experiences

- Make it possible for businesses to balance logic with emotion in decision-making

- Bring together effective combinations of individuals in collaborative groups to stimulate innovation

- Provide the route to increasingly intuitive and pleasing interactions with individuals

YOUR REFLECTIONS

Can you picture an individual customer, what their characteristics are, what they need?

Can you picture individuals in your company? What does the company need?

For those of you who prefer to start with a clean sheet . . .

. . . to Mind Map

Part 2

REALISING THE REWARDS

6 | MOVING FORWARD

CHAPTER 6

Moving forward

Mystery: *Why is customer experience constantly having to prove its worth,* *when we know it is the right approach to sustainable and profitable business?*

I am firmly of the view that customer experience can reach a level that I have called perpetual experience. In Part 2 of this book I'm going to examine how perpetual experience provides an effective response to the disruption described in Part 1.

Perpetual experience is a state of continuing, never-ceasing and self-enhancing experience where people are both fully conscious of, and valued for, their individuality. They participate because they feel that they can contribute, and are themselves valued. They share knowledge and experience in anticipation that other people will do the same, and for the same reasons. But we need to arrive at a point where the company doesn't create boundaries between customers and its people, but where both are part of a porous community. A point at which the company is a place where ideas flow freely and a range of emotions and opinions are expressed to enable creativity to prosper. This is also a company where I - and probably you - would like to work, as it is both personally engaging and rewarding. It cares about us, values our opinions and allows us to express our creativity.

In Part 1, I purposely looked at the disruptions that are taking place in businesses and society, and how they are driving fundamental changes in both people's behaviour and the business environment. Now we're going to look at how customer experience is developing in response to these disruptions. To achieve this, we need to quickly remind ourselves of how customer experience has evolved over the last fifteen years. This makes it possible to see how we can build on what we have, without damaging the foundations, and understand how perpetual experience can help companies at any point in their evolution.

Figure 8: The service buffer

The first stage of customer experience is what I have termed the 'service buffer', as depicted in Figure 8 above. This is a stage where the boundary between company and customers is impermeable and decision-making occurs in a management silo, surrounded by products and product knowledge. The emotional content is seen as 'in-the-moment' with no real concept of elongating the emotional attachment to enhance loyalty.

This stage is typified by the view that 'this is what we sell, take it or leave it'. The customer is on the outside of the company, and the only way they can contribute to decisions about products or management is through customer services. The company sets up a buffer between itself and its customers, and tasks the customer services function to handle complaints or queries such as, "my product doesn't work", "my bill is wrong", "how do I get spare parts?" "Why do I have to wait four weeks for delivery?" And so on.

The 'service buffer' approach drives the lowest cost-to-serve attitude, as the buffer isn't perceived as contributing to direct sales or more long-term revenue growth, such as loyalty. At best, the service buffer is dependent on investing in the right number of fully trained customer service staff. It is sufficiently flexible to meet seasonal trends and other ups and downs of business, but if the company so desires it can outsource the function to a lower cost country.

Under such a model there is little flow of information around the company about customer needs and product development. The key metrics are complaints, call waiting and handling times. You will not be surprised to hear that the service buffer mentality persists in many functions that are removed from customer interaction. But very few customer-facing functions retain this view of customer experience, and the people running the service centres often have very different outlooks and ambitions. The ability to change this mentality is one of the key benefits of perpetual experience.

The next stage is what I call 'service empowered by customer experience'. It has many of the features of the service buffer approach, and you will see in Figure 9 overleaf that the boundary between customers and the company remains relatively impermeable. Decision-making still occurs in silos around products and functions. Customers are still seen as being outside the company wall and customer services remain the main focus of interaction with customers. Query resolution and complaints still dominate the workflow.

But there are positive additions. Customers are segmented by products purchased and spend, leading to a greater understanding of customer needs and an improved ability to deliver a service recovery response that

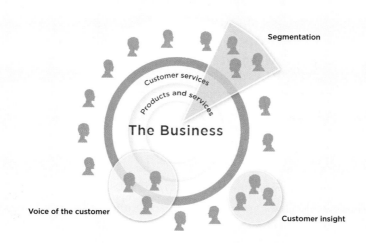

Figure 9: Service empowered by customer experience

meets customer expectations. Moreover, voice of the customer (as an extended market research concept, not as a customer experience trend) is introduced. In essence, the voice of the customer starts to reveal more detail about customer needs, wants, expectations, preferences and aversions, and can produce both qualitative and quantitative data. Generally, voice of the customer is implemented at the beginning or early stages of product development. We also start to see the introduction of customer insight as a service that may sit within or outside the company, although its impact is variable. This variability arises from a combination of the quality of the insight and the extent to which the company is prepared to listen, let alone understand or accept, the implications for the business.

The company now starts to take social media seriously. Customers' opinions and reactions penetrate further into the company, as you can see in the visual. The company has made itself much more aware of its customers' expectations and experiences. As a result, the financial imperative is often focused on customer satisfaction scores linked to reputation and, increasingly, regulatory commitments.

Figure 10: Independent customer experience

'Service empowered by customer experience' may well be an appropriate response for a company, depending on its products, services or market position. Overall, the flow of information is better - the company is much more aware of its customers and the effect of emotion on customer retention and future business. But the customer/company boundary and product management silos persist.

We now move on to what I call 'independent customer experience' shown in Figure 10 above. This is typified by increased segmentation, more refined methods of voice of the customer, and customer forums leading to the early stages of basic personalisation. The company also makes much greater use of customers' views and opinions from social media and these begin to have more impact on decision-making in the management silo. As we discussed earlier, the word management can over-state a company's effect on experience - I believe it is better to consider the ability to influence experiences, and therefore behaviours.

Most importantly, customers are beginning to be seen as individuals with individual needs. This is uncomfortable for the company due to the expectation in effort and cost, but nonetheless the idea is germinating.

The financial focus has shifted onto loyalty and advocacy, with an underlying theme of cost-saving, usually connected with omni-channel or multi-channel. Some companies start to look at selling through service models and linked advocacy programmes. In effect, the emotional and logical perspectives are starting to complement each other.

People experience

The next evolution of customer experience is often referred to as 'people experience'. This builds on 'independent customer experience' by introducing a very important resource, namely the employees of the company, in particular all the employees who are at the front line dealing with customers. It also includes, designers of products and services, staff in partner companies, and managers. Their precise function and seniority matters little, if they have contact with customers in a meaningful way then they are part of the customer experience team, and this includes the most senior managers and board directors. The company begins to act as a whole, as the visual below indicates. This is where you find some of the best UK companies with regard to customer experience, LV= General Insurance and First Direct bank being two good examples.

Figure 11: People experience

Before we go on to explore 'people experience' in more depth, I need to reference two people in particular. In 2008 I met Stewart Bromley, Head of People Experience for First Direct. Their move to people experience was way ahead of its time, and credit is due to both Stewart and First Direct for their foresight. Stewart recognised the positive effect that treating people as individuals would have on the whole organisation. He introduced the core value of playful, understanding its connection with emotional intelligence.

Then, a few years later, I met Peter Sinden, Sales and Service Director at LV= within General Insurance. In my view, Peter embodies people experience in a truly authentic way and his influence has an effect across the whole company. His title also reflects the fundamental observation that good experiences sell, and I'm sure you will either have met, or are yourself the type of person that has this type of influence. A key element of perpetual experience is replicating and scaling this effect.

With the move to people experience, we now have a much more porous company boundary. We also have fully defined customer segmentation with complete 'voice of the customer' information enhanced by customer relationship management (CRM). The analysis of Big Data includes email, live chat and social media, and results in a very high customer penetration into decision-making. Information flows both into and through customer-focused individuals and teams, and there a very high value is placed on their individual needs and expectations. Somewhat ironically, we can now see the introduction of tools such as artificial intelligence and automated learning beginning to blend voice, self and assisted service.

A company operating a people experience approach has evolved from a customer service company into a true customer experience company. It has successfully blended intellectual intelligence (IQ) and emotional intelligence (EQ), and its real metrics of success are business growth and financial security. Employees, customers and society all perceive it as an ethical and authentic company. Its values are never challenged, which is important, and something that we will return to in the chapter on authenticity.

All of the above iterations of customer and people experience have their place. Increasingly, the service buffer approach has limited applications, and service empowered customer experience or individual customer experience are likely to be the ambition for most companies. Interestingly, the people experience approach is currently most common in business-to-consumer environments, but in fact has great potential for B2B markets.

Perpetual experience

Wherever companies are, they can't afford to stand still, particularly in view of the disruptive innovation that we discussed in Part 1. If a company stands still, it will fail to keep pace with the connected world that is dramatically changing customers' expectations. This situation is highlighted by the challenges presented by providing effective self and assisted service. There is a train of thought that suggests the more a company has invested in its people, the harder it is to adopt a digital approach. But I disagree. Everything we have learned about recent technical and innovative developments is that they are people orientated. The companies that are people focused are already a long way down the road to addressing the challenges of disruption.

Perpetual experience can assist a company, whatever its ambition for customer experience. It can not only help the 'best in class' companies react to the future, but also companies who are trying hard to break the back of persistent service problems. Ultimately, perpetual experience will enable companies to harness the energy, talent and creativity of their customers, partners and employees.

Figure 12 opposite illustrates the changes that are required for a business to move to perpetual experience. In my view, the biggest change is that the company goes all the way with people experience and begins to value the needs and resulting experiences of everyone involved. You will also notice the visual includes partners, but could just have easily have referred to other suppliers or sub-contractors. There is almost no boundary between the company and the many voices both outside, within and connected to it. This is a truly people experience approach - these voices form groups around, not only problems and poor experiences, but also around creativity and suggestions for the development of new products, services and experiences. How these form, and the dynamics within them, we'll explore later.

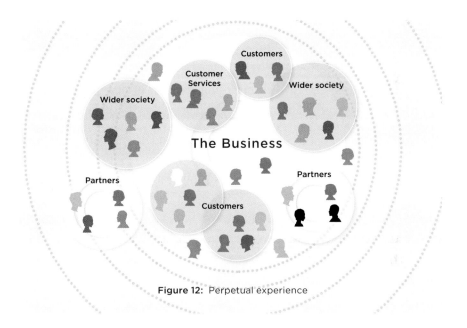

Figure 12: Perpetual experience

Under perpetual experience the flow of information is almost seamless and knowledge management moves into centre stage. Individuals come and go from specific perpetual experience groups, and the company benefits directly in the form of better problem resolution and enhanced creativity. By extracting knowledge, information and data from these interactions, the company can improve self and assisted service and observe the associated trends and patterns to evaluate future requirements.

Of course, you still have segments with generalised experiences, but each individual feels valued. They feel unique, as far as is possible to do so. This feeling is not simply created by placing greater focus on personalised or highly customised products and services, it also arises from the focus on emotional intelligence. Customer experience becomes business as usual. The business becomes inclusive, rather than exclusive, and people are instinctively drawn to the trusting, authentic and dynamic environment.

The company is highly engaged, constantly working to improve itself by addressing the needs and experience of its people. The people reciprocate with creativity and dedication. Technologies and sciences such as Big Data and AI can be deployed and embraced. The traditional customer interfaces such as call centres are now central to the creation of new products and services. They hand off transactional customer contact to self and assisted service channels. From a financial perspective, stability comes from reduced cost-to-serve and ensuring that the business remains perpetually relevant to customer needs.

Outcomes of perpetual experience

Knowledge, information and understanding have now become the keys to success, and a significant percentage of the knowledge generated by customer and service interaction becomes available to customers through self and assisted channels. Improvements in customer experience will be reflected in the workplace of the companies and it partners.

With perpetual experience, companies are in a position, not only to embrace but also to drive the future. They have moved into a proactive role and will reap the associated financial rewards. As I mentioned earlier, authenticity and trust will become driving forces, even more so than they are today. We will explore this more in the chapter on authenticity, but before that, in the next chapter I will return to how we facilitate the engagement of groups, larger communities of employees, and partners, and move to a sense of 'us', not 'them'.

MOVING FORWARD

Key points

- Customer experience takes many different forms as it matures

- The level or type of experience a company is looking to deliver should fit the product or service

- The move to people experience is inevitable as employees become more independent and less 'one company' career orientated

- Organisational boundaries are becoming more porous

- Capturing the knowledge from the interactions between customers, employees and partners can accumulate real-world knowledge

- Valuing individual opinions leads to improved problem resolution and enhances creativity and innovation

In summary, perpetual experience

- Is focused on delivering a consistent level of experience but recognises that it needs to evolve to stand still

- Brings employees into the information gathering, knowledge sharing and solution building processes within their company

- Provides a real-time real-world component to the ROI

- Identifies the causes that align to the symptoms of poor experience

- Shifts a company from a reactive to a proactive service position

- Provides a more comprehensive and inclusive picture of the challenges facing a business

- Stimulates agility, creativity, and innovation

YOUR REFLECTIONS

How mature is your delivery of customer experience?

How close is it to customer expectation, now and tomorrow?

For those of you who prefer to start with a clean sheet . . .

. . . to Mind Map

7 | Us, not them

CHAPTER 7

Us, not them

Mystery: Customer experience is easy, why can't everyone see it?

As I explored in the last chapter, at the core of perpetual experience is the idea that we treat people as individuals with individual needs. The basic proposition on customer experience has now evolved to a point where products or services address the needs of customers. Producing and delivering the products and services generates needs in employees, and the outcomes of customer and employee needs are expressed as experiences - good, bad or indifferent.

I've talked about the removal or diluting of boundaries to allow people to explore, share and resolve issues. It may seem obvious, but customers, employees and our partners' employees are all part of the same society. Inviting them to participate should be easy, but there are complications that we need to share and try to resolve.

Employees and partners

As we have discussed, the origins of perpetual experience can be found in the development of social communities, and we now need to take what we have learned from this into the business environment.

Individuals within a healthy group or community seek status and power and deploy different strategies to obtain these. They have to do this within what is acceptable to the group as, if not, they can be openly rebuked, ignored or challenged. The right type of challenge is of course productive, but aggression can be terminal, not only for the individual but also for the group. In a normal social situation, this is not as much of a problem as leaving the group is an easy option with few consequences. But once again we can see the difference between customer and people experience as, within the work environment, the consequences can be severe and challenges can quickly escalate. We also have a plethora of functional, professional and personal boundaries that interrupt the flow of sharing within the group. This makes the idea of generating and participating in overlapping groups tricky, but by no means impossible.

Employees want to be treated as true individuals and they want to be valued, not just by their immediate team, but by leaders and others from across the organisation. As we know, recognition is a powerful motivator. But many businesses are not aware of just how much the desire to be recognised and valued as an individual has grown as a result of the disruption discussed in Part 1 of the book. They see their employees just as people employed to do a job and, at best, people to be nurtured by the culture and objectives of the business. They certainly don't see them as individuals. This waste of talent and energy is something that many companies acknowledge needs to be addressed, but the question is how to go about it. You only need to look at all the initiatives taken by all sizes of organisations to address this waste - employee engagement programmes, team development initiatives, and so on. All recognise the fundamental problem of the waste of talent and productivity.

Sam Ellis's recent initiative at Atos is a good example of the growing trend for experienced customer experience professionals moving into human resources or people experience roles.

Atos is a global IT services provider. The customer experience journey started in our Managed Services service line in late 2009 when we set up the central customer experience function from scratch, reinvigorating the way we measured user and customer satisfaction.

It changed the way we gathered insight, making it quick and easy to leave feedback. We ditched old fashioned survey techniques (long surveys with multiple, often irrelevant questions) by using methods like voice and other online mechanisms. At the same time, we worked closely with research companies, such as Gartner and Forrester, to inspire our customer experience programme that included all customer stakeholders - from end users of IT to IT directors.The programme included the careful use of NPS by treating NPS scores as a by-product of continued service improvement and using other techniques, like predictive analytics and face to face client workshops. We saw steady, strong and credible improvement across all our key customer satisfaction metrics.

Using in house expertise these improvements have been matched by business growth, the increased number of client references and contract retention.

My move into employee engagement has helped us focus more on strategy in the areas of organisational culture and behaviours that underpin improvement initiatives, driven by the commitment and engagement of the Atos people. Other initiatives have been drastically reducing internal email, as well as developing a greater role for internal social networks and more open communication forums that have been essential to build trust and the associated connection with the company brand. The role of people engagement has impacted on customer engagement in terms of building that trust and is expected to significantly influence the company's success in a positive way.

Sam Ellis
Head of Customer Experience and Loyalty
Atos

Addressing people concerns has always been difficult for companies. There's a tendency to bundle the issue into a seemingly manageable single topic, and the most common is 'culture'. While attempts to improve culture aim to drive behavioural change, they often miss the basics. What people actually do is more often driven by the difficulty, or the experience, of completing a given task. Once again the company is confronted by the real world, rather than the world it thinks exists. This is probably one of the most important but hidden challenges of customer experience, and is just as relevant in the B2B environment as it is in consumer-led markets.

This real-world experience and effort required to complete the task will determine the quality and efficiency, rather than the values of the individual. Later, I'll be looking at this from the perspective of experiences that drive workarounds and the accumulation of experiences that lead to process failure.

In fact, the more the company pursues value-based initiatives, the more it risks turning off its employees as it can be seen to question the participants' values. Company initiatives would be better to demonstrate authenticity to enhance engagement. This is not to diminish the role of values. In fact, I see it as completely the opposite: to suggest that values can be so easily manipulated is to understate their importance to people. The importance of this approach is amplified in partner relationships, especially when the partner has the majority of the customer contact.

Rob's example on the next page highlights the problem, the solution and the reward.

Equally, if a company want customers to perceive it as an 'authentic business' or an 'ethical business' or a 'trusted business', then its employees have to really believe the company holds and respects these values. Ouch! Let's simplify this: if companies want to be seen as authentic, then they need to demonstrate it. In some cases, businesses need to change their outlook radically. Talent and productivity are never realised in full until the business fully accepts and acts on the fact that people are individuals. The business needs to appeal to their individual motivations.

At Overbury we recognised that a significant part of the practical customer experience was delivered by our sub-contractors. At the time their experience was dominated by cash flow concerns which was restricting their ability to deliver to the standards they aspired to. Overbury committed to a new and improved payment schedule and promoted a preferred supplier arrangement that included a 'no retentions' policy. This enabled Overbury to foster a relationship based on trust.

As a result, the contractors could return to delivering or even over delivering on behalf of Overbury, and to the benefit of customers. Customer measures improved and more business was secured. In effect, identifying and addressing the effects of poor experience and associated pressure within our delivery model helped us to achieve the best ROI on experience.

Rob Phillips
Overbury, part of the Morgan Sindall Group of Companies

Partner or supply chain companies also have the same issues and in many cases they become increasingly removed from customers. To overcome this, organisations have started to use phrases such as 'customers', 'customer', or 'we are all customers of someone' when referring to partners or suppliers. The principle is sound and the intention good, but unfortunately it can lead to even more distrust.

We now truly are looking at the problems and solutions from a people perspective. If all the customer and employee experiences are good, you have an efficient company producing products and services other people will pay for. And conversely, identifying a poor people experience will be a very quick and efficient way of finding weaknesses.

Effective representation

The image below (Figure 13) is a visualisation you have seen earlier but is now used in the context of the people experience journey. It's something we will look at in more detail in chapter ten. People experience journeys enable organisations to identify all the factors that generate a specific customer experience. If customer experience tells us what actually happens (rather than what we think happens), people experience journeys show us why it happens.

You are no doubt familiar with customer journey mapping, a process that helps us understand the experience of a customer across various touchpoints. People experience journeys follow the same principle, but they enable you to dig much deeper into the root causes of a particular customer experience. By exploring the needs of each individual involved in the creation and delivery of a product or service, a people experience journey reveals the many tensions, blockages and workarounds that can result in a poor experience for the customer.

By following a people experience journey through from initiation to outcome, we are able to reveal the pressures and weak links for teams, individuals and systems that hamper excellent customer experience. And just as importantly, the journey will also uncover localised knowledge and potentially invaluable solutions to problems that can be adapted or scaled up for broader use.

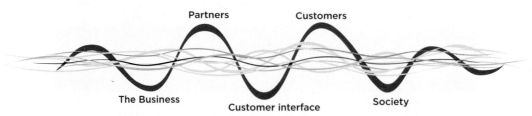

Figure 13: People experience journeys

The idea of connecting and sharing across silos isn't new. Many companies have tried to implement adaptations of society's social media platforms but, as we discussed earlier, the painful truth is that people quickly lose interest if there is nothing in it for them. People only enter and stay voluntarily in groups if they get something from them. However, in many people's working lives, this isn't the case. The same can be said for cross-function working groups and 'collaborative' teams. Naming the group 'collaborative' may set an expectation, but too often the way the group is run, and the dynamics within it, produces very little shared learning.

Watch out for the phrase "great meeting, no real disagreement". My question would be "why did you bother to meet"? Disagreement is great as long as everyone is aware of, and happy to recognise, the boundaries - as we discussed in the chapter on many voices.

Perpetual experience brings the thoughts and opinions from across the people experience journey together in a group discussion. It ensures that there is effective representation from all people involved in the journey, and the discussion needs to follow the principles of 'observe, share, reflect' to generate perpetual thinking.

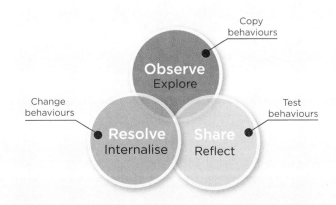

Figure 14: Changing behaviour through deliberately constructed debate

Are these meetings really that different from the day to day meetings we experience in the business world? A recent example captures the difference really well. After two hours of a stimulating and interactive perpetual thinking session a group returned to its established meeting format. Ten minutes in and the meeting was brought to a stop with a comment of "this is sucking the life out of me, can we go back to what we were doing before?"

It's a good analogy. Perpetual thinking brings life into a business.

So, we have to work harder to get people involved, and their motivations for participating will have to be driven by the promise of satisfying their individual needs. If the only way to get people to attend is fear, or the promise of doughnuts[3] , there is a problem.

You'll see below I have developed the visualisation shown earlier in this chapter (Figure 13) to highlight the engagement model of perpetual thinking resulting from people experience journeys.

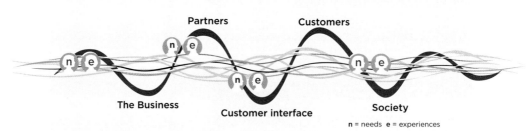

Figure 15: Needs and experiences

In this version of the visual each participant is accompanied by a need and experience, not just the customer. As a result, the perpetual thinking group can now function in a balanced environment because there is effective representation from all parties involved in the people experience journey. Something equally important is also happening - people are

---

[3] David Pearl: Will there be donuts? Better business one meeting at a time. 2012

starting to observe and reflect on each other's true circumstances which, as we will discover later, leads to more informed decisions and behaviours.

Think of forming a perpetual thinking group as inviting people to a new event. You need to explain what they will gain by attending, what will happen and the experience they can expect. In some cases, it's worth putting up small barriers to establish that they really do want to attend. If everyone declines, don't resort to manipulation or doughnuts, instead it would be better to consider whether the discussion is truly relevant to their needs.

I hope you're now getting the picture of how and why individuals participate in perpetual thinking groups. Let's now be a bit more specific about the benefits from the company's perspective.

The business perspective

Our conversation has now reached a point where we have explored people experience journeys and demonstrated how the knowledge, experience and participants contribute to perpetual thinking. From a business perspective, we're tackling two critical issues: how to work in the real world in real time, and how to address the problem of isolated thinking and decision-making. We know that these problems occur when people are not informed by a sufficiently broad range of information, experiences and opinions. Both ensure that businesses realise real-world, real-time benefits.

With perpetual thinking, many business disciplines and inputs - such as operational issues, regulatory issues, customer insight, artificial intelligence, and data analytics - all enter an environment that is more representative of what is actually happening in the real world. The company is elevated to a place where it is responding to real-world concerns and driving real behavioural change. This leads us into behavioural economics, where real-world behaviours can be interpreted quickly and efficiently into economic gains. These gains are not made at the expense of good people experience, but as a consequence of it. This shift will itself be perpetual as people will always move towards better experiences.

A good example of this is provided by Rod Sheriff's experience at Lebara where the real-world behaviours were translated into direct economic rewards.

At Lebara we faced a familiar challenge, proving that good customer experiences drive loyalty and advocacy. Proving this link, through measuring the loyalty of customers who contacted customer service in comparison to those that did not, allowed us to demonstrate the impact of great service and prove the return from investments that were made.

In effect, this allowed us to build and sustain an award winning service centre. It was essential that the business recognised that it contributed to profit rather than being an overhead to the business. It also assisted in building pride in the London based contact centre team, acknowledging they were a crucial part of the business.

Rod Sheriff
Founder and Director
In-gage

Rod was Customer Service Director at Lebara Mobile from September 2010 to October 2012

Once again we return to how decisions are often made in a business, and the lack of debate. The same data introduced into a balanced, open minded and contextually aware group will be viewed very differently than it will in a siloed, closed-minded group. Picking up on real time also introduces the subject of direct sales. Frequently, customer experience hands this problem to another department and fails to take the credit, or simply doesn't want to be associated with sales activity. But as we are discovering, customer experiences drive behaviours that result in direct sales as well as ongoing loyalty. Employee experiences can drive efficiency and innovation that transform a company's products, services, and even market position.

Companies are constantly seeking to reduce costs and make efficiency savings, but all too often their efforts focus on reducing customer service. This is self-defeating, as the information extracted from customer service interactions can drive effective self and assisted service. This is arguably one of the biggest challenges, and one I believe we are close to winning, but only if the business is operating in the real world. To achieve victory, internal workarounds will have to be reduced to allow customers to navigate self and assisted service effectively.

In summary, businesses will need to focus on the needs of individuals and on working in real time. Technology is the enabler. Perpetual thinking is the driving force. Companies that can embrace this will achieve a state of perpetual and profitable existence.

Us, not them

Key points

- Involving a wide and representative range of people in decision-making is an effective response to the challenges of silos and isolated thinking

- Individual needs and experiences mapped along the journey of a product or service expose the reality of what is actually happening

- Companies require a more sophisticated approach to people management and motivation

- There is a dichotomy between the benefits of decisive management style and involving everyone in decision making

- Inclusivity becomes a genuine invitation to participate in shaping the organisation

- Including thoughts and opinions from other organisations adds another dimension to the thinking that leads to a collective attitude

In summary, perpetual experience

- Brings life into a business by enabling people to share their experiences

- Is genuinely inclusive, because people are invited to participate and choose to opt-in

- Facilitates the sharing of circumstances to combat mistrust and siloed thinking

- Promotes a balance between a logical and emotional mind set

- Makes knowledge agile, fun, and engaging by valuing every individual's contribution

YOUR REFLECTIONS

What does your company like to be seen as? A group of individuals, a group of teams, a team or a community?

What would the people working in the company like it to be?

For those of you who prefer to start with a clean sheet . . .

. . . to Mind Map

8 | EXERTING INFLUENCE

CHAPTER 8

Exerting influence

Mystery: *Why is customer experience an objective that drives such variable outcomes?*

Customer service, customer experience, people experience and perpetual experience all have one thing in common: they are all looking to influence rather than direct a business. Organisations have historically tended to direct behaviour using authority, but as we have seen throughout this book, authority only affects behaviour to a certain degree. Exerting influence, and particularly authentic influence, is much more effective in achieving real and sustainable behaviour change. Once again, we are moving towards the need for real-world change, both within the company and in customer behaviour.

In fact, we have been relying on influence to change customer behaviour for many years. With perpetual experience, we are now bringing the same strategy into our companies and partners. Prior to the advent of customer experience, decisions were largely based on the economics of tangible business cases. Customer experience introduced emotion into the decisions and eventually into the business cases themselves. But as I described at the beginning of the book, there is too often a polarisation between these two extremes. A good example of the tangible would be companies moving call centres to culturally different countries, a trend that was especially popular in the late '90s. The decisions were made purely on a cost per call basis.

The opposite to the tangible is the emotional. An example is the use of emotionally charged video footage of a customer who missed talking to their grandmother on their birthday because the phone coverage was lost for the vital half hour when the call was to have been made. The consequences for the individual, and the consequences generated, were out of proportion to the relatively minor network outage. While the customer's emotion was real and justified, using it as an example to the logical-minded person is counter-productive.

Between logic and emotion

With perpetual experience, we can effectively blend facts and logic with emotion and intuition to better influence the plethora of decisions made within an organisation. The decision to move a call centre may be the right one if the customer experience can be maintained or improved. A reasonable emotional customer story would have provided the understanding of what the new call centre needed to deliver. In many ways, this middle ground of experiences is the most fertile for acquiring knowledge and creating sustainable customer relationships that will drive positive economic outcomes.

I'd like to come back to a phrase I used much earlier in the discussion, that of head space. I used it in connection with the conundrum of why technology that reduces time and effort for individual tasks still leaves us with less time - or head space. Add to this the vast increase in searchable knowledge and an increased capacity to perform a variety of actions quickly, and decision-making can become very pressured.

For example, as I am writing this book, people in the United Kingdom are being asked to decide if the country should stay in the European Union. The expectation is that people will make an informed decision, but it has become increasingly apparent that, as individuals, it is almost impossible to find and absorb all the facts. Everyone has access to powerful search engines and a vast amount of information to guide their decision, but a common complaint has been that people don't have the time to evaluate enough information to make a confident decision. The protagonists are promoting ideas that are a prediction of the future, and so by definition are rarely fact. To make matters worse, it seems that every new subject entering the debate is being interpreted to support both the leave and remain campaigns.

This situation highlights both the difficulty of having either too much or not enough information, and the dilemma that information doesn't always lead to understanding. Although this scenario is an extreme example, it is representative of the situations in which we often find ourselves when the connected world gives us information and opinion but may fail to increase our understanding. The purpose of this example is to highlight that people are now overloaded by knowledge. They don't have enough time to evaluate it, and they can feel insecure because they can't build a real, informed and confident understanding.

In some ways, the above example mirrors the dilemma that business leaders face when trying to exert influence. As we discussed earlier, influence is particularly relevant to the development of customer experience, as the latter is a business function that seeks to influence both company behaviours and those of individual employees.

For example, a customer experience team working in one of the UK's largest companies had just completed an extensive customer insight project. They had spent a great deal of time and money building a solid and logical business case. This included an external, non-industry, research-informed calculation of the financial rewards for every point increase in their chosen measure of trust, loyalty and advocacy. The insight was then analysed and the root causes of poor experiences identified. The team were ready to make the final decision on the actions that needed to be taken and seek approval for funding. As you can probably guess, it ended badly, although how and why baffled me for quite some time. Let me explain what happened - it may well be a situation with which you are familiar.

A planning meeting of eight people met to make the final decision on the actions required. The insight was laid out, figures checked, hypotheses explained and decisions agreed. The business case, written in their corporate language, was finalised in preparation for winning the budget and resource. At the budget meeting, the proposal was presented and the funding and resource were approved. Between the planning and the budget meeting a dilemma arose for the team leader. Everyone was happy when they left the planning meeting, but it only took each individual an hour or so to find another member of the team who confessed they thought that several of the decisions that had been made were wrong. The participants were unanimous in their doubt, but despite their reservations the budget meeting went ahead as planned and the budget was approved.

Why am I telling you this story? Let's reduce the story to its component parts:

1 The company required a purely logical business case.

2 Customer emotions were represented solely by figures and lacked any human interpretation.

3 The non-industry, research-informed economic calculations remained unchallenged.

4 The objective was to increase the score, not change behaviours.

All the participants were in a position where they were unable to influence the decision, even though they all had a conflicting personal view.

The company got what it asked for, which was an industrial approach to people issues. This is a great example of people feeling that they have no real influence over decision-making, despite their apparent authority. In such an environment, you can understand why everyone was looking for a defendable position. The decision making culture, even the language used, was devoid of any real emotion or intuition.

I am tempted to say we all recognise these meetings. But so often the participants are not conscious of the contrived nature of the decisions they make, and they over-estimate how much actual influence they have on outcomes.

The challenges of influencing

I would like to use another example to illustrate how difficult it is to influence people who are more used to authority. A man I'll call John worked for a slightly smaller subsidiary of a large multinational company. Both the subsidiary and John had an excellent and deserved reputation for customer experience, so John was asked to move to the multinational. He liked his new team and was looking forward to the challenges that lay ahead.

At their first team meeting, John shared his vision of what could be achieved over the coming months and asked for thoughts from his team. This was a genuine offer, as John fully intended to adjust his vision after listening to their suggestions. But instead of receiving suggestions, he was met with perplexed and slightly embarrassed expressions. He tried again, pointing out that the team had a better understanding of the multinational company than he did, and again indicating that he wanted them to voice their opinions.

This eventually had the desired effect, and they began to talk. The team worked in an environment where they expected to be instructed on what needed to be done, how to do it, and how to measure success. But John was more used to allowing his team to determine the best course of action, and then rely on his ability to influence team members to ensure their actions delivered the required outputs.

Let's not be too judgmental on this team. Their perceived lack of head space made the option of clear actions, objectives and measures very appealing. But John was in fact asking the individuals to commit the most precious resource of thinking time to the project, a resource that was scarce due to the pressures of their roles.

Inadvertently, the jump to actions and outcomes reduces - or completely eliminates - the ability to influence the project as it progresses. What we then have is a situation where the outcomes from projects are too pre-determined, with insufficient space for subtle changes where people can adapt the project to reflect real-world scenarios in which they have to operate.

The conclusion I have come to is that we should encourage ongoing influence as projects develop, even though it may take longer and require more effort. Often in companies, very little time is spent observing, sharing and reflecting on issues and so the prospect of doing so is greeted with an overwhelming feeling of 'where am I going to find the time?' How many companies are in a position where perceived effort and poor workplace experiences determine the decisions their people are making? It is encouraging to see that many companies are now making huge efforts to improve workplace experience. In doing so, they are reaping the benefits of creating more head space for their employees who are able to be more innovative and make more inclusive and effective decisions.

It's unfortunate that I can't name John as he is still at the same organisation and, with the help of others, is gradually changing the environment. He has demonstrated a great deal of what author Angela Duckworth has described as 'grit'. In her book 'Grit: The Power of Passion and Perseverance'[4], she describes the hypothesis that what really drives success is not genius but a unique combination of passion and long-term perseverance.

[4] Angela Duckworth: Grit, The Power of Passion and Perseverance. 2016.

John persevered and has built what he calls a network of collective influence. He has found this to be a much more effective way to drive sustainable change within the business. But whereas it took him a long time to build this network, perpetual experience enables a business to get to this outcome much more quickly and efficiently.

The role of trust in influence

In 2006, an article was published in the Harvard Business Review, it was entitled 'The Decision to Trust' by Robert Hurley. Hurley researched 450 executives around the world and found that about 50% didn't trust their leaders. Those that mistrusted their leaders rated their work environments as stressful, threatening, divisive, unproductive and tense. Conversely, Hurley's research also found that those executives who trusted their leaders rated their work environments as fun, supportive, motivating, productive and comfortable. It is obvious that those working in trusting environment are more likely to be responsive to influence, and by default the leaders more influential.

With this in mind, it is easier to see why UK bank First Direct's core value of 'playful' was effective at influencing the people and company. In a less authentic company, especially one in the financial services sector, such a value would have been dismissed as insincere and poorly thought through. But at First Direct, it guaranteed that employees at all levels could influence what, why and how things happened across the company.

So, trust creates a positive environment and mistrust creates a negative environment. Common sense leads us to this conclusion, but it seems leaders need to place greater importance on consciously creating a trusted, positive working environment if they are to exert effective influence. But what happens as we escalate this dynamic into partner and subcontractor relationships?

For example, the distribution of products may start with an international logistics company, but the final delivery could be a small independent business. Likewise, utility companies will rely on subcontractors to fit and read meters, retailers on franchised outlets. As mistrust develops, it is first experienced by the people involved in the interface between the companies or sub-contractors.

For others working in the company, remoteness or isolation can lead to misleading assessments of the actual levels of trust between the companies and individuals involved. Data, such as the number of exceptions, returns, delays and complaints will often highlight the issue, but then we have moved into a logical, data-driven understanding rather than one informed by intuition, diminishing the ability of people to influence. As a result, the company defaults to authoritative measures to correct the situation, rather than dealing more quickly with the issues as they arise through the people involved.

Of course, for everyone involved in the two organisations there would have been subtle signs that trust was being eroded. Whether these signs are acted on has a lot to do with the working environment, and the feeling that individuals don't have the authority or ownership that enables them to express their concerns. Essentially we are seeing the diminishing power of influence.

In the next chapter, we will explore how establishing an authentic environment can re-establish the role of influence. But for now it is important to acknowledge that perpetual experience provides an effective model for influencing as it is predicated on inclusivity, trust, and on the sharing of knowledge, experience and circumstances.

Influence and leadership

Everything we've discussed so far has led us to imagine a subtly different business world, one that is more in line with society. Inevitably our discussion needs to extend into how we drive change. But is drive change the right phrase? Do we want to drive change or influence evolution?

A discussion on influence wouldn't be complete without a consideration of leadership, for in the same way as culture, values and morality, leadership has an important role to play in influencing evolution. I would like to take you back to our earlier conversation on using the dynamics of groups, in chapter six. In these scenarios, influence is increased by authenticity, relevant knowledge and a willingness to share it openly and honestly.

At best, this is the dilemma facing today's leaders, at its worst a foreign language. This is not a criticism of any individual leader or leadership style as these tend to be a product of the environment in which they operate. Many would argue that the environment is set from the top, and to a certain degree this is true. But people talk about having a great leader, and then in the next breath describe the problems of sticky middle management or lack of engagement. As a result, we have to question the extent to which a leader is able to effectively influence the behaviour of individuals within their organisation.

The ability of a leader to influence is therefore related to the environment, and improving the environment would consequently support the leader's ability to influence. Customer experience often advocates the use of 'leaders, not a single leader' as a more effective model, with a better chance of influencing the environment. But we can improve on this. As we discussed earlier, there are two sides to influence: the ability to influence and the willingness to be influenced. Leaders of companies that break through the authority model into an open and trusting environment are therefore able to capitalise on the advantages of increased influence. The leader, or leaders, need to reciprocate the trust placed in them. Mutual respect is integral to developing such an environment, and perpetual experience is a way to make this transition to a more responsive organisation.

No measure of influence

A single measure is often introduced by leaders in the belief that it will drive the right behaviours and associated outcomes. In reality, companies are very efficient at finding ways to drive improvements in measures. When the outcomes are tangible and static this is less of a problem, but experiences are intangible and constantly evolving. It can often lead to a situation where people trying to improve the measure see the incompatibility of the score with the desired outcome.

In layman's terms, a company can have a measure of customer satisfaction as high as seventy percent and a churn rate of forty percent. Even worse, the frontline employees are still handling the complaints of those receiving poor experiences. Companies that use a blend of measures achieve significantly more influence for two reasons: firstly, the ability to cross-reference data helps build a more accurate picture of what is actually happening, and secondly a greater number of employees believe that they can make a difference to the score. Of course, this whole situation is further complicated if companies attach a reward - especially a global reward - to an increase in the single measure.

However, companies that are - for whatever reason - delivering consistently low scores, perhaps even negative figures, will initially benefit from a single measurement approach. This is because it provides them with a clear focus on the importance of customer experience. The challenge for them is to move away from this as soon as it starts to have a negative influence on behaviour. Another approach adopted by customer experience is to introduce the 'voice of the customer'. This can take many forms, from physically inviting customers into the organisation through to complex datasets and analytics. While voice of the customer can be invaluable to developing a better understanding of customer experience, its effect unfortunately tends to be lessened the further away it gets from the customer-facing functions. Often, voice of the customer projects are outsourced to third parties, and this can sometimes be beneficial if a company doesn't have a great connection with its customers. But conversely, outsourcing this activity can be detrimental as the outsourcer may be even further removed from the company's customers. Once again, perpetual experience can change the environment effectively so more of the company is receptive to the knowledge it is bringing in.

So what?

What could be more important than companies improving their ability to exert real influence? Leading by influence rather than by authority will inevitably lead to a more people-orientated environment. This will help companies become more proactive in their response to the needs of individuals, whether employees, customers, or partners, and will generate better experiences for everybody. It also frees a company from the shackles of slow and bureaucratic top down leadership. Perpetual thinking, by definition, relies on the fluidity and creativity that enables a company to keep pace - or even lead - the evolving environment.

Influence will thrive in an authentic company. Which is why our conversation now moves to authenticity.

Exerting influence

Key points

- The need for companies to understand the changing environment is becoming clear as they experiment with community and employee engagement

- The power of followers is becoming more evident as the effectiveness of authority diminishes

- Adopting these new skills requires conscious development

- Valuing people's needs and experiences, and understanding their context, enables more effective influence

- Leading by influence, rather than by authority, is a better way of driving sustainable behaviour change

- Influencing effectively requires a balance of logic and emotion

- Building trust is integral to exerting influence

In summary, perpetual experience

- Helps influence every decision across the company and its partners, and provides a continuing influence to enable an organisation to evolve

- Enables leaders to obtain much greater control over the operation and direction of the company

- Makes it possible to take a proactive approach to leading a company

- Positions an organisation to meet the challenges of the changing economic environment

YOUR REFLECTIONS

Does this chapter inspire you, or make you uneasy?

Who influences you? Who do you influence?

For those of you who prefer to start with a clean sheet . . .

. . . to Mind Map

9 | BUILDING AUTHENTICITY

CHAPTER 8

Building authenticity

Mystery: *How do we understand and influence what actually happens when we can't be everywhere at once?*

The authentic company

We have established the need for authenticity in how companies interact with people. But there is another element that we haven't previously discussed - people in the connected society, confronted by such a broad range of knowledge and opinion, have found it necessary to develop a shortcut to deciding who and what information they will trust.

The shortcut is commonly achieved in one of two ways: by accessing and triangulating different sources of information, or by taking a view on the historical performance of the source. Inconsistency then becomes a major issue, as a company giving a variety of opinions, data and information on its own products and services will start to appear inauthentic.

Interestingly, the response becomes the need to speak with one voice, rather than with many voices. The way to achieve this is to allow the power of many voices to establish and validate real-world truths. This potentially difficult concept can perhaps be demonstrated by Wikipedia, which through the collective efforts of many people is more continuously accurate than a moment-in-time encyclopaedia. The point is this: if you don't believe the source to be accurate, the answer is to cross-reference in order to confirm or challenge its authenticity and accuracy. Thanks to the internet, this is easy to achieve through knowledge search and accessing communities.

One of the mysteries of customer experience is how to close the gap between what the company thinks is happening and what customers and employees say is happening. In this case, a company will be assessing the authenticity of the people involved to establish what is actually happening. We can then see that authenticity is, at best, reciprocal - the employee and customers understand and accept the position of the company, and the company understands and accepts the position of its employees and customers.

This also explains one of the other mysteries of customer experience, which is why the problem of closing this gap is minimised for small companies. The advantage of a small company is that the leadership has an intuitive understanding of what is really happening. They can walk around and see and hear the discussions and interactions that are taking place. Large organisations can't do this, so the substitute is authenticity, and authentic organisations are better equipped to deal with the 'real-world' rather than the world they think they inhabit.

Why is the internal audience more difficult?

Compared to customers, employees can be a much tougher nut to crack. They see what actually happens and hear what is actually said, and often assume they know what others are thinking. Once again, to make the problem easier to address, there is a temptation to look for universal solutions.

A universal fix, especially to people related change, is very appealing for large organisations and would seem to be a logical approach. Looking back on my time at Lloyds, many really good initiatives were planned and implemented, but failed to get fully embedded as it was too easy to revert to previous behaviours, especially when the pressure was turned up.

On a similar note, the adoption of 'colleagues' as a general reference for 'people we work with' was intended to help bring two merged workforces together. The effect, however, was to further depersonalise the workplace with the inevitable effect on morale and engagement.

Lewis Ryden
Partner
Sybaris Chauffeurs

Lewis Ryden was Head of Call Management, Lloyds Banking Group from 2006 to 2008

As Lewis recalls above, the introduction of the word 'colleagues' at Lloyds was about as inauthentic as it gets.

Another financial services company correctly identified that customers would, on the whole, like a friendly service. This message was driven through a network of conversations and committees, and an action agreed. As it happened, one of the originators of the insight team walked into a branch of the bank several months later to be confronted by a very uncomfortable cashier. The discomfort was caused by a notice placed just beside the cashier. It read, 'as a minimum you will be greeted by a smile'. The look on the cashier's face was what was authentic: I hate my job. This is a good example of how a customer need, interpreted through customer insight, was then met with a company's desire to do something simple and tangible. It is easy to see that the real-time interaction between the cashier and the customer is a much more emotionally complex exchange. The customer could be in any number of emotional states, depending on his or her situation. Demonstrating an authentic emotional response is the solution, an instruction to smile is not.

Two further dimensions to authenticity are honesty and trust. But are they related, or in fact a completely separate issue? In his book 'Trust, Complexity and Control[5], Piotr Cofta refers to the understanding that trust cannot appear in the absence of evidence, and the significance of the evidence depends on the perceived honesty of such evidence. It is clear that we can't always be completely honest. Situations will develop where total honesty is destructive, or the current level of knowledge may not represent the final outcome. But where do we draw the line?

One answer to this dilemma is the development of a collective consciousness that, for many organisations, helps to establish this proverbial line in the sand, without the need for hard rules. As we've already discussed, it is almost impossible to set hard and fast rules that are effective around issues such trust and honesty. Karen expresses it well on the next page.

This idea of a collective consciousness has been explored in great depth in books. In Smart Swarms, Peter Miller[6] explains how members of a group, without being told to, can transform simple rules of thumb into meaningful patterns of collective behaviour. Scientists and psychologists may disagree on how it works, but agree that it does happen. What is important is that a collective consciousness can reveal otherwise hidden knowledge and collective opinions or beliefs. The outcomes of a collective consciousness have ranged from the toppling of governments to the promotion of artists into celebrities - and making vlogger Zoella an individual with considerable influence.

These examples also raise the question of control, and almost every company has experienced out-of-control groups that pursue a single minded and damaging agenda. So the last thing companies are likely to do is to invite these groups in. But the reality is that they already

---

[5] Piotr Cofta: Trust, Complexity and Control, Confidence in a Convergent World. 2007.

[6] Peter Miller: The Smart Swarm, How to work efficiently, communicate effectively and make better decisions using the secrets of flocks, schools and colonies. 2010.

Customer experience has undoubtedly come a long way in the last in the last 10 years, especially in the consumer market. Looking back, it's interesting to see how some of the challenges and solutions have changed, whilst others remain. Perhaps the biggest changes have been social connectivity, assisted and self-service expectations that have heightened customer expectations but also given companies new opportunities to deliver slick and efficient service. However, this development has only highlighted existing challenges around function and product silos, consistent investment and getting everyone on the same page.

Perhaps I've been lucky or, more likely, the two companies I've spent most time with working on customer experience have had an intuitive ability to tackle the same page issue. At Orange we could say, is this the Orange way, and the majority of people would know what was meant and expected. Now working in Virgin Media we say, is this what Richard would do, especially around people issues. Having this level of intuitive understanding among a large percentage of the people working for a company isn't an easy thing to develop but an essential ingredient when delivering consistent customer and employee experiences.

Karen Ingham
Customer Service Director
Virgin Media

Karen Ingham was Customer Service Director at Orange from 2000 to 2008

exist - ignoring them is no longer an option and controlling them is, in the most part, impossible. It's time to do what businesses often do well - turn a problem into an opportunity and engage with these groups. However, successful engagement and participation in any social or business group is only achievable if it is done with authenticity, as anything less than an authentic approach will result in the person or business being rejected by the group.

Values, morality, ethics and culture

Central to the many debates around customer experience has been discussion regarding the role of values, morality, ethics and culture. Views vary, from being the answer to all problems, to a convenient scapegoat for complicated staffing issues. It is often argued that culture encapsulates the other three and is demonstrated through behaviours, and I happen to agree. Culture has a palpable effect on society and companies, it influences the decisions we make and the actions we take.

The questions in my mind are - what decisions and what actions? Values, for instance, are very personal - so personal, in fact, that they change as we articulate them to strangers and again to close friends. Our values change again if we genuinely consider the values demonstrated through our actions and are not expected to share our conclusions with others. So proclaiming our values is difficult. How honest will we be? The evidence shows that the audience has a big effect on what we proclaim our values to be.

A similar dynamic exists with honesty. The complexity of daily life and business means that there will be the odd occasion where people will need to be sensitive regarding how and when they use the truth. Every time a decision or action is seen to contradict stated values, trust and authenticity is damaged. So how can an individual, let alone a company, talk about values with any real authenticity?

Morality is also an interesting subject, and can seem straightforward. But some of you may listen to programmes such as The Moral Maze on BBC's Radio 4 where you start with a firm view and within ten minutes you're confused and doubting your original position. You end up trying to judge the issue by the quality and, yes, the authenticity of people representing the differing standpoints. Ethics are very similar and often used to set minimal standards that then need further interpretation to put into practice.

So is culture and its derivatives the answer, or the scapegoat? Culture certainly seems to be questioned by customers, society and business leaders on a daily basis. Using culture, values, and morality can be a self-rewarding activity - there is often a great temptation to point the finger at other groups and proclaim that their values are inferior to our own. This was the underlying theme of 'them, not us' examined in chapter seven. We are often quite prepared to question the values, morality and culture of other individuals or groups, but less inclined to question our own or those of our group. What does this tell us about who is being authentic?

Which brings us to an interesting place. We don't see the recipient of our finger-pointing as someone in our group. In the case of customers, they are failing to see that people working for the company are the very people they live next door to. I've met hundreds of people working in a variety of companies, as have you, and we may like some of them more than others. But not many demonstrate behaviours that would lead us to question their values. So do they find it difficult to be authentic at work? Or is something else happening?

Even more difficult to understand is a leader who criticises company values. It may not be open criticism but any values-based training, workshop or initiative starts with an implied criticism. The assumption is that my values are better than yours. So what is happening and why? Praising values, morals, ethics and culture has the opposite effect in all regards. It promotes the recipient, implies they are part of our group, and is a very personal compliment. We are stating that they are one of us, not one of them.

In summary, the root cause of why values are so often questioned is a lack of understanding of others' circumstances. At their best, values can unify teams, help set a direction, bring hope, optimism and nourishment for the flagging soul and are accepted as authentic. When used to criticise, manipulate or assert leadership they are deceptively demotivating and often seen as inauthentic.

The conclusion I draw from this, is that companies would, on reflection, be better to use issues of culture, such as values, as subtle motivation. But once again this needs to be done in an authentic way to ensure the message has the desired effect. This leads us back to the opening of our conversation where we discussed the problems of putting the customer first and unrepresentative scoring. By this I am referring to companies that use a single measure that is too easily manipulated to misrepresent the true picture of what is actually happening. Many of us will have witnessed circumstances where an individual or team has been misled by such measures due to a lack of effective representation from other parts of the organisation. The solution again is for these people to be working in a broad and authentic environment.

There is yet another aspect to this issue which is that of cognitive bias. Most judgment calls will be subject to unconscious biases. In his book Thinking Fast and Slow[7], Daniel Kahneman argues that there are two systems that drive the way we think. System 1 is fast, intuitive, and emotional. System 2 is slower, more deliberative, and more logical. Kahneman exposes the extraordinary capabilities - and also the faults and biases - of fast thinking, and reveals the pervasive influence of intuitive impressions on our thoughts and behaviour.

Authenticity is primarily demonstrated through consistency and transparency, by doing what you say you will do, and by working within the boundaries set by social groups. So a business can be authentic when working with its own people, partners, customers and society. If the business shows that it understands and respects the unwritten social boundaries, it will be accepted, and if the business has something to contribute, it will be welcomed. How companies can begin to acquire this understanding is at the heart of perpetual experience, and the practicalities of this will be discussed in the final chapter.

Authenticity and perpetual experience

For the remainder of this chapter I will focus on why authenticity is integral to perpetual experience and consider some of the outcomes it can achieve.

---

[7] Daniel Kahneman, Nobel Laureate in Economics: Thinking Fast and Slow. 2011.

A fundamental principle of perpetual experience is that the authenticity of every participant in a perpetual thinking group is continually being assessed by the other participants. In fact, the participants in the group are practicing being authentic. The group coaches the participants in authenticity and, as an inevitable consequence, the outcomes produced are authentic. To make this work, it is essential to get the right people with the right knowledge, experience and breadth of opinion into the perpetual thinking groups, and in many cases this is achieved by undertaking people experience journeys, as explained in chapter six.

To demonstrate how this authenticity is achieved, I would like to examine how the dynamic works in practice. This dynamic is at the heart of how groups and communities can shape and influence ideas, and is best articulated by walking through how ideas are incubated in an authentic environment.

An idea or topic is proposed to the group, and crucially they all see it slightly differently. The idea is explored through an exchange of individual opinions and views that are a balance of emotional and logical debate.

During this process participants start to build a similar, but not uniform, picture of the topic, and it is important that they don't. What needs to be avoided are diagrams or lists that force people to conform to a single understanding, or the diversity of opinion will be lost along with the authenticity arising from individual views. Data-driven points of view can also be introduced and again tested in a balanced way by the experiences of the participants. This means that the data has no greater or lesser influence than the views of participants. At this stage the authentic points of view emerge.

The emergent thoughts and ideas will inevitably be challenged by individual participants within the group. It is important that any factor from outside the perpetual thinking group does not influence the emergent thoughts - by this I mean factors such as status, ego, personal or organisational agendas. A good way of achieving this is to have a significant representation from outside the company.

Chris Burton's experience below is a good example of this dynamic in action.

In British Gas Home Services, we had put together a programme to improve customer experience and field force performance which spanned the whole organisation and required cultural, structural, systems and technology changes. The scale of investment dictated that much time and effort was directed at ensuring all aspects of the plan had been fully considered before implementation, but after all the analysis was complete we felt that it would be helpful to have some objective and independent challenge.

The QoE discussion group provided an ideal forum for our ideas and thinking to be reviewed, tested and enhanced by people with diverse knowledge and experience. This stimulating environment provided a 'real-world' pool of creativity in which to assure plans and make any adjustments, prior to final decisions and implementation.

Chris Burton
Managing Director
DesigneD4Successs

Chris was Head of Business Design, British Gas Home Services 2004 - 2006

Chris's example also demonstrates perpetual thinking being used to validate an existing proposition, as the group will bring in new thoughts and circumstances that the originator had potentially missed. Perpetual thinking groups can of course be used to identify potential weaknesses in a proposition, theory or strategy.

To further illustrate the dynamic of authenticity in perpetual experience, let me use one final example. Imagine a product specialist working at a telecoms provider. Her task, and so need, is to resolve the ongoing issues with a product that generates a lot of customer contact. Some of these issues are complaints, and added to this the service department is seeing too many failures. Wouldn't she want a perpetual thinking group on her side to help her get to the bottom of the issues? Her role as an authentic participant with a desire to solve a persistent problem inspires commitment from others. These may be customers, but even more crucially they will be the people she needs to take the actions necessary to improve the product. The authenticity of perpetual thinking groups is just as useful for engineers, accountants and project managers.

While participants in a perpetual thinking group enjoy the process, they do need a reason to play. Why do I use the word play? Real play is authentic. Comedians on the stage at Wembley need to be authentic first, engaging and then funny. Which brings me to a final point on authenticity - just like our comedian who gradually builds a following until he is on the stage at Wembley, authenticity helps to build an audience. Probably the most common question I hear from customer experience practitioners is, "how do I engage with other parts of my organisation?" Authentic groups provide both the opportunity and, in the context of perpetual experience, the incentive to participate.

Authentic companies will have a truly differentiated position in their existing market that allows them to identify converging customer needs. We can see this starting to happen with the emergence of the internet of things. For companies to gain market share in this connected environment they must not only be trusted, but also be authentic as they cross traditional product boundaries.

Authenticity may well replace loyalty, advocacy and effort as the single measure of success in the connected economy. Of course, this doesn't all happen by accident - there are practical steps to be taken to establish an authentic environment, participants, and chairperson, and these steps are described in my final chapter - Making it happen.

Building authenticity

Key points

- People increasingly expect a more authentic relationship with a company

- The effort required for a customer to migrate to a competitor is reducing to a point where feelings such as authenticity are the deciding factor

- Being authentic makes companies better equipped to respond to the real world

- People want their opinion to be valued, and employees want to work for people who genuinely value their opinion

In summary, perpetual experience

- Provides a way to draw on the untapped talent and creativity in every organisation

- Gives customers, employees, and partners a voice in decision making, leading to a better experience for all involved

- Helps businesses understand what is really happening in the company, and an authentic organisation is then better equipped to drive real and sustainable change

- Delivers a real and authentic, rather than simulated, flow of knowledge and information - this allows companies to bridge the gap between what they think happens in the real world, and what actually happens

YOUR REFLECTIONS

Who do you see as authentic and why?

How authentic is your company and why?

For those of you who prefer to start with a clean sheet . . .

. . . to Mind Map

10 | MAKING IT HAPPEN

CHAPTER 10

Making it happen

Mystery: *Why does customer experience struggle to link cause with effect?*

Getting started

Hopefully our conversation and your reflections have given you some thoughts on how perpetual experience can be useful to you and your company. To help you get things started, this chapter will outline four different approaches to making it happen - the simplest requires only a group of people. We then scale up the number and variety of participants, and finally we bring things together in a searchable resource.

Perpetual thinking groups look at a subject in a new way and expand the understanding of the issues beyond the accepted remit of customer experience. The group identifies a wide range of stakeholders from within their own company or partner companies who need to be engaged.

People experience journeys engage these stakeholders and give them a reason to participate as the journey explores their specific experiences of the subject. These participants, and the insight they generate, are then brought back into an expanded perpetual thinking group.

Incubation hubs are used when ideas generated by perpetual thinking groups need to be tested through multiple customer interactions. The insight generated is often fed directly into self and assisted service channels.

Experience engines capture the learning and insight from all the above activities in a searchable database that connects people, ideas and contexts.

Each approach contains the fundamental principles of inclusivity, authenticity, developing and sharing knowledge. However, each focuses on a different aspect of perpetual experience development. All contain elements that people like you working in customer experience will recognise.

Perpetual Thinking

There are two sides to perpetual thinking: the first is about generating a mind set, and the second is how to use this mind set in a practical sense.

Perpetual thinking helps organisations tackle persistent issues in order to improve experiences. It is the foundation of perpetual experience, and involves bringing together diverse groups of people in a specifically orchestrated environment to undertake an authentic exploration of an issue. This is more than just a meeting - participants are taken through a deliberately constructed series of interventions that are designed to ensure that a full range of opinions and experiences emerges. As we have discussed earlier in our conversation, and as Natalie explains below, influencing decision-making is a key function of customer and perpetual experience as it balances logic with intuition, and data with emotion.

I've spent the last five years working with academics from various fields of behavioural science, including behavioural economics and social psychology. These fields excel at codifying and measuring different facets of decision-making. They help us appreciate the extent to which context influences behaviour.

Customers and employees are subject to a wide range of heuristics and cognitive biases. These both help and hinder everyday decision-making. While people rely upon heuristics for good reasons, they also get sabotaged by existing habits and fail to act upon their intentions. I'm fascinated by how we can apply these insights and experimental methods to businesses - especially in areas like customer experience and operations.

That said, while I would champion a more sophisticated, data-driven understanding of decision-making, I'm struck by how much companies gain from simply talking about behaviour. Asking simple questions like: What are people doing? Why? What could be different?

Focusing on behaviour takes people out of their particular silo and gets them thinking more holistically about the people within, and interacting with, their organisation. This is a simple change in perspective but can be hugely transformative.

Natalie Horne
BA Hons Oxford
Prime Decision

Perpetual thinking groups are deployed to address a variety of scenarios, from finding resolutions to evaluating propositions and guiding strategy. They are commonly used at the initiation and conclusion stages of the people experience journey that we will be exploring in a moment. A perpetual thinking group consists of a Chairperson and ideally between eight and twelve participants. The Chairperson has two key roles: to facilitate effective exploration of the topic, and to position him or herself as a trusted advisor. While the role of the Chairperson is crucial, the method we are about to explore supports and endorses the role, enabling a wider range of people to play the role of the Chairperson. A common mistake is for groups to rely on the natural charisma or authority of the Chairperson rather than following the methodology that makes the role work.

The role begins with the pre-group meeting exploration and ends with the post-group evaluation. While the Chairperson can be someone from within the business, perpetual thinking groups can be more effective if the Chairperson comes from outside the business as he or she is able to disrupt entrenched thinking by bringing in an outside influence.

During the group session, participants share their experiences of the topic under consideration in order to help the group develop new insights. They provide multiple perspectives on the topic, exposing diverse views that may well differ from their individual experience. The non-judgmental rationale of the group means that there are no 'wrong' views, and this makes it easier for participants to empathise with those who may hold differing opinions from their own.

Perpetual thinking groups are very different from the meetings that typically occur in businesses and organisations. Let's explore these in more detail.

Topic generation and invitation

Choosing the right topic for the group to discuss is essential, as the topic defines both the purpose of the group discussion and the ideal participants to invite. The topic description must have something for everyone, while still allowing enough flexibility to permit a full exploration of the subject. Inviting - rather than ordering - people to join the discussion is also crucial. We discussed earlier that people should want to participate because they see the value and not because they have been told to do so. By choosing to attend, the participants will be more engaged and inclined to invest in the discussion, and consequently this generates higher quality outputs.

Perpetual thinking sessions work with both a broad and a narrow focus. The multi-company sessions provided by The QoE tackle broad issues around experience management, whereas sessions run for individual companies can dig deep into a specific experience issue. Both have their place. For those new to perpetual thinking it can be helpful to participate in a multi-company session to experience the dynamics before moving to company-specific sessions. Although internal sessions are relatively easy to initiate and achieve quick wins, the guidelines we are discussing need to be followed for them to be effective.

Pre-session discussions between Chairperson and participant

Prior to the main group discussion, the Chairperson arranges a 1-2-1 discussion with each participant, either in person or over the phone. The opportunity for a 1-2-1 discussion with the Chairperson helps an individual to see how the topic relates to their specific circumstances, identifies the areas of the topic in which they feel confident, and those they would like to explore with the help of others. The primary function of the pre-session discussion is to engage the individual in the topic and uncover their personal views, rather than just the views of their company or organisation. The success of The QoE perpetual thinking group is testament to the validity of this approach. It has consistently focused on understanding participants' personal involvement in topics, encouraging them to bring their 'whole self' to the table, rather than just their 'company self'. This personal investment in the topic is key to generating transformational outputs.

The pre-session discussion also defuses the problem of individual egos trying to dominate the main discussion. In some cases, the Chairperson will need to build confidence in a participant so they feel more able to contribute their views on the topic. In other cases, the Chairperson will need to temper a participant's confidence to mitigate their desire to boost their ego by proving their knowledge to the group during the main discussion.

Importantly, the pre-session discussion provides the Chairperson with the context needed to gently challenge an individual during the main discussion if they begin to take the easy route of agreeing with the group before any real reason for the change has been presented. Just as importantly, the pre-session discussion helps the Chairperson identify aspects of the topic that may need to be introduced into the main group discussion. This ensures there will something of interest for every participant and leads to full engagement and higher quality insights.

On occasion, it is appropriate to introduce insight and data or a substantial proposal into the discussion, or it may even be the focus of the discussion. It is important that this is considered in the Chairperson's review and a synopsis is also circulated to other participants before the meeting. This gives others the opportunity to evaluate its implications from their perspective before the meeting.

Main Group Discussion

The ideal number of participants in a group discussion is between eight and twelve, with a focus on the diversity of role, knowledge, experience and personality. This will ensure that a full range of experiences emerges. To begin with, the Chairperson's role is to provide a solid base from which to launch the discussion by providing more context to the topic. The Chairperson must set the standard in authenticity for the group (see chapter nine for more on authenticity) and demonstrate that their role is that of a 'trusted advisor'.

From then on, the Chairperson's role is to facilitate the discussion by asking informed questions, guiding and nudging participants to consider and discuss ideas and concepts that may lay beyond their comfort zone. There are only two key rules that the Chairperson must enforce: firstly, that participants respect the opinions of everyone at the table, even if they differ from their own, and secondly that there is only one discussion at the table. This second point is essential to maintain focus, ensuring that all participants listen to and reflect on all viewpoints in turn, and leads to deeper insights.

It can be useful for the Chairperson to bring in thoughts, ideas and experiences from other companies. This is an effective way of encouraging participants to bring their whole selves into the discussion, as some feel more comfortable sharing their personal views on examples from outside their own organisation. The Chairperson can introduce these external perspectives him or herself, or might also consider inviting representatives from these companies to share their experiences in person.

Follow-up discussion between Chairperson and participant

A few days after the main group discussion, the Chairperson arranges 1-2-1 follow up calls with each participant. This stage is valuable for participants as it provides them with the opportunity to feed back, not only on the discussion, but also on how their own views and opinions have changed after a period of reflection. The 1-2-1 discussion helps to reinforce and internalise their new insights and is an important mechanism in helping them to modify and align their behaviour with their new perspective. The Chairperson's role in the follow-up discussion is often to gently challenge each participant to consider making a change based on their new knowledge.

The follow-up also brings value for the Chairperson as it enables him or her to understand what each individual took away from the discussion. These insights are then collated and used to draft a 'consolidated output' for the group.

Consolidated output

An essential feature of a perpetual thinking group is that each participant will take away their own unique insights from the discussion and use these to justify subsequent changes in behaviour. But it is also valuable for the Chairperson to draw together what he or she believes to be the key outcomes for the group arising from the discussion. This can be challenging, as the objective of the group is not necessarily to reach a consensus and it is important that the Chairperson takes care to minimise the influence of their personal bias on the consolidated output.

The consolidated output must articulate the differing opinions and themes that emerged and, if a consensus on a topic is reached, this must be reported accurately. Articulating recurring themes, patterns and experiences can add both real depth and richness to the output and be used as a basis for further groups.

To summarise, for a successful perpetual thinking group you need

- A topic that gives the participants a genuine reason to participate

- Individual engagement with elements of the topic

- A stimulating and authentic chairperson and environment

- Accurate and unbiased output that covers the session and the reflective thoughts of the participants

And amongst the outcomes you can expect are

- Fully contextualised and validated solutions and a working hypothesis to test, re-validate and implement

- Accumulated knowledge and a data view of the operating environment

- A comprehensive map of interacting factors, required actions and KPIs

- A proven method of addressing this type of issue in the future

- Patterns, trends and data for future sessions

To illustrate perpetual thinking groups in action, I would like to provide an example that builds as the chapter continues.

Example of a broken delivery - part 1
Perpetual thinking group examines a recurring problem

A customer orders a hand-delivered item via a call centre. A week later he heard the doorbell ring. By the time he reached the door, the fragile delivery lay damaged on the doorstep, and the delivery driver was already back in her van. As this was a persistent problem, it became the subject of a perpetual thinking group. The group needed to consider what the customer was promised, how the order was received, how the product was selected, packaged, dispatched and finally delivered.

People Experience Journeys

People experience journeys enable organisations to identify and explore people related factors that contribute to complex business problems. They often reveal the root causes of these problems and help a business develop solutions to these root causes, rather than simply deal with the symptoms.

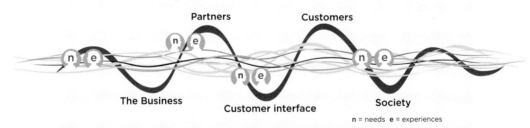

Figure 16: Needs and experiences

As we discussed in chapter six, and shown in the visualisation above, people experience journeys are based on the idea that every need generates an experience. When a need arises, whether for an employee or a customer, this generates an experience. To satisfy the need, knowledge is required - but where does this knowledge come from? And just as importantly, if someone learns something new through satisfying the need, how and where do they share this new knowledge?

People experience journeys enable companies to answer these questions, and in doing so they provide a way to dig much deeper into the complexity of a problem. By exploring the needs of each individual involved in the creation and delivery of a product or service, a people experience journey reveals the many tensions, blockages and workarounds that can result in a poor experience for employees, the business and the customer.

How do you do a people experience journey?

A people experience journey can be undertaken either through interviews or surveys, or a combination of both. The journey begins by asking the participants to consider a specific event, such as a stolen credit card or a delivery from a retailer. The participants then need to tell us the following:

1   What do they need to do in response to a given scenario?

    (Participants also rate how important they feel it is to perform the action)

2   What is their experience of what really happens?

    (Participants also rate how closely their experiences matches what they need)

3   What is their source of knowledge on how to proceed?

    (Participants also rate the extent to which this source influences their actions)

4   How do they share their thoughts on how to make improvements?

    (Again, participants also rate the extent to which this source influences their actions)

An example of a participant survey for a people experience journey

Before sending out the survey, the business would enter a short description of the event it wants participants to consider.

Participant Survey		
Business area (select from list)		
Your role		
Please think about the following event when answering the questions:		
The business description of the event, e.g. reporting a stolen card, or an Amazon delivery		
	Primary	**Secondary**
What are the top 2 things you really need to do in relation to this event?		
How important do you feel it is to do these? 0% - 100%		
In your personal experience what really happens?		
How closely does your experience match what you need? 0% - 100%		
What is your key source of information about this?		
How much does this source influence your actions? 0% - 100%		
What is your key way of sharing information about this?		
How much does this source influence your actions? 0% - 100%		

Figure 17: An example of a participant survey for a people experience journey

We are in effect taking what we know about surveying customers and applying it to our own people. As you know, survey techniques are ultimately scalable - from 1-2-1 interviews to online survey tools. The key is what do we ask and how to we analyse the responses? This could be assessing the outputs from interviews, or a more complex analysis of trends and underlying themes from surveys.

Your business may well have existing customer insight data, and this can be used to illustrate the customer perspective and the views of the wider society. The direct input comes from customer services, and any function within your company or your partners involved in the delivery of a product or service.

In the case of the B2B environment, the majority of people experience journeys will be based on face-to-face interviews. As with perpetual thinking, the person chosen to be the interviewer is important as they must strive to remain as neutral as possible. (For anyone interested in research methods, this approach to interviewing is similar to that used in phenomenography.)

The process exposes the pressures and weak links in teams, individuals and systems. And in doing so, a people experience journey will also uncover localised knowledge and potentially invaluable solutions to problems that can be adapted or scaled up for broader use.

Once the full people experience journey has been generated it can be aligned with other sources of information such as call and service centre metrics, process maps and system maps. Mapping the journey reveals poor experiences for both customers and employees that can both stem from, and lead to process failures. The business now has a clear understanding of what actually happens, where the weak points are, and who needs to be involved in designing and communicating a solution. Bringing people together to generate people experience journeys often results in unexpected connections that lead to new and innovative solutions. It is common for someone to say, "if only we could...", leading to a perplexed look across the table, quickly followed by, "but we can, we do this all the time using...".

In summary, people experience journeys

- Reinforce the move from customer to people experience
- Track the experiences and emotions of the customer, the business and its partners
- Enable people to share circumstances
- Permit powerful root cause analysis
- Provide a way to predict future issues and failures
- Facilitate alignment of process and real-world maps
- Generate knowledge to build and implement solutions
- Increase engagement and demonstrate authentic problem solving
- Are a great precursor to perpetual thinking groups and incubation hubs

Example - part 2
People experience journey investigates

The complaint used in the above example generated a need to process the order, select the product, dispatch and deliver the product. Fulfilling each of those needs generated an experience. By looking at those experiences, it quickly became evident that the driver's experience of trying to fulfil her quota of deliveries left no option but to place the product on the ground and run back to her van.

Example - part 3
Perpetual thinking group is re-convened

The journey was taken back into a perpetual thinking group. A more detailed investigation revealed a loyal driver who had been asked to temporarily cover another driver's commitments. But the company, seeing that she could manage this, made it a permanent arrangement. The resulting stress on the driver was responsible for both her and the customer's poor experience.

Incubation Hubs

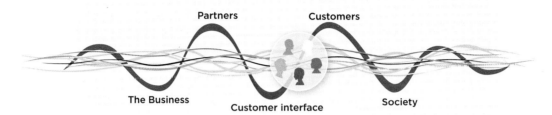

Figure 18: Positioning the incubator hub in the people experience journey

The purpose of the incubation hub is to get into the granular detail of the problem, examine the needs of everyone involved, test a hypothesis, and generate viable options for transformation. They are also used to generate the knowledge required to drive effective self and assisted service. The hub is set up within an area of the business, such as a call centre, with a representative group of participants, as illustrated in the people experience journey visual above, and runs for two to three months to enable effective monitoring of activity.

To tackle a complex problem with several stages, multiple mini incubation hubs are used to allow a focused exploration of each step of the problem. Each mini hub identifies and tests an alternative strategy for each stage and evaluates its effectiveness with participants. Incubation hubs give companies the opportunity to include inputs from a variety of sources and partners, depending on the issue being addressed. The temporary nature of the hub often makes this possible where a fixed line of connectivity would be impractical.

For example, if the people experience journeys have explored an issue to do with 'billing', an incubation hub would be assembled to unpack the problem. Each mini hub would examine a specific stage of the problem, such as receiving the bill, interpreting the bill, and understanding the implications for the device or tariff. Participants would then generate and test a different approach to each stage and evaluate its effectiveness. Whenever a hub is deployed, it generates a valuable and unique resource of knowledge, experience and understanding of real-world issues that can be fed into both the experience engine and into self and assisted service.

The participants for an incubation hub are chosen according to the hypothesis to be tested and according to the desired outcome. So if a call centre wants to extract the best resolutions to improve self and assisted service, the participants who are most effective at handling calls would be chosen. If, on the other hand, the purpose is to improve the day to day operation of the call centre, a more balanced sample would be used in order to reveal the full range of issues.

Importantly, if the hypothesis indicates that a major issue exists in another area of the business, the incubation hub would open a channel to an employee in that area to incorporate their experience. In this way, the incubation hub draws together relevant knowledge from across the business and uses real-world experiences to tackle complex problems.

An incubation hub also assesses the tools that are used in the business to understand how technology both helps and hinders participants in the people experience journey. This assessment may focus solely on the tools currently used, or may evaluate the benefits of accessing data available in other existing systems, such as Genesys, salesforce, eGain, Yammer, or other customer or product management systems. Establishing the current landscape of knowledge and data then makes it possible to determine whether any additional technology or functionality is needed, or whether existing tools just need to be used differently, in order to improve experiences.

By extracting the learning from customers' and employees' experiences, the incubation hub enables a business to respond to what actually happens by using this information to guide decision-making.

And by generating better ways for people to find and share the knowledge they need, the incubation hub reduces cost of service, reduces stress and workplace effort, increases operational efficiency, delivers marginal gains for customers and employees, and improves the experience of everyone involved.

Example - part 4
Resolution

The perpetual thinking group revealed that the company needed to change the delivery routes so all drivers had to pick up the slack. The group also discovered that the need for the item to be hand-delivered also added complications for the driver as a person needed to be available to receive the package. Crucially, participants from all stakeholder groups were part of the conversation, and a hypothesis was developed for testing: Can the agent book a time slot for the delivery? Will the customer commit to the time slot? How can the initial faults in the process be overcome?

An incubation hub was set up consisting of a select group of call centre agents. The agents were given the new scheduling tools with the ability to share their learning amongst the hub participants. This quickly revealed not only the answer, but also how to automate the process for the self-service environment. The outcome was to complete the picture so that the driver knew there was likely to be a person at home to receive the package. Her behaviour changed as a result.

Experience Engine

The experience engine makes it possible to search the knowledge and experiences generated by perpetual thinking, people experience journeys and incubation hubs. It contains searchable records of the experiences, legacy assets, themes and trends, and this enables people to access an understanding of both 'what happened', 'how it happened', and 'who was responsible for the thinking'.

While many customer experience functions identify a problem, develop a hypothesis, test and implement a solution, they often fail to record the process that was followed. On the occasions when the process has been recorded it is frequently written in the language of the company, rather than in natural, everyday language. This language barrier can make it difficult for others to understand the relevance of the solution, even though it may be what they are looking for. When the problem re-emerges, the lack of clarity and inability to search previous experiences can lead to a solution being developed from scratch, due to the inability to locate the right knowledge, often at significant cost.

Providing a searchable repository of legacy assets and experiences makes it possible to find out how a problem was addressed in the past. Importantly, the experience engine, as illustrated below in Figure 19, provides a social platform to enable a conversation with the person who

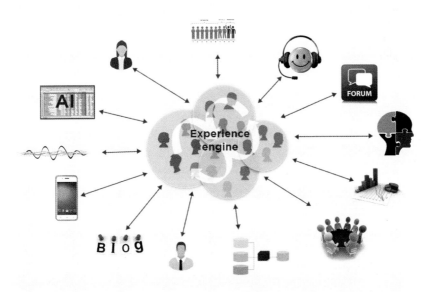

Figure 19: The experience engine sharing knowledge extracted from customer and employee interaction

solved the problem so that others can ask direct questions relating to their specific situation.

The ability to search the organisation's memory of experiences saves time, money and resources when seeking a solution to a problem. The knowledge can be reused to provide direction and content or future innovations in self and assisted service - and also the development of new products and services to meet the challenges of the changing business environment.

Making this happen will depend to a great extent on the existing capabilities and architecture of the business. Successful implementation requires that the experience engine can draw information from a comprehensive range of sources to facilitate effective search.

Example - part 5
Capturing the experience

The experience engine captures each of the pieces of information from our delivery example. A customer ordered a hand-delivered item via a call centre. The delivery was consistently poor.

The customer promise, how the order was received, how the product was selected, packaged, dispatched and finally delivered, all needed to be examined in detail. The needs and experiences revealed the cause of the decline and eventual failure of the delivery. Not valuing the driver's experience led to a decision that resulted in the change in behaviour. Resolving the issues required input from several functions and companies. The scenario needed testing in the real world. The people involved have the potential to recognise patterns in future investigations, so become a prime resource and willing participants for similar investigations.

The experience engine also captures a new, contextual dataset that can be used for designing future products and services and feeds directly into self and assisted service.

Conclusion

Working through these approaches helps us to build more than just good resolutions and datasets. It helps people in the company articulate why customer experience is important, what it means for them, and what 'good' looks like in a number of different scenarios. The message becomes authentic and engaging: customer experience has broken through to become business as usual.

MAKING IT HAPPEN

Key points

- Perpetual thinking helps organisations tackle persistent issues to improve experiences and outcomes

- People experience journeys uncover the root causes of problems and weak links in products and services

- Incubation hubs reveal the granular detail of a problem and provide the knowledge required for effective self and assisted service

- Experience engines make it possible to search the knowledge and experiences generated by perpetual thinking, people experience journeys and incubation hubs

In summary, perpetual experience will

- Enable organisations to move to a mind set of proactive influence

- Provide authentic interactions between companies and customers

- Help organisations engage with, and interpret the many voices of the connected society

- Allow employees to bring their whole selves to work, releasing new knowledge, insights and creativity that can be used to drive innovation

- Contextualise the vast quantities of data that a business can now collect, and help the business use this data to make more informed decisions

- Drive behaviours that contribute to real-time ROI

YOUR REFLECTIONS

What do you need to make a start?

What will you gain first?

For those of you who prefer to start with a clean sheet . . .

. . . to Mind Map

SUMMARY

Summary

I sincerely hope you have enjoyed our journey and our conversation. Unravelling the mysteries and evolution of customer experience in the context of rapid technical and social innovation has undoubtedly been a challenge. But I hope that you now have a clear understanding of both the underlying principles and practical applications of perpetual experience.

At the beginning of our conversation, I described companies being at a pivotal point where the knowledge and tools are available to transform their performance. Having reflected on this while writing the book, I now believe that the true pivotal point consists of the changing behaviours and expectations of people. People who increasingly value their individuality but also the opinions of their diverse social groups and communities. As the perceived power of the individual increases, we are beginning to see how people willingly participate in a range of activities and groups that stimulate a continuous creative flow of emotion, opinions, knowledge, experiences and innovations.

As we move further into the 21st century, I believe it is this perpetual flow of experiences that constitutes such an immense opportunity for companies. Perpetual experience provides a state of continuing, never-ceasing and self-enhancing experience, enabling businesses to take or regain their rightful place as trusted providers of the products and services that satisfy real, rather than perceived, needs. It enables businesses to gather and share the contextual knowledge that is required to make effective, people-oriented self and assisted service a reality. And it shows businesses how themes and trends combine with individual knowledge and understanding to create or enhance products and services, and guide strategic thinking.

Implementing perpetual experience will increase the scope and effectiveness of customer experience, increasing its ROI by harnessing the economics of real-world and real-time behaviour change. The move from customer experience, through people experience, and driven by the dynamics of perpetual experience, will elevate organisations to become authentic, proactive and powerful drivers of service and innovation. And as the connected society evolves, authentic leadership, managing by influence rather than by authority, and providing engaging environments, will become the keys to the current and future success of every company.

People like you will make perpetual experience happen: be an individual, be authentic, share your knowledge, and create a business that you and others are proud of.

Perpetual experience is the perpetual advantage.

Since its inception in 2005, The QoE has been a focal point for customer experience debate for leading brands and businesses across many sectors. I would like to thank all the companies listed overleaf for the experiences and insights they have brought to the table - they have been invaluable in shaping my thinking on the development of perpetual experience.

20:20	Cap Gemini
Airbus Defence and Space	Carlson Wagonlit Travel
Aol	Centrica
Atom Bank	Charles Tyrwhitt
Atos	Chorus Communications
Aurora Group	Cisco
Avaya	City & Guilds
AXA PPP	Colt
Barclays Bank	Consumer Intelligence
Beaverbrooks	Convergys
Beer Hawk	Crown Prosecution Service
Bibendum Wine	Deloitte
BMI Healthcare	Digital Headspace
Boots	Direct Line
BP	Dyfed Police
British Gas	E.on
BSkyB	e2v
BT	Eaga
BT 21C	EDF
Business Systems	Egg
Cable & Wireless	Emirates
CACI International	Europcar

First Data	KPMG
First Direct	Kwik-Fit Finance
Foster Denovo	Legal & General
F-Secure	L-3 Communications
Gartner	Lebara
Gmac	Lloyds Banking Group
Groupama	Lloyds Insurance
Hampshire Fire	LV=
Harding & Yorke	Macmillan Cancer Support
Henchards	Marks and Spencer
Home Group	Microlease
Honda	MS Fitout
HSBC	National Grid
Intelligent Finance	Nationwide
IFDS	NHS Direct
In-gage	Nokia
Intrepid	npower
Jaguar Land Rover	NTL
John Lewis Partnership	O2
JoHo Ventures	Onecom
KCOM	Orange
Kingston Communications	Overbury

Paradigm Services	T-Mobile
Park Leisure	Telewest
Pegasus Life	The Logic Group
Percepta	Thomson Airways
Personnel Dynamics	TNT
Platform	TomTom
Prime Decision	Totemic
QPC	Toyota
Roland DG	Travelport
Round	TUI
Salesforce	UCA
Scottish Water	UCAS
Shop Direct	Vidus
Simplyhealth	Virgin Media
Sony	Virgin Mobile
Sony Mobile	Vodafone Group
Spotify	Vodafone Enterprise
Stericycle	Von Essen Group
Sun Microsystems	Whitehouse Consulting
Sure Communications	Yorkshire Police
Sybaris	Zest Consultancy
Synovate	

perpetualexperience.com

THE FOUR PATHS OF
YOGA

Discovery Publisher

Author: Swami Vivekananda

616 Corporate Way
Valley Cottage, New York, 10989
www.discoverypublisher.com
edition@discoverypublisher.com
facebook.com/discoverypublisher
twitter.com/discoverypb

New York • Paris • Dublin • Tokyo • Hong Kong

TABLE OF CONTENTS

The Path of Devotion

THE FOUR PATHS OF
YOGA

From ancient times, people of India have practiced spiritual disciplines designed to clear the mind and support a state of serene, detached awareness. The practices for developing this desired state of balance, purity, wisdom, and peacefulness of mind are known collectively as yoga.

"Yoga" means "yoke" or "union"— referring to union with the true Self, the goal described in the Upanishads.

The sages distinguished four basic types of people and developed practices that are particularly suitable for each type, in order that each man can attain the desired union with the Self.

- For rational people, there is the Path of Knowledge.

- For meditative people, there is the Path of Self-Knowledge.

- For naturally active people, there is the Path of Selfless Action.

- For emotional people, there is the Path of Devotion.

—*Living Religions, 79*

I. The Path of Knowledge

—Jnana Yoga

An attempt to realize the Brahman-Atman identity through the study of the Vedas (i.e. the sacred texts of the Hindu tradition) and direct contemplation of the self:

> *After negating [one's identity with the body, the senses, and the mind] as "not this," "not this," that Awareness which alone remains — that I am. ...*
> *The thought "Who am I?" will destroy all other thoughts, and, like the stick used for stirring the burning pyre, it will itself in the end get destroyed. Then, there will arise Self-realization.*
>
> *—Living Religions, 81*

II. The Path of Self-Knowledge

—Raja Yoga

Various systems (such as those described in Patanjali's Yoga Sutras or the later system known as Kundalini) that focus on the use of techniques (including the adoption of physical postures, breath control, mantras and visualization) to bring the mind to a state of one-pointed concentration, known as samadhi, in which union with the absolute is attained.

> *Words and language are imperfect to describe this exalted state. ... Mind, intellect and the senses cease functioning. ... It is a state of eternal Bliss and eternal Wisdom. All dualities vanish in toto. ... All visible merge in the invisible or the Unseen. The individual soul becomes that which he contemplates.*
>
> *—Living Religions, 80*

III. The Path of Selfless Action

—Karma Yoga

Karma Yoga originally focused on varnasrama-dharma— the performance of actions in accordance with the duties (dharma) associated with one's caste (varna) and stage of life (asrama). By acting in accordance with the principles of varnasrama-dharma, one gradually worked through the four stages of life (student, householder, forest-dweller, renunciate) towards ultimate release from the cycle of rebirth (moksha)— though the process might take many lifetimes to complete.

In the Bhagavad-Gita, however, Krishna redefined Karma Yoga by combining it with the fundamental insight of Jnana Yoga— namely the ultimate identity of the individual self (atman) and the Universal Self (Brahman)— leading to the conclusion that "it is the Absolute who performs all actions." Through this realization, one is able to perform action "without any interest in its fruits and without any personal sense of giving." By relinquishing one's own attachment to the fruits of one's actions, one attains "liberation from the self in the very midst of work":

> *I pervade the entire universe in my unmanifested form. All creatures find their existence in me, but I am not limited by them. Behold my divine mystery!*
>
> *... The foolish do not look beyond physical appearances to see my true nature as the Lord of all creation. The knowledge of such deluded people is empty; their lives are fraught with disaster and evil and their work and hopes are all in vain.*
>
> *But truly great souls seek my divine nature. They worship me with a one-pointed mind, having realized that I am the eternal source of all. Constantly striving, they make firm their resolve and worship me without wavering. Full of devotion, they sing of my divine glory. ...*
>
> *Whatever I am offered in devotion with a pure heart— a leaf, a flower, fruit, or water— I partake of that love offering. Whatever you do, make it an offering to me— the food you eat, the sacrifices you make, the help you give, even your suffering. In this way you will be freed from the bondage of karma, and from its results both pleasant and painful. Then, firm in renunciation and yoga, with your heart free, you will come to me.*
>
> *I look upon all creatures equally; none are less dear to me and none more dear. But those who worship me with love live in me, and I come to life in them. ... All*

those who take refuge in me, whatever their birth, race, sex, or caste, will attain the supreme goal; this realization can be attained even by those whom society scorns. ... Therefore, having been born in this transient and forlorn world, give all your love to me. Fill your mind with me; love me; serve me; worship me always. Seeking me in your heart, you will at last be united with me.

—*Anthology of Living Religions, 66–68 (Bhagavad Gita, Chapter 9); cf. BG/9*

IV. The Path of Devotion

—*Bhakti Yoga*

Bhakti Yoga is closely related to the notion of Karma Yoga as presented in the Bhagavad-Gita, since it is precisely by performing action in a spirit of "devotion" to Krishna (rather than as a means of generating "good" karma that will benefit one either in this or some future life) that one attains release from the cycle of rebirth. This "devotion" is manifest as an intense feeling of love for God that is frequently expressed through poetry and song, such as the following offering from Mirabai:

> *Without Krishna I cannot sleep.*
> *Tortured by longing, I cannot sleep,*
> *And the fire of love*
> *Drives me to wander hither and thither.*
> *Without the light of the Beloved*
> *My house is dark,*
> *And lamps do not please me.*
> *Without the Beloved my bed is uninviting,*
> *And I pass the nights awake.*
> *When will my Beloved return home?*
> *... What shall I do? Where shall I go?*
> *Who can quench my pain?*
> *My body has been bitten*
> *By the snake of "absence,"*
> *And my life is ebbing away*
> *With every beat of the heart.*
> *... My Lord when will you come*

To meet your Mira?
... When, my Lord,
Will you come to laugh and talk with me?

—*Anthology of Living Religions, 79*

Since Bhakti Yoga is more easily pursued than either Raja or Jnana Yoga, it is by far the most common form of Hindu practice. Its appeal is nicely expressed in the following quote from Sri Ramakrishna:

As long as the I-sense lasts, so long are true knowledge and Liberation impossible. ... [But] how very few can obtain this Union [Samadhi] and free themselves from this "I"? It is very rarely possible. Talk as much as you want, isolate yourself continuously, still this "I" will always return to you. Cut down the poplar tree today, and you will find tomorrow it forms new shoots. When you ultimately find that this "I" cannot be destroyed, let it remain as "I" the servant.

—*Living Religions, 83*

JNANA YOGA
THE PATH OF KNOWLEDGE

Chapter I
The Necessity of Religion

Delivered in London

Of all the forces that have worked and are still working to mould the destinies of the human race, none, certainly, is more potent than that, the manifestation of which we call religion. All social organisations have as a background, somewhere, the workings of that peculiar force, and the greatest cohesive impulse ever brought into play amongst human units has been derived from this power. It is obvious to all of us that in very many cases the bonds of religion have proved stronger than the bonds of race, or climate, or even of descent. It is a well-known fact that persons worshipping the same God, believing in the same religion, have stood by each other, with much greater strength and constancy, than people of merely the same descent, or even brothers. Various attempts have been made to trace the beginnings of religion. In all the ancient religions which have come down to us at the present day, we find one claim made — that they are all supernatural, that their genesis is not, as it were, in the human brain, but that they have originated somewhere outside of it.

Two theories have gained some acceptance amongst modern scholars. One is the spirit theory of religion, the other the evolution of the idea of the Infinite. One party maintains that ancestor worship is the beginning of religious ideas; the other, that religion originates in the personification of the powers of nature. Man wants to keep up the memory of his dead relatives and thinks they are living even when the body is dissolved, and he wants to place food for them and, in a certain sense, to worship them. Out of that came the growth we call religion.

Studying the ancient religions of the Egyptians, Babylonians, Chinese, and many other races in America and elsewhere, we find very clear traces of this ancestor worship being the beginning of religion. With the ancient Egyptians, the first idea of the soul was that of a double. Every human body contained in it another being very similar to it; and when a man died, this double went out of the body and yet lived on. But the life of the double lasted only so long as the dead body remained intact, and that is why we find among the Egyptians so much solicitude to keep the body uninjured. And that is why they built those huge pyramids in which they preserved the bodies. For, if any portion of the external body was hurt, the double would be correspondingly injured. This is clearly ancestor worship. With the ancient Babylonians we find the same idea of the double, but with a variation. The double lost all sense of love; it frightened the living to give it food and drink, and to help it in various ways. It even lost all affection for its own children and its own wife. Among the ancient Hindus also, we find traces of this ancestor worship. Among the Chinese, the basis of their religion may also be said to be ancestor worship, and it still permeates the length and breadth of that vast country. In fact, the only religion that can really be said to flourish in China is that of ancestor worship. Thus it seems, on the one hand, a very good position is made out for those who hold the theory of ancestor worship as the beginning of religion.

On the other hand, there are scholars who from the ancient Aryan literature show that religion originated in nature worship. Although in India we find proofs of ancestor worship everywhere, yet in the oldest records there is no trace of it whatsoever. In the Rig-Veda Samhita, the most ancient record of the Aryan race, we do not find any trace of it. Modern scholars think, it is the worship of nature that they find there. The human mind seems to struggle to get a peep behind the scenes. The dawn, the evening, the hurricane, the stupendous and gigantic forces of nature, its beauties, these have exercised the human mind, and it aspires to go beyond, to understand something about them. In the struggle they endow these phenomena with personal attributes, giving them souls and bodies, sometimes beautiful, sometimes transcendent. Every attempt ends by these phenomena becoming abstractions whether personalised or not. So also it is found with the ancient Greeks; their whole mythology is simply this abstracted nature worship. So also with the ancient Germans, the Scandinavians, and all the other Aryan races. Thus, on this side, too, a very strong case has been made out, that religion has its origin in the personification of the powers of nature.

These two views, though they seem to be contradictory, can be reconciled on a third basis, which, to my mind, is the real germ of religion, and that I propose to call the struggle to transcend the limitations of the senses. Either, man goes to seek for the spirits of his ancestors, the spirits of the dead, that is, he wants to get a glimpse of what there is after the body is dissolved, or, he desires to understand the power working behind the stupendous phenomena of nature. Whichever of these is the case, one thing is certain, that he tries to transcend the limitations of the senses. He cannot remain satisfied with his senses; he wants to go beyond them. The explanation need not be mysterious. To me it seems very natural that the first glimpse of religion should come through dreams. The first idea of immortality man may well get through dreams. Is that not a most wonderful state? And we know that children and untutored minds find very little difference between dreaming and their awakened state. What can be more natural than that they find, as natural logic, that even during the sleep state when the body is apparently dead, the mind goes on with all its intricate workings? What wonder that men will at once come to the conclusion that when this body is dissolved for ever, the same working will go on? This, to my mind, would be a more natural explanation of the supernatural, and through this dream idea the human mind rises to higher and higher conceptions. Of course, in time, the vast majority of mankind found out that these dreams are not verified by their waking states, and that during the dream state it is not that man has a fresh existence, but simply that he recapitulates the experiences of the awakened state.

But by this time the search had begun, and the search was inward, arid man continued inquiring more deeply into the different stages of the mind and discovered higher states than either the waking or the dreaming. This state of things we find in all the organised religions of the world, called either ecstasy or inspiration. In all organised religions, their founders, prophets, and messengers are declared to have gone into states of mind that were neither waking nor sleeping, in which they came face to face with a new series of facts relating to what is called the spiritual kingdom. They realised things there much more intensely than we realise facts around us in our waking state. Take, for instance, the religions of the Brahmins. The Vedas are said to be written by Rishis. These Rishis were sages who realised certain facts. The exact definition of the Sanskrit word Rishi is a Seer of Mantras— of the thoughts conveyed in the Vedic hymns. These men declared that they had realised— sensed, if that word can be used with regard to the supersensuous— certain facts, and these facts they proceeded to put on record. We find the same truth declared amongst both the Jews and the Christians.

Some exceptions may be taken in the case of the Buddhists as represented by the Southern sect. It may be asked— if the Buddhists do not believe in any God or soul, how can their religion be derived from the supersensuous state of existence? The answer to this is that even the Buddhists find an eternal moral law, and that moral law was not reasoned out in our sense of the word But Buddha found it, discovered it, in a supersensuous state. Those of you who have studied the life of Buddha even as briefly given in that beautiful poem, The Light of Asia, may remember that Buddha is represented as sitting under the Bo-tree until he reached that supersensuous state of mind. All his teachings came through this, and not through intellectual cogitations.

Thus, a tremendous statement is made by all religions; that the human mind, at certain moments, transcends not only the limitations of the senses, but also the power of reasoning. It then comes face to face with facts which it could never have sensed, could never hive reasoned out. These facts are the basis of all the religions of the world. Of course we have the right to challenge these facts, to put them to the test of reason. Nevertheless, all the existing religions of the world claim for the human mind this peculiar power of transcending the limits of the senses and the limits of reason; and this power they put forward as a statement of fact.

Apart from the consideration of tie question how far these facts claimed by religions are true, we find one characteristic common to them all. They are all abstractions as contrasted with the concrete discoveries of physics, for instance; and in all the highly organised religions they take the purest form of Unit Abstraction, either in the form of an Abstracted Presence, as an Omnipresent Being, as an Abstract Personality called God, as a Moral Law, or in the form of an Abstract Essence underlying every existence. In modern times, too, the attempts made to preach religions without appealing to the supersensuous state if the mind have had to take up the old abstractions of the Ancients and give different names to them as "Moral Law", the "Ideal Unity", and so forth, thus showing that these abstractions are not in the senses. None of us have yet seen an "Ideal Human Being", and yet we are told to believe in it. None of us have yet seen an ideally perfect man, and yet without that ideal we cannot progress. Thus, this one fact stands out from all these different religions, that there is an Ideal Unit Abstraction, which is put before us, either in the form of a Person or an Impersonal Being, or a Law, or a Presence, or an Essence. We are always struggling to raise ourselves up to that ideal. Every human being, whosoever and wheresoever he may be, has an ideal of infinite power. Every human being has an ideal of infinite pleasure. Most of the works that we find around us, the activities displayed everywhere, are due to the struggle for this infinite power or this infinite pleasure. But a few quickly discover that although they are struggling for infinite power, it is not through the senses that it can be reached. They find out very soon that that infinite pleasure is not to be got through the senses, or, in other words, the senses are too limited, and the body is too limited, to express the Infinite. To manifest the Infinite through the finite is impossible, and sooner or later, man learns to give up the attempt to express the Infinite through the finite. This giving up, this renunciation of the attempt, is the background of ethics. Renunciation is the very basis upon which ethics stands. There never was an ethical code preached which had not renunciation for its basis.

Ethics always says, "Not I, but thou." Its motto is, "Not self, but non-self." The vain ideas of individualism, to which man clings when he is trying to find that Infinite Power or that Infinite Pleasure through the senses, have to be given up — say the laws of ethics. You have to put yourself last, and others before you. The senses say, "Myself first." Ethics says, "I must hold myself last." Thus, all codes of ethics are based upon this renunciation; destruction, not construction, of the individual on the material plane. That Infinite will never find expression upon the material plane, nor is it possible or thinkable.

So, man has to give up the plane of matter and rise to other spheres to seek a deeper expression of that Infinite. In this way the various ethical laws are being moulded, but all have that one central idea, eternal self-abnegation. Perfect self-annihilation is the ideal of ethics. People are startled if they are asked not to think of their individualities. They seem so very much afraid of losing what they call their individuality. At the same time, the same men would declare the highest ideals of ethics to be right, never for a moment thinking that the scope, the goal, the idea of all ethics is the destruction, and not the building up, of the individual.

Utilitarian standards cannot explain the ethical relations of men, for, in the first place, we cannot derive any ethical laws from considerations of utility. Without the supernatural sanction as it is called, or the perception of the superconscious as I prefer to term it, there can be no ethics. Without the struggle towards the Infinite there can be no ideal. Any system that wants to bind men down to the limits of their own societies is not able to find an explanation for the ethical laws of mankind. The Utilitarian wants us to give up the struggle after the Infinite, the reaching-out for the Supersensuous, as impracticable and absurd, and, in the same breath, asks us to take up ethics and do good to society. Why should we do good? Doing good is a secondary consideration. We must have an ideal. Ethics itself is not the end, but the means to the end. If the end is not there, why should we be ethical? Why should I do good to other men, and not injure them? If happiness is the goal of mankind, why should I not make myself happy and others unhappy? What prevents me? In the second place, the basis of utility is too narrow. All the current social forms and methods are derived from society as it exists, but what right has the Utilitarian to assume that society is eternal? Society did not exist ages ago, possibly will not exist ages hence. Most probably it is one of the passing stages through which we are going towards a higher evolution, and any law that is derived from society alone cannot be eternal, cannot cover the whole ground of man's nature. At best, therefore, Utilitarian theories can only work under present social conditions. Beyond that they have no value. But a morality an ethical code, derived from religion and spirituality, has the whole of infinite man for its scope. It takes up the individual, but its relations are to the Infinite, and it takes up society also — because society is nothing but numbers of these individuals grouped together; and as it applies to the individual and his eternal relations, it must necessarily apply to the whole of society, in whatever condition it may be at any given time. Thus we see that there is always the necessity of spiritual religion for mankind. Man cannot always think of matter, however pleasurable it may be.

It has been said that too much attention to things spiritual disturbs our practical relations in this world. As far back as in the days of the Chinese sage Confucius, it was said, "Let us take care of this world: and then, when we have finished with this world, we will take care of other world." It is very well that we should take care of this world. But if too much attention to the spiritual may affect a little our practical relations, too much attention to the so-called practical hurts us here and hereafter. It makes us materialistic. For man is not to regard nature as his goal, but something higher.

Man is man so long as he is struggling to rise above nature, and this nature is both internal and external. Not only does it comprise the laws that govern the particles of matter outside us and in our bodies, but also the more subtle nature within, which is, in fact, the motive power governing the external. It is good and very grand to conquer external nature, but grander still to conquer our internal nature. It is grand and good to know the laws that govern the stars and planets; it is infinitely grander and better to know the laws that govern the passions, the feelings, the will, of mankind. This conquering of the inner man, understanding the secrets of the subtle workings that are within the human mind, and knowing its wonderful secrets, belong entirely to religion. Human nature — the ordinary human nature, I mean — wants to see big material facts. The ordinary man cannot understand anything that is subtle. Well has it been said that the masses admire the lion that kills a thousand lambs, never for a moment thinking that it is death to the lambs. Although a momentary triumph for the lion; because they find pleasure only in manifestations of physical strength. Thus it is with the ordinary run of mankind. They understand and find pleasure in everything that is external. But in every society there is a section whose pleasures are not in the senses, but beyond, and who now and then catch glimpses of something higher than matter and struggle to reach it. And if we read the history of nations between the lines, we shall always find that the rise of a nation comes with an increase in the number of such men; and the fall begins when this pursuit after the Infinite, however vain Utilitarians may call it, has ceased. That is to say, the mainspring of the strength of every race lies in its spirituality, and the death of that race begins the day that spirituality wanes and materialism gains ground.

Thus, apart from the solid facts and truths that we may learn from religion, apart from the comforts that we may gain from it, religion, as a science, as a study, is the greatest and healthiest exercise that the human mind can have. This pursuit of the Infinite, this struggle to grasp the Infinite, this effort to get beyond the limitations of the senses — out of matter, as it were — and to evolve the spiritual man — this striving day and night to make the Infinite one with our being — this struggle itself is the grandest and most glorious that man can make. Some persons find the greatest pleasure in eating. We have no right to say that they should not. Others find the greatest pleasure in possessing certain things. We have no right to say that they should not. But they also have no right to say "no" to the man who finds his highest pleasure in spiritual thought. The lower the organisation, the greater the pleasure in the senses. Very few men can eat a meal with the same gusto as a dog or a wolf. But all the pleasures of the dog or the wolf have gone, as it were into the senses. The lower types of humanity in all nations find pleasure in the senses, while the cultured and the educated find it in thought, in philosophy, in arts and sciences. Spirituality is a still higher plane. The subject being infinite, that plane is the highest, and the pleasure there is the highest for those who can appreciate it. So, even on the utilitarian ground that man is to seek for pleasure, he should cultivate religious thought, for it is the highest pleasure that exists. Thus religion, as a study, seems to me to be absolutely necessary.

We can see it in its effects. It is the greatest motive power that moves the human mind. No other ideal can put into us the same mass of energy as the spiritual. So far as human history goes, it is obvious to all of us that this has been the case and that its powers are not dead. I do not deny that men, on simply utilitarian grounds, can be very good and moral. There have been many great men in this world perfectly sound, moral, and good, simply on utilitarian grounds. But the world-movers, men who bring, as it were, a mass of magnetism into the world whose spirit works in hundreds and in thousands, whose life ignites others with a spiritual fire — such men, we always find, have that spiritual background. Their

motive power came from religion. Religion is the greatest motive power for realising that infinite energy which is the birthright and nature of every man. In
building up character in making for everything that is good and great, in bringing peace to others and peace to one's own self, religion is the highest motive
power and, therefore, ought to be studied from that standpoint. Religion must
be studied on a broader basis than formerly. All narrow limited, fighting ideas
of religion have to go. All sect ideas and tribal or national ideas of religion must
be given up. That each tribe or nation should have its own particular God and
think that every other is wrong is a superstition that should belong to the past.
All such ideas must be abandoned.

As the human mind broadens, its spiritual steps broaden too. The time has
already come when a man cannot record a thought without its reaching to all
corners of the earth; by merely physical means, we have come into touch with
the whole world; so the future religions of the world have to become as universal, as wide.

The religious ideals of the future must embrace all that exists in the world and
is good and great, and, at the same time, have infinite scope for future development. All that was good in the past must be preserved; and the doors must
be kept open for future additions to the already existing store. Religions must
also be inclusive and not look down with contempt upon one another because
their particular ideals of God are different. In my life I have seen a great many
spiritual men, a great many sensible persons, who did not believe in God at all
that is to say, not in our sense of the word. Perhaps they understood God better
than we can ever do. The Personal idea of God or the Impersonal, the Infinite,
Moral Law, or the Ideal Man— these all have to come under the definition of
religion. And when religions have become thus broadened, their power for good
will have increased a hundredfold. Religions, having tremendous power in them,
have often done more injury to the world than good, simply on account of their
narrowness and limitations.

Even at the present time we find many sects and societies, with almost the same
ideas, fighting each other, because one does not want to set forth those ideas
in precisely the same way as another. Therefore, religions will have to broaden.
Religious ideas will have to become universal, vast, and infinite; and then alone
we shall have the fullest play of religion, for the power of religion has only just
begun to manifest in the world. It is sometimes said that religions are dying out,
that spiritual ideas are dying out of the world. To me it seems that they have
just begun to grow. The power of religion, broadened and purified, is going to

penetrate every part of human life. So long as religion was in the hands of a chosen few or of a body of priests, it was in temples, churches, books, dogmas, ceremonials, forms, and rituals. But when we come to the real, spiritual, universal concept, then, and then alone religion will become real and living; it will come into our very nature, live in our every movement, penetrate every pore of our society, and be infinitely more a power for good than it has ever been before.

What is needed is a fellow-feeling between the different types of religion, seeing that they all stand or fall together, a fellow-feeling which springs from mutual esteem and mutual respect, and not the condescending, patronising, niggardly expression of goodwill, unfortunately in vogue at the present time with many. And above all, this is needed between types of religious expression coming from the study of mental phenomena — unfortunately, even now laying exclusive claim to the name of religion — and those expressions of religion whose heads, as it were, are penetrating more into the secrets of heaven though their feet are clinging to earth, I mean the so-called materialistic sciences.

To bring about this harmony, both will have to make concessions, sometimes very large, nay more, sometimes painful, but each will find itself the better for the sacrifice and more advanced in truth. And in the end, the knowledge which is confined within the domain of time and space will meet and become one with that which is beyond them both, where the mind and senses cannot reach — the Absolute, the Infinite, the One without a second.

Chapter II
The Real Nature of Man

Delivered in London

Great is the tenacity with which man clings to the senses. Yet, however substantial he may think the external world in which he lives and moves, there comes a time in the lives of individuals and of races when, involuntarily, they ask, "Is this real?" To the person who never finds a moment to question the credentials of his senses, whose every moment is occupied with some sort of sense-enjoyment — even to him death comes, and he also is compelled to ask, "Is this real?" Religion begins with this question and ends with its answer. Even in the remote past, where recorded history cannot help us, in the mysterious light of mythology, back in the dim twilight of civilisation, we find the same question was asked, "What becomes of this? What is real?"

One of the most poetical of the Upanishads, the Katha Upanishad, begins with the inquiry: "When a man dies, there is a dispute. One party declares that he has gone for ever, the other insists that he is still living. Which is true?" Various answers have been given. The whole sphere of metaphysics, philosophy, and religion is really filled with various answers to this question. At the same time, attempts have been made to suppress it, to put a stop to the unrest of mind which asks, "What is beyond? What is real?" But so long as death remains, all these attempts at suppression will always prove to be unsuccessful. We may talk about seeing nothing beyond and keeping all our hopes and aspirations confined to the present moment, and struggle hard not to think of anything beyond the world of senses; and, perhaps, everything outside helps to keep us limited within its narrow bounds. The whole world may combine to prevent us from broadening out beyond the present. Yet, so long as there is death, the question must come again and again, "Is death the end of all these things to which we are clinging, as if they were the most real of all realities, the most substantial of all substances?" The world vanishes in a moment and is gone. Standing on the brink of a precipice beyond which is the infinite yawning chasm, every mind, however hardened, is bound to recoil and ask, "Is this real?" The hopes of a lifetime, built up little by little with all the energies of a great mind, vanish in a second. Are they real? This question must be answered. Time never lessens its power; on the other hand, it adds strength to it.

Then there is the desire to be happy. We run after everything to make ourselves happy; we pursue our mad career in the external world of senses. If you ask the young man with whom life is successful, he will declare that it is real; and he really thinks so. Perhaps, when the same man grows old and finds fortune ever eluding him, he will then declare that it is fate. He finds at last that his desires cannot be fulfilled. Wherever he goes, there is an adamantine wall beyond which he cannot pass. Every sense-activity results in a reaction. Everything is evanescent. Enjoyment, misery, luxury, wealth, power, and poverty, even life itself, are all evanescent.

Two positions remain to mankind. One is to believe with the nihilists that all is nothing, that we know nothing, that we can never know anything either about the future, the past, or even the present. For we must remember that he who denies the past and the future and wants to stick to the present is simply a madman. One may as well deny the father and mother and assert the child. It would be equally logical. To deny the past and future, the present must inevitably be denied also. This is one position, that of the nihilists. I have never seen a man who could really become a nihilist for one minute. It is very easy to talk.

Then there is the other position— to seek for an explanation, to seek for the real, to discover in the midst of this eternally changing and evanescent world whatever is real. In this body which is an aggregate of molecules of matter, is there anything which is real? This has been the search throughout the history of the human mind. In the very oldest times, we often find glimpses of light coming into men's minds. We find man, even then, going a step beyond this body, finding something which is not this external body, although very much like it, much more complete, much more perfect, and which remains even when this body is dissolved. We read in the hymns of the Rig-Veda, addressed to the God of Fire who is burning a dead body, "Carry him, O Fire, in your arms gently, give him a perfect body, a bright body, carry him where the fathers live, where there is no more sorrow, where there is no more death." The same idea you will find present in every religion. And we get another idea with it. It is a significant fact that all religions, without one exception, hold that man is a degeneration of what he was, whether they clothe this in mythological words, or in the clear language of philosophy, or in the beautiful expressions of poetry. This is the one fact that comes out of every scripture and of every mythology that the man that is, is a degeneration of what he was. This is the kernel of truth within the story of Adam's fall in the Jewish scripture. This is again and again repeated in the scriptures of the Hindus; the dream of a period which they call the Age of Truth, when no man died unless he wished to die, when he could keep his body as long as he liked, and his mind was pure and strong. There was no evil and no misery; and the present age is a corruption of that state of perfection. Side by side with this, we find the story of the deluge everywhere. That story itself is a proof that this present age is held to be a corruption of a former age by every religion. It went on becoming more and more corrupt until the deluge swept away a large portion of mankind, and again the ascending series began. It is going up slowly again to reach once more that early state of purity. You are all aware of the story of the deluge in the Old Testament. The same story was current among the ancient Babylonians, the Egyptians, the Chinese, and the Hindus. Manu, a great ancient sage, was praying on the bank of the Ganga, when a little minnow came to him for protection, and he put it into a pot of water he had before him. "What do you want?" asked Manu. The little minnow declared he was pursued by a bigger fish and wanted protection. Manu carried the little fish to his home, and in the morning he had become as big as the pot and said, "I cannot live in this pot any longer". Manu put him in a tank, and the next day he was as big as the tank and declared he could not live there any more. So Manu had to take him to a river, and in the morning the fish filled the river. Then Manu put him in the ocean, and he declared, "Manu, I am the Creator of the universe. I have taken this form to come and warn you that I will deluge the world. You build an ark and in it and put a pair of every kind of animal, and let your family enter the ark, and there will project out of the water my horn. Fasten the ark to it; and when the deluge subsides, come out and people the earth." So the world was deluged, and Manu saved his own family and two of every kind of animal and seeds of every plant. When the deluge subsided, he came and peopled the world; and we are all called "man", because we are the progeny of Manu.

Now, human language is the attempt to express the truth that is within. I am fully persuaded that a baby whose language consists of unintelligible sounds is attempting to express the highest philosophy, only the baby has not the organs to express it nor the means. The difference between the language of the highest philosophers and the utterances of babies is one of degree and not of kind. What you call the most correct, systematic, mathematical language of the present time, and the hazy, mystical, mythological languages of the ancients, differ only in degree. All of them have a grand idea behind, which is, as it were, struggling to express itself; and often behind these ancient mythologies are nuggets of truth; and often, I am sorry to say, behind the fine, polished phrases of the moderns is arrant trash. So, we need not throw a thing overboard because it is clothed in mythology, because it does not fit in with the notions of Mr. So-and-so or Mrs. So-and-so of modern times. If people should laugh at religion because most religions declare that men must believe in mythologies taught by such and such a prophet, they ought to laugh more at these moderns. In modern times, if a man quotes a Moses or a Buddha or a Christ, he is laughed at; but let him give the name of a Huxley, a Tyndall, or a Darwin, and it is swallowed without salt. "Huxley has said it", that is enough for many. We are free from superstitions indeed! That was a religious superstition, and this a scientific superstition; only, in and through that superstition came life-giving ideas of spirituality; in and through this modern superstition come lust and greed. That superstition was worship of God, and this superstition is worship of filthy lucre, of fame or power. That is the difference.

To return to mythology, behind all these stories we find one idea standing supreme— that man is a degeneration of what he was. Coming to the present times, modern research seems to repudiate this position absolutely. Evolutionists seem to contradict entirely this assertion. According to them, man is the evolution of the mollusc; and, therefore, what mythology states cannot be true. There is in India, however, a mythology which is able to reconcile both these positions. The Indian mythology has a theory of cycles, that all progression is in the form of waves. Every wave is attended by a fall, and that by a rise the next moment, that by a fall in the next, and again another rise. The motion is in cycles. Certainly it is true, even on the grounds of modern research, that man cannot be simply an evolution. Every evolution presupposes an involution. The modern scientific man will tell you that you can only get the amount of energy out of a machine which you have previously put into it. Something cannot be produced out of nothing. If a man is an evolution of the mollusc, then the perfect man— the Buddha-man, the Christ-man— was involved in the mollusc. If it is not so, whence come these gigantic personalities? Something cannot come out of nothing. Thus we are in the position of reconciling the scriptures with modern light. That energy which manifests itself slowly through various stages until it becomes the perfect man, cannot come out of nothing. It existed somewhere; and if the mollusc or the protoplasm is the first point to which you can trace it, that protoplasm, somehow or other, must have contained the energy.

There is a great discussion going on as to whether the aggregate of materials we call the body is the cause of manifestation of the force we call the soul, thought, etc., or whether it is the thought that manifests this body. The religions of the world of course hold that the force called thought manifests the body, and not the reverse. There are schools of modern thought which hold that what we call thought is simply the outcome of the adjustment of the parts of the machine which we call body. Taking the second position that the soul or the mass of thought, or however you may call it, is the outcome of this machine, the outcome of the chemical and physical combinations of matter making up the body and brain, leaves the question unanswered. What makes the body? What force combines the molecules into the body form? What force is there which takes up material from the mass of matter around and forms my body one way, another body another way, and so on? What makes these infinite distinctions? To say that the force called soul is the outcome of the combinations of the molecules of the body is putting the cart before the horse. How did the combinations come; where was the force to make them? If you say that some other force was the cause of these combinations, and soul was the outcome of that matter, and that soul — which combined a certain mass of matter — was itself the result of the combinations, it is no answer. That theory ought to be taken which explains most of the facts, if not all, and that without contradicting other existing theories. It is more logical to say that the force which takes up the matter and forms the body is the same which manifests through that body. To say, therefore, that the thought forces manifested by the body are the outcome of the arrangement of molecules and have no independent existence has no meaning; neither can force evolve out of matter. Rather it is possible to demonstrate that what we call matter does not exist at all. It is only a certain state of force. Solidity, hardness, or any other state of matter can be proved to be the result of motion. Increase of vortex motion imparted to fluids gives them the force of solids. A mass of air in vortex motion, as in a tornado, becomes solid-like and by its impact breaks or cuts through solids. A thread of a spider's web, if it could be moved at almost infinite velocity, would be as strong as an iron chain and would cut through an oak tree. Looking at it in this way, it would be easier to prove that what we call matter does not exist. But the other way cannot be proved.

What is the force which manifests itself through the body? It is obvious to all of us, whatever that force be, that it is taking particles up, as it were, and manipulating forms out of them — the human body. None else comes here to manipulate bodies for you and me. I never saw anybody eat food for me. I have to assimilate it, manufacture blood and bones and everything out of that food. What is this mysterious force? Ideas about the future and about the past seem to be terrifying to many. To many they seem to be mere speculation.

We will take the present theme. What is this force which is now working through us? We know how in old times, in all the ancient scriptures, this power, this manifestation of power, was thought to be a bright substance having the form of this body, and which remained even after this body fell. Later on, however, we find a higher idea coming— that this bright body did not represent the force. Whatsoever has form must be the result of combinations of particles and requires something else behind it to move it. If this body requires something which is not the body to manipulate it, the bright body, by the same necessity, will also require something other than itself to manipulate it. So, that something was called the soul, the Atman in Sanskrit. It was the Atman which through the bright body, as it were, worked on the gross body outside. The bright body is considered as the receptacle of the mind, and the Atman is beyond that. It is not the mind even; it works the mind, and through the mind the body. You have an Atman, I have another, each one of us has a separate Atman and a separate fine body, and through that we work on the gross external body. Questions were then asked about this Atman about its nature. What is this Atman, this soul of man which is neither the body nor the mind? Great discussions followed. Speculations were made, various shades of philosophic inquiry came into existence; and I shall try to place before you some of the conclusions that have been reached about this Atman.

The different philosophies seem to agree that this Atman, whatever it be, has neither form nor shape, and that which has neither form nor shape must be omnipresent. Time begins with mind, space also is in the mind. Causation cannot stand without time. Without the idea of succession there cannot be any idea of causation. Time, space and causation, therefore, are in the mind, and as this Atman is beyond the mind and formless, it must be beyond time, beyond space, and beyond causation. Now, if it is beyond time, space, and causation, it must be infinite. Then comes the highest speculation in our philosophy. The infinite cannot be two. If the soul be infinite, there can be only one Soul, and all ideas of various souls— you having one soul, and I having another, and so forth— are not real. The Real Man, therefore, is one and infinite, the omnipresent Spirit. And the apparent man is only a limitation of that Real Man. In that sense the mythologies are true that the apparent man, however great he may be, is only a dim reflection of the Real Man who is beyond. The Real Man, the Spirit, being beyond cause and effect, not bound by time and space, must, therefore, be free. He was never bound, and could not be bound. The apparent man, the reflection, is limited by time, space, and causation, and is, therefore, bound. Or in the language of some of our philosophers, he appears to be bound, but really is not. This is the reality in our souls, this omnipresence, this spiritual nature, this infinity. Every soul is infinite, therefore there is no question of birth and death.

Some children were being examined. The examiner put them rather hard questions, and among them was this one: "Why does not the earth fall?" He wanted to evoke answers about gravitation. Most of the children could not answer at all; a few answered that it was gravitation or something. One bright little girl answered it by putting another question: "Where should it fall?" The question is nonsense. Where should the earth fall? There is no falling or rising for the earth. In infinite space there is no up or down; that is only in the relative. Where is the going or coming for the infinite? Whence should it come and where should it go?

Thus, when people cease to think of the past or future, when they give up the idea of body, because the body comes and goes and is limited, then they have risen to a higher ideal. The body is not the Real Man, neither is the mind, for the mind waxes and wanes. It is the Spirit beyond, which alone can live forever. The body and mind are continually changing, and are, in fact, only names of series of changeful phenomena, like rivers whose waters are in a constant state of flux, yet presenting the appearance of unbroken streams. Every particle in this body is continually changing; no one has the same body for many minutes together, and yet we think of it as the same body. So with the mind; one moment it is happy, another moment unhappy; one moment strong, another weak; an ever-changing whirlpool. That cannot be the Spirit which is infinite. Change can only be in the limited. To say that the infinite changes in any way is absurd; it cannot be. You can move and I can move, as limited bodies; every particle in this universe is in a constant state of flux, but taking the universe as a unit, as one whole, it cannot move, it cannot change. Motion is always a relative thing. I move in relation to something else. Any particle in this universe can change in relation to any other particle; but take the whole universe as one, and in relation to what can it move? There is nothing besides it. So this infinite Unit is unchangeable, immovable, absolute, and this is the Real Man. Our reality, therefore, consists in the Universal and not in the limited. These are old delusions, however comfortable they are, to think that we are little limited beings, constantly changing. People are frightened when they are told that they are Universal Being, everywhere present. Through everything you work, through every foot you move, through every lip you talk, through every heart you feel.

People are frightened when they are told this. They will again and again ask you if they are not going to keep their individuality. What is individuality? I should like to see it. A baby has no moustache; when he grows to be a man, perhaps he has a moustache and beard. His individuality would be lost, if it were in the body. If I lose one eye, or if I lose one of my hands, my individuality would be lost if it were in the body. Then, a drunkard should not give up drinking because he would lose his individuality. A thief should not be a good man because he would thereby lose his individuality. No man ought to change his habits for fear of this. There is no individuality except in the Infinite. That is the only condition which does not change. Everything else is in a constant state of flux. Neither can individuality be in memory. Suppose, on account of a blow on the head I forget all about my past; then, I have lost all individuality; I am gone. I do not remember two or three years of my childhood, and if memory and existence are one, then whatever I forget is gone. That part of my life which I do not remember, I did not live. That is a very narrow idea of individuality.

We are not individuals yet. We are struggling towards individuality, and that is the Infinite, that is the real nature of man. He alone lives whose life is in the whole universe, and the more we concentrate our lives on limited things, the faster we go towards death. Those moments alone we live when our lives are in the universe, in others; and living this little life is death, simply death, and that is why the fear of death comes. The fear of death can only be conquered when man realises that so long as there is one life in this universe, he is living. When he can say, "I am in everything, in everybody, I am in all lives, I am the universe," then alone comes the state of fearlessness. To talk of immortality in constantly changing things is absurd. Says an old Sanskrit philosopher: It is only the Spirit that is the individual, because it is infinite. No infinity can be divided; infinity cannot be broken into pieces. It is the same one, undivided unit for ever, and this is the individual man, the Real Man. The apparent man is merely a struggle to express, to manifest this individuality which is beyond; and evolution is not in the Spirit. These changes which are going on — the wicked becoming good, the animal becoming man, take them in whatever way you like — are not in the Spirit. They are evolution of nature and manifestation of Spirit. Suppose there is a screen hiding you from me, in which there is a small hole through which I can see some of the faces before me, just a few faces. Now suppose the hole begins to grow larger and larger, and as it does so, more and more of the scene before me reveals itself and when at last the whole screen has disappeared, I stand face to face with you all. You did not change at all in this case; it was the hole that was evolving, and you were gradually manifesting yourselves. So it is with the Spirit.

No perfection is going to be attained. You are already free and perfect. What are these ideas of religion and God and searching for the hereafter? Why does man look for a God? Why does man, in every nation, in every state of society, want a perfect ideal somewhere, either in man, in God, or elsewhere? Because that idea is within you. It was your own heart beating and you did not know; you were mistaking it for something external. It is the God within your own self that is propelling you to seek for Him, to realise Him. After long searches here and there, in temples and in churches, in earths and in heavens, at last you come back, completing the circle from where you started, to your own soul and find that He for whom you have been seeking all over the world, for whom you have been weeping and praying in churches and temples, on whom you were looking as the mystery of all mysteries shrouded in the clouds, is nearest of the near, is your own Self, the reality of your life, body, and soul. That is your own nature. Assert it, manifest it. Not to become pure, you are pure already. You are not to be perfect, you are that already. Nature is like that screen which is hiding the reality beyond. Every good thought that you think or act upon is simply tearing the veil, as it were; and the purity, the Infinity, the God behind, manifests Itself more and more.

This is the whole history of man. Finer and finer becomes the veil, more and more of the light behind shines forth, for it is its nature to shine. It cannot be known; in vain we try to know it. Were it knowable, it would not be what it is, for it is the eternal subject. Knowledge is a limitation, knowledge is objectifying. He is the eternal subject of everything, the eternal witness in this universe, your own Self. Knowledge is, as it were, a lower step, a degeneration. We are that eternal subject already; how can we know it? It is the real nature of every man, and he is struggling to express it in various ways; otherwise, why are there so many ethical codes? Where is the explanation of all ethics? One idea stands out as the centre of all ethical systems, expressed in various forms, namely, doing good to others. The guiding motive of mankind should be charity towards men, charity towards all animals. But these are all various expressions of that eternal truth that, "I am the universe; this universe is one." Or else, where is the reason? Why should I do good to my fellowmen? Why should I do good to others? What compels me? It is sympathy, the feeling of sameness everywhere. The hardest hearts feel sympathy for other beings sometimes. Even the man who gets frightened if he is told that this assumed individuality is really a delusion, that it is ignoble to try to cling to this apparent individuality, that very man will tell you that extreme self-abnegation is the centre of all morality. And what is perfect self-abnegation? It means the abnegation of this apparent self, the abnegation of all selfishness. This idea of "me and mine"— Ahamkara and Mamata — is the result of past superstition, and the more this present self passes away, the more the real Self becomes manifest. This is true self-abnegation, the centre, the basis, the gist of all moral teaching; and whether man knows it or not the whole world is slowly going towards it, practicing it more or less. Only, the vast majority of mankind are doing it unconsciously. Let them do it consciously. Let then make the sacrifice, knowing that this "me and mine" is not the real Self, but only a limitation. But one glimpse Of that infinite reality which is behind — but one spark of that infinite fire that is the All — represents the present man; the Infinite is his true nature.

What is the utility, the effect, the result, of this knowledge? In these days, we have to measure everything by utility — by how many pounds shillings, and pence it represents. What right has a person to ask that truth should be judged by the standard of utility or money? Suppose there is no utility, will it be less true? Utility is not the test of truth. Nevertheless, there is the highest utility in this. Happiness, we see is what everyone is seeking for, but the majority seek it in things which are evanescent and not real. No happiness was ever found in the senses. There never was a person who found happiness in the senses or in enjoyment of the senses. Happiness is only found in the Spirit. Therefore the highest utility for mankind is to find this happiness in the Spirit. The next point is that ignorance is the great mother of all misery, and the fundamental ignorance is to think that the Infinite weeps and cries, that He is finite. This is the basis of all ignorance that we, the immortal, the ever pure, the perfect Spirit, think that we are little minds, that we are little bodies; it is the mother of all selfishness. As soon as I think that I am a little body, I want to preserve it, to protect it, to keep it nice, at the expense of other bodies; then you and I become separate. As soon as this idea of separation comes, it opens the door to all mischief and leads to all misery. This is the utility that if a very small fractional part of human beings living today can put aside the idea of selfishness, narrowness, and littleness, this earth will become a paradise tomorrow; but with machines and improvements of material knowledge only, it will never be. These only increase misery, as oil poured on fire increases the flame all the more. Without the knowledge of the Spirit, all material knowledge is only adding fuel to fire, only giving into the hands of selfish man one more instrument to take what belongs to others, to live upon the life of others, instead of giving up his life for them.

Is it practical? — is another question. Can it be practised in modern society?

Truth does not pay homage to any society, ancient or modern. Society has to pay homage to Truth or die. Societies should be moulded upon truth, and truth has not to adjust itself to society. If such a noble truth as unselfishness cannot be practiced in society, it is better for man to give up society and go into the forest. That is the daring man. There are two sorts of courage. One is the courage of facing the cannon. And the other is the courage of spiritual conviction. An Emperor who invaded India was told by his teacher to go and see some of the sages there. After a long search for one, he found a very old man sitting on a block of stone. The Emperor talked with him a little and became very much impressed by his wisdom. He asked the sage to go to his country with him. "No," said the sage, "I am quite satisfied with my forest here." Said the Emperor, "I will give you money, position, wealth. I am the Emperor of the world." "No," replied the man, "I don't care for those things." The Emperor replied, "If you do not go, I will kill you." The man smiled serenely and said, "That is the most foolish thing you ever said, Emperor. You cannot kill me. Me the sun cannot dry, fire cannot burn, sword cannot kill, for I am the birthless, the deathless, the ever-living omnipotent, omnipresent Spirit." This is spiritual boldness, while the other is the courage of a lion or a tiger. In the Mutiny of 1857 there was a Swami, a very great soul, whom a Mohammedan mutineer stabbed severely. The Hindu mutineers caught and brought the man to the Swami, offering to kill him. But the Swami looked up calmly and said, "My brother, thou art He, thou art He!" and expired. This is another instance. What good is it to talk of the strength of your muscles, of the superiority of your Western institutions, if you cannot make Truth square with your society, if you cannot build up a society into which the highest Truth will fit? What is the good of this boastful talk about your grandeur and greatness, if you stand up and say, "This courage is not practical." Is nothing practical but pounds, shillings, and pence? If so, why boast of your society? That society is the greatest, where the highest truths become practical. That is my opinion; and if society is; not fit for the highest truths, make it so; and the sooner, the better. Stand up, men and women, in this spirit, dare to believe in the Truth, dare to practice the Truth!

The world requires a few hundred bold men and women. Practise that boldness which dares know the Truth, which dares show the Truth in life, which does not quake before death, nay, welcomes death, makes a man know that he, is the Spirit, that, in the whole universe, nothing can kill him. Then you will be free. Then you will know your real Soul. "This Atman is first to be heard, then thoughts about and then meditated upon."

There is a great tendency in modern times to talk too much of work and decry thought. Doing is very good, but that comes from thinking. Little manifestations of energy through the muscles are called work. But where there is no thought, there will be no work. Fill the brain, therefore, with high thoughts, highest ideals, place them day and night before you, and out of that will come great work. Talk not about impurity, but say that we are pure. We have hypnotised ourselves into this thought that we are little, that we are born, and that we are going to die, and into a constant state of fear.

There is a story about a lioness, who was big with young, going about in search of prey; and seeing a flock of sheep, she jumped upon them. She died in the effort; and a little baby lion was born, motherless. It was taken care of by the sheep and the sheep brought it up, and it grew up with them, ate grass, and bleated like the sheep. And although in time it became a big, full-grown lion, it thought it was a sheep. One day another lion came in search of prey and was astonished to find that in the midst of this flock of sheep was a lion, fleeing like the sheep at the approach of danger. He tried to get near the sheep-lion, to tell it that it was not a sheep but a lion; but the poor animal fled at his approach. However, he watched his opportunity and one day found the sheep-lion sleeping. He approached it and said, "You are a lion." "I am a sheep," cried the other lion and could not believe the contrary but bleated. The lion dragged him towards a lake and said, "Look here, here is my reflection and yours." Then came the comparison. It looked at the lion and then at its own reflection, and in a moment came the idea that it was a lion. The lion roared, the bleating was gone. You are lions, you are souls, pure, infinite, and perfect. The might of the universe is within you. "Why weepest thou, my friend? There is neither birth nor death for thee. Why weepest thou? There is no disease nor misery for thee, but thou art like the infinite sky; clouds of various colours come over it, play for a moment, then vanish. But the sky is ever the same eternal blue." Why do we see wickedness? There was a stump of a tree, and in the dark, a thief came that way and said, "That is a policeman." A young man waiting for his beloved saw it and thought that it was his sweetheart. A child who had been told ghost stories took it for a ghost and began to shriek. But all the time it was the stump of a tree. We see the world as we are. Suppose there is a baby in a room with a bag of gold on the table and a thief comes and steals the gold. Would the baby know it was stolen? That which we have inside, we see outside. The baby has no thief inside and sees no thief outside. So with all knowledge. Do not talk of the wickedness of the world and all its sins. Weep that you are bound to see wickedness yet. Weep that you are bound to see sin everywhere, and if you want to help the world, do not condemn it. Do not weaken it more. For what is sin and what is misery, and what are all these, but the results of weakness? The world is made weaker and weaker every day by such teachings. Men are taught from childhood that they are weak and sinners. Teach them that they are all glorious children of immortality, even those who are the weakest in manifestation. Let positive, strong, helpful thought enter into their brains from very childhood. Lay yourselves open to these thoughts, and not to weakening and paralysing ones. Say to your own minds, "I am He, I am He." Let it ring day and night in your minds like a song, and at the point of death declare "I am He." That is the Truth; the infinite strength of the world is yours. Drive out the superstition that has covered your minds. Let us be brave. Know the Truth and practice the Truth. The goal may be distant, but awake, arise, and stop not till the goal is reached.

Chapter III
Maya and Illusion

Delivered in London

Almost all of you have heard of the word Maya. Generally it is used, though incorrectly, to denote illusion, or delusion, or some such thing. But the theory of Maya forms one of the pillars upon which the Vedanta rests; it is, therefore, necessary that it should be properly understood. I ask a little patience of you, for there is a great danger of it being misunderstood. The oldest idea of Maya that we find in Vedic literature is the sense of delusion; but then the real theory had not been reached. We find such passages as, "Indra through his Maya assumed various forms." Here it is true the word Maya means something like magic, and we find various other passages, always taking the same meaning. The word Maya then dropped out of sight altogether. But in the meantime the idea was developing. Later, the question was raised: "Why can't we know this secret of the universe?" And the answer given was very significant: "Because we talk in vain, and because we are satisfied with the things of the senses, and because we are running after desires; therefore, we, as it were, cover the Reality with a mist." Here the word Maya is not used at all, but we get the idea that the cause of our ignorance is a kind of mist that has come between us and the Truth. Much later on, in one of the latest Upanishads, we find the word Maya reappearing, but this time, a transformation has taken place in it, and a mass of new meaning has attached itself to the word. Theories had been propounded and repeated, others had been taken up, until at last the idea of Maya became fixed. We read in the Shvetashvatara Upanishad, "Know nature to be Maya and the Ruler of this Maya is the Lord Himself." Coming to our philosophers, we find that this word Maya has been manipulated in various fashions, until we come to the great Shankaracharya. The theory of Maya was manipulated a little by the Buddhists too, but in the hands of the Buddhists it became very much like what is called Idealism, and that is the meaning that is now generally given to the word Maya. When the Hindu says the world is Maya, at once people get the idea that the world is an illusion. This interpretation has some basis, as coming through the Buddhistic philosophers, because there was one section of philosophers who did not believe in the external world at all. But the Maya of the Vedanta, in its last developed form, is neither Idealism nor Realism, nor is it a theory. It is a simple statement of facts — what we are and what we see around us.

As I have told you before, the minds of the people from whom the Vedas came were intent upon following principles, discovering principles. They had no time to work upon details or to wait for them; they wanted to go deep into the heart of things. Something beyond was calling them, as it were, and they could not wait. Scattered through the Upanishads, we find that the details of subjects which we now call modern sciences are often very erroneous, but, at the same time, their principles are correct. For instance, the idea of ether, which is one of the latest theories of modern science, is to be found in our ancient literature in forms much more developed than is the modern scientific theory of ether today, but it was in principle. When they tried to demonstrate the workings of that principle, they made many mistakes. The theory of the all-pervading life principle, of which all life in this universe is but a differing manifestation, was understood in Vedic times; it is found in the Brahmanas. There is a long hymn in the Samhitas in praise of Prana of which all life is but a manifestation. By the by, it may interest some of you to know that there are theories in the Vedic philosophy about the origin of life on this earth very similar to those which have been advanced by some modern European scientists. You, of course, all know that there is a theory that life came from other planets. It is a settled doctrine with some Vedic philosophers that life comes in this way from the moon.

Coming to the principles, we find these Vedic thinkers very courageous and wonderfully bold in propounding large and generalised theories. Their solution of the mystery of the universe, from the external world, was as satisfactory as it could be. The detailed workings of modern science do not bring the question one step nearer to solution, because the principles have failed. If the theory of ether failed in ancient times to give a solution of the mystery of the universe, working out the details of that ether theory would not bring us much nearer to the truth. If the theory of all-pervading life failed as a theory of this universe, it would not mean anything more if worked out in detail, for the details do not change the principle of the universe. What I mean is that in their inquiry into the principle, the Hindu thinkers were as bold, and in some cases, much bolder than the moderns. They made some of the grandest generalizations that have yet been reached, and some still remain as theories, which modern science has yet to get even as theories. For instance, they not only arrived at the ether theory, but went beyond and classified mind also as a still more rarefied ether. Beyond that again, they found a still more rarefied ether. Yet that was no solution, it did not solve the problem. No amount of knowledge of the external world could solve the problem. "But", says the scientist, "we are just beginning to know a little : wait a few thousand years and we shall get the solution."" No," says the Vedantist, for he has proved beyond all doubt that the mind is limited, that it cannot go beyond certain limits — beyond time, space, and causation. As no man can jump out of his own self, so no man can go beyond the limits that have been put upon him by the laws of time and space. Every attempt to solve the laws of causation, time, and space would be futile, because the very attempt would have to be made by taking for granted the existence of these three. What does the statement of the existence of the world mean, then ? "This world has no existence." What is meant by that ? It means that it has no absolute existence. It exists only in relation to my mind, to your mind, and to the mind of everyone else. We see this world with the five senses but if we had another sense, we would see in it something more. If we had yet another sense, it would appear as something still different. It has, therefore, no real existence; it has no unchangeable, immovable, infinite existence. Nor can it be called non-existence, seeing that it exists, and we slave to work in and through it. It is a mixture of existence and non-existence.

Coming from abstractions to the common, everyday details of our lives, we find that our whole life is a contradiction, a mixture of existence and non-existence. There is this contradiction in knowledge. It seems that man can know everything, if he only wants to know; but before he has gone a few steps, he finds an adamantine wall which he cannot pass. All his work is in a circle, and he cannot go beyond that circle. The problems which are nearest and dearest to him are impelling him on and calling, day and night, for a solution, but he cannot solve them, because he cannot go beyond his intellect. And yet that desire is implanted strongly in him. Still we know that the only good is to be obtained by controlling and checking it. With every breath, every impulse of our heart asks us to be selfish. At the same time, there is some power beyond us which says that it is unselfishness alone which is good. Every child is a born optimist; he dreams golden dreams. In youth he becomes still more optimistic. It is hard for a young man to believe that there is such a thing as death, such a thing as defeat or degradation. Old age comes, and life is a mass of ruins. Dreams have vanished into the air, and the man becomes a pessimist. Thus we go from one extreme to another, buffeted by nature, without knowing where we are going. It reminds me of a celebrated song in the Lalita Vistara, the biography of Buddha. Buddha was born, says the book, as the saviour of mankind, but he forgot himself in the luxuries of his palace. Some angels came and sang a song to rouse him. And the burden of the whole song is that we are floating down the river of life which is continually changing with no stop and no rest. So are our lives, going on and on without knowing any rest. What are we to do? The man who has enough to eat and drink is an optimist, and he avoids all mention of misery, for it frightens him. Tell not to him of the sorrows and the sufferings of the world; go to him and tell that it is all good. "Yes, I am safe," says he. "Look at me! I have a nice house to live in. I do not fear cold and hunger; therefore do not bring these horrible pictures before me." But, on the other hand, there are others dying of cold and hunger. If you go and teach them that it is all good, they will not hear you. How can they wish others to be happy when they are miserable? Thus we are oscillating between optimism and pessimism.

Then, there is the tremendous fact of death. The whole world is going towards death; everything dies. All our progress, our vanities, our reforms, our luxuries, our wealth, our knowledge, have that one end— death. That is all that is certain. Cities come and go, empires rise and fall, planets break into pieces and crumble into dust, to be blown about by the atmospheres of other planets. Thus it has been going on from time without beginning. Death is the end of everything. Death is the end of life, of beauty, of wealth, of power, of virtue too. Saints die and sinners die, kings die and beggars die. They are all going to death, and yet this tremendous clinging on to life exists. Somehow, we do not know why, we cling to life; we cannot give it up. And this is Maya.

The mother is nursing a child with great care; all her soul, her life, is in that child. The child grows, becomes a man, and perchance becomes a blackguard and a brute, kicks her and beats her every day; and yet the mother clings to the child; and when her reason awakes, she covers it up with the idea of love. She little thinks that it is not love, that it is something which has got hold of her nerves, which she cannot shake off; however she may try, she cannot shake off the bondage she is in. And this is Maya.

We are all after the Golden Fleece. Every one of us thinks that this will be his. Every reasonable man sees that his chance is, perhaps, one in twenty millions, yet everyone struggles for it. And this is Maya.

Death is stalking day and night over this earth of ours, but at the same time we think we shall live eternally. A question was once asked of King Yudhishthira, "What is the most wonderful thing on this earth?" And the king replied, "Every day people are dying around us, and yet men think they will never die." And this is Maya.

These tremendous contradictions in our intellect, in our knowledge, yea, in all the facts of our life face us on all sides. A reformer arises and wants to remedy the evils that are existing in a certain nation; and before they have been remedied, a thousand other evils arise in another place. It is like an old house that is falling; you patch it up in one place and the ruin extends to another. In India, our reformers cry and preach against the evils of enforced widowhood. In the West, non-marriage is the great evil. Help the unmarried on one side; they are suffering. Help the widows on the other; they are suffering. It is like chronic rheumatism: you drive from the head, and it goes to the body; you drive it from there, and it goes to the feet. Reformers arise and preach that learning, wealth, and culture should not be in the hands of a select few; and they do their best to make them accessible to all. These may bring more happiness to some, but, perhaps, as culture comes, physical happiness lessens. The knowledge of happiness brings the knowledge of unhappiness. Which way then shall we go? The least amount of material prosperity that we enjoy is causing the same amount of misery elsewhere. This is the law. The young, perhaps, do not see it clearly, but those who have lived long enough and those who have struggled enough will understand it. And this is Maya. These things are going on, day and night, and to find a solution of this problem is impossible. Why should it be so? It is impossible to answer this, because the question cannot be logically formulated. There is neither how nor why in fact; we only know that it is and that we cannot help it. Even to grasp it, to draw an exact image of it in our own mind, is beyond our power. How can we solve it then?

Maya is a statement of the fact of this universe, of how it is going on. People generally get frightened when these things are told to them. But bold we must be. Hiding facts is not the way to find a remedy. As you all know, a hare hunted by dogs puts its head down and thinks itself safe; so, when we run into optimism, we do just like the hare, but that is no remedy. There are objections against this, but you may remark that they are generally from people who possess many of the good things of life. In this country (England) it is very difficult to become a pessimist. Everyone tells me how wonderfully the world is going on, how progressive; but what he himself is, is his own world. Old questions arise: Christianity must be the only true religion of the world because Christian nations are prosperous! But that assertion contradicts itself, because the prosperity of the Christian nation depends on the misfortune of non-Christian nations. There must be some to prey on. Suppose the whole world were to become Christian, then the Christian nations would become poor, because there would be no non-Christian nations for them to prey upon. Thus the argument kills itself. Animals are living upon plants, men upon animals and, worst of all, upon one another, the strong upon the weak. This is going on everywhere. And this is Maya. What solution do you find for this? We hear every day many explanations, and are told that in the long run all will be good. Taking it for granted that this is possible, why should there be this diabolical way of doing good? Why cannot good be done through good, instead of through these diabolical methods? The descendants of the human beings of today will be happy; but why must there be all this suffering now? There is no solution. This is Maya.

Again, we often hear that it is one of the features of evolution that it eliminates evil, and this evil being continually eliminated from the world, at last only good will remain. That is very nice to hear, and it panders to the vanity of those who have enough of this world's goods, who have not a hard struggle to face every clay and are not being crushed under the wheel of this so-called evolution. It is very good and comforting indeed to such fortunate ones. The common herd may surfer, but they do not care; let them die, they are of no consequence. Very good, yet this argument is fallacious from beginning to end. It takes for granted, in the first place, that manifested good and evil in this world are two absolute realities. In the second place, it make, at still worse assumption that the amount of good is an increasing quantity and the amount of evil is a decreasing quantity. So, if evil is being eliminated in this way by what they call evolution, there will come a time when all this evil will be eliminated and what remains will be all good. Very easy to say, but can it be proved that evil is a lessening quantity? Take, for instance, the man who lives in a forest, who does not know how to cultivate the mind, cannot read a book, has not heard of such a thing as writing. If he is severely wounded, he is soon all right again; while we die if we get a scratch. Machines are making things cheap, making for progress and evolution, but millions are crushed, that one may become rich; while one becomes rich, thousands at the same time become poorer and poorer, and whole masses of human beings are made slaves. That way it is going on. The animal man lives in the senses. If he does not get enough to eat, he is miserable; or if something happens to his body, he is miserable. In the senses both his misery and his happiness begin and end. As soon as this man progresses, as soon as his horizon of happiness increases, his horizon of unhappiness increases proportionately. The man in the forest does not know what it is to be jealous, to be in the law courts, to pay taxes, to be blamed by society, to be ruled over day and night by the most tremendous tyranny that human diabolism ever invented, which pries into the secrets of every human heart. He does not know how man becomes a thousand times more diabolical than any other animal, with all his vain knowledge and with all his pride. Thus it is that, as we emerge out of the senses, we develop higher powers of enjoyment, and at the same time we have to develop higher powers of suffering too. The nerves become finer and capable off more suffering. In every society, we often find that the ignorant, common man, when abused, does not feel much, but he feels a good thrashing. But the gentleman cannot bear a single word of abuse; he has become so finely nerved. Misery has increased with his susceptibility to happiness. This does not go much to prove the evolutionist's case. As we increase our power to be happy, we also increase our power to suffer, and sometimes I am inclined to think that if we increase our power to become happy in arithmetical progression, we shall increase, on the other hand, our power to become miserable in geometrical progression. We who are progressing know that the more we progress, the more avenues are opened to pain as well as to pleasure. And this is Maya.

Thus we find that Maya is not a theory for the explanation of the world; it is simply a statement of facts as they exist, that the very basis of our being is contradiction, that everywhere we have to move through this tremendous contradiction, that wherever there is good, there must also be evil, and wherever there is evil, there must be some good, wherever there is life, death must follow as its shadow, and everyone who smiles will have to weep, and vice versa. Nor can this state of things be remedied. We may verily imagine that there will be a place where there will be only good and no evil, where we shall only smile and never weep. This is impossible in the very nature of things; for the conditions will remain the same. Wherever there is the power of producing a smile in us, there lurks the power of producing tears. Wherever there is the power of producing happiness, there lurks somewhere the power of making us miserable.

Thus the Vedanta philosophy is neither optimistic nor pessimistic. It voices both these views and takes things as they are. It admits that this world is a mixture of good and evil, happiness and misery, and that to increase the one, one must of necessity increase the other. There will never be a perfectly good or bad world, because the very idea is a contradiction in terms. The great secret revealed by this analysis is that good and bad are not two cut-and-dried, separate existences. There is not one thing in this world of ours which you can label as good and good alone, and there is not one thing in the universe which you can label as bad and bad alone. The very same phenomenon which is appearing to be good now, may appear to be bad tomorrow. The same thing which is producing misery in one, may produce happiness in another. The fire that burns the child, may cook a good meal for a starving man. The same nerves that carry the sensations of misery carry also the sensations of happiness. The only way to stop evil, therefore, is to stop good also; there is no other way. To stop death, we shall have to stop life also. Life without death and happiness without misery are contradictions, and neither can be found alone, because each of them is but a different manifestation of the same thing. What I thought to be good yesterday, I do not think to be good now. When I look back upon my life and see what were my ideals at different times, I final this to be so. At one time my ideal was to drive a strong pair of horses; at another time I thought, if I could make a certain kind of sweetmeat, I should be perfectly happy; later I imagined that I should be entirely satisfied if I had a wife and children and plenty of money. Today I laugh at all these ideals as mere childish nonsense.

The Vedanta says, there must come a time when we shall look back and laugh at the ideals which make us afraid of giving up our individuality. Each one of us wants to keep this body for an indefinite time, thinking we shall be very happy, but there will come a time when we shall laugh at this idea. Now, if such be the truth, we are in a state of hopeless contradiction — neither existence nor non-existence, neither misery nor happiness, but a mixture of them. What, then, is the use of Vedanta and all other philosophies and religions? And, above all, what is the use of doing good work? This is a question that comes to the mind. If it is true that you cannot do good without doing evil, and whenever you try to create happiness there will always be misery, people will ask you, "What is the use of doing good?" The answer is in the first place, that we must work for lessening misery, for that is the only way to make ourselves happy. Every one of us finds it out sooner or later in our lives. The bright ones find it out a little earlier, and the dull ones a little later. The dull ones pay very dearly for the discovery and the bright ones less dearly. In the second place, we must do our part, because that is the only way of getting out of this life of contradiction. Both the forces of good and evil will keep the universe alive for us, until we awake from our dreams and give up this building of mud pies. That lesson we shall have to learn, and it will take a long, long time to learn it.

Attempts have been made in Germany to build a system of philosophy on the basis that the Infinite has become the finite. Such attempts are also made in England. And the analysis of the position of these philosophers is this, that the Infinite is trying to express itself in this universe, and that there will come a time when the Infinite will succeed in doing so. It is all very well, and we have used the words Infinite and manifestation and expression, and so on, but philosophers naturally ask for a logical fundamental basis for the statement that the finite can fully express the Infinite. The Absolute and the Infinite can become this universe only by limitation. Everything must be limited that comes through the senses, or through the mind, or through the intellect; and for the limited to be the unlimited is simply absurd and can never be. The Vedanta, on the other hand, says that it is true that the Absolute or the Infinite is trying to express itself in the finite, but there will come a time when it will find that it is impossible, and it will then have to beat a retreat, and this beating a retreat means renunciation which is the real beginning of religion. Nowadays it is very hard even to talk of renunciation. It was said of me in America that I was a man who came out of a land that had been dead and buried for five thousand years, and talked of renunciation. So says, perhaps, the English philosopher. Yet it is true that, that is the only path to religion. Renounce and give up. What did Christ say? "He that loseth his life for my sake shall find it." Again and again did he preach renunciation as the only way to perfection. There comes a time when the mind awakes from this long and dreary dream — the child gives up its play and wants to go back to its mother. It finds the truth of the statement, "Desire is never satisfied by the enjoyment of desires, it only increases the more, as fire, when butter is poured upon it."

This is true of all sense-enjoyments, of all intellectual enjoyments, and of all the enjoyments of which the human mind is capable. They are nothing, they are within Maya, within this network beyond which we cannot go. We may run therein through infinite time and find no end, and whenever we struggle to get a little enjoyment, a mass of misery falls upon us. How awful is this! And when I think of it, I cannot but consider that this theory of Maya, this statement that it is all Maya, is the best and only explanation. What an amount of misery there is in this world; and if you travel among various nations you will find that one nation attempts to cure its evils by one means, and another by another. The very same evil has been taken up by various races, and attempts have been made in various ways to check it, yet no nation has succeeded. If it has been minimised at one point, a mass of evil has been crowded at another point. Thus it goes. The Hindus, to keep up a high standard of chastity in the race, have sanctioned child-marriage, which in the long run has degraded the race. At the same time, I cannot deny that this child-marriage makes the race more chaste. What would you have? If you want the nation to be more chaste, you weaken men and women physically by child-marriage. On the other hand, are you in England any better off? No, because chastity is the life of a nation. Do you not find in history that the first death-sign of a nation has been unchastity? When that has entered, the end of the race is in sight. Where shall we get a solution of these miseries then? If parents select husbands and wives for their children, then this evil is minimised. The daughters of India are more practical than sentimental. But very little of poetry remains in their lives. Again, if people select their own husbands and wives, that does not seem to bring much happiness. The Indian woman is generally very happy; there are not many cases of quarrelling between husband and wife. On the other hand in the United States, where the greatest liberty obtains, the number of unhappy homes and marriages is large. Unhappiness is here, there, and everywhere. What does it show? That, after all, not much happiness has been gained by all these ideals. We all struggle for happiness and as soon as we get a little happiness on one side, on the other side there comes unhappiness.

Shall we not work to do good then? Yes, with more zest than ever, but what this knowledge will do for us is to break down our fanaticism. The Englishman will no more be a fanatic and curse the Hindu. He will learn to respect the customs of different nations. There will be less of fanaticism and more of real work. Fanatics cannot work, they waste three-fourths of their energy. It is the level-headed, calm, practical man who works. So, the power to work will increase from this idea. Knowing that this is the state of things, there will be more patience. The sight of misery or of evil will not be able to throw us off our balance and make us run after shadows. Therefore, patience will come to us, knowing that the world will have to go on in its own way. If, for instance, all men have become good, the animals will have in the meantime evolved into men, and will have to pass through the same state, and so with the plants. But only one thing is certain; the mighty river is rushing towards the ocean, and all the drops that constitute the stream will in time be drawn into that boundless ocean. So, in this life, with all its miseries and sorrows, its joys and smiles and tears, one thing is certain, that all things are rushing towards their goal, and it is only a question of time when you and I, and plants and animals, and every particles of life that exists must reach the Infinite Ocean of Perfection, must attain to Freedom, to God.

Let me repeat, once more, that the Vedantic position is neither pessimism nor optimism. It does not say that this world is all evil or all good. It says that our evil is of no less value than our good, and our good of no more value than our evil. They are bound together. This is the world, and knowing this, you work with patience. What for? Why should we work? If this is the state of things, what shall we do? Why not become agnostics? The modern agnostics also know there is no solution of this problem, no getting out of this evil of Maya, as we say in our language; therefore they tell us to be satisfied and enjoy life. Here, again, is a mistake, a tremendous mistake, a most illogical mistake. And it is this. What do you mean by life? Do you mean only the life of the senses? In this, every one of us differs only slightly from the brutes. I am sure that no one is present here whose life is only in the senses. Then, this present life means something more than that. Our feelings, thoughts, and aspirations are all part and parcel of our life; and is not the struggle towards the area, ideal, towards perfection, one of the most important components of what we call life? According to the agnostics, we must enjoy life as it is. But this life means, above all, this search after the ideal; the essence of life is going towards perfection. We must have that, and, therefore, we cannot be agnostics or take the world as it appears. The agnostic position takes this life, minus the ideal component, to be all that exists. And this, the agnostic claims, cannot be reached, therefore he must give up the search. This is what is called Maya— this nature, this universe.

All religions are more or less attempts to get beyond nature— the crudest or the most developed, expressed through mythology or symbology, stories of gods, angels or demons, or through stories of saints or seers, great men or prophets, or through the abstractions of philosophy— all have that one object, all are trying to get beyond these limitations. In one word, they are all struggling towards freedom. Man feels, consciously or unconsciously, that he is bound; he is not what he wants to be. It was taught to him at the very moment he began to look around. That very instant he learnt that he was bound, and be also found that there was something in him which wanted to fly beyond, where the body could not follow, but which was as yet chained down by this limitation. Even in the lowest of religious ideas, where departed ancestors and other spirits— mostly violent and cruel, lurking about the houses of their friends, fond of bloodshed and strong drink— are worshipped, even there we find that one common factor, that of freedom. The man who wants to worship the gods sees in them, above all things, greater freedom than in himself. If a door is closed, he thinks the gods can get through it, and that walls have no limitations for them. This idea of freedom increases until it comes to the ideal of a Personal God, of which the central concept is that He is a Being beyond the limitation of nature, of Maya. I see before me, as it were, that in some of those forest retreats this question is being, discussed by those ancient sages of India; and in one of them, where even the oldest and the holiest fail to reach the solutions a young man stands up in the midst of them, and declares, "Hear, ye children of immortality, hear, who live in the highest places, I have found the way.

By knowing Him who is beyond darkness we can go beyond death."

This Maya is everywhere. It is terrible. Yet we have to work through it. The man who says that he will work when the world has become all good and then he will enjoy bliss is as likely to succeed as the man who sits beside the Ganga and says, "I will ford the river when all the water has run into the ocean." The way is not with Maya, but against it. This is another fact to learn. We are not born as helpers of nature, but competitors with nature. We are its bond-masters, but we bind ourselves down. Why is this house here? Nature did not build it. Nature says, go and live in the forest. Man says, I will build a house and fight with nature, and he does so. The whole history of humanity is a continuous fight against the so-called laws of nature, and man gains in the end. Coming to the internal world, there too the same fight is going on, this fight between the animal man and the spiritual man, between light and darkness; and here too man becomes victorious. He, as it were, cuts his way out of nature to freedom.

We see, then, that beyond this Maya the Vedantic philosophers find something which is not bound by Maya; and if we can get there, we shall not be bound by Maya. This idea is in some form or other the common property of all religions. But, with the Vedanta, it is only the beginning of religion and not the end. The idea of a Personal God, the Ruler and Creator of this universe, as He has been styled, the Ruler of Maya, or nature, is not the end of these Vedantic ideas; it is only the beginning. The idea grows and grows until the Vedantist finds that He who, he thought, was standing outside, is he himself and is in reality within. He is the one who is free, but who through limitation thought he was bound.

Chapter IV
Maya and the Evolution of the Conception of God

Delivered in London, 20th October 1896

We have seen how the idea of Maya, which forms, as it were, one of the basic doctrines of the Advaita Vedanta, is, in its germs, found even in the Samhitas, and that in reality all the ideas which are developed in the Upanishads are to be found already in the Samhitas in some form or other. Most of you are by this time familiar with the idea of Maya, and know that it is sometimes erroneously explained as illusion, so that when the universe is said to be Maya, that also has to be explained as being illusion. The translation of the word is neither happy nor correct. Maya is not a theory; it is simply a statement of facts about the universe as it exists, and to understand Maya we must go back to the Samhitas and begin with the conception in the germ.

We have seen how the idea of the Devas came. At the same time we know that these Devas were at first only powerful beings, nothing more. Most of you are horrified when reading the old scriptures, whether of the Greeks, the Hebrews, the Persians, or others, to find that the ancient gods sometimes did things which, to us, are very repugnant. But when we read these books, we entirely forget that we are persons of the nineteenth century, and these gods were beings existing thousands of years ago. We also forget that the people who worshipped these gods found nothing incongruous in their characters, found nothing to frighten them, because they were very much like themselves. I may also remark that that is the one great lesson we have to learn throughout our lives. In judging others we always judge them by our own ideals. That is not as it should be. Everyone must be judged according to his own ideal, and not by that of anyone else. In our dealings with our fellow-beings we constantly labour under this mistake, and I am of opinion that the vast majority of our quarrels with one another arise simply from this one cause that we are always trying to judge others' gods by our own, others' ideals by our ideals, and others' motives by our motives. Under certain circumstances I might do a certain thing, and when I see another person taking the same course I think he has also the same motive actuating him, little dreaming that although the effect may be the same, yet many other causes may produce the same thing. He may have performed the action with quite a different motive from that which impelled me to do it. So in judging of those ancient religions we must not take the standpoint to which we incline, but must put ourselves into the position of thought and life of those early times.

The idea of the cruel and ruthless Jehovah in the Old Testament has frightened many— but why? What right have they to assume that the Jehovah of the ancient Jews must represent the conventional idea of the God of the present day? And at the same time, we must not forget that there will come men after us who will laugh at our ideas of religion and God in the same way that we laugh at those of the ancients. Yet, through all these various conceptions runs the golden thread of unity, and it is the purpose of the Vedanta to discover this thread. "I am the thread that runs through all these various ideas, each one of which is; like a pearl," says the Lord Krishna; and it is the duty of Vedanta to establish this connecting thread, how ever incongruous or disgusting may seem these ideas when judged according to the conceptions of today. These ideas, in the setting of past times, were harmonious and not more hideous than our present ideas. It is only when we try to take them out of their settings and apply to our own present circumstances that the hideousness becomes obvious. For the old surroundings are dead and gone. Just as the ancient Jew has developed into the keen, modern, sharp Jew, and the ancient Aryan into the intellectual Hindu similarly Jehovah has grown, and Devas have grown.

The great mistake is in recognising the evolution of the worshippers, while we do not acknowledge the evolution of the Worshipped. He is not credited with the advance that his devotees have made. That is to say, you and I, representing ideas, have grown; these gods also, as representing ideas, have grown. This may seem somewhat curious to you— that God can grow. He cannot. He is unchangeable. In the same sense the real man never grows. But man's ideas of God are constantly changing and expanding. We shall see later on how the real man behind each one of these human manifestations is immovable, unchangeable, pure, and always perfect; and in the same way the idea that we form of God is a mere manifestation, our own creation. Behind that is the real God who never changes, the ever pure, the immutable. But the manifestation is always changing revealing the reality behind more and more. When it reveals more of the fact behind, it is called progression, when it hides more of the fact behind, it is called retrogression. Thus, as we grow, so the gods grow. From the ordinary point of view, just as we reveal ourselves as we evolve, so the gods reveal themselves.

We shall now be in a position to understand the theory of Maya. In all the regions of the world the one question they propose to discuss is this : Why is there disharmony in the universe ? Why is there this evil in the universe ? We do not find this question in the very inception of primitive religious ideas, because the world did not appear incongruous to the primitive man. Circumstances were not inharmonious for him; there was no dash of opinions; to him there was no antagonism of good and evil. There was merely a feeling in his own heart of something which said yea, and something which said nay. The primitive man was a man of impulse. He did what occurred to him, and tried to bring out through his muscles whatever thought came into his mind, and he never stopped to judge, and seldom tried to check his impulses. So with the gods, they were also creatures of impulse. Indra comes and shatters the forces of the demons. Jehovah is pleased with one person and displeased with another, for what reason no one knows or asks. The habit of inquiry had not then arisen, and whatever he did was regarded as right. There was no idea of good or evil. The Devas did many wicked things in our sense of the word; again and again Indra and other gods committed very wicked deeds, but to the worshippers of Indra the ideas of wickedness and evil did not occur, so they did not question them.

With the advance of ethical ideas came the fight. There arose a certain sense in man, called in different languages and nations by different names. Call it the voice of God, or the result of past education, or whatever else you like, but the effect was this that it had a checking power upon the natural impulses of man. There is one impulse in our minds which says, do. Behind it rises another voice which says, do not. There is one set of ideas in our mind which is always struggling to get outside through the channels of the senses, and behind that, although it may be thin and weak, there is an infinitely small voice which says, do not go outside. The two beautiful Sanskrit words for these phenomena are Pravritti and Nivritti, " circling forward" and " circling inward". It is the circling forward which usually governs our actions. Religion begins with this circling inward. Religion begins with this " do not". Spirituality begins with this " do not". When the " do not" is not there, religion has not begun. And this " do not" came, causing men's ideas to grow, despite the fighting gods which they had worshipped.

A little love awoke in the hearts of mankind. It was very small indeed, and even now it is not much greater. It was at first confined to a tribe embracing perhaps members of the same tribe; these gods loved their tribes and each god was a tribal god, the protector of that tribe. And sometimes the members of a tribe would think of themselves as the descendants of their god, just as the clans in different nations think that they are the common descendants of the man who was the founder of the clan. There were in ancient times, and are even now, some people who claim to be descendants not only of these tribal gods, but also of the Sun and the Moon. You read in the ancient Sanskrit books of the great heroic emperors of the solar and the lunar dynasties. They were first worshippers of the Sun and the Moon, and gradually came to think of themselves as descendants of the god of the Sun of the Moon, and so forth. So when these tribal ideas began to grow there came a little love, some slight idea of duty towards each other, a little social organisation. Then, naturally, the idea came: How can we live together without bearing and forbearing? How can one man live with another without having some time or other to check his impulses, to restrain himself, to forbear from doing things which his mind would prompt him to do? It is impossible. Thus comes the idea of restraint. The whole social fabric is based upon that idea of restraint, and we all know that the man or woman who has not learnt the great lesson of bearing and forbearing leads a most miserable life.

Now, when these ideas of religion came, a glimpse of something higher, more ethical, dawned upon the intellect of mankind. The old gods were found to be incongruous — these boisterous, fighting, drinking, beef-eating gods of the ancients — whose delight was in the smell of burning flesh and libations of strong liquor. Sometimes Indra drank so much that he fell upon the ground and talked unintelligibly. These gods could no longer be tolerated. The notion had arisen of inquiring into motives, and the gods had to come in for their share of inquiry. Reason for such-and-such actions was demanded and the reason was wanting. Therefore man gave up these gods, or rather they developed higher ideas concerning them. They took a survey, as it were, of all the actions and qualities of the gods and discarded those which they could not harmonise, and kept those which they could understand, and combined them, labelling them with one name, Deva-deva, the God of gods. The god to be worshipped was no more a simple symbol of power; something more was required than that. He was an ethical god; he loved mankind, and did good to mankind. But the idea of god still remained. They increased his ethical significance, and increased also his power. He became the most ethical being in the universe, as well as almost almighty.

But all this patchwork would not do. As the explanation assumed greater proportions, the difficulty which it sought to solve did the same. If the qualities of the god increased in arithmetical progression, the difficulty and doubt increased in geometrical progression. The difficulty of Jehovah was very little beside the difficulty of the God of the universe, and this question remains to the present day. Why under the reign of an almighty and all-loving God of the universe should diabolical things be allowed to remain? Why so much more misery than happiness, and so much more wickedness than good? We may shut our eyes to all these things, but the fact still remains that this world is a hideous world. At best, it is the hell of Tantalus. Here we are with strong impulses and stronger cravings for sense-enjoyments, but cannot satisfy them. There rises a wave which impels us forward in spite of our own will, and as soon as we move one step, comes a blow. We are all doomed to live here like Tantalus. Ideals come into our head far beyond the limit of our sense-ideals, but when we seek to express them, we cannot do so. On the other hand, we are crushed by the surging mass around us. Yet if I give up all ideality and merely struggle through this world, my existence is that of a brute, and I degenerate and degrade myself. Neither way is happiness. Unhappiness is the fate of those who are content to live in this world, born as they are. A thousand times greater misery is the fate of those who dare to stand forth for truth and for higher things and who dare to ask for something higher than mere brute existence here. These are facts; but there is no explanation — there cannot be any explanation. But the Vedanta shows the way out. You must bear in mind that I have to tell you facts that will frighten you sometimes, but if you remember what I say, think of it, and digest it, it will be yours, it will raise you higher, and make you capable of understanding and living in truth.

Now, it is a statement of fact that this world is a Tantalus's hell, that we do not know anything about this universe, yet at the same time we cannot say that we do not know. I cannot say that this chain exists, when I think that I do not know it. It may be an entire delusion of my brain. I may be dreaming all the time. I am dreaming that I am talking to you, and that you are listening to me. No one can prove that it is not a dream. My brain itself may be a dream, and as to that no one has ever seen his own brain. We all take it for granted. So it is with everything. My own body I take for granted. At the same time I cannot say, I do not know. This standing between knowledge and ignorance, this mystic twilight, the mingling of truth and falsehood — and where they meet — no one knows. We are walking in the midst of a dream. Half sleeping, half waking, passing all our lives in a haze; this is the fate of everyone of us. This is the fate of all sense-knowledge. This is the fate of all philosophy, of all boasted science, of all boasted human knowledge. This is the universe.

What you call matter, or spirit, or mind, or anything else you may like to call them, the fact remains the same: we cannot say that they are, we cannot say that they are not. We cannot say they are one, we cannot say they are many. This eternal play of light and darkness — indiscriminate, indistinguishable, inseparable —

is always there. A fact, yet at the same time not a fact; awake and at the same time asleep. This is a statement of facts, and this is what is called Maya. We are born in this Maya, we live in it, we think in it, we dream in it. We are philosophers in it, we are spiritual men in it, nay, we are devils in this Maya, and we are gods in this Maya. Stretch your ideas as far as you can make them higher and higher, call them infinite or by any other name you please, even these ideas are within this Maya. It cannot be otherwise, and the whole of human knowledge is a generalization of this Maya trying to know it as it appears to be. This is the work of Nama-Rupa— name and form. Everything that has form, everything that calls up an idea in your mind, is within Maya; for everything that is bound by the laws of time, space, and causation is within Maya.

Let us go back a little to those early ideas of God and see what became of them. We perceive at once that the idea of some Being who is eternally loving us— eternally unselfish and almighty, ruling this universe— could not satisfy. "Where is the just, merciful God?" asked the philosopher. Does He not see millions and millions of His children perish, in the form of men and animals; for who can live one moment here without killing others? Can you draw a breath without destroying thousands of lives? You live, because, millions die. Every moment of your life, every breath that you breathe, is death to thousands; every movement that you make is death to millions. Every morsel that you eat is death to millions. Why should they die? There is an old sophism that they are very low existences. Supposing they are— which is questionable, for who knows whether the ant is greater than the man, or the man than the ant— who can prove one way or the other? Apart from that question, even taking it for granted that these are very low beings, still why should they die? If they are low, they have more reason to live. Why not? Because they live more in the senses, they feel pleasure and pain a thousandfold more than you or I can do. Which of us eats a dinner with the same gusto as a dog or wolf? None, because our energies are not in the senses; they are in the intellect, in the spirit. But in animals, their whole soul is in the senses, and they become mad and enjoy things which we human beings never dream of, and the pain is commensurate with the pleasure. Pleasure and pain are meted out in equal measure. If the pleasure felt by animals is so much keener than that felt by man, it follows that the animals' sense of pain is as keen, if not keener than man's. So the fact is, the pain and misery men feel in dying is intensified a thousandfold in animals, and yet we kill them without troubling ourselves about their misery. This is Maya. And if we suppose there is a Personal God like a human being, who made everything, these so-called explanations and theories which try to prove that out of evil comes good are not sufficient. Let twenty thousand good things come, but why should they come from evil? On that principle, I might cut the throats of others because I want the full pleasure of my five senses. That is no reason. Why should good come through evil? The question remains to be answered, and it cannot be answered. The philosophy of India was compelled to admit this.

The Vedanta was (and is) the boldest system of religion. It stopped nowhere, and it had one advantage. There was no body of priests who sought to suppress every man who tried to tell the truth. There was always absolute religious freedom. In India the bondage of superstition is a social one; here in the West society is very free. Social matters in India are very strict, but religious opinion is free. In England a man may dress any way he likes, or eat what he likes — no one objects; but if he misses attending church, then Mrs. Grundy is down on him. He has to conform first to what society says on religion, and then he may think of the truth. In India, on the other hand, if a man dines with one who does not belong to his own caste, down comes society with all its terrible powers and crushes him then and there. If he wants to dress a little differently from the way in which his ancestor dressed ages ago, he is done for. I have heard of a man who was cast out by society because he went several miles to see the first railway train. Well, we shall presume that was not true! But in religion, we find atheists, materialists, and Buddhists, creeds, opinions, and speculations of every phase and variety, some of a most startling character, living side by side. Preachers of all sects go about reaching and getting adherents, and at the very gates of the temples of gods, the Brahmins — to their credit be it said — allow even the materialists to stand and give forth their opinions.

Buddha died at a ripe old age. I remember a friend of mine, a great American scientist, who was fond of reading his life. He did not like the death of Buddha, because he was not crucified. What a false idea! For a man to be great he must be murdered! Such ideas never prevailed in India. This great Buddha travelled all over India, denouncing her gods and even the God of the universe, and yet he lived to a good old age. For eighty years he lived, and had converted half the country.

Then, there were the Charvakas, who preached horrible things, the most rank, undisguised materialism, such as in the nineteenth century they dare not openly preach. These Charvakas were allowed to preach from temple to temple, and city to city, that religion was all nonsense, that it was priestcraft, that the Vedas were the words and writings of fools, rogues, and demons, and that there was neither God nor an eternal soul. If there was a soul, why did it not come back after death drawn by the love of wife and child. Their idea was that if there was a soul it must still love after death, and want good things to eat and nice dress. Yet no one hurt these Charvakas.

Thus India has always had this magnificent idea of religious freedom, and you must remember that freedom is the first condition of growth. What you do not make free, will never grow. The idea that you can make others grow and help their growth, that you can direct and guide them, always retaining for yourself the freedom of the teacher, is nonsense, a dangerous lie which has retarded the growth of millions and millions of human beings in this world. Let men have the light of liberty. That is the only condition of growth.

We, in India, allowed liberty in spiritual matters, and we have a tremendous spiritual power in religious. Today, you grant the same liberty in social matters, and so have a splendid social organisation. We have not given any freedom to the expansion of social matters, and ours is a cramped society. You have never given any freedom in religious matters but with fire and sword have enforced your beliefs, and the result is that religion is a stunted, degenerated growth in the European mind. In India, we have to take off the shackles from society; in Europe, the chains must be taken from the feet of spiritual progress. Then will come a wonderful growth and development of man. If we discover that there is one unity running through all these developments, spiritual, moral, and social, we shall find that religion, in the fullest sense of the word, must come into society, and into our everyday life. In the light of Vedanta you will understand that all sciences are but manifestations of religion, and so is everything that exists in this world.

We see, then, that through freedom the sciences were built; and in them we have two sets of opinions; the one the materialistic and denouncing, and the other the positive and constructive. It is a most curious fact that in every society you find them. Supposing there is an evil in society, you will find immediately one group rise up and denounce it in vindictive fashion, which sometimes degenerates into fanaticism. There are fanatics in every society, and women frequently join in these outcries, because of their impulsive nature. Every fanatic who gets up and denounces something can secure a following. It is very easy to break down; a maniac can break anything he likes, but it would be hard for him to build up anything. These fanatics may do some good, according to their light, but much morn harm. Because social institutions are not made in a day, and to change them means removing the cause. Suppose there is an evil; denouncing it will not remove it, but you must go to work at the root. First find out the cause, then remove it, and the effect will be removed also. Mere outcry not produce any effect, unless indeed it produces misfortune.

There are others who had sympathy in their hearts and who understood the idea that we must go deep into the cause, these were the great saints. One fact you must remember, that all the great teachers of the world have declared that they came not to destroy but to fulfil. Many times his has not been understood, and their forbearance has been thought to be an unworthy compromise with existing popular opinions. Even now, you occasionally hear that these prophets and great teachers were rather cowardly, and dared not say and do what they thought was right; but that was not so. Fanatics little understand the infinite power of love in the hearts of these great sages who looked upon the inhabitants of this world as their children. They were the real fathers, the real gods, filled with infinite sympathy and patience for everyone; they were ready to bear and forbear. They knew how human society should grow, and patiently slowly, surely, went on applying their remedies, not by denouncing and frightening people, but by gently and kindly leading them upwards step by step. Such were the writers of the Upanishads. They knew full well how the old ideas of God were not reconcilable with the advanced ethical ideas of the time; they knew full well that what the atheists were preaching contained a good deal of truth, nay, great nuggets of truth; but at the same time, they understood that those who wished to sever the thread that bound the beads, who wanted to build a new society in the air, would entirely fail.

We never build anew, we simply change places; we cannot have anything new, we only change the position of things. The seed grows into the tree, patiently and gently; we must direct our energies towards the truth and fulfil the truth that exists, not try to make new truths. Thus, instead of denouncing these old ideas of God as unfit for modern times, the ancient sages began to seek out the reality that was in them. The result was the Vedanta philosophy, and out of the old deities, out of the monotheistic God, the Ruler of the universe, they found yet higher and higher ideas in what is called the Impersonal Absolute; they found oneness throughout the universe.

He who sees in this world of manifoldness that One running through all, in this world of death he who finds that One Infinite Life, and in this world of insentience and ignorance he who finds that One Light and Knowledge, unto him belongs eternal peace. Unto none else, unto none else.

Chapter V
Maya and Freedom

Delivered in London, 22nd October 1896

"Trailing clouds of glory we come," says the poet. Not all of us come as trailing clouds of glory however; some of us come as trailing black fogs; there can be no question about that. But every one of us comes into this world to fight, as on a battlefield. We come here weeping to fight our way, as well as we can, and to make a path for ourselves through this infinite ocean of life; forward we go, having long ages behind us and an immense expanse beyond. So on we go, till death comes and takes us off the field— victorious or defeated, we do not know. And this is Maya.

Hope is dominant in the heart of childhood. The whole world is a golden vision to the opening eyes of the child; he thinks his will is supreme. As he moves onward, at every step nature stands as an adamantine wall, barring his future progress. He may hurl himself against it again and again, striving to break through. The further he goes, the further recedes the ideal, till death comes, and there is release, perhaps. And this is Maya.

A man of science rises, he is thirsting after knowledge. No sacrifice is too great, no struggle too hopeless for him. He moves onward discovering secret after secret of nature, searching out the secrets from her innermost heart, and what for? What is it all for? Why should we give him glory? Why should he acquire fame? Does not nature do infinitely more than any human being can do?— and nature is dull, insentient. Why should it be glory to imitate the dull, the insentient? Nature can hurl a thunderbolt of any magnitude to any distance. If a man can do one small part as much, we praise him and laud him to the skies. Why? Why should we praise him for imitating nature, imitating death, imitating dullness imitating insentience? The force of gravitation can pull to pieces the biggest mass that ever existed; yet it is insentient. What glory is there in imitating the insentient? Yet we are all struggling after that. And this is maya.

The senses drag the human soul out. Man is seeking for pleasure and for happiness where it can never be found. For countless ages we are all taught that this is futile and vain, there is no happiness here. But we cannot learn; it is impossible for us to do so, except through our own experiences. We try them, and a blow comes. Do we learn then? Not even then. Like moths hurling themselves against the flame, we are hurling ourselves again and again into sense-pleasures, hoping to find satisfaction there. We return again and again with freshened energy; thus we go on, till crippled and cheated we die. And this is Maya.

So with our intellect. In our desire to solve the mysteries of the universe, we cannot stop our questioning, we feel we must know and cannot believe that no knowledge is to be gained. A few steps, and there arises the wall of beginningless and endless time which we cannot surmount. A few steps, and there appears a wall of boundless space which cannot be surmounted, and the whole is irrevocably bound in by the walls of cause and effect. We cannot go beyond them. Yet we struggle, and still have to struggle. And this is Maya.

With every breath, with every pulsation of the heart with every one of our movements, we think we are free, and the very same moment we are shown that we are not. Bound slaves, nature's bond-slaves, in body, in mind, in all our thoughts, in all our feelings. And this is Maya.

There was never a mother who did not think her child was a born genius, the most extraordinary child that was ever born; she dotes upon her child. Her whole soul is in the child. The child grows up, perhaps becomes a drunkard, a brute, ill-treats the mother, and the more he ill-treats her, the more her love increases. The world lauds it as the unselfish love of the mother, little dreaming that the mother is a born slave, she cannot help it. She would a thousand times rather throw off the burden, but she cannot. So she covers it with a mass of flowers, which she calls wonderful love. And this is Maya.

We are all like this in the world. A legend tells how once Narada said to Krishna, "Lord, show me Maya." A few days passed away, and Krishna asked Narada to make a trip with him towards a desert, and after walking for several miles, Krishna said, "Narada, I am thirsty; can you fetch some water for me?" "I will go at once, sir, and get you water." So Narada went. At a little distance there was a village; he entered the village in search of water and knocked at a door, which was opened by a most beautiful young girl. At the sight of her he immediately forgot that his Master was waiting for water, perhaps dying for the want of it. He forgot everything and began to talk with the girl. All that day he did not return to his Master. The next day, he was again at the house, talking to the girl. That talk ripened into love; he asked the father for the daughter, and they were married and lived there and had children. Thus twelve years passed. His father-in-law died, he inherited his property. He lived, as he seemed to think, a very happy life with his wife and children, his fields and his cattle and so forth. Then came a flood. One night the river rose until it overflowed its banks and flooded the whole village. Houses fell, men and animals were swept away and drowned, and everything was floating in the rush of the stream. Narada had to escape. With one hand be held his wife, and with the other two of his children; another child was on his shoulders, and he was trying to ford this tremendous flood. After a few steps he found the current was too strong, and the child on his shoulders fell and was borne away. A cry of despair came from Narada. In trying to save that child, he lost his grasp upon one of the others, and it also was lost. At last his wife, whom he clasped with all his might, was torn away by the current, and he was thrown on the bank, weeping and wailing in bitter lamentation. Behind him there came a gentle voice, "My child, where is the water? You went to fetch a pitcher of water, and I am waiting for you; you have been gone for quite half an hour." "Half an hour!" Narada exclaimed. Twelve whole years had passed through his mind, and all these scenes had happened in half an hour! And this is Maya.

In one form or another, we are all in it. It is a most difficult and intricate state of things to understand. It has been preached in every country, taught everywhere, but only believed in by a few, because until we get the experiences ourselves we cannot believe in it. What does it show? Something very terrible. For it is all futile. Time, the avenger of everything, comes, and nothing is left. He swallows up the saint and the sinner, the king and the peasant, the beautiful and the ugly; he leaves nothing. Everything is rushing towards that one goal destruction. Our knowledge, our arts, our sciences, everything is rushing towards it. None can stem the tide, none can hold it back for a minute. We may try to forget it, in the same way that persons in a plague-striker city try to create oblivion by drinking, dancing, and other vain attempts, and so becoming paralysed. So we are trying to forget, trying to create oblivion by all sorts of sense-pleasures. And this is Maya.

Two ways have been proposed. One method, which everyone knows, is very common, and that is: "It may be very true, but do not think of it. 'Make hay while the sun shines,' as the proverb says. It is all true, it is a fact, but do not mind it. Seize the few pleasures you can, do what little you can, do not look at tile dark side of the picture, but always towards the hopeful, the positive side." There is some truth in this, but there is also a danger. The truth is that it is a good motive power. Hope and a positive ideal are very good motive powers for our lives, but there is a certain danger in them. The danger lies in our giving up the struggle in despair. Such is the case with those who preach, "Take the world as it is, sit down as calmly and comfortably as you can and be contented with all these miseries. When you receive blows, say they are not blows but flowers; and when you are driven about like slaves, say that you are free. Day and night tell lies to others and to your own souls, because that is the only way to live happily." This is what is called practical wisdom, and never was it more prevalent in the world than in this nineteenth century; because never were harder blows hit than at the present time, never was competition keener, never were men so cruel to their fellow-men as now; and, therefore, must this consolation be offered. It is put forward in the strongest way at the present time; but it fails, as it always must fail. We cannot hide a carrion with roses; it is impossible. It would not avail long; for soon the roses would fade, and the carrion would be worse than ever before. So with our lives. We may try to cover our old and festering sores with cloth of gold, but there comes a day when the cloth of gold is removed, and the sore in all its ugliness is revealed.

Is there no hope then? True it is that we are all slaves of Maya, born in Maya, and live in Maya. Is there then no way out, no hope? That we are all miserable, that this world is really a prison, that even our so-called trailing beauty is but a prison-house, and that even our intellects and minds are prison-houses, have been known for ages upon ages. There has never been a man, there has never been a human soul, who has not felt this sometime or other, however he may talk. And the old people feel it most, because in them is the accumulated experience of a whole life, because they cannot be easily cheated by the lies of nature. Is there no way out? We find that with all this, with this terrible fact before us, in the midst of sorrow and suffering, even in this world where life and death are synonymous, even here, there is a still small voice that is ringing through all ages, through every country, and in every heart: "This My Maya is divine, made up of qualities, and very difficult to cross. Yet those that come unto Me, cross the river of life." "Come unto Me all ye that labour and are heavy laden and I will give you rest." This is the voice that is leading us forward. Man has heard it, and is hearing it all through the ages. This voice comes to men when everything seems to be lost and hope has fled, when man's dependence on his own strength has been crushed down and everything seems to melt away between his fingers, and life is a hopeless ruin. Then he hears it. This is called religion.

On the one side, therefore, is the bold assertion that this is all nonsense, that this is Maya, but along with it there is the most hopeful assertion that beyond Maya, there is a way out. On the other hand, practical men tell us, "Don't bother your heads about such nonsense as religion and metaphysics. Live here; this is a very bad world indeed, but make the best of it." Which put in plain language means, live a hypocritical, lying life, a life of continuous fraud, covering all sores in the best way you can. Go on putting patch after patch, until everything is lost, and you are a mass of patchwork. This is what is called practical life. Those that are satisfied with this patchwork will never come to religion. Religion begins with a tremendous dissatisfaction with the present state of things, with our lives, and a hatred, an intense hatred, for this patching up of life, an unbounded disgust for fraud and lies. He alone can be religious who dares say, as the mighty Buddha once said under the Bo-tree, when this idea of practicality appeared before him and he saw that it was nonsense, and yet could not find a way out. When the temptation came to him to give up his search after truth, to go back to the world and live the old life of fraud, calling things by wrong names, telling lies to one-self and to everybody, he, the giant, conquered it and said, "Death is better than a vegetating ignorant life; it is better to die on the battle-field than to live a life of defeat." This is the basis of religion. When a man takes this stand, he is on the way to find the truth, he is on the way to God. That determination must be the first impulse towards becoming religious. I will hew out a way for myself. I will know the truth or give up my life in the attempt. For on this side it is nothing, it is gone, it is vanishing every day. The beautiful, hopeful, young person of today is the veteran of tomorrow. Hopes and joys and pleasures will die like blossoms with tomorrow's frost. That is one side; on the other, there are the great charms of conquest, victories over all the ills of life, victory over life itself, the conquest of the universe. On that side men can stand. Those who dare, therefore, to struggle for victory, for truth, for religion, are in the right way; and that is what the Vedas preach: Be not in despair, the way is very difficult, like walking on the edge of a razor; yet despair not, arise, awake, and find the ideal, the goal.

Now all these various manifestations of religion, in whatever shape and form they have come to mankind, have this one common central basis. It is the preaching of freedom, the way out of this world. They never came to reconcile the world and religion, but to cut the Gordian knot, to establish religion in its own ideal, and not to compromise with the world. That is what every religion preaches, and the duty of the Vedanta is to harmonise all these aspirations, to make manifest the common ground between all the religions of the world, the highest as well as the lowest. What we call the most arrant superstition and the highest philosophy really have a common aim in that they both try to show the way out of the same difficulty, and in most cases this way is through the help of someone who is not himself bound by the laws of nature in one word, someone who is free. In spite of all the difficulties and differences of opinion about the nature of the one free agent, whether he is a Personal God, or a sentient being like man, whether masculine, feminine, or neuter— and the discussions have been endless— the fundamental idea is the same. In spite of the almost hopeless contradictions of the different systems, we find the golden thread of unity running through them all, and in this philosophy, this golden thread has been traced revealed little by little to our view, and the first step to this revelation is the common ground that all are advancing towards freedom.

One curious fact present in the midst of all our joys and sorrows, difficulties and struggles, is that we are surely journeying towards freedom. The question was practically this : "What is this universe ? From what does it arise ? Into what does it go ?" And the answer was: "In freedom it rises, in freedom it rests, and into freedom it melts away." This idea of freedom you cannot relinquish. Your actions, your very lives will be lost without it. Every moment nature is proving us to be slaves and not free. Yet, simultaneously rises the other idea, that still we are free At every step we are knocked down, as it were, by Maya, and shown that we are bound; and yet at the same moment, together with this blow, together with this feeling that we are bound, comes the other feeling that we are free. Some inner voice tells us that we are free. But if we attempt to realise that freedom, to make it manifest, we find the difficulties almost insuperable Yet, in spite of that it insists on asserting itself inwardly, "I am free, I am free." And if you study all the various religions of the world you will find this idea expressed. Not only religion— you must not take this word in its narrow sense— but the whole life of society is the assertion of that one principle of freedom. All movements are the assertion of that one freedom. That voice has been heard by everyone, whether he knows it or not, that voice which declares, "Come unto Me all ye that labour and are heavy laden." It may not be in the same language or the same form of speech, but in some form or other, that voice calling for freedom has been with us. Yes, we are born here on account of that voice; every one of our movements is for that. We are all rushing towards freedom, we are all following that voice, whether we know it or not; as the children of the village were attracted by the music of the flute-player, so we are all following the music of the voice without knowing it.

We are ethical when we follow that voice. Not only the human soul, but all creatures, from the lowest to the highest have heard the voice and are rushing towards it; and in the struggle are either combining with each other or pushing each other out of the way. Thus come competition, joys, struggles, life, pleasure, and death, and the whole universe is nothing but the result of this mad struggle to reach the voice. This is the manifestation of nature.

What happens then? The scene begins to shift. As soon as you know the voice and understand what it is, the whole scene changes. The same world which was the ghastly battle-field of Maya is now changed into something good and beautiful. We no longer curse nature, nor say that the world is horrible and that it is all vain; we need no longer weep and wail. As soon as we understand the voice, we see the reassert why this struggle should be here, this fight, this competition, this difficulty, this cruelty, these little pleasures and joys; we see that they are in the nature of things, because without them there would be no going towards the voice, to attain which we are destined, whether we know it or not. All human life, all nature, therefore, is struggling to attain to freedom. The sun is moving towards the goal, so is the earth in circling round the sun, so is the moon in circling round the earth. To that goal the planet is moving, and the air is blowing. Everything is struggling towards that. The saint is going towards that voice — he cannot help it, it is no glory to him. So is the sinner. The charitable man is going straight towards that voice, and cannot be hindered; the miser is also going towards the same destination: the greatest worker of good hears the same voice within, and he cannot resist it, he must go towards the voice; so with the most arrant idler. One stumbles more than another, and him who stumbles more we call bad, him who stumbles less we call good. Good and bad are never two different things, they are one and the same; the difference is not one of kind, but of degree.

Now, if the manifestation of this power of freedom is really governing the whole universe — applying that to religion, our special study — we find this idea has been the one assertion throughout. Take the lowest form of religion where there is the worship of departed ancestors or certain powerful and cruel gods; what is the prominent idea about the gods or departed ancestors? That they are superior to nature, not bound by its restrictions. The worshipper has, no doubt, very limited ideas of nature. He himself cannot pass through a wall, nor fly up into the skies, but the gods whom he worships can do these things. What is meant by that, philosophically? That the assertion of freedom is there, that the gods whom he worships are superior to nature as he knows it. So with those who worship still higher beings. As the idea of nature expands, the idea of the soul which is superior to nature also expands, until we come to what we call monotheism, which holds that there is Maya (nature), and that there is some Being who is the Ruler of this Maya.

Here Vedanta begins, where these monotheistic ideas first appear. But the

Vedanta philosophy wants further explanation. This explanation— that there is a Being beyond all these manifestations of Maya, who is superior to and independent of Maya, and who is attracting us towards Himself, and that we are all going towards Him— is very good, says the Vedanta, but yet the perception is not clear, the vision is dim and hazy, although it does not directly contradict reason. Just as in your hymn it is said, "Nearer my God to Thee," the same hymn would be very good to the Vedantin, only he would change a word, and make it, "Nearer my God to me." The idea that the goal is far off, far beyond nature, attracting us all towards it, has to be brought nearer and nearer, without degrading or degenerating it. The God of heaven becomes the God in nature, and the God in nature becomes the God who is nature, and the God who is nature becomes the God within this temple of the body, and the God dwelling in the temple of the body at last becomes the temple itself, becomes the soul and man— and there it reaches the last words it can teach. He whom the sages have been seeking in all these places is in our own hearts; the voice that you heard was right, says the Vedanta, but the direction you gave to the voice was wrong. That ideal of freedom that you perceived was correct, but you projected it outside yourself, and that was your mistake. Bring it nearer and nearer, until you find that it was all the time within you, it was the Self of your own self. That freedom was your own nature, and this Maya never bound you. Nature never has power over you. Like a frightened child you were dreaming that it was throttling you, and the release from this fear is the goal: not only to see it intellectually, but to perceive it, actualise it, much more definitely than we perceive this world. Then we shall know that we are free. Then, and then alone, will all difficulties vanish, then will all the perplexities of heart be smoothed away, all crookedness made straight, then will vanish the delusion of manifoldness and nature; and Maya instead of being a horrible, hopeless dream, as it is now will become beautiful, and this earth, instead of being a prison-house, will become our playground, and even dangers and difficulties, even all sufferings, will become deified and show us their real nature, will show us that behind everything, as the substance of everything, He is standing, and that He is the one real Self.

Chapter VI
The Absolute and Manifestation

Delivered in London, 1896

The one question that is most difficult to grasp in understanding the Advaita philosophy, and the one question that will be asked again and again and that will always remain is: How has the Infinite, the Absolute, become the finite? I will now take up this question, and, in order to illustrate it, I will use a figure.

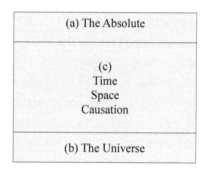

(a) The Absolute
(c) Time Space Causation
(b) The Universe

Here is the Absolute (a), and this is the universe (b). The Absolute has become the universe. By this is not only meant the material world, but the mental world, the spiritual world — heavens and earths, and in fact, everything that exists. Mind is the name of a change, and body the name of another change, and so on, and all these changes compose our universe. This Absolute (a) has become the universe (b) by coming through time, space, and causation (c). This is the central idea of Advaita. Time, space, and causation are like the glass through which the Absolute is seen, and when It is seen on the lower side, It appears as the universe. Now we at once gather from this that in the Absolute there is neither time, space, nor causation. The idea of time cannot be there, seeing that there is no mind, no thought. The idea of space cannot be there, seeing that there is no external change. What you call motion and causation cannot exist where there is only One. We have to understand this, and impress it on our minds, that what we call causation begins after, if we may be permitted to say so, the degeneration of the Absolute into the phenomenal, and not before; that our will, our desire and all these things always come after that. I think Schopenhauer's philosophy makes a mistake in its interpretation of Vedanta, for it seeks to make the will everything. Schopenhauer makes the will stand in the place of the Absolute. But the absolute cannot be presented as will, for will is something changeable and phenomenal, and over the line, drawn above time, space, and causation, there is no change, no motion; it is only below the line that external motion and internal motion, called thought begin. There can be no will on the other side, and will therefore, cannot be the cause of this universe. Coming nearer, we see in our own bodies that will is not the cause of every movement. I move this chair; my will is the cause of this movement, and this will becomes manifested as muscular motion at the other end. But the same power that moves the chair is moving the heart, the lungs, and so on, but not through will. Given that the power is the same, it only becomes will when it rises to the plane of consciousness, and to call it will before it has risen to this plane is a misnomer. This makes a good deal of confusion in Schopenhauer's philosophy.

A stone falls and we ask, why? This question is possible only on the supposition that nothing happens without a cause. I request you to make this very clear in your minds, for whenever we ask why anything happens, we are taking for granted that everything that happens must have a why, that is to say, it must have been preceded by something else which acted as the cause.

This precedence and succession are what we call the law of causation. It means that everything in the universe is by turn a cause and an effect. It is the cause of certain things which come after it, and is itself the effect of something else which has preceded it. This is called the law of causation and is a necessary condition of all our thinking. We believe that every particle in the universe, whatever it be, is in relation to every other particle. There has been much discussion as to how this idea arose. In Europe, there have been intuitive philosophers who believed that it was constitutional in humanity, others have believed it came from experience, but the question has never been settled. We shall see later on what the Vedanta has to say about it. But first we have to understand this that the very asking of the question "why" presupposes that everything round us has been preceded by certain things and will be succeeded by certain other things. The other belief involved in this question is that nothing in the universe is independent, that everything is acted upon by something outside itself. Interdependence is the law of the whole universe. In asking what caused the Absolute, what an error we are making! To ask this question we have to suppose that the Absolute also is bound by something, that It is dependent on something; and in making this supposition, we drag the Absolute down to the level of the universe. For in the Absolute there is neither time, space, nor causation; It is all one. That which exists by itself alone cannot have any cause. That which is free cannot have any cause; else it would not be free, but bound. That which has relativity cannot be free. Thus we see the very question, why the Infinite became the finite, is an impossible one, for it is self-contradictory. Coming from subtleties to the logic of our common plane, to common sense, we can see this from another side, when we seek to know how the Absolute has become the relative. Supposing we knew the answer, would the Absolute remain the Absolute? It would have become relative. What is meant by knowledge in our common-sense idea? It is only something that has become limited by our mind, that we know, and when it is beyond our mind, it is not knowledge. Now if the Absolute becomes limited by the mind, It is no more Absolute; It has become finite. Everything limited by the mind becomes finite. Therefore to know the Absolute is again a contradiction in terms. That is why this question has never been answered, because if it were answered, there would no more be an Absolute. A God known is no more God; He has become finite like one of us. He cannot be known He is always the Unknowable One.

But what Advaita says is that God is more than knowable. This is a great fact to learn. You must not go home with the idea that God is unknowable in the sense in which agnostics put it. For instance, here is a chair, it is known to us. But what is beyond ether or whether people exist there or not is possibly unknowable. But God is neither known nor unknowable in this sense. He is something still higher than known; that is what is meant by God being unknown and unknowable. The expression is not used in the sense in which it may be said that some questions are unknown ant unknowable. God is more than known. This chair is known, but God is intensely more than that because in and through Him we have to know this chair itself. He is the Witness, the eternal Witness of all knowledge. Whatever we know we have to know in and through Him. He is the Essence of our own Self. He is the Essence of this ego, this I and we cannot know anything excepting in and through that I. Therefore you have to know everything in and through the Brahman. To know the chair you have to know it in and through God. Thus God is infinitely nearer to us than the chair, but yet He is infinitely higher. Neither known, nor unknown, but something infinitely higher than either. He is your Self. "Who would live a second, who would breathe a second in this universe, if that Blessed One were not filling it?" Because in and through Him we breathe, in and through Him we exist. Not the

He is standing somewhere and making my blood circulate. What is meant is that He is the Essence of all this, tie Soul of my soul. You cannot by any possibility say you know Him; it would be degrading Him. You cannot get out of yourself, so you cannot know Him. Knowledge is objectification. For instance, in memory you are objectifying many things, projecting them out of yourself. All memory, all the things which I have seen and which I know are in my mind. The pictures, the impressions of all these things, are in my mind, and when I would try to think of them, to know them, the first act of knowledge would be to project them outside. This cannot be done with God, because He is the Essence of our souls, we cannot project Him outside ourselves. Here is one of the profoundest passages in Vedanta: "He that is the Essence of your soul, He is the Truth, He is the Self, thou art That, O Shvetaketu." This is what is meant by "Thou art God." You cannot describe Him by any other language. All attempts of language, calling Him father, or brother, or our dearest friend, are attempts to objectify God, which cannot be done. He is the Eternal Subject of everything. I am the subject of this chair; I see the chair; so God is the Eternal Subject of my soul. How can you objectify Him, the Essence of your souls, the Reality of everything? Thus, I would repeat to you once more, God is neither knowable nor unknowable, but something infinitely higher than either. He is one with us, and that which is one with us is neither knowable nor unknowable, as our own self. You cannot know your own self; you cannot move it out and make it an object to look at, because you are that and cannot separate yourself from it. Neither is it unknowable, for what is better known than yourself? It is really the centre of our knowledge. In exactly the same sense, God is neither unknowable nor known, but infinitely higher than both; for He is our real Self.

First, we see then that the question, "What caused the Absolute?" is a contradiction in terms; and secondly, we find that the idea of God in the Advaita is this Oneness; and, therefore, we cannot objectify Him, for we are always living and moving in Him, whether we know it or not. Whatever we do is always through Him. Now the question is: What are time, space, and causation? Advaita means non-duality; there are no two, but one. Yet we see that here is a proposition that the Absolute is manifesting Itself as many, through the veil of time, space, and causation. Therefore it seems that here are two, the Absolute and Maya (the sum total of time, space, and causation). It seems apparently very convincing that there are two. To this the Advaitist replies that it cannot be called two. To have two, we must have two absolute independent existences which cannot be caused. In the first place time, space, and causation cannot be said to be independent existences. Time is entirely a dependent existence; it changes with every change of our mind. Sometimes in dream one imagines that one has lived several years, at other times several months were passed as one second. So, time is entirely dependent on our state of mind. Secondly, the idea of time vanishes altogether, sometimes. So with space. We cannot know what space is. Yet it is there, indefinable, and cannot exist separate from anything else. So with causation.

The one peculiar attribute we find in time, space, and causation is that they cannot exist separate from other things. Try to think of space without colour, or limits, or any connection with the things around — just abstract space. You cannot; you have to think of it as the space between two limits or between three objects. It has to be connected with some object to have any existence. So with time; you cannot have any idea of abstract time, but you have to take two events, one preceding and the other succeeding, and join the two events by the idea of succession. Time depends on two events, just as space has to be related to outside objects. And the idea of causation is inseparable from time and space. This is the peculiar thing about them that they have no independent existence. They have not even the existence which the chair or the wall has. They are as shadows around everything which you cannot catch. They have no real existence; yet they are not non-existent, seeing that through them all things are manifesting as this universe. Thus we see, first, that the combination of time, space, and causation has neither existence nor non-existence. Secondly, it sometimes vanishes. To give an illustration, there is a wave on the ocean. The wave is the same as the ocean certainly, and yet we know it is a wave, and as such different from the ocean. What makes this difference? The name and the form, that is, the idea in the mind and the form. Now, can we think of a wave-form as something separate from the ocean? Certainly not. It is always associated with the ocean idea. If the wave subsides, the form vanishes in a moment, and yet the form was not a delusion. So long as the wave existed the form was there, and you were bound to see the form. This is Maya.

The whole of this universe, therefore, is, as it were, a peculiar form; the Absolute is that ocean while you and I, and suns and stars, and everything else are various waves of that ocean. And what makes the waves different? Only the form, and that form is time, space, and causation, all entirely dependent on the wave. As soon as the wave goes, they vanish. As soon as the individual gives up this Maya, it vanishes for him and he becomes free. The whole struggle is to get rid of this clinging on to time, space, and causation, which are always obstacles in our way. What is the theory of evolution? What are the two factors? A tremendous potential power which is trying to express itself, and circumstances which are holding it down, the environments not allowing it to express itself. So, in order to fight with these environments, the power is taking new bodies again and again. An amoeba, in the struggle, gets another body and conquers some obstacles, then gets another body and so on, until it becomes man. Now, if you carry this idea to its logical conclusion, there must come a time when that power that was in the amoeba and which evolved as man will have conquered all the obstructions that nature can bring before it and will thus escape from all its environments. This idea expressed in metaphysics will take this form; there are two components in every action, the one the subject, the other the object and the one aim of life is to make the subject master of the object. For instance, I feel unhappy because a man scolds me. My struggle will be to make myself strong enough to conquer the environment, so that he may scold and I shall not feel. That is how we are all trying to conquer. What is meant by morality? Making the subject strong by attuning it to the Absolute, so that finite nature ceases to have control over us. It is a logical conclusion of our philosophy that there must come a time when we shall have conquered all the environments, because nature is finite.

Here is another thing to learn. How do you know that nature is finite? You can only know this through metaphysics. Nature is that Infinite under limitations. Therefore it is finite. So, there must come a time when we shall have conquered all environments. And how are we to conquer them? We cannot possibly conquer all the objective environments. We cannot. The little fish wants to fly from its enemies in the water. How does it do so? By evolving wings and becoming a bird. The fish did not change the water or the air; the change was in itself. Change is always subjective. All through evolution you find that the conquest of nature comes by change in the subject. Apply this to religion and morality, and you will find that the conquest of evil comes by the change in the subjective alone. That is how the Advaita system gets its whole force, on the subjective side of man. To talk of evil and misery is nonsense, because they do not exist outside. If I am immune against all anger, I never feel angry. If I am proof against all hatred, I never feel hatred.

This is, therefore, the process by which to achieve that conquest— through the subjective, by perfecting the subjective. I may make bold to say that the only religion which agrees with, and even goes a little further than modern researches, both on physical and moral lines is the Advaita, and that is why it appeals to modern scientists so much. They find that the old dualistic theories are not enough for them, do not satisfy their necessities. A man must have not only faith, but intellectual faith too. Now, in this later part of the nineteenth century, such an idea as that religion coming from any other source than one's own hereditary religion must be false shows that there is still weakness left, and such ideas must be given up. I do not mean that such is the case in this country alone, it is in every country, and nowhere more than in my own. This Advaita was never allowed to come to the people. At first some monks got hold of it and took it to the forests, and so it came to be called the "Forest Philosophy". By the mercy of the Lord, the Buddha came and preached it to the masses, and the whole nation became Buddhists. Long after that, when atheists and agnostics had destroyed the nation again, it was found out that Advaita was the only way to save India from materialism.

Thus has Advaita twice saved India from materialism. Before the Buddha came, materialism had spread to a fearful extent, and it was of a most hideous kind, not like that of the present day, but of a far worse nature. I am a material-ist in a certain sense, because I believe that there is only One. That is what the materialist wants you to believe; only he calls it matter and I call it God. The materialists admit that out of this matter all hope, and religion, and everything have come. I say, all these have come out of Brahman. But the materialism that prevailed before Buddha was that crude sort of materialism which taught, "Eat, drink, and be merry; there is no God, soul or heaven; religion is a concoction of wicked priests." It taught the morality that so long as you live, you must try to live happily; eat, though you have to borrow money for the food, and never mind about repaying it. That was the old materialism, and that kind of philoso-phy spread so much that even today it has got the name of "popular philosophy". Buddha brought the Vedanta to light, gave it to the people, and saved India. A thousand years after his death a similar state of things again prevailed. The mobs, the masses, and various races, had been converted to Buddhism; natu-rally the teachings of the Buddha became in time degenerated, because most of the people were very ignorant. Buddhism taught no God, no Ruler of the universe, so gradually the masses brought their gods, and devils, and hobgob-lins out again, and a tremendous hotchpotch was made of Buddhism in India. Again materialism came to the fore, taking the form of licence with the higher classes and superstition with the lower. Then Shankaracharya arose and once more revivified the Vedanta philosophy. He made it a rationalistic philosophy. In the Upanishads the arguments are often very obscure. By Buddha the moral side of the philosophy was laid stress upon, and by Shankaracharya, the intel-lectual side. He worked out, rationalised, and placed before men the wonderful coherent system of Advaita.

Materialism prevails in Europe today. You may pray for the salvation of the modern sceptics, but they do not yield, they want reason. The salvation of Europe depends on a rationalistic religion, and Advaita — the non-duality, the Oneness, the idea of the Impersonal God — is the only religion that can have any hold on any intellectual people. It comes whenever religion seems to disappear and irreligion seems to prevail, and that is why it has taken ground in Europe and America.

I would say one thing more in connection with this philosophy. In the old Upanishads we find sublime poetry; their authors were poets. Plato says, inspiration comes to people through poetry, and it seems as if these ancient Rishis, seers of Truth, were raised above humanity to show these truths through poetry. They never preached, nor philosophised, nor wrote. Music came out of their hearts. In Buddha we had the great, universal heart and infinite patience, making religion practical and bringing it to everyone's door. In Shankaracharya we saw tremendous intellectual power, throwing the scorching light of reason upon everything. We want today that bright sun of intellectuality joined with the heart of Buddha, the wonderful infinite heart of love and mercy. This union will give us the highest philosophy. Science and religion will meet and shake hands. Poetry and philosophy will become friends. This will be the religion of the future, and if we can work it out, we may be sure that it will be for all times and peoples. This is the one way that will prove acceptable to modern science, for it has almost come to it. When the scientific teacher asserts that all things are the manifestation of one force, does it not remind you of the God of whom you hear in the Upanishads : " As the one fire entering into the universe expresses itself in various forms, even so that One Soul is expressing Itself in every soul and yet is infinitely more besides ?" Do you not see whither science is tending ? The Hindu nation proceeded through the study of the mind, through metaphysics and logic. The European nations start from external nature, and now they too are coming to the same results. We find that searching through the mind we at last come to that Oneness, that Universal One, the Internal Soul of everything, the Essence and Reality of everything, the Ever-Free, the Ever-Blissful, the Ever-Existing. Through material science we come to the same Oneness. Science today is telling us that all things are but the manifestation of one energy which is the sum total of everything which exists, and the trend of humanity is towards freedom and not towards bondage. Why should men be moral ? Because through morality is the path towards freedom, and immorality leads to bondage.

Another peculiarity of the Advaita system is that from its very start it is non-destructive. This is another glory, the boldness to preach, "Do not disturb the faith of any, even of those who through ignorance have attached themselves to lower forms of worship." That is what it says, do not disturb, but help everyone to get higher and higher; include all humanity. This philosophy preaches a God who is a sum total. If you seek a universal religion which can apply to everyone, that religion must not be composed of only the parts, but it must always be their sum total and include all degrees of religious development.

This idea is not clearly found in any other religious system. They are all parts equally struggling to attain to the whole. The existence of the part is only for this. So, from the very first, Advaita had no antagonism with the various sects existing in India. There are dualists existing today, and their number is by far the largest in India, because dualism naturally appeals to less educated minds. It is a very convenient, natural, common-sense explanation of the universe. But with these dualists, Advaita has no quarrel. The one thinks that God is outside the universe, somewhere in heaven, and the other, that He is his own Soul, and that it will be a blasphemy to call Him anything more distant. Any idea of sepa-ration would be terrible. He is the nearest of the near. There is no word in any language to express this nearness except the word Oneness. With any other idea the Advaitist is not satisfied just as the dualist is shocked with the concept of the Advaita, and thinks it blasphemous. At the same time the Advaitist knows that these other ideas must be, and so has no quarrel with the dualist who is on the right road. From his standpoint, the dualist will have to see many. It is a consti-tutional necessity of his standpoint. Let him have it. The Advaitist knows that whatever may be his theories, he is going to the same goal as he himself. There he differs entirely from dualist who is forced by his point of view to believe that all differing views are wrong. The dualists all the world over naturally believe in a Personal God who is purely anthropomorphic, who like a great potentate in this world is pleased with some and displeased with others. He is arbitrarily pleased with some people or races and showers blessing upon them. Naturally the dualist comes to the conclusion that God has favourites, and he hopes to be one of them. You will find that in almost every religion is the idea: "We are the favourites of our God, and only by believing as we do, can you be taken into fa-vour with Him." Some dualists are so narrow as to insist that only the few that have been predestined to the favour of God can be saved; the rest may try ever so hard, but they cannot be accepted. I challenge you to show me one dualistic religion which has not more or less of this exclusiveness. And, therefore, in the nature of things, dualistic religions are bound to fight and quarrel with each other, and this they have ever been doing. Again, these dualists win the popular favour by appealing to the vanity of the uneducated. They like to feel that they enjoy exclusive privileges. The dualist thinks you cannot be moral until you have a God with a rod in His hand, ready to punish you. The unthinking masses are generally dualists, and they, poor fellows, have been persecuted for thousands of years in every country; and their idea of salvation is, therefore, freedom from the fear of punishment. I was asked by a clergyman in America, "What! you have no Devil in your religion? How can that be?" But we find that the best and the greatest men that have been born in the world have worked with that high impersonal idea. It is the Man who said, "I and my Father are One", whose power has descended unto millions. For thousands of years it has worked for good. And we know that the same Man, because he was a nondualist, was merciful to others. To the masses who could not conceive of anything higher than a Personal God, he said, "Pray to your Father in heaven." To others who could grasp a higher idea, he said, "I am the vine, ye are the branches," but to his disciples to whom he revealed himself more fully, he proclaimed the highest truth, "I and my Father are One."

It was the great Buddha, who never cared for the dualist gods, and who has been called an atheist and materialist, who yet was ready to give up his body for a poor goat. That Man set in motion the highest moral ideas any nation can have. Whenever there is a moral code, it is ray of light from that Man. We cannot force the great hearts of the world into narrow limits, and keep them there, especially at this time in the history of humanity when there is a degree of intellectual development such as was never dreamed of even a hundred years ago, when a wave of scientific knowledge has arisen which nobody, even fifty years ago, would have dreamed of. By trying to force people into narrow limits you degrade them into animals and unthinking masses. You kill their moral life. What is now wanted is a combination of the greatest heart with the highest intellectuality, of infinite love with infinite knowledge. The Vedantist gives no other attributes to God except these three — that He is Infinite Existence, Infinite Knowledge, and Infinite Bliss, and he regards these three as One. Existence without knowledge and love cannot be; knowledge without love and love without knowledge cannot be. What we want is the harmony of Existence, Knowledge, and Bliss Infinite. For that is our goal. We want harmony, not one-sided development. And it is possible to have the intellect of a Shankara with the heart of a Buddha. I hope we shall all struggle to attain to that blessed combination.

Chapter VII
God in Everything

Delivered in London, 27th October 1896

We have seen how the greater portion of our life must of necessity be filled with evils, however we may resist, and that this mass of evil is practically almost infinite for us. We have been struggling to remedy this since the beginning of time, yet everything remains very much the same. The more we discover remedies, the more we find ourselves beset by subtler evils. We have also seen that all religions propose a God, as the one way of escaping these difficulties. All religions tell us that if you take the world as it is, as most practical people would advise us to do in this age, then nothing would be left to us but evil. They further assert that there is something beyond this world. This life in the five senses, life in the material world, is not all; it is only a small portion, and merely superficial. Behind and beyond is the Infinite in which there is no more evil. Some people call It God, some Allah, some Jehovah, Jove, and so on. The Vedantin calls It Brahman.

The first impression we get of the advice given by religions is that we had better terminate our existence. To the question how to cure the evils of life, the answer apparently is, give up life. It reminds one of the old story. A mosquito settled on the head of a man, and a friend, wishing to kill the mosquito, gave it such a blow that he killed both man and mosquito. The remedy of evil seems to suggest a similar course of action. Life is full of ills, the world is full of evils; that is a fact no one who is old enough to know the world can deny.

But what is remedy proposed by all the religions? That this world is nothing. Beyond this world is something which is very real. Here comes the difficulty. The remedy seems to destroy everything. How can that be a remedy? Is there no way out then? The Vedanta says that what all the religions advance is perfectly true, but it should be properly understood. Often it is misunderstood, because the religions are not very clear in their meaning. What we really want is head and heart combined. The heart is great indeed; it is through the heart that come the great inspirations of life. I would a hundred times rather have a little heart and no brain, than be all brains and no heart. Life is possible, progress is possible for him who has heart, but he who has no heart and only brains dies of dryness.

At the same time we know that he who is carried along by his heart alone has to undergo many ills, for now and then he is liable to tumble into pitfalls. The combination of heart and head is what we want. I do not mean that a man should compromise his heart for his brain or vice versa, but let everyone have an infinite amount of heart and feeling, and at the same time an infinite amount of reason. Is there any limit to what we want in this world? Is not the world infinite? There is room for an infinite amount of feeling, and so also for an infinite amount of culture and reason. Let them come together without limit, let them be running together, as it were, in parallel lines each with the other.

Most of the religions understand the fact, but the error into which they all seem to fall is the same; they are carried away by the heart, the feelings. There is evil in the world, give up the world; that is the great teaching, and the only teaching, no doubt. Give up the world. There cannot be two opinions that to understand the truth everyone of us has to give up error. There cannot be two opinions that everyone of us in order to have good must give up evil; there cannot be two opinions that everyone of us to have life must give up what is death.

And yet, what remains to us, if this theory involves giving up the life of the senses, the life as we know it? And what else do we mean by life? If we give this up, what remains?

We shall understand this better, when, later on, we come to the more philosophical portions of the Vedanta. But for the present I beg to state that in Vedanta alone we find a rational solution of the problem. Here I can only lay before you what the Vedanta seeks to teach, and that is the deification of the world. The Vedanta does not in reality denounce the world. The ideal of renunciation nowhere attains such a height as in the teachings of the Vedanta. But, at the same time, dry suicidal advice is not intended; it really means deification of the world— giving up the world as we think of it, as we know it, as it appears to us— and to know what it really is. Deify it; it is God alone. We read at the commencement of one of the oldest of the Upanishads, "Whatever exists in this universe is to be covered with the Lord."

We have to cover everything with the Lord Himself, not by a false sort of optimism, not by blinding our eyes to the evil, but by really seeing God in everything. Thus we have to give up the world, and when the world is given up, what remains? God. What is meant? You can have your wife; it does not mean that you are to abandon her, but that you are to see God in the wife. Give up your children; what does that mean? To turn them out of doors, as some human brutes do in every country? Certainly not. That is diabolism; it is not religion.

But see God in your children. So, in everything. In life and in death, in happiness and in misery, the Lord is equally present. The whole world is full of the Lord. Open your eyes and see Him. This is what Vedanta teaches. Give up the world which you have conjectured, because your conjecture was based upon a very partial experience, upon very poor reasoning, and upon your own weakness. Give it up; the world we have been thinking of so long, the world to which we have been clinging so long, is a false world of our own creation. Give that up; open your eyes and see that as such it never existed; it was a dream, Maya. What existed was the Lord Himself. It is He who is in the child, in the wife, and in the husband; it is He who is in the good and in the bad; He is in the sin and in the sinner; He is in life and in death.

A tremendous assertion indeed! Yet that is the theme which the Vedanta wants to demonstrate, to teach, and to preach. This is just the opening theme.

Thus we avoid the dangers of life and its evils. Do not desire anything. What makes us miserable? The cause of all miseries from which we suffer is desire. You desire something, and the desire is not fulfilled; the result is distress. If there is no desire, there is no suffering. But here, too, there is the danger of my being misunderstood. So it is necessary to explain what I mean by giving up desire and becoming free from all misery. The walls have no desire and they never suffer. True, but they never evolve. This chair has no desires, it never suffers; but it is always a chair. There is a glory in happiness, there is a glory in suffering. If I may dare to say so, there is a utility in evil too. The great lesson in misery we all know. There are hundreds of things we have done in our lives which we wish we had never done, but which, at the same time, have been great teachers. As for me, I am glad I have done something good and many things bad; glad I have done something right, and glad I have committed many errors, because every one of them has been a great lesson. I, as I am now, am the resultant of all I have done, all I have thought. Every action and thought have had their effect, and these effects are the sum total of my progress.

We all understand that desires are wrong, but what is meant by giving up desires? How could life go on? It would be the same suicidal advice, killing the desire and the man too. The solution is this. Not that you should not have property, not that you should not have things which are necessary and things which are even luxuries. Have all that you want, and more, only know the truth and realise it. Wealth does not belong to anybody. Have no idea of proprietorship, possessorship. You are nobody, nor am I, nor anyone else. All belongs to the Lord, because the opening verse told us to put the Lord in everything. God is in the wealth that you enjoy. He is in the desire that rises in your mind. He is in the things you buy to satisfy your desire; He is in your beautiful attire, in your beautiful ornaments. This is the line of thought. All will be metamorphosed as soon as you begin to see things in that light. If you put God in your every movement, in your conversation, in your form, in everything, the whole scene changes, and the world, instead of appearing as one of woe and misery, will become a heaven.

"The kingdom of heaven is within you," says Jesus; so says the Vedanta, and every great teacher. "He that hath eyes to see, let him see, and he that hath ears to hear, let him hear." The Vedanta proves that the truth for which we have been searching all this time is present, and was all the time with us. In our ignorance, we thought we had lost it, and went about the world crying and weeping, struggling to find the truth, while all along it was dwelling in our own hearts. There alone can we find it.

If we understand the giving up of the world in its old, crude sense, then it would come to this : that we must not work, that we must be idle, sitting like lumps of earth, neither thinking nor doing anything, but must become fatalists, driven about by every circumstance, ordered about by the laws of nature, drifting from place to place. That would be the result. But that is not what is meant. We must work. Ordinary mankind, driven everywhere by false desire, what do they know of work? The man propelled by his own feelings and his own senses, what does he know about work? He works, who is not propelled by his own desires, by any selfishness whatsoever. He works, who has no ulterior motive in view. He works, who has nothing to gain from work.

Who enjoys the picture, the seller or the seer? The seller is busy with his accounts, computing what his gain will be, how much profit he will realise on the picture. His brain is full of that. He is looking at the hammer, and watching the bids. He is intent on hearing how fast the bids are rising. That man is enjoying the picture who has gone there without any intention of buying or selling. He looks at the picture and enjoys it. So this whole universe is a picture, and when these desires have vanished, men will enjoy the world, and then this buying and selling and these foolish ideas of possession will be ended. The money-lender gone, the buyer gone, the seller gone, this world remains the picture, a beautiful painting. I never read of any more beautiful conception of God than the following : "He is the Great Poet, the Ancient Poet; the whole universe is His poem, coming in verses and rhymes and rhythms, written in infinite bliss." When we have given up desires, then alone shall we be able to read and enjoy this universe of God. Then everything will become deified. Nooks and corners, by-ways and shady places, which we thought dark and unholy, will be all deified. They will all reveal their true nature, and we shall smile at ourselves and think that all this weeping and crying has been but child's play, and we were only standing by, watching.

So, do your work, says the Vedanta. It first advises us how to work — by giving up — giving up the apparent, illusive world. What is meant by that? Seeing God everywhere. Thus do you work. Desire to live a hundred years, have all earthly desires, if you wish, only deify them, convert them into heaven. Have the desire to live a long life of helpfulness, of blissfulness and activity on this earth. Thus working, you will find the way out. There is no other way. If a man plunges headlong into foolish luxuries of the world without knowing the truth, he has missed his footing, he cannot reach the goal. And if a man curses the world, goes into a forest, mortifies his flesh, and kills himself little by little by starvation, makes his heart a barren waste, kills out all feelings, and becomes harsh, stern, and dried-up, that man also has missed the way. These are the two extremes, the two mistakes at either end. Both have lost the way, both have missed the goal.

So work, says the Vedanta, putting God in everything, and knowing Him to be in everything. Work incessantly, holding life as something deified, as God Himself, and knowing that this is all we have to do, this is all we should ask for. God is in everything, where else shall we go to find Him? He is already in every work, in every thought, in every feeling. Thus knowing, we must work — this is the only way, there is no other. Thus the effects of work will not bind us. We have seen how false desires are the cause of all the misery and evil we suffer, but when they are thus deified, purified, through God, they bring no evil, they bring no misery. Those who have not learnt this secret will have to live in a demoniacal world until they discover it. Many do not know what an infinite mine of bliss is in them, around them, everywhere; they have not yet discovered it. What is a demoniacal world? The Vedanta says, ignorance.

We are dying of thirst sitting on the banks of the mightiest river. We are dying of hunger sitting near heaps of food. Here is the blissful universe, yet we do not find it. We are in it all the time, and we are always mistaking it. Religion proposes to find this out for us. The longing for this blissful universe is in all hearts. It has been the search of all nations, it is the one goal of religion, and this ideal is expressed in various languages in different religions. It is only the difference of language that makes all these apparent divergences. One expresses a thought in one way, another a little differently, yet perhaps each is meaning exactly what the other is expressing in a different language.

More questions arise in connection with this. It is very easy to talk. From my childhood I have heard of seeing God everywhere and in everything, and then I can really enjoy the world, but as soon as I mix with the world, and get a few blows from it, the idea vanishes. I am walking in the street thinking that God is in every man, and a strong man comes along and gives me a push and I fall flat on the footpath. Then I rise up quickly with clenched fist, the blood has rushed to my head, and the reflection goes. Immediately I have become mad. Everything is forgotten; instead of encountering God I see the devil. Ever since we were born we have been told to see God in all. Every religion teaches that — see God in everything and everywhere. Do you not remember in the New Testament how Christ says so? We have all been taught that; but it is when we come to the practical side, that the difficulty begins. You all remember how in Aesop's Fables a fine stag is looking at his form reflected in a lake and is saying to his young one, "How powerful I am, look at my splendid head, look at my limbs, how strong and muscular they are; and how swiftly I can run." In the meantime he hears the barking of dogs in the distance, and immediately takes to his heels, and after he has run several miles, he comes back panting. The young one says, "You just told me how strong you were, how was it that when the dog barked, you ran away?" "Yes, my son; but when the dogs bark all my confidence vanishes." Such is the case with us. We think highly of humanity, we feel ourselves strong and valiant, we make grand resolves; but when the "dogs" of trial and temptation bark, we are like the stag in the fable. Then, if such is the case, what is the use of teaching all these things? There is the greatest use. The use is this, that perseverance will finally conquer. Nothing can be done in a day.

"This Self is first to be heard, then to be thought upon, and then meditated upon." Everyone can see the sky, even the very worm crawling upon the earth sees the blue sky, but how very far away it is! So it is with our ideal. It is far away, no doubt, but at the same time, we know that we must have it. We must even have the highest ideal. Unfortunately in this life, the vast majority of persons are groping through this dark life without any ideal at all. If a man with an ideal makes a thousand mistakes, I am sure that the man without an ideal makes fifty thousand. Therefore, it is better to have an ideal. And this ideal we must hear about as much as we can, till it enters into our hearts, into our brains, into our very veins, until it tingles in every drop of our blood and permeates every pore in our body. We must meditate upon it. "Out of the fullness of the heart the mouth speaketh," and out of the fullness of the heart the hand works too.

It is thought which is the propelling force in us. Fill the mind with the highest thoughts, hear them day after day, think them month after month. Never mind failures; they are quite natural, they are the beauty of life, these failures. What would life be without them? It would not be worth having if it were not for struggles. Where would be the poetry of life? Never mind the struggles, the mistakes. I never heard a cow tell a lie, but it is only a cow— never a man. So never mind these failures, these little backslidings; hold the ideal a thousand times, and if you fail a thousand times, make the attempt once more. The ideal of man is to see God in everything. But if you cannot see Him in everything, see Him in one thing, in that thing which you like best, and then see Him in another. So on you can go. There is infinite life before the soul. Take your time and you will achieve your end.

"He, the One, who vibrates more quickly than mind, who attains to more speed than mind can ever do, whom even the gods reach not, nor thought grasps, He moving, everything moves. In Him all exists. He is moving. He is also immovable. He is near and He is far. He is inside everything. He is outside everything, interpenetrating everything. Whoever sees in every being that same Atman, and whoever sees everything in that Atman, he never goes far from that Atman. When all life and the whole universe are seen in this Atman, then alone man has attained the secret. There is no more delusion for him. Where is any more misery for him who sees this Oneness in the universe?"

This is another great theme of the Vedanta, this Oneness of life, this Oneness of everything. We shall see how it demonstrates that all our misery comes through ignorance, and this ignorance is the idea of manifoldness, this separation between man and man, between nation and nation, between earth and moon, between moon and sun. Out of this idea of separation between atom and atom comes all misery. But the Vedanta says this separation does not exist, it is not real. It is merely apparent, on the surface. In the heart of things there is Unity still. If you go below the surface, you find that Unity between man and man, between races and races, high and low, rich and poor, gods and men, and men and animals. If you go deep enough, all will be seen as only variations of the One, and he who has attained to this conception of Oneness has no more delusion. What can delude him? He knows the reality of everything, the secret of everything. Where is there any more misery for him? What does he desire? He has traced the reality of everything to the Lord, the Centre, the Unity of everything, and that is Eternal Existence, Eternal Knowledge, Eternal Bliss. Neither death nor disease, nor sorrow, nor misery, nor discontent is there. All is Perfect Union and Perfect Bliss. For whom should he mourn then? In the Reality, there is no death, there is no misery; in the Reality, there is no one to mourn for, no one to be sorry for. He has penetrated everything, the Pure One, the Formless, the Bodiless, the Stainless. He the Knower, He the Great Poet, the Self-Existent, He who is giving to everyone what he deserves. They grope in darkness who worship this ignorant world, the world that is produced out of ignorance, thinking of it as Existence, and those who live their whole lives in this world, and never find anything better or higher, are groping in still greater darkness. But he who knows the secret of nature, seeing That which is beyond nature through the help of nature, he crosses death, and through the help of That which is beyond nature, he enjoys Eternal Bliss. "Thou sun, who hast covered the Truth with thy golden disc, do thou remove the veil, so that I may see the Truth that is within thee. I have known the Truth that is within thee, I have known what is the real meaning of thy rays and thy glory and have seen That which shines in thee; the Truth in thee I see, and That which is within thee is within me, and I am That."

Chapter VIII
Realisation

Delivered in London, 29th October 1896

I will read to you from one of the Upanishads. It is called the Katha Upanishad. Some of you, perhaps, have read the translation by Sir Edwin Arnold, called the Secret of Death. In our last [i.e. a previous] lecture we saw how the inquiry which started with the origin of the world, and the creation of the universe, failed to obtain a satisfactory answer from without, and how it then turned inwards. This book psychologically takes up that suggestion, questioning into the internal nature of man. It was first asked who created the external world, and how it came into being. Now the question is: What is that in man; which makes him live and move, and what becomes of that when he dies? The first philosophers studied the material substance, and tried to reach the ultimate through that. At the best, they found a personal governor of the universe, a human being immensely magnified, but yet to all intents and purposes a human being. But that could not be the whole of truth; at best, it could be only partial truth. We see this universe as human beings, and our God is our human explanation of the universe.

Suppose a cow were philosophical and had religion it would have a cow universe, and a cow solution of the problem, and it would not be possible that it should see our God. Suppose cats became philosophers, they would see a cat universe and have a cat solution of the problem of the universe, and a cat ruling it. So we see from this that our explanation of the universe is not the whole of the solution. Neither does our conception cover the whole of the universe. It would be a great mistake to accept that tremendously selfish position which man is apt to take. Such a solution of the universal problem as we can get from the outside labours under this difficulty that in the first place the universe we see is our own particular universe, our own view of the Reality. That Reality we cannot see through the senses; we cannot comprehend It. We only know the universe from the point of view of beings with five senses. Suppose we obtain another sense, the whole universe must change for us. Suppose we had a magnetic sense, it is quite possible that we might then find millions and millions of forces in existence which we do not now know, and for which we have no present sense or feeling. Our senses are limited, very limited indeed; and within these limitations exists what we call our universe; and our God is the solution of that universe, but that cannot be the solution of the whole problem. But man cannot stop there. He is a thinking being and wants to find a solution which will comprehensively explain all the universes. He wants to see a world which is at once the world of men, and of gods, and of all possible beings, and to find a solution which will explain all phenomena.

We see, we must first find the universe which includes all universes; we must find something which, by itself, must be the material running through all these various planes of existence, whether we apprehend it through the senses or not. If we could possibly find something which we could know as the common property of the lower as well as of the higher worlds, then our problem would be solved. Even if by the sheer force of logic alone we could understand that there must be one basis of all existence, then our problem might approach to some sort of solution; but this solution certainly cannot be obtained only through the world we see and know, because it is only a partial view of the whole.

Our only hope then lies in penetrating deeper. The early thinkers discovered that the farther they were from the centre, the more marked were the variations and differentiations; and that the nearer they approached the centre, the nearer they were to unity. The nearer we are to the centre of a circle, the nearer we are to the common ground in which all the radii meet; and the farther we are from the centre, the more divergent is our radial line from the others. The external world is far away from the centre, and so there is no common ground in it where all the phenomena of existence can meet. At best, the external world is but one part of the whole of phenomena. There are other parts, the mental, the moral, and the intellectual— the various planes of existence— and to take up only one, and find a solution of the whole out of that one, is simply impossible. We first, therefore, want to find somewhere a centre from which, as it were, all the other planes of existence start, and standing there we should try to find a solution. That is the proposition. And where is that centre? It is within us. The ancient sages penetrated deeper and deeper until they found that in the innermost core of the human soul is the centre of the whole universe. All the planes gravitate towards that one point. That is the common ground, and standing there alone can we find a common solution. So the question who made this world is not very philosophical, nor does its solution amount to anything.

This the Katha Upanishad speaks in very figurative language. There was, in ancient times, a very rich man, who made a certain sacrifice which required that he should give away everything that he had. Now, this man was not sincere. He wanted to get the fame and glory of having made the sacrifice, but he was only giving things which were of no further use to him — old cows, barren, blind, and lame. He had a boy called Nachiketas. This boy saw that his father was not doing what was right, that he was breaking his vow; but he did not know what to say to him. In India, father and mother are living gods to their children. And so the boy approached the father with the greatest respect and humbly inquired of him, "Father, to whom are you going to give me? For your sacrifice requires that everything shall be given away." The father was very much vexed at this question and replied, "What do you mean, boy? A father giving away his own son?" The boy asked the question a second and a third time, and then the angry father answered, "Thee I give unto Death (Yama)." And the story goes on to say that the boy went to Yama, the god of death. Yama was the first man who died. He went to heaven and became the governor of all the Pitris; all the good people who die, go, and live with him for a long time. He is a very pure and holy person, chaste and good, as his name (Yama) implies.

So the boy went to Yama's world. But even gods are sometimes not at home, and three days this boy had to wait there. After the third day Yama returned. "O learned one," said Yama, "you have been waiting here for three days without food, and you are a guest worthy of respect. Salutation to thee, O Brahmin, and welfare to me! I am very sorry I was not at home. But for that I will make amends. Ask three boons, one for each day." And the boy asked, "My first boon is that my father's anger against me may pass away; that he will be kind to me and recognise me when you allow me to depart." Yama granted this fully. The next boon was that he wanted to know about a certain sacrifice which took people to heaven. Now we have seen that the oldest idea which we got in the Samhita portion of the Vedas was only about heaven where they had bright bodies and lived with the fathers. Gradually other ideas came, but they were not satisfying; there was still need for something higher. Living in heaven would not be very different from life in this world. At best, it would only be a very healthy rich man's life, with plenty of sense-enjoyments and a sound body which knows no disease. It would be this material world, only a little more refined; and we have seen the difficulty that the external material world can never solve the problem. So no heaven can solve the problem. If this world cannot solve the problem, no multiplication of this world can do so, because we must always remember that matter is only an infinitesimal part of the phenomena of nature. The vast part of phenomena which we actually see is not matter. For instance, in every moment of our life what a great part is played by thought and feeling, compared with the material phenomena outside! How vast is this internal world with its tremendous activity! The sense-phenomena are very small compared with it. The heaven solution commits this mistake; it insists that the whole of phenomena is only in touch, taste, sight, etc. So this idea of heaven did not give full satisfaction to all. Yet Nachiketas asks, as the second boon, about some sacrifice through which people might attain to this heaven. There was an idea in the Vedas that these sacrifices pleased the gods and took human beings to heaven.

In studying all religions you will notice the fact that whatever is old becomes holy. For instance, our forefathers in India used to write on birch bark, but in time they learnt how to make paper. Yet the birch bark is still looked upon as very holy. When the utensils in which they used to cook in ancient times were improved upon, the old ones became holy; and nowhere is this idea more kept up than in India. Old methods, which must be nine or ten thousand years old, as of rubbing two sticks together to make fire, are still followed. At the time of sacrifice no other method will do. So with the other branch of the Asiatic Aryans. Their modern descendants still like to obtain fire from lightning, showing that they used to get fire in this way. Even when they learnt other customs, they kept up the old ones, which then became holy. So with the Hebrews. They used to write on parchment. They now write on paper, but parchment is very holy. So with all nations. Every rite which you now consider holy was simply an old custom, and the Vedic sacrifice were of this nature. In course of time, as they found better methods of life, their ideas were much improved; still these old forms remained, and from time to time they were practiced and received a holy significance.

Then, a body of men made it their business to carry on these sacrifices. These were the priests, who speculated on the sacrifices, and the sacrifices became everything to them. The gods came to enjoy the fragrance of the sacrifices, and it was considered that everything in this world could be got by the power of sacrifices. If certain oblations were made, certain hymns chanted, certain peculiar forms of altars made, the gods would grant everything. So Nachiketas asks by what form of sacrifice can a man go to heaven. The second boon was also readily granted by Yama who promised that this sacrifice should henceforth be named after Nachiketas.

Then the third boon comes, and with that the Upanishad proper begins. The boy said, "There is this difficulty: when a man dies some say he is, others that he is not. Instructed by you I desire to understand this." But Yama was frightened. He had been very glad to grant the other two boons. Now he said, "The gods in ancient times were puzzled on this point. This subtle law is not easy to understand. Choose some other boon, O Nachiketas, do not press me on this point, release me."

The boy was determined, and said, "What you have said is true, O Death, that even the gods had doubts on this point, and it is no easy matter to understand. But I cannot obtain another exponent like you and there is no other boon equal to this."

Death said, "Ask for sons and grandsons who will live one hundred years, many cattle, elephants, gold, and horses. Ask for empire on this earth and live as many ears as you like. Or choose any other boon which you think equal to these— wealth and long life. Or be thou a king, O Nachiketas, on the wide earth. I will make thee the enjoyer of all desires. Ask for all those desires which are difficult to obtain in the world. These heavenly maidens with chariots and music, which are not to be obtained by man, are yours. Let them serve you. O Nachiketas, but do not question me as to what comes after death."

Nachiketas said, "These are merely things of a day, O Death, they wear away the energy of all the sense-organs. Even the longest life is very short. These horses and chariots, dances and songs, may remain with Thee. Man cannot be satisfied by wealth. Can we retain wealth when we behold Thee? We shall live only so long as Thou desires". Only the boon which I have asked is chosen by me."

Yama was pleased with this answer and said, "Perfection is one thing and enjoyment another; these two having different ends, engage men differently. He who chooses perfection becomes pure. He who chooses enjoyment misses his true end. Both perfection and enjoyment present themselves to man; the wise man having examined both distinguishes one from the other. He chooses perfection as being superior to enjoyment, but the foolish man chooses enjoyment for the pleasure of his body. O Nachiketas, having thought upon the things which are only apparently desirable, thou hast wisely abandoned them." Death then proceeded to teach Nachiketas.

We now get a very developed idea of renunciation and Vedic morality, that until one has conquered the desires for enjoyment the truth will not shine in him. So long as these vain desires of our senses are clamouring and as it were dragging us outwards every moment, making us slaves to everything outside— to a little colour, a little taste, a little touch— notwithstanding all our pretensions, how can the truth express itself in our hearts?

Yama said, "That which is beyond never rises before the mind of a thoughtless child deluded by the folly of riches. 'This world exists, the other does not,' thinking thus they come again and again under my power. To understand this truth is very difficult. Many, even hearing it continually, do not understand it, for the speaker must be wonderful, so must be the hearer. The teacher must be wonderful, so must be the taught. Neither is the mind to be disturbed By vain arguments, for it is no more a question of argument, it is a question of fact." We have always heard that every religion insists on our having faith. We have been taught to believe blindly. Well, this idea of blind faith is objectionable, no doubt, but analysing it, we find that behind it is a very great truth. What it really means is what we read now. The mind is not to be ruffled by vain arguments, because argument will not help us to know God. It is a question of fact, and not of argument. All argument and reasoning must be based upon certain perceptions. Without these, there cannot be any argument. Reasoning is the method of comparison between certain facts which we have already perceived. If these perceived facts are not there already, there cannot be any reasoning. If this is true of external phenomena, why should it not be so of the internal? The chemist takes certain chemicals and certain results are produced. This is a fact; you see it, sense it, and make that the basis on which to build all your chemical arguments. So with the physicists, so with all other sciences. All knowledge must stand on perception of certain facts, and upon that we have to build our reasoning. But, curiously enough the vast majority of mankind think, especially at the present time, that no such perception is possible in religion, that religion can only be apprehended by vain arguments. Therefore we are told not to disturb the mind by vain arguments. Religion is a question of fact, not of talk. We have to analyse our own souls and to find what is there. We have to understand it and to realise what is understood. That is religion. No amount of talk will make religion. So the question whether there is a God or not can never be proved by argument, for the arguments are as much on one side as on the other. But if there is a God, He is in our own hearts. Have you ever seen Him? The question as to whether this world exists or not has not yet been decided, and the debate between the idealists and the realists is endless. Yet we know that the world exists, that it goes on. We only change the meaning of words. So, with all the questions of life, we must come to facts. There are certain religious facts which, as in external science, have to be perceived, and upon them religion will be built. Of course, the extreme claim that you must believe every dogma of a religion is degrading to the human mind. The man who asks you to believe everything, degrades himself, and, if you believe, degrades you too. The sages of the world have only the right to tell us that they have analysed their minds and have found these facts, and if we do the same we shall also believe, and not before. That is all that there is in religion. But you must always remember this, that as a matter of fact 99.9 per cent of those who attack religion have never analysed their minds, have never struggled to get at the facts. So their arguments do not have any weight against religion, any more than the words of a blind man who cries out, "You are all fools who believe in the sun," would affect us.

This is one great idea to learn and to hold on to, this idea of realisation. This turmoil and fight and difference in religions will cease only when we understand that religion is not in books and temples. It is an actual perception. Only the man who has actually perceived God and soul has religion. There is no real difference between the highest ecclesiastical giant who can talk by the volume, and the lowest, most ignorant materialist. We are all atheists; let us confess it. Mere intellectual assent does not make us religious. Take a Christian, or a Mohammedan, or a follower of any other religion in the world. Any man who truly realised the truth of the Sermon on the Mount would be perfect, and become a god immediately. Yet it is said that there are many millions of Christians in the world. What is meant is that mankind may at some time try to realise that Sermon. Not one in twenty millions is a real Christian.

So, in India, there are said to be three hundred millions of Vedantins. But if there were one in a thousand who had actually realised religion, this world would soon be greatly changed. We are all atheists, and yet we try to fight the man who admits it. We are all in the dark; religion is to us a mere intellectual assent, a mere talk, a mere nothing. We often consider a man religious who can talk well. But this is not religion. "Wonderful methods of joining words, rhetorical powers, and explaining texts of the books in various ways — these are only for the enjoyment of the learned, and not religion." Religion comes when that actual realisation in our own souls begins. That will be the dawn of religion; and then alone we shall be moral. Now we are not much more moral than the animals. We are only held down by the whips of society. If society said today, "I will not punish you if you steal", we should just make a rush for each other's property. It is the policeman that makes us moral. It is social opinion that makes us moral, and really we are little better than animals. We understand how much this is so in the secret of our own hearts. So let us not be hypocrites. Let us confess that we are not religious and have no right to look down on others. We are all brothers and we shall be truly moral when we have realised religion.

If you have seen a certain country, and a man forces you to say that you have not seen it, still in your heart of hearts you know you have. So, when you see religion and God in a more intense sense than you see this external world, nothing will be able to shake your belief. Then you have real faith. That is what is meant by the words in your Gospel, "He who has faith even as a grain of mustard seed." Then you will know the Truth because you have become the Truth.

This is the watchword of the Vedanta— realise religion, no talking will do. But it is done with great difficulty. He has hidden Himself inside the atom, this Ancient One who resides in the inmost recess of every human heart. The sages realised Him through the power of introspection, and got beyond both joy and misery, beyond what we call virtue and vice, beyond good and bad deeds, beyond being and non-being; he who has seen Him has seen the Reality. But what then about heaven? It was the idea of happiness minus unhappiness. That is to say, what we want is the joys of this life minus its sorrows. That is a very good idea, no doubt; it comes naturally; but it is a mistake throughout, because there is no such thing as absolute good, nor any such thing as absolute evil.

You have all heard of that rich man in Rome who learnt one day that he had only about a million pounds of his property left; he said, "What shall I do tomorrow?" and forthwith committed suicide. A million pounds was poverty to him. What is joy, and what is sorrow? It is a vanishing quantity, continually vanishing. When I was a child I thought if I could be a cabman, it would be the very acme of happiness for me to drive about. I do not think so now. To what joy will you cling? This is the one point we must all try to understand, and it is one of the last superstitions to leave us. Everyone's idea of pleasure is different. I have seen a man who is not happy unless he swallows a lump of opium every day. He may dream of a heaven where the land is made of opium. That would be a very bad heaven for me. Again and again in Arabian poetry we read of heaven with beautiful gardens, through which rivers run. I lived much of my life in a country where there is too much water; many villages are flooded and thousands of lives are sacrificed every year. So, my heaven would not have gardens through which rivers flow; I would have a land where very little rain falls. Our pleasures are always changing. If a young man dreams of heaven, he dreams of a heaven where he will have a beautiful wife. When that same man becomes old he does not want a wife. It is our necessities which make our heaven, and the heaven changes with the change of our necessities. If we had a heaven like that desired by those to whom sense-enjoyment is the very end of existence, then we would not progress. That would be the most terrible curse we could pronounce on the soul. Is this all we can come to? A little weeping and dancing, and then to die like a dog! What a curse you pronounce on the head of humanity when you long for these things! That is what you do when you cry after the joys of this world, for you do not know what true joy is. What philosophy insists on is not to give up joys, but to know what joy really is. The Norwegian heaven is a tremendous fighting place where they all sit before Odin; they have a wild boar hunt, and then they go to war and slash each other to pieces. But in some way or other, after a few hours of such fighting, the wounds are all healed up, and they go into a hall where the boar has been roasted, and have a carousal. And then the wild boar takes form again, ready to be hunted the next day. That is much the same thing as our heaven, not a whit worse, only our ideas may be a little more refined. We want to hunt wild boars, and get to a place where all enjoyments will continue, just as the Norwegian imagines that the wild boar is hunted and eaten every day, and recovers the next day.

Now, philosophy insists that there is a joy which is absolute, which never changes. That joy cannot be the joys and pleasures we have in this life, and yet Vedanta shows that everything that is joyful in this life is but a particle of that real joy, because that is the only joy there is. Every moment really we are enjoying the absolute bliss, though covered up, misunderstood, and caricatured. Wherever there is any blessing, blissfulness, or joy, even the joy of the thief in stealing, it is that absolute bliss coming out, only it has become obscured, muddled up, as it were, with all sorts of extraneous conditions, and misunderstood. But to understand that, we have to go through the negation, and then the positive side will begin. We have to give up ignorance and all that is false, and then truth will begin to reveal itself to us. When we have grasped the truth, things which we gave up at first will take new shape and form, will appear to us in a new light, and become deified. They will have become sublimated, and then we shall understand them in their true light. But to understand them, we have first to get a glimpse of truth; we must give them up at first, and then we get them back again, deified. We have to give up all our miseries and sorrows, all our little joys.

"That which all the Vedas declare, which is proclaimed by all penances, seeking which men lead lives of continence, I will tell you in one word — it is 'Om'." You will find this word "Om" praised very much in the Vedas, and it is held to be very sacred.

Now Yama answers the question: "What becomes of a man when the body dies?" "This Wise One never dies, is never born, It arises from nothing, and nothing arises from It. Unborn, Eternal, Everlasting, this Ancient One can never be destroyed with the destruction of the body.

If the slayer thinks he can slay, or if the slain thinks he is slain, they both do not know the truth, for the Self neither slays nor is slain." A most tremendous position. I should like to draw your attention to the adjective in the first line, which is "wise". As we proceed we shall find that the ideal of the Vedanta is that all wisdom and all purity are in the soul already, dimly expressed or better expressed — that is all the difference. The difference between man and man, and all things in the whole creation, is not in kind but only in degree. The background, the reality, of everyone is that same Eternal, Ever Blessed, Ever Pure, and Ever Perfect One. It is the Atman, the Soul, in the saint and the sinner, in the happy and the miserable, in the beautiful and the ugly, in men and in animals; it is the same throughout. It is the shining One. The difference is caused by the power of expression. In some It is expressed more, in others less, but this difference of expression has no effect upon the Atman. If in their dress one man shows more of his body than another, it does not make any difference in their bodies; the difference is in their dress. We had better remember here that throughout the Vedanta philosophy, there is no such thing as good and bad, they are not two different things; the same thing is good or bad, and the difference is only in degree. The very thing I call pleasurable today, tomorrow under better circumstances I may call pain. The fire that warms us can also consume us; it is not the fault of the fire. Thus, the Soul being pure and perfect, the man who does evil is giving the lie unto himself, he does not know the nature of himself. Even in the murderer the pure Soul is there; It dies not. It was his mistake; he could not manifest It; he had covered It up. Nor in the man who thinks that he is killed is the Soul killed; It is eternal. It can never be killed, never destroyed. "Infinitely smaller than the smallest, infinitely larger than the largest, this Lord of all is present in the depths of every human heart. The sinless, bereft of all misery, see Him through the mercy of the Lord; the Bodiless, yet dwelling in the body; the Spaceless, yet seeming to occupy space; Infinite, Omnipresent: knowing such to be the Soul, the sages never are miserable."

"This Atman is not to be realised by the power of speech, nor by a vast intellect, nor by the study of their Vedas." This is a very bold utterance. As I told you before, the sages were very bold thinkers, and never stopped at anything. You will remember that in India these Vedas are regarded in a much higher light than even the Christians regard their Bible. Your idea of revelation is that a man was inspired by God; but in India the idea is that things exist because they are in the Vedas. In and through the Vedas the whole creation has come. All that is called knowledge is in the Vedas. Every word is sacred and eternal; eternal as the soul, without beginning and without end. The whole of the Creator's mind is in this book, as it were. That is the light in which the Vedas are held. Why is this thing moral? Because the Vedas say so. Why is that thing immoral? Because the Vedas say so. In spite of that, look at the boldness of these sages whom proclaimed that the truth is not to be found by much study of the Vedas. "With whom the Lord is pleased, to that man He expresses Himself." But then, the objection may be advanced that this is something like partisanship. But as Yama explains, "Those who are evil-doers, whose minds area not peaceful, can never see the Light. It is to those who are true in heart, pure in deed, whose senses are controlled, that this Self manifests Itself."

Here is a beautiful figure. Picture the Self to be then rider and this body the chariot, the intellect to be the charioteer, mind the reins, and the senses the horses. He whose horses are well broken, and whose reins are strong and kept well in the hands of the charioteer (the intellect) reaches the goal which is the state of Him, the Omnipresent. But the man whose horses (the senses) are not controlled, nor the reins (the mind) well managed, goes to destruction. This Atman in all beings does not manifest Himself to the eyes or the senses, but those whose minds have become purified and refined realise Him. Beyond all sound, all sight, beyond form, absolute, beyond all taste and touch, infinite, without beginning and without end, even beyond nature, the Unchangeable; he who realises Him, frees himself from the jaws of death. But it is very difficult. It is, as it were, walking on the edge of a razor; the way is long and perilous, but struggle on, do not despair. Awake, arise, and stop not till the goal is reached.

The one central idea throughout all the Upanishads is that of realisation. A great many questions will arise from time to time, and especially to the modern man. There will be the question of utility, there will be various other questions, but in all we shall find that we are prompted by our past associations. It is association of ideas that has such a tremendous power over our minds. To those who from childhood have always heard of a Personal God and the personality of the mind, these ideas will of course appear very stern and harsh, but if they listen to them and think over them, they will become part of their lives and will no longer frighten them. The great question that generally arises is the utility of philosophy. To that there can be only one answer: if on the utilitarian ground it is good for men to seek for pleasure, why should not those whose pleasure is in religious speculation seek for that? Because sense-enjoyments please many, they seek for them, but there may be others whom they do not please, who want higher enjoyment. The dog's pleasure is only in eating and drinking. The dog cannot understand the pleasure of the scientist who gives up everything, and, perhaps, dwells on the top of a mountain to observe the position of certain stars. The dogs may smile at him and think he is a madman. Perhaps this poor scientist never had money enough to marry even, and lives very simply. May be, the dog laughs at him. But the scientist says, "My dear dog, your pleasure is only in the senses which you enjoy, and you know nothing beyond; but for me this is the most enjoyable life, and if you have the right to seek your pleasure in your own way, so have I in mine." The mistake is that we want to tie the whole world down to our own plane of thought and to make our mind the measure of the whole universe. To you, the old sense-things are, perhaps, the greatest pleasure, but it is not necessary that my pleasure should be the same, and when you insist upon that, I differ from you. That is the difference between the worldly utilitarian and the religious man. The first man says, " See how happy I am. I get money, but do not bother my head about religion. It is too unsearchable, and I am happy without it." So far, so good; good for all utilitarians. But this world is terrible. If a man gets happiness in any way excepting by injuring his fellow-beings, godspeed him; but when this man comes to me and says, "You too must do these things, you will be a fool if you do not," I say, "You are wrong, because the very things, which are pleasurable to you, have not the slightest attraction for me. If I had to go after a few handfuls of gold, my life would not be worth living! I should die." That is the answer the religious man would make. The fact is that religion is possible only for those who have finished with these lower things. We must have our own experiences, must have our full run. It is only when we have finished this run that the other world opens.

The enjoyments of the senses sometimes assume another phase which is dangerous and tempting. You will always hear the idea — in very old times, in every religion — that a time will come when all the miseries of life wills cease, and only its joys and pleasures will remain, and this earth will become a heaven. That I do not believe. This earth will always remain this same world. It is a most terrible thing to say, yet I do not see my way out of it. The misery in the world is like chronic rheumatism in the body; drive it from one part and it goes to another, drive it from there and you will feel it somewhere else. Whatever you do, it is still there. In olden times people lived in forests, and ate each other; in modern times they do not eat each other's flesh, but they cheat one another. Whole countries and cities are ruined by cheating. That does not show much progress. I do not see that what you call progress in the world is other than the multiplication of desires. If one thing is obvious to me it is this that desires bring all misery; it

is the state of the beggar, who is always begging for something, and unable to
see anything without the wish to possess it, is always longing, longing for more.
If the power to satisfy our desires is increased in arithmetical progression, the
power of desire is increased in geometrical progression. The sum total of happiness and misery in this world is at least the same throughout. If a wave rises
in the ocean it makes a hollow somewhere. If happiness comes to one man, unhappiness comes to another or, perhaps, to some animal. Men are increasing in
numbers and some animals are decreasing; we are killing them off, and taking
their land; we are taking all means of sustenance from them. How can we say,
then, that happiness is increasing? The strong race eats up the weaker, but do you
think that the strong race will be very happy? No; they will begin to kill each
other. I do not see on practical grounds how this world can become a heaven.
Facts are against it. On theoretical grounds also, I see it cannot be.

Perfection is always infinite. We are this infinite already, and we are trying to
manifest that infinity. You and I, and all beings, are trying to manifest it. So
far it is all right. But from this fact some German philosophers have started a
peculiar theory— that this manifestation will become higher and higher until
we attain perfect manifestation, until we have become perfect beings. What is
meant by perfect manifestation? Perfection means infinity, and manifestation
means limit, and so it means that we shall become unlimited limiteds, which is
self-contradictory. Such a theory may please children; but it is poisoning their
minds with lies, and is very bad for religion. But we know that this world is a
degradation, that man is a degradation of God, and that Adam fell. There is no
religion today that does not teach that man is a degradation. We have been degraded down to the animal, and are now going up, to emerge out of this bondage. But we shall never be able entirely to manifest the Infinite here. We shall
struggle hard, but there will come a time when we shall find that it is impossible
to be perfect here, while we are bound by the senses. And then the march back
to our original state of Infinity will be sounded.

This is renunciation. We shall have to get out of the difficulty by reversing the
process by which we got in, and then morality and charity will begin. What is
the watchword of all ethical codes? "Not I, but thou", and this "I" is the outcome of the Infinite behind, trying to manifest Itself on the outside world. This
little "I" is the result, and it will have to go back and join the Infinite, its own
nature. Every time you say, "Not I, my brother, but thou", you are trying to go
back, and every time you say "I, and not thou", you take the false step of trying
to manifest the Infinite through the sense-world. That brings struggles and evils

into the world, but after a time renunciation must come, eternal renunciation. The little "I" is dead and gone. Why care so much for this little life? All these vain desires of living and enjoying this life, here or in some other place, bring death.

If we are developed from animals, the animals also may be degraded men. How do you know it is not so? You have seen that the proof of evolution is simply this: you find a series of bodies from the lowest to the highest rising in a gradually ascending scale. But from that how can you insist that it is always from the lower upwards, and never from the higher downwards? The argument applies both ways, and if anything is true, I believe it is that the series is repeating itself in going up and down. How can you have evolution without involution? Our struggle for the higher life shows that we have been degraded from a high state. It must be so, only it may vary as to details. I always cling to the idea set forth with one voice by Christ, Buddha, and the Vedanta, that we must all come to perfection in time, but only by giving up this imperfection. This world is nothing. It is at best only a hideous caricature, a shadow of the Reality. We must go to the Reality. Renunciation will take us to It. Renunciation is the very basis of our true life; every moment of goodness and real life that we enjoy is when we do not think of ourselves. This little separate self must die. Then we shall find that we are in the Real, and that Reality is God, and He is our own true nature, and He is always in us and with us. Let us live in Him and stand in Him. It is the only joyful state of existence. Life on the plane of the Spirit is the only life, and let us all try to attain to this realisation.

Chapter IX
Unity in Diversity

Delivered in London, 3rd November 1896

"The Self-existent One projected the senses outwards and, therefore, a man looks outward, not within himself. A certain wise one, desiring immortality, with inverted senses, perceived the Self within." As I have already said, the first inquiry that we find in the Vedas was concerning outward things, and then a new idea came that the reality of things is not to be found in the external world; not by looking outwards, but by turning the eyes, as it is literally expressed, inwards. And the word used for the Soul is very significant: it is He who has gone inward, the innermost reality of our being, the heart centre, the core, from which, as it were, everything comes out; the central sun of which the mind, the body, the sense-organs, and everything else we have are but rays going outwards. "Men of childish intellect, ignorant persons, run after desires which are external, and enter the trap of far-reaching death, but the wise, understanding immortality, never seek for the Eternal in this life of finite things." The same idea is here made clear that in this external world, which is full of finite things, it is impossible to see and find the Infinite. The Infinite must be sought in that alone which is infinite, and the only thing infinite about us is that which is within us, our own soul. Neither the body, nor the mind, not even our thoughts, nor the world we see around us, are infinite. The Seer, He to whom they all belong, the Soul of man, He who is awake in the internal man, alone is infinite, and to seek for the Infinite Cause of this whole universe we must go there. In the Infinite Soul alone we can find it. "What is here is there too, and what is there is here also. He who sees the manifold goes from death to death." We have seen how at first there was the desire to go to heaven. When these ancient Aryans became dissatisfied with the world around them, they naturally thought that after death they would go to some place where there would be all happiness without any misery; these places they multiplied and called Svargas— the word may be translated as heavens— where there would be joy for ever, the body would become perfect, and also the mind, and there they would live with their forefathers. But as soon as philosophy came, men found that this was impossible and absurd. The very idea of an infinite in place would be a contradiction in terms, as a place must begin and continue in time. Therefore they had to give up that idea. They found out that the gods who lived in these heavens had once been human beings on earth, who through their good works had become gods, and the godhoods, as they call them, were different states, different positions; none of the gods spoken of in the Vedas are permanent individuals.

For instance, Indra and Varuna are not the names of certain persons, but the names of positions as governors and so on. The Indra who had lived before is not the same person as the Indra of the present day; he has passed away, and another man from earth has filled his place. So with all the other gods These are certain positions, which are filled successively by human souls who have raised themselves to the condition of gods, and yet even they die. In the old Rig-Veda we find the word "immortality" used with regard to these gods, but later on it is dropped entirely, for they found that immortality which is beyond time and space cannot be spoken of with regard to any physical form, however subtle it may be. However fine it may be, it must have a beginning in time and space, for the necessary factors that enter into the make-up of form are in space. Try to think of a form without space: it is impossible. Space is one of the materials, as it were, which make up the form, and this is continually changing Space and time are in Maya, and this idea is expressed in the line — "What is hole, that is there too." If there are these gods, they must be bound by the same laws that apply here, and all laws involve destruction and renewal again and again. These laws are moulding matter into different forms, and crushing them out again. Everything born must die; and so, if there are heavens, the same laws must hold good there.

In this world we find that all happiness is followed by misery as its shadow. Life has its shadow, death. They must go together, because they are not contradictory, not two separate existences, but different manifestations of the same unit, life and death, sorrow and happiness, good and evil. The dualistic conception that good and evil are two separate entities, and that they are both going on eternally is absurd on the face of it. They are the diverse manifestations of one and the same fact, one time appearing as bad, and at another time as good. The difference does not exist in kind, but only in degree. They differ from each other in degree of intensity. We find as a fact that the same nerve systems carry good and bad sensations alike, and when the nerves are injured, neither sensation comes to us. If a certain nerve is paralysed, we do not get the pleasurable feelings that used to come along that wires and at the same time we do not get the painful feelings either. They are never two, but the same. Again, the same thing produces pleasure and pain at different times of life. The same phenomenon will produce pleasure in one, and pain in another. The eating of meat produces pleasure to a man, but pain to the animal which is eaten. There has never been anything which gives pleasure to all alike. Some are pleased, others displeased. So on it will go. Therefore, this duality of existence is denied. And what follows? I told you in my last lecture that we can never have ultimately everything good on this earth and nothing bad. It may have disappointed and frightened some of you, but I cannot help it, and I am open to conviction when I am shown to the contrary; but until that can be proved to me, and I can find that it is true, cannot say so.

The general argument against my statement, and apparently a very convincing one, is this that in the course of evolution, all that is evil in what we see around us is gradually being eliminated, and the result is that if this elimination continues for millions of years, a time will come when all the evil will have been extirpated, and the good alone will remain. This is apparently a very sound argument. Would to God it were true! But there is a fallacy in it, and it is this that it takes for granted that both good and evil are things that are eternally fixed. It takes for granted that there is a definite mass of evil, which may be represented by a hundred, and likewise of good, and that this mass of evil is being diminished every day, leaving only the good. But is it so? The history of the world shows that evil is a continuously increasing quantity, as well as good. Take the lowest man; he lives in the forest. His sense of enjoyment is very small, and so also is his power to suffer. His misery is entirely on the sense-plane. If he does not get plenty of food, he is miserable; but give him plenty of food and freedom to rove and to hunt, and he is perfectly happy. His happiness consists only in the senses, and so does his misery also. But if that man increases in knowledge, his happiness will increase, the intellect will open to him, and his sense-enjoyment will evolve into intellectual enjoyment. He will feel pleasure in reading a beautiful poem, and a mathematical problem will be of absorbing interest to him. But, with these, the inner nerves will become more and more susceptible to miseries of mental pain, of which the savage does not think. Take a very simple illustration. In Tibet there is no marriage, and there is no jealousy, yet we know that marriage is a much higher state. The Tibetans have not known the wonderful enjoyment, the blessing of chastity, the happiness of having a chaste, virtuous wife, or a chaste, virtuous husband. These people cannot feel that. And similarly they do not feel the intense jealousy of the chaste wife or husband, or the misery caused by unfaithfulness on either side, with all the heart-burnings and sorrows which believers in chastity experience. On one side, the latter gain happiness, but on the other, they suffer misery too.

Take your country which is the richest in the world, and which is more luxurious than any other, and see how intense is the misery, how many more lunatics you have, compared with other races, only because the desires are so keen. A man must keep up a high standard of living, and the amount of money he spends in one year would be a fortune to a man in India. You cannot preach to him of simple living because society demands so much of him. The wheel of society is rolling on; it stops not for the widow's tears or the orphans' wails. This is the state of things everywhere. Your sense of enjoyment is developed, your society is very much more beautiful than some others. You have so many more things to enjoy. But those who have fewer have much less misery. You can argue thus throughout, the higher the ideal you have in the brain, the greater is your enjoyment, and the more profound your misery. One is like the shadow of the other. That the evils are being eliminated may be true, but if so, the good also must be dying out. But are not evils multiplying fast, and good diminishing, if I may so put it? If good increases in arithmetical progression, evil increase in geometrical progression. And this is Maya. This is neither optimism nor pessimism. Vedanta does not take he position that this world is only a miserable one. That would be untrue. At the same time, it is a mistake to say that this world is full of happiness and blessings. So it is useless to tell children that this world is all good, all flowers, all milk and honey. That is what we have all dreamt. At the same time it is erroneous to think, because one man has suffered more than another, that all is evil. It is this duality, this play of good and evil that makes our world of experiences. At the same time the Vedanta says, "Do not think that good and evil are two, are two separate essences, for they are one and the same thing, appearing in different degrees and in different guises and producing differences of feeling in the same mind." So, the first thought of the Vedanta is the finding of unity in the external; the One Existence manifesting Itself, however different It may appear in manifestation. Think of the old crude theory of the Persians — two gods creating this world, the good god doing everything that is good, and the bad one, everything bad. On the very face of it, you see the absurdity, for if it be carried out, every law of nature must have two parts, one of which is manipulated by one god, and then he goes away and the other god manipulates the other part. There the difficulty comes that both are working in the same world, and these two gods keep themselves in harmony by injuring one portion and doing good to another. This is a crude case, of course, the crudest way of expressing the duality of existence. But, take the more advanced, the more abstract theory that this world is partly good and partly bad. This also is absurd, arguing from the same standpoint. It is the law of unity that gives us our food, and it is the same law that kills many through accidents or misadventure.

We find, then, that this world is neither optimistic nor pessimistic; it is a mixture of both, and as we go on we shall find that the whole blame is taken away from nature and put upon our own shoulders. At the same time the Vedanta shows the way out, but not by denial of evil, because it analyses boldly the fact as it is and does not seek to conceal anything. It is not hopeless; it is not agnostic. It finds out a remedy, but it wants to place that remedy on adamantine foundations: not by shutting the child's mouth and blinding its eyes with something which is untrue, and which the child will find out in a few days. I remember when I was young, a young man's father died and left him poorly off, with a large family to support, and he found that his father's friends were unwilling to help him. He had a conversation with a clergyman who offered this consolation, "Oh, it is all good, all is sent for our good." That is the old method of trying to put a piece of gold leaf on an old sore. It is a confession of weakness, of absurdity. The young man went away, and six months afterwards a son was born to the clergyman, and he gave a thanksgiving party to which the young man was invited. The clergyman prayed, "Thank God for His mercies." And the young man stood up and said, "Stop, this is all misery." The clergyman asked, "Why?" "Because when my father died you said it was good, though apparently evil; so now, this is apparently good, but really evil." Is this the way to cure the misery of the world? Be good and have mercy on those who suffer. Do not try to patch it up, nothing will cure this world; go beyond it.

This is a world of good and evil. Wherever there is good, evil follows, but beyond and behind all these manifestations, all these contradictions, the Vedanta finds out that Unity. It says, "Give up what is evil and give up what is good." What remains then? Behind good and evil stands something which is yours, the real you, beyond every evil, and beyond every good too, and it is that which is manifesting itself as good and bad. Know that first, and then and then alone you will be a true optimist, and not before; for then you will be able to control everything. Control these manifestations and you will be at liberty to manifest the real "you". First be master of yourself, stand up and be free, go beyond the pale of these laws, for these laws do not absolutely govern you, they are only part of your being. First find out that you are not the slave of nature, never were and never will be; that this nature, infinite as you may think it, is only finite, a drop in the ocean, and your Soul is the ocean; you are beyond the stars, and the sun.

They are like mere bubbles compared with your infinite being. Know that, and you will control both good and evil. Then alone the whole vision will change and you will stand up and say, "How beautiful is good and how wonderful is evil!"

That is what the Vedanta teaches. It does not propose any slipshod remedy by covering wounds with gold leaf and the more the wound festers, putting on more gold leaf. This life is a hard fact; work your way through it boldly, though it may be adamantine; no matter, the soul is stronger. It lays no responsibility on little gods; for you are the makers of your own fortunes. You make yourselves suffer, you make good and evil, and it is you who put your hands before your eyes and say it is dark. Take your hands away and see the light; you are effulgent, you are perfect already, from the very beginning. We now understand the verse: "He goes from death to death who sees the many here." See that One and be free.

How are we to see it? This mind, so deluded, so weak, so easily led, even this mind can be strong and may catch a glimpse of that knowledge, that Oneness, which saves us from dying again and again. As rain falling upon a mountain flows in various streams down the sides of the mountain, so all the energies which you see here are from that one Unit. It has become manifold falling upon Maya. Do not run after the manifold; go towards the One. "He is in all that moves; He is in all that is pure; He fills the universe; He is in the sacrifice; He is the guest in the house; He is in man, in water, in animals, in truth; He is the Great One. As fire coming into this world is manifesting itself in various forms, even so, that one Soul of the universe is manifesting Himself in all these various forms. As air coming into this universe manifests itself in various forms, even so, the One Soul of all souls, of all beings, is manifesting Himself in all forms." This is true for you when you have understood this Unity, and not before Then is all optimism, because He is seen everywhere. The question is that if all this be true that that Pure One — the Self, the Infinite — has entered all this, how is it that He suffers, how is it that He becomes miserable, impure? He does not, says the Upanishad. "As the sun is the cause of the eyesight of every being, yet is not made defective by the defect in any eye, even so the Self of all is not affected by the miseries of the body, or by any misery that is around you." I may have some disease and see everything yellow, but the sun is not affected by it. "He is the One, the Creator of all, the Ruler of all, the Internal Soul of every being — He who makes His Oneness manifest. Thus sages who realise Him as the Soul of their souls, unto them belongs eternal peace; unto none else, unto none else. He who in this world of evanescence finds Him who never changes, he who in this universe of death finds that One Life, he who in this manifold finds that

Oneness, and all those who realise Him as the Soul of their souls, to them belongs eternal peace; unto none else, unto none else. Where to find Him in the external world, where to find Him in the suns, and moons, and stars? There the sun cannot illumine, nor the moon, nor the stars, the flash of lightning cannot illumine the place; what to speak of this mortal fire? He shining, everything else shines. It is His light that they have borrowed, and He is shining through them." Here is another beautiful simile. Those of you who have been in India and have seen how the banyan tree comes from one root and spreads itself far around, will understand this. He is that banyan tree; He is the root of all and has branched out until He has become this universe, and however far He extends, every one of these trunks and branches is connected.

Various heavens are spoken of in the Brahmana portions of the Vedas, but the philosophical teaching of the Upanishads gives up the idea of going to heaven. Happiness is not in this heaven or in that heaven, it is in the soul; places do not signify anything. Here is another passage which shows the different states of realisation "In the heaven of the forefathers, as a man sees things in a dream, so the Real Truth is seen." As in dreams we see things hazy and not so distinct, so we see the Reality there. There is another heaven called the Gandharva, in which it is still less clear; as a man sees his own reflection in the water, so is the Reality seen there. The highest heaven, of which the Hindus conceive is called the Brahmaloka; and in this, the Truth is seen much more clearly, like light and shade, but not yet quite distinctly. But as a man sees his own face in a mirror, perfect, distinct, and clear, so is the Truth shining in the soul of man. The highest heaven, therefore, is in our own souls; the greatest temple of worship is the human soul, greater than all heavens, says the Vedanta; for in no heaven anywhere, can we understand the reality as distinctly and clearly as in this life, in our own soul. Changing places does not help one much. I thought while I was in India that the cave would give me clearer vision. I found it was not so. Then I thought the forest would do so, then, Varanasi. But the same difficulty existed everywhere, because we make our own worlds. If I am evil, the whole world is evil to me. That is what the Upanishad says. And the same thing applies to all worlds. If I die and go to heaven, I should find the same, for until I am pure it is no use going to caves, or forests, or to Varanasi, or to heaven, and if I have polished my mirror, it does not matter where I live, I get the Reality just as It is. So it is useless, running hither and thither, and spending energy in vain, which should be spent only in polishing the mirror. The same idea is expressed again: "None sees Him, none sees His form with the eyes. It is in the mind, in the pure mind, that He is seen, and this immortality is gained."

Those who were at the summer lectures on Raja Yoga will be interested to know that what was taught then was a different kind of Yoga. The Yoga which we are now considering consists chiefly in controlling the senses. When the senses are held as slaves by the human soul, when they can no longer disturb the mind, then the Yogi has reached the goal. "When all vain desires of the heart have been given up, then this very mortal becomes immortal, then he becomes one with God even here. When all the knots of the heart are cut asunder, then the mortal becomes immortal, and he enjoys Brahman here." Here, on this earth, nowhere else.

A few words ought to be said here. You will generally hear that this Vedanta, this philosophy and other Eastern systems, look only to something beyond, letting go the enjoyments and struggle of this life. This idea is entirely wrong. It is only ignorant people who do not know anything of Eastern thought, and never had brain enough to understand anything of its real teaching, that tell you so. On the contrary, we read in our scriptures that our philosophers do not want to go to other worlds, but depreciate them as places where people weep and laugh for a little while only and then die. As long as we are weak we shall have to go through these experiences; but whatever is true, is here, and that is the human soul. And this also is insisted upon, that by committing suicide, we cannot escape the inevitable; we cannot evade it. But the right path is hard to find. The Hindu is just as practical as the Western, only we differ in our views of life. The one says, build a good house, let us have good clothes and food, intellectual culture, and so on, for this is the whole of life; and in that he is immensely practical. But the Hindu says, true knowledge of the world means knowledge of the soul, metaphysics; and he wants to enjoy that life. In America there was a great agnostic, a very noble man, a very good man, and a very fine speaker. He lectured on religion, which he said was of no use; why bother our heads about other worlds? He employed this simile; we have an orange here, and we want to squeeze all the juice out of it. I met him once and said, "I agree with you entirely. I have some fruit, and I too want to squeeze out the juice. Our difference lies in the choice of the fruit. You want an orange, and I prefer a mango. You think it is enough to live here and eat and drink and have a little scientific knowledge; but you have no right to say that that will suit all tastes. Such a conception is nothing to me. If I had only to learn how an apple falls to the ground, or how an electric current shakes my nerves, I would commit suicide. I want to understand the heart of things, the very kernel itself. Your study is the manifestation of life, mine is the life itself. My philosophy says you must know that and drive out from your mind all thoughts of heaven and hell and all other superstitions, even though they exist in the same sense that this world exists. I must know the heart of this life, its very essence, what it is, not only how it works and what are its manifestations. I want the why of everything, I leave the how to children. As one of your countrymen said, 'While I am smoking a cigarette, if I were to write a book, it would be the science of the cigarette.' It is good and great to be scientific, God bless them in their search; but when a man says that is all, he is talking foolishly, not caring to know the *raison d'être* of life, never studying existence itself. I may argue that all your knowledge is nonsense, without a basis. You are studying the manifestations of life, and when I ask you what life is, you say you do not know. You are welcome to your study, but leave me to mine."

I am practical, very practical, in my own way. So your idea that only the West is practical is nonsense. You are practical in one way, and I in another. There are different types of men and minds. If in the East a man is told that he will find out the truth by standing on one leg all his life, he will pursue that method. If in the West men hear that there is a gold mine somewhere in an uncivilised country, thousands will face the dangers there, in the hope of getting the gold; and, perhaps, only one succeeds. The same men have heard that they have souls but are content to leave the care of them to the church. The first man will not go near the savages, he says it may be dangerous. But if we tell him that on the top of a high mountain lives a wonderful sage who can give him knowledge of the soul, he tries to climb up to him, even if he be killed in the attempt. Both types of men are practical, but the mistake lies in regarding this world as the whole of life. Yours is the vanishing point of enjoyment of the senses — there is nothing permanent in it, it only brings more and more misery — while mine brings eternal peace.

I do not say your view is wrong, you are welcome to it. Great good and blessing come out of it, but do not, therefore, condemn my view. Mine also is practical in its own way. Let us all work on our own plans. Would to God all of us were equally practical on both sides. I have seen some scientists who were equally practical, both as scientists and as spiritual men, and it is my great hope that in course of time the whole of humanity will be efficient in the same manner. When a kettle of water is coming to the boil, if you watch the phenomenon, you find first one bubble rising, and then another and so on, until at last they all join, and a tremendous commotion takes place. This world is very similar. Each individual is like a bubble, and the nations, resemble many bubbles. Gradually these nations are joining, and I am sure the day will come when separation will vanish and that Oneness to which we are all going will become manifest. A time must come when every man will be as intensely practical in the scientific world as in the spiritual, and then that Oneness, the harmony of Oneness, will pervade the whole world. The whole of mankind will become Jivanmuktas — free whilst living. We are all struggling towards that one end through our jealousies and hatreds, through our love and co-operation. A tremendous stream is flowing towards the ocean carrying us all along with it; and though like straws and scraps of paper we may at times float aimlessly about, in the long run we are sure to join the Ocean of Life and Bliss.

Chapter X
The Freedom of the Soul

Delivered in London, 5th November 1896

The Katha Upanishad, which we have been studying, was written much later than that to which we now turn — the Chhandogya. The language is more modern, and the thought more organised. In the older Upanishads the language is very archaic, like that of the hymn portion of the Vedas, and one has to wade sometimes through quite a mass of unnecessary things to get at the essential doctrines. The ritualistic literature about which I told you which forms the second division of the Vedas, has left a good deal of its mark upon this old Upanishad, so that more than half of it is still ritualistic. There is, however, one great gain in studying the very old Upanishads. You trace, as it were, the historical growth of spiritual ideas. In the more recent Upanishads, the spiritual ideas have been collected and brought into one place; as in the Bhagavad Gita, for instance, which we may, perhaps, look upon as the last of the Upanishads, you do not find any inkling of these ritualistic ideas. The Gita is like a bouquet composed of the beautiful flowers of spiritual truths collected from the Upanishads. But in the Gita you cannot study the rise of the spiritual ideas, you cannot trace them to their source. To do that, as has been pointed out by many, you must study the Vedas. The great idea of holiness that has been attached to these books has preserved them, more than any other book in the world, from mutilation. In them, thoughts at their highest and at their lowest have all been preserved, the essential and the non-essential, the most ennobling teachings and the simplest matters of detail stand side by side; for nobody has dared to touch them. Commentators came and tried to smooth them down and to bring out wonderful new ideas from the old things; they tried to find spiritual ideas in even the most ordinary statements, but the texts remained, and as such, they are the most wonderful historical study. We all know that in the scriptures of every religion changes were made to suit the growing spirituality of later times; one word was changed here and another put in there, and so on. This, probably, has not been done with the Vedic literature, or if ever done, it is almost imperceptible. So we have this great advantage, we are able to study thoughts in their original significance, to note how they developed, how from materialistic ideas finer and finer spiritual ideas are evolved, until they attained their greatest height in the Vedanta. Descriptions of some of the old manners and customs are also there, but they do not appear much in the Upanishads. The language used is peculiar, terse, mnemonic.

The writers of these books simply jotted down these lines as helps to remember certain facts which they supposed were already well known. In a narrative, perhaps, which they are telling, they take it for granted that it is well known to everyone they are addressing. Thus a great difficulty arises, we scarcely know the real meaning of any one of these stories, because the traditions have nearly died out, and the little that is left of them has been very much exaggerated. Many new interpretations have been put upon them, so that when you find them in the Puranas they have already become lyrical poems. Just as in the West, we find this prominent fact in the political development of Western races that they cannot bear absolute rule, that they are always trying to prevent any one man from ruling over them, and are gradually advancing to higher and higher democratic ideas, higher and higher ideas of physical liberty, so, in Indian metaphysics, exactly the same phenomenon appears in the development of spiritual life. The multiplicity of gods gave place to one God of the universe, and in the Upanishads there is a rebellion even against that one God. Not only was the idea of many governors of the universe ruling their destinies unbearable, but it was also intolerable that there should be one person ruling this universe. This is the first thing that strikes us. The idea grows and grows, until it attains its climax. In almost all of the Upanishads, we find the climax coming at the last, and that is the dethroning of this God of the universe. The personality of God vanishes, the impersonality comes. God is no more a person, no more a human being, however magnified and exaggerated, who rules this universe, but He has become an embodied principle in every being, immanent in the whole universe. It would be illogical to go from the Personal God to the Impersonal, and at the same time to leave man as a person. So the personal man is broken down, and man as principle is built up. The person is only a phenomenon, the principle is behind it. Thus from both sides, simultaneously, we find the breaking down of personalities and the approach towards principles, the Personal God approaching the Impersonal, the personal man approaching the Impersonal Man. Then come the succeeding stages of the gradual convergence of the two advancing lines of the Impersonal God and the Impersonal Man. And the Upanishads embody the stages through which these two lines at last become one, and the last word of each Upanishad is, "Thou art That". There is but One Eternally Blissful Principle, and that One is manifesting Itself as all this variety.

Then came the philosophers. The work of the Upanishads seems to have ended at that point; the next was taken up by the philosophers. The framework was given them by the Upanishads, and they had to fill in the details. So, many questions would naturally arise. Taking for granted that there is but One Impersonal Principle which is manifesting Itself in all these manifold forms, how is it that the One becomes many? It is another way of putting the same old question which in its crude form comes into the human heart as the inquiry into the cause of evil and so forth. Why does evil exist in the world, and what is its cause? But the same question has now become refined, abstracted. No more is it asked from the platform of the senses why we are unhappy, but from the platform of philosophy. How is it that this One Principle becomes manifold? And the answer, as we have seen, the best answer that India has produced is the theory of Maya which says that It really has not become manifold, that It really has not lost any of Its real nature. Manifoldness is only apparent. Man is only apparently a person, but in reality he is the Impersonal Being. God is a person only apparently, but really He is the Impersonal Being.

Even in this answer there have been succeeding stages, and philosophers have varied in their opinions. All Indian philosophers did not admit this theory of Maya. Possibly most of them did not. There are dualists, with a crude sort of dualism, who would not allow the question to be asked, but stifled it at its very birth. They said, "You have no right to ask such a question, you have no right to ask for an explanation; it is simply the will of God, and we have to submit to it quietly. There is no liberty for the human soul. Everything is predestined — what we shall do, have, enjoy, and suffer; and when suffering comes, it is our duty to endure it patiently; if we do not, we shall be punished all the more. How do we know that? Because the Vedas say so." And thus they have their texts and their meanings and they want to enforce them.

There are others who, though not admitting the Maya theory, stand midway. They say that the whole of this creation forms, as it were, the body of God. God is the Soul of all souls and of the whole of nature. In the case of individual souls, contraction comes from evil doing. When a man does anything evil, his soul begins to contract and his power is diminished and goes on decreasing, until he does good works, when it expands again. One idea seems to be common in all the Indian systems, and I think, in every system in the world, whether they know it or not, and that is what I should call the divinity of man. There is no one system in the world, no real religion, which does not hold the idea that the human soul, whatever it be, or whatever its relation to God, is essentially pure and perfect, whether expressed in the language of mythology, allegory, or philosophy. Its real nature is blessedness and power, not weakness and misery. Somehow or other this misery has come. The crude systems may call it a personified evil, a devil, or an Ahriman, to explain how this misery came. Other systems may try to make a God and a devil in one, who makes some people miserable and others happy, without any reason whatever. Others again, more thoughtful, bring in the theory of Maya and so forth. But one fact stands out clearly, and it is with this that we have to deal. After all, these philosophical ideas and systems are but gymnastics of the mind, intellectual exercises. The one great idea that to me seems to be clear, and comes out through masses of superstition in every country and in every religion, is the one luminous idea that man is divine, that divinity is our nature.

Whatever else comes is a mere superimposition, as the Vedanta calls it. Something has been superimposed, but that divine nature never dies. In the most degraded as well as in the most saintly it is ever present. It has to be called out, and it will work itself out. We have to ask and it will manifest itself. The people of old knew that fire lived in the flint and in dry wood, but friction was necessary to call it out. So this fire of freedom and purity is the nature of every soul, and not a quality, because qualities can be acquired and therefore can be lost. The soul is one with Freedom, and the soul is one with Existence, and the soul is one with Knowledge. The Sat-Chit-Ananda— Existence-Knowledge-Bliss Absolute— is the nature, the birthright of the Soul, and all the manifestations that we see are Its expressions, dimly or brightly manifesting Itself. Even death is but a manifestation of that Real Existence. Birth and death, life and decay, degeneration and regeneration— are all manifestations of that Oneness. So, knowledge, however it manifests itself, either as ignorance or as learning, is but the manifestation of that same Chit, the essence of knowledge; the difference is only in degree, and not in kind. The difference in knowledge between the lowest worm that crawls under our feet and the highest genius that the world may produce is only one of degree, and not of kind. The Vedantin thinker boldly says that the enjoyments in this life, even the most degraded joys, are but manifestations of that One Divine Bliss, the Essence of the Soul.

This idea seems to be the most prominent in Vedanta, and, as I have said, it appears to me that every religion holds it. I have yet to know the religion which does not. It is the one universal idea working through all religions. Take the Bible for instance. You find there the allegorical statement that the first man Adam was pure, and that his purity was obliterated by his evil deeds afterwards. It is clear from this allegory that they thought that the nature of the primitive man was perfect. The impurities that we see, the weaknesses that we feel, are but super-impositions on that nature, and the subsequent history of the Christian religion shows that they also believe in the possibility, nay, the certainty of regaining that old state. This is the whole history of the Bible, Old and New Testaments together. So with the Mohammedans: they also believed in Adam and the purity of Adam, and through Mohammed the way was opened to regain that lost state. So with the Buddhists: they believe in the state called Nirvana which is beyond this relative world. It is exactly the same as the Brahman of the Vedantins, and the whole system of the Buddhists is founded upon the idea of regaining that lost state of Nirvana. In every system we find this doctrine present, that you cannot get anything which is not yours already. You are indebted to nobody in this universe. You claim your own birthright, as it has been most poetically expressed by a great Vedantin philosopher, in the title of one of his books — "The attainment of our own empire". That empire is ours; we have lost it and we have to regain it. The Mayavadin, however, says that this losing of the empire was a hallucination; you never lost it. This is the only difference.

Although all the systems agree so far that we had the empire, and that we have lost it, they give us varied advice as to how to regain it. One says that you must perform certain ceremonies, pay certain sums of money to certain idols, eat certain sorts of food, live in a peculiar fashion to regain that empire. Another says that if you weep and prostrate yourselves and ask pardon of some Being beyond nature, you will regain that empire. Again, another says if you love such a Being with all your heart, you will regain that empire. All this varied advice is in the Upanishads. As I go on, you will find it so. But the last and the greatest counsel is that you need not weep at all. You need not go through all these ceremonies, and need not take any notice of how to regain your empire, because you never lost it. Why should you go to seek for what you never lost? You are pure already, you are free already. If you think you are free, free you are this moment, and if you think you are bound, bound you will be. This is a very bold statement, and as I told you at the beginning of this course, I shall have to speak to you very boldly. It may frighten you now, but when you think over it, and realise it in your own life, then you will come to know that what I say is true. For, supposing that freedom is not your nature, by no manner of means can you become free. Supposing you were free and in some way you lost that freedom, that shows that you were not free to begin with. Had you been free, what could have made you lose it? The independent can never be made dependent; if it is really dependent, its independence was a hallucination.

Of the two sides, then, which will you take? If you say that the soul was by its own nature pure and free, it naturally follows that there was nothing in this universe which could make it bound or limited. But if there was anything in nature which could bind the soul, it naturally follows that it was not free, and your statement that it was free is a delusion. So if it is possible for us to attain to freedom, the conclusion is inevitable that the soul is by its nature free. It cannot be otherwise. Freedom means independence of anything outside, and that means that nothing outside itself could work upon it as a cause. The soul is causeless, and from this follow all the great ideas that we have. You cannot establish the immortality of the soul, unless you grant that it is by its nature free, or in other words, that it cannot be acted upon by anything outside. For death is an effect produced by some outside cause. I drink poison and I die, thus showing that my body can be acted upon by something outside that is called poison. But if it be true that the soul is free, it naturally follows that nothing can affect it, and it can never die. Freedom, immortality, blessedness, all depend upon the soul being beyond the law of causation, beyond this Maya. Of these two which will you take? Either make the first a delusion, or make the second a delusion. Certainly I will make the second a delusion. It is more consonant with all my feelings and aspirations. I am perfectly aware that I am free by nature, and I will not admit that this bondage is true and my freedom a delusion.

This discussion goes on in all philosophies, in some form or other. Even in the most modern philosophies you find the same discussion arising. There are two parties. One says that there is no soul, that the idea of soul is a delusion produced by the repeated transit of particles or matter, bringing about the combination which you call the body or brain; that the impression of freedom is the result of the vibrations and motions and continuous transit of these particles. There were Buddhistic sects who held the same view and illustrated it by this example: If young take a torch and whirl it round rapidly, there will be a circle of light. That circle does not really exist, because the torch is changing place every moment. We are but bundles of little particles, which in their rapid whirling produce the delusion of a permanent soul. The other party states that in the rapid succession of thought, matter occurs as a delusion, and does not really exist. So we see one side claiming that spirit is a delusion and the other, that matter is a delusion. Which side will you take? Of course, we will take the spirit and deny matter. The arguments are similar for both, only on the spirit side the argument is little stronger. For nobody has ever seen what matter is. We can only feel ourselves. I never knew a man who could feel matter outside of himself. Nobody was ever able to jump outside of himself. Therefore the argument is a little stronger on the side of the spirit. Secondly, the spirit theory explains the universe, whiles materialism does not. Hence the materialistic explanation is illogical. If you boil down all the philosophies and analyse them, you will find that they are reduced to one; or the other of these two positions. So here, too, in a more intricate form, in a more philosophical form, we find the same question about natural purity and freedom. Ones side says that the first is a delusion, and the other, that the second is a delusion. And, of course, we side with the second, in believing that our bondage is a delusion.

The solution of the Vedanta is that we are not bound, we are free already. Not only so, but to say or to think that we are bound is dangerous — it is a mistake, it is self-hypnotism. As soon as you say, "I am bound," "I am weak," "I am helpless," woe unto you; you rivet one more chain upon yourself. Do not say it, do not think it. I have heard of a man who lived in a forest and used to repeat day and night, "Shivoham"— I am the Blessed One— and one day a tiger fell upon him and dragged him away to kill him; people on the other side of the river saw it, and heard the voice so long as voice remained in him, saying, "Shivoham"— even in the very jaws of the tiger. There have been many such men. There have been cases of men who, while being cut to pieces, have blessed their enemies. "I am He, I am He; and so art thou. I am pure and perfect and so are all my enemies. You are He, and so am I." That is - the position of strength. Nevertheless, there are great and wonderful things in the religions of the dualists; wonderful is the idea of the Personal God apart from nature, whom we worship and love. Sometimes this idea is very soothing. But, says the Vedanta, the soothing is something like the effect that comes from an opiate, not natural. It brings weakness in the long run, and what this world wants today, more than it ever did before, is strength. It is weakness, says the Vedanta, which is the cause of all misery in this world. Weakness is the one cause of suffering. We become miserable because we are weak. We lie, steal, kill, and commit other crimes, because we are weak. We suffer because we are weak. We die because we are weak. Where there is nothing to weaken us, there is no death nor sorrow. We are miserable through delusion. Give up the delusion, and the whole thing vanishes. It is plain and simple indeed. Through all these philosophical discussions and tremendous mental gymnastics we come to this one religious idea, the simplest in the whole world.

The monistic Vedanta is the simplest form in which you can put truth. To teach dualism was a tremendous mistake made in India and elsewhere, because people did not look at the ultimate principles, but only thought of the process which is very intricate indeed. To many, these tremendous philosophical and logical propositions were alarming. They thought these things could not be made universal, could not be followed in everyday practical life, and that under the guise of such a philosophy much laxity of living would arise.

But I do not believe at all that monistic ideas preached to the world would produce immorality and weakness. On the contrary, I have reason to believe that it is the only remedy there is. If this be the truth, why let people drink ditch water when the stream of life is flowing by? If this be the truth, that they are all pure, why not at this moment teach it to the whole world? Why not teach it with the voice of thunder to every man that is born, to saints and sinners, men, women, and children, to the man on the throne and to the man sweeping the streets?

It appears now a very big and a very great undertaking; to many it appears very startling, but that is because of superstition, nothing else. By eating all sorts of bad and indigestible food, or by starving ourselves, we are incompetent to eat a good meal. We have listened to words of weakness from our childhood. You hear people say that they do not believe in ghosts, but at the same time, there are very few who do not get a little creepy sensation in the dark. It is simply superstition. So with all religious superstitions There are people in this country who, if I told them there was no such being as the devil, will think all religion is gone. Many people have said to me, how can there be religion without a devil? How can there be religion without someone to direct us? How can we live without being ruled by somebody? We like to be so treated, because we have become used to it. We are not happy until we feel we have been reprimanded by somebody every day. The same superstition! But however terrible it may seem now, the time will come when we shall look back, each one of us, and smile at every one of those superstitions which covered the pure and eternal soul, and repeat with gladness, with truth, and with strength, I am free, and was free, and always will be free. This monistic idea will come out of Vedanta, and it is the one idea that deserves to live. The scriptures may perish tomorrow. Whether this idea first flashed into the brains of Hebrews or of people living in the Arctic regions, nobody cares. For this is the truth and truth is eternal; and truth itself teaches that it is not the special property of any individual or nation. Men, animals, and gods are all common recipients of this one truth. Let them all receive it. Why make life miserable? Why let people fall into all sorts of superstitions? I will give ten thousand lives, if twenty of them will give up their superstition. Not only in this country, but in the land of its very birth, if you tell people this truth, they are frightened. They say, "This idea is for Sannyasins who give up the world and live in forests; for them it is all right. But for us poor householders, we must all have some sort of fear, we must have ceremonies," and so on.

Dualistic ideas have ruled the world long enough, and this is the result. Why not make a new experiment? It may take ages for all minds to receive monism, but why not begin now? If we have told it to twenty persons in our lives, we have done a great work.

There is one idea which often militates against it. It is this. It is all very well to say, "I am the Pure, the Blessed," but I cannot show it always in my life. That is true; the ideal is always very hard. Every child that is born sees the sky overhead very far away, but is that any reason why we should not look towards the sky? Would it mend matters to go towards superstition? If we cannot get nectar, would it mend matters for us to drink poison? Would it be any help for us, because we cannot realise the truth immediately, to go into darkness and yield to weakness and superstition?

I have no objection to dualism in many of its forms. I like most of them, but I have objections to every form of teaching which inculcates weakness. This is the one question I put to every man, woman, or child, when they are in physical, mental, or spiritual training. Are you strong? Do you feel strength? — for I know it is truth alone that gives strength. I know that truth alone gives life, and nothing but going towards reality will make us strong, and none will reach truth until he is strong. Every system, therefore, which weakens the mind, makes one superstitious, makes one mope, makes one desire all sorts of wild impossibilities, mysteries, and superstitions, I do not like, because its effect is dangerous. Such systems never bring any good; such things create morbidity in the mind, make it weak, so weak that in course of time it will be almost impossible to receive truth or live up to it. Strength, therefore, is the one thing needful. Strength is the medicine for the world's disease. Strength is the medicine which the poor must have when tyrannised over by the rich. Strength is the medicine that the ignorant must have when oppressed by the learned; and it is the medicine that sinners must have when tyrannised over by other sinners; and nothing gives such strength as this idea of monism. Nothing makes us so moral as this idea of monism. Nothing makes us work so well at our best and highest as when all the responsibility is thrown upon ourselves. I challenge everyone of you. How will you behave if I put a little baby in your hands? Your whole life will be changed for the moment; whatever you may be, you must become selfless for the time being. You will give up all your criminal ideas as soon as responsibility is thrown upon you— your whole character will change. So if the whole responsibility is thrown upon our own shoulders, we shall be at our highest and best; when we have nobody to grope towards, no devil to lay our blame upon, no Personal God to carry our burdens, when we are alone responsible, then we shall rise to our highest and best.

I am responsible for my fate, I am the bringer of good unto myself, I am the bringer of evil. I am the Pure and Blessed One. We must reject all thoughts that assert the contrary. "I have neither death nor fear, I have neither caste nor creed, I have neither father nor mother nor brother, neither friend nor foe, for I am Existence, Knowledge, and Bliss Absolute; I am the Blissful One, I am the Blissful One. I am not bound either by virtue or vice, by happiness or misery. Pilgrimages and books and ceremonials can never bind me. I have neither hunger nor thirst; the body is not mine, nor am I subject to the superstitions and decay that come to the body, I am Existence, Knowledge, and Bliss Absolute; I am the Blissful One, I am the Blissful One."

This, says the Vedanta, is the only prayer that we should have. This is the only way to reach the goal, to tell ourselves, and to tell everybody else, that we are divine. And as we go on repeating this, strength comes. He who falters at first will get stronger and stronger, and the voice will increase in volume until the truth takes possession of our hearts, and courses through our veins, and permeates our bodies. Delusion will vanish as the light becomes more and more effulgent, load after load of ignorance will vanish, and then will come a time when all else has disappeared and the Sun alone shines.

Chapter XI
The Cosmos: the Macrocosm

Delivered in New York, 19th January 1896

The flowers that we see all around us are beautiful; beautiful is the rising of the morning sun; beautiful are the variegated hues of nature. The whole universe is beautiful, and man has been enjoying it since his appearance on earth. Sublime and awe-inspiring are the mountains; the gigantic rushing rivers rolling towards the sea, the trackless deserts, the infinite ocean, the starry heavens — all these are awe-inspiring, sublime, and beautiful indeed. The whole mass of existence which we call nature has been acting on the human mind since time immemorial. It has been acting on the thought of man, and as its reaction has come out the question: What are these, whence are they? As far back as the time of the oldest portion of that most ancient human composition, the Vedas, we find the same question asked: "Whence is this? When there was neither aught nor naught, and darkness was hidden in darkness, who projected this universe? How? Who knows the secret?" And the question has come down to us at the present time. Millions of attempts have been made to answer it, yet millions of times it will have to be answered again. It is not that each answer was a failure; every answer to this question contained a part of truth, and this truth gathers strength as time rolls on. I will try to present before you the outline of the answer that I have gathered from the ancient philosophers of India; in harmony with modern knowledge.

We find that in this oldest of questions a few points had been already solved. The first is that there was a time when there was "neither aught nor naught", when this world did not exist; our mother earth with the seas and oceans, the rivers, and mountains, cities and villages human races, animals, plants, birds, and planets and luminaries, all this infinite variety of creation, had no existence. Are we sure of that? We will try to trace how this conclusion is arrived at. What does man see around him? Take a little plant. He puts a seed in the ground, and later, he finds a plant peep out, lift itself slowly above the ground, and grow and grow, till it becomes a gigantic tree. Then it dies, leaving only the seed. It completes the circle — it comes out of the seed, becomes the tree, and ends in the seed again. Look at a bird, how from the egg it springs, lives its life, and then dies, leaving other eggs, seeds of future birds. So with the animals, so with man. Everything in nature begins, as it were, from certain seeds, certain rudiments, certain fine forms, and becomes grosser and grosser, and develops, going on that way for a certain time, and then again goes back to that fine form, and subsides. The raindrop in which the beautiful sunbeam is playing was drawn in the form of vapour from the ocean, went far away into the air, and reached a region where it changed into water, and dropped down in its present form — to be converted into vapour again. So with everything in nature by which we are surrounded. We know that the huge mountains are being worked upon by glaciers and rivers, which are slowly but surely pounding them and pulverising them into sand, that drifts away into the ocean where it settles down on its bed, layer after layer, becoming hard as rocks, once more to be heaped up into mountains of a future generation. Again they will be pounded and pulverised, and thus the course goes on. From sand rise these mountains; unto sand they go.

If it be true that nature is uniform throughout, if it be true, and so far no human experience has contradicted it, that the same method under which a small grain of sand is created, works in creating the gigantic suns and stars and all this universe, if it be true that the whole of this universe is built on exactly the same plan as the atom, if it be true that the same law prevails throughout the universe, then, as it has been said in the Vedas, "Knowing one lump of clay we know the nature of all the clay that is in the universe." Take up a little plant and study its life, and we know the universe as it is. If we know one grain of sand, we understand the secret of the whole universe. Applying this course of reasoning to phenomena, we find, in the first place, that everything is almost similar at the beginning and the end. The mountain comes from the sand, and goes back to the sand; the river comes out of vapour, and goes back to vapour; plant life comes from the seed, and goes back to the seed; human life comes out of human germs, and goes back to human germs. The universe with its stars and planets has come out of a nebulous state and must go back to it. What do we learn from this? That the manifested or the grosser state is the effect, and the finer state the cause. Thousands of years ago, it was demonstrated by Kapila, the great father of all philosophy, that destruction means going back to the cause. If this table here is destroyed, it will go back to its cause, to those fine forms and particles which, combined, made this form which we call a table. If a man dies, he will go back to the elements which gave him his body; if this earth dies, it will go back to the elements which gave it form. This is what is called destruction, going back to the cause. Therefore we learn that the effect is the same as the cause, not different. It is only in another form. This glass is an effect, and it had its cause, and this cause is present in this form. A certain amount of the material called glass plus the force in the hands of the manufacturer, are the causes, the instrumental and the material, which, combined, produced this form called a glass. The force which was in the hands of the manufacturer is present in the glass as the power of adhesion, without which the particles would fall apart; and the glass material is also present. The glass is only a manifestation of these fine causes in a new shape, and if it be broken to pieces, the force which was present in the form of adhesion will go back and join its own element, and the particles of glass will remain the same until they take new forms.

Thus we find that the effect is never different from the cause. It is only that this effect is a reproduction of the cause in a grosser form. Next, we learn that all these particular forms which we call plants, animals, or men are being repeated ad infinitum, rising and falling. The seed produces the tree. The tree produces the seed, which again comes up as another tree, and so on and on; there is no end to it. Water-drops roll down the mountains into the ocean, and rise again as vapour, go back to the mountains and again come down to the ocean. So, rising and falling, the cycle goes on. So with all lives, so with all existence that we can see, feel, hear, or imagine. Everything that is within the bounds of our knowledge is proceeding in the same way, like breathing in and breathing out in the human body. Everything in creation goes on in this form, one wave rising, another falling, rising again, falling again. Each wave has its hollow, each hollow has its wave. The same law must apply to the universe taken as a whole, because of its uniformity. This universe must be resolved into its causes; the sun, moon, stars, and earth, the body and mind, and everything in this universe must return to their finer causes, disappear, be destroyed as it were. But they will live in the causes as fine forms. Out of these fine forms they will emerge again as new earths, suns, moons, and stars.

There is one fact more to learn about this rising and falling. The seed comes out of the tree; it does not immediately become a tree, but has a period of inactivity, or rather, a period of very fine unmanifested action. The seed has to work for some time beneath the soil. It breaks into pieces, degenerates as it were, and regeneration comes out of that degeneration. In the beginning, the whole of this universe has to work likewise for a period in that minute form, unseen and unmanifested, which is called chaos, and out of that comes a new projection. The whole period of one manifestation of this universe — its going down into the finer form, remaining there for some time, and coming out again — is, in Sanskrit, called a Kalpa or a Cycle. Next comes a very important question especially for modern; times. We see that the finer forms develop slowly and slowly, and gradually becomes grosser and grosser. We have seen that the cause is the same as the effect, and the effect is only the cause in another form. Therefore this whole universe cannot be produced out of nothing. Nothing comes without a cause, and the cause is the effect in another form.

Out of what has this universe been produced then? From a preceding fine universe. Out of what has men been produced? The preceding fine form. Out of what has the tree been produced? Out of the seed; the whole of the tree was there in the seed. It comes out and becomes manifest. So, the whole of this universe has been created out of this very universe existing in a minute form. It has been made manifest now. It will go back to that minute form, and again will be made manifest. Now we find that the fine forms slowly come out and become grosser and grosser until they reach their limit, and when they reach their limit they go back further and further, becoming finer and finer again. This coming out of the fine and becoming gross, simply changing the arrangements of its parts, as it were, is what in modern times called evolution. This is very true, perfectly true; we see it in our lives. No rational man can possibly quarrel with these evolutionists. But we have to learn one thing more. We have to go one step further, and what is that? That every evolution is preceded by an involution. The seed is the father of the tree, but another tree was itself the father of the seed. The seed is the fine form out of which the big tree comes, and another big tree was the form which is involved in that seed. The whole of this universe was present in the cosmic fine universe. The little cell, which becomes afterwards the man, was simply the involved man and becomes evolved as a man. If this is clear, we have no quarrel with the evolutionists, for we see that if they admit this step, instead of their destroying religion, they will be the greatest supporters of it.

We see then, that nothing can be created out of nothing. Everything exists through eternity, and will exist through eternity. Only the movement is in succeeding waves and hollows, going back to fine forms, and coming out into gross manifestations. This involution and evolution is going on throughout the whole of nature. The whole series of evolution beginning with the lowest manifestation of life and reaching up to the highest, the most perfect man, must have been the involution of something else. The question is: The involution of what? What was involved? God. The evolutionist will tell you that your idea that it was God is wrong. Why? Because you see God is intelligent, but we find that intelligence develops much later on in the course of evolution. It is in man and the higher animals that we find intelligence, but millions of years have passed in this world before this intelligence came. This objection of the evolutionists does not hold water, as we shall see by applying our theory. The tree comes out of the seed, goes back to the seed; the beginning and the end are the same. The earth comes out of its cause and returns to it. We know that if we can find the beginning we can find the end. E converso, if we find the end we can find the beginning. If that is so, take this whole evolutionary series, from the protoplasm at one end to the perfect man at the other, and this whole series is one life. In the end we find the perfect man, so in the beginning it must have been the same. Therefore, the protoplasm was the involution of the highest intelligence. You may not see it but that involved intelligence is what is uncoiling itself until it becomes manifested in the most perfect man. That can be mathematically demonstrated. If the law of conservation of energy is true, you cannot get anything out of a machine unless you put it in there first. The amount of work that you get out of an engine is exactly the same as you have put into it in the form of water and coal, neither more nor less. The work I am doing now is just what I put into me, in the shape of air, food, and other things. It is only a question of change and manifestation. There cannot be added in the economy of this universe one particle of matter or one foot-pound of force, nor can one particle of matter or one foot-pound of force be taken out. If that be the case, what is this intelligence? If it was not present in the protoplasm, it must have come all of a sudden, something coming out of nothing, which is absurd. It, therefore, follows absolutely that the perfect man, the free man, the God-man, who has gone beyond the laws of nature, and transcended everything, who has no more to go through this process of evolution, through birth and death, that man called the "Christ-man" by the Christians, and the "Buddha-man" by the Buddhists, and the "Free" by the Yogis — that perfect man who is at one end of the chain of evolution was involved in the cell of the protoplasm, which is at the other end of the same chain.

Applying the same reason to the whole of the universe, we see that intelligence must be the Lord of creation, the cause. What is the most evolved notion that man has of this universe? It is intelligence, the adjustment of part to part, the display of intelligence, of which the ancient design theory was an attempt at expression. The beginning was, therefore, intelligence. At the beginning that intelligence becomes involved, and in the end that intelligence gets evolved. The sum total of the intelligence displayed in the universe must, therefore, be the involved universal intelligence unfolding itself. This universal intelligence is what we call God. Call it by any other name, it is absolutely certain that in the beginning there is that Infinite cosmic intelligence. This cosmic intelligence gets involved, and it manifests, evolves itself, until it becomes the perfect man, the "Christ-man," the "Buddha-man." Then it goes back to its own source. That is why all the scriptures say, "In Him we live and move and have our being." That is why all the scriptures preach that we come from God and go back to God. Do not be frightened by theological terms; if terms frighten you, you are not fit to be philosophers. This cosmic intelligence is what the theologians call God.

I have been asked many times, "Why do you use that old word, God?" Because it is the best word for our purpose; you cannot find a better word than that, because all the hopes, aspirations, and happiness of humanity have been centred in that word. It is impossible now to change the word. Words like these were first coined by great saints who realised their import and understood their meaning. But as they become current in society, ignorant people take these words, and the result is that they lose their spirit and glory. The word God has been used from time immemorial, and the idea of this cosmic intelligence, and all that is great and holy, is associated with it. Do you mean to say that because some fool says it is not all right, we should throw it away? Another man may come and say, "Take my word," and another again, "Take my word." So there will be no end to foolish words. Use the old word, only use it in the true spirit, cleanse it of superstition, and realise fully what this great ancient word means. If you understand the power of the laws of association, you will know that these words are associated with innumerable majestic and powerful ideas; they have been used and worshipped by millions of human souls and associated by them with all that is highest and best, all that is rational, all that is lovable, and all that is great and grand in human nature. And they come as suggestions of these associations, and cannot be given up. If I tried to express all these by only telling you that God created the universe, it would have conveyed no meaning to you. Yet, after all this struggle, we have come back to Him, the Ancient and Supreme One.

We now see that all the various forms of cosmic energy, such as matter, thought, force, intelligence and so forth, are simply the manifestations of that cosmic intelligence, or, as we shall call it henceforth, the Supreme Lord. Everything that you see, feel, or hear, the whole universe, is His creation, or to be a little more accurate, is His projection; or to be still more accurate, is the Lord Himself. It is He who is shining as the sun and the stars, He is the mother earth. He is the ocean Himself. He comes as gentle showers, He is the gentle air that we breathe in, and He it is who is working as force in the body. He is the speech that is uttered, He is the man who is talking. He is the audience that is here. He is the platform on which I stand, He is the light that enables me to see your faces. It is all He. He Himself is both the material and the efficient cause of this universe, and He it is that gets involved in the minute cell, and evolves at the other end and becomes God again. He it is that comes down and becomes the lowest atom, and slowly unfolding His nature, rejoins Himself. This is the mystery of the universe. "Thou art the man, Thou art the woman, Thou art the strong man walking in the pride of youth, Thou art the old man tottering on crutches, Thou art in everything. Thou art everything, O Lord." This is the only solution of the Cosmos that satisfies the human intellect. In one word, we are born of Him, we live in Him, and unto Him we return.

Chapter XII
The Cosmos: the Microcosm

Delivered in New York, 26th January 1896

The human mind naturally wants to get outside, to peer out of the body, as it were, through the channels of the organs. The eye must see, the ear must hear, the senses must sense the external world — and naturally the beauties and sublimities of nature captivate the attention of man first. The first questions that arose in the human soul were about the external world. The solution of the mystery was asked of the sky, of the stars, of the heavenly bodies, of the earth, of the rivers, of the mountains, of the ocean; and in all ancient religions we find traces of how the groping human mind at first caught at everything external. There was a river-god, a sky-god, a cloud-god, a rain-god; everything external, all of which we now call the powers of nature, became metamorphosed, transfigured, into wills, into gods, into heavenly messengers. As the question went deeper and deeper, these external manifestations failed to satisfy the human mind, and finally the energy turned inward, and the question was asked of man's own soul. From the macrocosm the question was reflected back to the microcosm; from the external world the question was reflected to the internal. From analysing the external nature, man is led to analyse the internal; this questioning of the internal man comes with a higher state of civilisation, with a deeper insight into nature, with a higher state of growth.

The subject of discussion this afternoon is this internal man. No question is so near and dear to man's heart as that of the internal man. How many millions of times, in how many countries has this question been asked! Sages and kings, rich and poor, saints and sinners, every man, every woman, all have from time to time asked this question. Is there nothing permanent in this evanescent human life? Is there nothing, they have asked, which does not die away when this body dies? Is there not something living when this frame crumbles into dust? Is there not something which survives the fire which burns the body into ashes? And if so, what is its destiny? Where does it go? Whence did it come? These questions have been asked again and again, and so long as this creation lasts, so long as there are human brains to think, this question will have to be asked.

Yet, it is not that the answer did not come; each time the answer came, and as time rolls on, the answer will gain strength more and more. The question was answered once for all thousands of years ago, and through all subsequent time it is being restated, reillustrated, made clearer to our intellect. What we have to do, therefore, is to make a restatement of the answer. We do not pretend to throw any new light on those all-absorbing problems, but only to put before you the ancient truth in the language of modern times, to speak the thoughts of the ancients in the language of the moderns, to speak the thoughts of the philosophers in the language of the people, to speak the thoughts of the angels in the language of man, to speak the thoughts of God in the language of poor humanity, so that man will understand them; for the same divine essence from which the ideas emanated is ever present in man, and, therefore, he can always understand them.

I am looking at you. How many things are necessary for this vision? First, the eyes. For if I am perfect in every other way, and yet have no eyes, I shall not be able to see you. Secondly, the real organ of vision. For the eyes are not the organs. They are but the instruments of vision, and behind them is the real organ, the nerve centre in the brain. If that centre be injured, a man may have the clearest pair of eyes, yet he will not be able to see anything. So, it is necessary that this centre, or the real organ, be there. Thus, with all our senses. The external ear is but the instrument for carrying the vibration of sound inward to the centre. Yet, that is not sufficient. Suppose in your library you are intently reading a book, and the clock strikes, yet you do not hear it. The sound is there, the pulsations in the air are there, the ear and the centre are also there, and these vibrations have been carried through the ear to the centre, and yet you do not hear it. What is wanting? The mind is not there. Thus we see that the third thing necessary is, that the mind must be there. First the external instruments, then the organ to which this external instrument will carry the sensation, and lastly the organ it- self must be joined to the mind. When the mind is not joined to the organ, the organ and the ear may take the impression, and yet we shall not be conscious of it. The mind, too, is only the carrier; it has to carry the sensation still forward, and present it to the intellect. The intellect is the determining faculty and decides upon what is brought to it. Still this is not sufficient. The intellect must carry it forward and present the whole thing before the ruler in the body, the human soul, the king on the throne. Before him this is presented, and then from him comes the order, what to do or what not to do; and the order goes down in the same sequence to the intellect, to the mind, to the organs, and the organs convey it to the instruments, and the perception is complete.

The instruments are in the external body, the gross body of man; but the mind and the intellect are not. They are in what is called in Hindu philosophy the finer body; and what in Christian theology you read of as the spiritual body of man; finer, very much finer than the body, and yet not the soul. This soul is beyond them all. The external body perishes in a few years; any simple cause may disturb and destroy it. The finer body is not so easily perishable; yet it sometimes degenerates, and at other times becomes strong. We see how, in the old man, the mind loses its strength, how, when the body is vigorous, the mind becomes vigorous, how various medicines and drugs affect it, how everything external acts on it, and how it reacts on the external world. Just as the body has its progress and decadence, so also has the mind, and, therefore, the mind is not the soul, because the soul can neither decay nor degenerate. How can we know that? How can we know that there is something behind this mind? Because knowledge which is self-illuminating and the basis of intelligence cannot belong to dull, dead matter. Never was seen any gross matter which had intelligence as its own essence. No dull or dead matter can illumine itself. It is intelligence that illumines all matter. This hall is here only through intelligence because, as a hall, its existence would be unknown unless some intelligence built it. This body is not self-luminous; if it were, it would be so in a dead man also. Neither can the mind nor the spiritual body be self-luminous. They are not of the essence of intelligence. That which is self-luminous cannot decay. The luminosity of that which shines through a borrowed light comes and goes; but that which is light itself, what can make that come and go, flourish and decay? We see that the moon waxes and wanes, because it shines through the borrowed light of the sun. If a lump of iron is put into the fire and made red-hot, it glows and shines, but its light will vanish, because it is borrowed. So, decadence is possible only of that light which is borrowed and is not of its own essence.

Now we see that the body, the external shape, has no light as its own essence, is not self-luminous, and cannot know itself; neither can the mind. Why not? Because the mind waxes and wanes, because it is vigorous at one time and weak at another, because it can be acted upon by anything and everything. Therefore the light which shines through the mind is not its own. Whose is it then? It must belong to that which has it as its own essence, and as such, can never decay or die, never become stronger or weaker; it is self-luminous, it is luminosity itself. It cannot be that the soul knows, it is knowledge. It cannot be that the soul has existence, but it is existence. It cannot be that the soul is happy, it is happiness itself. That which is happy has borrowed its happiness; that which has knowledge has received its knowledge; and that which has relative existence has only a reflected existence. Wherever there are qualities these qualities have been reflected upon the substance, but the soul has not knowledge, existence, and blessedness as its qualities, they are the essence of the soul.

Again, it may be asked, why shall we take this for granted? Why shall we admit that the soul has knowledge, blessedness, existence, as its essence, and has not borrowed them? It may be argued, why not say that the soul's luminosity, the soul's blessedness, the soul's knowledge, are borrowed in the same way as the luminosity of the body is borrowed from the mind? The fallacy of arguing in this way will be that there will be no limit. From whom were these borrowed? If we say from some other source, the same question will be asked again. So, at last we shall have to come to one who is self-luminous; to make matters short then, the logical way is to stop where we get self-luminosity, and proceed no further.

We see, then, that this human being is composed first of this external covering, the body; secondly, the finer body, consisting of mind, intellect, and egoism. Behind them is the real Self of man. We have seen that all the qualities and powers of the gross body are borrowed from the mind, and the mind, the finer body, borrows its powers and luminosity from the soul, standing behind.

A great many questions now arise about the nature of this soul. If the existence of the soul is drawn from the argument that it is self-luminous, that knowledge, existence, blessedness are its essence, it naturally follows that this soul cannot have been created. A self-luminous existence, independent of any other existence, could never have been the outcome of anything. It always existed; there was never a time when it did not exist, because if the soul did not exist, where was time? Time is in the soul; it is when the soul reflects its powers on the mind and the mind thinks, that time comes. When there was no soul, certainly there was no thought, and without thought, there was no time. How can the soul, therefore, be said to be existing in time, when time itself exists in the soul? It has neither birth nor death, but it is passing through all these various stages. It is manifesting slowly and gradually from lower to higher, and so on. It is expressing its own grandeur, working through the mind on the body; and through the body it is grasping the external world and understanding it. It takes up a body and uses it; and when that body has failed and is used up, it takes another body; and so on it goes.

Here comes a very interesting question, that question which is generally known as the reincarnation of the soul. Sometimes people get frightened at the idea, and superstition is so strong that thinking men even believe that they are the outcome of nothing, and then, with the grandest logic, try to deduce the theory that although they have come out of zero, they will be eternal ever afterwards. Those that come out of zero will certainly have to go back to zero. Neither you, nor I nor anyone present, has come out of zero, nor will go back to zero. We have been existing eternally, and will exist, and there is no power under the sun or above the sun which can undo your or my existence or send us back to zero. Now this idea of reincarnation is not only not a frightening idea, but is most essential for the moral well-being of the human race. It is the only logical conclusion that thoughtful men can arrive at. If you are going to exist in eternity hereafter, it must be that you have existed through eternity in the past : it cannot be otherwise. I will try to answer a few objections that are generally brought against the theory. Although many of you will think they are very silly objections, still we have to answer them, for sometimes we find that the most thoughtful men are ready to advance the silliest ideas. Well has it been said that there never was an idea so absurd that it did not find philosophers to defend it. The first objection is, why do we not remember our past? Do we remember all our past in this life? How many of you remember what you did when you were babies? None of you remember your early childhood, and if upon memory depends your existence, then this argument proves that you did not exist as babies, because you do not remember your babyhood. It is simply unmitigated nonsense to say that our existence depends on our remembering it. Why should we remember the past? That brain is gone, broken into pieces, and a new brain has been manufactured. What has come to this brain is the resultant, the sum total of the impressions acquired in our past, with which the mind has come to inhabit the new body.

I, as I stand here, am the effect, the result, of all the infinite past which is tacked on to me. And why is it necessary for me to remember all the past? When a great ancient sage, a seer, or a prophet of old, who came face to face with the truth, says something, these modern men stand up and say, "Oh, he was a fool!" But just use another name, "Huxley says it, or Tyndall"; then it must be true, and they take it for granted. In place of ancient superstitions they have erected modern superstitions, in place of the old Popes of religion they have installed modern Popes of science. So we see that this objection as to memory is not valid, and that is about the only serious objection that is raised against this theory. Although we have seen that it is not necessary for the theory that there shall be the memory of past lives, yet at the same time, we are in a position to assert that there are instances which show that this memory does come, and that each one of us will get back this memory in that life in which he will become free. Then alone you will find that this world is but a dream; then alone you will realise in the soul of your soul that you are but actors and the world is a stage; then alone will the idea of non-attachment come to you with the power of thunder; then all this thirst for enjoyment, this clinging on to life and this world will vanish for ever; then the mind will see dearly as daylight how many times all these existed for you, how many millions of times you had fathers and mothers, sons and daughters, husbands and wives, relatives and friends, wealth and power. They came and went. How many times you were on the topmost crest of the wave, and how many times you were down at the bottom of despair! When memory will bring all these to you, then alone will you stand as a hero and smile when the world frowns upon you. Then alone will you stand up and say. "I care not for thee even, O Death, what terrors hast thou for me?" This will come to all.

Are there any arguments, any rational proofs for this reincarnation of the soul? So far we have been giving the negative side, showing that the opposite arguments to disprove it are not valid. Are there any positive proofs? There are; and most valid ones, too. No other theory except that of reincarnation accounts for the wide divergence that we find between man and man in their powers to acquire knowledge. First, let us consider the process by means of which knowledge is acquired. Suppose I go into the street and see a dog. How do I know it is a dog? I refer it to my mind, and in my mind are groups of all my past experiences, arranged and pigeon-holed, as it were. As soon as a new impression comes, I take it up and refer it to some of the old pigeon-holes, and as soon as I find a group of the same impressions already existing, I place it in that group, and I am satisfied. I know it is a dog, because it coincides with the impressions already there. When I do not find the cognates of this new experience inside, I become dissatisfied. When, not finding the cognates of an impression, we become dissatisfied, this state of the mind is called "ignorance"; but, when, finding the cognates of an impression already existing, we become satisfied, this is called "knowledge". When one apple fell, men became dissatisfied. Then gradually they found out the group. What was the group they found? That all apples fell, so they called it "gravitation". Now we see that without a fund of already existing experience, any new experience would be impossible, for there would be nothing to which to refer the new impression. So, if, as some of the European philosophers think, a child came into the world with what they call *tabula rasa*, such a child would never attain to any degree of intellectual power, because he would have nothing to which to refer his new experiences. We see that the power of acquiring knowledge varies in each individual, and this shows that each one of us has come with his own fund of knowledge. Knowledge can only be got in one way, the way of experience; there is no other way to know. If we have not experienced it in this life, we must have experienced it in other lives. How is it that the fear of death is everywhere? A little chicken is just out of an egg and an eagle comes, and the chicken flies in fear to its mother. There is an old explanation (I should hardly dignify it by such a name). It is called instinct. What makes that little chicken just out of the egg afraid to die? How is it that as soon as a duckling hatched by a hen comes near water, it jumps into it and swims? It never swam before, nor saw anything swim. People call it instinct. It is a big word, but it leaves us where we were before. Let us study this phenomenon of instinct. A child begins to play on the piano. At first she must pay attention to every key she is fingering, and as she goes on and on for months and years, the playing becomes almost involuntary, instinctive. What was first done with conscious will does not require later on an effort of the will. This is not yet a complete proof. One half remains, and that is that almost all the actions which are now instinctive can be brought under the control of the will. Each muscle of the body can be brought under control. This is perfectly well known. So the proof is complete by this double method, that what we now call instinct is degeneration of voluntary actions; therefore, if the analogy applies to the whole of creation, if all nature is uniform, then what is instinct in lower animals, as well as in men, must be the degeneration of will.

Applying the law we dwelt upon under macrocosm that each involution pre-supposes an evolution, and each evolution an involution, we see that instinct is involved reason. What we call instinct in men or animals must therefore be involved, degenerated, voluntary actions, and voluntary actions are impossible without experience. Experience started that knowledge, and that knowledge is there. The fear of death, the duckling taking to the water and all involuntary actions in the human being which have become instinctive, are the results of past experiences. So far we have proceeded very clearly, and so far the latest science is with us. But here comes one more difficulty. The latest scientific men are coming back to the ancient sages, and as far as they have done so, there is perfect agreement. They admit that each man and each animal is born with a fund of experience, and that all these actions in the mind are the result of past experience. "But what," they ask, "is the use of saying that that experience belongs to the soul? Why not say it belongs to the body, and the body alone? Why not say it is hereditary transmission?" This is the last question. Why not say that all the experience with which I am born is the resultant effect of all the past experience of my ancestors? The sum total of the experience from the little protoplasm up to the highest human being is in me, but it has come from body to body in the course of hereditary transmission. Where will the difficulty be? This question is very nice, and we admit some part of this hereditary transmission. How far? As far as furnishing the material. We, by our past actions, conform ourselves to a certain birth in a certain body, and the only suitable material for that body comes from the parents who have made themselves fit to have that soul as their offspring.

The simple hereditary theory takes for granted the most astonishing proposition without any proof, that mental experience can be recorded in matters, that mental experience can be involved in matter. When I look at you in the lake of my mind there is a wave. That wave subsides, but it remains in fine form, as an impression. We understand a physical impression remaining in the body. But what proof is there for assuming that the mental impression can remain in the body, since the body goes to pieces? What carries it? Even granting it were possible for each mental impression to remain in the body, that every impression, beginning from the first man down to my father, was in my father's body, how could it be transmitted to me? Through the bioplasmic cell? How could that be? Because the father's body does not come to the child in toto. The same parents may have a number of children; then, from this theory of hereditary transmission, where the impression and the impressed (that is to say, material) are one, it rigorously follows that by the birth of every child the parents must lose a part of their own impressions, or, if the parents should transmit the whole of their impressions, then, after the birth of the first child, their minds would be a vacuum.

Again, if in the bioplasmic cell the infinite amount of impressions from all time has entered, where and how is it? This is a most impossible position, and until these physiologists can prove how and where those impressions live in that cell, and what they mean by a mental impression sleeping in the physical cell, their position cannot be taken for granted. So far it is clear then, that this impression is in the mind, that the mind comes to take its birth and rebirth, and uses the material which is most proper for it, and that the mind which has made itself fit for only a particular kind of body will have to wait until it gets that material. This we understand. The theory then comes to this, that there is hereditary transmission so far as furnishing the material to the soul is concerned. But the soul migrates and manufactures body after body, and each thought we think, and each deed we do, is stored in it in fine forms, ready to spring up again and take a new shape. When I look at you a wave rises in my mind. It dives down, as it were, and becomes finer and finer, but it does not die. It is ready to start up again as a wave in the shape of memory. So all these impressions are in my mind, and when I die the resultant force of them will be upon me. A ball is here, and each one of us takes a mallet in his hands and strikes the ball from all sides; the ball goes from point to point in the room, and when it reaches the door it flies out. What does it carry out with it? The resultant of all these blows. That will give it its direction. So, what directs the soul when the body dies? The resultant, the sum total of all the works it has done, of the thoughts it has thought. If the resultant is such that it has to manufacture a new body for further experience, it will go to those parents who are ready to supply it with suitable material for that body. Thus, from body to body it will go, sometimes to a heaven, and back again to earth, becoming man, or some lower animal. This way it will go on until it has finished its experience, and completed the circle. It then knows its own nature, knows what it is, and ignorance vanishes, its powers become manifest, it becomes perfect; no more is there any necessity for the soul to work through physical bodies, nor is there any necessity for it to work through finer, or mental bodies. It shines in its own light, and is free, no more to be born, no more to die.

We will not go now into the particulars of this. But I will bring before you one more point with regard to this theory of reincarnation. It is the theory that advances the freedom of the human soul. It is the one theory that does not lay the blame of all our weakness upon somebody else, which is a common human fallacy. We do not look at our own faults; the eyes do not see themselves, they see the eyes of everybody else. We human beings are very slow to recognise our own weakness, our own faults, so long as we can lay the blame upon somebody else. Men in general lay all the blame of life on their fellow-men, or, failing that, on God, or they conjure up a ghost, and say it is fate. Where is fate, and who is fate? We reap what we sow. We are the makers of our own fate. None else has the blame, none has the praise. The wind is blowing; those vessels whose sails are unfurled catch it, and go forward on their way, but those which have their sails furled do not catch the wind. Is that the fault of the wind? Is it the fault of the merciful Father, whose wind of mercy is blowing without ceasing, day and night, whose mercy knows no decay, is it His fault that some of us are happy and some unhappy? We make our own destiny. His sun shines for the weak as well as for the strong. His wind blows for saint and sinner alike. He is the Lord of all, the Father of all, merciful, and impartial. Do you mean to say that He, the Lord of creation, looks upon the petty things of our life in the same light as we do? What a degenerate idea of God that would be! We are like little puppies, making life-and-death struggles here, and foolishly thinking that even God Himself will take it as seriously as we do. He knows what the puppies' play means. Our attempts to lay the blame on Him, making Him the punisher, and the rewarder, are only foolish. He neither punishes, nor rewards any. His infinite mercy is open to every one, at all times, in all places, under all conditions, unfailing, unswerving. Upon us depends how we use it. Upon us depends how we utilise it. Blame neither man, nor God, nor anyone in the world. When you find yourselves suffering, blame yourselves, and try to do better.

This is the only solution of the problem. Those that blame others — and, alas! the number of them is increasing every day — are generally miserable with helpless brains; they have brought themselves to that pass through their own mistakes and blame others, but this does not alter their position. It does not serve them in any way. This attempt to throw the blame upon others only weakens them the more. Therefore, blame none for your own faults, stand upon your own feet, and take the whole responsibility upon yourselves. Say, "This misery that I am suffering is of my own doing, and that very thing proves that it will have to be undone by me alone." That which I created, I can demolish; that which is created by some one else I shall never be able to destroy. Therefore, stand up, be bold, be strong. Take the whole responsibility on your own shoulders, and know that you are the creator of your own destiny. All the strength and succour you want is within yourselves. Therefore, make your own future. "Let the dead past bury its dead." The infinite future is before you, and you must always remember that each word, thought, and deed, lays up a store for you and that as the bad thoughts and bad works are ready to spring upon you like tigers, so also there is the inspiring hope that the good thoughts and good deeds are ready with the power of a hundred thousand angels to defend you always and for ever.

Chapter XIII
Immortality

Delivered in America

What question has been asked a greater number of times, what idea has led men more to search the universe for an answer, what question is nearer and dearer to the human heart, what question is more inseparably connected with our existence, than this one, the immortality of the human soul? It has been the theme of poets and sages, of priests and prophets; kings on the throne have discussed it, beggars in the street have dreamt of it. The best of humanity have approached it, and the worst of men have hoped for it. The interest in the theme has not died yet, nor will it die so long as human nature exists. Various answers have been presented to the world by various minds. Thousands, again, in every period of history have given up the discussion, and yet the question remains fresh as ever. Often in the turmoil and struggle of our lives we seem to forget it, but suddenly some one dies — one, perhaps, whom we loved, one near and dear to our hearts is snatched away from us — and the struggle, the din and turmoil of the world around us, cease for a moment, and the soul asks the old questions "What after this?" "What becomes of the soul?"

All human knowledge proceeds out of experience; we cannot know anything except by experience. All our reasoning is based upon generalised experience, all our knowledge is but harmonised experience. Looking around us, what do we find? A continuous change. The plant comes out of the seed, grows into the tree, completes the circle, and comes back to the seed. The animal comes, lives a certain time, dies, and completes the circle. So does man. The mountains slowly but surely crumble away, the rivers slowly but surely dry up, rains come out of the sea, and go back to the sea. Everywhere circles are being completed, birth, growth, development, and decay following each other with mathematical precision. This is our everyday experience. Inside of it all, behind all this vast mass of what we call life, of millions of forms and shapes, millions upon millions of varieties, beginning from the lowest atom to the highest spiritualised man, we find existing a certain unity. Every day we find that the wall that was thought to be dividing one thing and another is being broken down, and all matter is coming to be recognised by modern science as one substance, manifesting in different ways and in various forms; the one life that runs through all like a continuous chain, of which all these various forms represent the links, link after link, extending almost infinitely, but of the same one chain. This is what is called evolution. It is an old, old idea, as old as human society, only it is getting fresher and fresher as human knowledge is progressing. There is one thing more, which the ancients perceived, but which in modern times is not yet so clearly perceived, and that is involution. The seed is becoming the plant; a grain of sand never becomes a plant. It is the father that becomes a child; a lump of clay never becomes the child. From what does this evolution come, is the question. What was the seed? It was the same as the tree. All the possibilities of a future tree are in that seed; all the possibilities of a future man are in the little baby; all the possibilities of any future life are in the germ. What is this? The ancient philosophers of India called it involution. We find then, that every evolution presupposes an involution. Nothing can be evolved which is not already there. Here, again, modern science comes to our help. You know by mathematical reasoning that the sum total of the energy that is displayed in the universe is the same throughout. You cannot take away one atom of matter or one foot-pound of force. You cannot add to the universe one atom of matter or one foot-pound of force. As such, evolution does not come out of zero; then, where does it come from? From previous involution. The child is the man involved, and the man is the child evolved. The seed is the tree involved, and the tree is the seed evolved. All the possibilities of life are in the germ. The problem becomes a little clearer. Add to it the first idea of continuation of life. From the lowest protoplasm to the most perfect human being there is really but one life. Just as in one life we have so many various phases of expression, the protoplasm developing into the baby, the child, the young man, the old man, so, from that protoplasm up to the most perfect man we get one continuous life, one chain. This is evolution, but we have seen that each evolution presupposes an involution. The whole of this life which slowly manifests itself evolves itself from the protoplasm to the perfected human being— the Incarnation of God on earth— the whole of this series is but one life, and the whole of this manifestation must have been involved in that very protoplasm. This whole life, this very God on earth, was involved in it and slowly came out, manifesting itself slowly, slowly, slowly. The highest expression must have been there in the germ state in minute form; therefore this one force, this whole chain, is the involution of that cosmic life which is everywhere. It is this one mass of intelligence which, from the protoplasm up to the most perfected man, is slowly and slowly uncoiling itself. Not that it grows. Take off all ideas of growth from your mind. With the idea of growth is associated something coming from outside, something extraneous, which would give the lie to the truth that the Infinite which lies latent in every life is independent of all external conditions. It can never grow; It was always there, and only manifests Itself.

The effect is the cause manifested. There is no essential difference between the effect and the cause. Take this glass, for instance. There was the material, and the material plus the will of the manufacturer made the glass and these two were its causes and are present in it. In what form is the will present? As adhesion. If the force were not here, each particle would fall away. What is the effect then? It is the same as the cause, only taking; different form, a different composition. When the cause is changed and limited for a time, it becomes the effect We must remember this. Applying it to our idea of life the whole of the manifestation of this one series, from the protoplasm up to the most perfect man, must be the very same thing as cosmic life. First it got involved and became finer; and out of that fine something, which wet the cause, it has gone on evolving, manifesting itself, and becoming grosser.

But the question of immortality is not yet settled. We have seen that everything in this universe is indestructible. There is nothing new; there will be nothing new. The same series of manifestations are presenting themselves alternately like a wheel, coming up and going down. All motion in this universe is in the form of waves, successively rising and falling. Systems after systems are coming out of fine forms, evolving themselves, and taking grosser forms, again melting down, as it were, and going back to the fine forms. Again they rise out of that, evolving for a certain period and slowly going back to the cause. So with all life. Each manifestation of life is coming up and then going back again. What goes down? The form. The form breaks to pieces, but it comes up again. In one sense bodies and forms even are eternal. How? Suppose we take a number of dice and throw them, and they fall in this ratio— 6 — 5 — 3 — 4. We take the dice up and throw them again and again; there must be a time when the same numbers will come again; the same combination must come. Now each particle, each atom, that is in this universe, I take for such a die, and these are being thrown out and combined again and again. All these forms before you are one combination. Here are the forms of a glass, a table, a pitcher of water, and so forth. This is one combination; in time, it will all break. But there must come a time when exactly the same combination comes again, when you will be here, and this form will be here, this subject will be talked, and this pitcher will be here.

An infinite number of times this has been, and an infinite number of times this will be repeated. Thus far with the physical forms.

What do we find? That even the combination of physical forms is eternally repeated.

A most interesting conclusion that follows from this theory is the explanation of facts such as these: Some of you, perhaps, have seen a man who can read the past life of others and foretell the future. How is it possible for any one to see what the future will be, unless there is a regulated future? Effects of the past will recur in the future, and we see that it is so. You have seen the big Ferris Wheel in Chicago. The wheel revolves, and the little rooms in the wheel are regularly coming one after another; one set of persons gets into these, and after they have gone round the circle, they get out, and a fresh batch of people gets in. Each one of these batches is like one of these manifestations, from the lowest animals to the highest man. Nature is like the chain of the Ferris Wheel, endless and infinite, and these little carriages are the bodies or forms in which fresh batches of souls are riding, going up higher and higher until they become perfect and come out of the wheel. But the wheel goes on. And so long as the bodies are in the wheel, it can be absolutely and mathematically foretold where they will go, but not so of the souls. Thus it is possible to read the past and the future of nature with precision. We see, then, that there is recurrence of the same material phenomena at certain periods, and that the same combinations have been taking place through eternity. But that is not the immortality of the soul. No force can die, no matter can be annihilated. What becomes of it? It goes on changing, backwards and forwards, until it returns to the source from which it came. There is no motion in a straight line. Everything moves in a circle; a straight line, infinitely produced, becomes a circle. If that is the case, there cannot be eternal degeneration for any soul. It cannot be. Everything must complete the circle, and come back to its source. What are you and I and all these souls? In our discussion of evolution and involution, we have seen that you and I must be part of the cosmic consciousness, cosmic life, cosmic mind, which got involved and we must complete the circle and go back to this cosmic intelligence which is God. This cosmic intelligence is what people call Lord, or God, or Christ, or Buddha, or Brahman, what the materialists perceive as force, and the agnostics as that infinite, inexpressible beyond; and we are all parts of that.

This is the second idea, yet this is not sufficient; there will be still more doubts. It is very good to say that there is no destruction for any force. But all the forces and forms that we see are combinations. This form before us is a composition of several component parts, and so every force that we see is similarly compos-ite. If you take the scientific idea of force, and call it the sum total, the resul-tant of several forces, what becomes of your individuality? Everything that is a compound must sooner or later go back to its component parts. Whatever in this universe is the result of the combination of matter or force must sooner or later go back to its components. Whatever is the result of certain causes must die, must be destroyed. It gets broken up, dispersed, and resolved back into its components. Soul is not a force; neither is it thought. It is the manufacturer of thought, but not thought itself; it is the manufacturer of the body, but not the body. Why so? We see that the body cannot be the soul. Why not? Because it is not intelligent. A corpse is not intelligent, nor a piece of meat in a butcher's shop. What do we mean by intelligence? Reactive power. We want to go a little more deeply into this. Here is a pitcher; I see it. How? Rays of light from the pitcher enter my eyes, and make a picture in my retina, which is carried to the brain. Yet there is no vision. What the physiologists call the sensory nerves carry this impression inwards. But up to this there is no reaction. The nerve centre in the brain carries the impression to the mind, and the mind reacts, and as soon as this reaction comes, the pitcher flashes before it. Take a more commonplace example. Suppose you are listening to me intently and a mosquito is sitting on the tip of your nose and giving you that pleasant sensation which mosquitoes can give; but you are so intent on hearing me that you do not feel the mosquito at all. What has happened? The mosquito has bitten a certain part of your skin, and certain nerves are there. They have carried a certain sensation to the brain, and the impression is there, but the mind, being otherwise occupied, does not react, so you are not aware of the presence of the mosquito. When a new impression comes, if the mind does not react, we shall not be conscious of it, but when the reaction comes we feel, we see, we hear, and so forth. With this reaction comes illumination, as the Samkhya philosophers call it. We see that the body cannot illuminate, because in the absence of attention no sensation is possible. Cases have been known where, under peculiar conditions, a man who had never learnt a particular language was found able to speak it. Subsequent inquiries proved that the man had, when a child, lived among people who spoke that language and the impressions were left in his brain. These impressions remained stored up there, until through some cause the mind reacted, and illumination came, and then the man was able to speak the language. This shows that the mind alone is not sufficient, that the mind itself is an instrument in the hands of someone. In the case of that boy the mind contained that language, yet he did not know it,

but later there came a time when he did. It shows that there is someone besides
the mind; and when the boy was a baby, that someone did not use the power;
but when the boy grew up, he took advantage of it, and used it. First, here is the
body, second the mind, or instrument of thought, and third behind this mind
is the Self of man. The Sanskrit word is Atman. As modern philosophers have
identified thought with molecular changes in the brain, they do not know how to
explain such a case, and they generally deny it. The mind is intimately connected
with the brain which dies every time the body changes. The Self is the illumina-
tor, and the mind is the instrument in Its hands, and through that instrument
It gets hold of the external instrument, and thus comes perception. The external
instruments get hold of the impressions and carry them to the organs, for you
must remember always, that the eyes and ears are only receivers — it is the internal organs, the brain centres, which act. In Sanskrit these centres are called
Indriyas, and they carry sensations to the mind, and the mind presents them
further back to another state of the mind, which in Sanskrit is called Chitta,
and there they are organised into will, and all these present them to the King of
kings inside, the Ruler on His throne, the Self of man. He then sees and gives
His orders. Then the mind immediately acts on the organs, and the organs on
the external body. The real Perceiver, the real Ruler, the Governor, the Creator,
the Manipulator of all this, is the Self of man.

We see, then, that the Self of man is not the body, neither is It thought. It cannot be a compound. Why not? Because everything that is a compound can be
seen or imagined. That which we cannot imagine or perceive, which we cannot
bind together, is not force or matter, cause or effect, and cannot be a compound.
The domain of compounds is only so far as our mental universe, our thought
universe extends. Beyond this it does not hold good; it is as far as law reigns,
and if there is anything beyond law, it cannot be a compound at all. The Self of
man being beyond the law of causation, is not a compound. It is ever free and is
the Ruler of everything that is within law. It will never die, because death means
going back to the component parts, and that which was never a compound can
never die. It is sheer nonsense to say It dies.

We are now treading on finer and finer ground, and some of you, perhaps, will
be frightened. We have seen that this Self, being beyond the little universe of
matter and force and thought, is a simple; and as a simple It cannot die. That
which does not die cannot live. For life and death are the obverse and reverse of
the same coin. Life is another name for death, and death for life. One particular
mode of manifestation is what we call life; another particular mode of manifesta-

tion of the same thing is what we call death. When the wave rises on the top it is life; and when it falls into the hollow it is death. If anything is beyond death, we naturally see it must also be beyond life. I must remind you of the first conclusion that the soul of man is part of the cosmic energy that exists, which is God. We now find that it is beyond life and death. You were never born, and you will never die. What is this birth and death that we see around us? This belongs to the body only, because the soul is omnipresent. "How can that be?" you may ask. "So many people are sitting here, and you say the soul is omnipresent?" What is there, I ask, to limit anything that is beyond law, beyond causation? This glass is limited; it is not omnipresent, because the surrounding matter forces it to take that form, does not allow it to expand. It is conditioned be everything around it, and is, therefore, limited. But that which is beyond law, where there is nothing to act upon it, how can that be limited? It must be omnipresent. You are everywhere in the universe. How is it then that I am born and I am going to die, and all that? That is the talk of ignorance, hallucination of the brain. You were neither born, nor will you die. You have had neither birth, nor will have rebirth, nor life, nor incarnation, nor anything. What do you mean by coming and going? All shallow nonsense. You are everywhere. Then what is this coming and going? It is the hallucination produced by the change of this fine body which you call the mind. That is going on. Just a little speck of cloud passing before the sky. As it moves on and on, it may create the delusion that the sky moves. Sometimes you see a cloud moving before the moon, and you think that the moon is moving. When you are in a train you think the land is flying, or when you are in a boat, you think the water moves. In reality you are neither going nor coming, you are not being born, nor going to be reborn; you are infinite, ever-present, beyond all causation, and ever-free. Such a question is out of place, it is arrant nonsense. How could there be mortality when there was no birth?

One step more we will have to take to come to a logical conclusion. There is no half-way house. You are metaphysicians, and there is no crying quarter. If then we are beyond all law, we must be omniscient, ever-blessed; all knowledge must be in us and all power and blessedness. Certainly. You are the omniscient. Omnipresent being of the universe. But of such beings can there be many? Can there be a hundred thousand millions of omnipresent beings? Certainly not. Then, what becomes of us all? You are only one; there is only one such Self, and that One Self is you. Standing behind this little nature is what we call the Soul. There is only One Being, One Existence, the ever-blessed, the omnipresent, the omniscient, the birthless, deathless. "Through His control the sky expands, through His control the air breathes, through His control the sun shines, and through His control all live. He is the Reality in nature, He is the Soul of your soul, nay, more, you are He, you are one with Him." Wherever there are two, there is fear, there is danger, there is conflict, there is strife. When it is all One, who is there to hate, who is there to struggle with? When it is all He, with whom can you fight? This explains the true nature of life; this explains the true nature of being. This is perfection, and this is God. As long as you see the many, you are under delusion. "In this world of many he who sees the One, in this ever changing world he who sees Him who never changes, as the Soul of his own soul, as his own Self, he is free, he is blessed, he has reached the goal." Therefore know that thou art He; thou art the God of this universe, "Tat Tvam Asi" (That thou art). All these various ideas that I am a man or a woman, or sick or healthy, or strong or weak, or that I hate or I love, or have a little power, are but hallucinations. Away with them! What makes you weak? What makes you fear? You are the One Being in the universe. What frightens you? Stand up then and be free. Know that every thought and word that weakens you in this world is the only evil that exists. Whatever makes men weak and fear is the only evil that should be shunned. What can frighten you? If the suns come down, and the moons crumble into dust, and systems after systems are hurled into annihilation, what is that to you? Stand as a rock; you are indestructible. You are the Self, the God of the universe. Say— "I am Existence Absolute, Bliss Absolute, Knowledge Absolute, I am He," and like a lion breaking its cage, break your chain and be free for ever. What frightens you, what holds you down? Only ignorance and delusion; nothing else can bind you. You are the Pure One, the Ever-blessed.

Silly fools tell you that you are sinners, and you sit down in a corner and weep. It is foolishness, wickedness, downright rascality to say that you are sinners! You are all God. See you not God and call Him man? Therefore, if you dare, stand on that— mould your whole life on that. If a man cuts your throat, do not say no, for you are cutting your own throat. When you help a poor man, do not feel the least pride. That is worship for you, and not the cause of pride. Is not the whole universe you? Where is there any one that is not you? You are the Soul of this universe. You are the sun, moon, and stars, it is you that are shining everywhere. The whole universe is you. Whom are you going to hate or to fight? Know, then, that thou art He, and model your whole life accordingly; and he who knows this and models his life accordingly will no more grovel in darkness.

Chapter XIV
The Atman

Delivered in America

Many of you have read Max Muller's celebrated book, Three Lectures on the Vedanta Philosophy, and some of you may, perhaps, have read, in German, Professor Deussen's book on the same philosophy. In what is being written and taught in the West about the religious thought of India, one school of Indian thought is principally represented, that which is called Advaitism, the monistic side of Indian religion; and sometimes it is thought that all the teachings of the Vedas are comprised in that one system of philosophy. There are, however, various phases of Indian thought; and, perhaps, this non-dualistic form is in the minority as compared with the other phases. From the most ancient times there have been various sects of thought in India, and as there never was a formulated or recognised church or any body of men to designate the doctrines which should be believed by each school, people were very free to choose their own form, make their own philosophy and establish their own sects. We, therefore, find that from the most ancient times India was full of religious sects. At the present time, I do not know how many hundreds of sects we have in India, and several fresh ones are coming into existence every year. It seems that the religious activity of that nation is simply inexhaustible.

Of these various sects, in the first place, there can be made two main divisions, the orthodox and the unorthodox. Those that believe in the Hindu scriptures, the Vedas, as eternal revelations of truth, are called orthodox, and those that stand on other authorities, rejecting the Vedas, are the heterodox in India. The chief modern unorthodox Hindu sects are the Jains and the Buddhists. Among the orthodox some declare that the scriptures are of much higher authority than reason; others again say that only that portion of the scriptures which is rational should be taken and the rest rejected.

Of the three orthodox divisions, the Sankhyas, the Naiyayikas, and the Mimamsakas, the former two, although they existed as philosophical schools, failed to form any sect. The one sect that now really covers India is that of the later Mimamsakas or the Vedantists. Their philosophy is called Vedantism. All the schools of Hindu philosophy start from the Vedanta or Upanishads, but the monists took the name to themselves as a speciality, because they wanted to base the whole of their theology and philosophy upon the Vedanta and nothing else. In the course of time the Vedanta prevailed, and all the various sects of India that now exist can be referred to one or other of its schools. Yet these schools are not unanimous in their opinions.

We find that there are three principal variations among the Vedantists. On one point they all agree, and that is that they all believe in God. All these Vedantists also believe the Vedas to be the revealed word of God, not exactly in the same sense, perhaps, as the Christians or the Mohammedans believe, but in a very peculiar sense. Their idea is that the Vedas are an expression of the knowledge of God, and as God is eternal, His knowledge is eternally with Him, and so are the Vedas eternal. There is another common ground of belief: that of creation in cycles, that the whole of creation appears and disappears; that it is projected and becomes grosser and grosser, and at the end of an incalculable period of time it becomes finer and finer, when it dissolves and subsides, and then comes a period of rest. Again it: begins to appear and goes through the same process. They postulate the existence of a material which they call Akasha, which is something like the ether of the scientists, and a power which they call Prana. About; this Prana they declare that by its vibration the universe is produced. When a cycle ends, all this manifestation of nature becomes finer and finer and dissolves into that Akasha which cannot be seen or felt, yet out of which everything is manufactured. All the forces that we see in nature, such as gravitation, attraction, and repulsion, or as thought, feeling, and nervous motion — all these various forces resolve into that Prana, and the vibration of the Prana ceases. In that state it remains until the beginning of the next cycle. Prana then begins to vibrate, and that vibration acts upon the Akasha, and all these forms are thrown out in regular succession.

The first school I will tell you about is styled the dualistic school. The dualists believe that God, who is the creator of the universe and its ruler, is eternally separate from nature, eternally separate from the human soul. God is eternal; nature is eternal; so are all souls. Nature and the souls become manifested and change, but God remains the same. According to the dualists, again, this God is personal in that He has qualities, not that He has a body. He has human attributes; He is merciful, He is just, He is powerful, He is almighty, He can be approached, He can be prayed to, He can be loved, He loves in return, and so forth. In one word, He is a human God, only infinitely greater than man; He has none of the evil qualities which men have. "He is the repository of an infinite number of blessed qualities"— that is their definition. He cannot create without materials, and nature is the material out of which He creates the whole universe. There are some non-Vedantic dualists, called "Atomists", who believe that nature is nothing but an infinite number of atoms, and God's will, acting upon these atoms, creates. The Vedantists deny the atomic theory; they say it is perfectly illogical. The indivisible atoms are like geometrical points without parts or magnitude; but something without parts or magnitude, if multiplied an infinite number of times, will remain the same. Anything that has no parts will never make something that has parts; any number of zeros added together will not make one single whole number. So, if these atoms are such that they have no parts or magnitude, the creation of the universe is simply impossible out of such atoms. Therefore, according to the Vedantic dualists, there is what they call indiscrete or undifferentiated nature, and out of that God creates the universe. The vast mass of Indian people are dualists. Human nature ordinarily cannot conceive of anything higher. We find that ninety per cent of the population of the earth who believe in any religion are dualists. All the religions of Europe and Western Asia are dualistic; they have to be. The ordinary man cannot think of anything which is not concrete. He naturally likes to cling to that which his intellect can grasp. That is to say, he can only conceive of higher spiritual ideas by bringing them down to his own level. He can only grasp abstract thoughts by making them concrete. This is the religion of the masses all over the world. They believe in a God who is entirely separate from them, a great king, a high, mighty monarch, as it were. At the same time they make Him purer than the monarchs of the earth; they give Him all good qualities and remove the evil qualities from Him. As if it were ever possible for good to exist without evil; as if there could be any conception of light without a conception of darkness!

With all dualistic theories the first difficulty is, how is it possible that under the rule of a just and merciful God, the repository of an infinite number of good qualities, there can be so many evils in this world? This question arose in all dualistic religions, but the Hindus never invented a Satan as an answer to it. The Hindus with one accord laid the blame on man, and it was easy for them to do so. Why? Because, as I have just now told you, they did not believe that souls were created out of nothing We see in this life that we can shape and form our future every one of us, every day, is trying to shape the morrow; today we fix the fate of the morrow; tomorrow we shall fix the fate of the day after, and so on. It is quite logical that this reasoning can be pushed backward too. If by our own deeds we shape our destiny in the future why not apply the same rule to the past? If, in an infinite chain, a certain number of links are alternately repeated then, if one of these groups of links be explained, we can explain the whole chain. So, in this infinite length of time, if we can cut off one portion and explain that portion and understand it, then, if it be true that nature is uniform, the same explanation must apply to the whole chain of time. If it be true that we are working out our own destiny here within this short space of time if it be true that everything must have a cause as we see it now, it must also be true that that which we are now is the effect of the whole of our past; therefore, no other person is necessary to shape the destiny of mankind but man himself. The evils that are in the world are caused by none else but ourselves. We have caused all this evil; and just as we constantly see misery resulting from evil actions, so can we also see that much of the existing misery in the world is the effect of the past wickedness of man. Man alone, therefore, according to this theory, is respon-sible. God is not to blame. He, the eternally merciful Father, is not to blame at all. "We reap what we sow."

Another peculiar doctrine of the dualists is, that every soul must eventually come to salvation. No one will be left out. Through various vicissitudes, through vari-ous sufferings and enjoyments, each one of them will come out in the end. Come out of what? The one common idea of all Hindu sects is that all souls have to get out of this universe. Neither the universe which we see and feel, nor even an imaginary one, can be right, the real one, because both are mixed up with good and evil. According to the dualists, there is beyond this universe a place full of happiness and good only; and when that place is reached, there will be no more necessity of being born and reborn, of living and dying; and this idea is very dear to them. No more disease there, and no more death. There will be eternal happi-ness, and they will be in the presence of God for all time and enjoy Him for ever. They believe that all beings, from the lowest worm up to the highest angels and gods, will all, sooner or later, attain to that world where there will be no more misery. But our world will never end; it goes on infinitely, although moving in waves. Although moving in cycles it never ends. The number of souls that are to be saved, that are to be perfected, is infinite. Some are in plants, some are in the lower animals, some are in men, some are in gods, but all of them, even the highest gods, are imperfect, are in bondage. What is the bondage? The neces-sity of being born and the necessity of dying. Even the highest gods die. What are these gods? They mean certain states, certain offices. For instance, Indra the king of gods, means a certain office; some soul which was very high has gone to fill that post in this cycle, and after this cycle he will be born again as man and come down to this earth, and the man who is very good in this cycle will go and fill that post in the next cycle. So with all these gods; they are certain offices which have been filled alternately by millions and millions of souls, who, after filling those offices, came down and became men. Those who do good works in this world and help others, but with an eye to reward, hoping to reach heaven or to get the praise of their fellow-men, must when they die, reap the benefit of those good works — they become these gods. But that is not salvation; salvation never will come through hope of reward. Whatever man desires the Lord gives him. Men desire power, they desire prestige, they desire enjoyments as gods, and they get these desires fulfilled, but no effect of work can be eternal. The effect will be exhausted after a certain length of time; it may be aeons, but after that it will be gone, and these gods must come down again and become men and get another chance for liberation. The lower animals will come up and become men, become gods, perhaps, then become men again, or go back to animals, until the time when they will get rid of all desire for enjoyment, the thirst for life, this clinging on to the "me and mine". This "me and mine" is the very root of all the evil in the world. If you ask a dualist, "Is your child yours?" he will say, "It is God's. My property is not mine, it is God's." Everything should be held as God's.

Now, these dualistic sects in India are great vegetarians, great preachers of non-killing of animals. But their idea about it is quite different from that of the Buddhist. If you ask a Buddhist, "Why do you preach against killing any animal?" he will answer, "We have no right to take any life;" and if you ask a dualist, "Why do you not kill any animal?" he says, "Because it is the Lord's." So the dualist says that this "me and mine" is to be applied to God and God alone; He is the only "me" and everything is His. When a man has come to the state when he has no "me and mine," when everything is given up to the Lord, when he loves everybody and is ready even to give up his life for an animal, without any desire for reward, then his heart will be purified, and when the heart has been puri-fied, into that heart will come the love of God. God is the centre of attraction for every soul, and the dualist says, "A needle covered up with clay will not be attracted by a magnet, but as soon as the clay is washed off, it will be attracted." God is the magnet and human soul is the needle, and its evil works, the dirt and dust that cover it. As soon as the soul is pure it will by natural attraction come to God and remain with Him for ever, but remain eternally separate. The per-fected soul, if it wishes, can take any form; it is able to take a hundred bodies, if it wishes or have none at all, if it so desires. It becomes almost almighty, except that it cannot create; that power belongs to God alone. None, however perfect, can manage the affairs of the universe; that function belongs to God. But all souls, when they become perfect, become happy for ever and live eternally with God. This is the dualistic statement.

One other idea the dualists preach. They protest against the idea of praying to God, "Lord, give me this and give me that." They think that should not be done. If a man must ask some material gift, he should ask inferior beings for it; ask one of these gods, or angels or a perfected being for temporal things. God is only to be loved. It is almost a blasphemy to pray to God, "Lord, give me this, and give me that." According to the dualists, therefore, what a man wants, he will get sooner or later, by praying to one of the gods; but if he wants salvation, he must worship God. This is the religion of the masses of India.

The real Vedanta philosophy begins with those known as the qualified non-dualists. They make the statement that the effect is never different from the cause; the effect is but the cause reproduced in another form. If the universe is the effect and God the cause, it must be God Himself— it cannot be anything but that. They start with the assertion that God is both the efficient and the material cause of the universe; that He Himself is the creator, and He Himself is the material out of which the whole of nature is projected. The word "creation" in your language has no equivalent in Sanskrit, because there is no sect in India which believes in creation, as it is regarded in the West, as something coming out of nothing. It seems that at one time there were a few that had some such idea, but they were very quickly silenced. At the present time I do not know of any sect that believes this. What we mean by creation is projection of that which already existed. Now, the whole universe, according to this sect, is God Himself. He is the material of the universe. We read in the Vedas, "As the Urnanabhi (spider) spins the thread out of its own body, . . . even so the whole universe has come out of the Being."

If the effect is the cause reproduced, the question is: "How is it that we find this material, dull, unintelligent universe produced from a God, who is not material, but who is eternal intelligence? How, if the cause is pure and perfect, can the effect be quite different?" What do these qualified non-dualists say? Theirs is a very peculiar theory. They say that these three existences, God, nature, and the soul, are one. God is, as it were, the Soul, and nature and souls are the body of God. Just as I have a body and I have a soul, so the whole universe and all souls are the body of God, and God is the Soul of souls. Thus, God is the material cause of the universe. The body may be changed— may be young or old, strong or weak—but that does not affect the soul at all. It is the same eternal existence, manifesting through the body. Bodies come and go, but the soul does not change. Even so the whole universe is the body of God, and in that sense it is God. But the change in the universe does not affect God. Out of this material He creates the universe, and at the end of a cycle His body becomes finer, it contracts; at the beginning of another cycle it becomes expanded again, and out of it evolve all these different worlds.

Now both the dualists and the qualified non-dualists admit that the soul is by its nature pure, but through its own deeds it becomes impure. The qualified non-dualists express it more beautifully than the dualists, by saying that the soul's purity and perfection become contracted and again become manifest, and what we are now trying to do is to remanifest the intelligence, the purity, the power which is natural to the soul. Souls have a multitude of qualities, but not that of almightiness or all-knowingness. Every wicked deed contracts the nature of the soul, and every good deed expands it, and these souls, are all parts of God. "As from a blazing fire fly millions of sparks of the same nature, even so from this Infinite Being, God, these souls have come." Each has the same goal. The God of the qualified non-dualists is also a Personal God, the repository of an infinite number of blessed qualities, only He is interpenetrating everything in the universe. He is immanent in everything and everywhere; and when the scriptures say that God is everything, it means that God is interpenetrating everything, not that God has become the wall, but that God is in the wall. There is not a particle, not an atom in the universe where He is not. Souls are all limited; they are not omnipresent. When they get expansion of their powers and become perfect, there is no more birth and death for them; they live with God for ever.

Now we come to Advaitism, the last and, what we think, the fairest flower of philosophy and religion that any country in any age has produced, where human thought attains its highest expression and even goes beyond the mystery which seems to be impenetrable. This is the non-dualistic Vedantism. It is too abstruse, too elevated to be the religion of the masses. Even in India, its birthplace, where it has been ruling supreme for the last three thousand years, it has not been able to permeate the masses. As we go on we shall find that it is difficult for even the most thoughtful man and woman in any country to understand Advaitism. We have made ourselves so weak; we have made ourselves so low. We may make great claims, but naturally we want to lean on somebody else. We are like little, weak plants, always wanting a support. How many times I have been asked for a "comfortable religion!" Very few men ask for the truth, fewer still dare to learn the truth, and fewest of all dare to follow it in all its practical bearings. It is not their fault; it is all weakness of the brain. Any new thought, especially of a high kind, creates a disturbance, tries to make a new channel, as it were, in the brain matter, and that unhinges the system, throws men off their balance. They are used to certain surroundings, and have to overcome a huge mass of ancient superstitions, ancestral superstition, class superstition, city superstition, country superstition, and behind all, the vast mass of superstition that is innate in every human being. Yet there are a few brave souls in the world who dare to conceive the truth, who dare to take it up, and who dare to follow it to the end.

What does the Advaitist declare? He says, if there is a God, that God must be both the material and the efficient cause of the universe. Not only is He the creator, but He is also the created. He Himself is this universe. How can that be? God, the pure, the spirit, has become the universe? Yes; apparently so. That which all ignorant people see as the universe does not really exist. What are you and I and all these things we see? Mere self-hypnotism; there is but one Existence, the Infinite, the Ever-blessed One. In that Existence we dream all these various dreams. It is the Atman, beyond all, the Infinite, beyond the known, beyond the knowable; in and through That we see the universe. It is the only Reality. It is this table; It is the audience before me; It is the wall; It is everything, minus the name and form. Take away the form of the table, take away the name; what remains is It. The Vedantist does not call It either He or She — these are fictions, delusions of the human brain — there is no sex in the soul. People who are under illusion, who have become like animals, see a woman or a man; living gods do not see men or women. How can they who are beyond everything have any sex idea? Everyone and everything is the Atman — the Self — the sexless, the pure, the ever-blessed. It is the name, the form, the body, which are material, and they make all this difference. If you take away these two differences of name and form, the whole universe is one; there are no two, but one everywhere. You and I are one. There is neither nature, nor God, nor the universe, only that one Infinite Existence, out of which, through name and form, all these are manufactured. How to know the Knower? It cannot be known. How can you see your own Self? You can only reflect yourself. So all this universe is the reflection of that One Eternal Being, the Atman, and as the reflection falls upon good or bad reflectors, so good or bad images are cast up. Thus in the murderer, the reflector is bad and not the Self. In the saint the reflector is pure. The Self — the Atman — is by Its own nature pure. It is the same, the one Existence of the universe that is reflecting Itself from the lowest worm to the highest and most perfect being. The whole of this universe is one Unity, one Existence, physically, mentally, morally and spiritually. We are looking upon this one Existence in different forms and creating all these images upon It. To the being who has limited himself to the condition of man, It appears as the world of man. To the being who is on a higher plane of existence, It may seem like heaven. There is but one Soul in the universe, not two. It neither comes nor goes. It is neither born, nor dies, nor reincarnates. How can It die? Where can It go? All these heavens, all these earths, and all these places are vain imaginations of the mind. They do not exist, never existed in the past, and never will exist in the future.

I am omnipresent, eternal. Where can I go? Where am I not already? I am reading this book of nature. Page after page I am finishing and turning over, and one dream of life after another goes Away. Another page of life is turned over; another dream of life comes, and it goes away, rolling and rolling, and when I have finished my reading, I let it go and stand aside, I throw away the book, and the whole thing is finished. What does the Advaitist preach? He dethrones all the gods that ever existed, or ever will exist in the universe and places on that throne the Self of man, the Atman, higher than the sun and the moon, higher than the heavens, greater than this great universe itself. No books, no scriptures, no science can ever imagine the glory of the Self that appears as man, the most glorious God that ever was, the only God that ever existed, exists, or ever will exist. I am to worship, therefore, none but myself. "I worship my Self," says the Advaitist. To whom shall I bow down? I salute my Self. To whom shall I go for help? Who can help me, the Infinite Being of the universe? These are foolish dreams, hallucinations; who ever helped any one? None. Wherever you see a weak man, a dualist, weeping and wailing for help from somewhere above the skies, it is because he does not know that the skies also are in him. He wants help from the skies, and the help comes. We see that it comes; but it comes from within himself, and he mistakes it as coming from without. Sometimes a sick man lying on his bed may hear a tap on the door. He gets up and opens it and finds no one there. He goes back to bed, and again he hears a tap. He gets up and opens the door. Nobody is there. At last he finds that it was his own heartbeat which he fancied was a knock at the door. Thus man, after this vain search after various gods outside himself, completes the circle, and comes back to the point from which he started — the human soul, and he finds that the God whom he was searching in hill and dale, whom he was seeking in every brook, in every temple, in churches and heavens, that God whom he was even imagining as sitting in heaven and ruling the world, is his own Self. I am He, and He is I. None but I was God, and this little I never existed.

Yet, how could that perfect God have been deluded? He never was. How could a perfect God have been dreaming? He never dreamed. Truth never dreams. The very question as to whence this illusion arose is absurd. Illusion arises from illusion alone. There will be no illusion as soon as the truth is seen. Illusion always rests upon illusion; it never rests upon God, the Truth, the Atman. You are never in illusion; it is illusion that is in you, before you. A cloud is here; another comes and pushes it aside and takes its place. Still another comes and pushes that one away. As before the eternal blue sky, clouds of various hue and colour come, remain for a short time and disappear, leaving it the same eternal blue, even so are you, eternally pure, eternally perfect. You are the veritable Gods of the universe; nay, there are not two — there is but One. It is a mistake to say, "you and I"; say "I". It is I who am eating in millions of mouths; how can I be hungry? It is I who am working through an infinite number of hands; how can I be inactive? It is I who am living the life of the whole universe; where is death for me? I am beyond all life, beyond all death. Where shall I seek for freedom? I am free by my nature. Who can bind me — the God of this universe? The scriptures of the world are but little maps, wanting to delineate my glory, who am the only existence of the universe. Then what are these books to me? Thus says the Advaitist.

"Know the truth and be free in a moment." All the darkness will then vanish. When man has seen himself as one with the Infinite Being of the universe, when all separateness has ceased, when all men and women, an gods and angels, all animals and plants, and the whole universe have melted into that Oneness, then all fear disappears. Can I hurt myself? Can I kill myself? Can I injure myself? Whom to fear? Can you fear yourself? Then will all sorrow disappear. What can cause me sorrow? I am the One Existence of the universe. Then all jealousies will disappear; of whom to be jealous? Of myself? Then all bad feelings disappear. Against whom can I have bad feeling? Against myself? There is none in the universe but I. And this is the one way, says the Vedantist, to Knowledge. Kill out this differentiation, kill out this superstition that there are many. "He who in this world of many sees that One, he who in this mass of insentiency sees that one Sentient Being, he who in this world of shadows catches that Reality, unto him belongs eternal peace, unto none else, unto none else."

These are the salient points of the three steps which Indian religious thought has taken in regard to God. We have seen that it began with the Personal, the extra-cosmic God. It went from the external to the internal cosmic body, God immanent in the universe, and ended in identifying the soul itself with that God, and making one Soul, a unit of all these various manifestations in the universe. This is the last word of the Vedas. It begins with dualism, goes through a qualified monism and ends in perfect monism. We know how very few in this world can come to the last, or even dare believe in it, and fewer still dare act according to it. Yet we know that therein lies the explanation of all ethics, of all morality and all spirituality in the universe. Why is it that every one says, "Do good to others?" Where is the explanation? Why is it that all great men have preached the brotherhood of mankind, and greater men the brotherhood of all lives? Because whether they were conscious of it or not, behind all that, through all their irrational and personal superstitions, was peering forth the eternal light of the Self denying all manifoldness, and asserting that the whole universe is but one.

Again, the last word gave us one universe, which through the senses we see as matter, through the intellect as souls, and through the spirit as God. To the man who throws upon himself veils, which the world calls wickedness and evil, this very universe will change and become a hideous place; to another man, who wants enjoyments, this very universe will change its appearance and become a heaven, and to the perfect man the whole thing will vanish and become his own Self.

Now, as society exists at the present time, all these three stages are necessary; the one does not deny the other, one is simply the fulfilment of the other. The Advaitist or the qualified Advaitist does not say that dualism is wrong; it is a right view, but a lower one. It is on the way to truth; therefore let everybody work out his own vision of this universe, according to his own ideas. Injure none, deny the position of none; take man where he stands and, if you can, lend him a helping hand and put him on a higher platform, but do not injure and do not destroy. All will come to truth in the long run. "When all the desires of the heart will be vanquished, then this very mortal will become immortal"— then the very man will become God.

Chapter XV
The Atman: its Bondage and Freedom

Delivered in America

According to the Advaita philosophy, there is only one thing real in the universe, which it calls Brahman; everything else is unreal, manifested and manufactured out of Brahman by the power of Maya. To reach back to that Brahman is our goal. We are, each one of us, that Brahman, that Reality, plus this Maya. If we can get rid of this Maya or ignorance, then we become what we really are. According to this philosophy, each man consists of three parts — the body, the internal organ or the mind, and behind that, what is called the Atman, the Self. The body is the external coating and the mind is the internal coating of the Atman who is the real perceiver, the real enjoyer, the being in the body who is working the body by means of the internal organ or the mind.

The Atman is the only existence in the human body which is immaterial. Because it is immaterial, it cannot be a compound, and because it is not a compound, it does not obey the law of cause and effect, and so it is immortal. That which is immortal can have no beginning because everything with a beginning must have an end. It also follows that it must be formless; there cannot be any fond without matter. Everything that has form must have a beginning and an end. We have none of us seen a form which had not a beginning and will not have an end. A form comes out of a combination of force and matter. This chair has a peculiar form, that is to say a certain quantity of matter is acted upon by a certain amount of force and made to assume a particular shape. The shape is the result of a combination of matter and force. The combination cannot be eternal; there must come to every combination a time when it will dissolve. So all forms have a beginning and an end. We know our body will perish; it had a beginning and it will have an end. But the Self having no form, cannot be bound by the law of beginning and end. It is existing from infinite time; just as time is eternal, so is the Self of man eternal. Secondly, it must be all-pervading. It is only form that is conditioned and limited by space; that which is formless cannot be confined in space. So, according to Advaita Vedanta, the Self, the Atman, in you, in me, in every one, is omnipresent. You are as much in the sun now as in this earth, as much in England as in America. But the Self acts through the mind and the body, and where they are, its action is visible.

Each work we do, each thought we think, produces an impression, called in Sanskrit Samskara, upon the mind and the sum total of these impressions becomes the tremendous force which is called "character". The character of a man is what he has created for himself; it is the result of the mental and physical actions that he has done in his life. The sum total of the Samskaras is the force which gives a man the next direction after death. A man dies; the body falls away and goes back to the elements; but the Samskaras remain, adhering to the mind which, being made of fine material, does not dissolve, because the finer the material, the more persistent it is. But the mind also dissolves in the long run, and that is what we are struggling for. In this connection, the best illustration that comes to my mind is that of the whirlwind. Different currents of air coming from different directions meet and at the meeting-point become united and go on rotating; as they rotate, they form a body of dust, drawing in bits of paper, straw, etc., at one place, only to drop them and go on to another, and so go on rotating, raising and forming bodies out of the materials which are before them. Even so the forces, called Prana in Sanskrit, come together and form the body and the mind out of matter, and move on until the body falls down, when they raise other materials to make another body, and when this falls, another rises, and thus the process goes on. Force cannot travel without matter. So when the body falls down, the mind-stuff remains, Prana in the form of Samskaras acting on it; and then it goes on to another point, raises up another whirl from fresh materials, and begins another motion; and so it travels from place to place until the force is all spent; and then it falls down, ended. So when the mind will end, be broken to pieces entirely, without leaving any Samskara, we shall be entirely free, and until that time we are in bondage; until then the Atman is covered by the whirl of the mind, and imagines it is being taken from place to place. When the whirl falls down, the Atman finds that It is all-pervading. It can go where It likes, is entirely free, and is able to manufacture any number of minds or bodies It likes; but until then It can go only with the whirl. This freedom is the goal towards which we are all moving.

Suppose there is a ball in this room, and we each have a mallet in our hands and begin to strike the ball, giving it hundreds of blows, driving it from point to point, until at last it flies out of the room. With what force and in what direction will it go out? These will be determined by the forces that have been acting upon it all through the room. All the different blows that have been given will have their effects. Each one of our actions, mental and physical, is such a blow. The human mind is a ball which is being hit. We are being hit about this room of the world all the time, and our passage out of it is determined by the force of all these blows. In each case, the speed and direction of the ball is determined by the hits it has received; so all our actions in this world will determine our future birth. Our present birth, therefore, is the result of our past. This is one case: suppose I give you an endless chain, in which there is a black link and a white link alternately, without beginning and without end, and suppose I ask you the nature of the chain. At first you will find a difficulty in determining its nature, the chain being infinite at both ends, but slowly you find out it is a chain. You soon discover that this infinite chain is a repetition of the two links, black and white, and these multiplied infinitely become a whole chain. If you know the nature of one of these links, you know the nature of the whole chain, because it is a perfect repetition. All our lives, past, present, and future, form, as it were, an infinite chain, without beginning and without end, each link of which is one life, with two ends, birth and death. What we are and do here is being repeated again and again, with but little variation. So if we know these two links, we shall know all the passages we shall have to pass through in this world. We see, therefore, that our passage into this world has been exactly determined by our previous passages. Similarly we are in this world by our own actions. Just as we go out with the sum total of our present actions upon us, so we see that we come into it with the sum total of our past actions upon us; that which takes us out is the very same thing that brings us in. What brings us in? Our past deeds. What takes us out? Our own deeds here, and so on and on we go. Like the caterpillar that takes the thread from its own mouth and builds its cocoon and at last finds itself caught inside the cocoon, we have bound ourselves by our own actions, we have thrown the network of our actions around ourselves. We have set the law of causation in motion, and we find it hard to get ourselves out of it. We have set the wheel in motion, and we are being crushed under it. So this philosophy teaches us that we are uniformly being bound by our own actions, good or bad.

The Atman never comes nor goes, is never born nor dies. It is nature moving before the Atman, and the reflection of this motion is on the Atman; and the Atman ignorantly thinks it is moving, and not nature. When the Atman thinks that, it is in bondage; but when it comes to find it never moves, that it is omnipresent, then freedom comes. The Atman in bondage is called Jiva. Thus you see that when it is said that the Atman comes and goes, it is said only for facility of understanding, just as for convenience in studying astronomy you are asked to suppose that the sun moves round the earth, though such is not the case. So the Jiva, the soul, comes to higher or lower states. This is the well-known law of reincarnation; and this law binds all creation.

People in this country think it too horrible that man should come up from an animal. Why? What will be the end of these millions of animals? Are they nothing? If we have a soul, so have they, and if they have none, neither have we. It is absurd to say that man alone has a soul, and the animals none. I have seen men worse than animals.

The human soul has sojourned in lower and higher forms, migrating from one to another, according to the Samskaras or impressions, but it is only in the highest form as man that it attains to freedom. The man form is higher than even the angel form, and of all forms it is the highest; man is the highest being in creation, because he attains to freedom.

All this universe was in Brahman, and it was, as it were, projected out of Him, and has been moving on to go back to the source from which it was projected, like the electricity which comes out of the dynamo, completes the circuit, and returns to it. The same is the case with the soul. Projected from Brahman, it passed through all sorts of vegetable and animal forms, and at last it is in man, and man is the nearest approach to Brahman. To go back to Brahman from which we have been projected is the great struggle of life. Whether people know it or not does not matter. In the universe, whatever we see of motion, of struggles in minerals or plants or animals is an effort to come back to the centre and be at rest. There was an equilibrium, and that has been destroyed; and all parts and atoms and molecules are struggling to find their lost equilibrium again. In this struggle they are combining and re-forming, giving rise to all the wonderful phenomena of nature. All struggles and competitions in animal life, plant life, and everywhere else, all social struggles and wars are but expressions of that eternal struggle to get back to that equilibrium.

The going from birth to death, this travelling, is what is called Samsara in Sanskrit, the round of birth and death literally. All creation, passing through this round, will sooner or later become free. The question may be raised that if we all shall come to freedom, why should we struggle to attain it? If every one is going to be free, we will sit down and wait. It is true that every being will become free, sooner or later; no one can be lost. Nothing can come to destruction; everything must come up. If that is so, what is the use of our struggling? In the first place, the struggle is the only means that will bring us to the centre, and in the second place, we do not know why we struggle. We have to. "Of thousands of men some are awakened to the idea that they will become free." The vast masses of mankind are content with material things, but there are some who awake, and want to get back, who have had enough of this playing, down here. These struggle consciously, while the rest do it unconsciously.

The alpha and omega of Vedanta philosophy is to "give up the world," giving up the unreal and taking the real. Those who are enamoured of the world may ask, "Why should we attempt to get out of it, to go back to the centre? Suppose we have all come from God, but we find this world is pleasurable and nice; then why should we not rather try to get more and more of the world? Why should we try to get out of it?" They say, look at the wonderful improvements going on in the world every day, how much luxury is being manufactured for it. This is very enjoyable. Why should we go away, and strive for something which is not this? The answer is that the world is certain to die, to be broken into pieces and that many times we have had the same enjoyments. All the forms which we are seeing now have been manifested again and again, and the world in which we live has been here many times before. I have been here and talked to you many times before. You will know that it must be so, and the very words that you have been listening to now, you have heard many times before. And many times more it will be the same. Souls were never different, the bodies have been constantly dissolving and recurring. Secondly, these things periodically occur. Suppose here are three or four dice, and when we throw them, one comes up five, another four, another three, and another two. If you keep on throwing, there must come times when those very same numbers will recur. Go on throwing, and no matter how long may be the interval, those numbers must come again. It cannot be asserted in how many throws they will come again; this is the law of chance. So with souls and their associations. However distant may be the periods, the same combinations and dissolutions will happen again and again. The same birth, eating and drinking, and then death, come round again and again. Some never find anything higher than the enjoyments of the world, but those who want to soar higher find that these enjoyments are never final, are only by the way.

Every form, let us say, beginning from the little worm and ending in man, is like one of the cars of the Chicago Ferris Wheel which is in motion all the time, but the occupants change. A man goes into a car, moves with the wheel, and comes out. The wheel goes on and on. A soul enters one form, resides in it for a time, then leaves it and goes into another and quits that again for a third. Thus the round goes on till it comes out of the wheel and becomes free.

Astonishing powers of reading the past and the future of a man's life have been known in every country and every age. The explanation is that so long as the Atman is within the realm of causation— though its inherent freedom is not entirely lost and can assert itself, even to the extent of taking the soul out of the causal chain, as it does in the case of men who become free— its actions are greatly influenced by the causal law and thus make it possible for men, possessed with the insight to trace the sequence of effects, to tell the past and the future.

So long as there is desire or want, it is a sure sign that there is imperfection. A perfect, free being cannot have any desire. God cannot want anything. If He desires, He cannot be God. He will be imperfect. So all the talk about God desiring this and that, and becoming angry and pleased by turns is babies' talk, but means nothing. Therefore it has been taught by all teachers, "Desire nothing, give up all desires and be perfectly satisfied."

A child comes into the world crawling and without teeth, and the old man gets out without teeth and crawling. The extremes are alike, but the one has no experience of the life before him, while the other has gone through it all. When the vibrations of ether are very low, we do not see light, it is darkness; when very high, the result is also darkness. The extremes generally appear to be the same, though one is as distant from the other as the poles. The wall has no desires, so neither has the perfect man. But the wall is not sentient enough to desire, while for the perfect man there is nothing to desire. There are idiots who have no desires in this world, because their brain is imperfect. At the same time, the highest state is when we have no desires, but the two are opposite poles of the same existence. One is near the animal, and the other near to God.

Chapter XVI
The Real and the Apparent Man

Delivered in New York

Here we stand, and our eyes look forward sometimes miles ahead. Man has been doing that since he began to think. He is always looking forward, looking ahead. He wants to know where he goes even after the dissolution of his body. Various theories have been propounded, system after system has been brought forward to suggest explanations. Some have been rejected, while others have been accepted, and thus it will go on, so long as man is here, so long as man thinks. There is some truth in each of these systems. There is a good deal of what is not truth in all of them. I shall try to place before you the sum and substance, the result, of the inquiries in this line that have been made in India. I shall try to harmonise the various thoughts on the subject, as they have come up from time to time among Indian philosophers. I shall try to harmonise the psychologists and the metaphysicians, and, if possible, I shall harmonise them with modern scientific thinkers also.

The one theme of the Vedanta philosophy is the search after unity. The Hindu mind does not care for the particular; it is always after the general, nay, the universal. "What is that, by knowing which everything else is to be known?" That is the one theme. "As through the knowledge of one lump of clay all that is of clay is known, so, what is that, by knowing which this whole universe itself will be known?" That is the one search. The whole of this universe, according to the Hindu philosophers, can be resolved into one material, which they call Akasha. Everything that we see around us, feel, touch, taste, is simply a differentiated manifestation of this Akasha. It is all-pervading, fine. All that we call solids, liquids, or gases, figures, forms, or bodies, the earth, sun, moon, and stars — everything is composed of this Akasha.

What force is it which acts upon this Akasha and manufactures this universe out of it? Along with Akasha exists universal power; all that is power in the universe, manifesting as force or attraction — nay, even as thought — is but a different manifestation of that one power which the Hindus call Prana. This Prana, acting on Akasha, is creating the whole of this universe. In the beginning

156 · The Four Paths of Yoga

Swami Vivekananda

of a cycle, this Prana, as it were, sleeps in the infinite ocean of Akasha. It existed motionless in the beginning. Then arises motion in this ocean of Akasha by the action of this Prana, and as this Prana begins to move, to vibrate, out of this ocean come the various celestial systems, suns, moons, stars, earth, human beings, animals, plants, and the manifestations of all the various forces and phenomena. Every manifestation of power, therefore, according to them, is this Prana. Every material manifestation is Akasha. When this cycle will end, all that we call solid will melt away into the next form, the next finer or the liquid form; that will melt into the gaseous, and that into finer and more uniform heat vibrations, and all will melt back into the original Akasha, and what we now call attraction, repulsion, and motion, will slowly resolve into the original Prana. Then this Prana is said to sleep for a period, again to emerge and to throw out all those forms; and when this period will end, the whole thing will subside again. Thus this process of creation is going down, and coming up, oscillating backwards and forwards. In the language of modern science, it is becoming static during one period, and during another period it is becoming dynamic. At one time it becomes potential, and at the next period it becomes active. This alteration has gone on through eternity.

Yet, this analysis is only partial. This much has been known even to modern physical science. Beyond that, the research of physical science cannot reach. But the inquiry does not stop in consequence. We have not yet found that one, by knowing which everything else will be known. We have resolved the whole universe into two components, into what are called matter and energy, or what the ancient philosophers of India called Akasha and Prana. The next step is to resolve this Akasha and the Prana into their origin. Both can be resolved into the still higher entity which is called mind. It is out of mind, the Mahat, the universally existing thought-power, that these two have been produced. Thought is a still finer manifestation of being than either Akasha or Prana. It is thought that splits itself into these two. The universal thought existed in the beginning, and that manifested, changed, evolved itself into these two Akasha and Prana: and by the combination of these two the whole universe has been produced.

We next come to psychology. I am looking at you. The external sensations are brought to me by the eyes; they are carried by the sensory nerves to the brain. The eyes are not the organs of vision. They are but the external instruments, because if the real organ behind, that which carries the sensation to the brain, is destroyed, I may have twenty eyes, yet I cannot see you. The picture on the retina may be as complete as possible, yet I shall not see you. Therefore, the organ is different from its instruments; behind the instruments, the eyes, there must be the organ So it is with all the sensations. The nose is not the sense of smell; it is but the instrument, and behind it is the organ. With every sense we have, there is first the external instrument in the physical body; behind that in the same physical body, there is the organ; yet these are not sufficient. Suppose I am talking to you, and you are listening to me with close attention. Something happens, say, a bell rings; you will not, perhaps, hear the bell ring. The pulsations of that sound came to your ear, struck the tympanum, the impression was carried by the nerve into the brain; if the whole process was complete up to carrying the impulse to the brain, why did you not hear? Something else was wanting — the mind was not attached to the organ. When the mind detaches itself from the organ, the organ may bring any news to it, but the mind will not receive it. When it attaches itself to the organ, then alone is it possible for the mind to receive the news. Yet, even that does not complete the whole. The instruments may bring the sensation from outside, the organs may carry it inside, the mind may attach itself to the organ, and yet the perception may not be complete. One more factor is necessary; there must be a reaction within. With this reaction comes knowledge. That which is outside sends, as it were, the current of news into my brain. My mind takes it up, and presents it to the intellect, which groups it in relation to pre-received impressions and sends a current of reaction, and with that reaction comes perception. Here, then, is the will. The state of mind which reacts is called Buddhi, the intellect. Yet, even this does not complete the whole. One step more is required. Suppose here is a camera and there is a sheet of cloth, and I try to throw a picture on that sheet. What am I to do? I am to guide various rays of light through the camera to fall upon the sheet and become grouped there. Something is necessary to have the picture thrown upon, which does not move. I cannot form a picture upon something which is moving; that something must be stationary, because the rays of light which I throw on it are moving, and these moving rays of light, must be gathered, unified, co-ordinated, and completed upon something which is stationary. Similar is the case with the sensations which these organs of ours are carrying inside and presenting to the mind, and which the mind in its turn is presenting to the intellect. This process will not be complete unless there is something permanent in the background upon which the picture, as it were, may be formed, upon which we may unify all the different impressions. What is it that gives unity to the changing whole of our being? What is it that keeps up the identity of the moving thing moment after moment? What is it upon which all our different impressions are pieced together, upon which the perceptions, as it were, come together, reside, and form a united whole? We have found that to serve this end there must be something, and we also see that that something must be, relatively to the body and mind, motionless. The sheet of cloth upon which the camera throws the picture is, relatively to the rays of light, motionless, else there will be no picture. That is to say, the perceiver must be an individual. This something upon which the mind is painting all these pictures, this something upon which our sensations, carried by the mind and intellect, are placed and grouped and formed into a unity, is what is called the soul of man.

We have seen that it is the universal cosmic mind that splits itself into the Akasha and Prana, and beyond mind we have found the soul in us. In the universe, behind the universal mind, there is a Soul that exists, and it is called God. In the individual it is the soul of man. In this universe, in the cosmos, just as the universal mind becomes evolved into Akasha and Prana, even so, we may find that the Universal Soul Itself becomes evolved as mind. Is it really so with the individual man? Is his mind the creator of his body, and his soul the creator of his mind? That is to say, are his body, his mind, and his soul three different existences or are they three in one or, again, are they different states of existence of the same unit being? We shall gradually try to find an answer to this question. The first step that we have now gained is this: here is this external body, behind this external body are the organs, the mind, the intellect, and behind this is the soul. At the first step, we have found, as it were, that the soul is separate from the body, separate from the mind itself. Opinions in the religious world become divided at this point, and the departure is this. All those religious views which generally pass under the name of dualism hold that this soul is qualified, that it is of various qualities, that all feelings of enjoyment, pleasure, and pain really belong to the soul. The non-dualists deny that the soul has any such qualities; they say it is unqualified.

Let me first take up the dualists, and try to present to you their position with regard to the soul and its destiny; next, the system that contradicts them; and lastly, let us try to find the harmony which non-dualism will bring to us. This soul of man, because it is separate from the mind and body, because it is not composed of Akasha and Prana, must be immortal. Why? What do we mean by mortality? Decomposition. And that is only possible for things that are the result of composition; anything that is made of two or three ingredients must become decomposed. That alone which is not the result of composition can never become decomposed, and, therefore, can never die. It is immortal. It has been existing throughout eternity; it is uncreate. Every item of creation is simply a composition; no one ever saw creation come out of nothing. All that we know of creation is the combination of already existing things into newer forms. That being so, this soul of man, being simple, must have been existing for ever, and it will exist for ever. When this body falls off, the soul lives on. According to the Vedantists, when this body dissolves, the vital forces of the man go back to his mind and the mind becomes dissolved, as it were, into the Prana, and that Prana enters into the soul of man, and the soul of man comes out, clothed, as it were, with what they call the fine body, the mental body, or spiritual body, as you may like to call it. In this body are the Samskaras of the man. What are the Samskaras? This mind is like a lake, and every thought is like a wave upon that lake. Just as in the lake waves rise and then fall down and disappear, so these thought-waves are continually rising in the mind-stuff and then disappearing, but they do not disappear for ever. They become finer and finer, but they are all there, ready to start up at another time when called upon to do so. Memory is simply calling back into waveform some of those thoughts which have gone into that finer state of existence. Thus, everything that we have thought, every action that we have done, is lodged in the mind; it is all there in fine form, and when a man dies, the sum total of these impressions is in the mind, which again works upon a little fine material as a medium. The soul, clothed, as it were, with these impressions and the fine body, passes out, and the destiny of the soul is guided by the resultant of all the different forces represented by the different impressions. According to us, there are three different goals for the soul.

Those that are very spiritual, when they die, follow the solar rays and reach what is called the solar sphere, through which they reach what is called the lunar sphere, and through that they reach what is called the sphere of lightning, and there they meet with another soul who is already blessed, and he guides the new-comer forward to the highest of all spheres, which is called the Brahmaloka, the sphere of Brahma. There these souls attain to omniscience and omnipotence, become almost as powerful and all-knowing as God Himself; and they reside there for ever, according to the dualists, or, according to the non-dualists, they become one with the Universal at the end of the cycle. The next class of persons, who have been doing good work with selfish motives, are carried by the results of their good works, when they die, to what is called lunar sphere, where there are various heavens, and there they acquire fine bodies, the bodies of gods. They become gods and live there and enjoy the blessing of heaven for a long period; and after that period is finished, the old Karma is again upon them, and so they fall back again to the earth; they come down through the spheres of air and clouds and all these various regions, and, at last, reach the earth through raindrops. There on the earth they attach themselves to some cereal which is eventually eaten by some man who is fit to supply them with material to make a new body. The last class, namely, the wicked, when they die, become ghosts or demons, and live somewhere midway between the lunar sphere and this earth. Some try to disturb mankind, some are friendly; and after living there for some time they also fall back to the earth and become animals. After living for some time in an animal body they get released, and come back, and become men again, and thus get one more chance to work out their salvation. We see, then, that those who have nearly attained to perfection, in whom only very little of impurity remains, go to the Brahmaloka through the rays of the sun; those who were a middling sort of people, who did some good work here with the idea of going to heaven, go to the heavens in the lunar sphere and there obtain god-bodies; but they have again to become men and so have one more chance to become perfect. Those that are very wicked become ghosts and demons, and then they may have to become animals; after that they become men again and get another chance to perfect themselves. This earth is called the Karma-Bhumi, the sphere of Karma. Here alone man makes his good or bad Karma. When a man wants to go to heaven and does good works for that purpose, he becomes as good and does not as such store up any bad Karma. He just enjoys the effects of the good work he did on earth; and when this good Karma is exhausted, there come, upon him the resultant force of all the evil Karma he had previously stored up in life, and that brings him down again to this earth. In the same way, those that become ghosts remain in that state, not giving rise to fresh Karma, but suffer the evil results of their past misdeeds, and later on remain for a time in an animal body without causing any fresh Karma. When that period is finished, they too become men again. The states of reward and punishment due to good and bad Karmas are devoid of the force generating fresh Karmas; they have only to be enjoyed or suffered. If there is an extraordinarily good or an extraordinarily evil Karma, it bears fruit very quickly. For instance, if a man has been doing many evil things all his life, but does one good act, the result of that good act will immediately appear, but when that result has been gone through, all the evil acts must produce their results also. All men who do certain good and great acts, but the general tenor of whose lives has not been correct, will become gods; and after living for some time in god-bodies, enjoying the powers of gods, they will have again to become men; when the power of the good acts is thus finished, the old evil comes up to be worked out. Those who do extraordinarily evil acts have to put on ghost and devil bodies, and when the effect of those evil actions is exhausted, the little good action which remains associated with them, makes them again become men. The way to Brahmaloka, from which there is no more fall or return, is called the Devayana, i.e. the way to God; the way to heaven is known as Pitriyana, i.e. the way to the fathers.

Man, therefore, according to the Vedanta philosophy, is the greatest being that is in the universe, and this world of work the best place in it, because only herein is the greatest and the best chance for him to become perfect. Angels or gods, whatever you may call them, have all to become men, if they want to become perfect. This is the great centre, the wonderful poise, and the wonderful opportunity — this human life.

We come next to the other aspect of philosophy. There are Buddhists who deny the whole theory of the soul that I have just now been propounding. "What use is there," says the Buddhist, "to assume something as the substratum, as the background of this body and mind? Why may we not allow thoughts to run on? Why admit a third substance beyond this organism, composed of mind and body, a third substance called the soul? What is its use? Is not this organism sufficient to explain itself? Why take anew a third something?" These arguments are very powerful. This reasoning is very strong. So far as outside research goes, we see that this organism is a sufficient explanation of itself — at least, many of us see it in that light. Why then need there be a soul as substratum, as a something which is neither mind nor body but stands as a background for both mind and body? Let there be only mind and body. Body is the name of a stream of matter continuously changing. Mind is the name of a stream of consciousness or thought continuously changing. What produces the apparent unity between these two? This unity does not really exist, let us say. Take, for instance, a lighted torch, and whirl it rapidly before you. You see a circle of fire. The circle does not really exist, but because the torch is continually moving, it leaves the appearance of a circle. So there is no unity in this life; it is a mass of matter continually rushing down, and the whole of this matter you may call one unity, but no more. So is mind; each thought is separate from every other thought; it is only the rushing current that leaves behind the illusion of unity; there is no need of a third substance. This universal phenomenon of body and mind is all that really is; do not posit something behind it. You will find that this Buddhist thought has been taken up by certain sects and schools in modern times, and all of them claim that it is new — their own invention. This has been the central idea of most of the Buddhistic philosophies, that this world is itself all-sufficient; that you need not ask for any background at all; all that is, is this sense-universe: what is the use of thinking of something as a support to this universe? Everything is the aggregate of qualities; why should there be a hypothetical substance in which they should inhere? The idea of substance comes from the rapid interchange of qualities, not from something unchangeable which exists behind them. We see how wonderful some of these arguments are, and they appeal easily to the ordinary experience of humanity— in fact, not one in a million can think of anything other than phenomena. To the vast majority of men nature appears to be only a changing, whirling, combining, mingling mass of change. Few of us ever have a glimpse of the calm sea behind. For us it is always lashed into waves; this universe appears to us only as a tossing mass of waves. Thus we find these two opinions. One is that there is something behind both body and mind which is an unchangeable and immovable substance; and the other is that there is no such thing as immovability or unchangeability in the universe; it is all change and nothing but change. The solution of this difference comes in the next step of thought, namely, the non-dualistic.

It says that the dualists are right in finding something behind all, as a background which does not change; we cannot conceive change without there being something unchangeable. We can only conceive of anything that is changeable, by knowing something which is less changeable, and this also must appear more changeable in comparison with something else which is less changeable, and so on and on, until we are bound to admit that there must be something which never changes at all. The whole of this manifestation must have been in a state of non-manifestation, calm and silent, being the balance of opposing forces, so to say, when no force operated, because force acts when a disturbance of the equilibrium comes in. The universe is ever hurrying on to return to that state of equilibrium again. If we are certain of any fact whatsoever, we are certain of this. When the dualists claim that there is a something which does not change, they are perfectly right, but their analysis that it is an underlying something which is neither the body nor the mind, a something separate from both, is wrong. So far as the Buddhists say that the whole universe is a mass of change, they are perfectly right; so long as I am separate from the universe, so long as I stand back and look at something before me, so long as there are two things— the looker-on and the thing looked upon— it will appear always that the universe is one of change, continuously changing all the time. But the reality is that there is both change and changelessness in this universe. It is not that the soul and the mind and the body are three separate existences, for this organism made of these three is really one. It is the same thing which appears as the body, as the mind, and as the thing beyond mind and body, but it is not at the same time all these. He who sees the body does not see the mind even, he who sees the mind does not see that which he calls the soul — for him the body and mind have vanished. He who sees only motion never sees absolute calm, and he who sees absolute calm — for him motion has vanished. A rope is taken for a snake. He who sees the rope as the snake, for him the rope has vanished, and when the delusion ceases and he looks at the rope, the snake has vanished.

There is then but one all-comprehending existence, and that one appears as manifold. This Self or Soul or Substance is all that exists in the universe. That Self or Substance or Soul is, in the language of non-dualism, the Brahman appearing to be manifold by the interposition of name and form. Look at the waves in the sea. Not one wave is really different from the sea, but what makes the wave apparently different? Name and form; the form of the wave and the name which we give to it, "wave". This is what makes it different from the sea. When name and form go, it is the same sea. Who can make any real difference between the wave and the sea? So this whole universe is that one Unit Existence; name and form have created all these various differences. As when the sun shines upon millions of globules of water, upon each particle is seen a most perfect representation of the sun, so the one Soul, the one Self, the one Existence of the universe, being reflected on all these numerous globules of varying names and forms, appears to be various. But it is in reality only one. There is no "I" nor "you"; it is all one. It is either all "I" or all "you". This idea of duality, calf two, is entirely false, and the whole universe, as we ordinarily know it, is the result of this false knowledge. When discrimination comes and man finds there are not two but one, he finds that he is himself this universe. "It is I who am this universe as it now exists, a continuous mass of change. It is I who am beyond all changes, beyond all qualities, the eternally perfect, the eternally blessed."

There is, therefore, but one Atman, one Self, eternally pure, eternally perfect, unchangeable, unchanged; it has never changed; and all these various changes in the universe are but appearances in that one Self.

Upon it name and form have painted all these dreams; it is the form that makes the wave different from the sea. Suppose the wave subsides, will the form remain? No, it will vanish. The existence of the wave was entirely dependent upon the existence of the sea, but the existence of the sea was not at all dependent upon the existence of the wave. The form remains so long as the wave remains, but as soon as the wave leaves it, it vanishes, it cannot remain. This name and form is the outcome of what is called Maya. It is this Maya that is making individuals, making one appear different from another. Yet it has no existence. Maya cannot be said to exist. Form cannot be said to exist, because it depends upon the existence of another thing. It cannot be said as not to exist, seeing that it makes all this difference. According to the Advaita philosophy, then, this Maya or ignorance— or name and form, or, as it has been called in Europe, "time, space, and causality"— is out of this one Infinite Existence showing us the manifoldness of the universe; in substance, this universe is one. So long as any one thinks that there are two ultimate realities, he is mistaken. When he has come to know that there is but one, he is right. This is what is being proved to us every day, on the physical plane, on the mental plane, and also on the spiritual plane. Today it has been demonstrated that you and I, the sun, the moon, and the stars are but the different names of different spots in the same ocean of matter, and that this matter is continuously changing in its configuration. This particle of energy that was in the sun several months ago may be in the human being now; tomorrow it may be in an animal, the day after tomorrow it may be in a plant. It is ever coming and going. It is all one unbroken, infinite mass of matter, only differentiated by names and forms. One point is called the sun; another, the moon; another, the stars; another, man; another, animal; another, plant; and so on. And all these names are fictitious; they have no reality, because the whole is a continuously changing mass of matter. This very same universe, from another standpoint, is an ocean of thought, where each one of us is a point called a particular mind. You are a mind, I am a mind, everyone is a mind; and the very same universe viewed from the standpoint of knowledge, when the eyes have been cleared of delusions, when the mind has become pure, appears to be the unbroken Absolute Being, the ever pure, the unchangeable, the immortal.

What then becomes of all this threefold eschatology of the dualist, that when a man dies he goes to heaven, or goes to this or that sphere, and that the wicked persons become ghosts, and become animals, and so forth? None comes and none goes, says the non-dualist. How can you come and go? You are infinite; where is the place for you to go? In a certain school a number of little children were being examined. The examiner had foolishly put all sorts of difficult questions to the little children. Among others there was this question: "Why does not the earth fall?" His intention was to bring out the idea of gravitation or some other intricate scientific truth from these children. Most of them could not even understand the question, and so they gave all sorts of wrong answers. But one bright little girl answered it with another question: "Where shall it fall?" The very question of the examiner was nonsense on the face of it. There is no up and down in the universe; the idea is only relative. So it is with regard to the soul; the very question of birth and death in regard to it is utter nonsense. Who goes and who comes? Where are you not? Where is the heaven that you are not in already? Omnipresent is the Self of man. Where is it to go? Where is it not to go? It is everywhere. So all this childish dream and puerile illusion of birth and death, of heavens and higher heavens and lower worlds, all vanish immediately for the perfect. For the nearly perfect it vanishes after showing them the several scenes up to Brahmaloka. It continues for the ignorant.

How is it that the whole world believes in going to heaven, and in dying and being born? I am studying a book, page after page is being read and turned over. Another page comes and is turned over. Who changes? Who comes and goes? Not I, but the book. This whole nature is a book before the soul, chapter after chapter is being read and turned over, and every now and then a scene opens. That is read and turned over. A fresh one comes, but the soul is ever the same — eternal. It is nature that is changing, not the soul of man. This never changes. Birth and death are in nature, not in you. Yet the ignorant are deluded; just as we under delusion think that the sun is moving and not the earth, in exactly the same way we think that we are dying, and not nature. These are all, therefore, hallucinations. Just as it is a hallucination when we think that the fields are moving and not the railway train, exactly in the same manner is the hallucination of birth and death. When men are in a certain frame of mind, they see this very existence as the earth, as the sun, the moon, the stars; and all those who are in the same state of mind see the same things. Between you and me there may be millions of beings on different planes of existence. They will never see us, nor we them; we only see those who are in the same state of mind and on the same plane with us. Those musical instruments respond which have the same attunement of vibration, as it were; if the state of vibration, which they call "man-vibration", should be changed, no longer would men be seen here; the whole "man-universe" would vanish, and instead of that, other scenery would come before us, perhaps gods and the god-universe, or perhaps, for the wicked man, devils and the diabolic world; but all would be only different views of the one universe. It is this universe which, from the human plane, is seen as the earth, the sun, the moon, the stars, and all such things — it is this very universe which, seen from the plane of wickedness, appears as a place of punishment. And this very universe is seen as heaven by those who want to see it as heaven. Those who have been dreaming of going to a God who is sitting on a throne, and of standing there praising Him all their lives, when they die, will simply see a vision of what they have in their minds; this very universe will simply change into a vast heaven, with all sorts of winged beings flying about and a God sitting on a throne. These heavens are all of man's own making. So what the dualist says is true, says the Advaitin, but it is all simply of his own making. These spheres and devils and gods and reincarnations and transmigrations are all mythology; so also is this human life. The great mistake that men always make is to think that this life alone is true. They understand it well enough when other things are called mythologies, but are never willing to admit the same of their own position. The whole thing as it appears is mere mythology, and the greatest of all lies is that we are bodies, which we never were nor even can be. It is the greatest of all lies that we are mere men; we are the God of the universe. In worshipping God we have been always worshipping our own hidden Self. The worst lie that you ever tell yourself is that you were born a sinner or a wicked man. He alone is a sinner who sees a sinner in another man. Suppose there is a baby here, and you place a bag of gold on the table. Suppose a robber comes and takes the gold away. To the baby it is all the same; because there is no robber inside, there is no robber outside. To sinners and vile men, there is vileness outside, but not to good men. So the wicked see this universe as a hell, and the partially good see it as heaven, while the perfect beings realise it as God Himself. Then alone the veil falls from the eyes, and the man, purified and cleansed, finds his whole vision changed. The bad dreams that have been torturing him for millions of years, all vanish, and he who was thinking of himself either as a man, or a god, or a demon, he who was thinking of himself as living in low places, in high places, on earth, in heaven, and so on, finds that he is really omnipresent; that all time is in him, and that he is not in time; that all the heavens are in him, that he is not in any heaven; and that all the gods that man ever worshipped are in him, and that he is not in any one of those gods. He was the manufacturer of gods and demons, of men and plants and animals and stones, and the real nature of man now stands unfolded to him as being higher than heaven, more perfect than this universe of ours, more infinite than infinite time, more omnipresent than the omnipresent ether. Thus alone man becomes fearless, and becomes free. Then all delusions cease, all miseries vanish, all fears come to an end for ever. Birth goes away and with it death; pains fly, and with them fly away pleasures; earths vanish, and with them vanish heavens; bodies vanish, and with them vanishes the mind also. For that man disappears the whole universe, as it were. This searching, moving, continuous struggle of forces stops for ever, and that which was manifesting itself as force and matter, as struggles of nature, as nature itself, as heavens and earths and plants and animals and men and angels, all that becomes transfigured into one infinite, unbreakable, unchangeable existence, and the knowing man finds that he is one with that existence. "Even as clouds of various colours come before the sky, remain there for a second and then vanish away," even so before this soul are all these visions coming, of earths and heavens, of the moon and the gods, of pleasures and pains; but they all pass away leaving the one infinite, blue, unchangeable sky. The sky never changes; it is the clouds that change. It is a mistake to think that the sky is changed. It is a mistake to think that we are impure, that we are limited, that we are separate. The real man is the one Unit Existence.

Two questions now arise. The first is: "Is it possible to realise this? So far it is doctrine, philosophy, but is it possible to realise it?" It is. There are men still living in this world for whom delusion has vanished for ever. Do they immediately die after such realisation? Not so soon as we should think. Two wheels joined by one pole are running together. If I get hold of one of the wheels and, with an axe, cut the pole asunder, the wheel which I have got hold of stops, but upon the other wheel is its past momentum, so it runs on a little arid then falls down. This pure and perfect being, the soul, is one wheel, and this external hallucination of body and mind is the other wheel, joined together by the pole of work, of Karma. Knowledge is the axe which will sever the bond between the two, and the wheel of the soul will stop— stop thinking that it is coming and going, living and dying, stop thinking that it is nature and has wants and desires, and will find that it is perfect, desireless. But upon the other wheel, that of the body and mind, will be the momentum of past acts; so it will live for some time, until that momentum of past work is exhausted, until that momentum is worked away, and then the body and mind fall, and the soul becomes free. No more is there any going to heaven and coming back, not even any going to the Brahmaloka, or to any of the highest of the spheres, for where is he to come from, or to go to? The man who has in this life attained to this state, for whom, for a minute at least, the ordinary vision of the world has changed and the reality has been apparent, he is called the "Living Free". This is the goal of the Vedantin, to attain freedom while living.

Once in Western India I was travelling in the desert country on the coast of the Indian Ocean. For days and days I used to travel on foot through the desert, but it was to my surprise that I saw every day beautiful lakes, with trees all round them, and the shadows of the trees upside down and vibrating there. "How wonderful it looks and they call this a desert country!" I said to myself. Nearly a month I travelled, seeing these wonderful lakes and trees and plants. One day I was very thirsty and wanted to have a drink of water, so I started to go to one of these clear, beautiful lakes, and as I approached, it vanished. And with a flash it came to my brain, "This is the mirage about which I have read all my life," and with that came also the idea that throughout the whole of this month, every day, I had been seeing the mirage and did not know it. The next morning I began my march. There was again the lake, but with it came also the idea that it was the mirage and not a true lake. So is it with this universe. We are all travelling in this mirage of the world day after day, month after month, year after year, not knowing that it is a mirage. One day it will break up, but it will come back again; the body has to remain under the power of past Karma, and so the mirage will come back. This world will come back upon us so long as we are bound by Karma: men, women, animals, plants, our attachments and duties, all will come back to us, but not with the same power. Under the influence of the new knowledge the strength of Karma will be broken, its poison will be lost. It becomes transformed, for along with it there comes the idea that we know it now, that the sharp distinction between the reality and the mirage has been known.

This world will not then be the same world as before. There is, however, a danger here. We see in every country people taking up this philosophy and saying, "I am beyond all virtue and vice; so I am not bound by any moral laws; I may do anything I like." You may find many fools in this country at the present time, saying, "I am not bound; I am God Himself; let me do anything I like." This is not right, although it is true that the soul is beyond all laws, physical, mental, or moral. Within law is bondage; beyond law is freedom. It is also true that freedom is of the nature of the soul, it is its birthright: that real freedom of the soul shines through veils of matter in the form of the apparent freedom of man. Every moment of your life you feel that you are free. We cannot live, talk, or breathe for a moment without feeling that we are free; but, at the same time, a little thought shows us that we are like machines and not free. What is true then? Is this idea of freedom a delusion? One party holds that the idea of freedom is a delusion; another says that the idea of bondage is a delusion. How does this happen? Man is really free, the real man cannot but be free. It is when he comes into the world of Maya, into name and form, that he becomes bound. Free will is a misnomer. Will can never be free. How can it be? It is only when the real man has become bound that his will comes into existence, and not before. The will of man is bound, but that which is the foundation of that will is eternally free. So, even in the state of bondage which we call human life or god-life, on earth or in heaven, there yet remains to us that recollection of the freedom which is ours by divine right. And consciously or unconsciously we are all struggling towards it. When a man has attained his own freedom, how can he be bound by any law? No law in this universe can bind him, for this universe itself is his.

He is the whole universe. Either say he is the whole universe or say that to him there is no universe. How can he have then all these little ideas about sex and about country? How can he say, I am a man, I am a woman I am a child? Are they not lies? He knows that they are. How can he say that these are man's rights, and these others are woman's rights? Nobody has rights; nobody separately exists. There is neither man nor woman; the soul is sexless, eternally pure. It is a lie to say that I am a man or a woman, or to say that I belong to this country or that. All the world is my country, the whole universe is mine, because I have clothed myself with it as my body. Yet we see that there are people in this world who are ready to assert these doctrines, and at the same time do things which we should call filthy; and if we ask them why they do so, they tell us that it is our delusion and that they can do nothing wrong. What is the test by which they are to be judged? The test is here.

Though evil and good are both conditioned manifestations of the soul, yet evil is the most external coating, and good is the nearer coating of the real man, the Self. And unless a man cuts through the layer of evil he cannot reach the layer of good, and unless he has passed through both the layers of good and evil he cannot reach the Self. He who reaches the Self, what remains attached to him? A little Karma, a little bit of the momentum of past life, but it is all good momentum. Until the bad momentum is entirely worked out and past impurities are entirely burnt, it is impossible for any man to see and realise truth. So, what is left attached to the man who has reached the Self and seen the truth is the remnant of the good impressions of past life, the good momentum. Even if he lives in the body and works incessantly, he works only to do good; his lips speak only benediction to all; his hands do only good works; his mind can only think good thoughts; his presence is a blessing wherever he goes. He is himself a living blessing. Such a man will, by his very presence, change even the most wicked persons into saints. Even if he does not speak, his very presence will be a blessing to mankind. Can such men do any evil; can they do wicked deeds? There is, you must remember, all the difference of pole to pole between realisation and mere talking. Any fool can talk. Even parrots talk. Talking is one thing, and realising is another. Philosophies, and doctrines, and arguments, and books, and theories, and churches, and sects, and all these things are good in their own way; but when that realisation comes, these things drop away. For instance, maps are good, but when you see the country itself, and look again at the maps, what a great difference you find! So those that have realised truth do not require the ratiocinations of logic and all other gymnastics of the intellect to make them understand the truth; it is to them the life of their lives, concretised, made more than tangible. It is, as the sages of the Vedanta say, "even as a fruit in your hand"; you can stand up and say, it is here. So those that have realised the truth will stand up and say, "Here is the Self. You may argue with them by the year, but they will smile at you; they will regard it all as child's prattle; they will let the child prattle on. They have realised the truth and are full. Suppose you have seen a country, and another man comes to you and tries to argue with you that that country never existed, he may go on arguing indefinitely, but your only attitude of mind towards him must be to hold that the man is fit for a lunatic asylum. So the man of realisation says, "All this talk in the world about its little religions is but prattle; realisation is the soul, the very essence of religion." Religion can be realised. Are you ready? Do you want it? You will get the realisation if you do, and then you will be truly religious. Until you have attained realisation there is no difference between you and atheists. The atheists are sincere, but the man who says that he believes in religion and never attempts to realise it is not sincere.

The next question is to know what comes after realisation. Suppose we have realised this oneness of the universe, that we are that one Infinite Being, and suppose we have realised that this Self is the only Existence and that it is the same Self which is manifesting in all these various phenomenal forms, what becomes of us after that? Shall we become inactive, get into a corner and sit down there and die away? "What good will it do to the world?" That old question! In the first place, why should it do good to the world? Is there any reason why it should? What right has any one to ask the question, "What good will it do to the world?" What is meant by that? A baby likes candies. Suppose you are conducting investigations in connection with some subject of electricity and the baby asks you, "Does it buy candies?" "No" you answer. "Then what good will it do?" says the baby. So men stand up and say, "What good will this do to the world; will it give us money?" "No." "Then what good is there in it?" That is what men mean by doing good to the world. Yet religious realisation does all the good to the world. People are afraid that when they attain to it, when they realise that there is but one, the fountains of love will be dried up, that everything in life will go away, and that all they love will vanish for them, as it were, in this life and in the life to come. People never stop to think that those who bestowed the least thought on their own individualities have been the greatest workers in the world. Then alone a man loves when he finds that the object of his love is not any low, little, mortal thing. Then alone a man loves when he finds that the object of his love is not a clod of earth, but it is the veritable God Himself. The wife will love the husband the more when she thinks that the husband is God Himself. The husband will love the wife the more when he knows that the wife is God Himself. That mother will love the children more who thinks that the children are God Himself. That man will love his greatest enemy who knows that that very enemy is God Himself. That man will love a holy man who knows that the holy man is God Himself, and that very man will also love the unholiest of men because he knows the background of that unholiest of men is even He, the Lord. Such a man becomes a world-mover for whom his little self is dead and God stands in its place. The whole universe will become transfigured to him. That which is painful and miserable will all vanish; struggles will all depart and go. Instead of being a prison-house, where we every day struggle and fight and compete for a morsel of bread, this universe will then be to us a playground. Beautiful will be this universe then! Such a man alone has the right to stand up and say, "How beautiful is this world!" He alone has the right to say that it is all good. This will be the great good to the world resulting from such realisation, that instead of this world going on with all its friction and clashing, if all mankind today realise only a bit of that great truth, the aspect of the whole world will be changed, and, in place of fighting and quarrelling, there would be a reign of peace. This indecent and brutal hurry which forces us to go ahead of every one else will then vanish from the world. With it will vanish all struggle, with it will vanish all hate, with it will vanish all jealousy, and all evil will vanish away for ever. Gods will live then upon this earth. This very earth will then become heaven, and what evil can there be when gods are playing with gods, when gods are working with gods, and gods are loving gods? That is the great utility of divine realisation. Everything that you see in society will be changed and transfigured then. No more will you think of man as evil; and that is the first great gain. No more will you stand up and sneeringly cast a glance at a poor man or woman who has made a mistake. No more, ladies, will you look down with contempt upon the poor woman who walks the street in the night, because you will see even there God Himself. No more will you think of jealousy and punishments. They will all vanish; and love, the great ideal of love, will be so powerful that no whip and cord will be necessary to guide mankind aright.

If one millionth part of the men and women who live in this world simply sit down and for a few minutes say, "You are all God, O ye men and O ye animals and living beings, you are all the manifestations of the one living Deity!" the whole world will be changed in half an hour.

Instead of throwing tremendous bomb-shells of hatred into every corner, instead of projecting currents of jealousy and of evil thought, in every country people will think that it is all He. He is all that you see and feel. How can you see evil until there is evil in you? How can you see the thief, unless he is there, sitting in the heart of your heart? How can you see the murderer until you are yourself the murderer? Be good, and evil will vanish for you. The whole universe will thus be changed. This is the greatest gain to society. This is the great gain to the human organism. These thoughts were thought out, worked out amongst individuals in ancient times in India. For various reasons, such as the exclusiveness of the teachers and foreign conquest, those thoughts were not allowed to spread. Yet they are grand truths; and wherever they have been working, man has become divine. My whole life has been changed by the touch of one of these divine men, about whom I am going to speak to you next Sunday; and the time is coming when these thoughts will be cast abroad over the whole world. Instead of living in monasteries, instead of being confined to books of philosophy to be studied only by the learned, instead of being the exclusive possession of sects and of a few of the learned, they will all be sown broadcast over the whole world, so that they may become the common property of the saint and the sinner, of men and women and children, of the learned and of the ignorant. They will then permeate the atmosphere of the world, and the very air that we breathe will say with every one of its pulsations, "Thou art That". And the whole universe with its myriads of suns and moons, through everything that speaks, with one voice will say, "Thou art That".

RAJA YOGA

THE PATH OF SELF-KNOWLEDGE

Preface

Since the dawn of history, various extraordinary phenomena have been recorded as happening amongst human beings. Witnesses are not wanting in modern times to attest to the fact of such events, even in societies living under the full blaze of modern science. The vast mass of such evidence is unreliable, as coming from ignorant, superstitious, or fraudulent persons. In many instances the so-called miracles are imitations. But what do they imitate? It is not the sign of a candid and scientific mind to throw overboard anything without proper investigation. Surface scientists, unable to explain the various extraordinary mental phenomena, strive to ignore their very existence. They are, therefore, more culpable than those who think that their prayers are answered by a being, or beings, above the clouds, or than those who believe that their petitions will make such beings change the course of the universe. The latter have the excuse of ignorance, or at least of a defective system of education, which has taught them dependence upon such beings, a dependence which has become a part of their degenerate nature. The former have no such excuse.

For thousands of years such phenomena have been studied, investigated, and generalised, the whole ground of the religious faculties of man has been analysed, and the practical result is the science of Râja-Yoga. Raja-Yoga does not, after the unpardonable manner of some modern scientists, deny the existence of facts which are difficult to explain; on the other hand, it gently yet in no uncertain terms tells the superstitious that miracles, and answers to prayers, and powers of faith, though true as facts, are not rendered comprehensible through the superstitious explanation of attributing them to the agency of a being, or beings, above the clouds. It declares that each man is only a conduit for the infinite ocean of knowledge and power that lies behind mankind. It teaches that desires and wants are in man, that the power of supply is also in man; and that wherever and whenever a desire, a want, a prayer has been fulfilled, it was out of this infinite magazine that the supply came, and not from any supernatural being. The idea of supernatural beings may rouse to a certain extent the power of action in man, but it also brings spiritual decay. It brings dependence; it brings fear; it brings superstition. It degenerates into a horrible belief in the natural weakness of man. There is no supernatural, says the Yogi, but there are in nature gross manifestations and subtle manifestations. The subtle are the causes, the gross the effects. The gross can be easily perceived by the senses; not so the subtle. The practice of Raja-Yoga will lead to the acquisition of the more subtle perceptions.

All the orthodox systems of Indian philosophy have one goal in view, the liberation of the soul through perfection. The method is by Yoga. The word Yoga covers an immense ground, but both the Sânkhya and the Vedanta Schools point to Yoga in some form or other.

The subject of the present book is that form of Yoga known as Raja-Yoga. The aphorisms of Patanjali are the highest authority on Raja-Yoga, and form its textbook. The other philosophers, though occasionally differing from Patanjali in some philosophical points, have, as a rule, acceded to his method of practice a decided consent. The first part of this book comprises several lectures to classes delivered by the present writer in New York. The second part is a rather free translation of the aphorisms (Sutras) of Patanjali, with a running commentary. Effort has been made to avoid technicalities as far as possible, and to keep to the free and easy style of conversation. In the first part some simple and specific directions are given for the student who wants to practice, but all such are especially and earnestly reminded that, with few exceptions, Yoga can only be safely learnt by direct contact with a teacher. If these conversations succeed in awakening a desire for further information on the subject, the teacher will not be wanting.

The system of Patanjali is based upon the system of the Sankhyas, the points of difference being very few. The two most important differences are, first, that Patanjali admits a Personal God in the form of a first teacher, while the only God the Sankhyas admit is a nearly perfected being, temporarily in charge of a cycle of creation. Second, the Yogis hold the mind to be equally all-pervading with the soul, or Purusha, and the Sankhyas do not.

Swami Vivekananda

—*Each soul is potentially divine.*

—*The goal is to manifest this Divinity within by controlling nature, external and internal.*

—*Do this either by work, or worship, or psychic control, or philosophy— by one, or more, or all of these— and be free.*

—*This is the whole of religion. Doctrines, or dogmas, or rituals, or books, or temples, or forms, are but secondary details.*

Chapter I
Introduction

All our knowledge is based upon experience. What we call inferential knowledge, in which we go from the less to the more general, or from the general to the particular, has experience as its basis. In what are called the exact sciences, people easily find the truth, because it appeals to the particular experiences of every human being. The scientist does not tell you to believe in anything, but he has certain results which come from his own experiences, and reasoning on them when he asks us to believe in his conclusions, he appeals to some universal experience of humanity. In every exact science there is a basis which is common to all humanity, so that we can at once see the truth or the fallacy of the conclusions drawn therefrom. Now, the question is: Has religion any such basis or not? I shall have to answer the question both in the affirmative and in the negative.

Religion, as it is generally taught all over the world, is said to be based upon faith and belief, and, in most cases, consists only of different sets of theories, and that is the reason why we find all religions quarrelling with one another. These theories, again, are based upon belief. One man says there is a great Being sitting above the clouds and governing the whole universe, and he asks me to believe that solely on the authority of his assertion. In the same way, I may have my own ideas, which I am asking others to believe, and if they ask a reason, I cannot give them any. This is why religion and metaphysical philosophy have a bad name nowadays. Every educated man seems to say, "Oh, these religions are only bundles of theories without any standard to judge them by, each man preaching his own pet ideas." Nevertheless, there is a basis of universal belief in religion, governing all the different theories and all the varying ideas of different sects in different countries. Going to their basis we find that they also are based upon universal experiences.

In the first place, if you analyse all the various religions of the world, you will find that these are divided into two classes, those with a book and those without a book. Those with a book are the strongest, and have the largest number of followers. Those without books have mostly died out, and the few new ones have very small following. Yet, in all of them we find one consensus of opinion, that the truths they teach are the results of the experiences of particular persons. The Christian asks you to believe in his religion, to believe in Christ and to believe in him as the incarnation of God, to believe in a God, in a soul, and in a better state of that soul. If I ask him for reason, he says he believes in them. But if you go to the fountain-head of Christianity, you will find that it is based upon experience. Christ said he saw God; the disciples said they felt God; and so forth. Similarly, in Buddhism, it is Buddha's experience. He experienced certain truths, saw them, came in contact with them, and preached them to the world. So with the Hindus. In their books the writers, who are called Rishis, or sages, declare they experienced certain truths, and these they preach. Thus it is clear that all the religions of the world have been built upon that one universal and adamantine foundation of all our knowledge — direct experience. The teachers all saw God; they all saw their own souls, they saw their future, they saw their eternity, and what they saw they preached. Only there is this difference that by most of these religions especially in modern times, a peculiar claim is made, namely, that these experiences are impossible at the present day; they were only possible with a few men, who were the first founders of the religions that subsequently bore their names. At the present time these experiences have become obsolete, and, therefore, we have now to take religion on belief. This I entirely deny. If there has been one experience in this world in any particular branch of knowledge, it absolutely follows that that experience has been possible millions of times before, and will be repeated eternally. Uniformity is the rigorous law of nature; what once happened can happen always.

The teachers of the science of Yoga, therefore, declare that religion is not only based upon the experience of ancient times, but that no man can be religious until he has the same perceptions himself. Yoga is the science which teaches us how to get these perceptions. It is not much use to talk about religion until one has felt it. Why is there so much disturbance, so much fighting and quarrelling in the name of God? There has been more bloodshed in the name of God than for any other cause, because people never went to the fountain-head; they were content only to give a mental assent to the customs of their forefathers, and wanted others to do the same. What right has a man to say he has a soul if he does not feel it, or that there is a God if he does not see Him? If there is a God we must see Him, if there is a soul we must perceive it; otherwise it is better not to believe. It is better to be an outspoken atheist than a hypocrite. The modern idea, on the one hand, with the "learned" is that religion and metaphysics and all search after a Supreme Being are futile; on the other hand, with the semi-educated, the idea seems to be that these things really have no basis; their only value consists in the fact that they furnish strong motive powers for doing good to the world. If men believe in a God, they may become good, and moral, and so make good citizens. We cannot blame them for holding such ideas, seeing that all the teaching these men get is simply to believe in an eternal rigmarole of words, without any substance behind them. They are asked to live upon words; can they do it? If they could, I should not have the least regard for human nature. Man wants truth, wants to experience truth for himself; when he has grasped it, realised it, felt it within his heart of hearts, then alone, declare the Vedas, would all doubts vanish, all darkness be scattered, and all crookedness be made straight. "Ye children of immortality, even those who live in the highest sphere, the way is found; there is a way out of all this darkness, and that is by perceiving Him who is beyond all darkness; there is no other way."

The science of Râja-Yoga proposes to put before humanity a practical and scientifically worked out method of reaching this truth. In the first place, every science must have its own method of investigation. If you want to become an astronomer and sit down and cry "Astronomy! Astronomy!" it will never come to you. The same with chemistry. A certain method must be followed. You must go to a laboratory, take different substances, mix them up, compound them, experiment with them, and out of that will come a knowledge of chemistry. If you want to be an astronomer, you must go to an observatory, take a telescope, study the stars and planets, and then you will become an astronomer. Each science must have its own methods. I could preach you thousands of sermons, but they would not make you religious, until you practiced the method. These are the truths of the sages of all countries, of all ages, of men pure and unselfish, who had no motive but to do good to the world. They all declare that they have found some truth higher than what the senses can bring to us, and they invite verification. They ask us to take up the method and practice honestly, and then, if we do not find this higher truth, we will have the right to say there is no truth in the claim, but before we have done that, we are not rational in denying the truth of their assertions. So we must work faithfully using the prescribed methods, and light will come.

In acquiring knowledge we make use of generalisations, and generalisation is based upon observation. We first observe facts, then generalise, and then draw conclusions or principles. The knowledge of the mind, of the internal nature of man, of thought, can never be had until we have first the power of observing the facts that are going on within. It is comparatively easy to observe facts in the external world, for many instruments have been invented for the purpose, but in the internal world we have no instrument to help us. Yet we know we must observe in order to have a real science. Without a proper analysis, any science will be hopeless — mere theorising. And that is why all the psychologists have been quarrelling among themselves since the beginning of time, except those few who found out the means of observation.

The science of Raja-Yoga, in the first place, proposes to give us such a means of observing the internal states. The instrument is the mind itself. The power of attention, when properly guided, and directed towards the internal world, will analyse the mind, and illumine facts for us. The powers of the mind are like rays of light dissipated; when they are concentrated, they illumine. This is our only means of knowledge. Everyone is using it, both in the external and the internal world; but, for the psychologist, the same minute observation has to be directed to the internal world, which the scientific man directs to the external; and this requires a great deal of practice. From our childhood upwards we have been taught only to pay attention to things external, but never to things internal; hence most of us have nearly lost the faculty of observing the internal mechanism. To turn the mind as it were, inside, stop it from going outside, and then to concentrate all its powers, and throw them upon the mind itself, in order that it may know its own nature, analyse itself, is very hard work. Yet that is the only way to anything which will be a scientific approach to the subject.

What is the use of such knowledge? In the first place, knowledge itself is the highest reward of knowledge, and secondly, there is also utility in it. It will take away all our misery. When by analysing his own mind, man comes face to face, as it were, with something which is never destroyed, something which is, by its own nature, eternally pure and perfect, he will no more be miserable, no more unhappy. All misery comes from fear, from unsatisfied desire. Man will find that he never dies, and then he will have no more fear of death. When he knows that he is perfect, he will have no more vain desires, and both these causes being absent, there will be no more misery — there will be perfect bliss, even while in this body.

There is only one method by which to attain this knowledge, that which is called concentration. The chemist in his laboratory concentrates all the energies of his mind into one focus, and throws them upon the materials he is analysing, and so finds out their secrets. The astronomer concentrates all the energies of his mind and projects them through his telescope upon the skies; and the stars, the sun, and the moon, give up their secrets to him. The more I can concentrate my thoughts on the matter on which I am talking to you, the more light I can throw upon you. You are listening to me, and the more you concentrate your thoughts, the more clearly you will grasp what I have to say.

How has all the knowledge in the world been gained but by the concentration of the powers of the mind? The world is ready to give up its secrets if we only know how to knock, how to give it the necessary blow. The strength and force of the blow come through concentration. There is no limit to the power of the human mind. The more concentrated it is, the more power is brought to bear on one point; that is the secret.

It is easy to concentrate the mind on external things, the mind naturally goes outwards; but not so in the case of religion, or psychology, or metaphysics, where the subject and the object, are one. The object is internal, the mind itself is the object, and it is necessary to study the mind itself— mind studying mind. We know that there is the power of the mind called reflection. I am talking to you. At the same time I am standing aside, as it were, a second person, and knowing and hearing what I am talking. You work and think at the same time, while a portion of your mind stands by and sees what you are thinking. The powers of the mind should be concentrated and turned back upon itself, and as the darkest places reveal their secrets before the penetrating rays of the sun, so will this concentrated mind penetrate its own innermost secrets. Thus will we come to the basis of belief, the real genuine religion. We will perceive for ourselves whether we have souls, whether life is of five minutes or of eternity, whether there is a God in the universe or more. It will all be revealed to us. This is what Raja-Yoga proposes to teach. The goal of all its teaching is how to concentrate the minds, then, how to discover the innermost recesses of our own minds, then, how to generalise their contents and form our own conclusions from them. It, therefore, never asks the question what our religion is, whether we are Deists or Atheists, whether Christians, Jews, or Buddhists. We are human beings; that is sufficient. Every human being has the right and the power to seek for religion. Every human being has the right to ask the reason, why, and to have his question answered by himself, if he only takes the trouble.

So far, then, we see that in the study of this Raja-Yoga no faith or belief is necessary. Believe nothing until you find it out for yourself; that is what it teaches us. Truth requires no prop to make it stand. Do you mean to say that the facts of our awakened state require any dreams or imaginings to prove them? Certainly not. This study of Raja-Yoga takes a long time and constant practice. A part of this practice is physical, but in the main it is mental. As we proceed we shall find how intimately the mind is connected with the body. If we believe that the mind is simply a finer part of the body, and that mind acts upon the body, then it stands to reason that the body must react upon the mind. If the body is sick, the mind becomes sick also. If the body is healthy, the mind remains healthy and strong. When one is angry, the mind becomes disturbed. Similarly when the mind is disturbed, the body also becomes disturbed. With the majority of mankind the mind is greatly under the control of the body, their mind being very little developed. The vast mass of humanity is very little removed from the animals. Not only so, but in many instances, the power of control in them is little higher than that of the lower animals. We have very little command of our minds. Therefore to bring that command about, to get that control over body and mind, we must take certain physical helps. When the body is sufficiently controlled, we can attempt the manipulation of the mind. By manipulating the mind, we shall be able to bring it under our control, make it work as we like, and compel it to concentrate its powers as we desire.

According to the Raja-Yogi, the external world is but the gross form of the internal, or subtle. The finer is always the cause, the grosser the effect. So the external world is the effect, the internal the cause. In the same way external forces are simply the grosser parts, of which the internal forces are the finer. The man who has discovered and learned how to manipulate the internal forces will get the whole of nature under his control. The Yogi proposes to himself no less a task than to master the whole universe, to control the whole of nature. He wants to arrive at the point where what we call "nature's laws" will have no influence over him, where he will be able to get beyond them all. He will be master of the whole of nature, internal and external. The progress and civilisation of the human race simply mean controlling this nature.

Different races take to different processes of controlling nature. Just as in the same society some individuals want to control the external nature, and others the internal, so, among races, some want to control the external nature, and others the internal. Some say that by controlling internal nature we control everything. Others that by controlling external nature we control everything. Carried to the extreme both are right, because in nature there is no such division as internal or external. These are fictitious limitations that never existed. The externalists and the internalists are destined to meet at the same point, when both reach the extreme of their knowledge. Just as a physicist, when he pushes his knowledge to its limits, finds it melting away into metaphysics, so a metaphysician will find that what he calls mind and matter are but apparent distinctions, the reality being One.

The end and aim of all science is to find the unity, the One out of which the manifold is being manufactured, that One existing as many. Raja-Yoga proposes to start from the internal world, to study internal nature, and through that, control the whole— both internal and external. It is a very old attempt. India has been its special stronghold, but it was also attempted by other nations. In Western countries it was regarded as mysticism and people who wanted to practice it were either burned or killed as witches and sorcerers. In India, for various reasons, it fell into the hands of persons who destroyed ninety per cent of the knowledge, and tried to make a great secret of the remainder. In modern times many so-called teachers have arisen in the West worse than those of India, because the latter knew something, while these modern exponents know nothing.

Anything that is secret and mysterious in these systems of Yoga should be at once rejected. The best guide in life is strength. In religion, as in all other matters, discard everything that weakens you, have nothing to do with it. Mystery-mongering weakens the human brain. It has well-nigh destroyed Yoga— one of the grandest of sciences. From the time it was discovered, more than four thousand years ago, Yoga was perfectly delineated, formulated, and preached in India. It is a striking fact that the more modern the commentator the greater the mistakes he makes, while the more ancient the writer the more rational he is. Most of the modern writers talk of all sorts of mystery. Thus Yoga fell into the hands of a few persons who made it a secret, instead of letting the full blaze of daylight and reason fall upon it. They did so that they might have the powers to themselves.

In the first place, there is no mystery in what I teach. What little I know I will tell you. So far as I can reason it out I will do so, but as to what I do not know I will simply tell you what the books say. It is wrong to believe blindly. You must exercise your own reason and judgment; you must practice, and see whether these things happen or not. Just as you would take up any other science, exactly in the same manner you should take up this science for study. There is neither mystery nor danger in it. So far as it is true, it ought to be preached in the public streets, in broad daylight. Any attempt to mystify these things is productive of great danger.

Before proceeding further, I will tell you a little of the Sânkhya philosophy, upon which the whole of Raja-Yoga is based. According to the Sankhya philosophy, the genesis of perception is as follows: the affections of external objects are carried by the outer instruments to their respective brain centres or organs, the organs carry the affections to the mind, the mind to the determinative faculty, from this the Purusha (the soul) receives them, when perception results. Next he gives the order back, as it were, to the motor centres to do the needful. With the exception of the Purusha all of these are material, but the mind is much finer matter than the external instruments. That material of which the mind is composed goes also to form the subtle matter called the Tanmâtras. These become gross and make the external matter. That is the psychology of the Sankhya. So that between the intellect and the grosser matter outside there is only a difference in degree. The Purusha is the only thing which is immaterial. The mind is an instrument, as it were, in the hands of the soul, through which the soul catches external objects. The mind is constantly changing and vacillating, and can, when perfected, either attach itself to several organs, to one, or to none. For instance, if I hear the clock with great attention, I will not, perhaps, see anything although my eyes may be open, showing that the mind was not attached to the seeing organ, while it was to the hearing organ. But the perfected mind can be attached to all the organs simultaneously. It has the reflexive power of looking back into its own depths. This reflexive power is what the Yogi wants to attain; by concentrating the powers of the mind, and turning them inward, he seeks to know what is happening inside. There is in this no question of mere belief; it is the analysis arrived at by certain philosophers. Modern physiologists tell us that the eyes are not the organ of vision, but that the organ is in one of the nerve centres of the brain, and so with all the senses; they also tell us that these centres are formed of the same material as the brain itself. The Sankhyas also tell us the same thing The former is a statement on the physical side, and the latter on the psychological side; yet both are the same. Our field of research lies beyond this.

The Yogi proposes to attain that fine state of perception in which he can perceive all the different mental states. There must be mental perception of all of them. One can perceive how the sensation is travelling, how the mind is receiving it, how it is going to the determinative faculty, and how this gives it to the Purusha. As each science requires certain preparations and has its own method, which must be followed before it could be understood, even so in Raja-Yoga.

Certain regulations as to food are necessary; we must use that food which brings us the purest mind. If you go into a menagerie, you will find this demonstrated at once. You see the elephants, huge animals, but calm and gentle; and if you go towards the cages of the lions and tigers, you find them restless, showing how much difference has been made by food. All the forces that are working in this body have been produced out of food; we see that every day. If you begin to fast, first your body will get weak, the physical forces will suffer; then after a few days, the mental forces will suffer also. First, memory will fail. Then comes a point, when you are not able to think, much less to pursue any course of reasoning. We have, therefore, to take care what sort of food we eat at the beginning, and when we have got strength enough, when our practice is well advanced, we need not be so careful in this respect. While the plant is growing it must be hedged round, lest it be injured; but when it becomes a tree, the hedges are taken away. It is strong enough to withstand all assaults.

A Yogi must avoid the two extremes of luxury and austerity. He must not fast, nor torture his flesh. He who does so, says the Gita, cannot be a Yogi: He who fasts, he who keeps awake, he who sleeps much, he who works too much, he who does no work, none of these can be a Yogi (Gita, VI.16).

Chapter II
The First Steps

Râja-Yoga is divided into eight steps. The first is Yama — non-killing, truthfulness, non-stealing, continence, and non-receiving of any gifts. Next is Niyama — cleanliness, contentment, austerity, study, and self-surrender to God. Then comes Âsana, or posture; Prânâyâma, or control of Prâna; Pratyâhâra, or restraint of the senses from their objects; Dhâranâ, or fixing the mind on a spot; Dhyâna, or meditation; and Samâdhi, or superconsciousness. The Yama and Niyama, as we see, are moral trainings; without these as the basis no practice of Yoga will succeed. As these two become established, the Yogi will begin to realise the fruits of his practice; without these it will never bear fruit. A Yogi must not think of injuring anyone, by thought, word, or deed. Mercy shall not be for men alone, but shall go beyond, and embrace the whole world.

The next step is Asana, posture. A series of exercises, physical and mental, is to be gone through every day, until certain higher states are reached. Therefore it is quite necessary that we should find a posture in which we can remain long. That posture which is the easiest for one should be the one chosen. For thinking, a certain posture may be very easy for one man, while to another it may be very difficult. We will find later on that during the study of these psychological matters a good deal of activity goes on in the body. Nerve currents will have to be displaced and given a new channel. New sorts of vibrations will begin, the whole constitution will be remodelled as it were. But the main part of the activity will lie along the spinal column, so that the one thing necessary for the posture is to hold the spinal column free, sitting erect, holding the three parts — the chest, neck, and head — in a straight line. Let the whole weight of the body be supported by the ribs, and then you have an easy natural postures with the spine straight. You will easily see that you cannot think very high thoughts with the chest in. This portion of the Yoga is a little similar to the Hatha-Yoga which deals entirely with the physical body, its aim being to make the physical body very strong. We have nothing to do with it here, because its practices are very difficult, and cannot be learned in a day, and, after all, do not lead to much spiritual growth. Many of these practices you will find in Delsarte and other teachers, such as placing the body in different postures, but the object in these is physical, not psychological. There is not one muscle in the body over which a man cannot establish a perfect control. The heart can be made to stop or go on at his bidding, and each part of the organism can be similarly controlled.

The result of this branch of Yoga is to make men live long; health is the chief idea, the one goal of the Hatha-Yogi. He is determined not to fall sick, and he never does. He lives long; a hundred years is nothing to him; he is quite young and fresh when he is 150, without one hair turned grey. But that is all. A banyan tree lives sometimes 5000 years, but it is a banyan tree and nothing more. So, if a man lives long, he is only a healthy animal. One or two ordinary lessons of the Hatha-Yogis are very useful. For instance, some of you will find it a good thing for headaches to drink cold water through the nose as soon as you get up in the morning; the whole day your brain will be nice and cool, and you will never catch cold. It is very easy to do; put your nose into the water, draw it up through the nostrils and make a pump action in the throat.

After one has learned to have a firm erect seat, one has to perform, according to certain schools, a practice called the purifying of the nerves. This part has been rejected by some as not belonging to Raja-Yoga, but as so great an authority as the commentator Shankarâchârya advises it, I think fit that it should be mentioned, and I will quote his own directions from his commentary on the Shvetâshvatara Upanishad: "The mind whose dross has been cleared away by Pranayama, becomes fixed in Brahman; therefore Pranayama is declared. First the nerves are to be purified, then comes the power to practice Pranayama. Stopping the right nostril with the thumb, through the left nostril fill in air, according to capacity; then, without any interval, throw the air out through the right nostril, closing the left one. Again inhaling through the right nostril eject through the left, according to capacity; practicing this three or five times at four hours of the day, before dawn, during midday, in the evening, and at midnight, in fifteen days or a month purity of the nerves is attained; then begins Pranayama."

Practice is absolutely necessary. You may sit down and listen to me by the hour every day, but if you do not practice, you will not get one step further. It all depends on practice. We never understand these things until we experience them. We will have to see and feel them for ourselves. Simply listening to explanations and theories will not do. There are several obstructions to practice. The first obstruction is an unhealthy body: if the body is not in a fit state, the practice will be obstructed. Therefore we have to keep the body in good health; we have to take care of what we eat and drink, and what we do. Always use a mental effort, what is usually called "Christian Science," to keep the body strong. That is all— nothing further of the body. We must not forget that health is only a means to an end. If health were the end, we would be like animals; animals rarely become unhealthy.

The second obstruction is doubt; we always feel doubtful about things we do not see. Man cannot live upon words, however he may try. So, doubt comes to us as to whether there is any truth in these things or not; even the best of us will doubt sometimes: With practice, within a few days, a little glimpse will come, enough to give one encouragement and hope. As a certain commentator on Yoga philosophy says, "When one proof is obtained, however little that may be, it will give us faith in the whole teaching of Yoga." For instance, after the first few months of practice, you will begin to find you can read another's thoughts; they will come to you in picture form. Perhaps you will hear something happening at a long distance, when you concentrate your mind with a wish to hear. These glimpses will come, by little bits at first, but enough to give you faith, and strength, and hope. For instance, if you concentrate your thoughts on the tip of your nose, in a few days you will begin to smell most beautiful fragrance, which will be enough to show you that there are certain mental perceptions that can be made obvious without the contact of physical objects. But we must always remember that these are only the means; the aim, the end, the goal, of all this training is liberation of the soul. Absolute control of nature, and nothing short of it, must be the goal. We must be the masters, and not the slaves of nature; neither body nor mind must be our master, nor must we forget that the body is mine, and not I the body's.

A god and a demon went to learn about the Self from a great sage. They studied with him for a long time. At last the sage told them, "You yourselves are the Being you are seeking." Both of them thought that their bodies were the Self. They went back to their people quite satisfied and said, "We have learned everything that was to be learned; eat, drink, and be merry; we are the Self; there is nothing beyond us." The nature of the demon was ignorant, clouded; so he never inquired any further, but was perfectly contented with the idea that he was God, that by the Self was meant the body. The god had a purer nature. He at first committed the mistake of thinking: I, this body, am Brahman: so keep it strong and in health, and well dressed, and give it all sorts of enjoyments. But, in a few days, he found out that that could not be the meaning of the sage, their master; there must be something higher. So he came back and said, "Sir, did you teach me that this body was the Self? If so, I see all bodies die; the Self cannot die." The sage said, "Find it out; thou art That." Then the god thought that the vital forces which work the body were what the sage meant. But after a time, he found that if he ate, these vital forces remained strong, but, if he starved, they became weak. The god then went back to the sage and said, "Sir, do you mean that the vital forces are the Self?" The sage said, "Find out for yourself; thou art That." The god returned home once more, thinking that it was the mind, perhaps, that was the Self. But in a short while he saw that thoughts were so various, now good, again bad; the mind was too changeable to be the Self. He went back to the sage and said, "Sir, I do not think that the mind is the Self; did you mean that?" "No," replied the sage, "thou art That; find out for yourself." The god went home, and at last found that he was the Self, beyond all thought, one without birth or death, whom the sword cannot pierce or the fire burn, whom the air cannot dry or the water melt, the beginningless and endless, the immovable, the intangible, the omniscient, the omnipotent Being; that It was neither the body nor the mind, but beyond them all. So he was satisfied; but the poor demon did not get the truth, owing to his fondness for the body.

This world has a good many of these demoniac natures, but there are some gods too. If one proposes to teach any science to increase the power of sense-enjoyment, one finds multitudes ready for it. If one undertakes to show the supreme goal, one finds few to listen to him. Very few have the power to grasp the higher, fewer still the patience to attain to it. But there are a few also who know that even if the body can be made to live for a thousand years, the result in the end will be the same. When the forces that hold it together go away, the body must fall. No man was ever born who could stop his body one moment from changing. Body is the name of a series of changes. "As in a river the masses of water are changing before you every moment, and new masses are coming, yet taking similar form, so is it with this body." Yet the body must be kept strong and healthy. It is the best instrument we have.

This human body is the greatest body in the universe, and a human being the greatest being. Man is higher than all animals, than all angels; none is greater than man. Even the Devas (gods) will have to come down again and attain to salvation through a human body. Man alone attains to perfection, not even the Devas. According to the Jews and Mohammedans, God created man after creating the angels and everything else, and after creating man He asked the angels to come and salute him, and all did so except Iblis; so God cursed him and he became Satan. Behind this allegory is the great truth that this human birth is the greatest birth we can have. The lower creation, the animal, is dull, and manufactured mostly out of Tamas. Animals cannot have any high thoughts; nor can the angels, or Devas, attain to direct freedom without human birth. In human society, in the same way, too much wealth or too much poverty is a great impediment to the higher development of the soul. It is from the middle classes that the great ones of the world come. Here the forces are very equally adjusted and balanced.

Returning to our subject, we come next to Pranayarna, controlling the breathing. What has that to do with concentrating the powers of the mind? Breath is like the fly-wheel of this machine, the body. In a big engine you find the fly-wheel first moving, and that motion is conveyed to finer and finer machinery until the most delicate and finest mechanism in the machine is in motion. The breath is that fly-wheel, supplying and regulating the motive power to everything in this body.

There was once a minister to a great king. He fell into disgrace. The king, as a punishment, ordered him to be shut up in the top of a very high tower. This was done, and the minister was left there to perish. He had a faithful wife, however, who came to the tower at night and called to her husband at the top to know what she could do to help him. He told her to return to the tower the following night and bring with her a long rope, some stout twine, pack thread, silken thread, a beetle, and a little honey. Wondering much, the good wife obeyed her husband, and brought him the desired articles. The husband directed her to attach the silken thread firmly to the beetle, then to smear its horns with a drop of honey, and to set it free on the wall of the tower, with its head pointing upwards. She obeyed all these instructions, and the beetle started on its long journey. Smelling the honey ahead it slowly crept onwards, in the hope of reaching the honey, until at last it reached the top of the tower, when the minister grasped the beetle, and got possession of the silken thread. He told his wife to tie the other end to the pack thread, and after he had drawn up the pack thread, he repeated the process with the stout twine, and lastly with the rope. Then the rest was easy. The minister descended from the tower by means of the rope, and made his escape. In this body of ours the breath motion is the "silken thread"; by laying hold of and learning to control it we grasp the pack thread of the nerve currents, and from these the stout twine of our thoughts, and lastly the rope of Prana, controlling which we reach freedom.

We do not know anything about our own bodies; we cannot know. At best we can take a dead body, and cut it in pieces, and there are some who can take a live animal and cut it in pieces in order to see what is inside the body. Still, that has nothing to do with our own bodies. We know very little about them.

Why do we not? Because our attention is not discriminating enough to catch the very fine movements that are going on within. We can know of them only when the mind becomes more subtle and enters, as it were, deeper into the body. To get the subtle perception we have to begin with the grosser perceptions. We have to get hold of that which is setting the whole engine in motion. That is the Prana, the most obvious manifestation of which is the breath. Then, along with the breath, we shall slowly enter the body, which will enable us to find out about the subtle forces, the nerve currents that are moving all over the body. As soon as we perceive and learn to feel them, we shall begin to get control over them, and over the body. The mind is also set in motion: by these different nerve currents, so at last we shall reach the state of perfect control over the body and the mind, making both our servants. Knowledge is power. We have to get this power. So we must begin at the beginning, with Pranayama, restraining the Prana. This Pranayama is a long subject, and will take several lessons to illustrate it thoroughly. We shall take it part by part.

We shall gradually see the reasons for each exercise and what forces in the body are set in motion. All these things will come to us, but it requires constant practice, and the proof will come by practice. No amount of reasoning which I can give you will be proof to you, until you have demonstrated it for yourselves. As soon as you begin to feel these currents in motion all over you, doubts will vanish, but it requires hard practice every day. You must practice at least twice every day, and the best times are towards the morning and the evening. When night passes into day, and day into night, a state of relative calmness ensues. The early morning and the early evening are the two periods of calmness. Your body will have a like tendency to become calm at those times. We should take advantage of that natural condition and begin then to practice. Make it a rule not to eat until you have practiced; if you do this, the sheer force of hunger will break your laziness. In India they teach children never to eat until they have practiced or worshipped, and it becomes natural to them after a time; a boy will not feel hungry until he has bathed and practiced.

Those of you who can afford it will do better to have a room for this practice alone. Do not sleep in that room, it must be kept holy. You must not enter the room until you have bathed, and are perfectly clean in body and mind. Place flowers in that room always; they are the best surroundings for a Yogi; also pictures that are pleasing. Burn incense morning and evening. Have no quarrelling, nor anger, nor unholy thought in that room. Only allow those persons to enter it who are of the same thought as you. Then gradually there will be an

atmosphere of holiness in the room, so that when you are miserable, sorrowful, doubtful, or your mind is disturbed, the very fact of entering that room will
make you calm. This was the idea of the temple and the church, and in some
temples and churches you will find it even now, but in the majority of them the
very idea has been lost. The idea is that by keeping holy vibrations there the
place becomes and remains illumined. Those who cannot afford to have a room
set apart can practice anywhere they like. Sit in a straight posture, and the first
thing to do is to send a current of holy thought to all creation. Mentally repeat,
"Let all beings be happy; let all beings be peaceful; let all beings be blissful." So
do to the east, south, north and west. The more you do that the better you will
feel yourself. You will find at last that the easiest way to make ourselves healthy
is to see that others are healthy, and the easiest way to make ourselves happy is
to see that others are happy. After doing that, those who believe in God should
pray — not for money, not for health, nor for heaven; pray for knowledge and
light; every other prayer is selfish. Then the next thing to do is to think of your
own body, and see that it is strong and healthy; it is the best instrument you
have. Think of it as being as strong as adamant, and that with the help of this
body you will cross the ocean of life. Freedom is never to be reached by the weak.
Throw away all weakness. Tell your body that it is strong, tell your mind that it
is strong, and have unbounded faith and hope in yourself.

Chapter III
Prana

Prânâyâma is not, as many think, something about breath; breath indeed has very little to do with it, if anything. Breathing is only one of the many exercises through which we get to the real Pranayama. Pranayama means the control of Prâna. According to the philosophers of India, the whole universe is composed of two materials, one of which they call Âkâsha. It is the omnipresent, all-penetrating existence. Everything that has form, everything that is the result of combination, is evolved out of this Akasha. It is the Akasha that becomes the air, that becomes the liquids, that becomes the solids; it is the Akasha that becomes the sun, the earth, the moon, the stars, the comets; it is the Akasha that becomes the human body, the animal body, the plants, every form that we see, everything that can be sensed, everything that exists. It cannot be perceived; it is so subtle that it is beyond all ordinary perception; it can only be seen when it has become gross, has taken form. At the beginning of creation there is only this Akasha. At the end of the cycle the solids, the liquids, and the gases all melt into the Akasha again, and the next creation similarly proceeds out of this Akasha.

By what power is this Akasha manufactured into this universe? By the power of Prana. Just as Akasha is the infinite, omnipresent material of this universe, so is this Prana the infinite, omnipresent manifesting power of this universe. At the beginning and at the end of a cycle everything becomes Akasha, and all the forces that are in the universe resolve back into the Prana; in the next cycle, out of this Prana is evolved everything that we call energy, everything that we call force. It is the Prana that is manifesting as motion; it is the Prana that is manifesting as gravitation, as magnetism. It is the Prana that is manifesting as the actions of the body, as the nerve currents, as thought force. From thought down to the lowest force, everything is but the manifestation of Prana. The sum total of all forces in the universe, mental or physical, when resolved back to their original state, is called Prana. "When there was neither aught nor naught, when darkness was covering darkness, what existed then? That Akasha existed without motion." The physical motion of the Prana was stopped, but it existed all the same.

At the end of a cycle the energies now displayed in the universe quiet down and become potential. At the beginning of the next cycle they start up, strike upon the Akasha, and out of the Akasha evolve these various forms, and as the Akasha changes, this Prana changes also into all these manifestations of energy. The knowledge and control of this Prana is really what is meant by Pranayama.

This opens to us the door to almost unlimited power. Suppose, for instance, a man understood the Prana perfectly, and could control it, what power on earth would not be his? He would be able to move the sun and stars out of their places, to control everything in the universe, from the atoms to the biggest suns, because he would control the Prana. This is the end and aim of Pranayama. When the Yogi becomes perfect, there will be nothing in nature not under his control. If he orders the gods or the souls of the departed to come, they will come at his bidding. All the forces of nature will obey him as slaves. When the ignorant see these powers of the Yogi, they call them the miracles. One peculiarity of the Hindu mind is that it always inquires for the last possible generalisation, leaving the details to be worked out afterwards. The question is raised in the Vedas, "What is that, knowing which, we shall know everything?" Thus, all books, and all philosophies that have been written, have been only to prove that by knowing which everything is known. If a man wants to know this universe bit by bit he must know every individual grain of sand, which means infinite time; he cannot know all of them. Then how can knowledge be? How is it possible for a man to be all-knowing through particulars? The Yogis say that behind this particular manifestation there is a generalisation. Behind all particular ideas stands a generalised, an abstract principle; grasp it, and you have grasped everything. Just as this whole universe has been generalised in the Vedas into that One Absolute Existence, and he who has grasped that Existence has grasped the whole universe, so all forces have been generalised into this Prana, and he who has grasped the Prana has grasped all the forces of the universe, mental or physical. He who has controlled the Prana has controlled his own mind, and all the minds that exist. He who has controlled the Prana has controlled his body, and all the bodies that exist, because the Prana is the generalised manifestation of force.

How to control the Prana is the one idea of Pranayama. All the trainings and exercises in this regard are for that one end. Each man must begin where he stands, must learn how to control the things that are nearest to him. This body is very near to us, nearer than anything in the external universe, and this mind is the nearest of all. The Prana which is working this mind and body is the nearest to us of all the Prana in this universe. This little wave of the Prana which represents our own energies, mental and physical, is the nearest to us of all the waves of the infinite ocean of Prana. If we can succeed in controlling that little wave, then alone we can hope to control the whole of Prana. The Yogi who has done this gains perfection; no longer is he under any power. He becomes almost almighty, almost all-knowing. We see sects in every country who have attempted this control of Prana. In this country there are Mind-healers, Faith-healers, Spiritualists, Christian Scientists, Hypnotists, etc., and if we examine these different bodies, we shall find at the back of each this control of the Prana, whether they know it or not. If you boil all their theories down, the residuum will be that. It is the one and the same force they are manipulating, only unknowingly. They have stumbled on the discovery of a force and are using it unconsciously without knowing its nature, but it is the same as the Yogi uses, and which comes from Prana.

The Prana is the vital force in every being. Thought is the finest and highest action of Prana. Thought, again, as we see, is not all. There is also what we call instinct or unconscious thought, the lowest plane of action. If a mosquito stings us, our hand will strike it automatically, instinctively. This is one expression of thought. All reflex actions of the body belong to this plane of thought. There is again the other plane of thought, the conscious. I reason, I judge, I think, I see the pros and cons of certain things, yet that is not all. We know that reason is limited. Reason can go only to a certain extent, beyond that it cannot reach. The circle within which it runs is very very limited indeed. Yet at the same time, we find facts rush into this circle. Like the coming of comets certain things come into this circle; it is certain they come from outside the limit, although our reason cannot go beyond. The causes of the phenomena intruding themselves in this small limit are outside of this limit. The mind can exist on a still higher plane, the superconscious. When the mind has attained to that state, which is called Samâdhi— perfect concentration, superconsciousness— it goes beyond the limits of reason, and comes face to face with facts which no instinct or reason can ever know. All manipulations of the subtle forces of the body, the different manifestations of Prana, if trained, give a push to the mind, help it to go up higher, and become superconscious, from where it acts.

In this universe there is one continuous substance on every plane of existence. Physically this universe is one: there is no difference between the sun and you. The scientist will tell you it is only a fiction to say the contrary. There is no real difference between the table and me; the table is one point in the mass of matter, and I another point. Each form represents, as it were, one whirlpool in the infinite ocean of matter, of which not one is constant. Just as in a rushing stream there may be millions of whirlpools, the water in each of which is different every moment, turning round and round for a few seconds, and then passing out, replaced by a fresh quantity, so the whole universe is one constantly changing mass of matter, in which all forms of existence are so many whirlpools. A mass of matter enters into one whirlpool, say a human body, stays there for a period, becomes changed, and goes out into another, say an animal body this time, from which again after a few years, it enters into another whirlpool, called a lump of mineral. It is a constant change. Not one body is constant. There is no such thing as my body, or your body, except in words. Of the one huge mass of matter, one point is called a moon, another a sun, another a man, another the earth, another a plant, another a mineral. Not one is constant, but everything is changing, matter eternally concreting and disintegrating. So it is with the mind. Matter is represented by the ether; when the action of Prana is most subtle, this very ether, in the finer state of vibration, will represent the mind and there it will be still one unbroken mass. If you can simply get to that subtle vibration, you will see and feel that the whole universe is composed of subtle vibrations. Sometimes certain drugs have the power to take us, while as yet in the senses, to that condition. Many of you may remember the celebrated experiment of Sir Humphrey Davy, when the laughing gas overpowered him — how, during the lecture, he remained motionless, stupefied and after that, he said that the whole universe was made up of ideas. For, the time being, as it were, the gross vibrations had ceased, and only the subtle vibrations which he called ideas, were present to him. He could only see the subtle vibrations round him; everything had become thought; the whole universe was an ocean of thought, he and everyone else had become little thought whirlpools.

Thus, even in the universe of thought we find unity, and at last, when we get to the Self, we know that that Self can only be One. Beyond the vibrations of matter in its gross and subtle aspects, beyond motion there is but One. Even in manifested motion there is only unity. These facts can no more be denied. Modern physics also has demonstrated that the sum total of the energies in the universe is the same throughout. It has also been proved that this sum total of energy exists in two forms. It becomes potential, toned down, and calmed, and next it comes out manifested as all these various forces; again it goes back to the quiet state, and again it manifests. Thus it goes on evolving and involving through eternity. The control of this Prana, as before stated, is what is called Pranayama.

The most obvious manifestation of this Prana in the human body is the motion of the lungs. If that stops, as a rule all the other manifestations of force in the body will immediately stop. But there are persons who can train themselves in such a manner that the body will live on, even when this motion has stopped. There are some persons who can bury themselves for days, and yet live without breathing. To reach the subtle we must take the help of the grosser, and so, slowly travel towards the most subtle until we gain our point. Pranayama really means controlling this motion of the lungs and this motion is associated with the breath. Not that breath is producing it; on the contrary it is producing breath. This motion draws in the air by pump action. The Prana is moving the lungs, the movement of the lungs draws in the air. So Pranayama is not breathing, but controlling that muscular power which moves the lungs. That muscular power which goes out through the nerves to the muscles and from them to the lungs, making them move in a certain manner, is the Prana, which we have to control in the practice of Pranayama. When the Prana has become controlled, then we shall immediately find that all the other actions of the Prana in the body will slowly come under control. I myself have seen men who have controlled almost every muscle of the body; and why not? If I have control over certain muscles, why not over every muscle and nerve of the body? What impossibility is there? At present the control is lost, and the motion has become automatic. We cannot move our ears at will, but we know that animals can. We have not that power because we do not exercise it. This is what is called atavism.

Again, we know that motion which has become latent can be brought back to manifestation. By hard work and practice certain motions of the body which are most dormant can be brought back under perfect control. Reasoning thus we find there is no impossibility, but, on the other hand. every probability that each part of the body can be brought under perfect control. This the Yogi does through Pranayama. Perhaps some of you have read that in Pranayama, when drawing in the breath, you must fill your whole body with Prana. In the English translations Prana is given as breath, and you are inclined to ask how that is to be done. The fault is with the translator. Every part of the body can be filled with Prana, this vital force, and when you are able to do that, you can control the whole body. All the sickness and misery felt in the body will be perfectly controlled; not only so, you will be able to control another's body. Everything is infectious in this world, good or bad. If your body be in a certain state of tension, it will have a tendency to produce the same tension in others. If you are strong and healthy, those that live near you will also have the tendency to become strong and healthy, but if you are sick and weak, those around you will have the tendency to become the same. In the case of one man trying to heal another, the first idea is simply transferring his own health to the other. This is the primitive sort of healing. Consciously or unconsciously, health can be transmitted. A very strong man, living with a weak man, will make him a little stronger, whether he knows it or not. When consciously done, it becomes quicker and better in its action. Next come those cases in which a man may not be very healthy himself, yet we know that he can bring health to another. The first man, in such a case, has a little more control over the Prana, and can rouse, for the time being, his Prana, as it were, to a certain state of vibration, and transmit it to another person.

There have been cases where this process has been carried on at a distance, but in reality there is no distance in the sense of a break. Where is the distance that has a break? Is there any break between you and the sun? It is a continuous mass of matter, the sun being one part, and you another. Is there a break between one part of a river and another? Then why cannot any force travel? There is no reason against it. Cases of healing from a distance are perfectly true. The Prana can be transmitted to a very great distance; but to one genuine case, there are hundreds of frauds. This process of healing is not so easy as it is thought to be. In the most ordinary cases of such healing you will find that the healers simply take advantage of the naturally healthy state of the human body. An allopath comes and treats cholera patients, and gives them his medicines. The homoeopath comes and gives his medicines, and cures perhaps more than the allopath does, because the homoeopath does not disturb his patients, but allows nature to deal with them. The Faith-healer cures more still, because he brings the strength of his mind to bear, and rouses, through faith, the dormant Prana of the patient.

There is a mistake constantly made by Faith-healers: they think that faith directly heals a man. But faith alone does not cover all the ground. There are diseases where the worst symptoms are that the patient never thinks that he has that disease. That tremendous faith of the patient is itself one symptom of the disease, and usually indicates that he will die quickly. In such cases the principle that faith cures does not apply. If it were faith alone that cured, these patients also would be cured. It is by the Prana that real curing comes. The pure man, who has controlled the Prana, has the power of bringing it into a certain state of vibration, which can be conveyed to others, arousing in them a similar vibration. You see that in everyday actions. I am talking to you. What am I trying to do? I am, so to say, bringing my mind to a certain state of vibration, and the more I succeed in bringing it to that state, the more you will be affected by what I say. All of you know that the day I am more enthusiastic, the more you enjoy the lecture; and when I am less enthusiastic, you feel lack of interest.

The gigantic will powers of the world, the world movers, can bring their Prana into a high state of vibration, and it is so great and powerful that it catches others in a moment, and thousands are drawn towards them, and half the world think as they do. Great prophets of the world had the most wonderful control of the Prana, which gave them tremendous will-power; they had brought their Prana to the highest state of motion, and this is what gave them power to sway the world. All manifestations of power arise from this control. Men may not know the secret, but this is the one explanation. Sometimes in your own body the supply of Prana gravitates more or less to one part; the balance is disturbed, and when the balance of Prana is disturbed, what we call disease is produced. To take away the superfluous Prana, or to supply the Prana that is wanting, will be curing the disease. That again is Pranayama — to learn when there is more or less Prana in one part of the body than there should be. The feelings will become so subtle that the mind will feel that there is less Prana in the toe or the finger than there should be, and will possess the power to supply it. These are among the various functions of Pranayama. They have to be learned slowly and gradually, and as you see, the whole scope of Raja-Yoga is really to teach the control and direction in different planes of the Prana. When a man has concentrated his energies, he masters the Prana that is in his body. When a man is meditating, he is also concentrating the Prana.

In an ocean there are huge waves, like mountains, then smaller waves, and still smaller, down to little bubbles, but back of all these is the infinite ocean. The bubble is connected with the infinite ocean at one end, and the huge wave at the other end. So, one may be a gigantic man, and another a little bubble, but each is connected with that infinite ocean of energy, which is the common birthright of every animal that exists. Wherever there is life, the storehouse of infinite energy is behind it. Starting as some fungus, some very minute, microscopic bubble, and all the time drawing from that infinite store-house of energy, a form is changed slowly and steadily until in course of time it becomes a plant, then an animal, then man, ultimately God. This is attained through millions of aeons, but what is time? An increase of speed, an increase of struggle, is able to bridge the gulf of time. That which naturally takes a long time to accomplish can be shortened by the intensity of the action, says the Yogi. A man may go on slowly drawing in this energy from the infinite mass that exists in the universe, and, perhaps, he will require a hundred thousand years to become a Deva, and then, perhaps, five hundred thousand years to become still higher, and, perhaps, five millions of years to become perfect. Given rapid growth, the time will be lessened. Why is it not possible, with sufficient effort, to reach this very perfection in six months or six years? There is no limit. Reason shows that. If an engine, with a certain amount of coal, runs two miles an hour, it will run the distance in less time with a greater supply of coal. Similarly, why shall not the soul, by intensifying its action, attain perfection in this very life? All beings will at last attain to that goal, we know. But who cares to wait all these millions of aeons? Why not reach it immediately, in this body even, in this human form? Why shall I not get that infinite knowledge, infinite power, now?

The ideal of the Yogi, the whole science of Yoga, is directed to the end of teaching men how, by intensifying the power of assimilation, to shorten the time for reaching perfection, instead of slowly advancing from point to point and waiting until the whole human race has become perfect. All the great prophets, saints, and seers of the world— what did they do? In one span of life they lived the whole life of humanity, traversed the whole length of time that it takes ordinary humanity to come to perfection. In one life they perfect themselves; they have no thought for anything else, never live a moment for any other idea, and thus the way is shortened for them. This is what is meant by concentration, intensifying the power of assimilation, thus shortening the time. Raja-Yoga is the science which teaches us how to gain the power of concentration.

What has Pranayama to do with spiritualism? Spiritualism is also a manifestation of Pranayama. If it be true that the departed spirits exist, only we cannot see them, it is quite probable that there may be hundreds and millions of them about us we can neither see, feel, nor touch. We may be continually passing and repassing through their bodies, and they do not see or feel us. It is a circle within a circle, universe within universe. We have five senses, and we represent Prana in a certain state of vibration. All beings in the same state of vibration will see one another, but if there are beings who represent Prana in a higher state of vibration, they will not be seen. We may increase the intensity of a light until we cannot see it at all, but there may be beings with eyes so powerful that they can see such light. Again, if its vibrations are very low, we do not see a light, but there are animals that may see it, as cats and owls. Our range of vision is only one plane of the vibrations of this Prana. Take this atmosphere, for instance; it is piled up layer on layer, but the layers nearer to the earth are denser than those above, and as you go higher the atmosphere becomes finer and finer. Or take the case of the ocean; as you go deeper and deeper the pressure of the water increases, and animals which live at the bottom of the sea can never come up, or they will be broken into pieces.

Think of the universe as an ocean of ether, consisting of layer after layer of varying degrees of vibration under the action of Prana; away from the centre the vibrations are less, nearer to it they become quicker and quicker; one order of vibration makes one plane. Then suppose these ranges of vibrations are cut into planes, so many millions of miles one set of vibration, and then so many millions of miles another still higher set of vibration, and so on. It is, therefore, probable, that those who live on the plane of a certain state of vibration will have the power of recognising one another, but will not recognise those above them. Yet, just as by the telescope and the microscope we can increase the scope of our vision, similarly we can by Yoga bring ourselves to the state of vibration of another plane, and thus enable ourselves to see what is going on there. Suppose this room is full of beings whom we do not see. They represent Prana in a certain state of vibration while we represent another. Suppose they represent a quick one, and we the opposite. Prana is the material of which they are composed, as well as we. All are parts of the same ocean of Prana, they differ only in their rate of vibration. If I can bring myself to the quick vibration, this plane will immediately change for me: I shall not see you any more; you vanish and they appear. Some of you, perhaps, know this to be true. All this bringing of the mind into a higher state of vibration is included in one word in Yoga— Samadhi. All these states of higher vibration, superconscious vibrations of the mind, are grouped in that one word, Samadhi, and the lower states of Samadhi give us visions of these beings. The highest grade of Samadhi is when we see the real thing, when we see the material out of which the whole of these grades of beings are composed, and that one lump of clay being known, we know all the clay in the universe.

Thus we see that Pranayama includes all that is true of spiritualism even. Similarly, you will find that wherever any sect or body of people is trying to search out anything occult and mystical, or hidden, what they are doing is really this Yoga, this attempt to control the Prana. You will find that wherever there is any extraordinary display of power, it is the manifestation of this Prana. Even the physical sciences can be included in Pranayama. What moves the steam engine? Prana, acting through the steam. What are all these phenomena of electricity and so forth but Prana? What is physical science? The science of Pranayama, by external means. Prana, manifesting itself as mental power, can only be controlled by mental means. That part of Pranayama which attempts to control the physical manifestations of the Prana by physical means is called physical science, and that part which tries to control the manifestations of the Prana as mental force by mental means is called Raja-Yoga.

Chapter IV
The Psychic Prana

According to the Yogis, there are two nerve currents in the spinal column, called Pingalâ and Idâ, and a hollow canal called Sushumnâ running through the spinal cord. At the lower end of the hollow canal is what the Yogis call the "Lotus of the Kundalini". They describe it as triangular in form in which, in the symbolical language of the Yogis, there is a power called the Kundalini, coiled up. When that Kundalini awakes, it tries to force a passage through this hollow canal, and as it rises step by step, as it were, layer after layer of the mind becomes open and all the different visions and wonderful powers come to the Yogi. When it reaches the brain, the Yogi is perfectly detached from the body and mind; the soul finds itself free. We know that the spinal cord is composed in a peculiar manner. If we take the figure eight horizontally (∞) there are two parts which are connected in the middle. Suppose you add eight after eight, piled one on top of the other, that will represent the spinal cord. The left is the Ida, the right Pingala, and that hollow canal which runs through the centre of the spinal cord is the Sushumna. Where the spinal cord ends in some of the lumbar vertebrae, a fine fibre issues downwards, and the canal runs up even within that fibre, only much finer. The canal is closed at the lower end, which is situated near what is called the sacral plexus, which, according to modern physiology, is triangular in form. The different plexuses that have their centres in the spinal canal can very well stand for the different "lotuses" of the Yogi.

The Yogi conceives of several centres, beginning with the Mulâdhâra, the basic, and ending with the Sahasrâra, the thousand-petalled Lotus in the brain. So, if we take these different plexuses as representing these lotuses, the idea of the Yogi can be understood very easily in the language of modern physiology. We know there are two sorts of actions in these nerve currents, one afferent, the other efferent; one sensory and the other motor; one centripetal, and the other centrifugal. One carries the sensations to the brain, and the other from the brain to the outer body. These vibrations are all connected with the brain in the long run. Several other facts we have to remember, in order to clear the way for the explanation which is to come. This spinal cord, at the brain, ends in a sort of bulb, in the medulla, which is not attached to the brain, but floats in a fluid in the brain, so that if there be a blow on the head the force of that blow will be dissipated in the fluid, and will not hurt the bulb. This is an important fact to remember. Secondly, we have also to know that, of all the centres, we have particularly to remember three, the Muladhara (the basic), the Sahasrara (the thousand-petalled lotus of the brain) and the Manipura (the lotus of the navel).

Next we shall take one fact from physics. We all hear of electricity and various other forces connected with it. What electricity is no one knows, but so far as it is known, it is a sort of motion. There are various other motions in the universe; what is the difference between them and electricity? Suppose this table moves — that the molecules which compose this table are moving in different directions; if they are all made to move in the same direction, it will be through electricity. Electric motion makes the molecules of a body move in the same direction. If all the air molecules in a room are made to move in the same direction, it will make a gigantic battery of electricity of the room. Another point from physiology we must remember, that the centre which regulates the respiratory system, the breathing system, has a sort of controlling action over the system of nerve currents.

Now we shall see why breathing is practised. In the first place, from rhythmical breathing comes a tendency of all the molecules in the body to move in the same direction. When mind changes into will, the nerve currents change into a motion similar to electricity, because the nerves have been proved to show polarity under the action of electric currents. This shows that when the will is transformed into the nerve currents, it is changed into something like electricity. When all the motions of the body have become perfectly rhythmical, the body has, as it were, become a gigantic battery of will. This tremendous will is exactly what the Yogi wants. This is, therefore, a physiological explanation of the breathing exercise. It tends to bring a rhythmic action in the body, and helps us, through the respiratory centre, to control the other centres. The aim of Prânâyâma here is to rouse the coiled-up power in the Muladhara, called the Kundalini.

Everything that we see, or imagine, or dream, we have to perceive in space. This is the ordinary space, called the Mahâkâsha, or elemental space. When a Yogi reads the thoughts of other men, or perceives supersensuous objects he sees them in another sort of space called the Chittâkâsha, the mental space. When perception has become objectless, and the soul shines in its own nature, it is called the Chidâkâsha, or knowledge space. When the Kundalini is aroused, and enters the canal of the Sushumna, all the perceptions are in the mental space. When it has reached that end of the canal which opens out into the brain, the objectless perception is in the knowledge space. Taking the analogy of electricity, we find that man can send a current only along a wire, (The reader should remember that this was spoken before the discovery of wireless telegraphy.—Ed.) but nature requires no wires to send her tremendous currents. This proves that the wire is not really necessary, but that only our inability to dispense with it compels us to use it.

Similarly, all the sensations and motions of the body are being sent into the brain, and sent out of it, through these wires of nerve fibres. The columns of sensory and motor fibres in the spinal cord are the Ida and Pingala of the Yogis. They are the main channels through which the afferent and efferent currents travel. But why should not the mind send news without any wire, or react without any wire ? We see this is done in nature. The Yogi says, if you can do that, you have got rid of the bondage of matter. How to do it ? If you can make the current pass through the Sushumna, the canal in the middle of the spinal column, you have solved the problem. The mind has made this network of the nervous system, and has to break it, so that no wires will be required to work through. Then alone will all knowledge come to us— no more bondage of body; that is why it is so important that we should get control of that Sushumna. If we can send the mental current through the hollow canal without any nerve fibres to act as wires, the Yogi says, the problem is solved, and he also says it can be done.

This Sushumna is in ordinary persons closed up at the lower extremity; no action comes through it. The Yogi proposes a practice by which it can be opened, and the nerve currents made to travel through. When a sensation is carried to a centre, the centre reacts. This reaction, in the case of automatic centres, is followed by motion; in the case of conscious centres it is followed first by perception, and secondly by motion. All perception is the reaction to action from outside. How, then, do perceptions in dreams arise ? There is then no action from outside. The sensory motions, therefore, are coiled up somewhere. For instance, I see a city; the perception of that city is from the reaction to the sensations brought from outside objects comprising that city. That is to say, a certain motion in the brain molecules has been set up by the motion in the incarrying nerves, which again are set in motion by external objects in the city. Now, even after a long time I can remember the city. This memory is exactly the same phenomenon, only it is in a milder form. But whence is the action that sets up even the milder form of similar vibrations in the brain ? Not certainly from the primary sensations. Therefore it must be that the sensations are coiled up somewhere, and they, by their acting, bring out the mild reaction which we call dream perception.

Now the centre where all these residual sensations are, as it were, stored up, is called the Muladhara, the root receptacle, and the coiled-up energy of action is Kundalini, "the coiled up". It is very probable that the residual motor energy is also stored up in the same centre, as, after deep study or meditation on external objects, the part of the body where the Muladhara centre is situated (probably the sacral plexus) gets heated. Now, if this coiled-up energy be roused and made active, and then consciously made to travel up the Sushumna canal, as it acts upon centre after centre, a tremendous reaction will set in. When a minute portion of energy travels along a nerve fibre and causes reaction from centres, the perception is either dream or imagination. But when by the power of long internal meditation the vast mass of energy stored up travels along the Sushumna, and strikes the centres, the reaction is tremendous, immensely superior to the reaction of dream or imagination, immensely more intense than the reaction of sense-perception. It is super-sensuous perception. And when it reaches the metropolis of all sensations, the brain, the whole brain, as it were, reacts, and the result is the full blaze of illumination, the perception of the Self. As this Kundalini force travels from centre to centre, layer after layer of the mind, as it were, opens up, and this universe is perceived by the Yogi in its fine, or causal form. Then alone the causes of this universe, both as sensation and reaction, are known as they are, and hence comes all knowledge. The causes being known, the knowledge of the effects is sure to follow.

Thus the rousing of the Kundalini is the one and only way to attaining Divine Wisdom, superconscious perception, realisation of the spirit. The rousing may come in various ways, through love for God, through the mercy of perfected sages, or through the power of the analytic will of the philosopher. Wherever there was any manifestation of what is ordinarily called supernatural power or wisdom, there a little current of Kundalini must have found its way into the Sushumna. Only, in the vast majority of such cases, people had ignorantly stumbled on some practice which set free a minute portion of the coiled-up Kundalini. All worship, consciously or unconsciously, leads to this end. The man who thinks that he is receiving response to his prayers does not know that the fulfilment comes from his own nature, that he has succeeded by the mental attitude of prayer in waking up a bit of this infinite power which is coiled up within himself. What, thus, men ignorantly worship under various names, through fear and tribulation, the Yogi declares to the world to be the real power coiled up in every being, the mother of eternal happiness, if we but know how to approach her. And Râja-Yoga is the science of religion, the rationale of all worship, all prayers, forms, ceremonies, and miracles.

Chapter V
The Control of Psychic Prana

We have now to deal with the exercises in Prânâyâma. We have seen that the first step, according to the Yogis, is to control the motion of the lungs. What we want to do is to feel the finer motions that are going on in the body. Our minds have become externalised, and have lost sight of the fine motions inside. If we can begin to feel them, we can begin to control them. These nerve currents go on all over the body, bringing life and vitality to every muscle, but we do not feel them. The Yogi says we can learn to do so. How? By taking up and controlling the motion of the lungs; when we have done that for a sufficient length of time, we shall be able to control the finer motions.

We now come to the exercises in Pranayama. Sit upright; the body must be kept straight. The spinal cord, although not attached to the vertebral column, is yet inside of it. If you sit crookedly you disturb this spinal cord, so let it be free. Any time that you sit crookedly and try to meditate you do yourself an injury. The three parts of the body, the chest, the neck, and the head, must be always held straight in one line. You will find that by a little practice this will come to you as easy as breathing. The second thing is to get control of the nerves. We have said that the nerve centre that controls the respiratory organs has a sort of controlling effect on the other nerves, and rhythmical breathing is, therefore, necessary. The breathing that we generally use should not be called breathing at all. It is very irregular. Then there are some natural differences of breathing between men and women.

The first lesson is just to breathe in a measured way, in and out. That will harmonise the system. When you have practiced this for some time, you will do well to join to it the repetition of some word as "Om," or any other sacred word. In India we use certain symbolical words instead of counting one, two, three, four. That is why I advise you to join the mental repetition of the "Om," or some other sacred word to the Pranayama. Let the word flow in and out with the breath, rhythmically, harmoniously, and you will find the whole body is becoming rhythmical. Then you will learn what rest is. Compared with it, sleep is not rest. Once this rest comes the most tired nerves will be calmed down, and you will find that you have never before really rested.

The first effect of this practice is perceived in the change of expression of one's face; harsh lines disappear; with calm thought calmness comes over the face. Next comes beautiful voice. I never saw a Yogi with a croaking voice. These signs come after a few months' practice. After practicing the above mentioned breathing for a few days, you should take up a higher one. Slowly fill the lungs with breath through the Idâ, the left nostril, and at the same time concentrate the mind on the nerve current. You are, as it were, sending the nerve current down the spinal column, and striking violently on the last plexus, the basic lotus which is triangular in form, the seat of the Kundalini. Then hold the current there for some time. Imagine that you are slowly drawing that nerve current with the breath through the other side, the Pingalâ, then slowly throw it out through the right nostril. This you will find a little difficult to practice. The easiest way is to stop the right nostril with the thumb, and then slowly draw in the breath through the left; then close both nostrils with thumb and forefinger, and imagine that you are sending that current down, and striking the base of the Sushumnâ; then take the thumb off, and let the breath out through the right nostril. Next inhale slowly through that nostril, keeping the other closed by the forefinger, then close both, as before. The way the Hindus practice this would be very difficult for this country, because they do it from their childhood, and their lungs are prepared for it. Here it is well to begin with four seconds, and slowly increase. Draw in four seconds, hold in sixteen seconds, then throw out in eight seconds. This makes one Pranayama. At the same time think of the basic lotus, triangular in form; concentrate the mind on that centre. The imagination can help you a great deal. The next breathing is slowly drawing the breath in, and then immediately throwing it out slowly, and then stopping the breath out, using the same numbers. The only difference is that in the first case the breath was held in, and in the second, held out. This last is the easier one. The breathing in which you hold the breath in the lungs must not be practiced too much. Do it only four times in the morning, and four times in the evening. Then you can slowly increase the time and number. You will find that you have the power to do so, and that you take pleasure in it. So very carefully and cautiously increase as you feel that you have the power, to six instead of four. It may injure you if you practice it irregularly.

Of the three processes for the purification of the nerves, described above, the first and the last are neither difficult nor dangerous. The more you practice the first one the calmer you will be. Just think of "Om," and you can practice even while you are sitting at your work. You will be all the better for it. Some day, if you practice hard, the Kundalini will be aroused. For those who practice once or twice a day, just a little calmness of the body and mind will come, and beautiful voice; only for those who can go on further with it will Kundalini be aroused, and the whole of nature will begin to change, and the book of knowledge will open. No more will you need to go to books for knowledge; your own mind will have become your book, containing infinite knowledge. I have already spoken of the Ida and Pingala currents, flowing through either side of the spinal column, and also of the Sushumna, the passage through the centre of the spinal cord. These three are present in every animal; whatever being has a spinal column has these three lines of action. But the Yogis claim that in an ordinary man the Sushumna is closed; its action is not evident while that of the other two is carrying power to different parts of the body.

The Yogi alone has the Sushumna open. When this Sushumna current opens, and begins to rise, we get beyond the sense, our minds become supersensuous, superconscious— we get beyond even the intellect, where reasoning cannot reach. To open that Sushumna is the prime object of the Yogi. According to him, along this Sushumna are ranged these centres, or, in more figurative language, these lotuses, as they are called. The lowest one is at the lower end of the spinal cord, and is called Mulâdhara, the next higher is called Svâdhishthâna, the third Manipura, the fourth Anâhata, the fifth Vishuddha, the sixth Âjnâ and the last, which is in the brain, is the Sahasrâra, or "the thousand-petalled". Of these we have to take cognition just now of two centres only, the lowest, the Muladhara, and the highest, the Sahasrara. All energy has to be taken up from its seat in the Muladhara and brought to the Sahasrara. The Yogis claim that of all the energies that are in the human body the highest is what they call "Ojas". Now this Ojas is stored up in the brain, and the more Ojas is in a man's head, the more powerful he is, the more intellectual, the more spiritually strong. One man may speak beautiful language and beautiful thoughts, but they, do not impress people; another man speaks neither beautiful language nor beautiful thoughts, yet his words charm. Every movement of his is powerful. That is the power of Ojas.

Now in every man there is more or less of this Ojas stored up. All the forces that are working in the body in their highest become Ojas. You must remember that it is only a question of transformation. The same force which is working outside as electricity or magnetism will become changed into inner force; the same forces that are working as muscular energy will be changed into Ojas. The Yogis say that that part of the human energy which is expressed as sex energy, in sexual thought, when checked and controlled, easily becomes changed into Ojas, and as the Muladhara guides these, the Yogi pays particular attention to that centre. He tries to take up all his sexual energy and convert it into Ojas. It is only the chaste man or woman who can make the Ojas rise and store it in the brain; that is why chastity has always been considered the highest virtue. A man feels that if he is unchaste, spirituality goes away, he loses mental vigour and moral stamina. That is why in all the religious orders in the world which have produced spiritual giants you will always find absolute chastity insisted upon. That is why the monks came into existence, giving up marriage. There must be perfect chastity in thought, word, and deed; without it the practice of Raja-Yoga is dangerous, and may lead to insanity. If people practice Raja-Yoga and at the same time lead an impure life, how can they expect to become Yogis?

Chapter VI
Pratyahara and Dharana

The next step is called Pratyâhâra. What is this? You know how perceptions come. First of all there are the external instruments, then the internal organs acting in the body through the brain centres, and there is the mind. When these come together and attach themselves to some external object, then we perceive it. At the same time it is a very difficult thing to concentrate the mind and attach it to one organ only; the mind is a slave.

We hear "Be good," and "Be good," and "Be good," taught all over the world. There is hardly a child, born in any country in the world, who has not been told, "Do not steal," "Do not tell a lie," but nobody tells the child how he can help doing them. Talking will not help him. Why should he not become a thief? We do not teach him how not to steal; we simply tell him, "Do not steal." Only when we teach him to control his mind do we really help him. All actions, internal and external, occur when the mind joins itself to certain centres, called the organs. Willingly or unwillingly it is drawn to join itself to the centres, and that is why people do foolish deeds and feel miserable, which, if the mind were under control, they would not do. What would be the result of controlling the mind? It then would not join itself to the centres of perception, and, naturally, feeling and willing would be under control. It is clear so far. Is it possible? It is perfectly possible. You see it in modern times; the faith-healers teach people to deny misery and pain and evil. Their philosophy is rather roundabout, but it is a part of Yoga upon which they have somehow stumbled. Where they succeed in making a person throw off suffering by denying it, they really use a part of Pratyahara, as they make the mind of the person strong enough to ignore the senses. The hypnotists in a similar manner, by their suggestion, excite in the patient a sort of morbid Pratyahara for the time being. The so-called hypnotic suggestion can only act upon a weak mind. And until the operator, by means of fixed gaze or otherwise, has succeeded in putting the mind of the subject in a sort of passive, morbid condition, his suggestions never work.

Now the control of the centres which is established in a hypnotic patient or the patient of faith-healing, by the operator, for a time, is reprehensible, because it leads to ultimate ruin. It is not really controlling the brain centres by the power of one's own will, but is, as it were, stunning the patient's mind for a time by sudden blows which another's will delivers to it. It is not checking by means of reins and muscular strength the mad career of a fiery team, but rather by asking another to deliver heavy blows on the heads of the horses, to stun them for a time into gentleness. At each one of these processes the man operated upon loses a part of his mental energies, till at last, the mind, instead of gaining the power of perfect control, becomes a shapeless, powerless mass, and the only goal of the patient is the lunatic asylum.

Every attempt at control which is not voluntary, not with the controller's own mind, is not only disastrous, but it defeats the end. The goal of each soul is freedom, mastery— freedom from the slavery of matter and thought, mastery of external and internal nature. Instead of leading towards that, every will-current from another, in whatever form it comes, either as direct control of organs, or as forcing to control them while under a morbid condition, only rivets one link more to the already existing heavy chain of bondage of past thoughts, past superstitions. Therefore, beware how you allow yourselves to be acted upon by others. Beware how you unknowingly bring another to ruin. True, some succeed in doing good to many for a time, by giving a new trend to their propensities, but at the same time, they bring ruin to millions by the unconscious suggestions they throw around, rousing in men and women that morbid, passive, hypnotic condition which makes them almost soulless at last. Whosoever, therefore, asks any one to believe blindly, or drags people behind him by the controlling power of his superior will, does an injury to humanity, though he may not intend it.

Therefore use your own minds, control body and mind yourselves, remember that until you are a diseased person, no extraneous will can work upon you; avoid everyone, however great and good he may be, who asks you to believe blindly. All over the world there have been dancing and jumping and howling sects, who spread like infection when they begin to sing and dance and preach; they also are a sort of hypnotists. They exercise a singular control for the time being over sensitive persons, alas! often, in the long run, to degenerate whole races. Ay, it is healthier for the individual or the race to remain wicked than be made apparently good by such morbid extraneous control. One's heart sinks to think of the amount of injury done to humanity by such irresponsible yet well-meaning religious fanatics. They little know that the minds which attain to sudden spiritual upheaval under their suggestions, with music and prayers, are simply making themselves passive, morbid, and powerless, and opening themselves to any other suggestion, be it ever so evil. Little do these ignorant, deluded persons dream that whilst they are congratulating themselves upon their miraculous power to transform human hearts, which power they think was poured upon them by some Being above the clouds, they are sowing the seeds of future decay, of crime, of lunacy, and of death. Therefore, beware of everything that takes away your freedom. Know that it is dangerous, and avoid it by all the means in your power.

He who has succeeded in attaching or detaching his mind to or from the centres at will has succeeded in Pratyahara, which means, "gathering towards," checking the outgoing powers of the mind, freeing it from the thraldom of the senses. When we can do this, we shall really possess character; then alone we shall have taken a long step towards freedom; before that we are mere machines.

How hard it is to control the mind! Well has it been compared to the maddened monkey. There was a monkey, restless by his own nature, as all monkeys are. As if that were not enough some one made him drink freely of wine, so that he became still more restless. Then a scorpion stung him. When a man is stung by a scorpion, he jumps about for a whole day; so the poor monkey found his condition worse than ever. To complete his misery a demon entered into him. What language can describe the uncontrollable restlessness of that monkey? The human mind is like that monkey, incessantly active by its own nature; then it becomes drunk with the wine of desire, thus increasing its turbulence. After desire takes possession comes the sting of the scorpion of jealousy at the success of others, and last of all the demon of pride enters the mind, making it think itself of all importance. How hard to control such a mind!

The first lesson, then, is to sit for some time and let the mind run on. The mind is bubbling up all the time. It is like that monkey jumping about. Let the monkey jump as much as he can; you simply wait and watch. Knowledge is power, says the proverb, and that is true. Until you know what the mind is doing you cannot control it. Give it the rein; many hideous thoughts may come into it; you will be astonished that it was possible for you to think such thoughts. But you will find that each day the mind's vagaries are becoming less and less violent, that each day it is becoming calmer. In the first few months you will find that the mind will have a great many thoughts, later you will find that they have somewhat decreased, and in a few more months they will be fewer and fewer, until at last the mind will be under perfect control; but we must patiently practice every day. As soon as the steam is turned on, the engine must run; as soon as things are before us we must perceive; so a man, to prove that he is not a machine, must demonstrate that he is under the control of nothing. This controlling of the mind, and not allowing it to join itself to the centres, is Pratyahara. How is this practised? It is a tremendous work, not to be done in a day. Only after a patient, continuous struggle for years can we succeed.

After you have practised Pratyahara for a time, take the next step, the Dhâranâ, holding the mind to certain points. What is meant by holding the mind to certain points? Forcing the mind to feel certain parts of the body to the exclusion of others. For instance, try to feel only the hand, to the exclusion of other parts of the body. When the Chitta, or mind-stuff, is confined and limited to a certain place it is Dharana. This Dharana is of various sorts, and along with it, it is better to have a little play of the imagination. For instance, the mind should be made to think of one point in the heart. That is very difficult; an easier way is to imagine a lotus there. That lotus is full of light, effulgent light. Put the mind there. Or think of the lotus in the brain as full of light, or of the different centres in the Sushumna mentioned before.

The Yogi must always practice. He should try to live alone; the companionship of different sorts of people distracts the mind; he should not speak much, because to speak distracts the mind; not work much, because too much work distracts the mind; the mind cannot be controlled after a whole day's hard work. One observing the above rules becomes a Yogi. Such is the power of Yoga that even the least of it will bring a great amount of benefit. It will not hurt anyone, but will benefit everyone. First of all, it will tone down nervous excitement, bring calmness, enable us to see things more clearly. The temperament will be better, and the health will be better. Sound health will be one of the first signs, and a beautiful voice. Defects in the voice will be changed. This will be among the first of the many effects that will come. Those who practise hard will get many other signs. Sometimes there will be sounds, as a peal of bells heard at a distance, commingling, and falling on the ear as one continuous sound. Sometimes things will be seen, little specks of light floating and becoming bigger and bigger; and when these things come, know that you are progressing fast.

Those who want to be Yogis, and practice hard, must take care of their diet at first. But for those who want only a little practice for everyday business sort of life, let them not eat too much; otherwise they may eat whatever they please. For those who want to make rapid progress, and to practice hard, a strict diet is absolutely necessary. They will find it advantageous to live only on milk and cereals for some months. As the organisation becomes finer and finer, it will be found in the beginning that the least irregularity throws one out of balance. One bit of food more or less will disturb the whole system, until one gets perfect control, and then one will be able to eat whatever one likes.

When one begins to concentrate, the dropping of a pin will seem like a thunderbolt going through the brain. As the organs get finer, the perceptions get finer. These are the stages through which we have to pass, and all those who persevere will succeed. Give up all argumentation and other distractions. Is there anything in dry intellectual jargon? It only throws the mind off its balance and disturbs it. Things of subtler planes have to be realised. Will talking do that? So give up all vain talk. Read only those books which have been written by persons who have had realisation.

Be like the pearl oyster. There is a pretty Indian fable to the effect that if it rains when the star Svâti is in the ascendant, and a drop of rain falls into an oyster, that drop becomes a pearl. The oysters know this, so they come to the surface when that star shines, and wait to catch the precious raindrop. When a drop falls into them, quickly the oysters close their shells and dive down to the bottom of the sea, there to patiently develop the drop into the pearl. We should be like that. First hear, then understand, and then, leaving all distractions, shut your minds to outside influences, and devote yourselves to developing the truth within you. There is the danger of frittering away your energies by taking up an idea only for its novelty, and then giving it up for another that is newer. Take one thing up and do it, and see the end of it, and before you have seen the end, do not give it up. He who can become mad with an idea, he alone sees light. Those that only take a nibble here and a nibble there will never attain anything. They may titillate their nerves for a moment, but there it will end. They will be slaves in the hands of nature, and will never get beyond the senses.

Those who really want to be Yogis must give up, once for all, this nibbling at things. Take up one idea. Make that one idea your life— think of it, dream of it, live on that idea. Let the brain, muscles, nerves, every part of your body, be full of that idea, and just leave every other idea alone. This is the way to success, and this is the way great spiritual giants are produced. Others are mere talking machines. If we really want to be blessed, and make others blessed, we must go deeper. The first step is not to disturb the mind, not to associate with persons whose ideas are disturbing. All of you know that certain persons, certain places, certain foods, repel you. Avoid them; and those who want to go to the highest, must avoid all company, good or bad. Practise hard; whether you live or die does not matter. You have to plunge in and work, without thinking of the result. If you are brave enough, in six months you will be a perfect Yogi. But those who take up just a bit of it and a little of everything else make no progress. It is of no use simply to take a course of lessons. To those who are full of Tamas, ignorant and dull— those whose minds never get fixed on any idea, who only crave for something to amuse them— religion and philosophy are simply objects of entertainment. These are the unpersevering. They hear a talk, think it very nice, and then go home and forget all about it. To succeed, you must have tremendous perseverance, tremendous will. "I will drink the ocean," says the persevering soul, "at my will mountains will crumble up." Have that sort of energy, that sort of will, work hard, and you will reach the goal.

Chapter VII
Dhyana and Samadhi

We have taken a cursory view of the different steps in Râja-Yoga, except the finer ones, the training in concentration, which is the goal to which Raja-Yoga will lead us. We see, as human beings, that all our knowledge which is called rational is referred to consciousness. My consciousness of this table, and of your presence, makes me know that the table and you are here. At the same time, there is a very great part of my existence of which I am not conscious. All the different organs inside the body, the different parts of the brain— nobody is conscious of these.

When I eat food, I do it consciously; when I assimilate it, I do it unconsciously. When the food is manufactured into blood, it is done unconsciously. When out of the blood all the different parts of my body are strengthened, it is done unconsciously. And yet it is I who am doing all this; there cannot be twenty people in this one body. How do I know that I do it, and nobody else? It may be urged that my business is only in eating and assimilating the food, and that strengthening the body by the food is done for me by somebody else. That cannot be, because it can be demonstrated that almost every action of which we are now unconscious can be brought up to the plane of consciousness. The heart is beating apparently without our control. None of us here can control the heart; it goes on its own way. But by practice men can bring even the heart under control, until it will just beat at will, slowly, or quickly, or almost stop. Nearly every part of the body can be brought under control. What does this show? That the functions which are beneath consciousness are also performed by us, only we are doing it unconsciously. We have, then, two planes in which the human mind works. First is the conscious plane, in which all work is always accompanied with the feeling of egoism. Next comes the unconscious plane, where all work is unaccompanied by the feeling of egoism. That part of mind-work which is unaccompanied with the feeling of egoism is unconscious work, and that part which is accompanied with the feeling of egoism is conscious work. In the lower animals this unconscious work is called instinct. In higher animals, and in the highest of all animals, man, what is called conscious work prevails.

But it does not end here. There is a still higher plane upon which the mind can work. It can go beyond consciousness. Just as unconscious work is beneath consciousness, so there is another work which is above consciousness, and which also is not accompanied with the feeling of egoism. The feeling of egoism is only on the middle plane. When the mind is above or below that line, there is no feeling of "I", and yet the mind works. When the mind goes beyond this line of self-consciousness, it is called Samâdhi or superconsciousness. How, for instance, do we know that a man in Samadhi has not gone below consciousness, has not degenerated instead of going higher? In both cases the works are unaccompanied with egoism. The answer is, by the effects, by the results of the work, we know that which is below, and that which is above. When a man goes into deep sleep, he enters a plane beneath consciousness. He works the body all the time, he breathes, he moves the body, perhaps, in his sleep, without any accompanying feeling of ego; he is unconscious, and when he returns from his sleep, he is the same man who went into it. The sum total of the knowledge which he had before he went into the sleep remains the same; it does not increase at all. No enlightenment comes. But when a man goes into Samadhi, if he goes into it a fool, he comes out a sage.

What makes the difference? From one state a man comes out the very same man that he went in, and from another state the man comes out enlightened, a sage, a prophet, a saint, his whole character changed, his life changed, illumined. These are the two effects. Now the effects being different, the causes must be different. As this illumination with which a man comes back from Samadhi is much higher than can be got from unconsciousness, or much higher than can be got by reasoning in a conscious state, it must, therefore, be superconsciousness, and Samadhi is called the superconscious state.

This, in short, is the idea of Samadhi. What is its application? The application is here. The field of reason, or of the conscious workings of the mind, is narrow and limited. There is a little circle within which human reason must move. It cannot go beyond. Every attempt to go beyond is impossible, yet it is beyond this circle of reason that there lies all that humanity holds most dear. All these questions, whether there is an immortal soul, whether there is a God, whether there is any supreme intelligence guiding this universe or not, are beyond the field of reason. Reason can never answer these questions. What does reason say? It says, "I am agnostic; I do not know either yea or nay." Yet these questions are so important to us. Without a proper answer to them, human life will be purposeless. All our ethical theories, all our moral attitudes, all that is good and great in human nature, have been moulded upon answers that have come from beyond the circle. It is very important, therefore, that we should have answers to these questions. If life is only a short play, if the universe is only a "fortuitous combination of atoms," then why should I do good to another? Why should there be mercy, justice, or fellow-feeling? The best thing for this world would be to make hay while the sun shines, each man for himself. If there is no hope, why should I love my brother, and not cut his throat? If there is nothing beyond, if there is no freedom, but only rigorous dead laws, I should only try to make myself happy here. You will find people saying nowadays that they have utilitarian grounds as the basis of morality. What is this basis? Procuring the greatest amount of happiness to the greatest number. Why should I do this? Why should I not produce the greatest unhappiness to the greatest number, if that serves my purpose? How will utilitarians answer this question? How do you know what is right, or what is wrong? I am impelled by my desire for happiness, and I fulfil it, and it is in my nature; I know nothing beyond. I have these desires, and must fulfil them; why should you complain? Whence come all these truths about human life, about morality, about the immortal soul, about God, about love and sympathy, about being good, and, above all, about being unselfish?

All ethics, all human action and all human thought, hang upon this one idea of unselfishness. The whole idea of human life can be put into that one word, unselfishness. Why should we be unselfish? Where is the necessity, the force, the power, of my being unselfish? You call yourself a rational man, a utilitarian; but if you do not show me a reason for utility, I say you are irrational. Show me the reason why I should not be selfish. To ask one to be unselfish may be good as poetry, but poetry is not reason. Show me a reason. Why shall I be unselfish, and why be good? Because Mr. and Mrs. So-and-so say so does not weigh with me. Where is the utility of my being unselfish? My utility is to be selfish if utility means the greatest amount of happiness. What is the answer? The utilitarian can never give it. The answer is that this world is only one drop in an infinite ocean, one link in an infinite chain. Where did those that preached unselfishness, and taught it to the human race, get this idea? We know it is not instinctive; the animals, which have instinct, do not know it. Neither is it reason; reason does not know anything about these ideas. Whence then did they come?

We find, in studying history, one fact held in common by all the great teachers of religion the world ever had. They all claim to have got their truths from beyond, only many of them did not know where they got them from. For instance, one would say that an angel came down in the form of a human being, with wings, and said to him, "Hear, O man, this is the message." Another says that a Deva, a bright being, appeared to him. A third says he dreamed that his ancestor came and told him certain things. He did not know anything beyond that. But this is common that all claim that this knowledge has come to them from beyond, not through their reasoning power. What does the science of Yoga teach? It teaches that they were right in claiming that all this knowledge came to them from beyond reasoning, but that it came from within themselves.

The Yogi teaches that the mind itself has a higher state of existence, beyond reason, a superconscious state, and when the mind gets to that higher state, then this knowledge, beyond reasoning, comes to man. Metaphysical and transcendental knowledge comes to that man. This state of going beyond reason, transcending ordinary human nature, may sometimes come by chance to a man who does not understand its science; he, as it were, stumbles upon it. When he stumbles upon it, he generally interprets it as coming from outside. So this explains why an inspiration, or transcendental knowledge, may be the same in different countries, but in one country it will seem to come through an angel, and in another through a Deva, and in a third through God. What does it mean? It means that the mind brought the knowledge by its own nature, and that the finding of the knowledge was interpreted according to the belief and education of the person through whom it came. The real fact is that these various men, as it were, stumbled upon this superconscious state.

The Yogi says there is a great danger in stumbling upon this state. In a good many cases there is the danger of the brain being deranged, and, as a rule, you will find that all those men, however great they were, who had stumbled upon this superconscious state without understanding it, groped in the dark, and generally had, along with their knowledge, some quaint superstition. They opened themselves to hallucinations. Mohammed claimed that the Angel Gabriel came to him in a cave one day and took him on the heavenly horse, Harak, and he visited the heavens. But with all that, Mohammed spoke some wonderful truths. If you read the Koran, you find the most wonderful truths mixed with superstitions. How will you explain it? That man was inspired, no doubt, but that inspiration was, as it were, stumbled upon. He was not a trained Yogi, and did not know the reason of what he was doing. Think of the good Mohammed did to the world, and think of the great evil that has been done through his fanaticism! Think of the millions massacred through his teachings, mothers bereft of their children, children made orphans, whole countries destroyed, millions upon millions of people killed! So we see this danger by studying the lives of great teachers like Mohammed and others. Yet we find, at the same time, that they were all inspired. Whenever a prophet got into the superconscious state by heightening his emotional nature, he brought away from it not only some truths, but some fanaticism also, some superstition which injured the world as much as the greatness of the teaching helped. To get any reason out of the mass of incongruity we call human life, we have to transcend our reason, but we must do it scientifically, slowly, by regular practice, and we must cast off all superstition. We must take up the study of the superconscious state just as any other science. On reason we must have to lay our foundation, we must follow reason as far as it leads, and when reason fails, reason itself will show us the way to the highest plane. When you hear a man say, "I am inspired," and then talk irrationally, reject it. Why? Because these three states — instinct, reason, and superconsciousness, or the unconscious, conscious, and superconscious states — belong to one and the same mind. There are not three minds in one man, but one state of it develops into the others. Instinct develops into reason, and reason into the transcendental consciousness; therefore, not one of the states contradicts the others. Real inspiration never contradicts reason, but fulfils it. Just as you find the great prophets saying, "I come not to destroy but to fulfil," so inspiration always comes to fulfil reason, and is in harmony with it.

All the different steps in Yoga are intended to bring us scientifically to the superconscious state, or Samadhi. Furthermore, this is a most vital point to understand, that inspiration is as much in every man's nature as it was in that of the ancient prophets. These prophets were not unique; they were men as you or I. They were great Yogis. They had gained this superconsciousness, and you and I can get the same. They were not peculiar people. The very fact that one man ever reached that state, proves that it is possible for every man to do so. Not only is it possible, but every man must, eventually, get to that state, and that is religion. Experience is the only teacher we have. We may talk and reason all our lives, but we shall not understand a word of truth, until we experience it ourselves. You cannot hope to make a man a surgeon by simply giving him a few books. You cannot satisfy my curiosity to see a country by showing me a map; I must have actual experience. Maps can only create curiosity in us to get more perfect knowledge. Beyond that, they have no value whatever. Clinging to books only degenerates the human mind. Was there ever a more horrible blasphemy than the statement that all the knowledge of God is confined to this or that book? How dare men call God infinite, and yet try to compress Him within the covers of a little book! Millions of people have been killed because they did not believe what the books said, because they would not see all the knowledge of God within the covers of a book. Of course this killing and murdering has gone by, but the world is still tremendously bound up in a belief in books.

In order to reach the superconscious state in a scientific manner it is necessary to pass through the various steps of Raja-Yoga I have been teaching. After Pratyâhâra and Dhâranâ, we come to Dhyâna, meditation. When the mind has been trained to remain fixed on a certain internal or external location, there comes to it the power of flowing in an unbroken current, as it were, towards that point. This state is called Dhyana. When one has so intensified the power of Dhyana as to be able to reject the external part of perception and remain meditating only on the internal part, the meaning, that state is called Samadhi. The three— Dharana, Dhyana, and Samadhi— together, are called Samyama. That is, if the mind can first concentrate upon an object, and then is able to continue in that concentration for a length of time, and then, by continued concentration, to dwell only on the internal part of the perception of which the object was the effect, everything comes under the control of such a mind.

This meditative state is the highest state of existence. So long as there is desire, no real happiness can come. It is only the contemplative, witness-like study of objects that brings to us real enjoyment and happiness. The animal has its happiness in the senses, the man in his intellect, and the god in spiritual contemplation. It is only to the soul that has attained to this contemplative state that the world really becomes beautiful. To him who desires nothing, and does not mix himself up with them, the manifold changes of nature are one panorama of beauty and sublimity.

These ideas have to be understood in Dhyana, or meditation. We hear a sound. First, there is the external vibration; second, the nerve motion that carries it to the mind; third, the reaction from the mind, along with which flashes the knowledge of the object which was the external cause of these different changes from the ethereal vibrations to the mental reactions. These three are called in Yoga, Shabda (sound), Artha (meaning), and Jnâna (knowledge). In the language of physics and physiology they are called the ethereal vibration, the motion in the nerve and brain, and the mental reaction. Now these, though distinct processes, have become mixed up in such a fashion as to become quite indistinct. In fact, we cannot now perceive any of these, we only perceive their combined effect, what we call the external object. Every act of perception includes these three, and there is no reason why we should not be able to distinguish them.

When, by the previous preparations, it becomes strong and controlled, and has the power of finer perception, the mind should be employed in meditation. This meditation must begin with gross objects and slowly rise to finer and finer, until it becomes objectless. The mind should first be employed in perceiving the external causes of sensations, then the internal motions, and then its own reaction. When it has succeeded in perceiving the external causes of sensations by themselves, the mind will acquire the power of perceiving all fine material existences, all fine bodies and forms. When it can succeed in perceiving the motions inside by themselves, it will gain the control of all mental waves, in itself or in others, even before they have translated themselves into physical energy; and when he will be able to perceive the mental reaction by itself, the Yogi will acquire the knowledge of everything, as every sensible object, and every thought is the result of this reaction. Then will he have seen the very foundations of his mind, and it will be under his perfect control. Different powers will come to the Yogi, and if he yields to the temptations of any one of these, the road to his further progress will be barred. Such is the evil of running after enjoyments. But if he is strong enough to reject even these miraculous powers, he will attain to the goal of Yoga, the complete suppression of the waves in the ocean of the mind. Then the glory of the soul, undisturbed by the distractions of the mind, or motions of the body, will shine in its full effulgence; and the Yogi will find himself as he is and as he always was, the essence of knowledge, the immortal, the all-pervading.

Samadhi is the property of every human being— nay, every animal. From the lowest animal to the highest angel, some time or other, each one will have to come to that state, and then, and then alone, will real religion begin for him. Until then we only struggle towards that stage. There is no difference now between us and those who have no religion, because we have no experience. What is concentration good for, save to bring us to this experience? Each one of the steps to attain Samadhi has been reasoned out, properly adjusted, scientifically organised, and, when faithfully practiced, will surely lead us to the desired end. Then will all sorrows cease, all miseries vanish; the seeds for actions will be burnt, and the soul will be free for ever.

Chapter VIII
Raja Yoga in Brief

The following is a summary of Râja-Yoga freely translated from the Kurma-Purâna.

The fire of Yoga burns the cage of sin that is around a man. Knowledge becomes purified and Nirvâna is directly obtained. From Yoga comes knowledge; knowledge again helps the Yogi. He who combines in himself both Yoga and knowledge, with him the Lord is pleased. Those that practice Mahâyoga, either once a day, or twice a day, or thrice, or always, know them to be gods. Yoga is divided into two parts. One is called Abhâva, and the other, Mahayoga. Where one's self is meditated upon as zero, and bereft of quality, that is called Abhava. That in which one sees the self as full of bliss and bereft of all impurities, and one with God, is called Mahayoga. The Yogi, by each one, realises his Self. The other Yogas that we read and hear of, do not deserve to be ranked with the excellent Mahayoga in which the Yogi finds himself and the whole universe as God. This is the highest of all Yogas.

Yama, Niyama, Âsana, Prânâyâma, Pratyâhâra, Dhârâna, Dhyâna, and Samâdhi are the steps in Raja-Yoga, of which non-injury, truthfulness, non-covetousness, chastity, not receiving anything from another are called Yama. This purifies the mind, the Chitta. Never producing pain by thought, word, and deed, in any living being, is what is called Ahimsâ, non-injury. There is no virtue higher than non-injury. There is no happiness higher than what a man obtains by this attitude of non-offensiveness, to all creation. By truth we attain fruits of work. Through truth everything is attained. In truth everything is established. Relating facts as they are — this is truth. Not taking others' goods by stealth or by force, is called Asteya, non-covetousness. Chastity in thought, word, and deed, always, and in all conditions, is what is called Brahmacharya. Not receiving any present from anybody, even when one is suffering terribly, is what is called Aparigraha. The idea is, when a man receives a gift from another, his heart becomes impure, he becomes low, he loses his independence, he becomes bound and attached.

The following are helps to success in Yoga and are called Niyama or regular habits and observances; Tapas, austerity; Svâdhyâya, study; Santosha, contentment; Shaucha, purity; Ishvara-pranidhâna, worshipping God. Fasting, or in other ways controlling the body, is called physical Tapas. Repeating the Vedas and other Mantras, by which the Sattva material in the body is purified, is called study, Svadhyaya. There are three sorts of repetitions of these Mantras. One is called the verbal, another semi-verbal, and the third mental. The verbal or audible is the lowest, and the inaudible is the highest of all. The repetition which is loud is the verbal; the next one is where only the lips move, but no sound is heard. The inaudible repetition of the Mantra, accompanied with the thinking of its meaning, is called the "mental repetition," and is the highest. The sages have said that there are two sorts of purification, external and internal. The purification of the body by water, earth, or other materials is the external purification, as bathing etc. Purification of the mind by truth, and by all the other virtues, is what is called internal purification. Both are necessary. It is not sufficient that a man should be internally pure and externally dirty. When both are not attainable the internal purity is the better, but no one will be a Yogi until he has both. Worship of God is by praise, by thought, by devotion.

We have spoken about Yama and Niyama. The next is Asana (posture). The only thing to understand about it is leaving the body free, holding the chest, shoulders, and head straight. Then comes Pranayama. Prana means the vital forces in one's own body, Âyâma means controlling them. There are three sorts of Pranayama, the very simple, the middle, and the very high. Pranayama is divided into three parts: filling, restraining, and emptying. When you begin with twelve seconds it is the lowest Pranayama; when you begin with twenty-four seconds it is the middle Pranayama; that Pranayama is the best which begins with thirty-six seconds. In the lowest kind of Pranayama there is perspiration, in the medium kind, quivering of the body, and in the highest Pranayama levitation of the body and influx of great bliss. There is a Mantra called the Gâyatri. It is a very holy verse of the Vedas. "We meditate on the glory of that Being who has produced this universe; may He enlighten our minds." Om is joined to it at the beginning and the end. In one Pranayama repeat three Gayatris. In all books they speak of Pranayama being divided into Rechaka (rejecting or exhaling), Puraka (inhaling), and Kurnbhaka (restraining, stationary). The Indriyas, the organs of the senses, are acting outwards and coming in contact with external objects. Bringing them under the control of the will is what is called Pratyahara or gathering towards oneself. Fixing the mind on the lotus of the heart, or on the centre of the head, is what is called Dharana. Limited to one spot, making that spot the base, a particular kind of mental waves rises; these are not swallowed up by other kinds of waves, but by degrees become prominent, while all the others recede and finally disappear. Next the multiplicity of these waves gives place to unity and one wave only is left in the mind. This is Dhyana, meditation. When no basis is necessary, when the whole of the mind has become one wave, one-formedness, it is called Samadhi. Bereft of all help from places and centres, only the meaning of the thought is present. If the mind can be fixed on the centre for twelve seconds it will be a Dharana, twelve such Dharanas will be a Dhyana, and twelve such Dhyanas will be a Samadhi.

Where there is fire, or in water or on ground which is strewn with dry leaves, where there are many ant-hills, where there are wild animals, or danger, where four streets meet, where there is too much noise, where there are many wicked persons, Yoga must not be practiced. This applies more particularly to India. Do not practice when the body feels very lazy or ill, or when the mind is very miserable and sorrowful. Go to a place which is well hidden, and where people do not come to disturb you. Do not choose dirty places. Rather choose beautiful scenery, or a room in your own house which is beautiful. When you practice, first salute all the ancient Yogis, and your own Guru, and God, and then begin.

Dhyana is spoken of, and a few examples are given of what to meditate upon. Sit straight, and look at the tip of your nose. Later on we shall come to know how that concentrates the mind, how by controlling the two optic nerves one advances a long way towards the control of the arc of reaction, and so to the control of the will. Here are a few specimens of meditation. Imagine a lotus upon the top of the head, several inches up, with virtue as its centre, and knowledge as its stalk. The eight petals of the lotus are the eight powers of the Yogi. Inside, the stamens and pistils are renunciation. If the Yogi refuses the external powers he will come to salvation. So the eight petals of the lotus are the eight powers, but the internal stamens and pistils are extreme renunciation, the renunciation of all these powers. Inside of that lotus think of the Golden One, the Almighty, the Intangible, He whose name is Om, the Inexpressible, surrounded with effulgent light. Meditate on that. Another meditation is given. Think of a space in your heart, and in the midst of that space think that a flame is burning. Think of that flame as your own soul and inside the flame is another effulgent light, and that is the Soul of your soul, God. Meditate upon that in the heart. Chastity, non-injury, forgiving even the greatest enemy, truth, faith in the Lord, these are all different Vrittis. Be not afraid if you are not perfect in all of these; work, they will come. He who has given up all attachment, all fear, and all anger, he whose whole soul has gone unto the Lord, he who has taken refuge in the Lord, whose heart has become purified, with whatsoever desire he comes to the Lord, He will grant that to him. Therefore worship Him through knowledge, love, or renunciation.

"He who hates none, who is the friend of all, who is merciful to all, who has nothing of his own, who is free from egoism, who is even-minded in pain and pleasure, who is forbearing, who is always satisfied, who works always in Yoga, whose self has become controlled, whose will is firm, whose mind and intellect are given up unto Me, such a one is My beloved Bhakta. From whom comes no disturbance, who cannot be disturbed by others, who is free from joy, anger, fear, and anxiety, such a one is My beloved. He who does not depend on anything, who is pure and active, who does not care whether good comes or evil, and never becomes miserable, who has given up all efforts for himself; who is the same in praise or in blame, with a silent, thoughtful mind, blessed with what little comes in his way, homeless, for the whole world is his home, and who is steady in his ideas, such a one is My beloved Bhakta." Such alone become Yogis.

PATANJALI'S YOGA APHORISMS

There was a great god-sage called Nârada. Just as there are sages among mankind, great Yogis, so there are great Yogis among the gods. Narada was a good Yogi, and very great. He travelled everywhere. One day he was passing through a forest, and saw a man who had been meditating until the white ants had built a huge mound round his body — so long had he been sitting in that position. He said to Narada, "Where are you going?" Narada replied, "I am going to heaven." "Then ask God when He will be merciful to me; when I shall attain freedom." Further on Narada saw another man. He was jumping about, singing, dancing, and said, "Oh, Narada, where are you going?" His voice and his gestures were wild. Narada said, "I am going to heaven." "Then, ask when I shall be free." Narada went on. In the course of time he came again by the same road, and there was the man who had been meditating with the ant-hill round him. He said, "Oh, Narada, did you ask the Lord about me?" "Oh, yes." "What did He say?" "The Lord told me that you would attain freedom in four more births." Then the man began to weep and wail, and said, "I have meditated until an ant-hill has grown around me, and I have four more births yet!" Narada went to the other man. "Did you ask my question?" "Oh, yes. Do you see this tamarind tree? I have to tell you that as many leaves as there are on that tree, so many times, you shall be born, and then you shall attain freedom." The man began to dance for joy, and said, "I shall have freedom after such a short time!" A voice came, "My child, you will have freedom this minute." That was the reward for his perseverance. He was ready to work through all those births, nothing discouraged him. But the first man felt that even four more births were too long. Only perseverance, like that of the man who was willing to wait aeons brings about the highest result.

Introduction

Before going into the Yoga aphorisms I shall try to discuss one great question, upon which rests the whole theory of religion for the Yogis. It seems the consensus of opinion of the great minds of the world, and it has been nearly demonstrated by researches into physical nature, that we are the outcome and manifestation of an absolute condition, back of our present relative condition, and are going forward, to return to that absolute. This being granted, the question is: Which is better, the absolute or this state? There are not wanting people who think that this manifested state is the highest state of man. Thinkers of great calibre are of the opinion that we are manifestations of undifferentiated being and the differentiated state is higher than the absolute. They imagine that in the absolute there cannot be any quality; that it must be insensate, dull, and lifeless; that only this life can be enjoyed, and, therefore, we must cling to it. First of all we want to inquire into other solutions of life. There was an old solution that man after death remained the same; that all his good sides, minus his evil sides, remained for ever. Logically stated, this means that man's goal is the world; this world carried a stage higher, and eliminated of its evils, is the state they call heaven. This theory, on the face of it, is absurd and puerile, because it cannot be. There cannot be good without evil, nor evil without good. To live in a world where it is all good and no evil is what Sanskrit logicians call a "dream in the air". Another theory in modern times has been presented by several schools, that man's destiny is to go on always improving, always struggling towards, but never reaching the goal. This statement, though apparently very nice, is also absurd, because there is no such thing as motion in a straight line. Every motion is in a circle. If you can take up a stone, and project it into space, and then live long enough, that stone, if it meets with no obstruction, will come back exactly to your hand. A straight line, infinitely projected must end in a circle. Therefore, this idea that the destiny of man is progressing ever forward and forward, and never stopping, is absurd. Although extraneous to the subject, I may remark that this idea explains the ethical theory that you must not hate, and must love. Because, just as in the case of electricity the modern theory is that the power leaves the dynamo and completes the circle back to the dynamo, so with hate and love; they must come back to the source. Therefore do not hate anybody, because that hatred which comes out from you, must, in the long run, come back to you. If you love, that love will come back to you, completing the circle. It is as certain as can be, that every bit of hatred that goes out of the heart of a man comes back to him in full force, nothing can stop it; similarly every impulse of love comes back to him.

On other and practical grounds we see that the theory of eternal progression is untenable, for destruction is the goal of everything earthly. All our struggles and hopes and fears and joys, what will they lead to? We shall all end in death. Nothing is so certain as this. Where, then, is this motion in a straight line— this infinite progression? It is only going out to a distance, and coming back to the centre from which it started. See how, from nebulae, the sun, moon, and stars are produced; then they dissolve and go back to nebulae. The same is being done everywhere. The plant takes material from the earth, dissolves, and gives it back. Every form in this world is taken out of surrounding atoms and goes back to these atoms. It cannot be that the same law acts differently in different places. Law is uniform. Nothing is more certain than that. If this is the law of nature, it also applies to thought. Thought will dissolve and go back to its origin. Whether we will it or not, we shall have to return to our origin which is called God or Absolute. We all came from God, and we are all bound to go back to God. Call that by any name you like, God, Absolute, or Nature, the fact remains the same. "From whom all this universe comes out, in whom all that is born lives, and to whom all returns." This is one fact that is certain. Nature works on the same plan; what is being worked out in one sphere is repeated in millions of spheres. What you see with the planets, the same will it be with this earth, with men, and with all. The huge wave is a mighty compound of small waves, it may be of millions; the life of the whole world is a compound of millions of little lives, and the death of the whole world is the compound of the deaths of these millions of little beings.

Now the question arises: Is going back to God the higher state, or not? The philosophers of the Yoga school emphatically answer that it is. They say that man's present state is a degeneration. There is not one religion on the face of the earth which says that man is an improvement. The idea is that his beginning is perfect and pure, that he degenerates until he cannot degenerate further, and that there must come a time when he shoots upward again to complete the circle. The circle must be described. However low he may go, he must ultimately take the upward bend and go back to the original source, which is God. Man comes from God in the beginning, in the middle he becomes man, and in the end he goes back to God. This is the method of putting it in the dualistic form. The monistic form is that man is God, and goes back to Him again. If our present state is the higher one, then why is there so much horror and misery, and why is there an end to it? If this is the higher state, why does it end? That which corrupts and degenerates cannot be the highest state. Why should it be so diabolical, so unsatisfying? It is only excusable, inasmuch as through it we are taking a higher groove; we have to pass through it in order to become regenerate again. Put a seed into the ground and it disintegrates, dissolves after a time, and out of that dissolution comes the splendid tree. Every soul must disintegrate to become God. So it follows that the sooner we get out of this state we call "man" the better for us is it by committing suicide that we get out of this state? Not at all. That will be making it worse. Torturing ourselves, or condemning the world, is not the way to get out. We have to pass through the Slough of Despond, and the sooner we are through, the better. It must always be remembered that man-state is not the highest state.

The really difficult part to understand is that this state, the Absolute, which has been called the highest, is not, as some fear, that of the zoophyte or of the stone. According to them, there are only two states of existence, one of the stone, and the other of thought. What right have they to limit existence to these two? Is there not something infinitely superior to thought? The vibrations of light, when they are very low, we do not see; when they become a little more intense, they become light to us; when they become still more intense, we do not see them— it is dark to us. Is the darkness in the end the same darkness as in the beginning? Certainly not; they are different as the two poles. Is the thoughtlessness of the stone the same as the thoughtlessness of God? Certainly not. God does not think; He does not reason. Why should He? Is anything unknown to Him, that He should reason? The stone cannot reason; God does not. Such is the difference. These philosophers think it is awful if we go beyond thought; they find nothing beyond thought.

There are much higher states of existence beyond reasoning. It is really beyond the intellect that the first state of religious life is to be found. When you step beyond thought and intellect and all reasoning, then you have made the first step towards God; and that is the beginning of life. What is commonly called life is but an embryo state.

The next question will be: What proof is there that the state beyond thought and reasoning is the highest state? In the first place, all the great men of the world, much greater than those that only talk, men who moved the world, men who never thought of any selfish ends whatever, have declared that this life is but a little stage on the way towards Infinity which is beyond. In the second place, they not only say so, but show the way to every one, explain their methods, that all can follow in their steps. In the third place, there is no other way left. There is no other explanation. Taking for granted that there is no higher state, why are we going through this circle all the time; what reason can explain the world? The sensible world will be the limit to our knowledge if we cannot go farther, if we must not ask for anything more. This is what is called agnosticism. But what reason is there to believe in the testimony of the senses? I would call that man a true agnostic who would stand still in the street and die. If reason is all in all, it leaves us no place to stand on this side of nihilism. If a man is agnostic of everything but money, fame, and name, he is only a fraud. Kant has proved beyond all doubt that we cannot penetrate beyond the tremendous dead wall called reason. But that is the very first idea upon which all Indian thought takes its stand, and dares to seek, and succeeds in finding something higher than reason, where alone the explanation of the present state is to be found. This is the value of the study of something that will take us beyond the world. "Thou art our father, and wilt take us to the other shore of this ocean of ignorance." That is the science of religion, nothing else.

Chapter I
Concentration: its Spiritual Uses

अथ योगानुशासनम् ॥१॥

1. Now concentration is explained.

योगश्चित्तवृत्तिनिरोधः ॥२॥

2. Yoga is restraining the mind-stuff (Chitta)
from taking various forms (Vrittis).

A good deal of explanation is necessary here. We have to understand what Chitta is, and what the Vrittis are. I have eyes. Eyes do not see. Take away the brain centre which is in the head, the eyes will still be there, the retinae complete, as also the pictures of objects on them, and yet the eyes will not see. So the eyes are only a secondary instrument, not the organ of vision. The organ of vision is in a nerve centre of the brain. The two eyes will not be sufficient. Sometimes a man is asleep with his eyes open. The light is there and the picture is there, but a third thing is necessary— the mind must be joined to the organ. The eye is the external instrument; we need also the brain centre and the agency of the mind. Carriages roll down a street, and you do not hear them. Why? Because your mind has not attached itself to the organ of hearing. First, there is the instrument, then there is the organ, and third, the mind attached to these two. The mind takes the impression farther in, and presents it to the determinative faculty— Buddhi— which reacts. Along with this reaction flashes the idea of egoism. Then this mixture of action and reaction is presented to the Purusha, the real Soul, who perceives an object in this mixture. The organs (Indriyas), together with the mind (Manas), the determinative faculty (Buddhi), and egoism (Ahamkâra), form the group called the Antahkarana (the internal instrument). They are but various processes in the mind-stuff, called Chitta. The waves of thought in the Chitta are called Vrittis (literally "whirlpool"). What is thought? Thought is a force, as is gravitation or repulsion. From the infinite storehouse of force in nature, the instrument called Chitta takes hold of some, absorbs it and sends it out as thought. Force is supplied to us through food, and out of that food the body obtains the power of motion etc. Others, the finer forces, it throws out in what we call thought. So we see that the mind is not intelligent; yet it appears to be intelligent. Why? Because the intelligent soul is behind it. You are the only sentient being; mind is only the instrument through which you catch the external world. Take this book; as a book it does not exist outside, what exists outside is unknown and unknowable. The unknowable furnishes the suggestion that gives a blow to the mind, and the mind gives out the reaction in the form of a book, in the same manner as when a stone is thrown into the water, the water is thrown against it in the form of waves. The real universe is the occasion of the reaction of the mind. A book form, or an elephant form, or a man form, is not outside; all that we know is our mental reaction from the outer suggestion. "Matter is the permanent possibility of sensations," said John Stuart Mill. It is only the suggestion that is outside. Take an oyster for example. You know how pearls are made. A parasite gets inside the shell and causes irritation, and the oyster throws a sort of enamelling round it, and this makes the pearl. The universe of experience is our own enamel, so to say, and the real universe is the parasite serving as nucleus. The ordinary man will never understand it, because when he tries to do so, he throws out an enamel, and sees only his own enamel. Now we understand what is meant by these Vrittis. The real man is be-hind the mind; the mind is the instrument his hands; it is his intelligence that is percolating through the mind. It is only when you stand behind the mind that it becomes intelligent. When man gives it up, it falls to pieces and is nothing. Thus you understand what is meant by Chitta. It is the mind-stuff, and Vrittis are the waves and ripples rising in it when external causes impinge on it. These Vrittis are our universe.

The bottom of a lake we cannot see, because its surface is covered with ripples. It is only possible for us to catch a glimpse of the bottom, when the ripples have subsided, and the water is calm. If the water is muddy or is agitated all the time, the bottom will not be seen. If it is clear, and there are no waves, we shall see the bottom. The bottom of the lake is our own true Self; the lake is the Chitta and the waves the Vrittis. Again, the mind is in three states, one of which is dark-ness, called Tamas, found in brutes and idiots; it only acts to injure. No other idea comes into that state of mind. Then there is the active state of mind, Rajas, whose chief motives are power and enjoyment. "I will be powerful and rule oth-ers." Then there is the state called Sattva, serenity, calmness, in which the waves cease, and the water of the mind-lake becomes clear. It is not inactive, but rather intensely active. It is the greatest manifestation of power to be calm. It is easy to be active. Let the reins go, and the horses will run away with you. Anyone can do that, but he who can stop the plunging horses is the strong man. Which requires the greater strength, letting go or restraining? The calm man is not the man who is dull. You must not mistake Sattva for dullness or laziness. The calm man is the one who has control over the mind waves. Activity is the manifestation of inferior strength, calmness, of the superior.

The Chitta is always trying to get back to its natural pure state, but the organs draw it out. To restrain it, to check this outward tendency, and to start it on the return journey to the essence of intelligence is the first step in Yoga, because only in this way can the Chitta get into its proper course.

Although the Chitta is in every animal, from the lowest to the highest, it is only in the human form that we find it as the intellect. Until the mind-stuff can take the form of intellect it is not possible for it to return through all these steps, and liberate the soul. Immediate salvation is impossible for the cow or the dog, although they have mind, because their Chitta cannot as yet take that form which we call intellect.

The Chitta manifests itself in the following forms — scattering, darkening, gathering, one-pointed, and concentrated. The scattering form is activity. Its tendency is to manifest in the form of pleasure or of pain. The darkening form is dullness which tends to injury. The commentator says, the third form is natural to the Devas, the angels, and the first and second to the demons. The gathering form is when it struggles to centre itself. The one-pointed form is when it tries to concentrate, and the concentrated form is what brings us to Samâdhi.

तदा द्रष्टुः स्वरूपेऽवस्थानम् ॥३॥
3. At that time (the time of concentration) the seer (Purusha) rests in his own (unmodified) state.

As soon as the waves have stopped, and the lake has become quiet, we see its bottom. So with the mind; when it is calm, we see what our own nature is; we do not mix ourselves but remain our own selves.

वृत्तसारूप्यमितरत्र ॥४॥
4. At other times (other than that of concentration) the seer is identified with the modifications.

For instance, someone blames me; this produces a modification, Vritti, in my mind, and I identify myself with it and the result is misery.

वृत्तयः पंचतय्यः क्लष्टिटा अक्लष्टिटाः ॥५॥

5. There are five classes of modifications, (some) painful and (others) not painful.

प्रमाण-वपिर्यय-वकिल्प-नदि्रा-स्मृतयः ॥६॥

6. (These are) right knowledge, indiscrimination, verbal delusion, sleep, and memory.

प्रत्यक्षानुमानागमाः प्रमाणानि ॥७॥

7. Direct perception, inference, and competent evidence are proofs.

When two of our perceptions do not contradict each other, we call it proof. I hear something, and if it contradicts something already perceived, I begin to fight it out, and do not believe it. There are also three kinds of proof. Pratyaksha, direct perception; whatever we see and feel, is proof, if there has been nothing to delude the senses. I see the world; that is sufficient proof that it exists. Secondly, Anumâna, inference; you see a sign, and from the sign you come to the thing signified. Thirdly, Âptavâkya, the direct evidence of the Yogis, of those who have seen the truth. We are all of us struggling towards knowledge. But you and I have to struggle hard, and come to knowledge through a long tedious process of reasoning, but the Yogi, the pure one, has gone beyond all this. Before his mind, the past, the present, and the future are alike, one book for him to read; he does not require to go through the tedious processes for knowledge we have to; his words are proof, because he sees knowledge in himself. These, for instance, are the authors of the sacred scriptures; therefore the scriptures are proof. If any such persons are living now their words will be proof. Other philosophers go into long discussions about Aptavakya and they say, "What is the proof of their words?" The proof is their direct perception. Because whatever I see is proof, and whatever you see is proof, if it does not contradict any past knowledge. There is knowledge beyond the senses, and whenever it does not contradict reason and past human experience, that knowledge is proof. Any madman may come into this room and say he sees angels around him; that would not be proof. In the first place, it must be true knowledge, and secondly, it must not contradict past knowledge, and thirdly, it must depend upon the character of the man who gives it out. I hear it said that the character of the man is not of so much importance as what he may say; we must first hear what he says. This may be true in other things. A man may be wicked, and yet make an astronomical discovery, but in religion it is different, because no impure man will ever have the power to reach the truths of religion. Therefore we have first of all to see that the man who declares himself to be an Âpta is a perfectly unselfish and holy person; secondly, that he has reached beyond the senses; and thirdly, that what he says does not contradict the past knowledge of humanity. Any new discovery of truth does not contradict the past truth, but fits into it. And fourthly, that truth must have a possibility of verification. If a man says, "I have seen a vision," and tells me that I have no right to see it, I believe him not. Everyone must have the power to see it for himself. No one who sells his knowledge is an Apta. All these conditions must be fulfilled; you must first see that the man is pure, and that he has no selfish motive; that he has no thirst for gain or fame. Secondly, he must show that he is superconscious. He must give us something that we cannot get from our senses, and which is for the benefit of the world. Thirdly, we must see that it does not contradict other truths; if it contradicts other scientific truths reject it at once. Fourthly, the man should never be singular; he should only represent what all men can attain. The three sorts of proof are, then, direct sense-perception, inference, and the words of an Apta. I cannot translate this word into English. It is not the word "inspired", because inspiration is believed to come from outside, while this knowledge comes from the man himself. The literal meaning is "attained".

वपिर्ययो मथ्यिाज्ञानमतद्रूपप्रतष्पिठम् ॥ ८ ॥

8. Indiscrimination is false knowledge not established in real nature.

The next class of Vrittis that arises is mistaking one thing for another, as a piece of mother-of-pearl is taken for a piece of silver.

शब्दज्ञानानुपाती वस्तुश्न्यो वकिल्पः ॥ ९ ॥

9. Verbal delusion follows from words having no (corresponding) reality.

There is another class of Vrittis called Vikalpa. A word is uttered, and we do not wait to consider its meaning; we jump to a conclusion immediately. It is the sign of weakness of the Chitta. Now you can understand the theory of restraint. The weaker the man, the less he has of restraint. Examine yourselves always by that test. When you are going to be angry or miserable, reason it out how it is that some news that has come to you is throwing your mind into Vrittis.

अभाव-प्रत्ययालम्बना-वृत्तिर्निद्रा ॥१०॥

10. Sleep is a Vritti which embraces the feeling of voidness.

The next class of Vrittis is called sleep and dream. When we awake, we know that we have been sleeping; we can only have memory of perception. That which we do not perceive we never can have any memory of. Every reaction is a wave in the lake. Now, if, during sleep, the mind had no waves, it would have no perceptions, positive or negative, and, therefore, we would not remember them. The very reason of our remembering sleep is that during sleep there was a certain class of waves in the mind. Memory is another class of Vrittis which is called Smriti.

अनुभूतविषयासम्प्रमोषः स्मृतिः ॥११॥

11. Memory is when the (Vrittis of) perceived subjects do not slip away (and through impressions come back to consciousness).

Memory can come from direct perception, false knowledge, verbal delusion, and sleep. For instance, you hear a word. That word is like a stone thrown into the lake of the Chitta; it causes a ripple, and that ripple rouses a series of ripples; this is memory. So in sleep. When the peculiar kind of ripple called sleep throws the Chitta into a ripple of memory, it is called a dream. Dream is another form of the ripple which in the waking state is called memory.

अभ्यासवैराग्याभ्यां तन्निरोधः ॥१२॥

12. Their control is by practice and non-attachment.

The mind, to have non-attachment, must be clear, good, and rational. Why should we practice? Because each action is like the pulsations quivering over the surface of the lake. The vibration dies out, and what is left? The Samskâras, the impressions. When a large number of these impressions are left on the mind, they coalesce and become a habit. It is said, "Habit is second nature", it is first nature also, and the whole nature of man; everything that we are is the result of habit. That gives us consolation, because, if it is only habit, we can make and unmake it at any time. The Samskaras are left by these vibrations passing out of our mind, each one of them leaving its result. Our character is the sum-total of these marks, and according as some particular wave prevails one takes that tone. If good prevails, one becomes good; if wickedness, one becomes wicked; if joyfulness, one becomes happy. The only remedy for bad habits is counter habits; all the bad habits that have left their impressions are to be controlled by good habits. Go on doing good, thinking holy thoughts continuously; that is the only way to suppress base impressions. Never say any man is hopeless, because he only represents a character, a bundle of habits, which can be checked by new and better ones. Character is repeated habits, and repeated habits alone can reform character.

तत्र स्थितौ यत्नोऽभ्यासः ॥१३॥

13. Continuous struggle to keep them (the Vrittis) perfectly restrained is practice.

What is practice? The attempt to restrain the mind in Chitta form, to prevent its going out into waves.

स तु दीर्घकालनैरन्तर्यसत्कारासेवितो दृढभूमिः ॥१४॥

14. It becomes firmly grounded by long constant efforts with great love (for the end to be attained).

Restraint does not come in one day, but by long continued practice.

दृष्टानुश्रविकविषयवितृष्णस्य वशीकारसंज्ञा वैराग्यम् ॥१५॥

15. That effect which comes to these who have given up their thirst after objects, either seen or heard, and which wills to control the objects, is non–attachment.

The two motive powers of our actions are (1) what we see ourselves, (2) the experience of others. These two forces throw the mind, the lake, into various waves. Renunciation is the power of battling against these forces and holding the mind in check. Their renunciation is what see want. I am passing through a street, and a man comes and takes away my watch. That is my own experience. I see it myself, and it immediately throws my Chitta into a wave, taking the form of anger. Allow not that to come. If you cannot prevent that, you are nothing; if you can, you have Vairâgya. Again, the experience of the worldly-minded teaches us that sense-enjoyments are the highest ideal. These are tremendous temptations. To deny them, and not allow the mind to come to a wave form with regard to them, is renunciation; to control the twofold motive powers arising from my own experience and from the experience of others, and thus prevent the Chitta from being governed by them, is Vairagya. These should be controlled by me, and not I by them. This sort of mental strength is called renunciation. Vairagya is the only way to freedom.

ततपरं पुरुषख्यातेर्गुणावैतृष्णायम् ॥१६॥

16. That is extreme non-attachment which gives up even the qualities, and comes from the knowledge of (the real nature of) the Purusha.

It is the highest manifestation of the power of Vairagya when it takes away even our attraction towards the qualities. We have first to understand what the Purusha, the Self, is and what the qualities are. According to Yoga philosophy, the whole of nature consists of three qualities or forces; one is called Tamas, another Rajas, and the third Sattva. These three qualities manifest themselves in the physical world as darkness or inactivity, attraction or repulsion, and equilibrium of the two. Everything that is in nature, all manifestations, are combinations and recombinations of these three forces. Nature has been divided into various categories by the Sânkhyas; the Self of man is beyond all these, beyond nature. It is effulgent, pure, and perfect. Whatever of intelligence we see in nature is but the reflection of this Self upon nature. Nature itself is insentient. You must remember that the word nature also includes the mind; mind is in nature; thought is in nature; from thought, down to the grossest form of matter, everything is in nature, the manifestation of nature. This nature has covered the Self of man, and when nature takes away the covering, the self appears in Its own glory. The non-attachment, as described in aphorism 15 (as being control of objects or nature) is the greatest help towards manifesting the Self. The next aphorism defines Samadhi, perfect concentration which is the goal of the Yogi.

वितर्कवचिारानन्दास्मतिानुगमात् सम्परज्ञातः ॥१७॥

17. The concentration called right knowledge is that which is followed by reasoning, discrimination bliss, unqualified egoism.

Samadhi is divided into two varieties. One is called the Samprajnâta, and the other the Asamprajnâta. In the Samprajnata Samadhi come all the powers of controlling nature. It is of four varieties. The first variety is called the Savitarka, when the mind meditates upon an object again and again, by isolating it from other objects. There are two sorts of objects for meditation in the twenty-five categories of the Sankhyas, (1) the twenty-four insentient categories of Nature, and (2) the one sentient Purusha. This part of Yoga is based entirely on Sankhya philosophy, about which I have already told you. As you will remember, egoism and will and mind have a common basis, the Chitta or the mind stuff, out of which they are all manufactured. The mind-stuff takes in the forces of nature, and projects them as thought. There must be something, again, where both force and matter are one. This is called Avyakta, the unmanifested state of nature before creation, and to which, after the end of a cycle, the whole of nature returns, to come out again after another period. Beyond that is the Purusha, the essence of intelligence. Knowledge is power, and as soon as we begin to know a thing, we get power over it; so also when the mind begins to meditate on the different elements, it gains power over them. That sort of meditation where the external gross elements are the objects is called Savitarka. Vitarka means question; Savitarka, with question, questioning the elements, as it were, that they may give their truths and their powers to the man who meditates upon them. There is no liberation in getting powers. It is a worldly search after enjoyments, and there is no enjoyment in this life; all search for enjoyment is vain; this is the old, old lesson which man finds so hard to learn. When he does learn it, he gets out of the universe and becomes free. The possession of what are called occult powers is only intensifying the world, and in the end, intensifying suffering. Though as a scientist Patanjali is bound to point out the possibilities of this science, he never misses an opportunity to warn us against these powers.

Again, in the very same meditation, when one struggles to take the elements out of time and space, and think of them as they are, it is called Nirvitarka, without question. When the meditation goes a step higher, and takes the Tanmatras as its object, and thinks of them as in time and space, it is called Savichâra, with discrimination; and when in the same meditation one eliminates time and space, and thinks of the fine elements as they are, it is called Nirvichâra, without discrimination. The next step is when the elements are given up, both gross and fine, and the object of meditation is the interior organ, the thinking organ. When the thinking organ is thought of as bereft of the qualities of activity and dullness, it is then called Sânanda, the blissful Samadhi. When the mind itself is the object of meditation, when meditation becomes very ripe and concentrated, when all ideas of the gross and fine materials are given up, when the Sattva state only of the Ego remains, but differentiated from all other objects, it is called Sâsmita Samadhi. The man who has attained to this has attained to what is called in the Vedas "bereft of body". He can think of himself as without his gross body; but he will have to think of himself as with a fine body. Those that in this state get merged in nature without attaining the goal are called Prakritilayas, but those who do not stop even there reach the goal, which is freedom.

वरिमप्रत्ययाभ्यासपूर्वः संस्कारशेषोऽन्यः ॥१८॥

18. There is another Samadhi which is attained by the constant practice of cessation of all mental activity, in which the Chitta retains only the unmanifested impressions.

This is the perfect superconscious Asamprajnata Samadhi, the state which gives us freedom. The first state does not give us freedom, does not liberate the soul. A man may attain to all powers, and yet fall again. There is no safeguard until the soul goes beyond nature. It is very difficult to do so, although the method seems easy. The method is to meditate on the mind itself, and whenever thought comes, to strike it down, allowing no thought to come into the mind, thus making it an entire vacuum. When we can really do this, that very moment we shall attain liberation. When persons without training and preparation try to make their minds vacant, they are likely to succeed only in covering themselves with Tamas, the material of ignorance, which makes the mind dull and stupid, and leads them to think that they are making a vacuum of the mind. To be able to really do that is to manifest the greatest strength, the highest control. When this state, Asamprajnata, superconsciousness, is reached, the Samadhi becomes seedless. What is meant by that? In a concentration where there is consciousness, where the mind succeeds only in quelling the waves in the Chitta and holding them down, the waves remain in the form of tendencies. These tendencies (or seeds) become waves again, when the time comes. But when you have destroyed all these tendencies, almost destroyed the mind, then the Samadhi becomes seedless; there are no more seeds in the mind out of which to manufacture again and again this plant of life, this ceaseless round of birth and death.

You may ask, what state would that be in which there is no mind, there is no knowledge? What we call knowledge is a lower state than the one beyond knowledge. You must always bear in mind that the extremes look very much alike. If a very low vibration of ether is taken as darkness, an intermediate state as light, very high vibration will be darkness again. Similarly, ignorance is the lowest state, knowledge is the middle state, and beyond knowledge is the highest state, the two extremes of which seem the same. Knowledge itself is a manufactured something, a combination; it is not reality.

What is the result of constant practice of this higher concentration? All old tendencies of restlessness and dullness will be destroyed, as well as the tendencies of goodness too. The case is similar to that of the chemicals used to take the dirt and alloy off gold. When the ore is smelted down, the dross is burnt along with

the chemicals. So this constant controlling power will stop the previous bad tendencies, and eventually, the good ones also. Those good and evil tendencies will
suppress each other, leaving alone the Soul, in its own splendour untrammelled
by either good or bad, the omnipresent, omnipotent, and omniscient. Then the
man will know that he had neither birth nor death, nor need for heaven or earth.
He will know that he neither came nor went, it was nature which was moving,
and that movement was reflected upon the soul. The form of the light reflected
by the glass upon the wall moves, and the wall foolishly thinks it is moving. So
with all of us; it is the Chitta constantly moving making itself into various forms,
and we think that we are these various forms. All these delusions will vanish.
When that free Soul will command— not pray or beg, but command— then
whatever It desires will be immediately fulfilled; whatever It wants It will be
able to do. According to the Sankhya philosophy, there is no God. It says that
there can be no God of this universe, because if there were one, He must be a
soul, and a soul must be either bound or free. How can the soul that is bound
by nature, or controlled by nature, create? It is itself a slave. On the other hand,
why should the Soul that is free create and manipulate all these things? It has
no desires, so it cannot have any need to create. Secondly, it says the theory of
God is an unnecessary one; nature explains all. What is the use of any God? But
Kapila teaches that there are many souls, who, though nearly attaining perfection, fall short because they cannot perfectly renounce all powers. Their minds
for a time merge in nature, to re-emerge as its masters. Such gods there are. We
shall all become such gods, and, according to the Sankhyas, the God spoken of
in the Vedas really means one of these free souls. Beyond them there is not an
eternally free and blessed Creator of the universe. On the other hand, the Yogis
say, "Not so, there is a God; there is one Soul separate from all other souls, and
He is the eternal Master of all creation, the ever free, the Teacher of all teachers." The Yogis admit that those whom the Sankhyas call "the merged in nature"
also exist. They are Yogis who have fallen short of perfection, and though, for a
time, debarred from attaining the goal, remain as rulers of parts of the universe.

भव-प्रत्ययो विदेह-प्रकृतिलियानाम् ॥१९॥

19. (This Samadhi when not followed by extreme non-attachment) becomes the
cause of the re-manifestation of the gods and of those that become merged in nature.

The gods in the Indian systems of philosophy represent certain high offices
which are filled successively by various souls. But none of them is perfect.

श्रद्धा-वीर्य-स्मृति-समाधि-प्रज्ञा-पूर्वक इतरेषाम् ॥२०॥

20. To others (this Samadhi) comes through faith, energy, memory,
concentration, and discrimination of the real.

These are they who do not want the position of gods or even that of rulers of
cycles. They attain to liberation.

तीव्रसंवेगानामासन्नः ॥२१॥

21. Success is speedy for the extremely energetic.

मृदुमध्याधिमात्रत्वात्ततोऽपि विशेषः ॥२२॥

22. The success of Yogis differs according as the means they adopt are mild,
medium, or intense.

ईश्वरप्रणिधानाद्वा ॥२३॥

23. Or by devotion to Ishvara.

क्लेशकर्मविपाकाशयैरपरामृष्टः पुरुषविशेष ईश्वरः ॥२४॥

24. Ishvara (the Supreme Ruler) is a special Purusha, untouched by misery,
actions, their results, and desires.

We must again remember that the Pâtanjala Yoga philosophy is based upon the
Sankhya philosophy; only in the latter there is no place for God, while with the
Yogis God has a place. The Yogis, however, do not mention many ideas about
God, such as creating. God as the Creator of the universe is not meant by the
Ishvara of the Yogis. According to the Vedas, Ishvara is the Creator of the uni-
verse; because it is harmonious, it must be the manifestation of one will. The
Yogis want to establish a God, but they arrive at Him in a peculiar fashion of
their own. They say:

तत्र निरतिशयं सर्वज्ञत्वबीजम् ॥२५॥

25. In Him becomes infinite that all-knowingness which in others is (only) a germ.

The mind must always travel between two extremes. You can think of limited
space, but that very idea gives you also unlimited space. Close your eyes and think
of a little space; at the same time that you perceive the little circle, you have a
circle round it of unlimited dimensions. It is the same with time. Try to think of

a second; you will have, with the same act of perception, to think of time which is unlimited. So with knowledge. Knowledge is only a germ in man, but you will have to think of infinite knowledge around it, so that the very constitution of our mind shows us that there is unlimited knowledge, and the Yogis call that unlimited knowledge God.

स पूर्वेषामपि गुरुः कालेनानवच्छेदात् ॥२६॥

26. He is the Teacher of even the ancient teachers, being not limited by time.

It is true that all knowledge is within ourselves, but this has to be called forth by another knowledge. Although the capacity to know is inside us, it must be called out, and that calling out of knowledge can only be done, a Yogi maintains, through another knowledge. Dead, insentient matter never calls out knowledge, it is the action of knowledge that brings out knowledge. Knowing beings must be with us to call forth what is in us, so these teachers were always necessary. The world was never without them, and no knowledge can come without them. God is the Teacher of all teachers, because these teachers, however great they may have been — gods or angels — were all bound and limited by time, while God is not. There are two peculiar deductions of the Yogis. The first is that in thinking of the limited, the mind must think of the unlimited; and that if one part of that perception is true, so also must the other be, for the reason that their value as perceptions of the mind is equal. The very fact that man has a little knowledge shows that God has unlimited knowledge. If I am to take one, why not the other? Reason forces me to take both or reject both. If I believe that there is a man with a little knowledge, I must also admit that there is someone behind him with unlimited knowledge. The second deduction is that no knowledge can come without a teacher. It is true, as the modern philosophers say, that there is something in man which evolves out of him; all knowledge is in man, but certain environments are necessary to call it out. We cannot find any knowledge without teachers. If there are men teachers, god teachers, or angel teachers, they are all limited; who was the teacher before them? We are forced to admit, as a last conclusion, one teacher who is not limited by time; and that One Teacher of infinite knowledge, without beginning or end, is called God.

तस्य वाचकः प्रणवः ॥२७॥

27. His manifesting word is Om.

Every idea that you have in the mind has a counterpart in a word; the word and the thought are inseparable. The external part of one and the same thing is what we call word, and the internal part is what we call thought. No man can, by analysis, separate thought from word. The idea that language was created by men — certain men sitting together and deciding upon words, has been proved to be wrong. So long as man has existed there have been words and language. What is the connection between an idea and a word? Although we see that there must always be a word with a thought, it is not necessary that the same thought requires the same word. The thought may be the same in twenty different countries, yet the language is different. We must have a word to express each thought, but these words need not necessarily have the same sound Sounds will vary in different nations. Our commentator says, "Although the relation between thought and word is perfectly natural, yet it does not mean a rigid connection between one sound and one idea." These sounds vary, yet the relation between the sounds and the thoughts is a natural one. The connection between thoughts and sounds is good only if there be a real connection between the thing signified and the symbol; until then that symbol will never come into general use. A symbol is the manifester of the thing signified, and if the thing signified has already an existence, and if, by experience, we know that the symbol has expressed that thing many times, then we are sure that there is a real relation between them. Even if the things are not present, there will be thousands who will know them by their symbols. There must be a natural connection between the symbol and the thing signified; then, when that symbol is pronounced, it recalls the thing signified. The commentator says the manifesting word of God is Om. Why does he emphasise this word? There are hundreds of words for God. One thought is connected with a thousand words; the idea "God" is connected with hundreds of words, and each one stands as a symbol for God. Very good. But there must be a generalization among all time words, some substratum, some common ground of all these symbols, and that which is the common symbol will be the best, and will really represent them all. In making a sound we use the larynx and the palate as a sounding board. Is there any material sound of which all other sounds must be manifestations, one which is the most natural sound? Om (Aum) is such a sound, the basis of all sounds. The first letter, A, is the root sound, the key, pronounced without touching any part of the tongue or palate; M represents the last sound in the series, being produced by the closed lips, and the U rolls from the very root to the end of the sounding board of the mouth. Thus, Om represents the whole phenomena of sound-producing. As such, it must be the natural symbol, the matrix of all the various sounds. It denotes the whole range and possibility of all the words that can be made. Apart from these speculations, we see that around this word Om are centred all the different religious ideas in India; all the various religious ideas of the Vedas have gathered themselves round this word Om. What has that to do with America and England, or any other country? Simply this, that the word has been retained at every stage of religious growth in India, and it has been manipulated to mean all the various ideas about God. Monists, dualists, mono-dualists, separatists, and even atheists took up this Om. Om has become the one symbol for the religious aspiration of the vast majority of human beings. Take, for instance, the English word God. It covers only a limited function, and if you go beyond it, you have to add adjectives, to make it Personal, or Impersonal, or Absolute God. So with the words for God in every other language; their signification is very small. This word Om, however, has around it all the various significances. As such it should be accepted by everyone.

तज्जपस्तदर्थभावनम् ॥२८॥
28. The repetition of this (Om) and meditating on its meaning (is the way).

Why should there be repetition? We have not forgotten the theory of Samskaras, that the sum-total of impressions lives in the mind. They become more and more latent but remain there, and as soon as they get the right stimulus, they come out. Molecular vibration never ceases. When this universe is destroyed, all the massive vibrations disappear; the sun, moon, stars, and earth, melt down; but the vibrations remain in the atoms. Each atom performs the same function as the big worlds do. So even when the vibrations of the Chitta subside, its molecular vibrations go on, and when they get the impulse, come out again. We can now understand what is meant by repetition. It is the greatest stimulus that can be given to the spiritual Samskaras. "One moment of company with the holy makes a ship to cross this ocean of life." Such is the power of association. So this repetition of Om, and thinking of its meaning, is keeping good company in your own mind. Study, and then meditate on what you have studied. Thus light will come to you, the Self will become manifest.

But one must think of Om, and of its meaning too. Avoid evil company, because the scars of old wounds are in you, and evil company is just the thing that is necessary to call them out. In the same way we are told that good company will call out the good impressions that are in us, but which have become latent.

There is nothing holier in the world than to keep good company, because the good impressions will then tend to come to the surface.

ततः प्रत्यक्चेतनाधिगमोऽप्ययन्तरायाभावश्च ॥२९॥

29. From that is gained (the knowledge of) introspection, and the destruction of obstacles.

The first manifestation of the repetition and thinking of Om is that the introspective power will manifest more and more, all the mental and physical obstacles will begin to vanish. What are the obstacles to the Yogi?

व्याधि-स्त्यान-संशय-प्रमादालस्याविरति-भ्रान्तदिर्शनालब्धभूमिकित्वानवस्थितित्वा नि चित्तविक्षेपास्तेऽन्तरायाः ॥३०॥

30. Disease, mental laziness, doubt, lack of enthusiasm, lethargy, clinging to sense-enjoyments, false perception, non-attaining concentration, and falling away from the state when obtained, are the obstructing distractions.

Disease. This body is the boat which will carry us to the other shore of the ocean of life. It must be taken care of. Unhealthy persons cannot be Yogis. Mental laziness makes us lose all lively interest in the subject, without which there will neither be the will nor the energy to practise. Doubts will arise in the mind about the truth of the science, however strong one's intellectual conviction may be, until certain peculiar psychic experiences come, as hearing or seeing at a distance, etc. These glimpses strengthen the mind and make the student persevere. Falling away ... when obtained. Some days or weeks when you are practicing, the mind will be calm and easily concentrated, and you will find yourself progressing fast. All of a sudden the progress will stop one day, and you will find yourself, as it were, stranded. Persevere. All progress proceeds by such rise and fall.

दुःख-दौर्मनस्याङ्गमेजयत्व-श्वासप्रश्वासा विक्षेपसहभुवः ॥३१॥

31. Grief, mental distress, tremor of the body, irregular breathing, accompany non-retention of concentration.

Concentration will bring perfect repose to mind and body every time it is practised. When the practice has been misdirected, or not enough controlled, these disturbances come. Repetition of Om and self-surrender to the Lord will strengthen the mind, and bring fresh energy. The nervous shakings will come to almost everyone. Do not mind them at all, but keep on practising. Practice will cure them and make the seat firm.

तत्प्रतिषिधार्थमेकतत्त्वाभ्यासः ॥३२॥

32. To remedy this, the practice of one subject (should be made).

Making the mind take the form of one object for some time will destroy these obstacles. This is general advice. In the following aphorisms it will be expanded and particularized. As one practice cannot suit everyone, various methods will be advanced, and everyone by actual experience will find out that which helps him most.

मैत्री-करुणामुदितोपेक्षाणां सुख-दुःखपुण्यापुण्य-विषयाणां भावनातश्चित्तप्रसादनम् ॥३३॥

33. Friendship, mercy, gladness, and indifference, being thought of in regard to subjects, happy, unhappy, good, and evil respectively, pacify the Chitta.

We must have these four sorts of ideas. We must have friendship for all; we must be merciful towards those that are in misery; when people are happy, we ought to be happy; and to the wicked we must be indifferent. So with all subjects that come before us. If the subject is a good one, we shall feel friendly towards it; if the subject of thought is one that is miserable, we must be merciful towards it. If it is good, we must be glad; if it is evil, we must be indifferent. These attitudes of the mind towards the different subjects that come before it will make the mind peaceful. Most of our difficulties in our daily lives come from being unable to hold our minds in this way. For instance, if a man does evil to us, instantly we want to react evil, and every reaction of evil shows that we are not able to hold the Chitta down; it comes out in waves towards the object, and we lose our power. Every reaction in the form of hatred or evil is so much loss to the mind; and every evil thought or deed of hatred, or any thought of reaction, if it is controlled, will be laid in our favour. It is not that we lose by thus restraining ourselves; we are gaining infinitely more than we suspect. Each time we suppress hatred, or a feeling of anger, it is so much good energy stored up in our favour; that piece of energy will be converted into the higher powers.

प्रच्छर्दन-विधारणाभ्यां वा प्राणस्य ॥३४॥

34. By throwing out and restraining the Breath.

The word used is Prâna. Prana is not exactly breath. It is the name for the energy that is in the universe. Whatever you see in the universe, whatever moves or works, or has life, is a manifestation of this Prana. The sum-total of the energy displayed in the universe is called Prana. This Prana, before a cycle begins, remains in an almost motionless state; and when the cycle begins, this Prana begins to manifest itself. It is this Prana that is manifested as motion — as the nervous motion in human beings or animals; and the same Prana is manifesting as thought, and so on. The whole universe is a combination of Prana and Âkâsha; so is the human body. Out of Akasha you get the different materials that you feel and see, and out of Prana all the various forces. Now this throwing out and restraining the Prana is what is called Pranayama. Patanjali, the father of the Yoga philosophy, does not give very many particular directions about Pranayama, but later on other Yogis found out various things about this Pranayama, and made of it a great science. With Patanjali it is one of the many ways, but he does not lay much stress on it. He means that you simply throw the air out, and draw it in, and hold it for some time, that is all, and by that, the mind will become a little calmer. But, later on, you will find that out of this is evolved a particular science called Pranayama. We shall hear a little of what these later Yogis have to say.

Some of this I have told you before, but a little repetition will serve to fix it in your minds. First, you must remember that this Prana is not the breath; but that which causes the motion of the breath, that which is the vitality of the breath, is the Prana. Again, the word Prana is used for all the senses; they are all called Pranas, the mind is called Prana; and so we see that Prana is force. And yet we cannot call it force, because force is only the manifestation of it. It is that which manifests itself as force and everything else in the way of motion. The Chitta, the mind-stuff, is the engine which draws in the Prana from the surroundings, and manufactures out of Prana the various vital forces — those that keep the body in preservation — and thought, will, and all other powers. By the above-mentioned process of breathing we can control all the various motions in the body, and the various nerve currents that are running through the body. First we begin to recognise them, and then we slowly get control over them.

Now, these later Yogis consider that there are three main currents of this Prana in the human body. One they call Idâ, another Pingalâ, and the third Sushumnâ. Pingala, according to them, is on the right side of the spinal column, and the Ida on the left, and in the middle of the spinal column is the Sushumna, an empty channel. Ida and Pingala, according to them, are the currents working in every man, and through these currents, we are performing all the functions of life. Sushumna is present in all, as a possibility; but it works only in the Yogi. You must remember that Yoga changes the body. As you go on practising, your body changes; it is not the same body that you had before the practice. That is very rational, and can be explained, because every new thought that we have must make, as it were, a new channel through the brain, and that explains the tremendous conservatism of human nature. Human nature likes to run through the ruts that are already there, because it is easy. If we think, just for example's sake, that the mind is like a needle, and the brain substance a soft lump before it, then each thought that we have makes a street, as it were, in the brain, and this street would close up, but for the grey matter which comes and makes a lining to keep it separate. If there were no grey matter, there would be no memory, because memory means going over these old streets, retracing a thought as it were. Now perhaps you have marked that when one talks on subjects in which one takes a few ideas that are familiar to everyone, and combines and recombines them, it is easy to follow because these channels are present in everyone's brain, and it is only necessary to recur to them. But whenever a new subject comes, new channels have to be made, so it is not understood readily. And that is why the brain (it is the brain, and not the people themselves) refuses unconsciously to be acted upon by new ideas. It resists. The Prana is trying to make new channels, and the brain will not allow it. This is the secret of conservatism. The fewer channels there have been in the brain, and the less the needle of the Prana has made these passages, the more conservative will be the brain, the more it will struggle against new thoughts. The more thoughtful the man, the more complicated will be the streets in his brain, and the more easily he will take to new ideas, and understand them. So with every fresh idea, we make a new impression in the brain, cut new channels through the brain-stuff, and that is why we find that in the practice of Yoga (it being an entirely new set of thoughts and motives) there is so much physical resistance at first. That is why we find that the part of religion which deals with the world-side of nature is so widely accepted, while the other part, the philosophy, or the psychology, which clears with the inner nature of man, is so frequently neglected.

We must remember the definition of this world of ours; it is only the Infinite Existence projected into the plane of consciousness. A little of the Infinite is projected into consciousness, and that we call our world. So there is an Infinite beyond; and religion has to deal with both— with the little lump we call our world, and with the Infinite beyond. Any religion which deals with one only of these two will be defective. It must deal with both. The part of religion which deals with the part of the Infinite which has come into the plane of conscious-ness, got itself caught, as it were, in the plane of consciousness, in the cage of time, space, and causation, is quite familiar to us, because we are in that already, and ideas about this world have been with us almost from time immemorial. The part of religion which deals with the Infinite beyond comes entirely new to us, and getting ideas about it produces new channels in the brain, disturbing the whole system, and that is why you find in the practice of Yoga ordinary people are at first turned out of their grooves. In order to lessen these disturbances as much as possible, all these methods are devised by Patanjali, that we may prac-tice any one of them best suited to us.

वषियवती वा प्रवृत्तरि्तुपन्ना मनसः स्थतिनिबिन्धनी ॥३५॥

35. Those forms of concentration that bring extraordinary sense-perceptions cause perseverance of the mind.

This naturally comes with Dhâr, concentration; the Yogis say, if the mind becomes concentrated on the tip of the nose, one begins to smell, after a few days, wonderful perfumes. If it becomes concentrated at the root of the tongue, one begins to hear sounds; if on the tip of the tongue, one begins to taste won-derful flavours; if on the middle of the tongue, one feels as if one were coming in contact with something. If one concentrates one's mind on the palate, one begins to see peculiar things. If a man whose mind is disturbed wants to take up some of these practices of Yoga, yet doubts the truth of them, he will have his doubts set at rest when, after a little practice, these things come to him, and he will persevere.

वश्रिोका वा ज्योतष्मिती ॥३६॥

36. Or (by the meditation on) the Effulgent Light, which is beyond all sorrow.

This is another sort of concentration. Think of the lotus of the heart, with pet-als downwards, and running through it, the Sushumna; take in the breath, and while throwing the breath out imagine that the lotus is turned with the petals upwards, and inside that lotus is an effulgent light. Meditate on that.

वीतरागवषियं वा चति्तम् ॥३७॥

37. Or (by meditation on) the heart that has given up all attachment to sense-objects.

Take some holy person, some great person whom you revere, some saint whom you know to be perfectly nonattached, and think of his heart. That heart has become non-attached, and meditate on that heart; it will calm the mind. If you cannot do that, there is the next way:

स्वप्ननिद्राज्ञानालम्बनं वा ॥३८॥

38. Or by meditating on the knowledge that comes in sleep.

Sometimes a man dreams that he has seen angels coming to him and talking to him, that he is in an ecstatic condition, that he has heard music floating through the air. He is in a blissful condition in that dream, and when he wakes, it makes a deep impression on him. Think of that dream as real, and meditate upon it. If you cannot do that, meditate on any holy thing that pleases you.

यथाभिमितध्यानाद्वा ॥३९॥

39. Or by the meditation on anything that appeals to one as good.

This does not mean any wicked subject, but anything good that you like, any place that you like best, any scenery that you like best, any idea that you like best, anything that will concentrate the mind.

परमाणु परममहत्त्वान्तोऽस्य वशीकारः ॥४०॥

40. The Yogi's mind thus meditating, becomes unobstructed from the atomic to the infinite.

The mind, by this practice, easily contemplates the most minute, as well as the biggest thing. Thus the mindwaves become fainter.

क्षीणवृत्तेरभिजातस्येव मणेर्ग्रहीतृ ग्रहण-ग्राह्येषु तत्स्थ-तदञ्जनता समापत्तिः ॥४१॥

41. The Yogi whose Vrittis have thus become powerless (controlled) obtains in the receiver, (the instrument of) receiving, and the received (the Self, the mind, and external objects), concentratedness arid sameness like the crystal (before different coloured objects).

What results from this constant meditation? We must remember how in a previous aphorism Patanjali went into the various states of meditation, how the first would be the gross, the second the fine, and from them the advance was to still finer objects. The result of these meditations is that we can meditate as easily on the fine as on the gross objects. Here the Yogi sees the three things, the receiver, the received, and the receiving instrument, corresponding to the Soul, external objects, and the mind. There are three objects of meditation given us. First, the gross things, as bodies, or material objects ; second, fine things, as the mind, the Chitta ; and third, the Purusha qualified, not the Purusha itself, but the Egoism. By practice, the Yogi gets established in all these meditations. Whenever he meditates he can keep out all other thoughts ; he becomes identified with that on which he meditates. When he meditates, he is like a piece of crystal. Before flowers the crystal becomes almost identified with the flowers. If the flower is red, the crystal looks red, or if the flower is blue, the crystal looks blue.

तत्र शब्दार्थज्ञानविकिल्पैः सङ्कीर्णा सवितर्का समापत्तिः ॥४२॥

42. Sound, meaning, and resulting knowledge, being mixed up, is (called) Samadhi with question.

Sound here means vibration, meaning the nerve currents which conduct it ; and knowledge, reaction. All the various meditations we have had so far, Patanjali calls Savitarka (meditation with question). Later on he gives us higher and higher Dhyânas. In these that are called "with question," we keep the duality of subject and object, which results from the mixture of word, meaning, and knowledge. There is first the external vibration, the word. This, carried inward by the sense currents, is the meaning. After that there comes a reactionary wave in the Chitta, which is knowledge, but the mixture of these three makes up what we call knowledge. In all the meditations up to this we get this mixture as objects of meditation. The next Samadhi is higher.

स्मृतिपरिशुद्धौ स्वरूपशून्येवार्थमात्रनिर्भासा निर्वितर्का ॥४३॥

43. The Samadhi called "without question" (comes) when the memory is purified, or devoid of qualities, expressing only the meaning (of the meditated object).

It is by the practice of meditation of these three that we come to the state where these three do not mix. We can get rid of them. We will first try to understand what these three are. Here is the Chitta ; you will always remember the simile of the mind-stuff to a lake, and the vibration, the word, the sound, like a pulsation coming over it. You have that calm lake in you, and I pronounce a word, "Cow". As soon as it enters through your ears there is a wave produced in your Chitta along with it. So that wave represents the idea of the cow, the form or the meaning as we call it. The apparent cow that you know is really the wave in the mind-stuff that comes as a reaction to the internal and external sound vibrations. With the sound, the wave dies away; it can never exist without a word. You may ask how it is, when we only think of the cow, and do not hear a sound. You make that sound yourself. You are saying "cow" faintly in your mind, and with that comes a wave. There cannot be any wave without this impulse of sound; and when it is not from outside, it is from inside, and when the sound dies, the wave dies. What remains? The result of the reaction, and that is knowledge. These three are so closely combined in our mind that we cannot separate them. When the sound comes, the senses vibrate, and the wave rises in reaction; they follow so closely upon one another that there is no discerning one from the other. When this meditation has been practiced for a long time, memory, the receptacle of all impressions, becomes purified, and we are able clearly to distinguish them from one another. This is called Nirvitarka, concentration without question.

एतयैव सविचारा निर्विचारा च सूक्ष्मविषया व्याख्याता ॥४४॥

44. By this process (the concentrations) with discrimination and without discrimination, whose objects are finer, are (also) explained.

A process similar to the preceding is applied again; only, the objects to be taken up in the former meditations are gross; in this they are fine.

सूक्ष्मविषयत्वञ्चालिङ्ग-पर्यवसानम् ॥४५॥

45. The finer objects end with the Pradhâna.

The gross objects are only the elements and everything manufactured out of them. The fine objects begin with the Tanmatras or fine particles. The organs, the mind, (the mind, or common sensorium, the aggregate of all the senses), egoism, the mind-stuff (the cause of all manifestation), the equilibrium state of Sattva, Rajas, and Tamas materials — called Pradhâna (chief), Prakriti (nature), or Avyakta (unmanifest) — are all included within the category of fine objects, the Purusha (the Soul) alone being excepted.

ता एव सबीजः समाधिः ॥४६॥

46. These concentrations are with seed.

These do not destroy the seeds of past actions, and thus cannot give liberation, but what they bring to the Yogi is stated in the following aphorism.

नर्विचार-वैशारद्येऽध्यात्मप्रसादः ॥४७॥

47. The concentration "without discrimination" being purified, the Chitta becomes firmly fixed.

ऋतम्भरा तत्र प्रज्ञा ॥४८॥

48. The knowledge in that is called "filled with Truth".

The next aphorism will explain this.

श्रुतानुमानप्रज्ञाभ्यामन्यवषिया वशिषार्थत्वात् ॥४९॥

49. The knowledge that is gained from testimony and inference is about common objects. That from the Samadhi just mentioned is of a much higher order, being able to penetrate where inference and testimony cannot go.

The idea is that we have to get our knowledge of ordinary objects by direct perception, and by inference therefrom, and from testimony of people who are competent. By "people who are competent," the Yogis always mean the Rishis, or the Seers of the thoughts recorded in the scriptures — the Vedas. According to them, the only proof of the scriptures is that they were the testimony of competent persons, yet they say the scriptures cannot take us to realisation. We can read all the Vedas, and yet will not realise anything, but when we practise their teachings, then we attain to that state which realises what the scriptures say, which penetrates where neither reason nor perception nor inference can go, and where the testimony of others cannot avail. This is what is meant by the aphorism.

Realisation is real religion, all the rest is only preparation — hearing lectures, or reading books, or reasoning is merely preparing the ground; it is not religion. Intellectual assent and intellectual dissent are not religion. The central idea of the Yogis is that just as we come in direct contact with objects of the senses, so religion even can be directly perceived in a far more intense sense. The truths of religion, as God and Soul, cannot be perceived by the external senses. I cannot see God with my eyes, nor can I touch Him with my hands, and we also know that neither can we reason beyond the senses. Reason leaves us at a point quite indecisive; we may reason all our lives, as the world has been doing for thousands of years, and the result is that we find we are incompetent to prove or disprove the facts of religion. What we perceive directly we take as the basis, and upon that basis we reason. So it is obvious that reasoning has to run within these bounds of perception. It can never go beyond. The whole scope of realisation, therefore, is beyond sense-perception. The Yogis say that man can go beyond his direct sense-perception, and beyond his reason also. Man has in him the faculty, the power, of transcending his intellect even, a power which is in every being, every creature. By the practice of Yoga that power is aroused, and then man transcends the ordinary limits of reason, and directly perceives things which are beyond all reason.

तज्जः संस्कारोऽन्यसंस्कारप्रतबिन्धी ॥५०॥

50. The resulting impression from this Samadhi obstructs all other impressions.

We have seen in the foregoing aphorism that the only way of attaining to that superconsciousness is by concentration, and we have also seen that what hinder the mind from concentration are the past Samskaras, impressions. All of you have observed that, when you are trying to concentrate your mind, your thoughts wander. When you are trying to think of God, that is the very time these Samskaras appear. At other times they are not so active; but when you want them not, they are sure to be there, trying their best to crowd in your mind. Why should that be so? Why should they be much more potent at the time of concentration? It is because you are repressing them, and they react with all their force. At other times they do not react. How countless these old past impressions must be, all lodged somewhere in the Chitta, ready, waiting like tigers, to jump up! These have to be suppressed that the one idea which we want may arise, to the exclusion of the others. Instead they are all struggling to come up at the same time. These are the various powers of the Samskaras in hindering concentration of the mind. So this Samadhi which has just been given is the best to be practised, on account of its power of suppressing the Samskaras. The Samskara which will be raised by this sort of concentration will be so powerful that it will hinder the action of the others, and hold them in check.

तस्यापि निरोधे सर्वनिरोधान्निरिबीजः समाधिः ॥५१॥

51. By the restraint of even this (impression, which obstructs all other impressions), all being restrained, comes the "seedless" Samadhi.

You remember that our goal is to perceive the Soul itself. We cannot perceive the Soul, because it has got mingled up with nature, with the mind, with the body. The ignorant man thinks his body is the Soul. The learned man thinks his mind is the Soul. But both of them are mistaken. What makes the Soul get mingled up with all this? Different waves in the Chitta rise and cover the Soul; we only see a little reflection of the Soul through these waves; so, if the wave is one of anger, we see the Soul as angry; "I am angry," one says. If it is one of love, we see ourselves reflected in that wave, and say we are loving. If that wave is one of weakness, and the Soul is reflected in it, we think we are weak. These various ideas come from these impressions, these Samskaras covering the Soul. The real nature of the Soul is not perceived as long as there is one single wave in the lake of the Chitta; this real nature will never be perceived until all the waves have subsided. So, first, Patanjali teaches us the meaning of these waves; secondly, the best way to repress them; and thirdly, how to make one wave so strong as to suppress all other waves, fire eating fire as it were. When only one remains, it will be easy to suppress that also, and when that is gone, this Samadhi or concentration is called seedless. It leaves nothing, and the Soul is manifested just as It is, in Its own glory. Then alone we know that the Soul is not a compound; It is the only eternal simple in the universe, and as such, It cannot be born, It cannot die; It is immortal, indestructible, the ever-living essence of intelligence.

Chapter II
Concentration: its Practice

तपः-स्वाध्यायेश्वरप्रणिधानानि क्रियायोगः ॥१॥

1. Mortification, study, and surrendering fruits of work to God are called
Kriyâ-yoga.

Those Samâdhis with which we ended our last chapter are very difficult to attain; so we must take them up slowly. The first step, the preliminary step, is called Kriya-yoga. Literally this means work, working towards Yoga. The organs are the horses, the mind is the rein, the intellect is the charioteer, the soul is the rider, and the body is the chariot. The master of the household, the King, the Self of man, is sitting in this chariot. If the horses are very strong and do not obey the rein, if the charioteer, the intellect, does not know how to control the horses, then the chariot will come to grief. But if the organs, the horses, are well controlled, and if the rein, the mind, is well held in the hands of the charioteer, the intellect, the chariot reaches the goal. What is meant, therefore, by this mortification? Holding the rein firmly while guiding the body and the organs; not letting them do anything they like, but keeping them both under proper control. Study. What is meant by study in this case? No study of novels or story books, but study of those works which teach the liberation of the Soul. Then again this study does not mean controversial studies at all. The Yogi is supposed to have finished his period of controversy. He has had enough of that, and has become satisfied. He only studies to intensify his convictions. Vâda and Siddhânta— these are the two sorts of scriptural knowledge— Vada (the argumentative) and Siddhanta (the decisive). When a man is entirely ignorant he takes up the first of these, the argumentative fighting, and reasoning pro and con; and when he has finished that he takes up the Siddhanta, the decisive, arriving at a conclusion. Simply arriving at this conclusion will not do. It must be intensified. Books are infinite in number, and time is short; therefore the secret of knowledge is to take what is essential. Take that and try to live up to it. There is an old Indian legend that if you place a cup of milk and water before a Râja-Hamsa (swan), he will take all the milk and leave the water. In that way we should take what is of value in

Swami Vivekananda

knowledge, and leave the dross. Intellectual gymnastics are necessary at first. We must not go blindly into anything. The Yogi has passed the argumentative state, and has come to a conclusion, which is, like the rocks, immovable. The only thing he now seeks to do is to intensify that conclusion. Do not argue, he says; if one forces arguments upon you, be silent. Do not answer any argument, but go away calmly, because arguments only disturb the mind. The only thing necessary is to train the intellect, what is the use of disturbing it for nothing? The intellect is but a weak instrument, and can give us only knowledge limited by the senses. The Yogi wants to go beyond the senses, therefore intellect is of no use to him. He is certain of this and, therefore, is silent, and does not argue. Every argument throws his mind out of balance, creates a disturbance in the Chitta, and a disturbance is a drawback. Argumentations and searchings of the reason are only by the way. There are much higher things beyond them. The whole of life is not for schoolboy fights and debating societies. "Surrendering the fruits of work to God" is to take to ourselves neither credit nor blame, but to give up both to the Lord and be at peace.

समाधि-भावनार्थः क्लेश-तनूकरणार्थश्च ॥२॥

2. (It is for) the practice of Samadhi and minimising the pain-bearing obstructions.

Most of us make our minds like spoilt children, allowing them to do whatever they want. Therefore it is necessary that Kriya-yoga should be constantly practised, in order to gain control of the mind, and bring it into subjection. The obstructions to Yoga arise from lack of control, and cause us pain. They can only be removed by denying the mind, and holding it in check, through the means of Kriya-yoga.

अवदियास्मिता-राग-द्वेषाभिनिवेशाः क्लेशाः ॥३॥

3. The pain-bearing obstructions are— ignorance, egoism, attachment, aversion and clinging to life.

These are the five pains, the fivefold tie that binds us down, of which ignorance is the cause and the other four its effects. It is the only cause of all our misery. What else can make us miserable? The nature of the Soul is eternal bliss. What can make it sorrowful except ignorance, hallucination, delusion? All pain of the Soul is simply delusion.

अवदियाक्षेत्रमुत्तरेषां पुरसुपत-तनु-वचिछन्निनोदाःगाम् ॥४॥

4. Ignorance is the productive field of all these that follow, whether they are dormant, attenuated, overpowered, or expanded.

Ignorance is the cause of egoism, attachment, aversion, and clinging to life. These impressions exist in different states. They are sometimes dormant. You often hear the expression "innocent as a baby," yet in the baby may be the state of a demon or of a god, which will come out by degrees. In the Yogi, these impressions, the Samskâras left by past actions, are attenuated, that is, exist in a very fine state, and he can control them, and not allow them to become manifest. "Overpowered" means that sometimes one set of impressions is held down for a while by those that are stronger, but they come out when that repressing cause is removed. The last state is the "expanded," when the Samskaras, having helpful surroundings, attain to a great activity, either as good or evil.

अनतियाशुचि-दुःखानात्मसु नत्य-शुचि-सुखात्मख्यातिरिवदिया ॥५॥

5. Ignorance is taking the non-eternal, the impure, the painful, and the non-Self for the eternal, the pure, the happy, and the Âtman or Self (respectively).

All the different sorts of impressions have one source, ignorance. We have first to learn what ignorance is. All of us think, "I am the body, and not the Self, the pure, the effulgent, the ever blissful," and that is ignorance. We think of man, and see man as body. This is the great delusion.

दृग्दर्शनशक्त्योरेकात्मतेवास्मिता ॥६॥

6. Egoism is the identification of the seer with the instrument of seeing.

The seer is really the Self, the pure one, the ever holy, the infinite, the immortal. This is the Self of man. And what are the instruments? The Chitta or mind-stuff, the Buddhi or determinative faculty, the Manas or mind, and the Indriyas or sense-organs. These are the instruments for him to see the external world, and the identification of the Self with the instruments is what is called the ignorance of egoism. We say, "I am the mind," "I am thought," "I am angry," or "I am happy". How can we be angry and how can we hate? We should identify ourselves with the Self that cannot change. If It is unchangeable, how can It be one moment happy, and one moment unhappy? It is formless, infinite, omnipresent. What can change It? It is beyond all law. What can affect it? Nothing in the universe can produce an effect on It. Yet through ignorance, we identify ourselves with the mind-stuff, and think we feel pleasure or pain.

सुखानुशयी रागः ॥ ७ ॥

7. Attachment is that which dwells on pleasure.

We find pleasure in certain things, and the mind like a current flows towards them; and this following the pleasure centre, as it were, is what is called attachment. We are never attached where we do not find pleasure. We find pleasure in very queer things sometimes, but the principle remains: wherever we find pleasure, there we are attached.

दुःखानुशयी द्वेषः ॥ ८ ॥

8. Aversion is that which dwells on pain.

That which gives us pain we immediately seek to get away from.

स्वरसवाही विदुषोऽपि तथारूढोऽभिनिवेशः ॥ ९ ॥

9. Flowing through its own nature, and established even in the learned, is the clinging to life.

This clinging to life you see manifested in every animal. Upon it many attempts have been made to build the theory of a future life, because men are so fond of life that they desire a future life also. Of course it goes without saying that this argument is without much value, but the most curious part of it is, that, in Western countries, the idea that this clinging to life indicates a possibility of future life applies only to men, but does not include animals. In India this clinging to life has been one of the arguments to prove past experience and existence. For instance, if it be true that all our knowledge has come from experience, then it is sure that that which we never experienced we cannot imagine or understand. As soon as chickens are hatched they begin to pick up food. Many times it has been seen, where ducks have been hatched by hens, that, as soon as they came out of the eggs they flew to water, and the mother thought they would be drowned. If experience be the only source of knowledge, where did these chickens learn to pick up food, or the ducklings that the water was their natural element? If you say it is instinct, it means nothing — it is simply giving a word, but is no explanation. What is this instinct? We have many instincts in ourselves. For instance, most of you ladies play the piano, and remember, when you first learned, how carefully you had to put your fingers on the black and the white keys, one after the other, but now, after long years of practice, you can talk with your friends while your fingers play mechanically. It has become instinct. So with every work we do; by practice it becomes instinct, it becomes automatic; but so far as we know, all the cases which we now regard as automatic are degenerated reason. In the language of the Yogi, instinct is involved reason. Discrimination becomes involved, and gets to be automatic Samskaras. Therefore it is perfectly logical to think that all we call instinct in this world is simply involved reason. As reason cannot come without experience, all instinct is, therefore, the result of past experience. Chickens fear the hawk, and ducklings love the water; these are both the results of past experience. Then the question is whether that experience belongs to a particular soul, or to the body simply, whether this experience which comes to the duck is the duck's forefathers' experience, or the duck's own experience. Modern scientific men hold that it belongs to the body, but the Yogis hold that it is the experience of the mind, transmitted through the body. This is called the theory of reincarnation.

We have seen that all our knowledge, whether we call it perception, or reason, or instinct, must come through that one channel called experience, and all that we now call instinct is the result of past experience, degenerated into instinct and that instinct regenerates into reason again. So on throughout the universe, and upon this has been built one of the chief arguments for reincarnation in India. The recurring experiences of various fears, in course of time, produce this clinging to life. That is why the child is instinctively afraid, because the past experience of pain is there in it. Even in the most learned men, who know that this body will go, and who say "never mind, we have had hundreds of bodies, the soul cannot die"— even in them, with all their intellectual convictions, we still find this clinging on to life. Why is this clinging to life? We have seen that it has become instinctive. In the psychological language of the Yogis it has become a Samskara. The Samskaras, fine and hidden, are sleeping in the Chitta. All this past experience of death, all that which we call instinct, is experience become subconscious. It lives in the Chitta, and is not inactive, but is working underneath.

The Chitta-Vrittis, the mind-waves, which are gross, we can appreciate and feel; they can be more easily controlled, but what about the finer instincts? How can they be controlled? When I am angry, my whole mind becomes a huge wave of anger. I feel it, see it, handle it, can easily manipulate it, can fight with it; but I shall not succeed perfectly in the fight until I can get down below to its causes. A man says something very harsh to me, and I begin to feel that I am getting heated, and he goes on till I am perfectly angry and forget myself, identify myself with anger. When he first began to abuse me, I thought, "I am going to be angry". Anger was one thing, and I was another; but when I became angry, I was anger. These feelings have to be controlled in the germ, the root, in their fine forms, before even we have become conscious that they are acting on us. With the vast majority of mankind the fine states of these passions are not even known — the states in which they emerge from subconsciousness. When a bubble is rising from the bottom of the lake, we do not see it, nor even when it is nearly come to the surface; it is only when it bursts and makes a ripple that we know it is there. We shall only be successful in grappling with the waves when we can get hold of them in their fine causes, and until you can get hold of them, and subdue them before they become gross, there is no hope of conquering any passion perfectly. To control our passions we have to control them at their very roots; then alone shall we be able to burn out their very seeds. As fried seeds thrown into the ground will never come up, so these passions will never arise.

ते प्रतिप्रसवहेयाः सूक्ष्माः ॥१०॥

10. The fine Saskaras are to be conquered by resolving them into their causal state.

Samskaras are the subtle impressions that manifest themselves into gross forms later on. How are these fine Samskaras to be controlled? By resolving the effect into its cause. When the Chitta, which is an effect, is resolved into its cause, Asmitâ or Egoism, then only, the fine impressions die along with it. Meditation cannot destroy these.

ध्यानहेयास्तद्वृत्तयः ॥११॥

11. By meditation, their (gross) modifications are to be rejected.

Meditation is one of the great means of controlling the rising of these waves. By meditation you can make the mind subdue these waves, and if you go on practicing meditation for days, and months, and years, until it has become a habit, until it will come in spite of yourself, anger and hatred will be controlled and checked.

क्लेशमूलः कर्माशयो दृष्टादृष्टजन्मवेदनीयः ॥१२॥

12. The "receptacle of works" has its root in these pain-bearing obstructions, and their experience is in this visible life, or in the unseen life.

By the "receptacle of works" is meant the sum-total of Samskaras. Whatever work we do, the mind is thrown into a wave, and after the work is finished, we think the wave is gone. No. It has only become fine, but it is still there. When we try to remember the work, it comes up again and becomes a wave. So it was there; if not, there would not have been memory. Thus every action, every thought, good or bad, just goes down and becomes fine, and is there stored up. Both happy and unhappy thoughts are called pain-bearing obstructions, because according to the Yogis, they, in the long run, bring pain. All happiness which comes from the senses will, eventually, bring pain. All enjoyment will make us thirst for more, and that brings pain as its result. There is no limit to man's desires; he goes on desiring, and when he comes to a point where desire cannot be fulfilled, the result is pain. Therefore the Yogis regard the sum-total of the impressions, good or evil, as pain-bearing obstructions; they obstruct the way to freedom of the Soul.

It is the same with the Samskaras, the fine roots of all our works; they are the causes which will again bring effects, either in this life, or in the lives to come. In exceptional cases when these Samskaras are very strong, they bear fruit quickly; exceptional acts of wickedness, or of goodness, bring their fruits even in this life. The Yogis hold that men who are able to acquire a tremendous power of good Samskaras do not have to die, but, even in this life, can change their bodies into god-bodies. There are several such cases mentioned by the Yogis in their books. These men change the very material of their bodies; they re-arrange the molecules in such fashion that they have no more sickness, and what we call death does not come to them. Why should not this be? The physiological meaning of food is assimilation of energy from the sun. The energy has reached the plant, the plant is eaten by an animal, and the animal by man. The science of it is that we take so much energy from the sun, and make it part of ourselves. That being the case, why should there be only one way of assimilating energy? The plant's way is not the same as ours; the earth's process of assimilating energy differs from our own. But all assimilate energy in some form or other. The Yogis say that they are able to assimilate energy by the power of the mind alone, that they can draw in as much of it as they desire without recourse to the ordinary methods. As a spider makes its web out of its own substance, and becomes bound in it, and cannot go anywhere except along the lines of that web, so we have projected out of our own substance this network called the nerves, and we cannot work except through the channels of those nerves. The Yogi says we need not be bound by that.

Similarly, we can send electricity to any part of the world, but we have to send it by means of wires. Nature can send a vast mass of electricity without any wires at all. Why cannot we do the same? We can send mental electricity. What we call mind is very much the same as electricity. It is clear that this nerve fluid has some amount of electricity, because it is polarised, and it answers all electrical directions. We can only send our electricity through these nerve channels. Why not send the mental electricity without this aid? The Yogis say it is perfectly possible and practicable, and that when you can do that, you will work all over the universe. You will be able to work with any body anywhere, without the help of the nervous system. When the soul is acting through these channels, we say a man is living, and when these cease to work, a man is said to be dead. But when a man is able to act either with or without these channels, birth and death will have no meaning for him. All the bodies in the universe are made up of Tanmâtras, their difference lies in the arrangement of the latter. If you are the arranger, you can arrange a body in one way or another. Who makes up this body but you? Who eats the food? If another ate the food for you, you would not live long. Who makes the blood out of food? You, certainly. Who purifies the blood, and sends it through the veins? You. We are the masters of the body, and we live in it. Only we have lost the knowledge of how to rejuvenate it. We have become automatic, degenerate. We have forgotten the process of arranging its molecules. So, what we do automatically has to be done knowingly. We are the masters and we have to regulate that arrangement; and as soon as we can do that, we shall be able to rejuvenate just as we like, and then we shall have neither birth nor disease nor death.

सति मूले तद्विपाको जात्यायुर्भोगाः ॥१३॥

13. The root being there, the fruition comes (in the form of) species, life, and experience of pleasure and pain.

The roots, the causes, the Samskaras being there, they manifest and form the effects. The cause dying down becomes the effect; the effect getting subtler becomes the cause of the next effect. A tree bears a seed, which becomes the cause of another tree, and so on. All our works now are the effects of past Samskaras; again, these works becoming Samskaras will be the causes of future actions, and thus we go on. So this aphorism says that the cause being there, the fruit must come, in the form of species of beings: one will be a man, another an angel, another an animal, another a demon. Then there are different effects of Karma in life. One man lives fifty years, another a hundred, another dies in two years, and never attains maturity; all these differences in life are regulated by past Karma. One man is born, as it were, for pleasure; if he buries himself in a forest, pleasure will follow him there. Another man, wherever he goes, is followed by pain; everything becomes painful for him. It is the result of their own past. According to the philosophy of the Yogis, all virtuous actions bring pleasure, and all vicious actions bring pain. Any man who does wicked deeds is sure to reap their fruit in the form of pain.

ते हृलादपरितापफलाः पुण्यापुण्यहेतुत्वात् ॥१४॥

14. They bear fruit as pleasure or pain, caused by virtue or vice.

परिणामताप-संस्कारदुःखैर्गुणावृत्तविरोधाच्च दुःखमेव सर्वं विविकनिः ॥१५॥

15. To the discriminating, all is, as it were, painful on account of everything bringing pain either as consequence, or as anticipation of loss of happiness, or as fresh craving arising from impressions of happiness, and also as counteraction of qualities.

The Yogis say that the man who has discriminating powers, the man of good sense, sees through all that are called pleasure and pain, and knows that they come to all, and that one follows and melts into the other; he sees that men follow an ignis fatuus all their lives, and never succeed in fulfilling their desires. The great king Yudhishthira once said that the most wonderful thing in life is that every moment we see people dying around us, and yet we think we shall never die. Surrounded by fools on every side, we think we are the only exceptions, the only learned men. Surrounded by all sorts of experiences of fickleness, we think our love is the only lasting love. How can that be? Even love is selfish, and the Yogi says that in the end we shall find that even the love of husbands and wives, and children and friends, slowly decays. Decadence seizes everything in this life. It is only when everything, even love, fails, that, with a flash, man finds out how vain, how dream-like is this world. Then he catches a glimpse of Vairâgya (renunciation), catches a glimpse of the Beyond. It is only by giving up this world that the other comes; never through holding on to this one. Never yet was there a great soul who had not to reject sense-pleasures and enjoyments to acquire his greatness. The cause of misery is the clash between the different forces of nature, one dragging one way, and another dragging another, rendering permanent happiness impossible.

हेयं दुःखमनागतम् ॥१६॥

16. The misery which is not yet come is to be avoided.

Some Karma we have worked out already, some we are working out now in the present, and some are waiting to bear fruit in the future. The first kind is past and gone. The second we will have to work out, and it is only that which is waiting to bear fruit in the future that we can conquer and control, towards which end all our forces should be directed. This is what Patanjali means when he says that Samskaras are to be controlled by resolving them into their causal state (II.10).

द्रष्टृदृश्ययोः संयोगो हेयहेतुः ॥१७॥

17. The cause of that which is to be avoided is the junction of the seer and the seen.

Who is the seer? The Self of man, the Purusha. What is the seen? The whole of nature beginning with the mind, down to gross matter. All pleasure and pain arise from the junction between this Purusha and the mind. The Purusha, you must remember, according to this philosophy, is pure; when joined to nature, it appears to feel pleasure or pain by reflection.

प्रकाश-क्रिया-स्थितिशीलं भूतेन्द्रियात्मकं भोगापवर्गार्थं दृश्यमः ॥१८॥

18. The experienced is composed of elements and organs, is of the nature of illumination, action, and inertia, and is for the purpose of experience and release (of the experiencer).

The experienced, that is nature, is composed of elements and organs — the elements, gross and fine, which compose the whole of nature, and the organs of the senses, mind, etc.— and is of the nature of illumination (Sattva), action (Rajas), and inertia (Tamas). What is the purpose of the whole of nature? That the Purusha may gain experience. The Purusha has, as it were, forgotten its mighty, godly nature. There is a story that the king of the gods, Indra, once became a pig, wallowing in mire; he had a she-pig and a lot of baby pigs, and was very happy. Then some gods saw his plight, and came to him, and told him, "You are the king of the gods, you have all the gods under your command. Why are you here?" But Indra said, "Never mind; I am all right here; I do not care for heaven, while I have this sow and these little pigs." The poor gods were at their wits' end. After a time they decided to slay all the pigs one after another. When all were dead, Indra began to weep and mourn. Then the gods ripped his pig-body open and he came out of it, and began to laugh, when he realised what a hideous dream he had had—he, the king of the gods, to have become a pig, and to think that that pig-life was the only life! Not only so, but to have wanted the whole universe to come into the pig-life! The Purusha, when it identifies itself with nature, forgets that it is pure and infinite. The Purusha does not love, it is love itself. It does not exist, it is existence itself. The Soul does not know, It is knowledge itself. It is a mistake to say the Soul loves, exists, or knows. Love, existence, and knowledge are not the qualities of the Purusha, but its essence. When they get reflected upon something, you may call them the qualities of that something. They are not the qualities but the essence of the Purusha, the great Atman, the Infinite Being, without birth or death, established in its own glory. It appears to have become so degenerate that if you approach to tell it, "You are not a pig," it begins to squeal and bite.

Thus is it with us all in this Mâyâ, this dream world, where it is all misery, weeping and crying, where a few golden balls are rolled, and the world scrambles after them. You were never bound by laws, nature never had a bond for you. That is what the Yogi tells you. Have patience to learn it. And the Yogi shows how, by junction with nature, and identifying itself with the mind and the world, the Purusha thinks itself miserable. Then the Yogi goes on to show you that the way out is through experience. You have to get all this experience, but finish it quickly. We have placed ourselves in this net, and will have to get out. We have got ourselves caught in the trap, and we will have to work out our freedom. So get this experience of husbands, and wives, and friends, and little loves; you will get through them safely if you never forget what you really are. Never forget this is only a momentary state, and that we have to pass through it. Experience is the one great teacher—experience of pleasure and pain—but know it is only experience. It leads, step by step, to that state where all things become small, and the Purusha so great that the whole universe seems as a drop in the ocean and falls off by its own nothingness. We have to go through different experiences, but let us never forget the ideal.

वशिषावशिष-लङ्गिमात्रालङ्गिगानि गुणापर्वाणि ॥ १९ ॥

19. The states of the qualities are the defined, the undefined, the indicated only, and the signless.

The system of Yoga is built entirely on the philosophy of the Sânkhyas, as I told you before, and here again I shall remind you of the cosmology of the

Sankhya philosophy. According to the Sankhyas, nature is both the material and the efficient cause of the universe. In nature there are three sorts of materials, the Sattva, the Rajas, and the Tamas. The Tamas material is all that is dark, all that is ignorant and heavy. The Rajas is activity. The Sattva is calmness, light. Nature, before creation, is called by them Avyakta, undefined, or indiscrete; that is, in which there is no distinction of form or name, a state in which these three materials are held in perfect balance. Then the balance is disturbed, the three materials begin to mingle in various fashions, and the result is the universe. In every man, also, these three materials exist. When the Sattva material prevails, knowledge comes; when Rajas, activity; and when Tamas, darkness, lassitude, idleness, and ignorance. According to the Sankhya theory, the highest manifestation of nature, consisting of the three materials, is what they call Mahat or intelligence, universal intelligence, of which each human intellect is a part. In the Sankhya psychology there is a sharp distinction between Manas, the mind function, and the function of the Buddhi, intellect. The mind function is simply to collect and carry impressions and present them to the Buddhi, the individual Mahat, which determines upon it. Out of Mahat comes egoism, out of which again come the fine materials. The fine materials combine and become the gross materials outside — the external universe. The claim of the Sankhya philosophy is that beginning with the intellect down to a block of stone, all is the product of one substance, different only as finer to grosser states of existence. The finer is the cause, and the grosser is the effect. According to the Sankhya philosophy, beyond the whole of nature is the Purusha, which is not material at all. Purusha is not at all similar to anything else, either Buddhi, or mind, or the Tanmatras, or the gross materials. It is not akin to any one of these, it is entirely separate, entirely different in its nature, and from this they argue that the Purusha must be immortal, because it is not the result of combination. That which is not the result of combination cannot die. The Purushas or souls are infinite in number.

Now we shall understand the aphorism that the states of the qualities are defined, undefined, indicated only, and signess. By the "defined" are meant the gross elements, which we can sense. By the "undefined" are meant the very fine materials, the Tanmatras, which cannot be sensed by ordinary men. If you practise Yoga, however, says Patanjali, after a while your perceptions will become so fine that you will actually see the Tanmatras. For instance, you have heard how every man has a certain light about him; every living being emits a certain light, and this, he says, can be seen by the Yogi. We do not all see it, but we all throw out these Tanmatras, just as a flower continuously sends out fine particles which enable us to smell it. Every day of our lives we throw out a mass of good or evil, and everywhere we go the atmosphere is full of these materials. That is how there came to the human mind, unconsciously, the idea of building temples and churches. Why should man build churches in which to worship God? Why not worship Him anywhere? Even if he did not know the reason, man found that the place where people worshipped God became full of good Tanmatras. Every day people go there, and the more they go the holier they get, and the holier that place becomes. If any man who has not much Sattva in him goes there, the place will influence him and arouse his Sattva quality. Here, therefore, is the significance of all temples and holy places, but you must remember that their holiness depends on holy people congregating there. The difficulty with man is that he forgets the original meaning, and puts the cart before the horse. It was men who made these places holy, and then the effect became the cause and made men holy. If the wicked only were to go there, it would become as bad as any other place. It is not the building, but the people that make a church, and that is what we always forget. That is why sages and holy persons, who have much of this Sattva quality, can send it out and exert a tremendous influence day and night on their surroundings. A man may become so pure that his purity will become tangible. Whosoever comes in contact with him becomes pure.

Next "the indicated only" means the Buddhi, the intellect. "The indicated only" is the first manifestation of nature; from it all other manifestations proceed. The last is "the signless". There seems to be a great difference between modern science and all religions at this point. Every religion has the idea that the universe comes out of intelligence. The theory of God, taking it in its psychological significance, apart from all ideas of personality, is that intelligence is first in the order of creation, and that out of intelligence comes what we call gross matter. Modern philosophers say that intelligence is the last to come. They say that unintelligent things slowly evolve into animals, and from animals into men. They claim that instead of everything coming out of intelligence, intelligence itself is the last to come. Both the religious and the scientific statements, though seeming directly opposed to each other are true. Take an infinite series, A-B-A-B-A-B, etc. The question is — which is first, A or B? If you take the series as A-B. you will say that A is first, but if you take it as B-A, you will say that B is first. It depends upon the way we look at it. Intelligence undergoes modification and becomes the gross matter, this again merges into intelligence, and thus the process goes on. The Sankhyas, and other religionists, put intelligence first, and the series becomes intelligence, then matter. The scientific man puts his finger on matter, and says matter, then intelligence. They both indicate the same chain. Indian philosophy, however, goes beyond both intelligence and matter, and finds a Purusha, or Self, which is beyond intelligence, of which intelligence is but the borrowed light.

द्रष्टा दृशिमात्रः शुद्धोऽपि प्रत्ययानुपश्यः ॥२०॥

20. The seer is intelligence only, and though pure, sees through the colouring of the intellect.

This is, again, Sankhya philosophy. We have seen from the same philosophy that from the lowest form up to intelligence all is nature; beyond nature are Purushas (souls), which have no qualities. Then how does the soul appear to be happy or unhappy? By reflection. If a red flower is put near a piece of pure crystal, the crystal appears to be red, similarly the appearances of happiness or unhappiness of the soul are but reflections. The soul itself has no colouring. The soul is separate from nature. Nature is one thing, soul another, eternally separate. The Sankhyas say that intelligence is a compound, that it grows and wanes, that it changes, just as the body changes, and that its nature is nearly the same as that of the body. As a finger-nail is to the body, so is body to intelligence. The nail is a part of the body, but it can be pared off hundreds of times, and the body will still last. Similarly, the intelligence lasts aeons, while this body can be " pared off," thrown off. Yet intelligence cannot be immortal because it changes — growing and waning. Anything that changes cannot be immortal. Certainly intelligence is manufactured, and that very fact shows us that there must be something beyond that. It cannot be free, everything connected with matter is in nature, and, therefore, bound for ever. Who is free? The free must certainly be beyond cause and effect. If you say that the idea of freedom is a delusion, I shall say that the idea of bondage is also a delusion. Two facts come into our consciousness, and stand or fall with each other. These are our notions of bondage and freedom. If we want to go through a wall, and our head bumps against that wall, we see we are limited by that wall. At the same time we find a willpower, and think we can direct our will everywhere. At every step these contradictory ideas come to us. We have to believe that we are free, yet at every moment we find we are not free. If one idea is a delusion, the other is also a delusion, and if one is true, the other also is true, because both stand upon the same basis — consciousness. The Yogi says, both are true; that we are bound so far as intelligence goes, that we are free so far as the soul is concerned. It is the real nature of man, the soul, the Purusha, which is beyond all law of causation. Its freedom is percolating through layers of matter in various forms, intelligence, mind, etc. It is its light which is shining through all. Intelligence has no light of its own. Each organ has a particular centre in the brain; it is not that all the organs have one centre; each organ is separate. Why do all perceptions harmonise? Where do they get their unity? If it were in the brain, it would be necessary for all the organs, the eyes, the nose, the ears, etc., to have one centre only, while we know for certain that there are different centres for each. Both a man can see and hear at the same time, so a unity must be there at the back of intelligence. Intelligence is connected with the brain, but behind intelligence even stands the Purusha, the unit, where all different sensations and perceptions join and become one. The soul itself is the centre where all the different perceptions converge and become unified. That soul is free, and it is its freedom that tells you every moment that you are free. But you mistake, and mingle that freedom every moment with intelligence and mind. You try to attribute that freedom to the intelligence, and immediately find that intelligence is not free; you attribute that freedom to the body, and immediately nature tells you that you are again mistaken. That is why there is this mingled sense of freedom and bondage at the same time. The Yogi analyses both what is free and what is bound, and his ignorance vanishes. He finds that the Purusha is free, is the essence of that knowledge which, coming through the Buddhi, becomes intelligence, and, as such, is bound.

तदर्थ एव दृश्यस्यात्मा ॥२१॥

21. The nature of the experienced is for him.

Nature has no light of its own. As long as the Purusha is present in it, it appears as light. But the light is borrowed; just as the moon's light is reflected. According to the Yogis, all the manifestations of nature are caused by nature itself, but nature has no purpose in view, except to free the Purusha.

कृतार्थं प्रति नष्टमप्यनष्टं तदन्यसाधारणत्वात् ॥२२॥

22. Though destroyed for him whose goal has been gained, yet it is not destroyed, being common to others.

The whole activity of nature is to make the soul know that it is entirely separate from nature. When the soul knows this, nature has no more attractions for it. But the whole of nature vanishes only for that man who has become free. There will always remain an infinite number of others, for whom nature will go on working.

स्वस्वामिशक्त्योः स्वरूपोपलब्धिहेतुः संयोगः ॥२३॥

23. Junction is the cause of the realization of the nature of both the powers, the experienced and its Lord.

According to this aphorism, both the powers of soul and nature become manifest when they are in conjunction. Then all manifestations are thrown out. Ignorance is the cause of this conjunction. We see every day that the cause of our pain or pleasure is always our joining ourselves with the body. If I were perfectly certain that I am not this body, I should take no notice of heat and cold, or anything of the kind. This body is a combination. It is only a fiction to say that I have one body, you another, and the sun another. The whole universe is one ocean of matter, and you are the name of a little particle, and I of another, and the sun of another. We know that this matter is continuously changing. What is forming the sun one day, the next day may form the matter of our bodies.

तस्य हेतुरविद्या ॥२४॥

24. Ignorance is its cause.

Through ignorance we have joined ourselves with a particular body, and thus opened ourselves to misery. This idea of body is a simple superstition. It is superstition that makes us happy or unhappy. It is superstition caused by ignorance that makes us feel heat and cold, pain and pleasure. It is our business to rise above this superstition, and the Yogi shows us how we can do this. It has been demonstrated that, under certain mental conditions, a man may be burned, yet he will feel no pain. The difficulty is that this sudden upheaval of the mind comes like a whirlwind one minute, and goes away the next. If, however, we gain it through Yoga, we shall permanently attain to the separation of Self from the body.

तदभावात् संयोगाभावो हानं तद्दृशेः कैवल्यम् ॥२५॥

25. There being absence of that (ignorance) there is absence of junction, which is the thing-to-be avoided; that is the independence of the seer.

According to Yoga philosophy, it is through ignorance that the soul has been joined with nature. The aim is to get rid of nature's control over us. That is the goal of all religions. Each soul is potentially divine. The goal is to manifest this Divinity within, by controlling nature, external and internal. Do this either by work, or worship, or psychic control, or philosophy— by one or more or all of

these—and be free. This is the whole of religion. Doctrines, or dogmas, or rituals, or books, or temples, or forms, are but secondary details. The Yogi tries to
reach this goal through psychic control. Until we can free ourselves from nature, we are slaves; as she dictates so we must go. The Yogi claims that he who
controls mind controls matter also. The internal nature is much higher than the
external and much more difficult to grapple with, much more difficult to control. Therefore he who has conquered the internal nature controls the whole
universe; it becomes his servant. Raja-Yoga propounds the methods of gaining this control. Forces higher than we know in physical nature will have to be
subdued. This body is just the external crust of the mind. They are not two different things; they are just as the oyster and its shell. They are but two aspects
of one thing; the internal substance of the oyster takes up matter from outside,
and manufactures the shell. In the same way the internal fine forces which are
called mind take up gross matter from outside, and from that manufacture this
external shell, the body. If, then, we have control of the internal, it is very easy
to have control of the external. Then again, these forces are not different. It is
not that some forces are physical, and some mental; the physical forces are but
the gross manifestations of the fine forces, just as the physical world is but the
gross manifestation of the fine world.

विवेकख्यातिरविप्लवा हानोपायः ॥२६॥

26. The means of destruction of ignorance is unbroken practice of discrimination.

This is the real goal of practice—discrimination between the real and the unreal,
knowing that the Purusha is not nature, that it is neither matter nor mind, and
that because it is not nature, it cannot possibly change. It is only nature which
changes, combining and re-combining, dissolving continually. When through
constant practice we begin to discriminate, ignorance will vanish, and the Purusha
will begin to shine in its real nature—omniscient, omnipotent, omnipresent.

तस्य सप्तधा प्रान्तभूमिः प्रज्ञा ॥२७॥

27. His knowledge is of the sevenfold highest ground.

When this knowledge comes; it will come, as it were, in seven grades, one after
the other; and when one of these begins, we know that we are getting knowledge.
The first to appear will be that we have known what is to be known. The mind
will cease to be dissatisfied. While we are aware of thirsting after knowledge, we

begin to seek here and there, wherever we think we can get some truth, and failing to find it we become dissatisfied and seek in a fresh direction. All search is vain, until we begin to perceive that knowledge is within ourselves, that no one can help us, that we must help ourselves. When we begin to practise the power of discrimination, the first sign that we are getting near truth will be that that dissatisfied state will vanish. We shall feel quite sure that we have found the truth, and that it cannot be anything else but the truth. Then we may know that the sun is rising, that the morning is breaking for us, and taking courage, we must persevere until the goal is reached. The second grade will be the absence of all pains. It will be impossible for anything in the universe, external or internal, to give us pain. The third will be the attainment of full knowledge. Omniscience will be ours. The fourth will be the attainment of the end of all duty through discrimination. Next will come what is called freedom of the Chitta. We shall realise that all difficulties and struggles, all vacillations of the mind, have fallen down, just as a stone rolls from the mountain top into the valley and never comes up again. The next will be that the Chitta itself will realise that it melts away into its causes whenever we so desire. Lastly we shall find that we are established in our Self, that we have been alone throughout the universe, neither body nor mind was ever related, much less joined, to us. They were working their own way, and we, through ignorance, joined ourselves to them. But we have been alone, omnipotent, omnipresent, ever blessed ; our own Self was so pure and perfect that we required none else. We required none else to make us happy, for we are happiness itself. We shall find that this knowledge does not depend on anything else ; throughout the universe there can be nothing that will not become effulgent before our knowledge. This will be the last state, and the Yogi will become peaceful and calm, never to feel any more pain, never to be again deluded, never to be touched by misery. He will know he is ever blessed, ever perfect, almighty.

योगाङ्गानुष्ठानादशुद्धिक्षये ज्ञानदीप्तिरा विविकख्यातेः ॥२८॥

28. By the practice of the different parts of Yoga the impurities being destroyed, knowledge be comes effulgent up to discrimination.

Now comes the practical knowledge. What we have just been speaking about is much higher. It is away above our heads, but it is the ideal. It is first necessary to obtain physical and mental control. Then the realization will become steady in that ideal. The ideal being known, what remains is to practice the method of reaching it.

यम-नियमासन-प्राणायाम-प्रत्याहार-धारणा-ध्यान-समाधयोऽष्टावङ्गानि ॥२९॥

29. Yama, Niyama, Âsana, Prânâyâama, Pratyâhâra, Dhâranâ, Dhyâna, and
Samâdhi are the eight limbs of Yoga.

अहिंसा-सत्यास्तेय-ब्रह्मचर्यापरिग्रहा यमाः ॥३०॥

30. Non-killing, truthfulness, non-stealing, continence, and nor-receiving are
called Yamas.

A man who wants to be a perfect Yogi must give up the sex idea. The soul has
no sex; why should it degrade itself with sex ideas? Later on we shall understand
better why these ideas must be given up. The mind of the man who receives gifts
is acted on by the mind of the giver, so the receiver is likely to become degenerated. Receiving gifts is prone to destroy the independence of the mind, and
make us slavish. Therefore, receive no gifts.

एते जाति-देश-काल-समयानवच्छिन्नाः सार्वभौमा महाव्रतम् ॥३१॥

31. These, unbroken by time, place, purpose, and caste-rules, are (universal)
great vows.

These practices— non-killing, truthfulness, non-stealing, chastity, and non-
receiving— are to be practised by every man, woman, and child; by every soul,
irrespective of nation, country, or position.

शौच-सन्तोष-तपःस्वाध्यायेश्वरप्रणिधानानि नियमाः ॥३२॥

32. Internal and external purification, contentment, mortification, study, and
worship of God are the Niyamas.

External purification is keeping the body pure; a dirty man will never be a Yogi.
There must be internal purification also. That is obtained by the virtues named
in I.33. Of course, internal purity is of greater value than external, but both are
necessary, and external purity, without internal, is of no good.

वितर्कबाधने प्रतिपक्षभावनम् ॥३३॥

33. To obstruct thoughts which are inimical to Yoga, contrary thoughts should be brought.

That is the way to practise the virtues that have been stated. For instance, when
a big wave of anger has come into the mind, how are we to control that? Just

by raising an opposing wave. Think of love. Sometimes a mother is very angry with her husband, and while in that state, the baby comes in, and she kisses the baby; the old wave dies out and a new wave arises, love for the child. That suppresses the other one. Love is opposite to anger. Similarly, when the idea of stealing comes, non-stealing should be thought of; when the idea of receiving gifts comes, replace it by a contrary thought.

वितर्का हिंसादयः कृतकारितानुमोदिता लोभक्रोधमोहपूर्वका मृदुमध्याधिमात्रा
दुःखाज्ञानानन्तफला इति प्रतिपक्षभावनम् ॥३४॥

34. The obstructions to Yoga are killing, falsehood, etc., whether committed, caused, or approved; either through avarice, or anger, or ignorance; whether slight, middling, or great; and they result in infinite ignorance and misery. This is (the method of) thinking the contrary.

If I tell a lie, or cause another to tell one, or approve of another doing so, it is equally sinful. If it is a very mild lie, still it is a lie. Every vicious thought will rebound, every thought of hatred which you may have thought, in a cave even, is stored up, and will one day come back to you with tremendous power in the form of some misery here. If you project hatred and jealousy, they will rebound on you with compound interest. No power can avert them; when once you have put them in motion, you will have to bear them. Remembering this will prevent you from doing wicked things.

अहिंसाप्रतिष्ठायां तत्सन्निधौ वैरत्यागः ॥३५॥

35. Non-killing being established, in his presence all enmities cease (in others).

If a man gets the ideal of non-injuring others, before him even animals which are by their nature ferocious will become peaceful. The tiger and the lamb will play together before that Yogi. When you have come to that state, then alone you will understand that you have become firmly established in non-injuring.

सत्यप्रतिष्ठायां क्रियाफलाश्रयत्वम् ॥३६॥

36. By the establishment of truthfulness the Yogi gets the power of attaining for himself and others the fruits of work without the works.

When this power of truth will be established with you, then even in dream you will never tell an untruth. You will be true in thought, word, and deed. Whatever you say will be truth. You may say to a man, "Be blessed," and that man will be blessed. If a man is diseased, and you say to him, "Be thou cured," he will be cured immediately.

अस्तेयप्रतिष्ठायां सर्वरत्नोपस्थानम् ॥३७॥

37. By the establishment of non-stealing all wealth comes to the Yogi.

The more you fly from nature, the more she follows you; and if you do not care for her at all, she becomes your slave.

ब्रह्मचर्यप्रतिष्ठायां वीर्यलाभः ॥३८॥

38. By the establishment of continence energy is gained.

The chaste brain has tremendous energy and gigantic will-power. Without chastity there can be no spiritual strength. Continence gives wonderful control over mankind. The spiritual leaders of men have been very continent, and this is what gave them power. Therefore the Yogi must be continent.

अपरिग्रहस्थेर्ये जन्मकथन्तासंबोधः ॥३९॥

39. When he is fixed in non-receiving, he gets the memory of past life.

When a man does not receive presents, he does not become beholden to others, but remains independent and free. His mind becomes pure. With every gift, he is likely to receive the evils of the giver. If he does not receive, the mind is purified, and the first power it gets is memory of past life. Then alone the Yogi becomes perfectly fixed in his ideal. He sees that he has been coming and going many times, so he becomes determined that this time he will be free, that he will no more come and go, and be the slave of Nature.

शौचात्स्वाङ्गजुगुप्सा परैरसंसर्गः ॥४०॥

40. Internal and external cleanliness being established, there arises disgust for
one's own body, and non-intercourse with others.

When there is real purification of the body, external and internal, there arises neglect of the body, and the idea of keeping it nice vanishes. A face which others call most beautiful will appear to the Yogi as merely animal, if there is not intelligence behind it. What the world calls a very common face he regards as heavenly, if the spirit shines behind it. This thirst after body is the great bane of human life. So the first sign of the establishment of purity is that you do not care to think you are a body. It is only when purity comes that we get rid of the body idea.

सत्त्वशुद्धि-सौमनस्यैकाग्र्येन्द्रियजयात्मदर्शन-योग्यत्वानि च ॥४१॥

41. There also arises purification of the Sattva, cheerfulness of the mind, concentration, conquest of the organs, and fitness for the realisation of the Self.

By the practice of cleanliness, the Sattva material prevails, and the mind becomes concentrated and cheerful. The first sign that you are becoming religious is that you are becoming cheerful. When a man is gloomy, that may be dyspepsia, but it is not religion. A pleasurable feeling is the nature of the Sattva. Everything is pleasurable to the Sâttvika man, and when this comes, know that you are progressing in Yoga. All pain is caused by Tamas, so you must get rid of that; moroseness is one of the Exults of Tamas. The strong, the well knit, the young, the healthy, the daring alone are fit to be Yogis. To the Yogi everything is bliss, every human face that he sees brings cheerfulness to him. That is the sign of a virtuous man. Misery is caused by sin, and by no other cause. What business have you with clouded faces? It is terrible. If you have a clouded face, do not go out that day, shut yourself up in your room. What right have you to carry this disease out into the world? When your mind has become controlled, you have control over the whole body; instead of being a slave to this machine, the machine is your slave. Instead of this machine being able to drag the soul down, it becomes its greatest helpmate.

सन्तोषादनुत्तमः सुखलाभः ॥४२॥

42. From contentment comes superlative happiness.

कायेन्द्रियसिद्धिरशुद्धिक्षयात्तपसः ॥४३॥

43. The result of mortification is bringing powers to the organs and the body, by destroying the impurity.

The results of mortification are seen immediately, sometimes by heightened powers of vision, hearing things at a distance, and so on.

स्वाध्यायादिष्टदेवतासंप्रयोगः ॥४४॥

44. By the repetition of the Mantra comes the realisation of the intended deity.

The higher the beings that you want to get the harder is the practice.

समाधिसिद्धिरीश्वरप्रणिधानात् ॥४५॥

45. By sacrificing all to Ishvara comes Samadhi.

By resignation to the Lord, Samadhi becomes perfect.

स्थिरसुखमासनम् ॥४६॥

46. Posture is that which is firm and pleasant.

Now comes Asana, posture. Until you can get a firm seat you cannot practice the breathing and other exercises. Firmness of seat means that you do not feel the body at all. In the ordinary way, you will find that as soon as you sit for a few minutes all sorts of disturbances come into the body; but when you have got beyond the idea of a concrete body, you will lose all sense of the body. You will feel neither pleasure nor pain. And when you take your body up again, it will feel so rested. It is only perfect rest that you can give to the body. When you have succeeded in conquering the body and keeping it firm, your practice will remain firm, but while you are disturbed by the body, your nerves become disturbed, and you cannot concentrate the mind.

प्रयत्नशैथिल्यानन्तसमापत्तिभ्याम् ॥४७॥

47. By lessening the natural tendency (for restlessness) and meditating on the unlimited, posture becomes firm and pleasant.

We can make the seat firm by thinking of the infinite. We cannot think of the Absolute Infinite, but we can think of the infinite sky.

ततो द्वन्द्वानभिघातः ॥४८॥

48. Seat being conquered, the dualities do not obstruct.

The dualities, good and bad, heat and cold, and all the pairs of opposites, will not then disturb you.

तस्मिन् सति श्वासप्रश्वासयोर्गतविच्छेदः प्राणायामः ॥४९॥

49. Controlling the motion of the exhalation and the inhalation follows after this.

When posture has been conquered, then the motion of the Prana is to be broken and controlled. Thus we come to Pranayama, the controlling of the vital forces of the body. Prana is not breath, though it is usually so translated. It is the sum total of the cosmic energy. It is the energy that is in each body, and its most apparent manifestation is the motion of the lungs. This motion is caused by Prana drawing in the breath, and it is what we seek to control in Pranayama. We begin by controlling the breath, as the easiest way of getting control of the Prana.

बाह्याभ्यन्तरस्तम्भवृत्तिर्देशकालसंख्याभिः परिदृष्टो दीर्घसूक्ष्मः ॥५०॥

50. Its modifications are either external or internal, or motionless, regulated by place, terns, and number, either long or short.

The three sorts of motion of Pranayama are, one by which we draw the breath in, another by which we throw it out, and the third action is when the breath is held in the lungs, or stopped from entering the lungs. These, again, are varied by place and time. By place is meant that the Prana is held to some particular part of the body. By time is meant how long the Prana should be confined to a certain place, and so we are told how many seconds to keep one motion, and how many seconds to keep another. The result of this Pranayama is Udghâta, awakening the Kundalini.

बाह्याभ्यन्तरविषयाक्षेपी चतुर्थः ॥५१॥

51. The fourth is restraining the Prana by reflecting on external or internal object.

This is the fourth sort of Pranayama, in which the Kumbhaka is brought about by long practice attended with reflection, which is absent in the other three.

ततः क्षीयते प्रकाशावरणम् ॥५२॥

52. From that, the covering to the light of the Chitta is attenuated.

The Chitta has, by its own nature, all knowledge. It is made of Sattva particles, but is covered by Rajas and Tamas particles, and by Pranayama this covering is removed.

भारणासु च योग्यता मनसः ॥५३॥

53. The mind becomes fit for Dharana.

After this covering has been removed, we are able to concentrate the mind.

स्वस्ववषियासम्परयोगे चतितस्वरूपानुकार इवेन्द्रयियाणां परत्याहारः ॥५४॥

54. The drawing in of the organs is by their giving up their own objects and taking the form of the mind-stuff, as it were.

The organs are separate states of the mind-stuff. I see a book; the form is not in the book, it is in the mind. Something is outside which calls that form up. The real form is in the Chitta. The organs identify themselves with, and take the forms of, whatever comes to them. If you can restrain the mind-stuff from taking these forms, the mind will remain calm. This is called Pratyahara.

ततः परमा वश्यतेन्द्रयियाणाम् ॥५५॥

55. Thence arises supreme control of the organs.

When the Yogi has succeeded in preventing the organs from taking the forms of external objects, and in making them remain one with the mind-stuff, then comes perfect control of the organs. When the organs are perfectly under control, every muscle and nerve will be under control, because the organs are the centres of all the sensations, and of all actions. These organs are divided into organs of work and organs of sensation. When the organs are controlled, the Yogi can control all feeling and doing; the whole of the body comes under his control. Then alone one begins to feel joy in being born; then one can truthfully say, "Blessed am I that I was born." When that control of the organs is obtained, we feel how wonderful this body really is.

Chapter III

Powers

We have now come to the chapter in which the Yoga powers are described.

देश्वबन्धश्चचित्तस्य धारणा ॥१॥

1. Dhâranâ is holding the mind on to some particular object.

Dharana (concentration) is when the mind holds on to some object, either in the body, or outside the body, and keeps itself in that state.

तत्र प्रत्ययैकतानता ध्यानम् ॥२॥

2. An unbroken flow of knowledge in that object is Dhyâna.

The mind tries to think of one object, to hold itself to one particular spot, as the top of the head, the heart, etc., and if the mind succeeds in receiving the sensations only through that part of the body, and through no other part, that would be Dharana, and when the mind succeeds in keeping itself in that state for some time, it is called Dhyana (mediation).

तदेवार्थमात्रनिर्भासं स्वरूपश्रून्यमिव समाधिः ॥३॥

3. When that, giving up all forms, reflects only the meaning, it is Samâdhi.

That comes when in meditation the form or the external part is given up. Suppose I were meditating on a book, and that I have gradually succeeded in concentrating the mind on it, and perceiving only the internal sensations, the meaning, unexpressed in any form— that state of Dhyana is called Samadhi.

त्रयमेकत्र संयमः ॥४॥

4. (These) three (when practiced) in regard to one object is Samyama.

When a man can direct his mind to any particular object and fix it there, and then keep it there for a long time, separating the object from the internal part, this is Samyama; or Dharana, Dhyana, and Samadhi, one following the other, and making one. The form of the thing has vanished, and only its meaning remains in the mind.

तज्जयात् प्रज्ञाऽऽलोकः ॥५॥

5. By the conquest of that comes light of knowledge.

When one has succeeded in making this Samyama, all powers come under his control. This is the great instrument of the Yogi. The objects of knowledge are infinite, and they are divided into the gross, grosser, grossest and the fine, finer, finest and so on. This Samyama should be first applied to gross things, and when you begin to get knowledge of this gross, slowly, by stages, it should be brought to finer things.

तस्य भूमिषु विनियोगः ॥६॥

6. That should be employed in stages.

This is a note of warning not to attempt to go too fast.

त्रयमन्तरङ्गं पूर्वेभ्यः ॥७॥

7. These three are more internal than those that precede.

Before these we had the Pratyâhâra, the Prânâyâma, the Âsana, the Yama and Niyama; they are external parts of the three— Dharana, Dhyana and Samadhi. When a man has attained to them, he may attain to omniscience and omnipotence, but that would not be salvation. These three would; not make the mind Nirvikalpa, changeless, but would leave the seeds for getting bodies again. Only when the seeds are, as the Yogi says, "fried", do they lose the possibility of producing further plants. These powers cannot fry the seed.

तदपि बहिरङ्गं निर्बीजस्य ॥८॥

8. But even they are external to the seedless (Samadhi).

Compared with that seedless Samadhi, therefore, even these are external. We have not yet reached the real Samadhi, the highest, but a lower stage, in which this universe still exists as we see it, and in which are all these powers.

व्युत्थान-निरोधसंस्कारयोरभिभव-प्रादुर्भावौ निरोधक्षणचित्तान्वयो निरोध-परिणामः ॥९॥

9. By the suppression of the disturbed impressions of the mind, and by the rise of impressions of control, the mind, which persists in that moment of control, is said to attain the controlling modifications.

That is to say, in this first state of Samadhi the modifications of the mind have been controlled, but not perfectly, because if they were, there would be no modifications. If there is a modification which impels the mind to rush out through the senses, and the Yogi tries to control it, that very control itself will be a modification. One wave will be checked by another wave, so it will not be real Samadhi in which all the waves subside, as control itself will be a wave. Yet this lower Samadhi is very much nearer to the higher Samadhi than when the mind comes bubbling out.

तस्य प्रशान्तवाहिता संस्कारात् ॥१०॥

10. Its flow becomes steady by habit.

The flow of this continuous control of the mind becomes steady when practiced day after day, and the mind obtains the faculty of constant concentration.

सर्वार्थतैकाग्रतयोः क्षयोदयौ चित्तस्य समाधि-परिणामः ॥११॥

11. Taking in all sorts of objects, and concentrating upon one object, these two powers being destroyed and manifested respectively, the Chitta gets the modification called Samadhi.

The mind takes up various objects, runs into all sorts of things. That is the lower state. There is a higher state of the mind, when it takes up one object and excludes all others, of which Samadhi is the result.

शान्तोदितौ तुल्यप्रत्ययौ चित्तस्यैकाग्रता-परिणामः ॥१२॥

12. The one-pointedness of the Chitta is when the impression that is past and that which is present are similar.

How are we to know that the mind has become concentrated? Because the idea of time will vanish. The more time passes unnoticed the more concentrated we are. In common life we see that when we are interested in a book we do not note the time at all, and when we leave the book, we are often surprised to find

how many hours have passed. All time will have the tendency to come and stand
in the one present. So the definition is given: When the past and present come
and stand in one, the mind is said to be concentrated[1].

एतेन भूतेन्द्रियेषु धर्मलक्षणावस्थापरिणामा व्याख्याताः ॥१३॥

*13. By this is explained the threefold transformation of form, time and
state, in fine or gross matter and in the organs.*

By the threefold changes in the mind-stuff as to form, time and state are explained the corresponding changes in gross and subtle matter and in the organs.
Suppose there is a lump of gold. It is transformed into a bracelet and again into
an ear-ring. These are changes as to form. The same phenomena looked at from
the standpoint of time give us change as to time. Again, the bracelet or the ear-
ring may be bright or dull, thick or thin, and so on. This is change as to state.
Now referring to the aphorisms 9, 11 and 12, the mind-stuff is changing into
Vrittis — this is change as to form. That it passes through past, present and future
moments of time is change as to time. That the impressions vary as to intensity
within one particular period, say, present, is change as to state. The concentrations taught in the preceding aphorisms were to give the Yogi a voluntary control over the transformations of his mind-stuff, which alone will enable him to
make the Samyama named in III.4.

ज्ञान्तोदितिाव्यपदेश्ययधर्मानुपातो धर्मी ॥१४॥

*14. That which is acted upon by transformations, either past, present, or yet to
be manifested is the qualified.*

That is to say, the qualified is the substance which is being acted upon by time
and by the Samskâras, and getting changed and being manifested always.

क्रमान्यत्वं परिणामान्यत्वे हेतुः ॥१५॥

15. The succession of changes is the cause of manifold evolution.

परिणामत्रयसंयमादतीतानागतज्ज्ञानम् ॥१६॥

*16. By making Samyama on the three sorts of changes comes the knowledge of
past and future.*

We must not lose sight of the first definition of Samyama. When the mind has attained to that state when it identifies itself with the internal impression of the object, leaving the external, and when, by long practice, that is retained by the mind and the mind can get into that state in a moment, that is Samyama. If a man in that state wants to know the past and future, he has to make a Samyama on the changes in the Samskaras (III.13). Some are working now at present, some have worked out, and some are waiting to work. So by making a Samyama on these he knows the past and future.

शब्दार्थप्रत्ययानामितरेतराध्यासात्सङ्करस्तत्प्रविभागसंयमात् सर्वभूतरुतज्ञानम् ॥१७॥

17. By making Samyama on word, meaning and knowledge, which are ordinarily confused, comes the knowledge of all animal sounds.

The word represents the external cause, the meaning represents the internal vibration that travels to the brain through the channels of the Indriyas, conveying the external impression to the mind, and knowledge represents the re-action of the mind, with which comes perception. These three, confused, make our sense-objects. Suppose I hear a word; there is first the external vibration, next the internal sensation carried to the mind by the organ of hearing, then the mind reacts, and I know the word. The word I know is a mixture of the three — vibration, sensation, and reaction. Ordinarily these three are inseparable; but by practice the Yogi can separate them. When a man has attained to this, if he makes a Samyama on any sound, he understands the meaning which that sound was intended to express, whether it was made by man or be any other animal.

संस्कारसाक्षात्करणात् पूर्वजातिज्ञानम् ॥१८॥

18. By perceiving the impressions, (comes) the knowledge of past life.

Each experience that we have, comes in the form of a wave in the Chitta, and this subsides and becomes finer and finer, but is never lost. It remains there in minute form, and if we can bring this wave up again, it becomes memory. So, if the Yogi can make a Samyama on these past impressions in the mind, he will begin to remember all his past lives.

प्रत्ययस्य परचित्तज्ञानम् ॥१९॥

19. By making Samyama on the signs in another's body, knowledge of his mind comes.

Each man has particular signs on his body, which differentiate him from others; when the Yogi makes a Samyama on these signs he knows the nature of the mind of that person.

न च तत् सालम्बनं तस्यावषियीभूततत्वात् ॥२०॥

20. But not its contents, that not being the object of the Samyama.

He would not know the contents of the mind by making a Samyama on the body. There would be required a twofold Samyama, first on the signs in the body, and then on the mind itself. The Yogi would then know everything that is in that mind.

कायरूपसंयमात्तद्ग्राह्यशक्ति-स्तम्भे चक्षुःप्रकाशासंप्रयोगेऽन्तर्धानम् ॥२१॥

21. By making Samyama on the form of the body, the perceptibility of the form being obstructed and the power of manifestation in the eye being separated, the Yogi's body becomes unseen.

A Yogi standing in the midst of this room can apparently vanish. He does not really vanish, but he will not be seen by anyone. The form and the body are, as it were, separated. You must remember that this can only be done when the Yogi has attained to that power of concentration when form and the thing formed have been separated. Then he makes a Samyama on that, and the power to perceive forms is obstructed, because the power of perceiving forms comes from the junction of form and the thing formed.

एतेन शब्दाद्यन्तर्धानमुक्तम् ॥२२॥

22. By this the disappearance or concealment of words which are being spoken and such other things are also explained.

सोपक्रमं निरुपक्रमं च कर्म तत्संयमादपरान्तज्ञानमरिष्टेभ्यो वा ॥२३॥

23. Karma is of two kinds— soon to be fructified and late to be fructified. By making Samyana on these, or by the signs called Arishta, portents, the Yogis know the exact time of separation from their bodies.

When a Yogi makes a Samyama on his own Karma, upon those impressions in his mind which are now working, and those which are just waiting to work, he knows exactly by those that are waiting when his body will fall. He knows when he will die, at what hour, even at what minute. The Hindus think very much of that knowledge or consciousness of the nearness of death, because it is taught in the Gita that the thoughts at the moment of departure are great powers in determining the next life.

मैत्र्यादिषु बलानि ॥२४

24. *By making Samyama on friendship, mercy, etc. (I.33), the Yogi excels in the respective qualities.*

बलेषु हस्तिबिलादीनि ॥२५॥

25. *By making Samyama on the strength of the elephant and others, their respective strength comes to the Yogi.*

When a Yogi has attained to this Samyama and wants strength, he makes a Samyama on the strength of the elephant and gets it. Infinite energy is at the disposal of everyone if he only knows how to get it. The Yogi has discovered the science of getting it.

प्रवृत्त्यालोकन्यासात् सूक्ष्म-व्यवहति-विप्रकृष्टज्ञानम् ॥२६॥

26. *By making Samyama on the Effulgent Light (I.36), comes the knowledge of the fine, the obstructed, and the remote.*

When the Yogi makes Samyama on that Effulgent Light in the heart, he sees things which are very remote, things, for instance, that are happening in a distant place, and which are obstructed by mountain barriers, and also things which are very fine.

भुवनज्ञानं सूर्ये संयमात् ॥२७॥

27. *By making Samyama on the sun, (comes) the knowledge of the world.*

चन्द्रे ताराव्यूहज्ञानम् ॥२८॥

28. *On the moon, (comes) the knowledge of the cluster of stars.*

ध्रुवे तद्गतिज्ञानम् ॥२९॥

29. *On the pole-star, (comes) the knowledge of the motions of the stars.*

नाभिचक्रे कायव्यूहज्ञानम् ॥३०॥

30. *On the navel circle, (comes) the knowledge of the constitution of the body.*

कण्ठकूपे क्षुत्पपिासानिवृत्ततिः ॥ ३१॥

31. On the hollow of the throat, (comes) cessation of hunger.

When a man is very hungry, if he can make Samyama on the hollow of the throat, hunger ceases.

कूर्मनाड्यां स्थैर्यम् ॥ ३२॥

32. On the nerve called Kurma, (comes) fixity of the body.

When he is practising, the body is not disturbed.

मूर्धज्योतिषि सिद्धदर्शनम् ॥ ३३॥

33. On the light emanating from the top of the head, sight of the Siddhas.

The Siddhas are beings who are a little above ghosts. When the Yogi concentrates his mind on the top of his head, he will see these Siddhas. The word Siddha does not refer to those men who have become free — a sense in which it is often used.

प्रातिभाद्वा सर्वम् ॥ ३४॥

34. Or by the power of Prâtibha, all knowledge.

All these can come without any Samyama to the man who has the power of Pratibha (spontaneous enlightenment from purity). When a man has risen to a high state of Pratibha, he has that great light. All things are apparent to him. Everything comes to him naturally without making Samyama.

हृदये चित्त-संवित् ॥ ३५॥

35. In the heart, knowledge of minds.

सत्त्वपुरुषयोरत्यन्तासंकीर्णयोः प्रत्ययाविशेषाद् भोगः परार्थत्वात् स्वार्थसंयमात्
पुरुषज्ञानम् ॥ ३६॥

36. Enjoyment comes from the non-discrimination of the soul and Sattva
which are totally different because the latter's actions are for another.
Samyama on the self-centred one gives knowledge of the Purusha.

All action of Sattva, a modification of Prakriti characterised by light and happiness, is for the soul. When Sattva is free from egoism and illuminated with the pure intelligence of Purusha, it is called the self-centred one, because in that state it becomes independent of all relations.

ततः प्रातिभश्रावणवेदनादर्शास्वादवार्ता जायन्ते ॥ ३७॥

37. From that arises the knowledge belonging to Pratibha and (supernatural) hearing, touching, seeing, tasting and smelling.

ते समाधावुपसर्गा व्युत्थाने सिद्धयः ॥ ३८॥

38. These are obstacles to Samadhi; but they are powers in the worldly state.

To the Yogi knowledge of the enjoyments of the world comes by the junction of the Purusha and the mind. If he wants to make Samyama on the knowledge that they are two different things, nature and soul, he gets knowledge of the Purusha. From that arises discrimination. When he has got that discrimination, he gets the Pratibha, the light of supreme genius. These powers, however, are obstructions to the attainment of the highest goal, the knowledge of the pure Self, and freedom. These are, as it were, to be met in the way; and if the Yogi rejects them, he attains the highest. If he is tempted to acquire these, his further progress is barred.

बन्धकारणशैथिल्यात् प्रचारसंवेदनाच्च चित्तस्य परशरीरावेशः ॥ ३९॥

39. When the cause of bondage of the Chitta has become loosened, the Yogi, by his knowledge of its channels of activity (the nerves), enters another's body.

The Yogi can enter a dead body and make it get up and move, even while he himself is working in another body. Or he can enter a living body and hold that man's mind and organs in check, and for the time being act through the body of that man. That is done by the Yogi coming to this discrimination of Purusha and nature. If he wants to enter another's body, he makes a Samyama on that body and enters it, because, not only is his soul omnipresent, but his mind also, as the Yogi teaches. It is one bit of the universal mind. Now, however, it can only work; through the nerve currents in this body, but when the Yogi has loosened himself from these nerve currents, he can work through other things.

उदानजयाज्जलपङ्ककण्टकादिष्वसङ्ग उत्क्रान्तिश्च ॥ ४०॥

40. By conquering the current called Udâna the Yogi does not sink in water or in swamps, he can walk on thorns etc., and can, die at will.

Udana is the name of the nerve current that governs the lungs and all the up-
per parts of the body, and when he is master of it, he becomes light in weight.
He does not sink in water; he can walk on thorns and sword blades, and stand
in fire, and can depart this life whenever he likes.

समानजयात् परज्वलनम् ॥४१॥

41. By the conquest of the current Samâna he is surrounded by a blaze of light.

Whenever he likes, light flashes from his body.

श्रोत्राकाशयोः सम्बन्धसंयमाद्दिव्यं श्रोत्रम् ॥४२॥

*42. By making Samyama on the relation between the ear and the Akâsha comes
divine hearing.*

There is the Akasha, the ether, and the instrument, the ear. By making Samyama
on them the Yogi gets supernormal hearing; he hears everything. Anything spoken or sounded miles away he can hear.

कायाकाशयोः सम्बन्धसंयमाल्लघुतूलसमापत्तेश्चाकाशगमनम् ॥४३॥

*43. By making Samyama on the relation between the Akasha and the
body and becoming light as cotton-wool etc., through meditation on them,
the yogi goes through the skies.*

This Akasha is the material of this body; it is only Akasha in a certain form
that has become the body. If the Yogi makes a Sanyama on this Akasha material
of his body, it acquires the lightness of Akasha, and he can go anywhere through
the air. So in the other case also.

बहिरकल्पिता वृत्तिर्महाविदेहा ततः प्रकाशावरणक्षयः ॥४४॥

*44. By making Samyama on the "real modifications" of the mind,
outside of the body, called great disembodiedness, comes disappearance of
the covering to light.*

The mind in its foolishness thinks that it is working in this body. Why should
I be bound by one system of nerves, and put the Ego only in one body, if the

mind is omnipresent? There is no reason why I should. The Yogi wants to feel the Ego wherever he likes. The mental waves which arise in the absence of egoism in the body are called "real modifications" or "great disembodiedness". When he has succeeded in making Samyama on these modifications, all covering to light goes away, and all darkness and ignorance vanish. Everything appears to him to be full of knowledge.

स्थूल-स्वरूप-सूक्ष्मान्वयार्थवत्त्वसंयमाद्भूतजयः ॥४५॥

45. *By making Samyama on the gross and fine forms of the elements, their essential traits, the inherence of the Gunas in them and on their contributing to the experience of the soul, comes mastery of the elements.*

The Yogi makes Samyama on the elements, first on the gross, and then on the finer states. This Samyama is taken up more by a sect of the Buddhists. They take a lump of clay and make Samyama on that, and gradually they begin to see the fine materials of which it is composed, and when they have known all the fine materials in it, they get power over that element. So with all the elements. The Yogi can conquer them all.

ततोऽणिमादिप्रादुर्भावः कायसम्पत्तद्धर्मानभिघातश्च ॥४६॥

46. *From that comes minuteness and the rest of the powers, "glorification of the body," and indestructibleness of the bodily qualities.*

This means that the Yogi has attained the eight powers. He can make himself as minute as a particle, or as huge as a mountain, as heavy as the earth, or as light as the air; he can reach anything he likes, he can rule everything he wants, he can conquer everything he wants, and so on. A lion will sit at his feet like a lamb, and all his desires will be fulfilled at will.

रूप-लावण्य-बल-वज्रसंहननत्वानि कायसम्पत् ॥४७॥

47. *The "glorification of the body" is beauty, complexion, strength, adamantine hardness.*

The body becomes indestructible. Nothing can injure it. Nothing can destroy it until the Yogi wishes. "Breaking the rod of time he lives in this universe with his body." In the Vedas it is written that for that man there is no more disease, death or pain.

गर्हणा-स्वरूपास्मितान्वयार्थबत्त्वसंयमादिन्द्रियजय: ॥४८॥

48. By making Samyama on the objectivity and power of illumination of the
organs, on egoism, the inherence of the Gunas in them and on their contributing
to the experience of the soul, comes the conquest of the organs.

In the perception of external objects the organs leave their place in the mind
and go towards the object; this is followed by knowledge. Egoism also is present in the act. When the Yogi makes Samyama on these and the other two by
gradation, he conquers the organs. Take up anything that you see or feel, a book
for instance; first concentrate the mind on it, then on the knowledge that is in
the form of a book, and then on the Ego that sees the book, and so on. By that
practice all the organs will be conquered.

ततो मनोजवित्वं विकिरणभाव: प्रधानजयश्च ॥४९॥

49. From that comes to the body the power of rapid movement like the mind,
power of the organs independently of the body, and conquest of nature.

Just as by the conquest of the elements comes glorified body, so from the conquest of the organs will come the above-mentioned powers.

सत्त्वपुरुषान्यताख्यातिमात्रस्य सर्वभावाधिष्ठातृत्वं सर्वज्ञातृत्वञ्च ॥५०॥

50. By making Samyama on the discrimination between the Sattva and
the Purusha come omnipotence and omniscience.

When nature has been conquered, and the difference between the Purusha and
nature realised— that the Purusha is indestructible, pure and perfect— then
come omnipotence and omniscience.

तद्वैराग्यादपि दोषबीजक्षये कैवल्यम् ॥५१॥

51. By giving up even these powers comes the destruction of the very
seed of evil, which leads to Kaivalya.

He attains aloneness, independence, and becomes free. When one gives up
even the ideas of omnipotence and omniscience, there comes entire rejection of
enjoyment, of the temptations from celestial beings. When the Yogi has seen
all these wonderful powers, and rejected them, he reaches the goal. What are
all these powers? Simply manifestations. They are no better than dreams. Even

omnipotence is a dream. It depends on the mind. So long as there is a mind it can be understood, but the goal is beyond even the mind.

स्थान्युपनमिन्तररो सङ्गस्मयाकररां पुनरनष्टिपरसङ्गात् ॥५२॥

52. The Yogi should not feel allured or flattered by the overtures of celestial beings for fear of evil again.

There are other dangers too; gods and other beings come to tempt the Yogi. They do not want anyone to be perfectly free. They are jealous, just as we are, and worse than us sometimes. They are very much afraid of losing their places. Those Yogis who do not reach perfection die and become gods; leaving the direct road they go into one of the side streets, and get these powers. Then, again, they have to be born. But he who is strong enough to withstand these temptations and go straight to the goal, becomes free.

कषरा-ततक्रमयोः संयमाद्वविकजं ज्ञानम् ॥५३॥

53. By making Samyama on a particle of time and its precession and succession comes discrimination.

How are we to avoid all these things, these Devas, and heavens, and powers? By discrimination, by knowing good from evil. Therefore a Samyama is given by which the power of discrimination can be strengthened. This by making a Samyama on a particle of time, and the time preceding and following it.

जाति-लक्षरा-देश्रैरन्यताऽनवच्छेदात्तुल्ययोस्ततः परतपित्तिः ॥५४॥

54. Those things which cannot be differentiated by species, sign, and place, even they will be discriminated by the above Samyama.

The misery that we suffer comes from ignorance, from non-discrimination between the real and the unreal. We all take the bad for the good, the dream for the reality. Soul is the only reality, and we have forgotten it. Body is an unreal dream, and we think we are all bodies. This non-discrimination is the cause of misery. It is caused by ignorance. When discrimination comes, it brings strength, and then alone can we avoid all these various ideas of body, heavens, and gods. This ignorance arises through differentiating by species, sign, and place. For instance, take a cow. The cow is differentiated from the dog by species. Even with the cows alone how do we make the distinction between one cow and another?

By signs. If two objects are exactly similar, they can be distinguished if they are in different places. When objects are so mixed up that even these differential will not help us, the power of discrimination acquired by the above-mentioned practice will give us the ability to distinguish them. The highest philosophy of the Yogi is based upon this fact, that the Purusha is pure and perfect, and is the only "simple" that exists in this universe. The body and mind are compounds, and yet we are ever identifying ourselves with them This is the great mistake that the distinction has been lost. When this power of discrimination has been attained, man sees that everything in this world, mental and physical, is a compound, and, as such, cannot be the Purusha.

तारकं सर्ववषियं सर्वथावषियमक्रमञ्चेति विविकजं ज्ञानम् ॥५५॥

55. *The saving knowledge is that knowledge of discrimination which simultaneously covers all objects, in all their variations.*

Saving, because the knowledge takes the Yogi across the ocean of birth and death. The whole of Prakriti in all its states, subtle and gross, is within the grasp of this knowledge. There is no succession in perception by this knowledge; it takes in all things simultaneously, at a glance.

सत्त्वपुरुषयोः शुद्धसिाम्ये केवल्यमिति ॥५६॥

56. *By the similarity of purity between the Sattva and the Purusha comes Kaivalya.*

When the soul realises that it depends on nothing in the universe, from gods to the lowest atom, that is called Kaivalya (isolation) and perfection. It is attained when this mixture of purity and impurity called Sattva (intellect) has been made as pure as the Purusha itself; then the Sattva reflects only the unqualified essence of purity, which is the Purusha.

Note:

1: The distinction among the three kinds of concentration mentioned in aphorisms 9, 11 and 12 is as follows: In the first, the disturbed impressions are merely held back, but not altogether obliterated by the impressions of control which just come in; in the second, the former are completely suppressed by the latter which stand in bold relief, while in the third, which is the highest, there is no question of suppressing, but only similar impressions succeed each other in a stream.

Chapter IV

Independence

जन्मौषधि-मन्त्र-तपः-समाधिजाः सिद्धयः ॥१॥

1. The Siddhis (powers) are attained by birth, chemical means, power of words,
mortification, or concentration.

Sometimes a man is born with the Siddhis, powers, of course, those he had earned in his previous incarnation. This time he is born, as it were, to enjoy the fruits of them. It is said of Kapila, the great father of the Sânkhya philosophy, that he was a born Siddha, which means literally a man who has attained to success.

The Yogis claim that these powers can be gained by chemical means. All of you know that chemistry originally began as alchemy; men went in search of the philosopher's stone and elixirs of life, and so forth. In India there was a sect called the Râsâyanas. Their idea was that ideality, knowledge, spirituality, and religion were all very right, but that the body was the only instrument by which to attain to all these. If the body came to an end every now and again, it would take so much more time to attain to the goal. For instance, a man wants to practice Yoga, or wants to become spiritual. Before he has advanced very far he dies. Then he takes another body and begins again, then dies, and so on. In this way much time will be lost in dying and being born again. If the body could be made strong and perfect, so that it would get rid of birth and death, we should have so much more time to become spiritual. So these Rasayanas say, first make the body very strong. They claim that this body can be made immortal. Their idea is that if the mind manufactures the body, and if it be true that each mind is only one outlet to the infinite energy, there should be no limit to each outlet getting any amount of power from outside. Why is it impossible to keep our bodies all the time? We have to manufacture all the bodies that we ever have. As soon as this body dies, we shall have to manufacture another. If we can do that, why cannot we do it just here and now, without getting out of the present body? The theory is perfectly correct. If it is possible that we live after death, and make other bodies, why is it impossible that we should have the power of making bodies here, without entirely dissolving this body, simply changing it continually? They also thought that in mercury and in sulphur was hidden the most wonderful power, and that by certain preparations of these a man could keep the body as long as he liked. Others believed that certain drugs could bring powers, such as flying through the air. Many of the most wonderful medicines of the present day we owe to the Rasayanas, notably the use of metals in medicine. Certain sects of Yogis claim that many of their principal teachers are still living in their old bodies. Patanjali, the great authority on Yoga, does not deny this.

The power of words. There are certain sacred words called Mantras, which have power, when repeated under proper conditions, produce these extraordinary powers. We are living in the midst of such a mass of miracles, day and night, that we do not think anything of them. There is no limit to man's power, the power of words and the power of mind.

Mortification. You find that in every religion mortification and asceticisms have been practised. In these religious conceptions the Hindus always go to the extremes. You will find men with their hands up all their lives, until their hands wither and die. Men keep standing, day and night, until their feet swell, and if they live, the legs become so stiff in this position that they can no more bend them, but have to stand all their lives. I once saw a man who had kept his hands raised in this way, and I asked him how it felt when he did it first. He said it was awful torture. It was such torture that he had to go to a river and put himself in water, and that allayed the pain for a little while. After a month he did not suffer much. Through such practices powers (Siddhis) can be attained.

Concentration. Concentration is Samâdhi, and that is Yoga proper; that is the principal theme of this science, and it is the highest means. The preceding ones are only secondary, and we cannot attain to the highest through them. Samadhi is the means through which we can gain anything and everything, mental, moral, or spiritual.

जात्यन्तरपरिणामः प्रकृत्यापूरात् ॥२॥

2. The change into another species is by the filling in of nature.

Patanjali has advanced the proposition that these powers come by birth, sometimes by chemical means, or through mortification. He also admits that this body can be kept for any length of time. Now he goes on to state what is the cause of the change of the body into another species. He says this is done by the filling in of nature, which he explains in the next aphorism.

नमित्तितमप्रयोजकं प्रकृतीनां वरणभेदस्तु ततः क्षेत्रिकवत् ॥३॥

3. Good and bad deeds are not the direct causes in the transformations of nature,
but they act as breakers of obstacles to the evolutions of nature: as a farmer breaks
the obstacles to the course of water, which then runs down by its own nature.

The water for irrigation of fields is already in the canal, only shut in by gates. The farmer opens these gates, and the water flows in by itself, by the law of gravitation. So all progress and power are already in every man; perfection is man's nature, only it is barred in and prevented from taking its proper course. If anyone can take the bar off, in rushes nature. Then the man attains the powers which are his already. Those we call wicked become saints, as soon as the bar is broken and nature rushes in. It is nature that is driving us towards perfection, and eventually she will bring everyone there. All these practices and struggles to become religious are only negative work, to take off the bars, and open the doors to that perfection which is our birthright, our nature.

Today the evolution theory of the ancient Yogis will be better understood in the light of modern research. And yet the theory of the Yogis is a better explanation. The two causes of evolution advanced by the moderns, namely, sexual selection and survival of the fittest, are inadequate. Suppose human knowledge to have advanced so much as to eliminate competition, both from the function of acquiring physical sustenance and of acquiring a mate. Then, according to the moderns, human progress will stop and the race will die. The result of this theory is to furnish every oppressor with an argument to calm the qualms of conscience. Men are not lacking, who, posing as philosophers, want to kill out all wicked and incompetent persons (they are, of course, the only judges of competency) and thus preserve the human race! But the great ancient evolutionist, Patanjali, declares that the true secret of evolution is the manifestation of the perfection which is already in every being; that this perfection has been barred and the infinite tide behind is struggling to express itself. These struggles and competitions are but the results of our ignorance, because we do not know the proper way to unlock the gate and let the water in. This infinite tide behind must express itself; it is the cause of all manifestation. Competitions for life or sex-gratification are only momentary, unnecessary, extraneous effects, caused by ignorance. Even when all competition has ceased, this perfect nature behind will make us go forward until everyone has become perfect. Therefore there is no reason to believe that competition is necessary to progress. In the animal the man was suppressed, but as soon as the door was opened, out rushed man. So

in man there is the potential god, kept in by the locks and bars of ignorance.
When knowledge breaks these bars, the god becomes manifest.

नरिमाणाचत्तितान्यस्मितामात्रात् ॥४॥

4. From egoism alone proceed the created minds.

The theory of Karma is that we suffer for our good or bad deeds, and the whole
scope of philosophy is to reach the glory of man. All the scriptures sing the glory
of man, of the soul, and then, in the same breath, they preach Karma. A good
deed brings such a result, and a bad deed such another, but if the soul can be
acted upon by a good or a bad deed, the soul amounts to nothing. Bad deeds
put a bar to the manifestation of the nature of the Purusha; good deeds take
the obstacles off, and the glory of the Purusha becomes manifest. The Purusha
itself is never changed. Whatever you do never destroys your own glory, your
own nature, because the soul cannot be acted upon by anything, only a veil is
spread before it, hiding its perfection.

With a view to exhausting their Karma quickly, Yogis create Kâya-vyuha, or
groups of bodies, in which to work it out. For all these bodies they create minds
from egoism. These are called "created minds", in contradistinction to their
original minds.

परवृत्तभिदे प्रयोजकं चतितमेकमनेकेषाम् ॥५॥

5. Though the activities of the different created minds are various, the
one original mind is the controller of them all.

These different minds, which act in these different bodies are called made-minds,
and the bodies, made-bodies; that is, manufactured bodies and minds. Matter
and mind are like two inexhaustible storehouses. When you become a Yogi, you
learn the secret of their control. It was yours all the time, but you had forgotten
it. When you become a Yogi, you recollect it. Then you can do anything with it,
manipulate it in every way you like. The material out of which a manufactured
mind is created is the very same material which is used for the macrocosm. It is not
that mind is one thing and matter another, they are different aspects of the same
thing. Asmitâ, egoism, is the material, the fine state of existence out of which
these made-minds and made-bodies of the Yogi are manufactured. Therefore,
when the Yogi has found the secret of these energies of nature, he can manufacture any number of bodies or minds out of the substance known as egoism.

तत्र ध्यानजमनाश्रयम् ॥ ६ ॥

6. Among the various Chittas, that which is attained by Samadhi is desireless.

Among all the various minds that we see in various men, only that mind which has attained to Samadhi, perfect concentration, is the highest. A man who has attained certain powers through medicines, or through words, or through mortifications, still has desires, but that man who has attained to Samadhi through concentration is alone free from all desires.

कर्माशुक्लाकृष्णं योगनिस्त्रविधिमितरेषाम् ॥ ७ ॥

7. Works are neither black nor white for the Yogis; for others they are threefold — black, white, and mixed.

When the Yogi has attained perfection, his actions, and the Karma produced by those actions, do not bind him, because he did not desire them. He just works on; he works to do good, and he does good, but does not care for the result, and it will not come to him. But, for ordinary men, who have not attained to the highest state, works are of three kinds, black (evil actions), white (good actions), and mixed.

ततस्तद्विपाकानुगुणानामेवाभिव्यक्तिर्वासनानाम् ॥ ८ ॥

8. From these threefold works are manifested in each state only those desires (which are) fitting to that state alone. (The others are held in abeyance for the time being.)

Suppose I have made the three kinds of Karma, good, bad, and mixed, and suppose I die and become a god in heaven. The desires in a god body are not the same as the desires in a human body; the god body neither eats nor drinks. What becomes of my past unworked Karmas which produce as their effect the desire to eat and drink? Where would these Karmas go when I become a god? The answer is that desires can only manifest themselves in proper environments. Only those desires will come out for which the environment is fitted; the rest will remain stored up. In this life we have many godly desires, many human desires, many animal desires. If I take a god body, only the good desires will come up, because for them the environments are suitable. And if I take an animal body, only the animal desires will come up, and the good desires will wait. What does this show? That by means of environment we can check these desires. Only that Karma which is suited to and fitted for the environments will come out. This shows that the power of environment is the great check to control even Karma itself.

जाति-देश-काल-व्यवहितानामप्यानन्तर्यं स्मृतिसंस्कारयोरेकरूपत्वात् ॥९॥

9. *There is consecutiveness in desires, even though separated by species, space, and time, there being identification of memory and impressions.*

Experiences becoming fine become impressions; impressions revivified become memory. The word memory here includes unconscious co-ordination of past experiences, reduced to impressions, with present conscious action. In each body, the group of impressions acquired in a similar body only becomes the cause of action in that body. The experiences of a dissimilar body are held in abeyance. Each body acts as if it were a descendant of a series of bodies of that species only; thus, consecutiveness of desires is not to be broken.

तासामनादित्वं चाशिषो नित्यत्वात् ॥१०॥

10. *Thirst for happiness being eternal, desires are without beginning.*

All experience is preceded by desire for happiness. There was no beginning of experience, as each fresh experience is built upon the tendency generated by past experience; therefore desire is without beginning.

हेतुफलाश्रयालम्बनैः संगृहीतत्वादेषामभावे तदभावः ॥११॥

11. *Being held together by cause, effect, support, and objects, in the absence of these is its absence.*

Desires are held together by cause and effect; (The causes are the "pain-bearing obstructions" (II.3) and actions (IV.7), and the effects are "species, life, and experience of pleasure and pain" (II.13). if a desire has been raised, it does not die without producing its effect. Then, again, the mind-stuff is the great storehouse, the support of all past desires reduced to Samskara form; until they have worked themselves out, they will not die. Moreover, so long as the senses receive the external objects, fresh desires will arise. If it be possible to get rid of the cause, effect, support, and objects of desire, then alone it will vanish.

अतीतानागतं स्वरूपतोऽस्त्यध्वभेदाद्धर्माणाम् ॥१२॥

12. The past and future exist in their own nature, qualities having different ways.

The idea is that existence never comes out of nonexistence. The past and future, though not existing in a manifested form, yet exist in a fine form.

ते व्यक्त-सूक्ष्मा गुणात्मानः ॥१३॥

13. They are manifested or fine, being of the nature of the Gunas.

The Gunas are the three substances, Sattva, Rajas, and Tamas, whose gross state is the sensible universe. Past and future arise from the different modes of manifestation of these Gunas.

परिणामैकत्वाद्वस्तुतत्त्वम् ॥१४॥

14. The unity in things is from the unity in changes.

Though there are three substances, their changes being co-ordinated, all objects have their unity.

वस्तुसाम्ये चित्तभेदात्तयोर्विभक्तः पन्थाः ॥१५॥

15. Since perception and desire vary with regard to the same object, mind and object are of different nature.

That is, there is an objective world independent of our minds. This is a refutation of Buddhistic Idealism. Since different people look at the same thing differently, it cannot be a mere imagination of any particular individual.

न चैकचित्ततन्त्रं वस्तु तदप्रमाणकं तदा किं स्यात् ॥

The object cannot be said to be dependent on a single mind. There being no proof of its existence, it would then become nonexistent.

If the perception of an object were the only criterion of its existence, then when the mind is absorbed in anything or is in Samadhi, it would not be perceived by anybody and might as well be said to be non-existent. This is an undesirable conclusion.

तदुपरागापेक्षत्तिवाच्चत्तितम्रग वरात् ज्ञाताज्ञातम् ॥१६॥

16. *Things are known on unknown to the mind, being dependent on the colouring which they give to the mind.*

सदा ज्ञाताश्चत्तितवृत्तयस्तत्पर्भोः पुरुषस्यापरगिामत्तिवात् ॥१७॥

17. *The states of the mind are always known, because the lord of the mind, the Purusha, is unchangeable.*

The whole gist of this theory is that the universe is both mental and material. Both of these are in a continuous state of flux. What is this book? It is a combination of molecules in constant change. One lot is going out, and another coming in; it is a whirlpool, but what makes the unity? What makes it the same book? The changes are rhythmical; in harmonious order they are sending impressions to my mind, and these pieced together make a continuous picture, although the parts are continuously changing. Mind itself is continuously changing. The mind and body are like two layers in the same substance, moving at different rates of speed. Relatively, one being slower and the other quicker, we can distinguish between the two motions. For instance, a train is in motion, and a carriage is moving alongside it. It is possible to find the motion of both these to a certain extent. But still something else is necessary. Motion can only be perceived when there is something else which is not moving. But when two or three things are relatively moving, we first perceive the motion of the faster one, and then that of the slower ones. How is the mind to perceive? It is also in a flux. Therefore another thing is necessary which moves more slowly, then you must get to something in which the motion is still slower, and so on, and you will find no end. Therefore logic compels you to stop somewhere. You must complete the series by knowing something which never changes. Behind this never-ending chain of motion is the Purusha, the changeless, the colourless, the pure. All these impressions are merely reflected upon it, as a magic lantern throws images upon a screen, without in any way tarnishing it.

न तत् स्वाभासं दृश्यत्वात् ॥१८॥

18. *The mind is not self-luminous, being an object.*

Tremendous power is manifested everywhere in nature, but it is not self-luminous, not essentially intelligent. The Purusha alone is self-luminous, and gives its light to everything. It is the power of the Purusha that is percolating through all matter and force.

एकसमये चोभयानवधारणम् ॥१९॥

19. From its being unable to cognise both at the same time.

If the mind were self-luminous it would be able to cognise itself and its objects at the same time, which it cannot. When it cognises the object, it cannot reflect on itself. Therefore the Purusha is self-luminous, and the mind is not.

चित्तान्तरदृश्ये बुद्धिबुद्धेरतिप्रसङ्गः स्मृतिसङ्करश्च ॥२०॥

20. Another cognising mind being assumed, there will be no end to such assumptions, and confusion of memory will be the result.

Let us suppose there is another mind which cognises the ordinary mind, then there will have to be still another to cognise the former, and so there will be no end to it. It will result in confusion of memory, there will be no storehouse of memory.

चितेरप्रतिसंक्रमायास्तदाकारापत्तौ स्वबुद्धि-संवेदनम् ॥२१॥

21. The essence of knowledge (the Purusha) being unchangeable, when the mind takes its form, it becomes conscious.

Patanjali says this to make it more clear that knowledge is not a quality of the Purusha. When the mind comes near the Purusha it is reflected, as it were, upon the mind, and the mind, for the time being, becomes knowing and seems as if it were itself the Purusha.

द्रष्टृदृश्योपरक्तं चित्तं सर्वार्थम् ॥२२॥

22. Coloured by the seer and the seen the mind is able to understand everything.

On one side of the mind the external world, the seen, is being reflected, and on the other, the seer is being reflected. Thus comes the power of all knowledge to the mind.

तदसंख्येयवासनाभिश्चित्रमपि परार्थं संहत्यकारित्वात् ॥२३॥

23. The mind, though variegated by innumerable desires, acts for another (the Purusha), because it acts in combination.

The mind is a compound of various things and therefore it cannot work for itself. Everything that is a combination in this world has some object for that combination, some third thing for which this combination is going on. So this combination of the mind is for the Purusha.

विशेषदर्शिन आत्मभाव-भावनाविनिवृत्तिः ॥२४॥

24. For the discriminating, the perception of the mind as Atman ceases.

Through discrimination the Yogi knows that the Purusha is not mind.

तदा विवेकनिम्नं कैवल्यप्राग्भारं चित्तम् ॥२५॥

25. Then, bent on discriminating, the mind attains the previous state of Kaivalya (isolation). (There is another reading— कैवल्यप्राग्भारं। *The meaning then would be: "Then the mind becomes deep in discrimination and gravitates towards Kaivalya.")*

Thus the practice of Yoga leads to discriminating power, to clearness of vision. The veil drops from the eyes, and we see things as they are. We find that nature is a compound, and is showing the panorama for the Purusha, who is the witness; that nature is not the Lord, that all the combinations of nature are simply for the sake of showing these phenomena to the Purusha, the enthroned king within. When discrimination comes by long practice, fear ceases, and the mind attains isolation.

तच्छिद्रेषु प्रत्ययान्तराणि संस्कारेभ्यः ॥२६॥

26. The thoughts that arise as obstructions to that are from impressions.

All the various ideas that arise, making us believe that we require something external to make us happy, are obstructions to that perfection. The Purusha is happiness and blessedness by its own nature. But that knowledge is covered over by past impressions. These impressions have to work themselves out.

हानमेषां क्लेशवदुक्तम् ॥२७॥

27. Their destruction is in the same manner as of ignorance, egoism, etc., as said before (II.10).

परसंख्यानेऽप्यकुसीदस्य सर्वथा विवेकख्यातेर्धर्ममेघः समाधिः ॥२८॥

28. Even when arriving at the right discriminating knowledge of the essences,
he who gives up the fruits, unto him comes, as the result of perfect domination,
the Samadhi called the cloud of virtue.

When the Yogi has attained to this discrimination, all the powers mentioned
in the last chapter come to him, but the true Yogi rejects them all. Unto him
comes a peculiar knowledge, a particular light, called the Dharma-megha, the
cloud of virtue. All the great prophets of the world whom history has recorded
had this. They had found the whole foundation of knowledge within themselves.
Truth to them had become real. Peace and calmness, and perfect purity became
their own nature, after they had given up the vanities of powers.

ततः क्लेश्रकर्मनिवृत्तिः ॥२९॥

29. From that comes cessation of pain and works.

When that cloud of virtue has come, then no more is there fear of falling, nothing can drag the Yogi down. No more will there be evils for him. No more pains.

तदा सर्वावरणमलापेतस्य ज्ञानस्याऽनन्त्याज्ज्ञेयमल्पम् ॥३०॥

30. The knowledge, bereft of covering and impurities, becoming infinite, the
knowable becomes small.

Knowledge itself is there; its covering is gone. One of the Buddhistic scriptures
defines what is meant by the Buddha (which is the name of a state) as infinite
knowledge, infinite as the sky. Jesus attained to that and became the Christ.
All of you will attain to that state. Knowledge becoming infinite, the knowable
becomes small. The whole universe, with all its objects of knowledge, becomes
as nothing before the Purusha. The ordinary man thinks himself very small, because to him the knowable seems to be infinite.

ततः कृतार्थानां परिणामक्रमसमाप्तिर्गुणानाम् ॥३१॥

31. Then are finished the successive transformations of the qualities, they having
attained the end.

Then all these various transformations of the qualities, which change from species to species, cease for ever.

क्षणप्रतियोगी परिणामापरान्ततनिर्ग्राह्यः क्रमः ॥३२॥

32. The changes that exist in relation to moments and which are perceived at the other end (at the end of a series) are succession.

Patanjali here defines the word succession, the changes that exist in relation to moments. While I think, many moments pass, and with each moment there is a change of idea, but I only perceive these changes at the end of a series. This is called succession, but for the mind that has realised omnipresence there is no succession. Everything has become present for it; to it the present alone exists, the past and future are lost. Time stands controlled, all knowledge is there in one second. Everything is known like a flash.

पुरुषार्थशून्यानां गुणानां प्रतिप्रसवः कैवल्यं स्वरूपप्रतिष्ठा वा चितिशक्तेरिति ॥३३॥

33. The resolution in the inverse order of the qualities, bereft of any motive of action for the Purusha, is Kaivalya, or it is the establishment of the power of knowledge in its own nature.

Nature's task is done, this unselfish task which our sweet nurse, nature, had imposed upon herself. She gently took the self-forgetting soul by the hand, as it were, and showed him all the experiences in the universe, all manifestations, bringing him higher and higher through various bodies, till his lost glory came back, and he remembered his own nature. Then the kind mother went back the same way she came, for others who also have lost their way in the trackless desert of life. And thus is she working, without beginning and without end. And thus through pleasure and pain, through good and evil, the infinite river of souls is flowing into the ocean of perfection, of self-realisation.

Glory unto those who have realised their own nature. May their blessings be on us all!

KARMA YOGA
THE PATH OF SELFLESS ACTION

Chapter I
Karma in Its Effect on Character

The word Karma is derived from the Kri, to do; all action is Karma. Technically, this word also means the effects of actions. In connection with metaphysics, it sometimes means the effects, of which our past actions were the causes. But in Karma Yoga we have simply to do with the word Karma as meaning work. The goal of mankind is knowledge; that is the one ideal placed before us by Eastern philosophy. Pleasure is not the goal of man, but knowledge. Pleasure and happiness come to an end. It is a mistake to suppose that pleasure is the goal; the cause of all the miseries we have in the world is that men foolishly think pleasure to be the ideal to strive for. After a time man finds that it is not happiness, but knowledge, towards which he is going, and that both pleasure and pain are great teachers, and that he learns as much from evil as from good. As pleasure and pain pass before his soul they leave upon it different pictures, and the result of these combined impressions is what is called man's "character." If you take the character of any man it really is but the aggregate of tendencies, the sum-total of the bent of his mind; you will find that misery and happiness are equal factors in the formation of that character. Good and evil have an equal share in moulding character, and in some instances misery is a greater teacher than happiness. In studying the great characters the world has produced, I dare say, in the vast majority of cases, it would be found that it was misery that taught more than happiness, it was poverty that taught more than wealth, it was blows that brought out their inner fire more than praise.

Now this knowledge, again, is inherent in man; no knowledge comes from outside; it is all inside. What we say a man "knows," should, in strict psychological language, be what he "discovers" or "unveils"; what a man "learns" is really what he "discovers," by taking the cover off his own soul, which is a mine of infinite knowledge. We say Newton discovered gravitation. Was it sitting anywhere in a corner waiting for him? It was in his own mind; the time came and he found it out. All knowledge that the world has ever received comes from the mind; the infinite library of the universe is in your own mind. The external world is simply the suggestion, the occasion, which sets you to study your own mind, but the object of your study is always your own mind. The falling of an apple gave the suggestion to Newton, and he studied his own mind; he rearranged all the previous links of thought in his mind and discovered a new link among them, which we call the law of gravitation. It was not in the apple nor in anything in the centre of the earth. All knowledge therefore, secular or spiritual, is in the human mind. In many cases it is not discovered, but remains covered, and when the covering is being slowly taken off we say "we are learning," and the advance of knowledge is made by the advance of this process of uncovering. The man from whom this veil is being lifted is the more knowing man; the man upon whom it lies thick is ignorant, and the man from whom it has entirely gone is all-knowing, omniscient. There have been omniscient men, and, I believe, there will be yet; and that there will be myriads of them in the cycles to come. Like fire in a piece of flint, knowledge exists in the mind; suggestion is the friction which brings it out. So with all our feelings and actions— our tears and our smiles, our joys and our griefs, our weeping and our laughter, our curses and our blessings, our praises and our blames— every one of these we may find, if we calmly study our own selves, to have been brought out from within ourselves by so many blows. The result is what we are; all these blows taken together are called Karma,— work, action. Every mental and physical blow that is given to the soul, by which, as it were, fire is struck from it, and by which its own power and knowledge are discovered, is Karma, this word being used in its widest sense; thus we are all doing Karma all the time. I am talking to you: that is Karma. You are listening: that is Karma. We breathe: that is Karma. We walk: Karma. Everything we do, physical or mental, is Karma, and it leaves its marks on us.

There are certain works which are, as it were, the aggregate, the sum-total, of a large number of smaller works. If we stand near the seashore and hear the waves dashing against the shingle we think it is such a great noise; and yet we know that one wave is really composed of millions and millions of minute waves: each one of these is making a noise, and yet we do not catch it; it is only when they become the big aggregate that we hear. Similarly every pulsation of the heart is work; certain kinds of work we feel and they become tangible to us; they are, at the same time, the aggregate of a number of small works. If you really want to judge of the character of a man look not at his great performances. Every fool may become a hero at one time or another. Watch a man do his most common actions; those are indeed the things which will tell you the real character of a great man. Great occasions rouse even the lowest of human beings to some kind of greatness, but he alone is the really great man whose character is great always, the same wherever he be.

Karma in its effect on character is the most tremendous power that man has to deal with. Man is, as it were, a centre, and is attracting all the powers of the universe towards himself, and in this centre is fusing them all and again sending them off in a big current. Such a centre is the real man, the almighty, the omniscient, and he draws the whole universe towards him; good and bad, misery and happiness, all are running towards him and clinging round him; and out of them he fashions the mighty stream of tendency called character and throws it outwards. As he has the power of drawing in anything, so has he the power of throwing it out.

All the actions that we see in the world, all the movements in human society, all the works that we have around us, are simply the display of thought, the manifestation of the will of man. Machines or instruments, cities, ships, or men-of-war, all these are simply the manifestation of the will of man; and this will is caused by character and character is manufactured by Karma. As is Karma, so is the manifestation of the will. The men of mighty will the world has produced have all been tremendous workers— gigantic souls, with wills powerful enough to overturn worlds, wills they got by persistent work, through ages and ages. Such a gigantic will as that of a Buddha or a Jesus could not be obtained in one life, for we know who their fathers were. It is not known that their fathers ever spoke a word for the good of mankind. Millions and millions of carpenters like Joseph had gone; millions are still living. Millions and millions of petty kings like Buddha's father had been in the world. If it was only a case of hereditary transmission, how do you account for this petty prince, who was not, perhaps, obeyed by his own servants, producing this son, whom half a world worships? How do you explain the gulf between the carpenter and his son, whom millions of human beings worship as God? It cannot be solved by the theory of heredity. The gigantic will which Buddha and Jesus threw over the world, whence did it come? Whence came this accumulation of power? It must have been there through ages and ages, continually growing bigger and bigger, until it burst on society in a Buddha or a Jesus, even rolling down to the present day.

All this is determined by Karma, work. No one can get anything unless he earns it; this is an eternal law; we may sometimes think it is not so, but in the long run we become convinced of it. A man may struggle all his life for riches; he may cheat thousands, but he finds at last that he did not deserve to become rich and his life becomes a trouble and a nuisance to him. We may go on accumulating things for our physical enjoyment, but only what we earn is really

ours. A fool may buy all the books in the world, and they will be in his library;
but he will be able to read only those that he deserves to; and this deserving is
produced by Karma. Our Karma determines what we deserve and what we can
assimilate. We are responsible for what we are; and whatever we wish ourselves
to be, we have the power to make ourselves. If what we are now has been the
result of our own past actions, it certainly follows that whatever we wish to be
in future can be produced by our present actions; so we have to know how to
act. You will say, "What is the use of learning how to work? Every one works in
some way or other in this world." But there is such a thing as frittering away our
energies. With regard to Karma Yoga, the Gita says that it is doing work with
cleverness and as a science: by knowing how to work, one can obtain the greatest results. You must remember that all work is simply to bring out the power of
the mind which is already there, to wake up the soul. The power is inside every
man, so is knowledge; the different works are like blows to bring them out, to
cause these giants to wake up.

Man works with various motives; there cannot be work without motive. Some
people want to get fame, and they work for fame. Others want money, and they
work for money. Others want to have power, and they work for power. Others
want to get to heaven, and they work for the same. Others want to leave a name
when they die, as they do in China, where no man gets a title until he is dead;
and that is a better way, after all, than with us. When a man does something very
good there, they give a title of nobility to his father, who is dead, or to his grandfather. Some people work for that. Some of the followers of certain Mahomedan
sects work all their lives to have a big tomb built for them when they die. I know
sects among whom as soon as a child is born a tomb is prepared for it; that is
among them the most important work a man has to do, and the bigger and the
finer the tomb the better off the man is supposed to be. Others work as a pen-
ance: do all sorts of wicked things, then erect a temple, or give something to the
priests to buy them off and obtain from them a passport to heaven. They think
that this kind of beneficence will clear them and they will go scot-free in spite
of their sinfulness. Such are some of the various motives for work.

Work for work's sake. There are some who are really the salt of the earth in every country and who work for work's sake, who do not care for name, or fame,
or even to go to heaven. They work just because good will come of it. There are
others who do good to the poor and help mankind from still higher motives, because they believe in doing good and love good. The motive for name and fame
seldom brings immediate results, as a rule; they come to us when we are old and

have almost done with life. If a man works without any selfish motive in view, does he not gain anything? Yes, he gains the highest. Unselfishness is more paying, only people have not the patience to practise it. It is more paying from the point of view of health also. Love, truth and unselfishness are not merely moral figures of speech, but they form our highest ideal, because in them lies such a manifestation of power. In the first place, a man who can work for five days, or even for five minutes, without any selfish motive whatever, without thinking of future, of heaven, of punishment, or anything of the kind, has in him the capacity to become a powerful moral giant. It is hard to do it, but in the heart of our hearts we know its value, and the good it brings. It is the greatest manifestation of power — this tremendous restraint; self-restraint is a manifestation of greater power than all outgoing action. A carriage with four horses may rush down a hill unrestrained, or the coachman may curb the horses. Which is the greater manifestation of power, to let them go or to hold them? A cannon-ball flying through the air goes a long distance and falls. Another is cut short in its flight by striking against a wall, and the impact generates intense heat. All outgoing energy following a selfish motive is frittered away; it will not cause power to return to you, but if restrained it will result in development of power. This self-control will tend to produce a mighty will, a character which makes a Christ or a Buddha. Foolish men do not know this secret; they nevertheless want to rule mankind. Even a fool may rule the whole world if he works and waits. Let him wait a few years, restrain that foolish idea of governing; and when that idea is wholly gone, he will be a power in the world. The majority of us cannot see beyond a few years, just as some animals cannot see beyond a few steps. Just a little narrow circle; that is our world. We have not the patience to look beyond, and thus become immoral and wicked. This is our weakness, our powerlessness.

Even the lowest forms of work are not to be despised. Let the man who knows no better, work for selfish ends, for name and fame; but everyone should always try to get towards higher and higher motives and to understand them. "To work we have the right, but not to the fruits thereof." Leave the fruits alone. Why care for results? If you wish to help a man, never think what that man's attitude should be towards you. If you want to do a great or a good work, do not trouble to think what the result will be.

There arises a difficult question in this ideal of work. Intense activity is necessary; we must always work. We cannot live a minute without work. What then becomes of rest? Here is one side of the life-struggle,— work, in which we are whirled rapidly round. And here is the other, that of calm, retiring renunciation:

everything is peaceful around, there is very little of noise and show, only nature with her animals and flowers and mountains. Neither of them is a perfect picture. A man used to solitude, if brought in contact with the surging whirlpool of the world, will be crushed by it; just as the fish that lives in the deep sea water, as soon as it is brought to the surface, breaks into pieces, deprived of the weight of water on it that had kept it together. Can a man who, has been used to the turmoil and the rush of life live at ease if he comes to a quiet place? He suffers and perchance may lose his mind. The ideal man is he who, in the midst of the greatest silence and solitude, finds the intensest activity, and in the midst of the intensest activity finds the silence and solitude of the desert. He has learned the secret of restraint; he has controlled himself. He goes through the streets of a big city with all its traffic, and his mind is as calm as if he were in a cave, where not a sound could reach him; and he is intensely working all the time. That is the ideal of Karma Yoga, and if you have attained to that you have really learned the secret of work.

But we have to begin from the beginning, to take up the works as they come to us and slowly make ourselves, more unselfish every day. We must do the work and find out the motive power that prompts us; and, almost without exception, in the first years, we shall find that our motives are always selfish; but gradually this selfishness will melt by persistence, till at last will come the time when we shall be able to do really unselfish work. We may all hope that some day or other, as we struggle through the paths of life, there will come a time when we shall become perfectly unselfish; and the moment we attain to that, all our powers will be concentrated, and the knowledge which is ours will be manifest.

Chapter II
Each is Great in His Own Place

According to the Sankhya philosophy, nature is composed of three forces called, in Sanskrit, Sattva, Rajas and Tamas. These as manifested in the physical world are what we may call equilibrium, activity and inertness. Tamas is typified as darkness or inactivity; Rajas is activity, expressed as attraction or repulsion; and Sattva is the equilibrium of the two.

In every man there are these three forces. Sometimes Tamas prevails; we become lazy; we cannot move; we are inactive, bound down by certain ideas or by mere dullness. At other times activity prevails and at still other times that calm balancing of both. Again, in different men, one of these forces is generally predominant. The characteristic of one man is inactivity, dullness and laziness; that of another, activity, power, manifestation of energy; and in still another we find the sweetness, calmness and gentleness, which are due to the balancing of both action and inaction. So in all creation — in animals, plants and men — we find the more or less typical manifestation of all these different forces.

Karma Yoga has specially to deal with these three factors. By teaching what they are and how to employ them it helps us to do our work better. Human society is a graded organisation. We all know about morality, and we all know about duty, but at the same time we find that in different countries the significance of morality varies greatly. What is regarded as moral in one country, may in another be considered perfectly immoral. For instance, in one country cousins may marry; in another, it is thought to be very immoral; in one, men may marry their sisters-in-law; in another, it is regarded as immoral; in one country people may marry only once; in another, many times; and so forth. Similarly in all other departments of morality we find the standard varies greatly; yet we have the idea that there must be a universal standard of morality.

So it is with duty. The idea of duty varies much among different nations: in one country, if a man does not do certain things, people will say he has acted wrongly; while if he does those very things in another country, people will say that he did not act rightly; and yet we know that there must be some universal idea of duty. In the same way, one class of society thinks that certain things are among its duty, while another class thinks quite the opposite and would be horrified if it had to do those things. Two ways are left open to us,— the way of the ignorant, who think that there is only one way to truth and that all the rest are wrong,— and the way of the wise, who admit that, according to our mental constitution or the different planes of existence in which we are, duty and morality may vary. The important thing is to know that there are gradations of duty and of morality— that the duty of one state of life, in one set of circumstances will not and cannot be that of another.

To illustrate:— All great teachers have taught, "Resist not evil," that non-resistance is the highest moral ideal. We all know that, if a certain number of us attempted to put that maxim fully into practice, the whole social fabric would fall to pieces, the wicked would take possession of our properties and our lives, and would do whatever they liked with us. Even if only one day of such non-resistance were practised it would lead to disaster. Yet, intuitively, in our heart of hearts we feel the truth of the teaching, "Resist not evil." This seems to us to be the highest ideal; yet to teach this doctrine only would be equivalent to condemning a vast portion of mankind. Not only so, it would be making men feel that they were always doing wrong, cause in them scruples of conscience in all their actions; it would weaken them, and that constant self-disapproval would breed more vice than any other weakness would. To the man who has begun to hate himself the gate to degeneration has already opened; and the same is true of a nation.

Our first duty is not to hate ourselves; because to advance we must have faith in ourselves first and then in God. He who has no faith in himself can never have faith in God. Therefore, the only alternative remaining to us is to recognise that duty and morality vary under different circumstances; not that the man who resists evil is doing what is always and in itself wrong, but that in the different circumstances in which he is placed it may become even his duty to resist evil.

In reading the Bhagavad-Gita, many of you in Western countries may have felt astonished at the second chapter, wherein Sri Krishna calls Arjuna a hypocrite and a coward because of his refusal to fight, or offer resistance, on account of his adversaries being his friends and relatives, making the plea that non-resistance was the highest ideal of love. This is a great lesson for us all to learn, that in all matters the two extremes are alike; the extreme positive and the extreme negative are always similar; when the vibrations of light are too slow we do not see them, nor do we see them when they are too rapid. So with sound; when very low in pitch we do not hear it, when very high we do not hear it either. Of like nature is the difference between resistance and non-resistance. One man does not resist because he is weak, lazy, and cannot because he will not; the other man knows that he can strike an irresistible blow if he likes; yet he not only does not strike, but blesses his enemies. The one who from weakness resists not commits a sin, and as such cannot receive any benefit from the non-resistance; while the other would commit a sin by offering resistance. Buddha gave up his throne and renounced his position, that was true renunciation; but there cannot be any question of renunciation in the case of a beggar who has nothing to renounce. So we must always be careful about what we really mean when we speak of this non-resistance and ideal love. We must first take care to understand whether we have the power of resistance or not. Then, having the power, if we renounce it and do not resist, we are doing a grand act of love; but if we cannot resist, and yet, at the same time, try to deceive ourselves into the belief that we are actuated by motives of the highest love, we are doing the exact opposite. Arjuna became a coward at the sight of the mighty array against him; his "love" made him forget his duty towards his country and king. That is why Sri Krishna told him that he was a hypocrite:— Thou talkest like a wise man, but thy actions betray thee to be a coward; therefore stand up and fight!

Such is the central idea of Karma Yoga. The Karma-Yogin is the man who understands that the highest ideal is non-resistance, and who also knows that this nonresistance is the highest manifestation of power in actual possession, also what is called the resisting of evil is but a step on the way towards the manifestation of this highest power, namely, non-resistance. Before reaching this highest ideal, man's duty is to resist evil; let him work, let him fight, let him strike straight from the shoulder. Then only, when he has gained the power to resist, will non-resistance be a virtue.

I once met a man in my country whom I had known before as a very stupid, dull person, who knew nothing and had not the desire to know anything, and was living the life of a brute. He asked me what he should do to know God, how he was to get free. "Can you tell a lie?" I asked him. "No," he replied. "Then you must learn to do so. It is better to tell a lie than to be a brute, or a log of wood; you are inactive; you have not certainly reached the highest state, which is beyond all actions, calm and serene; you are too dull even to do something wicked." That was an extreme case, of course, and I was joking with him; but what I meant was, that a man must be active, in order to pass through activity to perfect calmness.

Inactivity should be avoided by all means. Activity always means resistance.

Resist all evils, mental and physical; and when you have succeeded in resisting, then will calmness come. It is very easy to say, "Hate nobody, resist not evil," but we know what that kind generally means in practice. When the eyes of society are turned towards us we may make a show of non-resistance, but in our hearts it is canker all the time. We feel the utter want of the calm of non-resistance; we feel that it would be better for us to resist. If you desire wealth, and know at the same time that the whole world regards him who aims at wealth as a very wicked man, you, perhaps, will not dare to plunge into the struggle for wealth, yet your mind will be running day and night after money. This is hypocrisy and will serve no purpose. Plunge into the world, and then, after a time, when you have suffered and enjoyed all that is in it, will renunciation come; then will calmness come. So fulfil your desire for power and everything else, and after you have fulfilled the desire, will come the time when you will know that they are all very little things; but until you have fulfilled this desire, until you have passed through that activity, it is impossible for you to come to the state of calmness, serenity and self-surrender. These ideas of serenity and renunciation have been preached for thousands of years; everybody has heard of them from childhood, and yet we see very few in the world who have really reached that stage. I do not know if I have seen twenty persons in my life who are really calm and non-resisting, and I have travelled over half the world.

Every man should take up his own ideal and endeavour to accomplish it; that is a surer way of progress than taking up other men's ideals, which he can never hope to accomplish. For instance, we take a child and at once give him the task of walking twenty miles; either the little one dies, or one in a thousand crawls the twenty miles, to reach the end exhausted and half-dead. That is like what we generally try to do with the world. All the men and women, in any society, are not of the same mind, capacity, or of the same power to do things; they must have different ideals, and we have no right to sneer at any ideal. Let every one do the best he can for realising his own ideal. Nor is it right that I should be judged by your standard or you by mine. The apple tree should not be judged by the standard of the oak, nor the oak by that of the apple. To judge the apple tree you must take the apple standard; and for the oak its own standard.

Unity in variety is the plan of creation. However men and women may vary individually, there is unity in the background. The different individual characters and classes of men and women are natural variations in creation. Hence, we ought not to judge them by the same standard or put the same ideal before them. Such a course creates an unnatural struggle only and the result is that man begins to hate himself and is hindered from becoming religious and good. Our duty is to encourage every one in his struggle to live up to his own highest ideal, and strive at the same time to make the ideal as near as possible to the truth.

In the Hindu system of morality we find that this fact has been recognised from very ancient times; and in their scriptures and books on ethics different rules are laid down for the different classes of men,— the householder, the Sannyasin (the man who has renounced the world), and the student.

The life of every individual, according to the Hindu scriptures, has its peculiar duties apart from what belongs in common to universal humanity. The Hindu begins life as a student; then he marries and becomes a householder; in old age he retires, and lastly he gives up the world and becomes a Sannyasin. To each of these stages of life certain duties are attached. No one of these stages is intrinsically superior to another; the life of the married man is quite as great as that of the celibate who has devoted himself to religious work. The scavenger in the street is quite as great and glorious as the king on his throne. Take him off his throne, make him do the work of the scavenger, and see how he fares. Take up the scavenger and see how he will rule. It is useless to say that the man who lives out of the world is a greater man than he who lives in the world; it is much more difficult to live in the world and worship God than to give it up and live a free and easy life. The four stages of life in India have in later times been reduced to two,— that of the householder and of the monk. The householder marries and carries on his duties as a citizen, and the duty of the other is to devote his energies wholly to religion, to preach and to worship God. I shall read to you a few passages from the Maha-Nirvana-Tantra, which treats of this subject and you will see that it is a very difficult task for a man to be a householder, and perform all his duties perfectly:

The householder should be devoted to God; the knowledge of God should be his goal of life. Yet he must work constantly, perform all his duties; he must give up the fruits of his actions to God.

It is the most difficult thing in this world, to work and not care for the result, to help a man and never think that he ought to be grateful, to do some good work and at the same time never look to see whether it brings you name or fame, or nothing at all. Even the most arrant coward becomes brave when the world praises him. A fool can do heroic deeds when the approbation of society is upon him, but for a man to constantly do good without caring for the approbation of his fellow-men is indeed the highest sacrifice man can perform. The great duty of the householder is to earn a living, but he must take care that he does not do it by telling lies, or by cheating, or by robbing others; and he must remember that his life is for the service of God, and the poor.

Knowing that mother and father are the visible representatives of God, the householder, always and by all means, must please them. If the mother is pleased, and the father, God is pleased with that man. That child is really a good child who never speaks harsh words to his parents.

Before parents one must not utter jokes, must not show restlessness, must not show anger or temper. Before mother or father, a child must bow down low, and stand up in their presence, and must not take a seat until they order him to sit.

If the householder has food and drink and clothes without first seeing that his mother and his father, his children, his wife, and the poor, are supplied, he is committing a sin. The mother and the father are the causes of this body, so a man must undergo a thousand troubles in order to do good to them.

Even so is his duty to his wife; no man should scold his wife, and he must always maintain her as if she were his own mother. And even when he is in the greatest difficulties and troubles, he must not show anger to his wife.

He who thinks of another woman besides his wife, if he touches her even with his mind—that man goes to dark hell.

Before women he must not talk improper language, and never brag of his powers. He must not say, 'I have-done this, and I have done that.'

The householder must always please his wife with money, clothes, love, faith, and words like nectar, and never do anything to disturb her. That man who has succeeded in getting the love of a chaste wife has succeeded in his religion and has all the virtues.

The following are duties towards children:

A son should be lovingly reared up to his fourth year he should be educated till he is sixteen. When he is twenty years of age he should be employed in some work; he should then be treated affectionately by his father as his equal. Exactly in the same manner the daughter should be brought up, and should be educated with the greatest care. And when she marries, the father ought to give her jewels and wealth.

Then the duty of the man is towards his brothers and sisters, and towards the children of his brothers and sisters, if they are poor, and towards his other relatives, his friends and his servants. Then his duties are towards the people of the same village, and the poor, and any one that comes to him for help. Having sufficient means, if the householder does not take care to give to his relatives and to the poor, know him to be only a brute; he is not a human being.

Excessive attachment to food, clothes, and the tending of the body, and dressing of the hair should be avoided. The householder must be pure in heart and clean in body, always active and always ready for work.

To his enemies the householder must be a hero. Then he must resist. That is the duty of the householder. He must not sit down in a corner and weep, and talk non-sense about non-resistance. If he does not show himself a hero to his enemies he has not done his duty. And to his friends and relatives he must be as gentle as a lamb.

It is the duty of the householder not to pay reverence to the wicked; because, if he reverences the wicked people of the world, he patronises wickedness; and it will be a great mistake if he disregards those who are worthy of respect, the good people. He must not be gushing in his friendship; he must not go out of the way making friends everywhere; he must watch the actions of the men he wants to make friends with, and their dealings with other men, reason upon them, and then make friends.

These three things he must not talk of. He must not talk in public of his own fame; he must not preach his own name or his own powers; he must not talk of his wealth, or of anything that has been told to him privately.

A man must not say he is poor, or that he is wealthy— he must not brag of his wealth. Let him keep his own counsel; this is his religious duty. This is not mere worldly wisdom; if a man does not do so, he may be held to be immoral.

The householder is the basis, the prop, of the whole society; he is the principal earner. The poor, the weak, the children and the women who do not work— all live upon the householder; so there must be certain duties that he has to per-form, and these duties must make him feel strong to perform them, and not make him think that he is doing things beneath his ideal. Therefore, if he has done something weak, or has made some mistake, he must not say so in public; and if he is engaged in some enterprise and knows he is sure to fail in it he must not speak of it. Such self-exposure is not only uncalled-for, but also unnerves the man and makes him unfit for the performance of his legitimate duties in life. At the same time, he must struggle hard to acquire these things— firstly, knowledge, and secondly, wealth. It is his duty, and if he does not do his duty he is nobody. A householder who does not struggle to get wealth is immoral. If he is lazy, and content to lead an idle life, he is immoral, because upon him depend hundreds. If he gets riches hundreds of others will be thereby supported.

If there were not in this city hundreds who had striven to become rich, and who had acquired wealth, where would all this civilisation, and these almshouses and great houses be?

Going after wealth in such a case is not bad, because that wealth is for distribution. The householder is the centre of life and society. It is a worship for him to acquire and spend wealth nobly, for the householder who struggles to become rich by good means and for good purposes is doing practically the same thing for the attainment of salvation as the anchorite does in his cell when he is praying, for in them we see only the different aspects of the same virtue of self-surrender and self-sacrifice prompted by the feeling of devotion to God and to all that is His.

He must struggle to acquire a good name by all means; he must not gamble; he must not move in the company of the wicked; he must not tell lies, and must not be the cause of trouble to others.

Often people enter into things they have not the means to accomplish, with the result that they cheat others to attain their own ends. Then there is in all things the time factor to be taken into consideration; what at one time might be a failure, would perhaps at another time be a very great success.

The householder must speak the truth, and speak gently, using words which people like, which will do good to others; nor should he talk of the business of other men.

The householder by digging tanks, by planting trees on the roadsides, by establishing rest-houses for men and animals, by making roads and building bridges, goes towards the same goal as the greatest Yogin.

This is one part of the doctrine of Karma Yoga— activity, the duty of the householder. There is a passage later on, where it says that "if the householder dies in battle, fighting for his country or his religion, he comes to the same goal as the Yogin by meditation," showing thereby that what is duty for one is not duty for another; at the same time, it does not say that this duty is lowering and the other elevating; each duty has its own place, and according to the circumstances in which we are placed, must we perform our duties.

One idea comes out of all this, the condemnation of all weakness. This is a particular idea in all our teachings which I like, either in philosophy, or in religion, or in work. If you read the Vedas you will find this word always repeated— "fearlessness"— fear nothing. Fear is a sign of weakness. A man must go about his duties without taking notice of the sneers and the ridicule of the world.

If a man retires from the world to worship God, he must not think that those who live in the world and work for the good of the world are not worshipping God; neither must those who live in the world, for wife and children, think that those who give up the world are low vagabonds. Each is great in his own place. This thought I will illustrate by a story.

A certain king used to inquire of all the Sannyasins that came to his country, "Which is the greater man— he who gives up the world and becomes a Sannyasin, or he who lives in the world and performs his duties as a householder?" Many wise men sought to solve the problem. Some asserted that the Sannyasin was the greater, upon which the king demanded that they should prove their assertion. When they could not, he ordered them to marry and become householders. Then others came and said, "The householder who performs his duties is the greater man." Of them, too, the king demanded proofs. When they could not give them, he made them also settle down as householders.

At last there came a young Sannyasin, and the king similarly inquired of him also. He answered, "Each, O king, is equally great in his place." "Prove this to me," asked the king. "I will prove it to you," said the Sannyasin, "but you must first come and live as I do for a few days, that I may be able to prove to you what I say." The king consented and followed the Sannyasin out of his own territory and passed through many other countries until they came to a great kingdom. In the capital of that kingdom a great ceremony was going on. The king and the Sannyasin heard the noise of drums and music, and heard also the criers; the people were assembled in the streets in gala dress, and a great proclamation was being made. The king and the Sannyasin stood there to see what was going on. The crier was proclaiming loudly that the princess, daughter of the king of that country, was about to choose a husband from among those assembled before her.

It was an old custom in India for princesses to choose husbands in this way, each princess had certain ideas of the sort of man she wanted for a husband; some would have the handsomest man; others would have only the most learned; others again the richest, and so on. All the princes of the neighbourhood put on their bravest attire and presented themselves before her. Sometimes they too had their own criers to enumerate their advantages and the reasons why they hoped the princess would choose them. The princess was taken round on a throne, in the most array and looked at and heard about them. If she was not pleased with what she saw and heard, she said to her bearers, "Move on," and no more notice was taken of the rejected suitors. If, however, the princess was pleased with any one of them she threw a garland of flowers over him and he became her husband.

The princess of the country to which our king and the Sannyasin had come was having one of these interesting ceremonies. She was the most beautiful princess in the world, and the husband of the princess would be ruler of the kingdom after her father's death. The idea of this princess was to marry the handsomest man, but she could not find the right one to please her. Several times these meetings had taken place, but the princess could not select a husband. This meeting was the most splendid of all; more people than ever had come to it. The princess came in on a throne, and the bearers carried her from place to place. She did not seem to care for any one, and every one became disappointed that this meeting also was going to be a failure. Just then came a young man, a Sannyasin, handsome as if the sun had come down to the earth, and stood in one corner of the assembly, watching what was going on. The throne with the princess came near him, and as soon as she saw the beautiful Sannyasin, she stopped and threw the garland over him. The young Sannyasin seized the garland and threw it off, exclaiming, "What nonsense is this? I am a Sannyasin. What is marriage to me?" The king of that country thought that perhaps this man was poor and so dared not marry the princess, and said to him, "With my daughter goes half my kingdom now, and the whole kingdom after my death!" and put the garland again on the Sannyasin. The young man threw it off once more, saying, "Nonsense. I do not want to marry," and walked quickly away from the assembly.

Now the princess had fallen so much in love with this young man that she said, "I must marry this man or I shall die;" and she went after him to bring him back. Then our other Sannyasin, who had brought the king there, said to him, "King, let us follow this pair;" so they walked after them, but at a good distance behind. The young Sannyasin who had refused to marry the princess walked out into the country for several miles; when he came to a forest and entered into it, the princess followed him, and the other two followed them. Now this young Sannyasin was well acquainted with that forest and knew all the intricate paths in it, he suddenly passed into one of these and disappeared, and the princess could not discover him. After trying for a long time to find him she sat down under a tree and began to weep, for she did not know the way out. Then our king and the other Sannyasin came up to her and said, "Do not weep; we will show you the way out of this forest, but it is too dark for us to find it now. Here is a big tree; let us rest under it, and in the morning we will go early and show you the road."

Now a little bird and his wife and their three little ones lived on that tree, in a nest. This little bird looked down and saw the three people under the tree and said to his wife, "My dear, what shall we do; here are some guests in the house, and it is winter, and we have no fire?" So he flew away and got a bit of burning firewood in his beak and dropped it before the guests, to which they added fuel and made a blazing fire. But the little bird was not satisfied. He said again to his wife, "My dear, what shall we do? There is nothing to give these people to eat, and they are hungry. We are householders; it is our duty to feed any one who comes to the house. I must do what I can, I will give them my body." So he plunged into the midst of the fire and perished. The guests saw him falling and tried to save him, but he was too quick for them.

The little bird's wife saw what her husband did, and she said, "Here are three persons and only one little bird for them to eat. It is not enough; it is my duty as a wife not to let my husband's effort go in vain; let them have my body also;" then she fell into the fire and was burned to death.

Then the three baby-birds, when they saw what was done and that there was still not enough food for the three guests, said, "Our parents have done what they could and still it is not enough. It is our duty to carry on the work of our parents; let our bodies go too." And they all dashed down into the fire also.

Amazed at what they saw, the three people could not of course eat these birds. They passed the night without food and in the morning the king and the Sannyasin showed the princess the way, and she went back to her father.

Then the Sannyasin said to the king, "King, you have seen that each is great in his own place. If you want to live in the world live like those birds, ready at any moment to sacrifice yourself for others. If you want to renounce the world be like that young man to whom the most beautiful woman and a kingdom were as nothing. If you want to be a householder hold your life a sacrifice for the welfare of others; and if you choose the life of renunciation do not even look at beauty, and money and power. Each is great in his own place, but the duty of the one is not the duty of the other."

Chapter III
The Secret of Work

Helping others physically, by removing their physical needs, is indeed great; but the help is greater, according as the need is greater and according as the help is far-reaching. If a man's wants can be removed for an hour, it is helping him indeed; if his wants can be removed for a year it will be more help to him; but if his wants can be removed for ever, it is surely the greatest help that can be given him. Spiritual knowledge is the only thing that can destroy our miseries for ever; any other knowledge satisfies wants only for a time. It is only with the knowledge of the spirit that the faculty of want is annihilated for ever; so helping man spiritually is the highest help that can be given to him; he who gives man spiritual knowledge is the greatest benefactor of mankind, and as such we always find that those were the most powerful of men who helped man in his spiritual needs; because spirituality is the true basis of all our activities in life. A spiritually strong and sound man will be strong in every other respect, if he so wishes; until there is spiritual strength in man even physical needs cannot be well satisfied. Next to spiritual comes intellectual help; the gift of knowledge is a far higher gift than that of food and clothes; it is even higher than giving life to a man, because the real life of man consists of knowledge; ignorance is death, knowledge is life. Life is of very little value, if it is a life in the dark, groping through ignorance and misery. Next in order comes, of course, helping a man physically. Therefore, in considering the question of helping others. We must always strive not to commit the mistake of thinking that physical help is the only help that can be given, it is not only the last but the least, because it cannot bring about permanent satisfaction. The misery that I feel when I am hungry is satisfied by eating, but hunger returns; my misery can cease only when I am satisfied beyond all want. Then hunger will not make me miserable; no distress, no sorrow will be able to move me. So that help which tends to make us strong spiritually is the highest, next to it comes intellectual help, and after that physical help.

The miseries of the world cannot be cured by physical help only; until man's nature changes, these physical needs will always arise, and miseries will always be felt, and no amount of physical help will cure them completely. The only solution of this problem is to make mankind pure. Ignorance is the mother of all the evil and all the misery we see. Let men have light, let them be pure and spiritually strong and educated, then alone will misery cease in the world, not before. We may convert every house in the country into a charity asylum; we may fill the land with hospitals, but the misery of man will still continue to exist until man's character changes.

We read in the Bhagavad-Gita again and again that we must all work incessantly. All work is by nature composed of good and evil. We cannot do any work which will not do some good somewhere; there cannot be any work which will not cause some harm somewhere. Every work must necessarily be a mixture of good and evil; yet we are commanded to work incessantly. Good and evil will both have their results, will produce their Karma. Good action will entail upon us good effect; bad action, bad. But good and bad are both bondages of the soul. The solution reached in the Gita in regard to this bondage-producing nature of work is, that if we do not attach ourselves to the work we do, it will not have any binding effect on our soul. We shall try to understand what is meant by this "non-attachment" to work.

This is the one central idea in the Gita; work incessantly, but be not attached to it. "Samskara" can be translated very nearly by inherent tendency. Using the simile of a lake for the mind, every ripple, every wave that rises in the mind, when it subsides, does not die out entirely, but leaves a mark and a future possibility of that wave coming out again. This mark, with the possibility of the wave reappearing, is what is called Samskara. Every work that we do, every movement of the body, every thought that we think, leaves such an impression on the mind-stuff, and even when such impressions are not obvious on the surface they are sufficiently strong to work beneath the surface, subconsciously. What we are every moment is determined by the sum-total of these impressions on the mind. What I am just at this moment is the effect of the sum-total of all the impressions of my past life. This is really what is meant by character; each man's character is determined by the sum-total of these impressions. If good impressions prevail, the character becomes good; if bad, it becomes bad. If a man continuously hears bad words, thinks bad thoughts, does bad actions, his mind will be full of bad impressions; and they will influence his thought and work without his being conscious of the fact. In fact, these bad impressions are always working, and their resultant must be evil; and that man will be a bad man; he cannot help it; the sum-total of these impressions in him will create the strong motive power for doing bad actions; he will be like a machine in the hands of his impressions, and they will force him to do evil. Similarly, if a man thinks good thoughts and does good works, the sum-total of these impressions will be good; and they, in a similar manner, will force him to do good even in spite of himself. When a man has done so much good work and thought so many good thoughts that there is an irresistible tendency in him to do good, in spite of himself and even if he wishes to do evil, his mind, as the sum-total of his tendencies, will not allow him to do so; the tendencies will turn him back; he is completely under the influence of the good tendencies. When such is the case, a man's good character is said to be established.

As the tortoise tucks its feet and head inside the shell, and you may kill it and break it in pieces, and yet it will not come out, even so the character of that man who has control over his motives and organs is unchangeably established. He controls his own inner forces, and nothing can draw them out against his will. By this continuous reflex of good thoughts, good impressions moving over the surface of the mind, the tendency for doing good becomes strong, and as the result we feel able to control the indriyas (the sense-organs, the nerve centres). Thus alone will character be established; then alone a man gets to truth; such a man is safe for ever; he cannot do any evil; you may place him in any company; there will be no danger for him. There is a still higher state than having this good tendency, and that is the desire for liberation. You must remember that freedom of the soul is the goal of all Yogas, and each one equally leads to the same result. By work alone men may get to where Buddha got largely by meditation or Christ by prayer. Buddha was a working Jnani; Christ was a Bhakta, but the same goal was reached by both of them. The difficulty is here. Liberation means entire freedom—freedom from the bondage of good, as well as from the bondage of evil. A golden chain is as much a chain as an iron one. There is a thorn in my finger, and I use another to take the first one out, and when I have taken it out I throw both of them aside; I have no necessity for keeping the second thorn, because both are thorns after all. So the bad tendencies are to be counteracted by the good ones, and the bad impressions on the mind should be removed by the fresh waves of good ones, until all that is evil almost disappears, or is subdued and held in control in a corner of the mind; but after that, the good tendencies have also to be conquered. Thus the "attached" becomes the "unattached." Work, but let not the action or the thought produce a deep impression on the mind; let the ripples come and go; let huge actions proceed from the muscles and the brain, but let them not make any deep impression on the soul.

How can this be done? We see that the impression of any action to which we attach ourselves, remains. I may meet hundreds of persons during the day, and among them meet also one whom I love; and when I retire at night I may try to think of all the faces I saw, but only that face comes before the mind— the face which I met perhaps only for one minute, and which I loved; all the others have vanished. My attachment to this particular person caused a deeper impression on my mind than all the other faces. Physiologically, the impressions have all been the same; every one of the faces that I saw pictured itself on the retina, and the brain took the pictures in, and yet there was no similarity of effect upon the mind. Most of the faces, perhaps, were entirely new faces, about which I had never thought before, but that one face of which I got only a glimpse, found associations inside. Perhaps I had pictured him in my mind for years, knew hundreds of things about him, and this one new vision of him awakened hundreds of sleeping memories in my mind; and this one impression having been repeated perhaps a hundred times more than those of the different faces together, will produce a great effect on the mind.

Therefore, be "unattached;" let things work; let brain centres work; work incessantly, but let not a ripple conquer the mind. Work as if you were a stranger in this land, a sojourner; work incessantly, but do not bind yourselves; bondage is terrible. This world is not our habitation, it is only one of the many stages through which we are passing. Remember that great saying of the Sankhya, "The whole of nature is for the soul, not the soul for nature." The very reason of nature's existence is for the education of the soul; it has no other meaning; it is there because the soul must have knowledge, and through knowledge free itself. If we remember this always, we shall never be attached to nature; we shall know that nature is a book in which we are to read, and that when we have gained the required knowledge the book is of no more value to us. Instead of that, however, we are identifying ourselves with nature; we are thinking that the soul is for nature, that the spirit is for the flesh. and, as the common saying has it, we think that man "lives to eat" and not "eats to live," we are continually making this mistake; we are regarding nature as ourselves and are becoming attached to it; and as soon as this attachment comes, there is the deep impression on the soul, which binds us down and makes us work not from freedom but like slaves.

The whole gist of this teaching is that you should work like a master and not as a slave; work incessantly, but do not do slave's work. Do you not see how everybody works? Nobody can be altogether at rest; ninety-nine per cent. of mankind work like slaves, and the result is misery; it is all selfish work. Work through freedom! Work through love! The word 'love' is very difficult to understand; love never comes until there is freedom. There is no true love possible in the slave. If you buy a slave and tie him down in chains and make him work for you, he will work like a drudge, but there will be no love in him. So when we ourselves work for the things of the world as slaves, there can be no love in us, and our work is not true work. This is true of work done for relatives and friends, and is true of work done for our own selves. Selfish work is slave's work; and here is a test. Every act of love brings happiness; there is no act of love which does not bring peace and blessedness as its reaction. Real existence, real knowledge, and real love are eternally connected with one another, the three in one: where one of them is, the others also must be; they are the three aspects of the One without a second — the Existence-Knowledge-Bliss. When that existence becomes relative, we see it as the world; that knowledge becomes in its turn modified into the knowledge of the things of the world; and that bliss forms the foundation of all true love known to the heart of man. Therefore true love can never react so as to cause pain either to the lover or to the beloved. Suppose a man loves a woman; he wishes to have her all to himself and feels extremely jealous about her every movement; he wants her to sit near him, to stand near him, and to eat and move at his bidding. He is a slave to her and wishes to have her as his slave. That is not love; it is a kind of morbid affection of the slave, insinuating itself as love. It cannot be love, because it is painful; if she does not do what he wants, it brings him pain. With love there is no painful reaction; love only brings a reaction of bliss; if it does not, it is not love; it is a mistaking something else for love. When you have succeeded in loving your husband, your wife, your children, the whole world, the universe, in such a manner that there is no reaction of pain or jealousy, no selfish feeling, then you are in a fit state to be unattached.

Krishna says: Look at Me, Arjuna! If I stop from work for one moment the whole universe will die. I have nothing to gain from work; I am the one Lord, but why do I work? Because I love the world. God is unattached because He loves; that real love makes us unattached. Wherever there is attachment, the clinging to the things of the world, you must know that it is all physical, attraction between sets of particles of matter; something that attracts two bodies nearer and nearer all the time, and if they cannot get near enough produces pain; but where there is real love it does not rest on physical attachment at all. Such lovers may be a thousand miles away from one another, but their love will be all the same; it does not die; and will never produce any painful reaction.

To attain this unattachment is almost a life-work, but as soon as we have reached this point we have attained the goal of love and become free; the bondage of nature falls from us, and we see nature as she is; she forges no more chains for us; we stand entirely free and take not the results of work into consideration; who then cares for what the results may be?

Do you ask anything from your children in return for what you have given them? It is your duty to work for them, and there the matter ends. In whatever you do for a particular person, a city, or a state, assume the same attitude towards it as you have towards your children — expect nothing in return. If you can invariably take the position of a giver, in which everything given by you is a free offering to the world, without any thought of return, then will your work bring you no attachment. Attachment comes only where we expect a return.

If working like slaves result in selfishness and attachment, working as masters of our own mind gives rise to the bliss of non-attachment. We often talk of right and justice, but we find that in the world right and justice are mere baby's talk. There are two things which guide the conduct of men: might and mercy. The exercise of might is invariably the exercise of selfishness. All men and women try to make the most of whatever power or advantage they have. Mercy is heaven itself; to be good we have all to be merciful. Even justice and right should stand on mercy. All thought of obtaining return for the work we do hinders our spiritual progress; nay, in the end it brings misery. There is another way in which this idea of mercy and selfless charity can be put into practice; that is, by looking upon works as "worship" in case we believe in a personal God. Here we give up all the fruits of our work unto the Lord; and, worshipping Him thus, we have no right to expect anything from mankind for the work we do. The Lord Himself works incessantly and is ever without attachment. Just as water cannot wet the lotus leaf, so work cannot bind the unselfish man by giving rise to attachment to results. The selfless and unattached man may live in the very heart of a crowded and sinful city; he will riot be touched by sin.

This idea of complete self-sacrifice is illustrated in the following story:— After the battle of Kurukshetra the five Pandava brothers performed a great sacrifice and made very large gifts to the poor. All people expressed amazement at the greatness and richness of the sacrifice, and said that such a sacrifice the world had never seen before. But, after the ceremony, there came a little mongoose; half his body was golden, and the other half was brown; and he began to roll on the floor of the sacrificial hall. He said to those around, "You are all liars; this is no sacrifice." "What!" they exclaimed, "you say this is no sacrifice; do you not know how money and jewels were poured out to the poor and every one became rich and happy? This was the most wonderful sacrifice any man ever performed." But the mongoose said, "There was once a little village, and in it there dwelt a poor Brahman, with his wife, his son and his son's wife. They were very poor and lived on small gifts made to them for preaching and teaching. There came in that land a three years' famine, and the poor Brahman suffered more than ever. At last when the family had starved for days, the father brought home one morning a little barley flour, which he had been fortunate enough to obtain, and he divided it into four parts, one for each member of the family. They prepared it for their meal, and just as they were about to eat there was a knock at the door. The father opened it, and there stood a guest. Now in India a guest is a sacred person; he is as a god for the time being, and must be treated as such. So the poor Brahman said, 'Come in, sir; you are welcome.' He set before the guest his own portion of the food, which the guest quickly ate and said, 'Oh, sir, you have killed me; I have been starving for ten days, and this little bit has but increased my hunger.' Then the wife said to her husband, 'Give him my share,' but the husband said, 'Not so.' The wife however insisted, saying, 'Here is a poor man, and it is our duty as householders to see that he is fed, and it is my duty as a wife to give him my portion, seeing that you have no more to offer him.' Then she gave her share to the guest, which he ate, and said he was still burning with hunger. So the son said, 'Take my portion also; it is the duty of a son to help his father to fulfil his obligations.' The guest ate that, but remained still unsatisfied; so the son's wife gave him her portion also. That was sufficient, and the guest departed, blessing them. That night those four people died of starvation. A few granules of that flour had fallen on the floor, and when I rolled my body on them half of it became golden, as you see. Since then I have been travelling all over the world, hoping to find another sacrifice like that, but nowhere have I found one; nowhere else has the other half of my body been turned into gold. That is why I say this is no sacrifice.

This idea of charity is going out of India; great men are becoming fewer and fewer. When I was first learning English I read an English story book, in which there was a story about a dutiful boy who had gone out to work and had given some of his money to his old mother, and this was praised in three or four pages. What was that? No Hindu boy can ever understand the moral of that story. Now I understand it when I hear the Western idea— every man for himself. And some men take everything for themselves, and fathers and mothers and wives and children go to the wall. That should never and nowhere be the ideal of the householder.

Now you see what Karma Yoga means; even at the point of death to help any one, without asking questions. Be cheated millions of times and never ask a question, and never think of what you are doing. Never vaunt of your gifts to the poor or expect their gratitude, but rather be grateful to them for giving you the occasion of practising charity to them. Thus it is plain that to be an ideal householder is a much more difficult task than to be an ideal Sannyasin; the true life of work is indeed as hard as, if not harder than, the equally true life of renunciation.

Chapter IV
What is Duty?

It is necessary in the study of Karma Yoga to know what duty is. If I have to do something I must first know that it is my duty, and then I can do it. The idea of duty again is different in different nations. The Mahommedan says what is written in his book, the Koran, is his duty; the Hindu says what is in the Vedas is his duty; and the Christian says what is in the Bible is his duty. We find that there are varied ideas of duty, differing according to different states in life, different historical periods and different nations. The term 'duty,' like every other universal abstract term, is impossible clearly to define; we can only get an idea of it by knowing its practical operations and results. When certain things occur before us we have all a natural or trained impulse to act in a certain manner towards them; when this impulse comes, the mind begins to think about the situation; sometimes it thinks that it is good to act in a particular manner under the given conditions, at other times it thinks that it is wrong to act in the same manner even in the very same circumstances. The ordinary idea of duty everywhere is that every good man follows the dictates of his conscience. But what is it that makes an act a duty? If a Christian finds a piece of beef before him and does not eat it to save his own life, or will not give it to save the life of another man, he is sure to feel that he has not done his duty. But if a Hindu dares to eat that piece of beef or to give it to another Hindu, he is equally sure to feel that he too has not done his duty; the Hindu's training and education make him feel that Way. In the last century there were notorious bands of robbers in India called Thugs; they thought it their duty to kill any man they could and take away his money the larger the number of men they killed, the better they thought they were. Ordinarily if a man goes out into the street and shoots down another man, he is apt to feel sorry for it, thinking that he has done wrong. But if the very same man, as a soldier in his regiment, kills not one but twenty, he is certain to feel glad and think that he has done his duty remarkably well. Therefore we see that it is not the thing done that defines a duty. To give an objective definition of duty is thus entirely impossible. Yet there is duty from the subjective side. Any action that makes us go Godward is a good action, and is our duty; any action that makes us go downward is evil, and is not our duty. From the subjective standpoint we may see that certain acts have a tendency to exalt and ennoble us, while certain other acts have a tendency to degrade and to brutalise us. But it is not possible to make out with certainty which acts have which kind of tendency in relation to all persons, of all sorts and conditions. There is, however, only one idea of duty which has been universally accepted by all mankind, of all ages and sects and countries, and that has been summed up in a Sanskrit aphorism thus:— "Do not injure any being; not injuring any being is virtue; injuring any being is sin."

The Bhagavad-Gita frequently alludes to duties dependent upon birth and position in life. Birth and position in life and in society largely determine the mental and moral attitude of individuals towards the various activities of life. It is therefore our duty to do that work which will exalt and ennoble us in accordance with the ideals and activities of the society in which we are born. But it must be particularly remembered that the same ideals and activities do not prevail in all societies and countries; our ignorance of this is the main cause of much of the hatred of one nation towards another. An American thinks that whatever an American does in accordance with the custom of his country is the best thing to do, and that whoever does not follow his custom must be a very wicked man. A Hindu thinks that his customs are the only right ones and are the best in the world, and that whosoever does not obey them must be the most wicked man living. This is quite a natural mistake which all of us are apt to make. But it is very harmful; it is the cause of half the uncharitableness found in the world. When I came to this country and was going through the Chicago Fair, a man from behind pulled at my turban. I looked back and saw that he was a very gentlemanly-looking man, neatly dressed. I spoke to him and when he found that I knew English he became very much abashed. On another occasion in the same Fair another man gave me a push. When I asked him the reason, he also was ashamed and stammered out an apology saying, "Why do you dress that way!" The sympathies of these men were limited within the range of their own language and their own fashion of dress. Much of the oppression of powerful nations on weaker ones are caused by this prejudice. It dries up their fellow — feeling for fellow-men. That very man who asked me why I did not dress as he did and wanted to ill-treat me because of my dress, may have been a very good man, a good father and a good citizen; but the kindliness of his nature died out as soon as he saw a man in a different dress. Strangers are exploited in all countries, because they do not know how to defend themselves; thus they carry home false impressions of the peoples they have seen. Sailors, soldiers and traders behave in foreign lands in very queer ways, although they would not dream of doing so in their own country; perhaps this is why the Chinese call Europeans and Americans "foreign devils." They could not have done this if they had met the good, the kindly sides of Western life.

Therefore the one point we ought to remember is that we should always try to see the duty of others through their own eyes, and never judge the customs of other peoples by our own standard. I am not the standard of the universe. I have to accommodate myself to the world, and not the world to me. So we see that environments change the nature of our duties, and doing the duty which is ours at any particular time is the best thing we can do in this world. Let us do that duty which is ours by birth; and when we have done that, let us do the duty which is ours by our position in life and in society. There is, however, one great danger in human nature, viz., that man never examines himself. He thinks he is quite as fit to be on the throne as the king. Even if he is, he must first show that he has done the duty of his own position; and then higher duties will come to him. When we begin to work earnestly in the world, nature gives us blows right and left and soon enables us to find out our position. No man can long occupy satisfactorily a position for which he is not fit. There is no use in grumbling against nature's adjustment. He who does the lower work is not therefore a lower man. No man is to be judged by the mere nature of his duties, but all should be judged by the manner and the spirit in which they perform them.

Later on we shall find that even this idea of duty undergoes change, and that the greatest work is done only when there is no selfish motive to prompt it. Yet it is work through the sense of duty that leads us to work without any idea of duty; when work will become worship—nay, something higher, then will work be done for its own sake. We shall find that the philosophy of duty, whether it be in the form of ethics or of love, is the same as in every other Yoga—the object being the attenuating of the lower self, so that the real higher Self may shine forth; to lessen the frittering away of energies on the lower plane of existence, so that the soul may manifest itself on the higher ones. This is accomplished by the continuous denial of low desires, which duty rigorously requires. The whole organisation of society has thus been developed consciously or unconsciously in the realms of action and experience, where, by limiting selfishness, we open the way to an unlimited expansion of the real nature of man.

Duty is seldom sweet. It is only when love greases its wheels that it runs smoothly; it is a continuous friction otherwise. How else could parents do their duties to their children, husbands to their wives and vice versa? Do we not meet with cases of friction every day in our lives? Duty is sweet only through love, and love shines alone in freedom. Yet is it freedom to be a slave to the senses, to anger, to jealousies and a hundred other petty things that must occur every day in human life? In all these little roughnesses that we meet with in life, the highest expression of freedom is to forbear. Women, slaves to their own irritable, jealous tempers, are apt to blame their husbands, and assert their own 'freedom', as they think, not knowing that thereby they only prove that they are slaves. So it is with husbands who eternally find fault with their wives.

Chastity is the first virtue in man or woman, and the man who, however he may have strayed away, cannot be brought to the right path by a gentle and loving and chaste wife, is indeed very rare. The world is not yet as bad as that. We hear much about brutal husbands all over the "world and about the impurity of men, but is it not true that there are quite as many brutal and impure women as men? If all women were as good and pure as their own constant assertions would lead one to believe, I am perfectly satisfied that there would not be one impure man in the world. What brutality is there which purity and chastity cannot conquer? A good, chaste wife, who thinks of every other man except her own husband as her child and has the attitude of a mother towards all men, will grow so great in the power of her purity that there cannot be a single man, however brutal, who will not breathe an atmosphere of holiness in her presence. Similarly every husband must look upon all women, except his own wife, in the light of his own mother or daughter or sister. That man, again, who wants to be a teacher of religion must look upon every woman as his mother, and always behave towards her as such.

The position of the mother is the highest in the world, as it is the one place in which to learn and exercise the greatest unselfishness. The love of God is the only love that is higher than a mother's love; all others are lower. It is the duty of the mother to think of her children first and then of herself. But, instead of that, if the parents are always thinking of themselves first, the result is that the relation between parents and children becomes the same as that between birds and their offspring which, as soon as they are fledged, do not recognise any parents. Blessed, indeed, is the man who is able to look upon woman as the representative of the motherhood of God. Blessed, indeed, is the woman to whom man represents the fatherhood of God. Blessed are the children who look upon their parents as Divinity manifested on earth.

The only way to rise is by doing the duty next to us, and thus gathering strength go on until we reach the highest state. A young Sannyasin went to a forest; there he meditated, worshipped and practised Yoga for a long time. After years of hard work and practice, he was one day sitting under a tree, when some dry leaves fell upon his head. He looked up and saw a crow and a crane fighting on the top of the tree, which made him very angry. He said, "What! Dare you throw these dry leaves upon my head!" As with these words he angrily glanced at them a flash of fire went out of his head— such was the Yogin's power— and burnt the birds to ashes. He was very glad, almost overjoyed at this development of power,— he could burn the crow and the crane by a look. After a time he had to go to the town to beg his bread. He went, stood at a door and said :— "Mother, give me food." A voice came from inside the house :"Wait a little, my son." The young man thought :— "You wretched woman, how dare you make me wait! You do not know my power yet." While he was thinking thus the voice came again :— "Boy, don't be thinking too much of yourself. Here is neither crow nor crane." He was astonished; still he had to wait. At last the woman came, and he fell at her feet and said :— "Mother how did you know that?" She said :— "My boy, I do not know your Yoga or your practices. I am a common everyday woman. I made you wait because my husband is ill, and I was nursing him. All my life I have struggled to do my duty. When I was unmarried, I did my duty to my parents; now that I am married, I do my duty to my husband; that is all the Yoga I practise. But by doing my duty I have become illumined; thus I could read your thoughts and know what you had done in the forest. If you want to know something higher than this, go to the market of such and such a town where you will find a Vyadha* who will tell you something that you will be very glad to learn." The Sannyasin thought :— "Why should I go to that town and to a Vyadha!" But after what he had seen his mind opened a little, so he went. When he came near the town he found the market, and there saw, at a distance, a big fat Vyadha cutting meat with big knives, talking and bargaining with different people. The young man said, "Lord help me! Is this the man from whom I am going to learn? He is the incarnation of a demon, if he is anything." In the meantime this man looked up and said, "O Swamin, did that lady send you here? Take a seat until I have done my business." The Sannyasin thought, "What comes to me here?" He took his seat; the man went on with his work and after he had finished he took his money and said to the Sannyasin, "Come, sir, come to my home." On reaching home the Vyadha gave him a seat, saying, "Wait here," and went into the house. He then washed his old father and mother, fed them and did all he could to please them, after which he came to the Sannyasin and said, "Now, sir, you have come here to see me; what can I do for you?" The Sannyasin asked him a few questions about soul and about God, and the Vyadha gave him a lecture which forms a part of the Mahabharata, called the Vyadha-Gita. It contains one of the highest flights of the Vedanta. When the Vyadha finished his teaching the Sannyasin felt astonished. He said, "Why are you in that body? With such knowledge as yours why are you in a Vyadha's body, and doing such filthy, ugly work?" "My son," replied the Vyadha, "no duty is ugly, no duty is impure. My birth placed me in these circumstances and environments. In my boyhood I learnt the trade; I am unattached, and I try to do my duty well. I try to do my duty as a householder, and I try to do all I can to make my father and mother happy. I neither know your Yoga, nor have I become a Sannyasin, nor did I go out of the world into a forest; nevertheless, all that you have heard and seen has come to me through the unattached doing of the duty which belongs to my position."

There is a sage in India, a great Yogin, one of the most wonderful men I have ever seen in my life. He is a peculiar man, he will not teach any one; if you ask him a question he will not answer. It is too much for him to take up the position of a teacher, he will not do it. If you ask a question, and wait for some days, in the course of conversation he will bring up the subject, and wonderful light will he throw on it. He told me once the secret of work, "Let the end and the means be joined into one." When you are doing any work, do not think of anything beyond. Do it as worship, as the highest worship, and devote your whole life to it for the time being. Thus, in the story, the Vyadha and the woman did their duty with cheerfulness and whole-heartedness; and the result was that they became illuminated; clearly showing that the right performance of the duties of any station in life, without attachment to results, leads us to the highest realisation of the perfection of the soul.

It is the worker who is attached to results that grumbles about the nature of the duty which has fallen to his lot; to the unattached worker all duties are equally good, and form efficient instruments with which selfishness and sensuality may be killed, and the freedom of the soul secured. We are all apt to think too highly of ourselves. Our duties are determined by our deserts to a much larger extent than we are willing to grant. Competition rouses envy, and it kills the kindliness of the heart. To the grumbler all duties are distasteful; nothing will ever satisfy him, and his whole life is doomed to prove a failure. Let us work on, doing as we go whatever happens to be our duty, and being ever ready to put our shoulders to the wheel. Then surely shall we see the Light!

* The lowest class of people in India who used to live as hunters and butchers.

Chapter V
We Help Ourselves, Not the World

Before considering further how devotion to duty helps us in our spiritual progress, let me place before you in a brief compass another aspect of what we in India mean by Karma. In every religion there are three parts; philosophy, mythology and ritual. Philosophy of course is the essence of every religion; mythology explains and illustrates it by means of the more or less legendary lives of great men, stories and fables of wonderful things and so on; ritual gives to that philosophy a still more concrete form, so that every one may grasp it — ritual is in fact concretised philosophy. This ritual is Karma; it is necessary in every religion, because most of us cannot understand abstract spiritual things until we grow much spiritually. It is easy for men to think that they can understand anything, but when it comes to practical experience they find that abstract ideas are often very hard to comprehend. Therefore symbols are of great help and we cannot dispense with the symbolical method of putting things before us. From time immemorial symbols have been used by all kinds of religions. In one sense we cannot think but in symbols; words themselves are symbols of thought. In another sense everything in the universe may be looked upon as a symbol. The whole universe is a symbol and God is the essence behind. This kind of symbology is not simply the creation of man; it is not that certain people belonging to a religion sit down together and think out certain symbols, and bring them into existence out of their own minds. The symbols of religion have a natural growth. Otherwise, why is it that certain symbols are associated with certain ideas in the mind of almost every one? Certain symbols are universally prevalent. Many of you may think that the cross first came into existence as a symbol in connection with the Christian religion; but as a matter of fact it existed before Christianity was, before Moses was born, before the Vedas were given out, before there was any human record of human things. The cross may be found to have been in existence among the Aztecs and the Phoenicians: every race seems to have had the cross. Again the symbol of the crucified Saviour, of a man crucified upon a cross, appears to have been known to almost every nation. The circle has been a great symbol throughout the world. Then there is the most universal of all symbols, the Swastika. At one time it was thought that the Buddhists carried it all over the world with them, but it has been found out that ages before Buddhism it was used among nations. In old Babylon and in Egypt it was to be found. What does this show? All these symbols could not have been purely conventional. There must be some reason for them, some natural association between them and the human mind. Language is not the result of convention; it is not that people ever agreed to represent certain ideas by certain words; there never was an idea without a corresponding word or a word without a corresponding idea; ideas and words are in their nature inseparable. The symbols to represent ideas may be sound symbols or colour symbols. Deaf and dumb people have to think with other than sound symbols. Every thought in the mind has a form as its counterpart; this is called in Sanskrit philosophy nama-rupa— name and form. It is as impossible to create by convention a system of symbols as it is to create a language. In the world's ritualistic symbols we have an expression of the religious thought of humanity. It is easy to say that there is no use of rituals and temples and all such paraphernalia; every baby says that in modern times. But it must be easy for all to see that those who worship inside a temple are in many respects different from those who will not worship there. Therefore the association of particular temples, rituals and other concrete forms with particular religions has a tendency to bring into the mind of the followers of those religions the thoughts for which those concrete things stand as symbols; and it is not wise to ignore rituals and symbology altogether. The study and practice of these things form naturally a part of Karma Yoga.

There are many other aspects of this science of work. One among them is to know the relation between thought and word and what can be achieved by the power of the word. In every religion the power of the word is recognised, so much so that in some of them creation itself is said to have come out of the word. The external aspect of the thought of God is the Word, and, as God thought and willed before He created, creation came out of the Word. In this stress and hurry of our materialistic life our nerves lose sensibility and become hardened. The older we grow, the longer we are knocked about in the world, the more callous we become; and we are apt to neglect things that even happen persistently and prominently around us. Human nature, however, asserts itself sometimes and we are led to inquire into and wonder at some of these common occurrences; wondering thus is the first step in the acquisition of light. Apart from the higher philosophic and religious value of the Word we may see that sound symbols play a prominent part in the drama of human life. I am talking to you. I am not touching you; the pulsations of the air caused by my speaking go into your ear, they touch your nerves and produce effects in your minds. You cannot resist this. What can be more wonderful than this? One man calls another a fool, and this other stands up and clenches his fist and lands a blow on his nose. Look at the power of the word! There is a woman weeping and miserable; another woman comes along and speaks to her a few gentle words; the doubled up frame of the weeping woman becomes straightened at once, her sorrow is gone and she already begins to smile. Think of the power of words! They are a great force in higher philosophy as well as in common life. Day and night we manipulate this force without thought and without enquiry. To know the nature of this force and to use it well is also a part of Karma Yoga.

Our duty to others means helping others; doing good to the world. Why should we do good to the world? Apparently to help the world, but really to help ourselves. We should always try to help the world, that should be the highest motive in us; but if we consider well, we find that the world does not require our help at all. This world was not made that you or I should come and help it. I once read a sermon in which was said:— "All this beautiful world is very good, because it gives us time and opportunity to help others." Apparently, this is a very beautiful sentiment, but is it not a blasphemy to say that the world needs our help? We cannot deny that there is much misery in it; to go out and help others is, therefore, the best thing we can do, although, in the long run, we shall find that helping others is only helping ourselves. As a boy I had some white mice. They were kept in a little box which had little wheels made for them, and when the mice tried to cross the wheels, the wheels turned and turned, and the mice never got anywhere. So it is with the world and our helping it. The only help is that we get moral exercise. This world is neither good nor evil; each man manufactures a world for himself. If a blind man begins to think of the world, it is either as soft or hard, or as cold or hot. We are a mass of happiness or misery; we have seen that hundreds of times in our lives. As a rule, the young are optimistic and the old pessimistic. The young have life before them; the old complain their day is gone; hundreds of desires, which they cannot fulfil, struggle in their hearts. Both are foolish nevertheless. Life is good or evil according to the state of mind in which we look at it; it is neither by itself. Fire, by itself, is neither good nor evil. When it keeps us warm we say:— "How beautiful is fire!" When it burns our fingers we blame it. Still, in itself it is neither good nor bad. According as we use it, it produces in us the feeling of good or bad; so also is this world. It is perfect. By perfection is meant that it is perfectly fitted to meet its ends. We may all be perfectly sure that it will go on beautifully well without us, and we need not bother our heads wishing to help it.

Yet we must do good; the desire to do good is the highest motive power we have, if we know all the time that it is a privilege to help others. Do not stand on a high pedestal and take five cents in your hand and say, "Here, my poor man," but be grateful that the poor man is there, so that by making a gift to him you are able to help yourself. It is not the receiver that is blessed, but it is the giver. Be thankful that you are allowed to exercise your power of benevolence and mercy in the world, and thus become pure and perfect. All good acts tend to make us pure and perfect. What can we do at best? Build a hospital, make roads, or erect charity asylums! We may organise a charity and collect two or three millions of dollars, build a hospital with one million, with the second give balls and drink champagne, and of the third let the officers steal half, and leave the rest finally to reach the poor; but what are all these? One mighty wind in five minutes can break all your buildings up. What shall we do then? One volcanic eruption may sweep away all our roads and hospitals and cities and buildings. Let us give up all this foolish talk of doing good to the world. It is not waiting for your or my help; yet we must work and constantly do good, because it is a blessing to ourselves. That is the only way we can become perfect. No beggar whom we have helped has ever owed a single cent to us; we owe everything to him, because he has allowed us to exercise our charity on him. It is entirely wrong to think that we have done, or can do, good to the world, or to think that we have helped such and such people. It is a foolish thought, and all foolish thoughts bring misery. We think that we have helped some man and expect him to thank us; and because he does not, unhappiness comes to us. Why should we expect anything in return for what we do? Be grateful to the man you help, think of him as God. Is it not a great privilege to be allowed to worship God by helping our fellow-man? If we were really unattached, we should escape all this pain of vain expectation, and could cheerfully do good work in the world. Never will unhappiness or misery come through work done without attachment. The world will go on with its happiness and misery through eternity.

There was a poor man who wanted some money; and, somehow, he had heard that if he could get hold of a ghost, he might command him to bring money or anything else he liked; so he was very anxious to get hold of a ghost. He went about searching for a man who would give him a ghost; and at last he found a sage, with great powers, and besought his help. The sage asked him what he would do with a ghost. "I want a ghost to work for me; teach me how to get hold of one, sir; I desire it very much," replied the man. But the sage said, "Don't disturb yourself, go home." The next day the man went again to the sage and began to weep and pray, "Give me a ghost; I must have a ghost, sir, to help me." At last the sage was disgusted, and said, "Take this charm, repeat this magic word and a ghost will come, and whatever you say to him he will do. But beware they are terrible beings, and must be kept continually busy. If you fail to give him work he will take your life." The man replied, "That is easy; I can give him work for all his life." Then he went to a forest, and after long repetition of the magic word, a huge ghost appeared before him, and said, "I am a ghost; I have been conquered by your magic; but you must keep me constantly employed the moment you fail to give me work I will kill you." The man said, "Build me a palace," and the ghost said, "It is done; the palace is built." "Bring me money," said the man. "Here is your money," said the ghost. "Cut this forest down, and build a city in its place." "That is done," said the ghost; "anything more?" Now the man began to be frightened and thought he could give him nothing more to do; he does everything in a trice. The ghost said, "Give me something to do or I will eat you up." The poor man could find no further occupation for him, and was frightened. So he ran and ran and at last reached the sage, and said, "Oh sir protect my life!" The sage asked him what the matter was, and the man replied "I have nothing to give the ghost to do. Everything I tell him to do he does in a moment, and he threatens to eat me up if I do not give him work." Just then the ghost arrived, saying, "I'll eat you up," and he would have swallowed the man. The man began to shake, and begged the sage to save his life. The sage said, "I will find you a way out. Look at that dog with a curly tail. Draw your sword quickly and cut the tail off and give it to the ghost to straighten out." The man cut off the dog's tail and gave it to the ghost, saying, "Straighten that out for me." The ghost took it and slowly and carefully straightened it out, but as soon as he let it go, it instantly curled up again. Once more he laboriously straightened it out only to find it again curled up as soon as he attempted to let go of it. Again he patiently straightened it out but as soon as he let it go, it curled up again. So he went on for days and days, until he was exhausted and said, "I was never in such trouble before in my life. I am an old veteran ghost, but never before was I in such trouble. I will make a compromise with you," he said to the man. "You let me off and I will let you keep all I have given you and will promise not to harm you. The man was much pleased, and accepted the offer gladly.

This world is like a dog's curly tail, and people have been striving to straighten it out, for hundreds of years; but when they let it go, it has curled up again. How could it be otherwise? One must first know how to work without attachment, then he will not be a fanatic. When we know that this world is like a dog's curly tail and will never get , we shall not become fanatics. If there were no fanaticism in the world it would make much more progress than it does now. It is a mistake to think that fanaticism can make for the progress of mankind. On the contrary it is a retarding element creating hatred and anger, and causing people to fight each other, and making them unsympathetic. We think that whatever we do or possess is the best in the world, and what we do not do or possess is of no value. So, always remember the instance of the curly tail of the dog whenever you have a tendency to become a fanatic. You need not worry or make yourself sleepless about the world; it will go on without you. When you have avoided fanaticism then alone will you work well. It is the level-headed man, the calm man, of good judgment and cool nerves, of great sympathy and love, who does good work and so does good to himself. The fanatic is foolish and has no sympathy; he can never straighten the world, nor himself become pure and perfect.

To recapitulate the chief points in today's lecture:

- Firstly, we have to bear in mind that we are all debtors to the world and the world does not owe us anything. It is a great privilege for all of us to be allowed to do anything for the world. In helping the world we really help ourselves.
- The second point is that there is a God in this universe. It is not true that this universe is drifting and stands in need of help from you and me. God is ever present therein, He is undying and eternally active and infinitely watchful. When the whole universe sleeps He sleeps not; He is working incessantly; all the changes and manifestations of the world are His.
- Thirdly, we ought not to hate any one. This world will always continue to be a mixture of good and evil. Our duty is to sympathise with the weak and to love even the wrongdoer. The world is a grand moral gymnasium wherein we have all to take exercise so as to become stronger and stronger spiritually.
- Fourthly, we ought not to be fanatics of any kind because fanaticism is opposed to love. You hear fanatics glibly saying, "I do not hate the sinner, I hate the sin;" but I am prepared to go any distance to see the face of that man who can really make a distinction between the sin and the sinner. It is easy to say so.

If we can distinguish well between quality and substance we may become perfect men. It is not easy to do this. And further, the calmer we are and the less disturbed our nerves, the more shall we love and the better will our work be.

Chapter VI
Non-Attachment is Complete Self-Abnegation

Just as every action that emanates from us comes back to us as reaction, even so our actions may act on other people and theirs on us. Perhaps all of you have observed it as a fact that when persons do evil actions they become more and more evil, and when they begin to do good they become stronger and stronger and learn to do good at all times. This intensification of the influence of action cannot be explained on any other ground, than that we can act and react upon each other. To take an illustration from physical science, when I am doing a certain action, my mind may be said to be in a certain state of vibration; all minds which are in similar circumstances will have the tendency to be affected by my mind. If there are different musical instruments tuned alike in one room, all of you may have noticed that when one is struck the others have the tendency to vibrate so as to give the same note. So all minds that have the same tension, so to say, will be equally affected by the same thought. Of course, this influence of thought on mind will vary, according to distance and other causes, but the mind is always open to affection. Suppose I am doing an evil act, my mind is in a certain state of vibration, and all minds in the universe, which are in a similar state, have the possibility of being affected by the vibration of my mind. So, when I am doing a good action, my mind is in another state of vibration; and all minds similarly strung have the possibility of being affected by my mind; and this power of mind upon mind is more or less according as the force of the tension is greater or less.

Following this simile further, it is quite possible that, just as light waves may travel for millions of years before they reach any object, so thought waves may also travel hundreds of years before they meet an object with which they vibrate in unison. It is quite possible, therefore, that this atmosphere of ours is full of such thought pulsations, both good and evil. Every thought projected from every brain goes on pulsating, as it were, until it meets a fit object that will receive it. Any mind which is open to receive some of these impulses will take them immediately. So, when a man is doing evil actions, he has brought his mind to a certain state of tension and all the waves which correspond to that state of tension, and which may be said to be already in the atmosphere, will struggle to enter into his mind. That is why an evil-doer generally goes on doing more and more evil. His actions become intensified. Such, also, will be the case with the doer of good; he will open himself to all the good waves that are in the atmosphere, and his good actions also will become intensified. We run, therefore, a twofold danger in doing evil: first, we open ourselves to all the evil influences surrounding us; secondly, we create evil which affects others, may be, hundreds of years hence. In doing evil we injure ourselves and others also. In doing good we do good to ourselves and to others as well; and, like all other forces in man, these forces of good and evil also gather strength from outside.

According to Karma Yoga, the action one has done cannot be destroyed, until it has borne its fruit; no power in nature can stop it from yielding its results. If I do an evil action, I must suffer for it; there is no power in this universe to stop or stay it. Similarly if I do a good action, there is no power in the universe which can stop its bearing good results. The cause must have its effect; nothing can prevent or restrain this. Now comes a very fine and serious question about Karma Yoga— namely, that these actions of ours, both good and evil, are intimately connected with each other. We cannot put a line of demarcation and say, this action is entirely good and this entirely evil. There is no action which does not bear good and evil fruits at the same time. To take the nearest example: I am talking to you, and some of you, perhaps, think I am doing good; and at the same time I am, perhaps, killing thousands of microbes in the atmosphere; I am thus doing evil to something else. When it is very near to us and affects those we know, we say that it is very good action, if it affects them in a good manner. For instance, you may call my speaking to you very good, but the microbes will not; the microbes you do not see, but yourselves you do see. The way in which my talk affects you is obvious to you, but how it affects the microbes is not so obvious. And so, if we analyse our evil actions also we may find that some good possibly results from them somewhere. He who in good action sees that there is something evil in it, and in the midst of evil sees that there is something good in it somewhere,— has known the secret of work.

But what follows from it? That, howsoever we may try, there cannot be any action which is perfectly pure, or any which is perfectly impure, taking purity and impurity in the sense of injury and non-injury. We cannot breathe or live without injuring others, and every bit of the food we eat is taken away from another's mouth: our very lives are crowding out other lives. It may be men, or animals, or small microbes, but some one or other of these we have to crowd out. That being the case, it naturally follows that perfection can never be attained by work. We may work through all eternity, but there will be no way out of this intricate maze; you may work on, and on, and on; there will be no end to this inevitable association of good and evil in the results of work.

The second point to consider is, what is the end of work? We find the vast majority of people in every country believing that there will be a time when this world will become perfect, when there will be no disease, or death, or unhappiness, or wickedness. That is a very good idea, a very good motive power to inspire and uplift the ignorant; but if we think for a moment we shall find on the very face of it that it cannot be so. How can it be, seeing that good and evil are the obverse and reverse of the same coin? How can you have good without evil at the same time? What is meant by perfection? A perfect life is a contradiction in terms. Life itself is a state of continuous struggle between ourselves and everything outside. Every moment we are fighting actually with external nature, and if we are defeated our life has to go. It is, for instance, a continuous struggle for food and air. If food or air fails we die. Life is not a simple and smoothly flowing thing, but it is a compound effect. This complex struggle between something inside and the external world is what we call life. So it is clear that when this struggle ceases, there will be an end of life.

What is meant by ideal happiness is that,— when there is the cessation of this struggle. But then life will cease, for the struggle can only cease when life itself has ceased. We have seen already that in helping the world we help ourselves. The main effect of work done for others is to purify ourselves. By means of the constant effort to do good to others we are trying to forget ourselves; this forgetfulness of self is the one great lesson we have to learn in life. Man thinks foolishly that he can make himself happy, and after years of struggle finds out at last that true happiness consists in killing selfishness and that no one can make him happy except himself. Every act of charity, every thought of sympathy, every action of help, every good deed, is taking so much of self-importance away from our little selves and making us think of ourselves as the lowest and the least; and, therefore, it is all good. Here we find that Jnana, Bhakti, and Karma, all come to one point. The highest ideal is eternal and entire self-abnegation, where there is no "I," but all is "thou"; and whether he is conscious, or unconscious of it Karma Yoga leads man to that end. A religious preacher may become horrified at the idea of an impersonal God; he may insist on a personal God and wish to keep up his own identity and individuality, whatever he may mean by that. But his ideas of ethics, if they are really good, cannot but be based on the highest self-abnegation. It is the basis of all morality; you may extend it to men, or animals, or angels, it is the one basic idea, the one fundamental principle running through all ethical systems.

You will find various classes of men in this world. First, there are the God-men whose self-abnegation is complete, and who do only good to others even at the sacrifice of their own lives. These are the highest of men. If there are a hundred of such in any country, that country need never despair. But they are unfortunately too few. Then there are the good men who do good to others so long as it does not injure themselves; and there is a third class, who, to do good to themselves injure others. It is said by a Sanskrit poet that there is a fourth unnameable class of people who injure others merely for injury's sake. Just as there are at one pole of existence the highest good men, who do good for the sake of doing good, so at the other pole, there are others who injure others just for the sake of the injury. They do not gain anything thereby, but it is their nature to do evil.

Here are two Sanskrit words. The one is "Pravritti," which means revolving towards, and the other is "Nivritti," which means revolving away. The "revolving towards" is what we call the world, the "I and mine"; it includes all those things which are always enriching that "me" by wealth and money and power and name and fame, and which are of a grasping nature, always tending to accumulate everything in one centre, that centre being "myself." That is the "Pravatti," the natural tendency of every human being; taking everything from everywhere and heaping it around one centre, that centre being man's own sweet self. When this tendency begins to break, when it is "Nivritti" or "going away from," then begin morality and religion. Both "Pravritti" and "Nivritti" are of the nature of work: the former is evil work, and the latter is good work. This "Nivritti" is the fundamental basis of all morality and all religion, and the very perfection of it is entire self-abnegation, readiness to sacrifice mind and body and everything for another being. When a man has reached that state he has attained to the perfection of Karma Yoga. This is the highest result of good works. Although a man has not studied a single system of philosophy, although he does not believe in any God, and never has believed, although he has not prayed even once in his whole life, if the simple power of good actions has brought him to that state where he is ready to give up his life and all else for others, he has arrived at the same point to which the religious man will come through his prayers and the philosopher through his knowledge; and so you may find that the philosopher, the worker, and the devotee, all meet at one point, that one point being self-abnegation. However much their systems of philosophy and religion may differ, all mankind stand in reverence and awe before the man who is ready to sacrifice himself for others. Here, it is not at all any question of creed, or doctrine — even men who are very much opposed to all religious ideas, when they see one of these acts of complete self-sacrifice, feel that they must revere it. Have you not seen even a most bigoted Christian, when he reads Edwin Arnold's "Light of Asia," stand in reverence of Buddha, who preached no God, preached nothing but self-sacrifice? The only thing is that the bigot does not know that his own end and aim in life is exactly the same as that of those from whom he differs. The worshipper, by keeping constantly before him the idea of God and a surrounding of good, comes to the same point at last and says, "Thy will be done," and keeps nothing to himself. That is self-abnegation. The philosopher, with his knowledge, sees that the seeming self is a delusion and easily gives it up; it is self-abnegation. So Karma, Bhakti and Jnana all meet here; and this is what was meant by all the great preachers of ancient times, when they taught that God is not the world. There is one thing which is the world and another which is God; and this distinction is very true; what they mean by world is selfishness. Unselfishness is God. One may live on a throne, in a golden palace, and be perfectly unselfish; and then he is in God. Another may live in a hut and wear rags, and have nothing in the world; yet, if he is selfish, he is intensely merged in the world.

To come back to one of our main points, we say that we cannot do good without at the same time doing some evil, or do evil without doing some good. Knowing this, how can we work? There have therefore been sects in this world who have in an astoundingly way preached slow suicide as the only means to get out of the world; because, if a man lives he has to kill poor little animals and plants or do injury to something or some one. So, according to them the only way out of the world is to die. The Jainas have preached this doctrine as their highest ideal. This teaching seems to be very logical. But the true solution is found in the Gita. It is the theory of non-attachment, to be attached to nothing while doing our work of life. Know that you are separated entirely from the world; that you are in the world, and that whatever you may be doing in it, you are not doing that for your own sake. Any action that you do for yourself will bring its effect to bear upon you. If it is a good action you will have to take the good effect, and, if bad, you will have to take the bad effect; but any action that is not done for your own sake, whatever it be, will have no effect on you. There is to be found a very expressive sentence in our scriptures embodying this idea:— "Even if he kill the whole universe (or be himself killed) he is neither the killer nor the killed, when he knows that he is not acting for himself at all." Therefore Karma Yoga teaches, "Do not give up the world; live in the world, imbibe its influences as much as you can; but if it be for your own enjoyment's sake— work not at all. Enjoyment should not be the goal. First kill your self and then take the whole world as yourself; as the old Christians used to say, "the old man must die." This old man is the selfish idea that the whole world is made for our enjoyment. Foolish parents teach their children to pray, "O Lord, Thou hast created this sun for me and this moon for me," as if the Lord has had nothing else to do than to create everything for these babies. Do not teach your children such nonsense. Then again, there are people who are foolish in another way; they teach us that all these animals were created for us to kill and eat, and that this universe is for the enjoyment of men. That is all foolishness. A tiger may say, "Man was created for me," and pray, "O Lord, how wicked are these men, who do not come and place themselves before me to be eaten; they are breaking Your law." If the world is created for us we are also created for the world. That this world is created for our enjoyment is the most wicked idea that holds us down. This world is not for our sake; millions pass out of it every year; the world does not feel it; millions of others are supplied in their place. Just as much as the world is for us, so we are also for the world.

To work properly, therefore, you have first to give up the idea of attachment. Secondly, do not mix in the fray, hold yourself as a witness and go on working. My master used to say, "Look upon your children as a nurse does." The nurse will take your baby and fondle it and play with it and behave towards it as gently as if it were her own child; but as soon as you give her notice to quit, she is ready to start off with bag and baggage from the house. Everything in the shape of attachment is forgotten; it will not give the ordinary nurse the least pang to leave your children and take up other children. Even so are you to be with all that you consider your own. You are the nurse, and if you believe in God, believe that all these things which you consider yours are really His. The greatest weakness often insinuates itself as the greatest good and strength. It is a weakness to think that any one is dependent on me, and that I can do good to another. This belief is the mother of all our attachment, and through this attachment comes all our pain. We must inform our minds that no one in this universe depends upon us; not one beggar depends on our charity; not one soul on our kindness; not one living thing on our help. All are helped on by nature, and will be so helped even though millions of us were not here. The course of nature will not stop for such as you and me; it is, as already pointed out, only a blessed privilege to you and to me that we are allowed, in the way of helping others, to educate ourselves. This is a great lesson to learn in life, and when we have learned it fully we shall never be unhappy; we can go and mix without harm in society anywhere and everywhere. You may have wives and husbands, and regiments of servants, and kingdoms to govern; if only you act on the principle that the world is not for you and does not inevitably need you, they can do you no harm. This very year some of your friends may have died. Is the world waiting without going on, for them to come again. Is its current stopped? No, it goes on. So drive out of your mind the idea that you have to do something for the world; the world does not require any help from you. It is sheer nonsense on the part of any man to think that he is born to help the world; it is simply pride, it is selfishness insinuating itself in the form of virtue. When you have trained your mind and your nerves to realise this idea of the world's non-dependence on you or on anybody, there will then be no reaction in the form of pain resulting from work. When you give something to a man and expect nothing— do not even expect the man to be grateful— his ingratitude will not tell upon you, because you never expected anything, never thought you had any right to anything in the way of a return; you gave him what he deserved; his own Karma got it for him; your Karma made you the carrier thereof. Why should you be proud of having given away something? You are the porter that carried the money or other kind of gift, and the world deserved it by its own Karma. Where is then the reason for pride in you? There is nothing very great in what you give to the world. When you have acquired the feeling of non-attachment, there will then be neither good nor evil for you. It is only selfishness that causes the difference between good and evil. It is a very hard thing to understand, but you will come to learn in time that nothing in the universe has power over you until you allow it to exercise such a power. Nothing has power over the Self of man, until the Self becomes a fool and loses independence. So, by non-attachment, you overcome and deny the power of anything to act upon you. It is very easy to say that nothing has the right to act upon you until you allow it to do so; but what is the true sign of the man who really does not allow anything to work upon him, who is neither happy nor unhappy when acted upon by the external world? The sign is that good or ill fortune causes no change in his mind; in all conditions he continues to remain the same.

There was a great sage in India called Vyasa. This Vyasa is known as the author of the Vedanta aphorisms, and was a holy man. His father had tried to become a very perfect man and had failed. His grandfather had also tried and failed. His great-grandfather had similarly tried and failed. He himself did not succeed perfectly, but his son, Shuka, was born perfect. Vyasa taught his son wisdom; and after teaching him the knowledge of truth himself, he sent him to the court of King Janaka. He was a great king and was called Janaka Videha. Videha means "without a body." Although a king, he had entirely forgotten that he was a body; he felt that he was a spirit all the time. This boy Shuka was sent to be taught by him. The king knew that Vyasa's son was coming to him to learn wisdom; so he made certain arrangements beforehand; and when the boy presented himself at the gates of the palace, the guards took no notice of him whatsoever. They only gave him a seat, and he sat there for three days and nights, nobody speaking to him, nobody asking him who he was or whence he was. He was the son of a very great sage; his father was honoured by the whole country, and he himself was a most respectable person; yet the low, vulgar guards of the palace would take no notice of him. After that, suddenly, the ministers of the king and all the big officials came there and received him with the greatest honours. They conducted him in and showed him into splendid rooms, gave him the most fragrant baths and wonderful dresses, and for eight days they kept him there in all kinds of luxury. That solemnly serene face of Shuka did not change even to the smallest extent by the change in the treatment accorded to him; he was the same in the midst of this luxury as when waiting at the door. Then he was brought before the king. The king was on his throne, music was playing, and dancing and other amusements were going on. The king then gave him a cup of milk, full to the brim, and asked him to go seven times round the hall without spilling even a drop. The boy took the scup and proceeded in the midst of the music and the attraction of the beautiful faces. As desired by the king, seven times did he go round, and not a drop of the milk was spilt. The boy's mind could not be attracted by anything in the world, unless he allowed it to affect him. And when he brought the cup to the king, the king said to him. "What your father has taught you, and what you have learned yourself, I can only repeat; you have known the truth; go home."

Thus the man that has practised control over himself cannot be acted upon by anything outside; there is no more slavery for him. His mind has become free; such a man alone is fit to live well in the world. We generally find men holding two opinions regarding the world. Some are pessimists and say, "How horrible this world is, how wicked!" Some others are optimists and say, "How beautiful this world is, how wonderful!" To those who have not controlled their own minds, the world is either full of evil or at best a mixture of good and evil. This very world will become to us an optimistic world when we become masters of our own minds. Nothing will then work upon us as good or evil; we shall find everything to be in its proper place, to be harmonious. Some men, who begin by saying that the world is a hell, often end by saying that it is a heaven when they succeed in the practice of self-control. If we are genuine Karma-Yogis and wish to train ourselves to the attainment of this state, wherever we may begin we are sure to end in perfect self-abnegation; and as soon as this seeming self has gone, the whole world, which at first appears to us to be filled with evil, will appear to be heaven itself and full of blessedness. Its very atmosphere will be blessed; every human face there will be good. Such is the end and aim of Karma Yoga, and such is its perfection in practical life.

Our various Yogas do not conflict with each other; each of them leads us to the same goal and makes us perfect; only each has to be strenuously practised. The whole secret is in practising. First you have to hear, then think, and then practise. This is true of every Yoga. You have first to hear about it and understand what it is; and many things which you do not understand will be made clear to you by constant hearing and thinking. It is hard to understand everything at once. The explanation of everything is after all in yourself. No one was ever really taught by another; each of us has to teach himself. The external teacher offers only the suggestion which rouses the internal teacher to work to understand things. Then things will be made clearer to us by our own power of perception and thought, and we shall realise them in our own souls; and that realisation will grow into the intense power of will. First it is feeling, then it becomes willing, and out of that willing comes the tremendous force for work that will go through every vein and nerve and muscle, until the whole mass of your body is changed into an instrument of the unselfish Yoga of work, and the desired result of perfect self-abnegation and utter unselfishness is duly attained. This attainment does not depend on any dogma, or doctrine, or belief. Whether one is Christian, or Jew, or Gentile, it does not matter. Are you unselfish? That is the question. If you are, you will be perfect without reading a single religious book, without go-ing into a single church or temple. Each one of our Yogas is fitted to make man perfect even without the help of the others, because they have all the same goal in view. The Yogas of work, of wisdom, and of devotion are all capable of serving as direct and independent means for the attainment of Moksha. "Fools alone say that work and philosophy are different, not the learned." The learned know that, though apparently different from each other, they at last lead to the same goal of human perfection.

Chapter VII
Freedom

In addition to meaning work, we have stated that psychologically the word Karma also implies causation. Any work, any action, any thought that produces an effect is called a Karma. Thus the law of Karma means the law of causation, of inevitable cause and sequence. Wheresoever there is a cause, there an effect must be produced; this necessity cannot be resisted, and this law of Karma, according to our philosophy, is true throughout the whole universe. Whatever we see, or feel, or do, whatever action there is anywhere in the universe, while being the effect of past work on the one hand, becomes, on the other, a cause in its turn, and produces its own effect. It is necessary, together with this, to consider what is meant by the word 'law.' By law is meant the tendency of a series to repeat itself. When we see one event followed by another, or sometimes happening simultaneously with another, we expect this sequence or co-existence to recur. Our old logicians and philosophers of the Nyaya school call this law by the name of Vyapti. According to them all our ideas of law are due to association. A series of phenomena becomes associated with things in our mind in a sort of invariable order, so that whatever we perceive at any time is immediately referred to other facts in the mind. Any one idea or, according to our psychology, any one wave that is produced in the mind-stuff, chitta, must always give rise to many similar waves. This is the psychological idea of association, and causation is only an aspect of this grand pervasive principle of association. This pervasiveness of association is what is, in Sanskrit, called Vyapti. In the external world the idea of law is the same as in the internal,— the expectation that a particular phenomenon will be followed by another, and that the series will repeat itself. Really speaking, therefore, law does not exist in nature. Practically it is an error to say that gravitation exists in the earth, or that there is any law existing objectively anywhere in nature. Law is the method, the manner in which our mind grasps a series of phenomena; it is all in the mind. Certain phenomena, happening one after another or together, and followed by the conviction of the regularity of their recurrence, thus enabling our minds to grasp the method of the whole series, constitute what we call law.

The next question for consideration is what we mean by law being universal. Our universe is that portion of existence which is characterised by what the Sanskrit psychologists call desa-kala-nimitta, or what is known to European psychology as space, time and causation. This universe is only a part of infinite existence, thrown into a peculiar mould, composed of space, time and causation. It necessarily follows that law is possible only within this conditioned universe; beyond it there cannot be any law. When we speak of the universe we only mean that portion of existence which is limited by our mind; the universe of the senses, which we can see, feel, touch, hear, think of, imagine; this alone is under law; but beyond it existence cannot be subject to law, because causation does not extend beyond the world of our minds. Anything beyond the range of our mind and our senses is not bound by the law of causation, as there is no mental association of things in the region beyond the senses, and no causation without association of ideas. It is only when 'being' or existence gets moulded into name and form that it obeys the law of causation, and is said to be under law; because all law has its essence in causation. Therefore, we see at once that there cannot be any such thing as free will; the very words are a contradiction, because will is what we know, and everything that we know is within our universe, and everything within our universe is moulded by the conditions of space, time and causation. Everything that we know, or can possibly know, must be subject to causation, and that which obeys the law of causation cannot be free. It is acted upon by other agents, and becomes a cause in its turn. But that which has become converted into the will, which was not the will before, but which, when it fell into this mould of space, time and causation, became converted into the human will, is free; and when this will gets out of this mould of space, time and causation, it will be free again. From freedom it comes, and becomes moulded into this bondage, and it gets out and goes back to freedom again.

The question has been raised as to from whom this universe comes, in whom it rests, and to whom it goes; and the answer has been given that from freedom it comes, in bondage it rests, and goes back into that freedom again. So, when we speak of man as no other than that infinite being which is manifesting itself, we mean that only one very small part thereof is man; this body and this mind which we see are only one part of the whole, only one spot of the infinite being. This whole universe is only one speck of the infinite being; and all our laws, our bondages, our joys and our sorrows, our happinesses and our expectations, are only within this small universe; all our progression and digression are within its small compass. So you see how childish it is to expect a continuation of this universe— the creation of our minds— and to expect to go to heaven, which after all must mean only a repetition of this world that we know. You see at once that it is an impossible and childish desire to make the whole of infinite existence conform to the limited and conditioned existence which we know. When a man says that he will have again and again this same thing which he is having now, or, as I sometimes put it, when he asks for a comfortable religion, you may know that he has become so degenerate that he cannot think of anything higher than what he is now; he is just his little present surroundings and nothing more. He has forgotten his infinite nature, and his whole idea is confined to these little joys, and sorrows, and heart-jealousies of the moment. He thinks that this finite thing is the infinite; and not only so, he will not let this foolishness go. He clings on desperately unto Trishna, the thirst after life, what the Buddhists call Tanha and Trissa. There may be millions of kinds of happiness, and beings, and laws, and progress, and causation, all acting outside the little universe that we know, and after all the whole of this comprises but one section of our infinite nature.

To acquire freedom we have to get beyond the limitations of this universe; it cannot be found here. Perfect equilibrium, or what the Christians call the peace that passes all understanding, cannot be had in this universe, nor in heaven, nor in any place where our mind and thoughts can go, where the senses can feel, or which the imagination can conceive. No such place can give us that freedom, because all such places would be within our universe, and it is limited by space, time and causation. There may be places that are more etherial than this earth of ours, where enjoyments may be keener, but even those places must be in the universe, and therefore in bondage to law; so we have to go beyond, and real religion begins where this little universe ends. These little joys, and sorrows, and knowledge of things end there, and the reality begins. Until we give up the thirst after life, the strong attachment to this our transient conditioned existence, we have no hope of catching even a glimpse of that infinite freedom beyond. It stands to reason then that there is only one way to attain to that freedom which is the goal of all the noblest aspirations of mankind, and that is by giving up this little life, giving up this little universe, giving up this earth, giving up heaven, giving up the body, giving up the mind, giving up everything that is limited and conditioned. If we give up our attachment to this little universe of the senses, or of the mind, we shall be free immediately. The only way to come out of bondage is to go beyond the limitations of law, to go beyond causation.

But it is a most difficult thing to give up the clinging to this universe; few ever attain to that. There are two ways to do that, mentioned in our books. One is called the 'neti, neti' (not this, not this), the other is called the 'iti' (this); the former is the negative, and the latter is the positive way. The negative way is the most difficult. It is only possible to the men of the very highest, exceptional minds and gigantic wills who simply stand up and say, "No, I will not have this," and the mind and body obey their will, and they come out successful. But such people are very rare. The vast majority of mankind choose the positive way, the way through the world, making use of all the bondages themselves to break those very bondages. This is also a kind of giving up; only it is done slowly and gradually, by knowing things, enjoying things and thus obtaining experience, and knowing the nature of things until the mind lets them all go at last and becomes unattached. The former way of obtaining non-attachment is by reasoning, and the latter way is through work and experience. The first is the path of Jnana Yoga, and is characterised by the refusal to do any work; the second is that of Karma Yoga, in which there is no cessation from work. Every one must work in the universe. Only those who are perfectly satisfied with the Self, whose desires do not go beyond the Self, whose mind never strays out of the Self, to whom the Self is all in all, only those do not work. The rest must work. A current rushing down of its own nature falls into a hollow and makes a whirlpool, and, after running a little in that whirlpool, it emerges again in the form of the free current to go on unchecked. Each human life is like that current. It gets into the whirl, gets involved in this world of space, time and causation, whirls round a little, crying out 'my father, my brother, my name, my fame,' and so on, and at last emerges out of it and regains its original freedom. The whole universe is doing that. Whether we know it or not, whether we are conscious or unconscious of it, we are all working to get out of the dream of the world. Man's experience in the world is to enable him to get out of its whirlpool.

What is Karma Yoga? The knowledge of the secret of work. We see that the whole universe is working. For what? For salvation, for liberty; from the atom to the highest being working for the one end, liberty for the mind, for the body, for the spirit. All things are always trying to get freedom, flying away from bondage. The sun, the moon, the earth, the planets, all are trying to fly away from bondage. The centrifugal and the centripetal forces of nature are indeed typical of our universe. Instead of being knocked about in this universe, and after long delay and thrashing, getting to know things as they are, we learn from Karma Yoga the secret of work, the method of work, the organising power of work. A vast mass of energy may be spent in vain, if we do not know how to utilise it. Karma Yoga makes a science of work, you learn by it how best to utilise all the working of this world. Work is inevitable, it must be so; but we should work to the highest purpose. Karma Yoga makes us admit that this world is a world of five minutes; that it is a something we have to pass through; and that freedom is not here, but is only to be found beyond. To find the way out of the bondages of the world we have to go through it slowly and surely. There may be those exceptional persons about whom I just spoke, those who can stand aside and give up the world, as a snake casts off its skin and stands aside and looks at it. There are no doubt these exceptional beings; but the rest of mankind have to go slowly through the world of work; Karma Yoga shows the process, the secret and the method of doing it to the best advantage.

What does it say? "Work incessantly, but give up all attachment to work." Do not identify yourself with anything. Hold your mind free. All this that you see, the pains and the miseries are but the necessary conditions of this world; poverty and wealth and happiness are but momentary; they do not belong to our real nature at all. Our nature is far beyond misery and happiness, beyond every object of the senses, beyond the imagination; and yet we must go on working all the time. "Misery comes through attachment, not through work." As soon as we identify ourselves with the work we do, we feel miserable; but if we do not identify ourselves with it we do not feel that misery. If a beautiful picture belonging to another is burnt, a man does not generally become miserable; but when his own picture is burnt how miserable he feels Why? Both were beautiful pictures, perhaps copies of the same original; but in one case very much more misery is felt than in the other. It is because in one case he identifies himself with the picture, and not in the other. This 'I and mine' causes the whole misery. With the sense of possession comes selfishness, and selfishness brings on misery. Every act of selfishness or thought of selfishness makes us attached to something, and immediately we are made slaves. Each wave in the chitta that says 'I and mine,' immediately puts a chain round us and makes us slaves; and the more we say 'I and mine' the more slavery grows, the more misery increases. Therefore, Karma Yoga tells us to enjoy the beauty of all the pictures in the world, but not to identify ourselves with any of them. Never say 'mine.' Whenever we say a thing is mine, misery will immediately come. Do not even say 'my child' in your mind. Possess the child, but do not say 'mine.' If you do, then will come the misery. Do not say 'my house,' do not say 'my body.' The whole difficulty is there. The body is neither yours, nor mine, nor anybody's. These bodies are coming and going by the laws of nature but we are free, standing as witness. This body is no more free than a picture, or a wall. Why should we be attached so much to a body? If somebody paints a picture, he does it and passes on. Do not project that tentacle of selfishness, "I must possess it." As soon as that is projected, misery will begin.

So Karma Yoga says, first destroy the tendency to project this tentacle of selfishness, and when you have the power of checking it, hold it in and do not allow the mind to get into the wave of selfishness. Then you may go out into the world and work as much as you can. Mix everywhere; go where you please; you will never be contaminated with evil. There is the lotus leaf in the water; the water cannot touch and adhere to it; so will you be in the world. This is called 'Vairagya,' dispassion or non-attachment. I believe I have told you that without non-attachment there cannot be any kind of Yoga. Non-attachment is the basis of all the Yogas. The man who gives up living in houses, wearing fine clothes, and eating good food, and goes into the desert, may be a most attached person. His only possession, his own body, may become everything to him; and as he lives he will be simply struggling for the sake of his body. Non-attachment does not mean anything that we may do in relation to our external body, it is all in the mind. The binding link of 'I and mine' is in the mind. If we have not this link with the body and with the things of the senses, we are nonattached, wherever and whatever we may be. A man may be on a throne and perfectly non-attached; another man may be in rags and still very much attached. First, we have to attain this state of non-attachment, and then to work incessantly. Karma Yoga gives us the method that will help us in giving up all attachment, though it is indeed very hard.

Here are the two ways of giving up all attachment. The one is for those who do not believe in God, or in any outside help. They are left to their own devices; they have simply to work with their own will, with the powers of their mind and discrimination, saying, "I must be nonattached." For those who believe in God there is another way, which is much less difficult. They give up the fruits of work unto the Lord, they work and are never attached to the results. Whatever they see, feel, hear, or do, is for Him. For whatever good work we may do, let us not claim any praise or benefit. It is the Lord's; give up the fruits unto Him. Let us stand aside and think that we are only servants obeying the Lord, our Master, and that every impulse for action comes from Him every moment. Whatever thou worshippest, whatever thou perceivest, whatever thou doest, give up all unto Him and be at rest. Let us be at peace, perfect peace, with ourselves, and give up our whole body and mind and everything as an eternal sacrifice unto the Lord. Instead of the sacrifice of pouring oblations into the fire, perform this one great sacrifice day and night— the sacrifice of your little self. "In search of wealth in

this world, Thou art the only wealth I have found; I sacrifice myself unto Thee
In search of some one to be loved, Thou art the only one beloved I have found
I sacrifice myself unto Thee." Let us repeat this day and night, and say, "Nothing
for me; no matter whether the thing is good, bad, or indifferent; I do not care
for it; I sacrifice all unto Thee." Day and night let us renounce our seeming self
until it becomes a habit with us to do so, until it gets into the blood, the nerves
and the brain, and the whole body is every moment obedient to this idea of self-
renunciation. Go then into the midst of the battlefield, with the roaring cannon
and the din of war, and you will find yourself to be free and at peace.

Karma Yoga teaches us that the ordinary idea of duty is on the lower plane
nevertheless, all of us have to do our duty. Yet we may see that this peculiar sense
of duty is very often a great cause of misery. Duty becomes a disease with us; it
drags us ever forward. It catches hold of us and makes our whole life miserable
It is the bane of human life. This duty, this idea of duty is the midday summer
sun which scorches the innermost soul of mankind. Look at those poor slaves
to duty! Duty leaves them no time to say prayers, no time to bathe. Duty is ever
on them. They go out and work. Duty is on them! They come home and think
of the work for the next day. Duty is on them! It is living a slave's life, at last
dropping down in the street and dying in harness, like a horse. This is duty as it
is understood. The only true duty is to be unattached and to work as free beings
to give up all work unto God. All our duties are His. Blessed are we that we are
ordered out here. We serve our time; whether we do it ill or well, who knows? If
we do it well, we do not get the fruits. If we do it ill, neither do we get the care
Be at rest, be free, and work. This kind of freedom is a very hard thing to attain
How easy it is to interpret slavery as duty—the morbid attachment of flesh for
flesh as duty! Men go out into the world and struggle and fight for money or
for any other thing to which they get attached. Ask them why they do it. They
say, "It is a duty." It is the absurd greed for gold and gain, and they try to cover
it with a few flowers.

What is duty after all? It is really the impulsion of the flesh, of our attachment
and when an attachment has become established, we call it duty. For instance
in countries where there is no marriage, there is no duty between husband and
wife; when marriage comes, husband and wife live together on account of attachment; and that kind of living together becomes settled after generations
and when it becomes so settled, it becomes a duty. It is, so to say, a sort of chronic
disease. When it is acute we call it disease, when it is chronic we call it nature. It
is a disease. So when attachment becomes chronic, we baptise it with the high-

sounding name of duty. We strew flowers upon it, trumpets sound for it, sacred texts are said over it, and then the whole world fights, and men earnestly rob each other for this duty's sake. Duty is good to the extent that it checks brutality. To the lowest kinds of men, who cannot have any other ideal, it is of some good ; but those who want to be Karma-Yogis must throw this idea of duty overboard. There is no duty for you and me. Whatever you have to give to the world, do give by all means, but not as a duty. Do not take any thought of that. Be not compelled. Why should you be compelled ? Everything that you do under compulsion goes to build up attachment. Why should you have any duty ? Resign everything unto God. In this tremendous fiery furnace where the fire of duty scorches everybody, drink this cup of nectar and be happy. We are all simply working out His will, and have nothing to do with rewards and punishments. If you want the reward you must also have the punishment ; the only way to get out of the punishment is to give up the reward. The only way of getting out of misery is by giving up the idea of happiness, because these two are linked to each other. On one side there is happiness, on the other there is misery. On one side there is life, on the other there is death. The only way to get beyond death is to give up the love of life. Life and death are the same thing, looked at from different points. So the idea of happiness without misery, or of life without death, is very good for school-boys and children ; but the thinker sees that it is all a contradiction in terms and gives up both. Seek no praise, no reward, for anything you do. No sooner do we perform a good action than we begin to desire credit for it. No sooner do we give money to some charity than we want to see our names blazoned in the papers. Misery must come as the result of such desires. The greatest men in the world have passed away unknown. The Buddhas and the Christs that we know are but second rate heroes in comparison with the greatest men of whom the world knows nothing. Hundreds of these unknown heroes have lived in every country working silently. Silently they live and silently they pass away ; and in time their thoughts find expression in Buddhas or Christs, and it is these latter that become known to us. The highest men do not seek to get any name or fame from their knowledge. They leave their ideas to the world ; they put forth no claims for themselves and establish no schools or systems in their name. Their whole nature shrinks from such a thing. They are the pure Sattvikas, who can never make any stir, but only melt down in love. I have seen one such Yogi who lives in a cave in India. He is one of the most wonderful men I have ever seen. He has so completely lost the sense of his own individuality that we may say that the man in him is completely gone, leaving behind only the all-comprehending sense of the divine. If an animal bites one of his arms, he is ready to give it his other arm also, and say that it is the Lord's will. Everything that comes to him is from the Lord. He does not show himself to men, and yet he is a magazine of love and of true and sweet ideas.

Next in order come the men with more Rajas, or activity, combative natures, who take up the ideas of the perfect ones and preach them to the world. The highest kind of men silently collect true and noble ideas, and others — the Buddhas and Christs — go from place to place preaching them and working for them. In the life of Gautama Buddha we notice him constantly saying that he is the twenty-fifth Buddha. The twenty-four before him are unknown to history, although the Buddha known to history must have built upon foundations laid by them. The highest men are calm, silent and unknown. They are the men who really know the power of thought; they are sure that, even if they go into a cave and close the door and simply think five true thoughts and then pass away, these five thoughts of their will live through eternity. Indeed such thoughts will penetrate through the mountains, cross the oceans, and travel through the world. They will enter deep into human hearts and brains and raise up men and women who will give them practical expression in the workings of human life. These Sattvika men are too near the Lord to be active and to fight, to be working, struggling, preaching and doing good, as they say, here on earth to humanity. The active workers, however good, have still a little remnant of ignorance left in them. When our nature has yet some impurities left in it, then alone can we work. It is in the nature of work to be impelled ordinarily by motive and by attachment. In the presence of an ever active Providence who notes even the sparrows fall, how can man attach any importance to his own work? Will it not be a blasphemy to do so when we know that He is taking care of the minutest things in the world? We have only to stand in awe and reverence before Him saying, "Thy will be done." The highest men cannot work, for in them there is no attachment. Those whose whole soul is gone into the Self, those whose desires are confined in the Self, who have become ever associated with the Self, for them there is no work. Such are indeed the highest of mankind; but apart from them every one else has to work. In so working we should never think that we can help on even the least thing in this universe. We cannot. We only help ourselves in this gymnasium of the world. This is the proper attitude of work. If we work in this way, if we always remember that our present opportunity to work thus is a privilege which has been given to us, we shall never be attached to anything.

Millions like you and me think that we are great people in the world; but we all die, and in five minutes the world will have forgotten us. But the life of God is infinite. "Who can live a moment, breathe a moment, if this all-powerful One does not will it?" He is the ever active Providence. All power is His and within His command. Through His command the winds blow, the sun shines, the earth lives, and death stalks upon the earth. He is the all in all; He is all and in all. We can only worship Him. Give up all fruits of work; do good for its own sake; then alone will come perfect non-attachment. The bonds of the heart will thus break, and we shall reap perfect freedom. This freedom is indeed the goal of Karma Yoga.

Chapter VIII
The Ideal of Karma Yoga

The grandest idea in the religion of the Vedanta is that: we may reach the same goal by different paths; and these paths I have generalised into four — viz., those of work, love, psychology and knowledge. But you must, at the same time, remember that these divisions are not very marked and quite exclusive of each other. Each blends into the other. But according to the type which prevails we name the divisions. It is not that you cannot find a man who has no other faculty than that of work, nor that you cannot find men who are more than devoted worshippers only, nor that there are not men who have more than mere knowledge. These divisions are made in accordance with the type or the tendency that may be seen to prevail in a man. We have found that, in the end, all these four paths converge and become one. All religions and all methods of work and worship lead us to one and the same goal.

I have already tried to point out that goal. It is freedom as I understand it. Everything that we perceive around us is struggling towards freedom, from the atom to the man, from the insentient, lifeless particle of matter to the highest existence on earth, the human soul. The whole universe is in fact the result of this struggle for freedom. In all combinations every particle is trying to go on its own way, to fly from the other particles; but the others are holding it in check. Our earth is trying to fly away from the sun, and the moon from the earth. Everything has a tendency to infinite dispersion. All that we see in the universe has for its basis this one struggle towards freedom; it is under the impulse of this tendency that the saint prays and the robber robs. When the line of action taken is not a proper one we call it evil, and when the manifestation of it is proper and high we call it good. But the impulse is the same, the struggle towards freedom. The saint is oppressed with the knowledge of his condition of bondage, and he wants to get rid of it; so he worships God. The thief is oppressed with the idea that he does not possess certain things, and he tries to get rid of that want, to obtain freedom from it; so he steals. Freedom is the one goal of all nature, sentient or insentient; and, consciously or , everything is struggling towards that goal. The freedom which the saint seeks is very different from that which the robber seeks; the freedom loved by the saint leads him to the enjoyment of infinite, unspeakable bliss, while that on which the robber has set his heart only forges other bonds for his soul.

There is to be found in every religion the manifestation of this struggle towards freedom. It is the groundwork of all morality, of unselfishness, which means getting rid of the idea that men are the same as their little body. When we see a man doing good work, helping others, it means that he cannot be confined within the limited circle of 'me and mine'. There is no limit to this getting out of selfishness. All the great systems of ethics preach absolute unselfishness as the goal. Supposing this absolute unselfishness can be reached by a man, what becomes of him? He is no more the little Mr. So-and-so; he has acquired infinite expansion. That little personality which he had before is now lost to him for ever; he has become infinite, and the attainment of this infinite expansion is indeed the goal of all religions and of all moral and philosophical teachings. The personalist, when he hears this idea philosophically put, gets frightened. At the same time, if he preaches morality, he after all teaches the very same idea himself. He puts no limit to the unselfishness of man. Suppose a man becomes perfectly unselfish under the personalistic system, how are we to distinguish him from the perfected ones in other systems? He has become one with the universe and to become that is the goal of all; only the poor personalist has not the courage to follow out his own reasoning to its right conclusion. Karma Yoga is the attaining through unselfish work of that freedom which is the goal of all human nature. Every selfish action, therefore, retards our reaching the goal, and every unselfish action takes us towards the goal; that is why the only definition that can be given of morality is this:— That which is selfish is immoral, and that which is unselfish is moral.

But, if you come to details, the matter will not be seen to be quite so simple. For instance, environment often makes the details different as I have already mentioned. The same action under one set of circumstances may be unselfish, and under another set quite selfish. So we can give only a general definition, and leave the details to be worked out by taking into consideration the differences in time, place and circumstances. In one country one kind of conduct is considered moral, and in another the very same is immoral, because the circumstances differ. The goal of all nature is freedom, and freedom is to be attained only by perfect unselfishness; every thought, word or deed that is unselfish takes us towards the goal, and, as such, is called moral. That definition, you will find, holds good in every religion and every system of ethics. In some systems of thought morality is derived from a Superior Being— God. If you ask why a man ought to do this and not that, their answer is: "Because such is the command of God." But whatever be the source from which it is derived, their code of ethics also has the same central idea— not to think of self but to give up self. And yet some persons, in spite of this high ethical idea, are frightened at the thought of having to give up their little personalities. We may ask the man who clings to the idea of little personalities to consider the case of a person who has become perfectly unselfish, who has no thought for himself, who does no deed for himself, who speaks no word for himself, and then say where his 'himself' is. That 'himself' is known to him only so long as he thinks, acts or speaks for himself. If he is only conscious of others, of the universe, and of the all, where is his 'himself'? It is gone for ever.

Karma Yoga, therefore, is a system of ethics and religion intended to attain freedom through unselfishness, and by good works. The Karma-Yogi need not believe in any doctrine whatever. He may not believe even in God, may not ask what his soul is, nor think of any metaphysical speculation. He has got his own special aim of realising selflessness; and he has to work it out himself. Every moment of his life must be realisation because he has to solve by mere work, without the help of doctrine or theory, the very same problem to which the Jnani applies his reason and inspiration and the Bhakta his love.

Now comes the next question: What is this work? What is this doing good to the world? Can we do good to the world? In an absolute sense, 'no' in a relative sense, 'yes'. No permanent or everlasting good can be done to the world; if it could be done, the world would not be this world. We may satisfy the hunger of a man for five minutes, but he will be hungry again. Every pleasure with which we supply a man may be seen to be momentary. No one can permanently cure this ever-recurring fever of pleasure and pain. Can any permanent happiness be given to the world? In the ocean we cannot raise a wave without causing a hollow somewhere else. The sum-total of the good things in the world has been the same throughout in its relation to man's need and greed. It cannot be increased or decreased. Take the history of the human race as we know today. Do we not find the same miseries and the same happiness, the same pleasures and pains, the same differences in position? Are not some rich, some poor, some high, some low, some healthy, some unhealthy?

All this was just the same with the Egyptians, the Greeks, and the Romans in ancient times as it is with the Americans today. So far as history is known it has always been the same; yet at the same time we find, that running along with all these incurable differences of pleasure and pain, there has ever been the struggle to alleviate them. Every period of history has given birth to thousands of men and women who have worked hard to smooth the passage of life for others. And how far have they succeeded? We can only play at driving the ball from one place to another. We take away pain from the physical plane, and it goes to the mental one. It is like that picture in Dante's hell where the misers were given a mass of gold to roll up a hill. Every time they rolled it up a little, it again rolled down. All our talks about the millennium are very nice as school-boys' stories, but they are no better than that. All nations that dream of the millennium also think, that of all peoples in the world, they will have the best of it then for themselves. This is the wonderfully unselfish idea of the millennium!

We cannot add happiness to this world; similarly, we cannot add pain to it either. The sum-total of the energies of pleasure and pain displayed here on earth will be the same throughout. We just push it from this side to the other side, and from that side to this, but it will remain the same, because to remain so is its very nature. This ebb and flow, this rising and falling, is in the world's very nature; it would be as logical to hold otherwise as to say that we may have life without death. This is complete nonsense, because the very idea of life implies death and the very idea of pleasure implies pain. The lamp is constantly burning out, and that is its life. If you want to have life you have to die every moment for it. Life and death are only different expressions of the same thing, looked at from different standpoints; they are the falling and the rising of the same wave, and the two form one whole. One looks at the 'fall' side and becomes a pessimist, another looks at the 'rise' side and becomes an optimist. When a boy is going to school and his father and mother are taking care of him, everything seems blessed to him; his wants are simple, he is a great optimist. But the old man, with his varied experience, becomes calmer, and is sure to have his warmth considerably cooled down. So, old nations, with signs of decay all around them, are apt to be less hopeful than new nations. There is a proverb in India. "A thousand years a city, and a thousand years forest." This change of city into forest and vice versa is going on everywhere, and it makes people optimists or pessimists according to the side they see of it.

The next idea we take up is the idea of equality. These millennium ideas have been great motive powers to work. Many religions preach this as an element in them, — that God is coming to rule the universe, and that then there will be no difference at all in conditions. The people who preach this doctrine are mere fanatics, and fanatics are indeed the sincerest of mankind. Christianity was preached just on the basis of the fascination of this fanaticism, and that is what made it so attractive to the Greek and the Roman slaves. They believed that under the millennial religion there would be no more slavery, that there would be plenty to eat and drink; and therefore, they flocked round the Christian standard. Those who preached the idea first were of course ignorant fanatics, but very sincere. In modern times this millennial aspiration takes the form of equality— of liberty, equality and fraternity. This is also fanaticism. True equality has never been and never can be on earth. How can we all be equal here? This impossible kind of equality implies total death. What makes this world what it is? Lost balance. In the primal state, which is called chaos, there is perfect balance. How do all the formative forces of the universe come then? By struggling, competition, conflict.

Suppose that all the particles of matter were held in equilibrium, would there be then any process of creation? We know from science that it is impossible. Disturb a sheet of water, and there you find every particle of the water trying to become calm again, one rushing against the other; and in the same way all the phenomena which we call the universe— all things therein— are struggling to get back to the state of perfect balance. Again a disturbance comes, and again we have combination and creation. Inequality is the very basis of creation. At the same time the forces struggling to obtain equality are as much a necessity of creation as those which destroy it.

Absolute equality, that which means a perfect balance of all the struggling forces in all the planes, can never be in this world. Before you attain that state, the world will have become quite unfit for any kind of life, and no one will be there. We find, therefore, that all these ideas of the millennium and of absolute equality are not only impossible but also that, if we try to carry them out, they will lead us surely enough to the day of destruction. What makes the difference between man and man? It is largely the difference in the brain. Nowadays no one but a lunatic will say that we are all born with the same brain power. We come into the world with unequal endowments; we come as greater men or as lesser men, and there is no getting away from that pre-natally determined condition. The American Indians were in this country for thousands of years, and a few handfuls of your ancestors came to their land. What difference have they caused in the appearance of the country! Why did not the Indians make improvements and build cities, if all were equal? With your ancestors a different sort of brain power came into the land, different bundles of past impressions came, and they worked out and manifested themselves. Absolute non-differentiation is death. So long as this world lasts, differentiation there will and must be, and the millennium of perfect equality will come only when a cycle of creation comes to its end. Before that equality cannot be. Yet this idea of realising the millennium is a great motive power. Just as inequality is necessary for creation itself, so the struggle to limit it is also necessary. If there were no struggle to become free and get back to God, there would be no creation either. It is the difference between these two forces that determines the nature of the motives of men. There will always be these motives to work, some tending towards bondage and others towards freedom.

This world's wheel within wheel is terrible mechanism; if we put our hands in it, as soon as we are caught we are gone. We all think that when we have done a certain duty, we shall be at rest; but before we have done a part of that duty another is already in waiting. We are all being dragged along by this mighty, complex world-machine. There are only two ways out of it; one is to give up all concern with the machine, to let it go and stand aside, to give up our desires. That is very easy to say, but is almost impossible to do. I do not know whether in twenty millions of men one can do that. The other way is to plunge into the world and learn the secret of work, and that is the way of Karma Yoga. Do not fly away from the wheels of the world-machine, but stand inside it and learn the secret of work. Through proper work done inside, it is also possible to come out. Through this machinery itself is the way out.

We have now seen what work is. It is a part of nature's foundation, and goes on always. Those that believe in God understand this better, because they know that God is not such an incapable being as will need our help. Although this universe will go on always, our goal is freedom; our goal is unselfishness; and according to Karma Yoga that goal is to be reached through work. All ideas of making the world perfectly happy may be good as motive powers for fanatics; but we must know that fanaticism brings forth as much evil as good. The Karma-Yogi asks why you require any motive to work other than the inborn love of freedom. Be beyond the common worthy motives; "To work you have the right, but not to the fruits thereof." Man can train himself to know and to practise that, says the Karma-Yogi. When the idea of doing good becomes a part of his very being, then he will not seek for any motive outside. Let us do good because it is good to do good; he who does good work even in order to get to heaven binds himself down, says the Karma-Yogi. Any work that is done with any the least selfish motive, instead of making us free, forges one more chain for our feet.

So the only way is to give up all the fruits of work, to be unattached to them. Know that this world is not we, nor are we this world; that we are really not the body; that we really do not work. We are the Self, eternally at rest and at peace. Why should we be bound by anything? It is very good to say that we should be perfectly nonattached, but what is the way to do it? Every good work we do without any ulterior motive, instead of forging a new chain, will break one of the links in the existing chains. Every good thought that we send to the world without thinking of any return, will be stored up there and break one link in the chain, and make us purer and purer, until we become the purest of mortals. Yet all this may seem to be rather quixotic and too philosophical, more theoretical than practical. I have read many arguments against the Bhagavad-Gita, and many have said that without motives you cannot work. They have never seen unselfish work except under the influence of fanaticism, and therefore they speak in that way.

Let me tell you in conclusion a few words about one man who actually carried this teaching of Karma Yoga into practice. That man is Buddha. He is the one man who ever carried this into perfect practice. All the prophets of the world, except Buddha, had external motives to move them to unselfish action. The prophets of the world, with this single exception, may be divided into two sets, one set holding that they are incarnations of God come down on earth, and the other holding that they are only messengers from God; and both draw their impetus for work from outside, expect reward from outside, however highly spiritual may be the language they use. But Buddha is the only prophet who said, "I do not care to know your various theories about God. What is the use of discussing all the subtle doctrines about the soul? Do good and be good. And this will take you to freedom and to whatever truth there is." He was, in the conduct of his life, absolutely without personal motives; and what man worked more than he? Show me in history one character who has soared so high above all. The whole human race has produced but one such character, such high philosophy, such wide sympathy. This great philosopher, preaching the highest philosophy, yet had the deepest sympathy for the lowest of animals, and never put forth any claims for himself. He is the ideal Karma-Yogi, acting entirely without motive, and the history of humanity shows him to have been the greatest man ever born; beyond compare the greatest combination of heart and brain that ever existed, the greatest soul-power that has ever been manifested. He is the first great reformer the world has seen. He was the first who dared to say, "Believe not because some old manuscripts are produced, believe not because it is your national belief, because you have been made to believe it from your childhood; but reason it all out, and after you have analysed it, then, if you find that it will do good to one and all believe it, live up to it, and help others to live up to it."

He works best who works without any motive, neither for money, nor for fame, nor for anything else; and when a man can do that, he will be a Buddha, and out of him will come the power to work in such a manner as will transform the world. This man represents the very highest ideal of Karma Yoga.

BHAKTI YOGA
THE PATH OF DEVOTION

Chapter I
Prayer

स तन्मयो ह्यमृत ईशसंस्थो ज्ञः सर्वगो भुवनस्यास्य गोप्ता।
य ईशेऽस्य जगतो नतियमेव नान्यो हेतुर्वदियत ईशनाय॥
यो ब्रह्माणां विदिधाति पूर्व यो वै वेदांश्च प्रहिणोति तस्मै।
तं ह देवं आत्मबुध्दप्रकाशं मुमुक्षुर्वे शरणमहं प्रपद्ये॥

*He is the Soul of the Universe; He is Immortal; His is the Rulership;
He is the All-knowing, the All-pervading, the Protector of the
Universe, the Eternal Ruler. None else is there efficient to govern the
world eternally. He who at the beginning of creation projected Brahmâ
(i.e. the universal consciousness), and who delivered the Vedas unto
him—seeking liberation I go for refuge unto that effulgent One, whose
light turns the understanding towards the Âtman.*

—Shvetâshvatara-Upanishad, VI. 17-18.

Definition Of Bhakti

Bhakti Yoga is a real, genuine search after the Lord, a search beginning, continuing, and ending in love. One single moment of the madness of extreme love to God brings us eternal freedom. "Bhakti", says Nârada in his explanation of the Bhakti-aphorisms, "is intense love to God"; "When a man gets it, he loves all, hates none; he becomes satisfied for ever"; "This love cannot be reduced to any earthly benefit", because so long as worldly desires last, that kind of love does not come; "Bhakti is greater than karma, greater than Yoga, because these are intended for an object in view, while Bhakti is its own fruition, its own means and its own end."

Bhakti has been the one constant theme of our sages. Apart from the special writers on Bhakti, such as Shândilya or Narada, the great commentators on the Vyâsa-Sutras, evidently advocates of knowledge (Jnâna), have also something very suggestive to say about love. Even when the commentator is anxious to explain many, if not all, of the texts so as to make them import a sort of dry knowledge, the Sutras, in the chapter on worship especially, do not lend themselves to be easily manipulated in that fashion.

There is not really so much difference between knowledge (Jnana) and love (Bhakti) as people sometimes imagine. We shall see, as we go on, that in the end they converge and meet at the same point. So also is it with Râja-Yoga, which when pursued as a means to attain liberation, and not (as unfortunately it frequently becomes in the hands of charlatans and mystery-mongers) as an instrument to hoodwink the unwary, leads us also to the same goal.

The one great advantage of Bhakti is that it is the easiest and the most natural way to reach the great divine end in view; its great disadvantage is that in its lower forms it oftentimes degenerates into hideous fanaticism. The fanatical crew in Hinduism, or Mohammedanism, or Christianity, have always been almost exclusively recruited from these worshippers on the lower planes of Bhakti. That singleness of attachment (Nishthâ) to a loved object, without which no genuine love can grow, is very often also the cause of the denunciation of everything else. All the weak and undeveloped minds in every religion or country have only one way of loving their own ideal, i.e. by hating every other ideal. Herein is the explanation of why the same man who is so lovingly attached to his own ideal of God, so devoted to his own ideal of religion, becomes a howling fanatic as soon as he sees or hears anything of any other ideal. This kind of love is somewhat like the canine instinct of guarding the master's property from intrusion; only, the instinct of the dog is better than the reason of man, for the dog never mistakes its master for an enemy in whatever dress he may come before it. Again, the fanatic loses all power of judgment. Personal considerations are in his case of such absorbing interest that to him it is no question at all what a man says — whether it is right or wrong; but the one thing he is always particularly careful to know is who says it. The same man who is kind, good, honest, and loving to people of his own opinion, will not hesitate to do the vilest deeds when they are directed against persons beyond the pale of his own religious brotherhood.

But this danger exists only in that stage of Bhakti which is called the preparatory (Gauni). When Bhakti has become ripe and has passed into that form which is called the supreme (Parâ), no more is there any fear of these hideous manifestations of fanaticism; that soul which is overpowered by this higher form of Bhakti is too near the God of Love to become an instrument for the diffusion of hatred.

It is not given to all of us to be harmonious in the building up of our characters in this life : yet we know that, that character is of the noblest type in which all these three — knowledge and love and Yoga — are harmoniously fused. Three things are necessary for a bird to fly — the two wings and the tail as a rudder for steering. Jnana (Knowledge) is the one wing, Bhakti (Love) is the other, and Yoga is the tail that keeps up the balance. For those who cannot pursue all these three forms of worship together in harmony and take up, therefore, Bhakti alone as their way, it is necessary always to remember that forms and ceremonials, though absolutely necessary for the progressive soul, have no other value than taking us on to that state in which we feel the most intense love to God.

There is a little difference in opinion between the teachers of knowledge and those of love, though both admit the power of Bhakti. The Jnanis hold Bhakti to be an instrument of liberation, the Bhaktas look upon it both as the instrument and the thing to be attained. To my mind this is a distinction without much difference. In fact, Bhakti, when used as an instrument, really means a lower form of worship, and the higher form becomes inseparable from the lower form of realisation at a later stage. Each seems to lay a great stress upon his own peculiar method of worship, forgetting that with perfect love true knowledge is bound to come even unsought, and that from perfect knowledge true love is inseparable.

Bearing this in mind let us try to understand what the great Vedantic commentators have to say on the subject. In explaining the Sutra Âvrittirasakridupadeshât[1], Bhagavân Shankara says, "Thus people say, 'He is devoted to the king, he is devoted to the Guru'; they say this of him who follows his Guru, and does so,

having that following as the one end in view. Similarly they say, 'The loving wife
meditates on her loving husband'; here also a kind of eager and continuous remembrance is meant."This is devotion according to Shankara.

"Meditation again is a constant remembrance (of the thing meditated upon,
flowing like an unbroken stream of oil poured out from one vessel to another.
When this kind of remembering has been attained (in relation to God) all bandages break. Thus it is spoken of in the scriptures regarding constant remembering as a means to liberation. This remembering again is of the same form as
seeing, because it is of the same meaning as in the passage, 'When He who is
far and near is seen, the bonds of the heart are broken, all doubts vanish, and all
effects of work disappear' He who is near can be seen, but he who is far can only
be remembered. Nevertheless the scripture says that he have to see Him who is
near as well as Him who, is far, thereby indicating to us that the above kind of
remembering is as good as seeing. This remembrance when exalted assumes the
same form as seeing... Worship is constant remembering as may be seen from
the essential texts of scriptures. Knowing, which is the same as repeated worship,
has been described as constant remembering... Thus the memory, which has attained to the height of what is as good as direct perception, is spoken of in the
Shruti as a means of liberation. 'This Atman is not to be reached through various sciences, nor by intellect, nor by much study of the Vedas. Whomsoever this
Atman desires, by him is the Atman attained, unto him this Atman discover
Himself.' Here, after saying that mere hearing, thinking and meditating are no
the means of attaining this Atman, it is said, 'Whom this Atman desires, by him
the Atman is attained.' The extremely beloved is desired; by whomsoever this
Atman is extremely beloved, he becomes the most beloved of the Atman. So tha
this beloved may attain the Atman, the Lord Himself helps. For it has been said
by the Lord: 'Those who are constantly attached to Me and worship Me with
love—I give that direction to their will by which they come to Me.' Therefore
it is said that, to whomsoever this remembering, which is of the same form as
direct perception, is very dear, because it is dear to the Object of such memory
perception, he is desired by the Supreme Atman, by him the Supreme Atman
is attained. This constant remembrance is denoted by the word Bhakti." So says
Bhagavân Râmânuja in his commentary on the Sutra Athâto Brahma-jijnâsâ[2]

In commenting on the Sutra of Patanjali, Ishvara pranidhânâdvâ, i.e. "Or by the
worship of the Supreme Lord"—Bhoja says, "Pranidhâna is that sort of Bhakti
in which, without seeking results, such as sense-enjoyments etc., all works are
dedicated to that Teacher of teachers." Bhagavan Vyâsa also, when commenting

on the same, defines Pranidhana as "the form of Bhakti by which the mercy of the Supreme Lord comes to the Yogi, and blesses him by granting him his desires". According to Shândilya, "Bhakti is intense love to God." The best definition is, however, that given by the king of Bhaktas, Prahlâda:

या प्रीतिरविविकानां विषयेष्वनपायिनी।त्वामनुस्मरतः सा मे हृदयान्मापसर्पतु॥

That deathless love which the ignorant have for the fleeting objects of the senses — as I keep meditating on Thee — may not that love slip away from my heart!

Love! For whom? For the Supreme Lord Ishvara. Love for any other being, however great cannot be Bhakti; for, as Ramanuja says in his Shri Bhâshya, quoting an ancient Âchârya, i.e. a great teacher:

आब्रह्मस्तम्बपर्यन्ताः जगदन्तर्व्यवस्थिताः। पुराणानि
कर्मजनितिसंसारवश्ववर्तनिः॥यतस्ततो न ते ध्याने ध्यानिनामुपकारकाः।
अवदियान्तर्गतास्सर्वे ते हि संसारगोचराः॥

From Brahmâ to a clump of grass, all things that live in the world are slaves of birth and death caused by Karma; therefore they cannot be helpful as objects of meditation, because they are all in ignorance and subject to change.

In commenting on the word Anurakti used by Shandilya, the commentator Svapneshvara says that it means Anu, after, and Rakti, attachment; i.e. the attachment which comes after the knowledge of the nature and glory of God; else a blind attachment to any one, e.g. to wife or children, would be Bhakti. We plainly see, therefore, that Bhakti is a series or succession of mental efforts at religious realisation beginning with ordinary worship and ending in a supreme intensity of love for Ishvara.

Notes:

1- Meditation is necessary, that having been often enjoined.
2- Hence follows a dissertation on Brahman.

Chapter II
The Philosophy of Ishvara

Who is Ishvara? Janmâdyasya yatah — "From whom is the birth, continuation, and dissolution of the universe," — He is Ishvara — "the Eternal, the Pure, the Ever-Free, the Almighty, the All-Knowing, the All-Merciful, the Teacher of all teachers"; and above all, Sa Ishvarah anirvachaniya-premasvarupah — "He the Lord is, of His own nature, inexpressible Love." These certainly are the definitions of a Personal God. Are there then two Gods — the "Not this, not this," the Sat-chit-ânanda, the Existence-Knowledge-Bliss of the philosopher, and this God of Love of the Bhakta? No, it is the same Sat-chit-ananda who is also the God of Love, the impersonal and personal in one. It has always to be understood that the Personal God worshipped by the Bhakta is not separate or different from the Brahman. All is Brahman, the One without a second; only the Brahman, as unity or absolute, is too much of an abstraction to be loved and worshipped; so the Bhakta chooses the relative aspect of Brahman, that is, Ishvara, the Supreme Ruler. To use a simile: Brahman is as the clay or substance out of which an infinite variety of articles are fashioned. As clay, they are all one; but form or manifestation differentiates them. Before every one of them was made, they all existed potentially in the clay, and, of course, they are identical substantially; but when formed, and so long as the form remains, they are separate and different; the clay-mouse can never become a clay-elephant, because, as manifestations, form alone makes them what they are, though as unformed clay they are all one. Ishvara is the highest manifestation of the Absolute Reality, or in other words, the highest possible reading of the Absolute by the human mind. Creation is eternal, and so also is Ishvara.

In the fourth Pâda of the fourth chapter of his Sutras, after stating the almost infinite power and knowledge which will come to the liberated soul after the attainment of Moksha, Vyâsa makes the remark, in an aphorism, that none, however, will get the power of creating, ruling, and dissolving the universe, because that belongs to God alone. In explaining the Sutra it is easy for the dualistic commentators to show how it is ever impossible for a subordinate soul, Jiva, to have the infinite power and total independence of God. The thorough dualistic commentator Madhvâchârya deals with this passage in his usual summary method by quoting a verse from the Varâha Purâna.

In explaining this aphorism the commentator Râmânuja says, "This doubt being raised, whether among the powers of the liberated souls is included that unique power of the Supreme One, that is, of creation etc. of the universe and even the Lordship of all, or whether, without that, the glory of the liberated consists only in the direct perception of the Supreme One, we get as an argument the following : It is reasonable that the liberated get the Lordship of the universe, because the scriptures say, 'He attains to extreme sameness with the Supreme One and all his desires are realised.' Now extreme sameness and realisation of all desires cannot be attained without the unique power of the Supreme Lord, namely, that of governing the universe. Therefore, to attain the realisation of all desires and the extreme sameness with the Supreme, we must all admit that the liberated get the power of ruling the whole universe. To this we reply, that the liberated get all the powers except that of ruling the universe. Ruling the universe is guiding the form and the life and the desires of all the sentient and the non-sentient beings. The liberated ones from whom all that veils His true nature has been removed, only enjoy the unobstructed perception of the Brahman, but do not possess the power of ruling the universe. This is proved from the scriptural text, " From whom all these things are born, by which all that are born live, unto whom they, departing, return—ask about it. That is Brahman.' If this quality of ruling the universe be a quality common even to the liberated then this text would not apply as a definition of Brahman defining Him through His ruler-ship of the universe. The uncommon attributes alone define a thing ; therefore in texts like—'My beloved boy, alone, in the beginning there existed the One without a second. That saw and felt, "I will give birth to the many." That projected heat.'—'Brahman indeed alone existed in the beginning. That One evolved. That projected a blessed form, the Kshatra. All these gods are Kshatras : Varuna, Soma, Rudra, Parjanya, Yama, Mrityu, Ishâna.'—'Atman indeed existed alone in the beginning ; nothing else vibrated ; He thought of projecting the world ; He projected the world after.'—'Alone Nârâyana existed ; neither Brahmâ, nor Ishana, nor the Dyâvâ-Prithivi, nor the stars, nor water, nor fire, nor Soma, nor the sun. He did not take pleasure alone. He after His meditation had one daughter, the ten organs, etc.'—and in others as, 'Who living in the earth is separate from the earth, who living in the Atman, etc.'—the Shrutis speak of the Supreme One as the subject of the work of ruling the universe... Nor in these descriptions of the ruling of the universe is there any position for the liberated soul, by which such a soul may have the ruling of the universe ascribed to it."

In explaining the next Sutra, Râmânuja says, "If you say it is not so, because there are direct texts in the Vedas in evidence to the contrary, these texts refer to the glory of the liberated in the spheres of the subordinate deities." This also is an easy solution of the difficulty. Although the system of Ramanuja admits the unity of the total, within that totality of existence there are, according to him, eternal differences. Therefore, for all practical purposes, this system also being dualistic, it was easy for Ramanuja to keep the distinction between the personal soul and the Personal God very clear.

We shall now try to understand what the great representative of the Advaita School has to say on the point. We shall see how the Advaita system maintains all the hopes and aspirations of the dualist intact, and at the same time propounds its own solution of the problem in consonance with the high destiny of divine humanity. Those who aspire to retain their individual mind even after liberation and to remain distinct will have ample opportunity of realising their aspirations and enjoying the blessing of the qualified Brahman. These are they who have been spoken of in the Bhâgavata Purâna thus: "O king, such are the, glorious qualities of the Lord that the sages whose only pleasure is in the Self, and from whom all fetters have fallen off, even they love the Omnipresent with the love that is for love's sake." These are they who are spoken of by the Sânkhyas as getting merged in nature in this cycle, so that, after attaining perfection, they may come out in the next as lords of world-systems. But none of these ever becomes equal to God (Ishvara). Those who attain to that state where there is neither creation, nor created, nor creator, where there is neither knower, nor knowable, nor knowledge, where there is neither I, nor thou, nor he, where there is neither subject, nor object, nor relation, "there, who is seen by whom?"—such persons have gone beyond everything to "where words cannot go nor mind", gone to that which the Shrutis declare as "Not this, not this"; but for those who cannot, or will not reach this state, there will inevitably remain the triune vision of the one undifferentiated Brahman as nature, soul, and the interpenetrating sustainer of both—Ishvara. So, when Prahlâda forgot himself, he found neither the universe nor its cause; all was to him one Infinite, undifferentiated by name and form; but as soon as he remembered that he was Prahlada, there was the universe before him and with it the Lord of the universe—"the Repository of an infinite number of blessed qualities". So it was with the blessed Gopis. So long as they had lost sense of their own personal identity and individuality, they were all Krishnas, and when they began again to think of Him as the One to be worshipped, then they were Gopis again, and immediately

तासामाविरभूच्छौरिः स्मयमानमुखाम्बुजः।पीताम्बरधरः स्तरग्वी
साखान्मन्मथमन्मथः॥ (Bhagavata)

Unto them appeared Krishna with a smile on His lotus face, clad in yellow robes
and having garlands on, the embodied conqueror (in beauty) of the god of love.

Now to go back to our Acharya Shankara : "Those", he says, "who by worshipping the qualified Brahman attain conjunction with the Supreme Ruler, preserv-
ing their own mind—is their glory limited or unlimited ? This doubt arising,
we get as an argument : Their glory should be unlimited because of the scriptural texts, 'They attain their own kingdom', 'To him all the gods offer worship',
Their desires are fulfilled in all the worlds'. As an answer to this, Vyasa writes,
Without the power of ruling the universe.' Barring the power of creation etc. of
the universe, the other powers such as Animâ etc. are acquired by the liberated.
As to ruling the universe, that belongs to the eternally perfect Ishvara. Why ?
Because He is the subject of all the scriptural texts as regards creation etc., and
the liberated souls are not mentioned therein in any connection whatsoever. The
Supreme Lord indeed is alone engaged in ruling the universe. The texts as to
creation etc. all point to Him. Besides, there is given the adjective 'ever-perfect'.
Also the scriptures say that the powers Anima etc. of the others are from the
search after and the worship of God. Therefore they have no place in the ruling of the universe. Again, on account of their possessing their own minds, it is
possible that their wills may differ, and that, whilst one desires creation, another
may desire destruction. The only way of avoiding this conflict is to make all wills
subordinate to some one will. Therefore the conclusion is that the wills of the
liberated are dependent on the will of the Supreme Ruler."
Bhakti, then, can be directed towards Brahman, only in His personal aspect.

क्लेशोऽधिकितरस्तेषामव्यक्तासक्तचेतसाम्
The way is more difficult for those whose mind is attached to the Absolute!

Bhakti has to float on smoothly with the current of our nature. True it is that
we cannot have; any idea of the Brahman which is not anthropomorphic, but is
it not equally true of everything we know ? The greatest psychologist the world
has ever known, Bhagavan Kapila, demonstrated ages ago that human consciousness is one of the elements in the make-up of all the objects of our per-

ception and conception, internal as well as external. Beginning with our bodies and going up to Ishvara, we may see that every object of our perception is this consciousness plus something else, whatever that may be; and this unavoidable mixture is what we ordinarily think of as reality. Indeed it is, and ever will be, all of the reality that is possible for the human mind to know. Therefore to say that Ishvara is unreal, because He is anthropomorphic, is sheer nonsense. It sounds very much like the occidentals squabble on idealism and realism, which fearful-looking quarrel has for its foundation a mere play on the word "real". The idea of Ishvara covers all the ground ever denoted and connoted by the word real, and Ishvara is as real as anything else in the universe; and after all, the word real means nothing more than what has now been pointed out. Such is our philosophical conception of Ishvara.

Chapter III
Spiritual Realisation, the Aim of Bhakti Yoga

To the Bhakta these dry details are necessary only to strengthen his will; beyond that they are of no use to him. For he is treading on a path which is fitted very soon to lead him beyond the hazy and turbulent regions of reason, to lead him to the realm of realisation. He, soon, through the mercy of the Lord, reaches a plane where pedantic and powerless reason is left far behind, and the mere intellectual groping through the dark gives place to the daylight of direct perception. He no more reasons and believes, he almost perceives. He no more argues, he senses. And is not this seeing God, and feeling God, and enjoying God higher than everything else? Nay, Bhaktas have not been wanting who have maintained that it is higher than even Moksha — liberation. And is it not also the highest utility? There are people — and a good many of them too — in the world who are convinced that only that is of use and utility which brings to man creature-comforts. Even religion, God, eternity, soul, none of these is of any use to them, as they do not bring them money or physical comfort. To such, all those things which do not go to gratify the senses and appease the appetites are of no utility. In every mind, utility, however, is conditioned by its own peculiar wants. To men, therefore, who never rise higher than eating, drinking, begetting progeny, and dying, the only gain is in sense enjoyments; and they must wait and go through many more births and reincarnations to learn to feel even the faintest necessity for anything higher. But those to whom the eternal interests of the soul are of much higher value than the fleeting interests of this mundane life, to whom the gratification of the senses is but like the thoughtless play of the baby, to them God and the love of God form the highest and the only utility of human existence. Thank God there are some such still living in this world of too much worldliness.

Bhakti Yoga, as we have said, is divided into the Gauni or the preparatory, and the Parâ or the supreme forms. We shall find, as we go on, how in the preparatory stage we unavoidably stand in need of many concrete helps to enable us to get on; and indeed the mythological and symbological parts of all religions are natural growths which early environ the aspiring soul and help it Godward. It is also a significant fact that spiritual giants have been produced only in those systems of religion where there is an exuberant growth of rich mythology and ritualism. The dry fanatical forms of religion which attempt to eradicate all that is poetical, all that is beautiful and sublime, all that gives a firm grasp to the infant mind tottering in its Godward way—the forms which attempt to break down the very ridge-poles of the spiritual roof, and in their ignorant and superstitious conceptions of truth try to drive away all that is life-giving, all that furnishes the formative material to the spiritual plant growing in the human soul—such forms of religion too soon find that all that is left to them is but an empty shell, a contentless frame of words and sophistry with perhaps a little flavour of a kind of social scavengering or the so-called spirit of reform.

The vast mass of those whose religion is like this, are conscious or unconscious materialists—the end and aim of their lives here and hereafter being enjoyment, which indeed is to them the alpha and the omega of human life, and which is their Ishtâpurta; work like street-cleaning and scavengering, intended for the material comfort of man is, according to them, the be-all and end-all of human existence; and the sooner the followers of this curious mixture of ignorance and fanaticism come out in their true colours and join, as they well deserve to do, the ranks of atheists and materialists, the better will it be for the world. One ounce of the practice of righteousness and of spiritual Self-realisation outweighs tons and tons of frothy talk and nonsensical sentiments. Show us one, but one gigantic spiritual genius growing out of all this dry dust of ignorance and fanaticism; and if you cannot, close your mouths, open the windows of your hearts to the clear light of truth, and sit like children at the feet of those who know what they are talking about—the sages of India. Let us then listen attentively to what they say.

Chapter IV
The Need of Guru

Every soul is destined to be perfect, and every being, in the end, will attain the state of perfection. Whatever we are now is the result of our acts and thoughts in the past; and whatever we shall be in the future will be the result of what we think end do now. But this, the shaping of our own destinies, does not preclude our receiving help from outside; nay, in the vast majority of cases such help is absolutely necessary. When it comes, the higher powers and possibilities of the soul are quickened, spiritual life is awakened, growth is animated, and man becomes holy and perfect in the end.

This quickening impulse cannot be derived from books. The soul can only receive impulses from another soul, and from nothing else. We may study books all our lives, we may become very intellectual, but in the end we find that we have not developed at all spiritually. It is not true that a high order of intellectual development always goes hand in hand with a proportionate development of the spiritual side in Man. In studying books we are sometimes deluded into thinking that thereby we are being spiritually helped; but if we analyse the effect of the study of books on ourselves, we shall find that at the utmost it is only our intellect that derives profit from such studies, and not our inner spirit. This inadequacy of books to quicken spiritual growth is the reason why, although almost every one of us can speak most wonderfully on spiritual matters, when it comes to action and the living of a truly spiritual life, we find ourselves so awfully deficient. To quicken the spirit, the impulse must come from another soul.

The person from whose soul such impulse comes is called the Guru—the teacher; and the person to whose soul the impulse is conveyed is called the Shishya—the student. To convey such an impulse to any soul, in the first place, the soul from which it proceeds must possess the power of transmitting it, as it were, to another; and in the second place, the soul to which it is transmitted must be fit to receive it. The seed must be a living seed, and the field must be ready ploughed; and when both these conditions are fulfilled, a wonderful growth of genuine religion takes place. "The true preacher of religion has to be of wonderful capabilities, and clever shall his hearer be" आश्चर्यो वक्ता कुशलोऽस्य

लब्धा—and when both of these are really wonderful and extraordinary, then will a splendid spiritual awakening result, and not otherwise. Such alone are the real teachers, and such alone are also the real students, the real aspirants. All others are only playing with spirituality. They have just a little curiosity awakened, just a little intellectual aspiration kindled in them, but are merely standing on the outward fringe of the horizon of religion. There is no doubt some value even in that, as it may in course of time result in the awakening of a real thirst for religion; and it is a mysterious law of nature that as soon as the field is ready, the seed must and does come; as soon as the soul earnestly desires to have religion, the transmitter of the religious force must and does appear to help that soul. When the power that attracts the light of religion in the receiving soul is full and strong, the power which answers to that attraction and sends in light does come as a matter of course.

There are, however, certain great dangers in the way. There is, for instance, the danger to the receiving soul of its mistaking momentary emotions for real religious yearning. We may study that in ourselves. Many a time in our lives, somebody dies whom we loved; we receive a blow; we feel that the world is slipping between our fingers, that we want something surer and higher, and that we must become religious. In a few days that wave of feeling has passed away, and we are left stranded just where we were before. We are all of us often mistaking such impulses for real thirst after religion; but as long as these momentary emotions are thus mistaken, that continuous, real craving of the soul for religion will not come, and we shall not find the true transmitter of spirituality into our nature. So whenever we are tempted to complain of our search after the truth that we desire so much, proving vain, instead of so complaining, our first duty ought to be to look into our own souls and find whether the craving in the heart is real. Then in the vast majority of cases it would be discovered that we were not fit for receiving the truth, that there was no real thirst for spirituality.

There are still greater dangers in regard to the transmitter, the Guru. There are many who, though immersed in ignorance, yet, in the pride of their hearts, fancy they know everything, and not only do not stop there, but offer to take others on their shoulders; and thus the blind leading the blind, both fall into the ditch.

अविद्यायामन्तरे वर्तमानाः स्वयं धीराः पण्डितम्मन्यमानाः । दन्द्रम्यमाणाः
परियन्ति मूढा अन्धेनैव नीयमाना यथान्धाः ॥

Fools dwelling in darkness, wise in their own conceit, and puffed up with vain knowledge, go round and round staggering to and fro, like blind men led by the blind. (Katha Up., I. ii. 5).

The world is full of these. Every one wants to be a teacher, every beggar wants to make a gift of a million dollars! Just as these beggars are ridiculous, so are these teachers.

Chapter V
Qualifications of the Aspirant and the Teacher

How are we to know a teacher, then? The sun requires no torch to make him visible, we need not light a candle in order to see him. When the sun rises, we instinctively become aware of the fact, and when a teacher of men comes to help us, the soul will instinctively know that truth has already begun to shine upon it. Truth stands on its own evidence, it does not require any other testimony to prove it true, it is self effulgent. It penetrates into the innermost corners of our nature, and in its presence the whole universe stands up and says, "This is truth." The teachers whose wisdom and truth shine like the light of the sun are the very greatest the world has known, and they are worshipped as God by the major portion of mankind. But we may get help from comparatively lesser ones also; only we ourselves do not possess intuition enough to judge properly of the man from whom we receive teaching and guidance; so there ought to be certain tests, certain conditions, for the teacher to satisfy, as there are also for the taught.

The conditions necessary for the taught are purity, a real thirst after knowledge, and perseverance. No impure soul can be really religious. Purity in thought, speech, and act is absolutely necessary for any one to be religious. As to the thirst after knowledge, it is an old law that we all get whatever we want. None of us can get anything other than what we fix our hearts upon. To pant for religion truly is a very difficult thing, not at all so easy as we generally imagine. Hearing religious talks or reading religious books is no proof yet of a real want felt in the heart; there must be a continuous struggle, a constant fight, an unremitting grappling with our lower nature, till the higher want is actually felt and the victory is achieved. It is not a question of one or two days, of years, or of lives; the struggle may have to go on for hundreds of lifetimes. The success sometimes may come immediately, but we must be ready to wait patiently even for what may look like an infinite length of time. The student who sets out with such a spirit of perseverance will surely find success and realisation at last.

In regard to the teacher, we must see that he knows the spirit of the scriptures. The whole world reads Bibles, Vedas, and Korans; but they are all only words, syntax, etymology, philology, the dry bones of religion. The teacher who deals too much in words and allows the mind to be carried away by the force of words loses the spirit. It is the knowledge of the spirit of the scriptures alone that constitutes the true religious teacher. The network of the words of the scriptures is like a huge forest in which the human mind often loses itself and finds no way out.

शब्दजालं महारण्यं चित्तभ्रमणकारणम्।

The network of words is a big forest; it is the cause of a curious wandering of the mind.

The various methods of joining words, the various methods of speaking in beautiful language, the various methods of explaining the diction of the scriptures are only for the disputations and enjoyment of the learned, they do not conduce to the development of spiritual perception.

वाग्वैखरी शब्दझरी शास्त्रव्याख्यानकौशलम्। वैदुष्यं विदुषां तद्वद् भुक्तये न तु मुक्तये॥

Those who employ such methods to impart religion to others are only desirous to show off their learning, so that the world may praise them as great scholars.

You will find that no one of the great teachers of the world ever went into these various explanations of the text; there is with them no attempt at "text-torturing", no eternal playing upon the meaning of words and their roots. Yet they nobly taught, while others who have nothing to teach have taken up a word sometimes and written a three-volume book on its origin, on the man who used it first, and on what that man was accustomed to eat, and how long he slept, and so on. Bhagavân Ramakrishna used to tell a story of some men who went into a mango orchard and busied themselves in counting the leaves, the twigs, and the branches, examining their colour, comparing their size, and noting down everything most carefully, and then got up a learned discussion on each of these topics, which were undoubtedly highly interesting to them. But one of them, more sensible than the others, did not care for all these things, and instead thereof, began to eat the mango fruit. And was he not wise? So leave this counting of leaves and twigs and note-taking to others. This kind of work has its proper place, but not here in the spiritual domain. You never see a strong spiritual man among these "leaf counters". Religion, the highest aim, the highest glory of man, does not require so much labour. If you want to be a Bhakta, it is not at all necessary for you to know whether Krishna was born in Mathurâ or in Vraja, what he was doing, or just the exact date on which he pronounced the teachings of the Gitä. You only require to feel the craving for the beautiful lessons of duty and love in the Gita. All the other particulars about it and its author are for the enjoyment of the learned. Let them have what they desire. Say "Shântih, Shântih" to their learned controversies, and let us "eat the mangoes".

The second condition necessary in the teacher is — sinlessness. The question is often asked, "Why should we look into the character and personality of a teacher? We have only to judge of what he says, and take that up." This is not right. If a man wants to teach me something of dynamics, or chemistry, or any other physical science, he may be anything he likes, because what the physical sciences require is merely an intellectual equipment; but in the spiritual sciences it is impossible from first to last that there can be any spiritual light in the soul that is impure. What religion can an impure man teach? The sine qua non of acquiring spiritual truth for one's self or for imparting it to others is the purity of heart and soul. A vision of God or a glimpse of the beyond never comes until the soul is pure. Hence with the teacher of religion we must see first what he is, and then what he says. He must be perfectly pure, and then alone comes the value of his words, because he is only then the true "transmitter". What can he transmit if he has not spiritual power in himself? There must be the worthy vibration of spirituality in the mind of the teacher, so that it may be sympathetically conveyed to the mind of the taught. The function of the teacher is indeed an affair of the transference of something, and not one of mere stimulation of the existing intellectual or other faculties in the taught. Something real and appreciable as an influence comes from the teacher and goes to the taught. Therefore the teacher must be pure.

The third condition is in regard to the motile. The teacher must not teach with any ulterior selfish motive — for money, name, or fame; his work must be simply out of love, out of pure love for mankind at large. The only medium through which spiritual force can be transmitted is love. Any selfish motive, such as the desire for gain or for name, will immediately destroy this conveying median. God is love, and only he who has known God as love can be a teacher of godliness and God to man.

When you see that in your teacher these conditions are all fulfilled, you are safe; if they are not, it is unsafe to allow yourself to be taught by him, for there is the great danger that, if he cannot convey goodness to your heart, he may convey wickedness. This danger must by all means be guarded against.

श्रोत्रियोऽवृजिनोऽकामहतो यो ब्रह्मवित्तमः

*He who is learned in the scriptures, sinless, unpolluted by lust, and is the
greatest knower of the Brahman, is the real teacher.*

From what has been said, it naturally follows that we cannot be taught to love, appreciate, and assimilate religion everywhere and by everybody. The "books in the running brooks, sermons in stones, and good in everything" is all very true as a poetical figure: but nothing can impart to a man a single grain of truth unless he has the undeveloped germs of it in himself. To whom do the stones and brooks preach sermons? To the human soul, the lotus of whose inner holy shrine is already quick with life. And the light which causes the beautiful opening out of this lotus comes always from the good and wise teacher. When the heart has thus been opened, it becomes fit to receive teaching from the stones or the brooks, the stars, or the sun, or the moon, or from any thing which has its existence in our divine universe; but the unopened heart will see in them nothing but mere stones or mere brooks. A blind man may go to a museum, but he will not profit by it in any way; his eyes must be opened first, and then alone he will be able to learn what the things in the museum can teach.

This eye-opener of the aspirant after religion is the teacher. With the teacher, therefore, our relationship is the same as that between an ancestor and his descendant. Without faith, humility, submission, and veneration in our hearts towards our religious teacher, there cannot be any growth of religion in us; and it is a significant fact that, where this kind of relation between the teacher and the taught prevails, there alone gigantic spiritual men are growing; while in those countries which have neglected to keep up this kind of relation the religious teacher has become a mere lecturer, the teacher expecting his five dollars and the person taught expecting his brain to be filled with the teacher's words, and each going his own way after this much has been done. Under such circumstances spirituality becomes almost an unknown quantity. There is none to transmit it and none to have it transmitted to. Religion with such people becomes business; they think they can obtain it with their dollars. Would to God that religion could be obtained so easily! But unfortunately it cannot be.

Religion, which is the highest knowledge and the highest wisdom, cannot be bought, nor can it be acquired from books. You may thrust your head into all the corners of the world, you may explore the Himalayas, the Alps, and the Caucasus, you may sound the bottom of the sea and pry into every nook of Tibet and the desert of Gobi, you will not find it anywhere until your heart is ready for receiving it and your teacher has come. And when that divinely appointed teacher comes serve him with childlike confidence and simplicity, freely open your heart to his influence, and see in him God manifested. Those who come to seek truth with such a spirit of love and veneration, to them the Lord of Truth reveals the most wonderful things regarding truth, goodness, and beauty.

Chapter VI
Incarnate Teachers and Incarnation

Wherever His name is spoken, that very place is holy. How much more so is the man who speaks His name, and with what veneration ought we to approach that man out of whom comes to us spiritual truth! Such great teachers of spiritual truth are indeed very few in number in this world, but the world is never altogether without them. They are always the fairest flowers of human life — अहेतुकदयासिन्धुः — *the ocean of mercy without any motive.*

आचार्यं मां विजानीयात्
Know the Guru to be Me

says Shri Krishna in the Bhagavata.

The moment the world is absolutely bereft of these, it becomes a hideous hell and hastens on to its destruction.

Higher and nobler than all ordinary ones are another set of teachers, the Avatâras of Ishvara, in the world. They can transmit spirituality with a touch, even with a mere wish. The lowest and the most degraded characters become in one second saints at their command. They are the Teachers of all teachers, the highest manifestations of God through man. We cannot see God except through them. We cannot help worshipping them; and indeed they are the only ones whom we are bound to worship.

No man can really see God except through these human manifestations. If we try to see God otherwise, we make for ourselves a hideous caricature of Him and believe the caricature to be no worse than the original. There is a story of an ignorant man who was asked to make an image of the God Shiva, and who, after days of hard struggle, manufactured only the image of a monkey. So whenever we try to think of God as He is in His absolute perfection, we invariably meet with the most miserable failure, because as long as we are men, we cannot conceive Him as anything higher than man. The time will come when we shall transcend our human nature and know Him as He is; but as long as we are men, we must worship Him in man and as man. Talk as you may, try as you may, you

cannot think of God except as a man. You may deliver great intellectual dis
courses on God and on all things under the sun, become great rationalists and
prove to your satisfaction that all these accounts of the Avataras of God as man
are nonsense. But let us come for a moment to practical common sense. What
is there behind this kind of remarkable intellect? Zero, nothing, simply so much
froth. When next you hear a man delivering a great intellectual lecture against
this worship of the Avataras of God, get hold of him and ask what his idea of
God is, what he understands by "omnipotence", "omnipresence", and all simi
lar terms, beyond the spelling of the words. He really means nothing by them,
he cannot formulate as their meaning any idea unaffected by his own human
nature; he is no better off in this matter than the man in the street who has not
read a single book. That man in the street, however, is quiet and does not dis
turb the peace of the world, while this big talker creates disturbance and misery
among mankind. Religion is, after all, realisation, and we must make the sharpest
distinction between talk; and intuitive experience. What we experience in the
depths of our souls is realisation. Nothing indeed is so uncommon as common
sense in regard to this matter.

By our present constitution we are limited and bound to see God as man. If,
for instance the buffaloes want to worship God, they will, in keeping with their
own nature, see Him as a huge buffalo; if a fish wants to worship God, it will
have to form an Idea of Him as a big fish, and man has to think of Him as man.
And these various conceptions are not due to morbidly active imagination. Man,
the buffalo, and the fish all may be supposed to represent so many different ves
sels, so to say. All these vessels go to the sea of God to get filled with water, each
according to its own shape and capacity; in the man the water takes the shape
of man, in the buffalo, the shape of a buffalo and in the fish, the shape of a fish.
In each of these vessels there is the same water of the sea of God. When men
see Him, they see Him as man, and the animals, if they have any conception of
God at all, must see Him as animal each according to its own ideal. So we can
not help seeing God as man, and, therefore, we are bound to worship Him as
man. There is no other way.

Two kinds of men do not worship God as man—the human brute who has
no religion, and the Paramahamsa who has risen beyond all the weaknesses of
humanity and has transcended the limits of his own human nature. To him all
nature has become his own Self. He alone can worship God as He is. Here, too,
as in all other cases, the two extremes meet. The extreme of ignorance and the
other extreme of knowledge—neither of these go through acts of worship. The

human brute does not worship because of his ignorance, and the Jivanmuktas (free souls) do not worship because they have realised God in themselves. Being between these two poles of existence, if any one tells you that he is not going to worship God as man, take kindly care of that man; he is, not to use any harsher term, an irresponsible talker; his religion is for unsound and empty brains.

God understands human failings and becomes man to do good to humanity:

यदा यदा हि धर्मस्य ग्लानिर्भवति भारत। अभ्युत्थानमधर्मस्य तदात्मानं
सृजाम्यहम्॥ परित्राणाय साधूनां विनाशाय च दुष्कृताम्। धर्मसंस्थापनार्थाय
समभवामि युगे युगे॥

Whenever virtue subsides and wickedness prevails, I manifest Myself. To establish virtue, to destroy evil, to save the good I come from Yuga (age) to Yuga.

अवजानन्ति मां मूढा मानुषीं तनुमाश्रितम्।परं भावमजानन्तो मम भूतमहेश्वरम्॥
Fools deride Me who have assumed the human form, without knowing My real nature as the Lord of the universe.

Such is Shri Krishna's declaration in the Gita on Incarnation. "When a huge tidal wave comes," says Bhagavan Shri Ramakrishna, "all the little brooks and ditches become full to the brim without any effort or consciousness on their own part; so when an Incarnation comes, a tidal wave of spirituality breaks upon the world, and people feel spirituality almost full in the air."

Chapter VII
The Mantra: Om, Word and Wisdom

But we are now considering not these Mahâ-purushas, the great Incarnations, but only the Siddha-Gurus (teachers who have attained the goal); they, as a rule, have to convey the gems of spiritual wisdom to the disciple by means of words (Mantras) to be meditated upon. What are these Mantras? The whole of this universe has, according to Indian philosophy, both name and form (Nâma-Rupa) as its conditions of manifestation. In the human microcosm, there cannot be a single wave in the mind-stuff (Chittavritti) unconditioned by name and form. If it be true that nature is built throughout on the same plan, this kind of conditioning by name and form must also be the plan of the building of the whole of the cosmos.

यथा एकेन मृत्पशिण्डेन सर्वं मृन्मयं वज्ञिातं स्यात्
As one lump of clay being known, all things of clay are known

so the knowledge of the microcosm must lead to the knowledge of the macrocosm. Now form is the outer crust, of which the name or the idea is the inner essence or kernel. The body is the form, and the mind or the Antahkarana is the name, and sound-symbols are universally associated with Nâma (name) in all beings having the power of speech. In the individual man the thought-waves rising in the limited Mahat or Chitta (mind-stuff), must manifest themselves, first as words, and then as the more concrete forms.

In the universe, Brahmâ or Hiranyagarbha or the cosmic Mahat first manifested himself as name, and then as form, i.e. as this universe. All this expressed sensible universe is the form, behind which stands the eternal inexpressible Sphota, the manifester as Logos or Word. This eternal Sphota, the essential eternal material of all ideas or names is the power through which the Lord creates the universe, nay, the Lord first becomes conditioned as the Sphota, and then evolves Himself out as the yet more concrete sensible universe.

This Sphota has one word as its only possible symbol, and this is the ओं (Om). And as by no possible means of analysis can we separate the word from the idea this Om and the eternal Sphota are inseparable; and therefore, it is out of this holiest of all holy words, the mother of all names and forms, the eternal Om, that the whole universe may be supposed to have been created. But it may be said that, although thought and word are inseparable, yet as there may be various word-symbols for the same thought, it is not necessary that this particular word Om should be the word representative of the thought, out of which the universe has become manifested. To this objection we reply that this Om is the only possible symbol which covers the whole ground, and there is none other like it. The Sphota is the material of all words, yet it is not any definite word in its fully formed state. That is to say, if all the peculiarities which distinguish one word from another be removed, then what remains will be the Sphota; therefore this Sphota is called the Nâda-Brahma, the Sound-Brahman.

Now, as every word-symbol, intended to express the inexpressible Sphota, will so particularise it that it will no longer be the Sphota, that symbol which particularises it the least and at the same time most approximately expresses its nature, will be the truest symbol thereof; and this is the Om, and the Om only; because these three letters अ उ म (A.U.M.), pronounced incombination as Om, may well be the generalised symbol of all possible sounds. The letter A is the least differentiated of all sounds, therefore Krishna says in the Gita अक्षराणां अकारोऽस्मि—*I am A among the letters.*

Again, all articulate sounds are produced in the space within the mouth beginning with the root of the tongue and ending in the lips—the throat sound is A, and M is the last lip sound, and the U exactly represents the rolling forward of the impulse which begins at the root of the tongue till it ends in the lips. If properly pronounced, this Om will represent the whole phenomenon of sound-production, and no other word can do this; and this, therefore, is the fittest symbol of the Sphota, which is the real meaning of the Om. And as the symbol can never be separated from the thing signified, the Om and the Sphota are one. And as the Sphota, being the finer side of the manifested universe, is nearer to God and is indeed that first manifestation of divine wisdom this Om is truly symbolic of God. Again, just as the "One only" Brahman, the Akhanda-Sachchidânanda, the undivided Existence-Knowledge-Bliss, can be conceived by imperfect human souls only from particular standpoints and associated with particular qualities, so this universe, His body, has also to be thought of along the line of the thinker's mind.

This direction of the worshipper's mind is guided by its prevailing elements or Tattvas. The result is that the same God will be seen in various manifestations as the possessor of various predominant qualities, and the same universe will appear as full of manifold forms. Even as in the case of the least differentiated and the most universal symbol Om, thought and sound-symbol are seen to be insepa- rably associated with each other, so also this law of their inseparable association applies to the many differentiated views of God and the universe: each of them therefore must have a particular word-symbol to express it. These word-symbols evolved out of the deepest spiritual perception of sages, symbolise and express as nearly as possible the particular view of God and the universe they stand for. And as the Om represents the Akhanda, the undifferentiated Brahman, the others represent the Khanda or the differentiated views of the same Being; and they are all helpful to divine meditation and the acquisition of true knowledge.

Chapter VIII
Worship of Substitutes and Images

The next points to be considered are the worship of Pratikas or of things more or less satisfactory as substitutes for God, and the worship of Pratimâs or images. What is the worship of God through a Pratika?

It is अब्रह्मणि ब्रह्मदृष्ट्यऽनुसन्धानम् *Joining the mind with devotion to that which is not Brahman, taking it to be Brahman*, says Bhagavân Râmânuja. "Worship the mind as Brahman this is internal; and the Âkâsha as Brahman, this is with regard to the Devas", says Shankara. The mind is an internal Pratika, the Akasha is an external one, and both have to be worshipped as substitutes of God. He continues, "Similarly, 'the Sun is Brahman, this is the command', 'He who worships Name as Brahman'—in all such passages the doubt arises as to the worship of Pratikas." The word Pratika means going towards; and worshipping a Pratika is worshipping something as a substitute which is, in some one or more respects, like Brahman more and more, but is not Brahman. Along with the Pratikas mentioned in the Shrutis there are various others to be found in the Purânas and the Tantras. In this kind of Pratika-worship may be included all the various forms of Pitri-worship and Deva-worship.

Now worshipping Ishvara and Him alone is Bhakti; the worship of anything else—Deva, or Pitri, or any other being—cannot be Bhakti. The various kinds of worship of the various Devas are all to be included in ritualistic Karma, which gives to the worshipper only a particular result in the form of some celestial enjoyment, but can neither give rise to Bhakti nor lead to Mukti. One thing, therefore, has to be carefully borne in mind. If, as it may happen in some cases, the highly philosophic ideal, the supreme Brahman, is dragged down by Pratika-worship to the level of the Pratika, and the Pratika itself is taken to be the Atman of the worshipper or his Antaryâmin (Inner Ruler), the worshipper gets entirely misled, as no Pratika can really be the Atman of the worshipper.

But where Brahman Himself is the object of worship, and the Pratika stands only as a substitute or a suggestion thereof, that is to say, where, through the Pratika the omnipresent Brahman is worshipped—the Pratika itself being idealised into the cause of all, Brahman—the worship is positively beneficial; nay, it is absolutely necessary for all mankind until they have all got beyond the primary or preparatory state of the mind in regard to worship. When, therefore, any gods or other beings are worshipped in and for themselves, such worship is only a ritualistic Karma; and as a Vidyâ (science) it gives us only the fruit belonging to that particular Vidya; but when the Devas or any other beings are looked upon as Brahman and worshipped, the result obtained is the same as by the worshipping of Ishvara. This explains how, in many cases, both in the Shruti and the Smritis, a god, or a sage, or some other extraordinary being is taken up and lifted, as it were, out of his own nature and idealised into Brahman, and is then worshipped. Says the Advaitin, "Is not everything Brahman when the name and the form have been removed from it?" "Is not He, the Lord, the innermost Self of every one?" says the Vishishtâdvaitin.

फलम् आदित्याद्युपासनेषु ब्रह्मैव दास्यति सर्वाध्यक्षत्वात्

The fruition of even the worship of Adityas etc. Brahman Himself bestows, because He is the Ruler of all. Says Shankara in his Brahma-Sutra-Bhâsya

ईदृशं चात्र ब्रह्मणा उपास्यत्वं यतः प्रतीकेषु तद्दृष्ट्याध्यारोपणं प्रतिमादिषु इव विष्णुवादीनाम्।

Here in this way does Brahman become the object of worship, because He, as Brahman, is superimposed on the Pratikas, just as Vishnu etc. are superimposed upon images etc.

The same ideas apply to the worship of the Pratimas as to that of the Pratikas; that is to say, if the image stands for a god or a saint, the worship is not the result of Bhakti, and does not lead to liberation; but if it stands for the one God, the worship thereof will bring both Bhakti and Mukti. Of the principal religions of the world we see Vedantism, Buddhism, and certain forms of Christianity freely using images; only two religions, Mohammedanism and Protestantism, refuse such help. Yet the Mohammedans use the grave of their saints and martyrs almost in the place of images; and the Protestants, in rejecting all concrete help to religion, are drifting away every year farther and farther from spirituality till at present there is scarcely any difference between the advanced Protestants and the followers of August Comte, or agnostics who preach ethics alone. Again, in Christianity and Mohammedanism whatever exists of image worship is made to fall under that category in which the Pratika or the Pratima is worshipped in itself, but not as a "help to the vision" (Drishtisaukaryam) of God; therefore it is at best only of the nature of ritualistic Karmas and cannot produce either Bhakti or Mukti. In this form of image-worship, the allegiance of the soul is given to other things than Ishvara, and, therefore, such use of images, or graves, or temples, or tombs, is real idolatry; it is in itself neither sinful nor wicked—it is a rite—a Karma, and worshippers must and will get the fruit thereof.

Chapter IX
The Chosen Ideal

The next thing to be considered is what we know as Ishta-Nishthâ. One who aspires to be a Bhakta must know that "so many opinions are so many ways". He must know that all the various sects of the various religions are the various manifestations of the glory of the same Lord. "They call You by so many names; they divide You, as it were, by different names, yet in each one of these is to be found Your omnipotence. ...You reach the worshipper through all of these, neither is there any special time so long as the soul has intense love for You. You are so easy of approach; it is my misfortune that I cannot love You." Not only this, the Bhakta must take care not to hate, nor even to criticise those radiant sons of light who are the founders of various sects; he must not even hear them spoken ill of. Very few indeed are those who are at once the possessors of an extensive sympathy and power of appreciation, as well as an intensity of love. We find, as a rule, that liberal and sympathetic sects lose the intensity of religious feeling, and in their hands, religion is apt to degenerate into a kind of politico-social club life. On the other hand, intensely narrow sectaries, whilst displaying a very commendable love of their own ideals, are seen to have acquired every particle of that love by hating every one who is not of exactly the same opinions as themselves. Would to God that this world was full of men who were as intense in their love as worldwide in their sympathies! But such are only few and far between. Yet we know that it is practicable to educate large numbers of human beings into the ideal of a wonderful blending of both the width and the intensity of love; and the way to do that is by this path of the Istha-Nishtha or "steadfast devotion to the chosen ideal". Every sect of every religion presents only one ideal of its own to mankind, but the eternal Vedantic religion opens to mankind an infinite number of doors for ingress into the inner shrine of divinity, and places before humanity an almost inexhaustible array of ideals, there being in each of them a manifestation of the Eternal One. With the kindest solicitude, the Vedanta points out to aspiring men and women the numerous roads, hewn out of the solid rock of the realities of human life, by the glorious sons, or human manifestations, of God, in the past and in the present, and stands

Swami Vivekananda

with outstretched arms to welcome all — to welcome even those that are yet to be — to that Home of Truth and that Ocean of Bliss, wherein the human soul, liberated from the net of Mâyâ, may transport itself with perfect freedom and with eternal joy.

Bhakti Yoga, therefore, lays on us the imperative command not to hate or deny any one of the various paths that lead to salvation. Yet the growing plant must be hedged round to protect it until it has grown into a tree. The tender plant of spirituality will die if exposed too early to the action of a constant change of ideas and ideals. Many people, in the name of what may be called religious liberalism, may be seen feeding their idle curiosity with a continuous succession of different ideals. With them, hearing new things grows into a kind of disease, a sort of religious drink-mania. They want to hear new things just by way of getting a temporary nervous excitement, and when one such exciting influence has had its effect on them, they are ready for another. Religion is with these people a sort of intellectual opium-eating, and there it ends. "There is another sort of man", says Bhagavan Ramakrishna, "who is like the pearl-oyster of the story. The pearl-oyster leaves its bed at the bottom of the sea, and comes up to the surface to catch the rain-water when the star Svâti is in the ascendant. It floats about on the surface of the sea with its shell wide open, until it has succeeded in catching a drop of the rain-water, and then it dives deep down to its sea-bed, and there rests until it has succeeded in fashioning a beautiful pearl out of that rain-drop."

This is indeed the most poetical and forcible way in which the theory of Ishta-Nishtha has ever been put. This Eka-Nishtha or devotion to one ideal is absolutely necessary for the beginner in the practice of religious devotion. He must say with Hanuman in the Râmâyana, "Though I know that the Lord of Shri and the Lord of Jânaki are both manifestations of the same Supreme Being, yet my all in all is the lotus-eyed Râma." Or, as was said by the sage Tulasidâsa, he must say, "Take the sweetness of all, sit with all, take the name of all, say yea, yea, but keep your seat firm." Then, if the devotional aspirant is sincere, out of this little seed will come a gigantic tree like the Indian banyan, sending out branch after branch and root after root to all sides, till it covers the entire field of religion. Thus will the true devotee realise that He who was his own ideal in life is worshipped in all ideals by all sects, under all names, and through all forms.

In regard to the method and the means of Bhakti Yoga we read in the commentary of Bhagavan Ramanuja on the Vedanta-Sutras: "*The attaining of That comes through discrimination, controlling the passions, practice, sacrificial work, purity, strength, and suppression of excessive joy.*" Viveka or discrimination is, according to Ramanuja, discriminating, among other things, the pure food from the impure. According to him, food becomes impure from three causes: (1) by the nature of the food itself, as in the case of garlic etc.; (2) owing to its coming from wicked and accursed persons; and (3) from physical impurities, such as dirt, or hair, etc. The Shrutis say, When the food is pure, the Sattva element gets purified, and the memory becomes unwavering", and Ramanuja quotes this from the Chhândogya Upanishad.

The question of food has always been one of the most vital with the Bhaktas Apart from the extravagance into which some of the Bhakti sects have run, there is a great truth underlying this question of food. We must remember that, according to the Sankhya philosophy, the Sattva, Rajas, and Tamas, which in the state of homogeneous equilibrium form the Prakriti, and in the heterogeneous disturbed condition form the universe—are both the substance and the quality of Prakriti. As such they are the materials out of which every human form has been manufactured, and the predominance of the Sattva material is what is absolutely necessary for spiritual development. The materials which we receive through our food into our body-structure go a great way to determine our mental constitution; therefore the food we eat has to be particularly taken care of. However, in this matter, as in others, the fanaticism into which the disciples invariably fall is not to be laid at the door of the masters.

And this discrimination of food is, after all, of secondary importance. The very same passage quoted above is explained by Shankara in his Bhâshya on the Upanishads in a different way by giving an entirely different meaning to the word Âhâra, translated generally as food. According to him, "That which is gathered in is Ahara. The knowledge of the sensations, such as sound etc., is gathered in for the enjoyment of the enjoyer (self); the purification of the knowledge which gathers in the perception of the senses is the purifying of the food (Ahara). The word 'purification-of-food' means the acquiring of the knowledge of sensations untouched by the defects of attachment, aversion, and delusion; such is the meaning. Therefore such knowledge or Ahara being purified, the Sattva material of the possessor it — the internal organ — will become purified, and the Sattva being purified, an unbroken memory of the Infinite One, who has been known in His real nature from scriptures, will result."

These two explanations are apparently conflicting, yet both are true and necessary. The manipulating and controlling of what may be called the finer body, viz the mood, are no doubt higher functions than the controlling of the grosser body of flesh. But the control of the grosser is absolutely necessary to enable one to arrive at the control of the finer. The beginner, therefore, must pay particular attention to all such dietetic rules as have come down from the line of his accredited teachers; but the extravagant, meaningless fanaticism, which has driven religion entirely to the kitchen, as may be noticed in the case of many of our sects, without any hope of the noble truth of that religion ever coming out to the sunlight of spirituality, is a peculiar sort of pure and simple materialism. It is neither Jnâna, nor Bhakti, nor Karma; it is a special kind of lunacy, and those who pin their souls to it are more likely to go to lunatic asylums than to Brahmaloka. So it stands to reason that discrimination in the choice of food is necessary for the attainment of this higher state of mental composition which cannot be easily obtained otherwise.

Controlling the passions is the next thing to be attended to. To restrain the Indriyas (organs) from going towards the objects of the senses, to control them and bring them under the guidance of the will, is the very central virtue in religious culture. Then comes the practice of self-restraint and self-denial. All the immense possibilities of divine realisation in the soul cannot get actualised without struggle and without such practice on the part of the aspiring devotee. "The mind must always think of the Lord." It is very hard at first to compel the mind to think of the Lord always, but with every new effort the power to do so grows stronger in us. "By practice, O son of Kunti, and by non-attachment is it attained", says Shri Krishna in the Gita. And then as to sacrificial work, it is understood that the five great sacrificed[1] (Panchamahâyajna) have to be performed as usual.

Purity is absolutely the basic work, the bed-rock upon which the whole Bhakti-building rests. Cleansing the external body and discriminating the food are both easy, but without internal cleanliness and purity, these external observances are

of no value whatsoever. In the list of qualities conducive to purity, as given b
Ramanuja, there are enumerated, Satya, truthfulness; Ârjava, sincerity; Day;
doing good to others without any gain to one's self; Ahimsâ, not injuring other
by thought, word, or deed; Anabhidhyâ, not coveting others' goods, not think
ing vain thoughts, and not brooding over injuries received from another. In thi
list, the one idea that deserves special notice is Ahimsa, non-injury to other:
This duty of non-injury is, so to speak, obligatory on us in relation to all being:
As with some, it does not simply mean the non-injuring of human beings an
mercilessness towards the lower animals; nor, as with some others, does it mea:
the protecting of cats and dogs and feeding of ants with sugar—with libert
to injure brother-man in every horrible way! It is remarkable that almost ever
good idea in this world can be carried to a disgusting extreme. A good prac
tice carried to an extreme and worked in accordance with the letter of the lav
becomes a positive evil. The stinking monks of certain religious sects, who d
not bathe lest the vermin on their bodies should be killed, never think of th
discomfort and disease they bring to their fellow human beings. They do no
however, belong to the religion of the Vedas!

The test of Ahimsa is absence of jealousy. Any man may do a good deed o
make a good gift on the spur of the moment or under the pressure of some su
perstition or priestcraft; but the real lover of mankind is he who is jealous c
none. The so-called great men of the world may all be seen to become jealous c
each other for a small name, for a little fame, and for a few bits of gold. So lon,
as this jealousy exists in a heart, it is far away from the perfection of Ahims;
The cow does not eat meat, nor does the sheep. Are they great Yogis, great non
injurers (Ahimsakas)? Any fool may abstain from eating this or that; surel
that gives him no more distinction than to herbivorous animals. The man wh
will mercilessly cheat widows and orphans and do the vilest deeds for mone
is worse than any brute even if he lives entirely on grass. The man whose hear
never cherishes even the thought of injury to any one, who rejoices at the pros
perity of even his greatest enemy, that man is the Bhakta, he is the Yogi, he i
the Guru of all, even though he lives every day of his life on the flesh of swine
Therefore we must always remember that external practices have value only a
helps to develop internal purity. It is better to have internal purity alone whe:
minute attention to external observances is not practicable. But woe unto th
man and woe unto the nation that forgets the real, internal, spiritual essential
of religion and mechanically clutches with death-like grasp at all external form
and never lets them go. The forms have value only so far as they are expressions c

the life within. If they have ceased to express life, crush them out without mercy.

The next means to the attainment of Bhakti Yoga is strength (Anavasâda). "This Atman is not to be attained by the weak", says the Shruti. Both physical weakness and mental weakness are meant here. "The strong, the hardy" are the only fit students. What can puny, little, decrepit things do ? They will break to pieces whenever the mysterious forces of the body and mind are even slightly awakened by the practice of any of the Yogas. It is "the young, the healthy, the strong" that can score success. Physical strength, therefore, is absolutely necessary. It is the strong body alone that can bear the shock of reaction resulting from the attempt to control the organs. He who wants to become a Bhakta must be strong, must be healthy. When the miserably weak attempt any of the Yogas, they are likely to get some incurable malady, or they weaken their minds. Voluntarily weakening the body is really no prescription for spiritual enlightenment.

The mentally weak also cannot succeed in attaining the Atman. The person who aspires to be a Bhakta must be cheerful. In the Western world the idea of a religious man is that he never smiles, that a dark cloud must always hang over his face, which, again, must be long drawn with the jaws almost collapsed. People with emaciated bodies and long faces are fit subjects for the physician, they are not Yogis. It is the cheerful mind that is persevering. It is the strong mind that hews its way through a thousand difficulties. And this, the hardest task of all, the cutting of our way out of the net of Maya, is the work reserved only for giant wills.

Yet at the same time excessive mirth should be avoided (Anuddharsha). Excessive mirth makes us unfit for serious thought. It also fritters away the energies of the mind in vain. The stronger the will, the less the yielding to the sway of the emotions. Excessive hilarity is quite as objectionable as too much of sad seriousness, and all religious realisation is possible only when the mind is in a steady, peaceful condition of harmonious equilibrium.

It is thus that one may begin to learn how to love the Lord.

Note :

1 : To gods, sages, manes, guests, and all creatures.

PARA-BHAKTI OR SUPREME DEVOTION

Chapter I
The Preparatory Renunciation

We have now finished the consideration of what may be called the preparatory Bhakti, and are entering on the study of the Parâ-Bhakti or supreme devotion. We have to speak of a preparation to the practice of this Para-Bhakti. All such preparations are intended only for the purification of the soul. The repetition of names, the rituals, the forms, and the symbols, all these various things are for the purification of the soul. The greatest purifier among all such things, a purifier without which no one can enter the regions of this higher devotion (Para-Bhakti), is renunciation. This frightens many; yet, without it, there cannot be any spiritual growth. In all our Yogas this renunciation is necessary. This is the stepping-stone and the real centre and the real heart of all spiritual culture—renunciation. This is religion—renunciation.

When the human soul draws back from the things of the world and tries to go into deeper things; when man, the spirit which has here somehow become concretised and materialised, understands that he is thereby going to be destroyed and to be reduced almost into mere matter, and turns his face away from matter—then begins renunciation, then begins real spiritual growth. The Karma-Yogi's renunciation is in the shape of giving up all the fruits of his action; he is not attached to the results of his labour; he does not care for any reward here or hereafter. The Râja-Yogi knows that the whole of nature is intended for the soul to acquire experience, and that the result of all the experiences of the soul is for it to become aware of its eternal separateness from nature. The human soul has to understand and realise that it has been spirit, and not matter, through eternity, and that this conjunction of it with matter is and can be only for a time. The Raja-Yogi learns the lesson of renunciation through his own experience of nature. The Jnâna-Yogi has the harshest of all renunciations to go through, as he has to realise from the very first that the whole of this solid-looking nature is all an illusion. He has to understand that all that is any kind of manifestation of power in nature belongs to the soul, and not to nature. He has to know from the very start that all knowledge and all experience are in the soul and not in nature; so he has at once and by the sheer force of rational conviction to tear himself away from all bondage to nature. He lets nature and all that belongs t her go, he lets them vanish and tries to stand alone!

Of all renunciations, the most natural, so to say, is that of the Bhakti-Yogi. Her there is no violence, nothing to give up, nothing to tear off, as it were, from our selves, nothing from which we have violently to separate ourselves. The Bhakta renunciation is easy, smooth flowing, and as natural as the things around us. W see the manifestation of this sort of renunciation, although more or less in th form of caricatures, every day around us. A man begins to love a woman; afte a while he loves another, and the first woman he lets go. She drops put of hi mind smoothly, gently, without his feeling the want of her at all. A woman love a man; she then begins to love another man, and the first one drops off from he mind quite naturally. A man loves his own city, then he begins to love his coun try, and the intense love for his little city drops off smoothly, naturally. Again, man learns to love the whole world; his love for his country, his intense, fanatica patriotism drops off without hurting him, without any manifestation of violence An uncultured man loves the pleasures of the senses intensely; as he become cultured, he begins to love intellectual pleasures, and his sense-enjoyments be come less and less. No man can enjoy a meal with the same gusto or pleasure a a dog or a wolf, but those pleasures which a man gets from intellectual experi ences and achievements, the dog can never enjoy. At first, pleasure is in associa tion with the lowest senses; but as soon as an animal reaches a higher plane o existence, the lower kind of pleasures becomes less intense. In human societ the nearer the man is to the animal, the stronger is his pleasure in the senses and the higher and the more cultured the man is, the greater is his pleasure i intellectual and such other finer pursuits. So when a man gets even higher tha the plane of the intellect, higher than that of mere thought, when he gets t the plane of spirituality and of divine inspiration, he finds there a state of blis compared with which all the pleasures of the senses, or even of the intellect, ar as nothing. When the moon shines brightly, all the stars become dim; and whe the sun shines, the moon herself becomes dim. The renunciation necessary fo the attainment of Bhakti is not obtained by killing anything, but just comes i as naturally as in the presence of an increasingly stronger light, the less intens ones become dimmer and dimmer until they vanish away completely. So thi love of the pleasures of the senses and of the intellect is all made dim and throw aside and cast into the shade by the love of God Himself.

That love of God grows and assumes a form which is called Para-Bhakti o supreme devotion. Forms vanish, rituals fly away, books are superseded; image temples, churches, religions and sects, countries and nationalities — all these little limitations and bondages fall off by their own nature from him who knows this love of God. Nothing remains to bind him or fetter his freedom. A ship, all of a sudden, comes near a magnetic rock, and its iron bolts and bars are all attracted and drawn out, and the planks get loosened and freely float on the water. Divine grace thus loosens the binding bolts and bars of the soul, and it becomes free. So in this renunciation auxiliary to devotion, there is no harshness, no dryness no struggle, nor repression nor suppression. The Bhakta has not to suppress any single one of his emotions, he only strives to intensify them and direct them to God.

Chapter II
The Bhakta's Renunciation Results from Love

We see love everywhere in nature. Whatever in society is good and great and sublime is the working out of that love; whatever in society is very bad, nay diabolical, is also the ill-directed working out of the same emotion of love. It is this same emotion that gives us the pure and holy conjugal love between husband and wife as well as the sort of love which goes to satisfy the lowest forms of animal passion. The emotion is the same, but its manifestation is different in different cases. It is the same feeling of love, well or ill directed, that impels one man to do good and to give all he has to the poor, while it makes another man cut the throats of his brethren and take away all their possessions. The former loves others as much as the latter loves himself. The direction of the love is bad in the case of the latter, but it is right and proper in the other case. The same fire that cooks a meal for us may burn a child, and it is no fault of the fire if it does so; the difference lies in the way in which it is used. Therefore love, the intense longing for association, the strong desire on the part of two to become one — and it may be, after all, of all to become merged in one — is being manifested everywhere in higher or lower forms as the case may be.

Bhakti Yoga is the science of higher love. It shows us how to direct it; it shows us how to control it, how to manage it, how to use it, how to give it a new aim, as it were, and from it obtain the highest and most glorious results, that is, how to make it lead us to spiritual blessedness. Bhakti Yoga does not say, "Give up"; it only says, "Love; love the Highest!"—and everything low naturally falls off from him, the object of whose love is the Highest.

"I cannot tell anything about Thee except that Thou art my love. Thou art beautiful, Oh, Thou art beautiful! Thou art beauty itself." What is after all really required of us in this Yoga is that our thirst after the beautiful should be directed to God. What is the beauty in the human face, in the sky, in the stars, and in the moon? It is only the partial apprehension of the real all-embracing Divine Beauty. "He shining, everything shines. It is through His light that all things shine." Take this high position of Bhakti which makes you forget at once all your little personalities. Take yourself away from all the world's little selfish clingings. Do not look upon humanity as the centre of all your human and higher interests. Stand as a witness, as a student, and observe the phenomena of nature. Have the feeling of personal non-attachment with regard to man, and see how this mighty feeling of love is working itself out in the world. Sometimes a little friction is produced, but that is only in the course of the struggle to attain the higher real love. Sometimes there is a little fight or a little fall; but it is all only by the way. Stand aside, and freely let these frictions come. You feel the frictions only when you are in the current of the world, but when you are outside of it simply as a witness and as a student, you will be able to see that there are millions and millions of channels in which God is manifesting Himself as Love.

"Wherever there is any bliss, even though in the most sensual of things, there is a spark of that Eternal Bliss which is the Lord Himself." Even in the lowest kinds of attraction there is the germ of divine love. One of the names of the Lord in Sanskrit is Hari, and this means that He attracts all things to Himself. His is in fact the only attraction worthy of human hearts. Who can attract a soul really? Only He! Do you think dead matter can truly attract the soul? It never did, and never will. When you see a man going after a beautiful face, do you think that it is the handful of arranged material molecules which really attracts the man? Not at all. Behind those material particles there must be and is the play of divine influence and divine love. The ignorant man does not know it, but yet, consciously or unconsciously, he is attracted by it and it alone. So even the lowest forms of attraction derive their power from God Himself. "None, O beloved, ever loved the husband for the husband's sake; it is the Âtman, the Lord who is within, for whose sake the husband is loved." Loving wives may know this or they may not; it is true all the same. "None, O beloved, ever loved the wife for the wife's sake, but it is the Self in the wife that is loved." Similarly, no one loves a child or anything else in the world except on account of Him who is within. The Lord is the great magnet, and we are all like iron filings; we are being constantly attracted by Him, and all of us are struggling to reach Him. All this struggling of ours in this world is surely not intended for selfish ends. Fools do not know what they are doing: the work of their life is, after all, to approach the great magnet. All the tremendous struggling and fighting in life is intended to make us go to Him ultimately and be one with Him.

The Bhakti-Yogi, however, knows the meaning of life's struggles; he understands it. He has passed through a long series of these struggles and knows what they mean and earnestly desires to be free from the friction thereof; he wants to avoid the clash and go direct to the centre of all attraction, the great Hari

This is the renunciation of the Bhakta. This mighty attraction in the direction of God makes all other attractions vanish for him. This mighty infinite love of God which enters his heart leaves no place for any other love to live there. How can it be otherwise" Bhakti fills his heart with the divine waters of the ocean of love, which is God Himself; there is no place there for little loves. That is to say the Bhakta's renunciation is that Vairâgya or non-attachment for all things that are not God which results from Anurâga or great attachment to God.

This is the ideal preparation for the attainment of the supreme Bhakti. When this renunciation comes, the gate opens for the soul to pass through and reach the lofty regions of supreme devotion or Para-Bhakti. Then it is that we begin to understand what Para-Bhakti is; and the man who has entered into the inner shrine of the Para-Bhakti alone has the right to say that all forms and symbols are useless to him as aids to religious realisation. He alone has attained that supreme state of love commonly called the brotherhood of man; the rest only talk. He sees no distinctions; the mighty ocean of love has entered into him, and he sees not man in man, but beholds his Beloved everywhere. Through every face shines to him his Hari. The light in the sun or the moon is all His manifestation. Wherever there is beauty or sublimity, to him it is all His. Such Bhaktas are still living; the world is never without them. Such, though bitten by a serpent only say that a messenger came to them from their Beloved. Such men alone have the right to talk of universal brotherhood. They feel no resentment; their minds never react in the form of hatred or jealousy. The external, the sensuous has vanished from them for ever. How can they be angry, when, through their love, they are always able to see the Reality behind the scenes?

Chapter III
The Naturalness of Bhakti Yoga and its Central Secret

Those who with constant attention always worship You, and those who worship the Undifferentiated, the Absolute, of these who are the greatest Yogis? — Arjuna asked of Shri Krishna. The answer was: *Those who concentrating their minds on Me worship Me with eternal constancy and are endowed with the highest faith, they are My best worshippers, they are the greatest Yogis. Those that worship the Absolute, the Indescribable, the Undifferentiated, the Omnipresent, the Unthinkable, the All-comprehending, the Immovable, and the Eternal, by controlling the play of their organs and having the conviction of sameness in regard to all things, they also, being engaged in doing good to all beings, come to Me alone. But to those whose minds have been devoted to the unmanifested Absolute, the difficulty of the struggle along the way is much greater, for it is indeed with great difficulty that the path of the unmanifested Absolute is trodden by any embodied being. Those who, having offered up all their work unto Me, with entire reliance on Me, meditate on Me and worship Me without any attachment to anything else — them, I soon lift up from the ocean of ever-recurring births and deaths, as their mind is wholly attached to Me.* (Gita, XII).

Jnâna-Yoga and Bhakti Yoga are both referred to here. Both may be said to have been defined in the above passage. Jnana-Yoga is grand; it is high philosophy; and almost every human being thinks, curiously enough, that he can surely do everything required of him by philosophy; but it is really very difficult to live truly the life of philosophy. We are often apt to run into great dangers in trying to guide our life by philosophy. This world may be said to be divided between persons of demoniacal nature who think the care-taking of the body to be the be-all and the end-all of existence, and persons of godly nature who realise that the body is simply a means to an end, an instrument intended for the culture of the soul. The devil can and indeed does cite the scriptures for his own purpose; and thus the way of knowledge appears to offer justification to what the bad man does, as much as it offers inducements to what the good man does. This is the great danger in Jnana-Yoga. But Bhakti Yoga is natural, sweet, and gentle; the Bhakta does not take such high flights as the Jnana-Yogi, and, therefore, he is not apt to have such big falls. Until the bandages of the soul pass away, it can not of course be free, whatever may be the nature of the path that the religiou man takes.

Here is a passage showing how, in the case of one of the blessed Gopis, th soul-binding chains of both merit and demerit were broken. *The intense pleasur in meditating on God took away the binding effects of her good deeds. Then her intens misery of soul in not attaining unto Him washed off all her sinful propensities; an then she became free.*

तच्चिन्तावपुलाह्लादक्षीणापुण्यचया तथा। तदप्राप्ति महद्दुःखविलीनाशेषपातका॥
निरुच्छ्वासतया मुक्तिं गतान्या गोपकन्यका॥ (Vishnu-Purâna)

In Bhakti Yoga the central secret is, therefore, to know that the various pas sions and feelings and emotions in the human heart are not wrong in them selves; only they have to be carefully controlled and given a higher and highe direction, until they attain the very highest condition of excellence. The highes direction is that which takes us to God; every other direction is lower. We fin that pleasures and pains are very common and oft-recurring feelings in our live When a man feels pain because he has not wealth or some such worldly thing he is giving a wrong direction to the feeling. Still pain has its uses. Let a ma feel pain that he has not reached the Highest, that he has not reached God, an that pain will be to his salvation. When you become glad that you have a hand ful of coins, it is a wrong direction given to the faculty of joy; it should be give a higher direction, it must be made to serve the Highest Ideal. Pleasure in tha kind of ideal must surely be our highest joy. This same thing is true of all ou other feelings. The Bhakta says that not one of them is wrong, he gets hold c them all and points them unfailingly towards God.

Chapter IV
The Forms of Love: Manifestation

Here are some of the forms in which love manifests itself. First there is reverence. Why do people show reverence to temples and holy places? Because He is worshipped there, and His presence is associated with all such places. Why do people in every country pay reverence to teachers of religion? It is natural for the human heart to do so, because all such teachers preach the Lord. At bottom, reverence is a growth out of love; we can none of us revere him whom we do not love. Then comes Priti—pleasure in God. What an immense pleasure men take in the objects of the senses. They go anywhere, run through any danger, to get the thing which they love, the thing which their senses like. What is wanted of the Bhakta is this very kind of intense love which has, however, to be directed to God. Then there is the sweetest of pains, Viraha, the intense misery due to the absence of the beloved. When a man feels intense misery because he has not attained to God, has not known that which is the only thing worthy to be known, and becomes in consequence very dissatisfied and almost mad—then there is Viraha; and this state of the mind makes him feel disturbed in the presence of anything other than the beloved (Ekarativichikitsâ). In earthly love we see how often this Viraha comes. Again, when men are really and intensely in love with women or women with men, they feel a kind of natural annoyance in the presence of all those whom they do not love. Exactly the same state of impatience in regard to things that are not loved comes to the mind when Para-Bhakti holds sway over it; even to talk about things other than God becomes distasteful then. "Think of Him, think of Him alone, and give up all other vain words" अन्या वाचो वमुंचथ।—Those who talk of Him alone, the Bhakta finds to be friendly to him; while those who talk of anything else appear to him to be unfriendly. A still higher stage of love is reached when life itself is maintained for the sake of the one Ideal of Love, when life itself is considered beautiful and worth living only on account of that Love (तदर्थप्राणसंस्थानं). Without it, such a life would not remain even for a moment. Life is sweet, because it thinks of the Beloved. Tadiyatâ (His-ness) comes when a man becomes perfect according to Bhakti—when he has become blessed, when he has attained God, when he has touched the feet of God, as it were. Then his whole nature is purified and completely changed. All his purpose in life then becomes fulfilled. Yet many such Bhaktas live on just to worship Him. That is the bliss, the only pleasure in life which they will not give up. "O king, such is the blessed quality of Hari that even those who have become satisfied with everything, all the knots of whose hearts have been cut asunder, even they love the Lord for love's sake"—the Lord "Whom all the gods worship—all the lovers of liberation, and all the knowers of the Brahman"—यं सर्वे देवा नमन्ति मुमुक्षवो ब्रह्मवादनिश्चेति (Nri. Tap. Up.). Such is the power of love. When a man has forgotten himself altogether, and does not feel that anything belongs to him, then he acquires the state of Tadiyata; everything is sacred to him, because it belongs to the Beloved. Even in regard to earthly love, the lover thinks that everything belonging to his beloved is sacred and so dear to him. He loves even a piece of cloth belonging to the darling of his heart In the same way, when a person loves the Lord, the whole universe becomes dear to him, because it is all His.

Chapter V
Universal Love and How it Leads to Self-Surrender

How can we love the Vyashti, the particular, without first loving the Samashti, the universal? God is the Samashti, the generalised and the abstract universal whole; and the universe that we see is the Vyashti, the particularised thing. To love the whole universe is possible only by way of loving the Samashti—the universal—which is, as it were, the one unity in which are to be found millions and millions of smaller unities. The philosophers of India do not stop at the particulars; they cast a hurried glance at the particulars and immediately start to find the generalised forms which will include all the particulars. The search after the universal is the one search of Indian philosophy and religion. The Jnâni aims at the wholeness of things, at that one absolute and; generalised Being, knowing which he knows everything. The Bhakta wishes to realise that one generalised abstract Person, in loving whom he loves the whole universe. The Yogi wishes to have possession of that one generalised form of power, by controlling which he controls this whole universe. The Indian mind, throughout its history, has been directed to this kind of singular search after the universal in everything—in science, in psychology, in love, in philosophy. So the conclusion to which the Bhakta comes is that, if you go on merely loving one person after another, you may go on loving them so for an infinite length of time, without being in the least able to love the world as a whole. When, at last, the central idea is, however, arrived at that the sum total of all love is God, that the sum total of the aspirations of all the souls in the universe, whether they be free, or bound, or struggling towards liberation, is God, then alone it becomes possible for any one to put forth universal love. God is the Samashti, and this visible universe is God differentiated and made manifest. If we love this sum total, we love everything. Loving the world doing it good will all come easily then; we have to obtain this power only by loving God first; otherwise it is no joke to do good to the world. "Everything is His and He is my Lover; I love Him," says the Bhakta. In this way everything becomes sacred to the Bhakta, because all things are His. All are His children, His body, His manifestation. How then may we hurt any one? How then may we not love any one? With the love of God will come, as a sure effect, the love of every one in the universe. The nearer we approach God, the more do we begin to see that all things are in Him. When the soul succeeds in appropriating the bliss of this supreme love, it also begins to see Him in everything. Our heart will thus become an eternal fountain of love. And when we reach even higher states of this love, all the little differences between the things of the world are entirely lost; man is seen no more as man, but only as God; the animal is seen no more as animal, but as God; even the tiger is no more a tiger, but a manifestation of God. Thus in this intense state of Bhakti, worship is offered to every one, to every life, and to every being.

एवं सर्वेषु भूतेषु भक्तिरिव्यभिचारिणी। कर्तव्या पण्डितैर्ज्ञात्वा सर्वभूतमयं हरिम्॥

Knowing that Hari, the Lord, is in every being, the wise have thus to manifest unswerving love towards all beings.

As a result of this kind of intense all-absorbing love, comes the feeling of perfect self-surrender, the conviction that nothing that happens is against us, Aprâtikulya. Then the loving soul is able to say, if pain comes, "Welcome pain. If misery comes, it will say, "Welcome misery, you are also from the Beloved." If a serpent comes, it will say, "Welcome serpent." If death comes, such a Bhakta will welcome it with a smile. "Blessed am I that they all come to me; they are all welcome." The Bhakta in this state of perfect resignation, arising out of intense love to God and to all that are His, ceases to distinguish between pleasure and pain in so far as they affect him. He does not know what it is to complain of pain or misery; and this kind of uncomplaining resignation to the will of God who is all love, is indeed a worthier acquisition than all the glory of grand and heroic performances.

To the vast majority of mankind, the body is everything; the body is all the universe to them; bodily enjoyment is their all in all. This demon of the worship of the body and of the things of the body has entered into us all. We may indulge in tall talk and take very high flights, but we are like vultures all the same; our mind is directed to the piece of carrion down below. Why should our body be saved, say, from the tiger? Why may we not give it over to the tiger? The tiger will thereby be pleased, and that is not altogether so very far from self-sacrifice and worship. Can you reach the realization of such an idea in which all sense of self is completely lost? It is a very dizzy height on the pinnacle of the religion of love, and few in this world have ever climbed up to it; but until a man

eaches that highest point of ever-ready and ever-willing self-sacrifice, he cannot become a perfect Bhakta. We may all manage to maintain our bodies more
or less satisfactorily and for longer or shorter intervals of time. Nevertheless, our
bodies have to go; there is no permanence about them. Blessed are they whose
bodies get destroyed in the service of others. "Wealth, and even life itself, the
sage always holds ready for the service of others. In this world, there being one
thing certain, viz death, it is far better that this body dies in a good cause than
in a bad one." We may drag our life on for fifty years or a hundred years; but
after that, what is it that happens? Everything that is the result of combination
must get dissolved and die. There must and will come a time for it to be decomposed. Jesus and Buddha and Mohammed are all dead; all the great Prophets
and Teachers of the world are dead.

"In this evanescent world, where everything is falling to pieces, we have to make
the highest use of what time we have," says the Bhakta; and really the highest
use of life is to hold it at the service of all beings. It is the horrible body-idea
that breeds all the selfishness in the world, just this one delusion that we are
wholly the body we own, and that we must by all possible means try our very
best to preserve and to please it. If you know that you are positively other than
your body, you have then none to fight with or struggle against; you are dead
to all ideas of selfishness. So the Bhakta declares that we have to hold ourselves
as if we are altogether dead to all the things of the world; and that is indeed
self-surrender. Let things come as they may. This is the meaning of "Thy will
be done"—not going about fighting and struggling and thinking all the while
that God wills all our own weaknesses and worldly ambitions. It may be that
good comes even out of our selfish struggles; that is, however, God's look-out.
The perfected Bhakta's idea must be never to will and work for himself. "Lord,
they build high temples in Your name; they make large gifts in Your name; I
am poor; I have nothing; so I take this body of mine and place it at Your feet.
Do not give me up, O Lord." Such is the prayer proceeding out of the depths
of the Bhakta's heart. To him who has experienced it, this eternal sacrifice of
the self unto the Beloved Lord is higher by far than all wealth and power, than
even all soaring thoughts of renown and enjoyment. The peace of the Bhakta's
calm resignation is a peace that passeth all understanding and is of incomparable
value. His Apratikulya is a state of the mind in which it has no interests and
naturally knows nothing that is opposed to it. In this state of sublime resignation everything in the shape of attachment goes away completely, except that
one all-absorbing love to Him in whom all things live and move and have their

being. This attachment of love to God is indeed one that does not bind the sou but effectively breaks all its bondages.

Chapter VI
The Higher Knowledge and the Higher Love Are One to the True Lover

The Upanishads distinguish between a higher knowledge and a lower knowledge; and to the Bhakta there is really no difference between this higher knowledge and his higher love (Parâ-Bhakti). The Mundaka Upanishad says:

वेदे विद्ये वेदितव्ये इति ह स्म यद्ब्रह्मविदो वदन्ती परा चैवापरा च॥ तत्रापरा ऋग्वेदो यजुर्वदः सामवेदोऽथर्ववेदः शिक्षा कल्पो व्याकरणं निरुक्तं छन्दो ज्योतिषमिती अथ परा यया तदक्षरमधिगम्यते॥

The knowers of the Brahman declare that there are two kinds of knowledge worthy to be known, namely, the Higher (Parâ) and the lower (Aparâ). Of these the lower (knowledge) consists of the Rig-Veda, the Yajur-Veda, the Sâma-Veda, the Atharva-Veda, the Shikshâ (or the science dealing with pronunciation and accent), the Kalpa (or the sacrificial liturgy), grammar, the Nirukta (or the science dealing with etymology and the meaning of words), prosody, and astronomy; and the higher (knowledge) is that by which that Unchangeable is known.

The higher knowledge is thus clearly shown to be the knowledge of the Brahman; and the Devi-Bhâgavata gives us the following definition of the higher love (Para-Bhakti): "As oil poured from one vessel to another falls in an unbroken line, so, when the mind in an unbroken stream thinks of the Lord, we have what is called Para-Bhakti or supreme love." This kind of undisturbed and ever-steady direction of the mind and the heart to the Lord with an inseparable attachment is indeed the highest manifestation of man's love to God. All other forms of Bhakti are only preparatory to the attainment of this highest form thereof, viz the Para-Bhakti which is also known as the love that comes after attachment (Râgânugâ). When this supreme love once comes into the heart of man, his mind will continuously think of God and remember nothing else. He will give no room in himself to thoughts other than those of God, and his soul will be unconquerably pure and will alone break all the bonds of mind and matter and become serenely free. He alone can worship the Lord in his own heart; to him forms, symbols, books, and doctrines are all unnecessary and are incapable of proving serviceable in any way. It is not easy to love the Lord thus. Ordinarily human love is seen to flourish only in places where it is returned; where love is not returned for love, cold indifference is the natural result. There are, however rare instances in which we may notice love exhibiting itself even where there is no return of love. We may compare this kind of love, far purposes of illustration, to the love of the moth for the fire; the insect loves the fire, falls into it, and dies. It is indeed in the nature of this insect to love so. To love because it is the nature of love to love is undeniably the highest and the most unselfish manifestation of love that may be seen in the world. Such love, working itself out on the plane of spirituality, necessarily leads to the attainment of Para-Bhakti.

Chapter VII
The Triangle of Love

We may represent love as a triangle, each of the angles of which corresponds to one of its inseparable characteristics. There can be no triangle without all its three angles; and there can be no true love without its three following characteristics. The first angle of our triangle of love is that love knows no bargaining. Wherever there is any seeking for something in return, there can, be no real love; it becomes a mere matter of shop-keeping. As long as there is in us any idea of deriving this or that favour from God in return for our respect and allegiance to Him, so long there can be no true love growing in our hearts. Those who worship God because they wish Him to bestow favours on them are sure not to worship Him if those favours are not forthcoming. The Bhakta loves the Lord because He is lovable, there is no other motive originating or directing this divine emotion of the true devotee.

We have heard it said that a great king once went into a forest and there met a sage. He talked with the sage a little and was very much pleased with his purity and wisdom. The king then wanted the sage to oblige him by receiving a present from him. The sage refused to do so, saying, "The fruits of the forest are enough food for me; the pure streams of water flowing down from the mountains give enough drink for me; the barks of the trees supply me with enough covering; and the caves of the mountains form my home. Why should I take any present from you or from anybody?" The king said, "Just to benefit me, sir, please take something from my hands and please come with me to the city and to my palace." After much persuasion, the sage at last consented to do as the king desired and went with him to his palace. Before offering the gift to the sage, the king repeated his prayers, saying, "Lord, give me more children; Lord, give me more wealth; Lord, give me more territory; Lord, keep my body in better health", and so on. Before the king finished saying his prayer, the sage had got up and walked away from the room quietly. At this the king became perplexed and began to follow him, crying aloud, "Sir, you are going away, you have not received my gifts." The sage turned round to him and said, "I do not beg of beggars. You are yourself nothing but a beggar, and how can you give me anything? I am no fool to think of taking anything from a beggar like you. Go away, do not follow me.

There is well brought out the distinction between mere beggars and the real lovers of God. Begging is not the language of love. To worship God even for the sake of salvation or any other rewards equally degenerate. Love knows no reward. Love is always for love's sake. The Bhakta loves because he cannot help loving. When you see a beautiful scenery and fall in love with it, you do not demand anything in the way of favour from the scenery, nor does the scenery demand anything from you. Yet the vision thereof brings you to a blissful state of the mind; it tones down all the friction in your soul, it makes you calm, almost raises you, for the time being, beyond your mortal nature and places you in a condition of quite divine ecstasy. This nature of real love is the first angle of our triangle. Ask not anything in return for your love; let your position be always that of the giver; give your love unto God, but do not ask anything in return even from Him.

The second angle of the triangle of love is that love knows no fear. Those that love God through fear are the lowest of human beings, quite undeveloped as men. They worship God from fear of punishment. He is a great Being to them, with a whip in one hand and the sceptre in the other; if they do not obey Him they are afraid they will be whipped. It is a degradation to worship God through fear of punishment; such worship is, if worship at all, the crudest form of the worship of love. So long as there is any fear in the heart, how can there be love also? Love conquers naturally all fear. Think of a young mother in the street and a dog barking at her; she is frightened and flies into nearest house. But suppose the next day she is in the street with her child, and a lion springs upon the child. Where will be her position now? Of course, in the very mouth of the lion, protecting her child. Love conquers all fear. Fear comes from the selfish idea of cutting one's self off from the universe. The smaller and the more selfish I make myself, the more is my fear. If a man thinks he is a little nothing, fear will surely come upon him. And the less you think of yourself as an insignificant person, the less fear there will be for you. So long as there is the least spark of fear in you there can be no love there. Love and fear are incompatible; God is never to be feared by those who love Him. The commandment, "Do not take the name of the Lord thy God in vain", the true lover of God laughs at. How can there be any blasphemy in the religion of love? The more you take the name of the Lord, the better for you, in whatever way you may do it. You are only repeating His name because you love Him.

The third angle of the love-triangle is that love knows no rival, for in it is always embodied the lover's highest ideal. True love never comes until the object of our love becomes to us our highest ideal. It may be that in many cases human love is misdirected and misplaced, but to the person who loves, the thing he loves is always his own highest idea. One may see his ideal in the vilest of beings, and another in the highest of beings; nevertheless, in every case it is the ideal alone that can be truly and intensely loved. The highest ideal of every man is called God. Ignorant or wise, saint or sinner, man or woman, educated or uneducated, cultivated or uncultivated, to every human being the highest ideal is God. The synthesis of all the highest ideals of beauty, of sublimity, and of power gives us the completest conception of the loving and lovable God.

These ideals exist in some shape or other in every mind naturally; they form a part and parcel of all our minds. All the active manifestations of human nature are struggles of those ideals to become realised in practical life. All the various movements that we see around us in society are caused by the various ideals in various souls trying to come out and become concretised; what is inside presses on to come outside. This perennially dominant influence of the ideal is the one force, the one motive power, that may be seen to be constantly working in the midst of mankind. It may be after hundreds of births, after struggling through thousands of years, that man finds that it is vain to try to make the inner ideal mould completely the external conditions and square well with them; after realising this he no more tries to project his own ideal on the outside world, but worships the ideal itself as ideal from the highest standpoint of love. This ideally perfect ideal embraces all lower ideals. Every one admits the truth of the saying that a lover sees Helen's beauty on an Ethiop's brow. The man who is standing aside as a looker-on sees that love is here misplaced, but the lover sees his Helen all the same and does not see the Ethiop at all. Helen or Ethiop, the objects of our love are really the centres round which our ideals become crystallised. What is it that the world commonly worships? Not certainly this all-embracing, ideally perfect ideal of the supreme devotee and lover. That ideal which men and women commonly worship is what is in themselves; every person projects his or her own ideal on the outside world and kneels before it. That is why we find that men who are cruel and blood-thirsty conceive of a bloodthirsty God, because they can only love their own highest ideal. That is why good men have a very high ideal of God, and their ideal is indeed so very different from that of others.

Chapter VII

The God of Love Is His Own Proof

What is the ideal of the lover who has quite passed beyond the idea of selfishness, of bartering and bargaining, and who knows no fear? Even to the great God such a man will say, "I will give You my all, and I do not want anything from You; indeed there is nothing that I can call my own." When a man has acquired this conviction, his ideal becomes one of perfect love, one of perfect fearlessness of love. The highest ideal of such a person has no narrowness of particularity about it; it is love universal, love without limits and bonds, love itself, absolute love. This grand ideal of the religion of love is worshipped and loved absolutely as such without the aid of any symbols or suggestions. This is the highest form of Para-Bhakti—the worship of such an all-comprehending ideal as the ideal; all the other forms of Bhakti are only stages on the way to reach it.

All our failures and all our successes in following the religion of love are on the road to the realisation of that one ideal. Object after object is taken up, and the inner ideal is successively projected on them all; and all such external objects are found inadequate as exponents of the ever-expanding inner ideal and are naturally rejected one after another. At last the aspirant begins to think that it is vain to try to realise the ideal in external objects, that all external objects are as nothing when compared with the ideal itself; and, in course of time, he acquires the power of realising the highest and the most generalised abstract idea entirely as an abstraction that is to him quite alive and real. When the devotee has reached this point, he is no more impelled to ask whether God can be demonstrated or not, whether He is omnipotent and omniscient or not. To him He is only the God of Love; He is the highest ideal of love, and that is sufficient for all his purposes. He, as love, is self-evident. It requires no proofs to demonstrate the existence of the beloved to the lover. The magistrate-Gods of other forms of religion may require a good deal of proof to prove Them, but the Bhakta does not and cannot think of such Gods at all. To him God exists entirely as love. "None, O beloved, loves the husband for the husband's sake, but it is for the sake of the Self who is in the husband that the husband is loved; none, O beloved, loves the wife for the wife's sake, but it is for the sake of the Self who is in the wife that the wife is loved."

It is said by some that selfishness is the only motive power in regard to all human activities. That also is love lowered by being particularised. When I think of myself as comprehending the Universal, there can surely be no selfishness in me; but when I, by mistake, think that I am a little something, my love becomes particularized and narrowed. The mistake consists in making the sphere of love narrow and contracted. All things in the universe are of divine origin and deserve to be loved; it has, however, to be borne in mind that the love of the whole includes the love of the parts. This whole is the God of the Bhaktas, and all the other Gods, Fathers in Heaven, or Rulers, or Creators, and all theories and doctrines and books have no purpose and no meaning for them, seeing that they have through their supreme love and devotion risen above those things altogether. When the heart is purified and cleansed and filled to the brim with the divine nectar of love, all other ideas of God become simply puerile and are rejected as being inadequate or unworthy. Such is indeed the power of Para-Bhakti or Supreme Love; and the perfected Bhakta no more goes to see God in temples and churches; he knows no place where he will not find Him. He finds Him in the temple as well as out of the temple, he finds Him in the saint's saintliness as well as in the wicked man's wickedness, because he has Him already seated in glory in his own heart as the one Almighty inextinguishable Light of Love which is ever shining and eternally present.

Chapter IX
Human Representations of the Divine Ideal of Love

It is impossible to express the nature of this supreme and absolute ideal of love in human language. Even the highest flight of human imagination is incapable of comprehending it in all its infinite perfection and beauty. Nevertheless, the followers of the religion of love, in its higher as well as its lower forms, in all countries, have all along had to use the inadequate human language to comprehend and to define their own ideal of love. Nay more, human love itself, in all its varied forms has been made to typify this inexpressible divine love. Man can think of divine things only in his own human way, to us the Absolute can be expressed only in our relative language. The whole universe is to us a writing of the Infinite in the language of the finite. Therefore Bhaktas make use of all the common terms associated with the common love of humanity in relation to God and His worship through love.

Some of the great writers on Para-Bhakti have tried to understand and experience this divine love in so many different ways. The lowest form in which this love is apprehended is what they call the peaceful—the Shânta. When a man worships God without the fire of love in him, without its madness in his brain, when his love is just the calm commonplace love, a little higher than mere forms and ceremonies and symbols, but not at all characterized by the madness of intensely active love, it is said to be Shanta. We see some people in the world who like to move on slowly, and others who come and go like the whirlwind. The Shânta-Bhakta is calm, peaceful, gentle.

The next higher type is that of Dâsya, i.e. servantship; it comes when a man thinks he is the servant of the Lord. The attachment of the faithful servant unto the master is his ideal.

The next type of love is Sakhya, friendship—"Thou art our beloved friend." Just as a man opens his heart to his friend and knows that the friend will never chide him for his faults but will always try to help him, just as there is the idea of equality between him and his friend, so equal love flows in and out between the worshipper and his friendly God. Thus God becomes our friend, the friend who is near, the friend to whom we may freely tell all the tales of our lives. The innermost secrets of our hearts we may place before Him with the great assurance of safety and support. He is the friend whom the devotee accepts as an equal. God is viewed here as our playmate. We may well say that we are all playing in this universe. Just as children play their games, just as the most glorious kings and emperors play their own games, so is the Beloved Lord Himself in sport with this universe. He is perfect; He does not want anything. Why should He create? Activity is always with us for the fulfilment of a certain want, and want always presupposes imperfection. God is perfect; He has no wants. Why should He go on with this work of an ever-active creation? What purpose has He in view? The stories about God creating this world for some end or other that we imagine are good as stories, but not otherwise. It is all really in sport; the universe is His play going on. The whole universe must after all be a big piece of pleasing fun to Him. If you are poor, enjoy that as fun; if you are rich, enjoy the fun of being rich; if dangers come, it is also good fun; if happiness comes, there is more good fun. The world is just a playground, and we are here having good fun, having a game; and God is with us playing all the while, and we are with Him playing. God is our eternal playmate. How beautifully He is playing! The play is finished when the cycle: comes to an end. There is rest for a shorter or longer time; again all come out and play. It is only when you forget that it is all play and that you are also helping in the play, it is only then that misery and sorrows come. Then the heart becomes heavy, then the world weighs upon you with tremendous power. But as soon as you give up the serious idea of reality as the characteristic of the changing incidents of the three minutes of life and know it to be but a stage on which we are playing, helping Him to play, at once misery ceases for you. He plays in every atom; He is playing when He is building up earths, and suns, and moons; He is playing with the human heart, with animals, with plants. We are His chessmen; He puts the chessmen on the board and shakes them up. He arranges us first in one way and then in another, and we are consciously or unconsciously helping in His play. And, oh, bliss! we are His playmates!

The next is what is known as Vâtsalya, loving God not as our Father but as our Child. This may look peculiar, but it is a discipline to enable us to detach all ideas of power from the concept of God. The idea of power brings with it awe. There should be no awe in love. The ideas of reverence and obedience are necessary for the formation of character; but when character is formed, when the lover has tasted the calm, peaceful love and tasted also a little of its intense madness, then he need talk no more of ethics and discipline. To conceive God as mighty, majestic, and glorious, as the Lord of the universe, or as the God of gods, the lover says he does not care. It is to avoid this association with God of the fear-creating sense of power that he worships God as his own child. The mother and the father are not moved by awe in relation to the child; they cannot have any reverence for the child. They cannot think of asking any favour from the child. The child's position is always that of the receiver, and out of love for the child the parents will give up their bodies a hundred times over. A thousand lives they will sacrifice for that one child of theirs, and, therefore, God is loved as a child. This idea of loving God as a child comes into existence and grows naturally among those religious sects which believe in the incarnation of God. For the Mohammedans it is impossible to have this idea of God as a child; they will shrink from it with a kind of horror. But the Christian and the Hindu can realise it easily, because they have the baby Jesus and the baby Krishna. The women in India often look upon themselves as Krishna's mother; Christian mothers also may take up the idea that they are Christ's mothers, and it will bring to the West the knowledge of God's Divine Motherhood which they so much need. The superstitions of awe and reverence in relation to God are deeply rooted in the bears of our hearts, and it takes long years to sink entirely in love our ideas of reverence and veneration, of awe and majesty and glory with regard to God.

There is one more human representation of the divine ideal of love. It is known as Madhura, sweet, and is the highest of all such representations. It is indeed based on the highest manifestation of love in this world, and this love is also the strongest known to man. What love shakes the whole nature of man, what love runs through every atom of his being—makes him mad, makes him forget his own nature, transforms him, makes him either a God or a demon—as the love between man and woman. In this sweet representation of divine love God is our husband. We are all women; there are no men in this world; there is but One man, and this is He, our Beloved. All that love which man gives to woman or woman to man, has her to be given up to the Lord.

All the different kinds of love which we see in the world, and with which we are more or less playing merely, have God as the one goal; but unfortunately, man does not know the infinite ocean into which this mighty river of love is constantly flowing, and so, foolishly, he often tries to direct it to little dolls of human beings. The tremendous love for the child that is in human nature is not for the little doll of a child; if you bestow it blindly and exclusively on the child, you will suffer in consequence. But through such suffering will come the awakening by which you are sure to find out that the love which is in you, if it s given to any human being, will sooner or later bring pain and sorrow as the esult. Our love must, therefore, be given to the Highest One who never dies nd never changes, to Him in the ocean of whose love there is neither ebb nor low. Love must get to its right destination, it must go unto Him who is really he infinite ocean of love. All rivers flow into the ocean. Even the drop of wa- er coming down from the mountain side cannot stop its course after reaching . brook or a river, however big it may be; at last even that drop somehow does ind its way to the ocean. God is the one goal of all our passions and emotions. f you want to be angry, be angry with Him. Chide your Beloved, chide your 'riend. Whom else can you safely chide? Mortal man will not patiently put up vith your anger; there will be a reaction. If you are angry with me I am sure quickly to react, because I cannot patiently put up with your anger. Say unto he Beloved, "Why do You not come to me; why do You leave me thus alone?" Vhere is there any enjoyment but in Him? What enjoyment can there be in ittle clods of earth? It is the crystallised essence of infinite enjoyment that we 1ave to seek, and that is in God. Let all our passions and emotions go up unto Jim They are meant for Him, for if they miss their mark and go lower, they be- :ome vile; and when they go straight to the mark, to the Lord, even the lowest)f them becomes transfigured. All the energies of the human body and mind, 1owsoever they may express themselves, have the Lord as their one goal, as their Ekâyana. All loves and all passions of the human heart must go to God. He is he Beloved. Whom else can this heart love? He is the most beautiful, the most ublime, He is beauty itself, sublimity itself. Who in this universe is more beauti- ul than He? Who in this universe is more fit to become the husband than He? Vho in this universe is fitter to be loved than He? So let Him be the husband, et Him be the Beloved.

Often it so happens that divine lovers who sing of this divine love accept the anguage of human love in all its aspects as adequate to describe it. Fools do not inderstand this; they never will. They look at it only with the physical eye. They lo not understand the mad throes of this spiritual love. How can they? "For one ciss of Thy lips, O Beloved! One who has been kissed by Thee, has his thirst for Thee increasing for ever, all his sorrows vanish, and he forgets all things except Thee alone." Aspire after that kiss of the Beloved, that touch of His lips which nakes the Bhakta mad, which makes of man a god. To him, who has been blessed vith such a kiss, the whole of nature changes, worlds vanish, suns and moons lie out, and the universe itself melts away into that one infinite ocean of love. That is the perfection of the madness of love.

Ay, the true spiritual lover does not rest even there; even the love of husban and wife is not mad enough for him. The Bhaktas take up also the idea of ille gitimate love, because it is so strong; the impropriety of it is not at all the thin they have in view. The nature if this love is such that the more obstructions ther are for its free play, the more passionate it becomes. The love between husban and wife is smooth, there are no obstructions there. So the Bhaktas take up th idea of a girl who is in love with her own beloved, and her mother or father o husband objects to such love; and the more anybody obstructs the course of he love, so much the more is her love tending to grow in strength. Human languag cannot describe how Krishna in the groves of Vrindâ was madly loved, how a the sound of his voice the ever-blessed Gopis rushed out to meet him, forgettin everything, forgetting this world and its ties, its duties, its joys, and its sorrow Man, O man, you speak of divine love and at the same time are able to atten to all the vanities of this world—are you sincere? "Where Râma is, there is n room for any desire—where desire is, there is no room for Rama; these neve coexist—like light and darkness they are never together."

Chapter X
Conclusion

When this highest ideal of love is reached, philosophy is thrown away; who will then care for it? Freedom, Salvation, Nirvâna — all are thrown away; who cares to become free while in the enjoyment of divine love? "Lord, I do not want wealth, nor friends, nor beauty, nor learning, nor even freedom; let me be born again and again, and be Thou ever my Love. Be Thou ever and ever my Love." "Who cares to become sugar?" says the Bhakta, "I want to taste sugar." Who will then desire to become free and one with God? "I may know that I am He; yet will I take myself away from Him and become different, so that I may enjoy the Beloved." That is what the Bhakta says. Love for love's sake is his highest enjoyment. Who will not be bound hand and foot a thousand times over to enjoy the Beloved? No Bhakta cares for anything except love, except to love and to be loved. His unworldly love is like the tide rushing up the river; this lover goes up the river against the current. The world calls him mad I know one whom the world used to call mad, and this was his answer: "My friends, the whole world is a lunatic asylum. Some are mad after worldly love, some after name, some after fame, some after money, some after salvation and going to heaven. In this big lunatic asylum I am also mad, I am mad after God. If you are mad after money, I am mad after God. You are mad; so am I. I think my madness is after all the best." The true Bhakta's love is this burning madness before which everything else vanishes for him. The whole universe is to him full of love and love alone; that is how it seems to the lover. So when a man has this love in him, he becomes eternally blessed, eternally happy. This blessed madness of divine love alone can cure for ever the disease of the world that is in us. With desire, selfishness has vanished. He has drawn near to God, he has thrown off all those vain desires of which he was full before.

We all have to begin as dualists in the religion of love. God is to us a separate Being, and we feel ourselves to be separate beings also. Love then comes in the middle, and man begins to approach God, and God also comes nearer and nearer to man. Man takes up all the various relationships of life, as father, as mother, as son, as friend, as master, as lover, and projects them on his ideal of love, on his

God. To him God exists as all these, and the last point of his progress is reached when he feels that he has become absolutely merged in the object of his worship. We all begin with love for ourselves, and the unfair claims of the little self make even love selfish. At last, however, comes the full blaze of light, in which this little self is seen to have become one with the Infinite. Man himself is transfigured in the presence of this Light of Love, and he realises at last the beautiful and inspiring truth that Love, the Lover, and the Beloved are One.

Lightning Source UK Ltd.
Milton Keynes UK
UKHW010750190919
350075UK00001B/247/P